Old Wheelways

Old Wheelways

TRACES OF BICYCLE HISTORY ON THE LAND

ROBERT L. MCCULLOUGH

The MIT Press
Cambridge, Massachusetts
London, England

MIT Press books may be purchased at special quantity discounts for business or sales promotional use. For information, please email special_sales@mitpress.mit.edu.

This book was set in ITC Stone Serif, Gotham Narrow, and Bauer Bodoni Std by the MIT Press. Printed and bound in the United States of America.

Library of Congress Cataloging-in-Publication Data

McCullough, Robert, 1949–
Old wheelways : traces of bicycle history on the land / Robert L. McCullough.
  pages cm
Includes bibliographical references and index.
ISBN 978-0-262-02946-9 (hardcover : alk. paper)
1. Bicycle touring—United States—History—19th century. 2. Bicycle trails—United States—History—19th century. 3. Landscapes—United States—History—19th century. 4. United States—Historical geography. 5. United States—Description and travel. I. Title.
GV1045.M38 2015
796.6'40973—dc23

2015009276

10 9 8 7 6 5 4 3 2 1

To Montpelier's indomitable cyclists,
and to its noon peleton, with gratitude.

Contents

Bicycle Landseeërs

In 1894, a group of Baltimore wheelmen formed an association called The Thirteen Cyclers, hoping to explore as much new territory as possible given the topography of the surrounding countryside and the time at members' disposal. The group's travels are recorded in two small, handwritten volumes titled *Route Book* and *Book of Runs*; together, they are an archive that revels in discovery—and one noticeably different from the records of many other bicycle clubs, because the entries contain few references to social activities or reports of racing. Charles Rhodes served as captain, and his year-ending missive, written shortly before the club's anniversary ride in April 1895, became a proclamation of the club's founding purpose. Noting that they had covered much ground that had been little known to the cycling fraternity during the preceding year, Rhodes outlined his ambitious objectives for the coming year, an itinerary that stretched across most of Maryland and steered toward locations in Pennsylvania, reaching as far as Steelton and Gettysburg.

Rhodes observed that the greatest difficulty for touring in new districts was to find suitable points to obtain meals, but on more than one occasion the group also had trouble finding its way, venturing along cow paths of dubious outcome, into thick woods, across fields of high weeds, or through deep pockets of sand. Although some narratives capture the appeal of special outings—for instance, a moonlight ride "of the old kind" to Ridgeville—or point to notable land features, such as a windmill-like signal for a ferry crossing on the Little Choptank River, with red blades for passengers and white for teams, the books are most valuable as unadorned impressions of travel by bicycle during the late nineteenth century, best read with a willingness to tarry if one hopes to imagine those journeys. Possessing a heightened awareness of their surroundings and stirred by the compositional elements inherent in those landscapes, these Baltimore wheelmen had become discerning landseeërs.[1]

As commonly used, the word *seer* describes a person or mystic who is gifted with profound spiritual insight or one for whom divine revelations are made known through visions. However, a few notable writers have altered the word's spelling to *seeër* in order to avoid the customary interpretations. Instead, they have used the term to apply to persons whose sense of sight is penetrating and who employ that capacity to achieve understanding, whether through contemplation or imagination. For example, while discussing the romantic writing of Sir Walter Scott, Robert Louis Stevenson described Scott as "a great daydreamer, a seeër of fit and beautiful and humorous visions."[2]

The word *landseeër* is particularly apt for late nineteenth-century bicyclists, who, having mastered a newly engineered means of independence, awaken to their environs with a sense of anticipation and are able to observe those settings from a fresh perspective. Often, bicycle landseeërs travel close to home, suggesting that the word's meaning should encompass not only exotic travel experiences but also a newly found familiarity with the nearby unknown, where much has been overlooked. Charles Pratt, one of the founding members of the League of American Wheelmen (LAW) in 1880 and a frequent contributor to cycling's touring literature, reminded his readers that although distance lends enchantment, true enchantments are not all distant: "Ten to one you, Reader, unless you be a wheelman, do not know your own county."[3]

As landseeërs, bicyclists observe what others are unable to see, but the explanation is hardly mystical. In his thoughtful little book titled *Outside Lies Magic*, landscape historian John Stilgoe notices that pedestrians moving past a picket fence see only narrow segments of features located behind the fence and are unable to visualize a complete picture. However, a bicyclist, moving effortlessly at just the right speed, mentally assembles those glimpses rapidly enough to create a composite view to remarkable effect. Yet Stilgoe could extend his observation beyond just picket fences. The ability to move at a distinct pace endows cyclists with the ability to record mental images of various land features, recalling and connecting them in creative ways and forming visual prospects that remain invisible to others—panoramas unseen by those whose views are confined to fleeting glances that offer little insight about cultural imprints on the land. Today, bicycling's landseeërs can spot the traces of history that others disregard in our built and cultural environments and can offer imaginative and fitting visions for reclaiming those forgotten places.

The vanishing remnants of nineteenth-century bicycling heritage are as good a place as any to start that process of discovery. For roughly two decades, from 1880 to 1900, bicycles and bicyclists shaped and reshaped American social, cultural, economic, and industrial history; introduced an independent and dependable means of overland travel; propelled a campaign to improve the nation's pitiful network of roads; influenced the appearance of cities in subtle ways; swayed park planners; and set into motion the modern machine and engineering technology essential to the development of automobiles and airplanes.

Wheelmen and wheelwomen also assembled a substantial and today greatly underutilized body of geographical literature, illustration, photography, and vivid descriptions of American places, becoming in the process some of country's keenest observers of suburban and rural landscapes—and skillful landseeërs. These cyclists also financed and built a surprisingly extensive network of bicycle paths to satisfy their exploratory impulses—more than two thousand miles in New York State alone—and accomplished that feat in less than a decade, a remarkably short time when one considers today's short, five- or six-mile projects that can consume years of planning or debate and cost enormous sums.

Unfortunately, today we can point to very few landmarks or monuments that nurture the public's collective memory of cyclists' important contributions. Clearly, those disciplines that speak for our built and cultural environments should correct this poor record of recognition accorded to cycling heritage.

With those thoughts in mind, I set about the task of turning the pages of as many of cycling's journals as possible—and there are a great number—in an effort to trace the direction of cyclists' nineteenth- and early-twentieth-century

FIGURE 0.2

Charlotte sidepath in Monroe County, New York. Cyclists seeking scenic or unusual locale moved freely from urban centers, to streetcar suburbs, to open countryside. Sidepaths for bicycles often shared existing travel corridors used by vehicles, trolleys, and pedestrians. Placement of those paths adjacent to sidewalks or tracks—or between the two—often created conflict when property owners, teamsters, and streetcar workers damaged path surfaces. Photograph by Cline Rogers in an album titled *Sidepaths: Monroe County (1899)*. Courtesy Rochester (N.Y.) Public Library, Local History and Genealogy Division.

wanderings; to seek the vestiges, land marks, imprints, or traces of cyclists' former journeys; and where possible to reclaim the paths, wheelways, or thin bicycle traces that once formed a vast system of dendritic-like travel corridors that made country riding possible. Rather than beaten trails through wild or unknown regions, however, those narrow, tire-worn passages instead signal the start of searches through a different type of uncharted terrain: the urban, suburban, and rural locales where bicycles can function safely, both as vehicles for recreation and as a means of transportation. Charting a course for those investigations, or taking one's trace, is as uncertain today as it was a century ago.[4]

Establishing manageable geographic boundaries for the project also became necessary, and I have been traveling across fourteen states—New England's six states, New York, New Jersey, Pennsylvania, Delaware, Maryland, Ohio, Indiana, and a small portion of Kentucky—ever since the project began about twelve years ago. Temporally, the period of study begins shortly before the Philadelphia Centennial Exposition in 1876, at which the American public first inspected

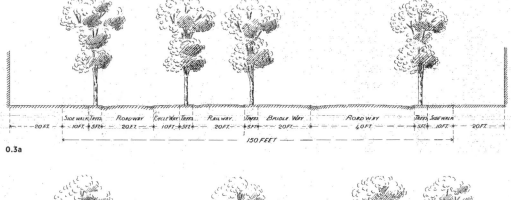

0.3a

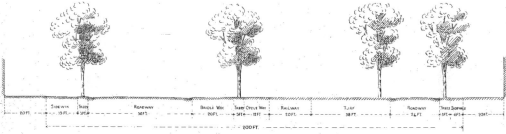

ALTERNATIVE SECTION FOR AVENUE, EXCEPT THAT PORTION BETWEEN HARVARD AND WASHINGTON STREETS.

0.3b

FIGURE 0.3a, b

In 1886, Frederick Law Olmsted offered alternative designs for widening Boston's Beacon Street, designating specific corridors for vehicles, trolleys, horses, bicycles, and pedestrians and seeming to study the relationship between bicycles and trolleys. During the ensuing years, cyclists in a number of cities offered creative ideas for combining bicycle paths with trolley lines, recognizing that the two types of transportation are not inherently incompatible. Courtesy National Park Service, Frederick Law Olmsted National Historic Site.

high-wheel bicycles, a stately English invention, and concludes with the onset of World War II, when a reviving interest in bicycles and bicycle paths—pointing to a modern era—is forestalled by that conflict.

The resulting work seeks a better acquaintance among landscape historians—who ponder the subtle weave of place, time, and public memory on the land—and bicycle historians, who study the far-reaching influences of one of humankind's great inventions. From that acquaintance, hopefully, a fruitful dialogue will emerge and diffuse among those who investigate a wide range of closely related disciplines: the cultural geographer who interprets the meaning evident in the layered traces of human activity on the land; the historical geographer or urban historian who seeks to reconstruct and understand the ever-shifting edges separating suburban and rural environments during the closing decades of the nineteenth century; the urban planner or historic preservationist who today seeks to reclaim those same lands, now densely urban and often forsaken; the *odologist* (landscape historian John Brinkerhoff Jackson's word)

FIGURE 0.4

View of Blue Hills Parkway, looking toward Mattapan from Brook Road, August 1914. The Metropolitan Park Commission engaged the Olmsted firm to plan large public reservations in Boston's suburbs and to connect those parks to the city's central districts by means of parkways. Acknowledging that those outlying lands would be inaccessible to city residents unable to afford carriages, the firm designed parkways with wide, shaded medians for use by electrified trolleys. The firm thus modified parkway design to address not only the relationship between scenery and pleasure travel but also different modes of transportation traveling at different speeds. John Charles Olmsted specifically explored ways to design park-like corridors for rapid transit without destroying scenic quality, a far more challenging task than designing similarly pleasing corridors for bicycle traffic. What remains for today's transportation planners is to incorporate scenic experience into corridors designed exclusively for alternative modes of transportation; our parkways of the future will have separate roads for light rail, bicycles, and pedestrians. Courtesy Massachusetts State Archives.

who studies the irrepressible transformation of our roads from connective corridors into complex public spaces; the ecologist who is intent upon assessing the changes caused by human interaction with the environment; the historian of tourism who unravels the complex role of travel in shaping modern society; or the enlightened transportation engineer who must transform concept into a practical physical form.

Although many portions of this study are deeply grounded in bicycle history, the point of view is always aligned to emphasize the ways that bicycles have shaped American landscapes and to record impressions of those places. That outlook has governed the overall organization of the work and the development of the various historic contexts that illuminate the scarce remnants of bicycle history on the land. The first chapter, *Awheel*, introduces the principal and related disciplines to one another.

Thematically, the obvious ties to travel, the importance of bicycles to mobility, and the closely related roles of cyclists as both geographic explorers and path builders—the former providing a partial context for the latter—all help to unify the separate chapters, as do the many connections to American places, and so the bicycle becomes a vehicle capable of crossing the numerous disciplines that touch American landscape-related studies. Those themes traverse time as well as distance, and today's cyclists can exercise the skills inherited from their nineteenth-century brethren, becoming landseeërs who can reclaim neglected places or path builders who devise useful routes for urban, suburban, and country riding.

One of the most distressing aspects of the history of bicycle path building from the late nineteenth century is that those early campaigns offer a prologue to nearly every obstacle faced by those who are engaged in the building of bicycle paths and bicycle lanes today. Although more than a century has elapsed, we are no closer to resolving the conflict over use of public roads by bicycles and other vehicles. Automobiles are only the current—and most dangerous—vehicles on that long list.

Remarkably, some of the creative ideas that cyclists proposed for resolving those conflicts, such as travel ways that combined two very different but compatible types of transportation (trolleys and bicycles), remain relevant today. Those nineteenth-century plans could be adapted to parkways designed for alternative means of transportation—light rail, bicycles, and pedestrians—with each travelway carefully separated by grade, berms, bridges, landscaping or other design features but nevertheless engineered into a fully integrated transportation corridor that also incorporates worthy cultural or natural resources into the daily travel experience: our parkways of the future.

CHAPTER ONE
Awheel

Gallant travelers *awheel* in 1880, perched astride bicycles with enormous front wheels, pedaled adventurously beyond commercial avenues or suburban streets and into open countryside, intent upon observing America, its people, and its cultural and natural resources from a distinctive pace and view—far removed from those who traveled *afoot* or by train or horse. Wheeling's popularity flourished after 1890, when safety bicycles superseded the high-wheel versions, and wheelmen and wheelwomen traced out new vicinages or ventured toward more remote horizons. These geographic observers also viewed America at an important moment in its history: the close of a dynamic era, in which an agrarian society flourishes but is challenged—and in many regions surpassed—by expanding industrial and commercial sectors. Urban and rural are often juxtaposed, a contrast that moves evermore sharply into focus, but also blurs as suburban peripheries edge toward open country.

A century before cyclists began their peregrinations, Yale president Timothy Dwight had begun his travels through New England and New York, determined to observe an experiment then taking place, unprecedented in human history: conversion of a wilderness (albeit a landscape legible to Native Americans) into a desirable residence for European civilizations. One hundred years later, cyclists ventured across that same terrain, but by then the land had been shaped exhaustively by human activity. Far from being a wilderness, the countryside had become a cultural landscape, a document explaining human toil on the land. Cyclists' accounts provide insightful commentary on the state and evolution of the experiment that captivated Dwight, and their descriptions can aid those who contemplate the changes wrought during the preceding century. The writings are even more valuable because they offer a glimpse of landscapes that would soon be altered forever by the automobile.

Wheelway Views: A Concise Compilation

The published and unpublished observations by bicycling's landseeërs can be organized into several categories. Articles and illustrations in a wide array of periodicals are an especially important group, promoting bicycle touring for both men and women and offering tempting day trips, week-long excursions, or extended summer vacations. The earliest illustrations are often reproduced through wood engravings, linking cycling to an important period in American art during which American wood engravers excel, making it possible for cyclist, artist, and engraver to collaborate in the exploration and creative interpretations of landscapes or places. The distinctive imagery that results is one of the many neglected topics long hidden at the juncture of cycling and geographic exploration.

Books and diaries by solitary overland wheelmen represent another genre, the labor of venturesome souls hoping to conquer then-astounding distances in carefully recorded time, reliant only on machine, stamina, wits, and the generosity of rural society. For some, descriptive essays were probably incidental to the daily mileage quotas needed to reach far-off destinations that promised public acclaim, yet most provide explicit descriptions of roads, signboards, food, and overnight accommodations. Other long-distance cyclists were unconcerned with speed or fame and preferred to focus on surroundings, immersing themselves in discovery. In particular, Karl Kron's 1887 tome, *Ten Thousand Miles on a Bicycle*, is an encyclopedic diary of travel and should be a reference work for any historical geographer studying the tenor of urban or rural America—mostly its eastern states—during this period. Kron's book also offers opportunity for comparison to Timothy Dwight's portrayal of New England and New York a century earlier: two very different journeys, but each remarkable as a tribute to travel and observation.

Road books prepared by state divisions of the League of American Wheelmen are a third type of published resource. These books are unique compilations of tabulated routes, maps, and detailed land descriptions, brimming with information about roads or sidepaths, including type, surface, grade, condition, distances, recommended routes, obstacles (such as hills or ravines), bordering landmarks, and opportunities to view scenery. Many offer information about roads that have long since become obscure, and much of the information provided in these books is available nowhere else.[1]

Articles in newspapers, which are able to reach a broad sampling of local readers, are a fourth category. Editors drew from cycling's popularity, sponsoring long-distance quests and local races or printing weekly columns and special cycling editions. Some newspapers published road books similar to those prepared by the LAW and also promoted the building of bicycle paths.

Cyclists' photographs are a discrete category of geographical evidence. Like illustrations, photographs contain useful historical information, and their content and composition can tell us much about the aims of photographer, author, or editor. A few compositional studies thematically linked to places on the land are especially valuable—for instance, those focusing on the shifting edges of nineteenth-century suburbs, a common theme among contributors to cycling journals. In 1882, one prescient wheelman anticipated that the bicycle would advance the merger of country and city life, predicting that "the present pedestrian limits of our suburban homes will ere long radiate from one and two miles to ten and fifteen." Moreover, the rapid rise to popularity of photography and cycling coincided, leaving us with visual references that mark a shifting outlook closely tied to independent travel. For example, during his tenure as editor of the *LAW Bulletin and Good Roads* journal, Sterling Elliott introduced a column titled "The Camera," which offered advice for amateur photographers roaming the countryside by bicycle.[2]

Other evidence of cycling's contributions to historical geography exists in various forms. During the 1880s and 1890s, cycling's popularity centered on bicycle clubs, and members often kept records of their travels, transposing field notes into narratives that club secretaries then submitted to cycling's many journals. The resulting news columns offer useful information about local roads or about buildings and places explored along the way; many such places are sought for reasons of historic interest. Accounts by women are of particular value in terms of perspective and impression.

Yet the published versions of club runs may be less important to historians of landscape and geography than the unedited diaries and field notes that occasionally survive, such as those by Baltimore's Thirteen Cyclers. Although entries are sometimes brief, the accounts can give today's readers an especially clear view of overland travel by bicycle during the nineteenth century. Field notes often mark places familiar to roving cyclists—crucial locations, such as the conclusion of one carefully judged distance or the beginning of another—usually with food or rest in the offing. The meaning once inherent in those place names and locations—and readily communicated among wheelmen and wheelwomen—is usually beyond the grasp of current travelers, even if such places survive.

Interdisciplinary Wheeling: An Introduction

In general, cyclists' literature, imagery, maps, and other evidence of geographic discoveries can be useful to a number of often-overlapping disciplines that explore the relationships between land and culture. Yet few practitioners of these disciplines have pursued the far-flung travels and observations of nineteenth-century cyclists. In truth, the omissions can be glaring, and the topic is ripe for continued investigation.

Historical and cultural geographers who study cultural landscapes, our most revealing biographies of human activity on the land and the equivalent of written texts, can borrow extensively from travel writing and illustration by cyclists. Geographer Carl Sauer, who chaired the Department of Geography at the University of California for several decades and who with his "Berkeley School" disciples forged cultural geography into an important branch of geographic science in America, acknowledged the critical relationship between historical geography and travel. Sauer noted that the accounts of America's late eighteenth- and early nineteenth-century travelers constituted the greater part of our country's literature essential both to the study of cultural or historical geography and to the deciphering of land imprints left by human activity. For Sauer, justification for historical geography rests on the ability to identify events or influences that are geographically important, and he cautions that retrospection is a concern for origins—and for the knowledge that flows from those origins—not a form of antiquarianism. He also laments both the loss of curiosity about the unknown and the absence of contemporary writing in historical geography. Yet he completely overlooks the substantial body of geographic writing by bicycle travelers, narratives that are pregnant with the very curiosity and exploratory zeal that he proclaims is absent from his own generation.[3]

Opportunities abound to draw from the writing of cycling's nineteenth-century travelers, and historical and cultural geographers who explore the dramatic physical growth of late nineteenth-century cities toil in especially productive

FIGURE 1.2

Streetcar companies sometimes preceded public utility companies in supplying electricity to urban fringes. However, both were selective in locating electric service, a means to assure profit. As a result, electrical service influenced the direction and places of suburban growth, and sidepaths often confirmed those trends. The light at the entrance to the Elmwood Avenue Bridge across the Genesee River in this 1899 image is probably incandescent rather than electric arc and verifies the distribution of electrical power to this outlying area near Genesee Valley Park, about three miles from the center of Rochester, New York. Cyclists traveling along the sidepath in the foreground could cross the three-span, mostly wrought-iron bridge, probably manufactured by New York's Groton Bridge Company (evident from its decorative plate) and described as a riveted-lattice truss with quadruple sets of diagonals, also known as a Hilton truss. Today, the University of Rochester campus borders the river near this heavily urban crossing. Photograph by Cline Rogers, in an album titled *Sidepaths: Monroe County (1899)*. Courtesy Rochester (N.Y.) Public Library, Local History and Genealogy Division.

terrain. In that urban realm, advances in structural, material, and building technology transformed modestly sized commercial buildings into towering architectural expressions of urbanity, augmenting the divide between metropolitan and provincial societies in the process. Beset by the noise, congestion, soot, and chaos of the industrialized metropolis, civic groups began campaigns to beautify, encouraged by public and philanthropic investment that presented a burnished facade but also concealed underlying unrest and growing malady. Railroads sped newly fashioned prospects to other cities along narrow corridors of connectivity, offering rural America glimpses of cosmopolitan glitter. Urban expansion coalesced near arteries, where electrified trolleys replaced those drawn by horses,

FIGURE 1.3

Once across the river, cyclists could continue easterly along the Elmwood Avenue sidepath. There, utility poles likely anticipated telephone service, evident from the different sizes of insulating spools. During the late nineteenth century, two closely spaced cross-arms of equal length mounted on the same side of the pole had begun to replace earlier poles with multiple cross-arms; they were tapered from bottom to top and alternately mounted on opposite sides of the pole, suggesting that the poles in this image were recently installed. The sidepath commission's partially visible sign explains the rules for use of the paths. Photograph by Cline Rogers, in an album titled *Sidepaths: Monroe County (1899)*. Courtesy Rochester (N.Y.) Public Library, Local History and Genealogy Division.

steadily transforming rural dominion into suburban borderland. New factory zones expanded in other directions, well beyond the urban core but still accessible from labor's sometimes troubling environs. Architects cast colossal, coal-fired, steam-generated electrical power plants into monumental symbols of industry and progress.[4]

Although these trends advanced relentlessly, urban growth remained an organic, complex process shaped by countless local and regional factors. Countryside was within easy reach, if not sight, of even the largest American cities, and places edging toward irrevocable change were most closely watched by those who harbored speculative intent. Yet such places also became familiar terrain to local adventurers who held exploratory aims. Into these shifting margins between the urban and rural wheeled the cyclist, always seeking and marking convenient paths to scenic or unusual locale but usually tethered in some way to the city. These cyclists became keen observers of that era's physical and temporal balance between urban and rural. The routes they carefully documented can tell

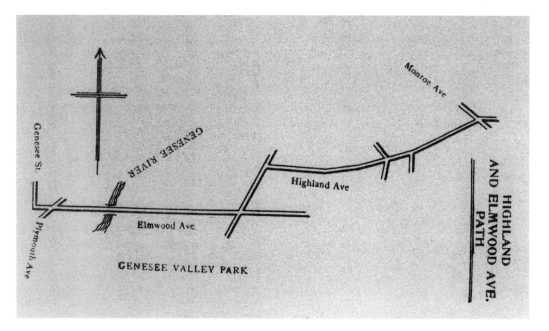

FIGURE 1.4
The bridge, utility lines, and paths foretell suburban growth along Rochester's Elmwood Avenue and Highland Avenue in 1899, a corridor that was dominated by agriculture and where barbed-wire fences still provided an adequate means of separation between field and traveler. Courtesy New York State Library, Manuscripts and Special Collections.

us much about the murky sequence of growth occurring at the edges of cities, both large and small, where suburban villas were gradually surrounded by grids of vacant lots, transformed in turn into compact communities of Queen Anne cottages, as one wheelman described such settings. So too can we learn from the race routes carefully selected for scenic occasions, many of them popular Memorial Day events.[5]

Cultural and historical geographers also can borrow from itinerant cyclists who penetrated territory far beyond the metropolis and its suburban periphery. There, Middle America remained isolated by its great distances, detached from urban society and accessible via roads of doubtful condition and conclusion—land features familiar only to local populations. From these remote regions, rural citizenry could imagine cities most easily through the articles, illustrations, photographs, and advertisements circulated in popular journals. In such realms, the cyclist traveler became a host for cultural cross-pollination, forerunners to a phenomenon that shaped much of America's cultural landscape during the twentieth century as the tempo of motorized travel accelerated. The sameness of today's automobile-connected geography points to the pivotal relationship between travel and cultural imitation.

For geographers and historians, a cardinal significance should attach to cyclists' depictions of America's suburban borderlands and provincial countryside immediately before arrival of the automobile, the twentieth-century conveyance that would shape land forms as thoroughly as nearly every human agent before it. Ironically, at precisely the moment when Carl Sauer began encouraging the study of cultural geography, the automobile had just begun to announce its influence. Sauer acknowledges that the introduction of the Model T Ford represented one of the two most important geographical events of his lifetime (settlement of the last surviving prairie became the other). Adding to that irony, accounts by cyclists are some of the best descriptions of land features long-since erased by automobiles. In many places today, efforts to reconstruct or even imagine that late nineteenth-century countryside are already very difficult. True, today we have the benefit of maps or atlases from that earlier period; the first United States Geological Surveys are particularly useful and coincide very closely to this time of travel by bicycle. Useful too is compositional imagery—when available. However, cyclists' written descriptions add substantial depth to these two-dimensional forms. A century from now, as other generations weigh the merits of motor travel against its human, economic, and environmental costs, accurate perceptions of our pre-automobile landscape will be essential and should draw from all available historical resources, including those watchfully recorded by wheelmen and wheelwomen.[6]

Landscape historians will discover that cyclists contemplated the picturesque qualities of American landscapes, and the writing, illustration, and photography by touring wheelmen and wheelwomen joins the romanticism prevalent in literature, art, architecture, landscape architecture, and park planning during the last quarter of the nineteenth century. Cyclists also contributed to changing perceptions concerning the visual qualities of that era's landscapes, insights encouraged by the artist–illustrators commissioned to join wheelmen on travel-writing expeditions. Both artist and cyclist found worthy subjects in what, by standards of that day, would have been regarded as scenes too commonplace for artistic merit: ramshackle truck farms, tidal shanties, or industrial buildings. Yet such settings captured the attention of perceptive wheelmen and wheelwomen and invited closer study, free from the constraints imposed by the appointed arbiters of aesthetic values—a liberation closely tied to the independent mobility made possible by bicycles. As imaginative observers, these cyclists and artists found a shared appreciation for ordinary places, redefining artistic values and foretelling a similar but more universal shift in outlook that would unfold following the arrival of automobiles.[7]

Cyclists' awareness of the crucial relationship between pace of travel and the ability to observe one's surroundings adds an important dimension to landscape studies, today a broad field of inquiry that stretches beyond cultural or historical geography. Wheelmen traveling in 1885 understood the salience of that relationship, and our ability to apply a similar awareness holds enormous import for

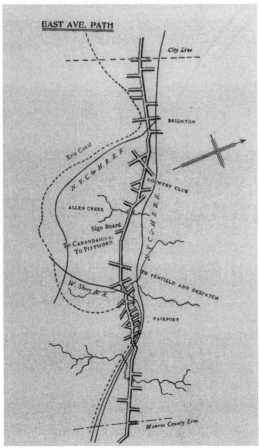

FIGURES 1.5 AND 1.6

In Monroe County, rural electrification, highway improvements, and sidepath construction coincided, here extending southeasterly along East Avenue, evidence of the city's growth in that direction. Cyclists could travel through open countryside for about eight miles en route to Fairport near the county line, twice crossing the Erie Canal. Courtesy New York State Library, Manuscripts and Special Collections. Photograph by Cline Rogers, in an album titled *Sidepaths: Monroe County (1899)*. Courtesy Rochester (N.Y.) Public Library, Local History and Genealogy Division.

the future of our built, cultural, and natural environments. A subtle connection exists between the pace of bicycle travel and our sense of place—an awareness shaped by space, architectural form, view, or memory, but also capable of being lengthened in both time and distance along a linear path.

Any discussion about the interwoven relationships among cycling, landscapes, and responses to our physical surroundings also can borrow from cultural geography and the writing of Carl Sauer and from those who enlarged his ideas, including J. B. Jackson and John Stilgoe. Although Sauer always stressed the importance of rigorous standards for cultural geography as a science, his writing nevertheless generated conflict about the proper boundaries of geographic investigation and about the inherent value of cultural landscapes as a definable field of science. Sauer may have furthered this divide by acknowledging that certain aspects of landscape, its "symphonic quality," might lead to a level of understanding beyond the reach of science.[8]

If such ideas were anathema among some geographers, Sauer's approach nevertheless appealed to generations of geographers, historians, writers, and artists who turned to the magical or indefinable aspects of landscapes but also to the ordinary qualities of our surrounding environments that fuse place, time, and memory, expanding the dialogue far beyond purely aesthetic considerations— and giving structure to what roving cyclists of the nineteenth century instinctively understood. A genre of literature began to take shape, anchored in America by eloquent writers, such as Jackson, who readily embraced the idea of landscapes as cultural texts but who sought to interpret and give meaning to the features of everyday landscapes that serve as symbols of how we, as a society, shape our land and how in turn such places shape us. Such writing helped to broaden the environmental movement, shifting attention to cultural resources and to human and nonhuman ecologies. The study of American landscapes also acquired its own loosely defined, multidisciplinary garb, advanced by the journal *Landscape*, founded by Jackson in 1951. As the inaugural issue proclaims: "A rich and beautiful book is always open before us. We have but to learn to read it."[9]

As keen observers of nineteenth-century tableaus, cyclists join many other writers and artists who discern a subtle weave of time, place, and memory in landscapes. Sauer used the phrase *sense of place* in his pivotal 1925 essay, "The Morphology of Landscape," but by the close of the twentieth century the expression had gained such widespread usage that Jackson complained it had little meaning. Yet sense of place often alludes to a harmony between humans and their surroundings, an accord that can depend upon many factors. To some people, sense of place embodies an architectonic quality, capturing features such as light and shadow, reflection, scale, the shape and weight or mass of buildings, spatial relationships among structures and open spaces, color, arboreal canopy, or axial views. Jackson, instead, points to a temporal aspect associated with memorable events, "a lively awareness of the familiar environment, a ritual repetition, a sense of fellowship based on a shared experience." Awareness of place, time, and memory can give sensory accent

FIGURE 1.7

Just beyond city boundaries, legislatively chartered turnpike companies often retained control of principal roads long after the era of turnpike construction had yielded to railroads. Anticipating profit in 1888, the Rochester, Charlotte, and Turnpike Toll Company financed construction of a bicycle path linking Rochester with Charlotte to the north and with Lake Ontario. The company charged a five-cent toll but failed to keep the path in repair, eventually provoking litigation by cyclists who disputed the fee. When that challenge failed, the Monroe County Sidepath Commission rebuilt the path, but cyclists grudgingly continued to pay a toll, circumstances suggested by the closed hand of the keeper and the pose of the cyclist at the gate. The city's proximity is also evident from the gas-light standard. Photograph by Cline Rogers, in an album titled *Sidepaths: Monroe County (1899)*. Courtesy Rochester (N.Y.) Public Library, Local History and Genealogy Division.

to many other points of view, far removed from matters of aesthetics. For many nineteenth-century cyclists, memories of these experiences could be distilled into uncomplicated prose: *the paradise of open country*.[10]

Able to move at distinctive speeds, a cyclist can lengthen a sense of place in both distance and time, allowing sensory perception to linger in thought or memory and providing opportunities to revisit places imaginatively from a distance. That type of experience might occur in a geographically expansive setting, such as that recounted by three wheelmen in 1879, during one of America's first bicycle tours. The trio, Charles Pratt from the Boston Bicycle Club and Edward W. Pope and Winfield S. Slocum from the Massachusetts Bicycle Club, journeyed from Watertown, Massachusetts, to Portland, Maine, returning to Boston by steamer on the evening of the fourth day. In New Hampshire, en route from Portsmouth to Dover, the riders became spellbound in the especially scenic valley of the Cocheco River, climbing gradually for several miles to a summit, from which they could gaze back upon their ascent, captivated by a spell-binding panorama of mountain, river, forest, fields, and villages. Today, cyclists who have experienced quiet, tree-sheltered, car-free passages in open countryside understand that a sense of place can linger for mile after mile.[11]

Sense of place can be as varied as our own creative and individual interpretations of landscape. To the informed and exploring eye, an abandoned, decaying bicycle factory bearing the grit of productivity (for instance, the Emblem Bicycle Company plant in the small village of Angola, New York) can still possess strong sensory appeal for those whose pride of work and economic livelihood once were bound to factory benches—the type of shared awareness that Jackson describes. Or an ordinary commercial shop reclaimed from obscurity can become an anchor for a nearby neighborhood of modest homes, reversing the downward spiral of urban decay. The Wright Cycle Shop, one of several used by Orville and Wilbur Wright in Dayton, Ohio, but the last still standing in its original location, is now a National Historic Landmark and a centerpiece for its renewed community.[12]

The discipline of historic preservation has embraced sense of place and has made its own contributions to cultural landscapes. The National Park Service, which keeps the National Register of Historic Places and oversees management of national historic sites, has developed a large body of specialized literature and guidelines for evaluating and interpreting historic cultural landscapes. Concern for sense of place has become a central theme in efforts to rehabilitate downtown business districts and urban neighborhoods or to preserve fragile village centers and rural landscapes. Documenting and protecting the remnants of cycling heritage is one way of benefiting those campaigns, but instilling greater awareness of nineteenth-century cyclists' quests to discover historic sites is another. These cyclists energetically investigated historic buildings and places as part of their recreational and educational touring, roughly fifty years before a few American cities turned to the economic benefits of heritage tourism as a legal justification for the conservation of historic resources. Curiously, historians in this field have yet to recognize the contributions of cyclists. Even worse, those who seek to preserve the scarce physical remnants of cycling history may face concern that the period of cycling's influence was too short to add historic significance to specific landmarks that may have been designed originally for other purposes or were long since devoted to different uses. For example, in 1975, when the New York City Landmarks Preservation Commission designated Ocean Parkway in Brooklyn as a scenic landmark, the designation overlooked the important Coney Island bicycle path, opened to celebration in 1895 and one of the country's very few nineteenth-century bicycle paths to survive.[13]

Sense of time is also fundamental to the field of historic preservation, but those who engage in the many disciplines that touch landscape studies sometimes disagree about the value or methods of capturing historic features of the built and cultural environment in carefully protected periods of time. Jackson and many other thoughtful writers, including urban planner Kevin Lynch and historical geographer David Lowenthal, have voiced such concerns, but without abandoning a sense of dismay at the often-destructive process of change. Lynch, in particular, emphasizes the need for a mechanism to dispose of the obsolete past and to avoid an inflexible reverence for the tangle of history. In its place, he urges creativity in the weaving of a temporal collage, true to the heart of our sense of time: *the sense of now.* Yet our present perceptions of time and place—and by implication obsolescence—are closely tied to our pace of travel, and those who are propelled by bicycle will likely create a temporal collage very different from that by people whose awareness of surroundings is more confined, whether by distance, speed, or means of travel.[14]

As we try to assess the present and future value of cyclists' writing and imagery in this broader vein of landscape studies, sense of place, and sense of time, the relationship between pace of travel and awareness of surroundings is salient. Although Karl Kron is a quixotic figure, his observations are often perceptive, particularly when he explains the advantages of travel by bicycle: "A tourist on foot moves too slowly to see the country on a grand scale; a tourist by train moves too swiftly to see the individual significance of any particular features of it; and a tourist on horseback or in a carriage would probably find more physical pain than intellectual pleasure."[15]

A subtle temporal relationship exists between the pace of travel, whether bicycle or automobile, and the pace of change taking place around us. That relationship becomes visible in many ways, but consider the increasing speed with which cities expanded outward during the time following World War II, a tempo influenced by numerous factors but nevertheless corresponding directly to the speed of automobiles. By contrast, the rate of urban expansion during the final decades of the nineteenth century (also the consequence of varied causes) was limited by the speed of transport then available, principally trolley or railroad. To the extent that choices about our current modes (and pace) of travel can influence the extent or rate of change in our surrounding environments, those choices become weighty indeed. Moreover, when one considers Kron's all-important relationship between pace of travel and awareness of one's surroundings, the temporal relationship between speed of travel and rate of change to our environments gains greater dimension. In this context, cyclists' cognizance of our cultural landscapes holds considerable import for the future as we struggle to manage current and future change.

Today's cyclists who build upon their own enthusiasm for cycling heritage and delve more deeply into the countless texts visible in our cultural landscapes can contribute two special skills as landseeërs. In addition to their instinctive grasp for the relationship between pace of travel and awareness of surroundings, these cyclists can identify, interpret, and translate important resources in our built and cultural environments in ways that create, shape, or sustain a sense of place or sense of time. Cyclists' ability to move freely from place to place at a unique pace and thus lengthen, both temporally and in distance, the fleeting facility of sensory recall is part of that process. That same freedom to move about and to explore cultural landscapes as a form of text also creates in cyclists an awareness of places warranting connection—for example, a series of mills or factories built initially at the edges of an urban district, then swallowed by suburban expansion, and now densely urban again but also desolate. Such places can be joined by various means—paths, view corridors, physical landmarks, or other creative designs—but through such connectivity the temporal collage that Kevin Lynch commends is enriched.

Environmental historians have affirmed Carl Sauer's emphasis on the important relationship between travel and geography, and authors such as Roderick Nash and William Cronon have cited Dwight and Swedish scientist Peter Kalm as among the most reliable providers of accounts of our country's ecosystems during the late eighteenth century and, either expressly or by implication, of descriptions of the changes to ecologies then occurring. Yet environmental historians also omit mention of nineteenth-century cyclists and the concern for environmental quality evident in their writing and explorations, particularly among illustrator–journalists, who often display a strong conservation ethic. Skilled in visual and sensory perception and sharply aware of the rapid pace of change occurring then (as now) in America, these artist–wanderers reckoned with the casual destruction that often accompanies change, joining other travelers in history who have elevated recreational travel into heightened awareness of the impact of human activity on our environments. Remarkably, cycling's illustrators often chose to depict farmsteads, architectural or engineering landmarks, places of historic interest, or quiet village settings rather than natural features. In those built and cultural environments, we find counterparts to the country's natural geography explored by a different group of recreational travelers—mountain hikers—who also wandered throughout the Northeast during the closing decades of the nineteenth century. These hikers and their clubs became instrumental in shaping conservation policy in America and invite comparison to the country's roaming cyclists. Differences exist, but the critical relationship between exploratory travel and the impulse to conserve and protect is present in both.[16]

The ties between cycling and conservation or environmental history also lead in other directions. In Baltimore, naturalist Frank C. Kirkwood first experimented with high-wheel bicycles on Thanksgiving Day in 1883, and by the following summer he had acquired a Columbia Expert model that served as a vehicle for studying Maryland's birds. Although he joined one of the city's clubs, the Druid Cyclists, Kirkwood became an itinerant explorer, meticulously recording his solo bicycle trips into remote regions to examine migratory and nesting patterns and to collect eggs. Those excursions span both the high-wheel and safety eras and led to his book, *A List of the Birds of Maryland*, published in 1895. He later became a member of the American Ornithologists Union Committee on the

Protection of North American Birds and also served as the Secretary of the Maryland Game and Fish Association.[17]

The literature of cycling will also interest ecologists and historians who study the transformation of roads and paths from mundane corridors between two places to superhighways in an infinitely complex technological, political, social, commercial, and industrial society. Our system of highways is already so multifaceted that we may have built it far beyond the capacity of our economy to sustain it or even our own willingness to understand it in its entirety. As J. B. Jackson discerns, "Roads no longer merely lead to places; they *are* places." Roads are public spaces where the means of travel distinguishes the prosperous from the disadvantaged. They can be gateways to freedom and escape; locales of social intercourse or of privacy and solitude; or places of metaphorical journey. Roads are also open passages of human disturbance where certain ecologies can thrive and evolve, free from shadow. Especially important, roads are corridors through which change finds its way onto the land. Those who attribute such versatility principally to the automobile have yet to investigate travels by nineteenth-century cyclists, historically among the country's most perceptive observers of roads. Although Jackson deserves credit for recognizing the significance of roads in so many varied contexts, the lexicon for roads that he offered in an early issue of *Landscape* could have benefited from LAW road books.[18]

Cultural and historical geography, landscape studies, environmental history, and historic preservation are among many fields of study intersected by the wanderings of late nineteenth- and early twentieth-century cyclists. In turn, these disciplines touch many other related fields, including ecology, anthropology, urban planning, architecture and architectural history, landscape architecture, transportation, and travel and tourism. The shifting and constant adjustments occurring in many of these specific fields pushes inquiry in new directions, adding layers of complexity. Cultural observers have confronted a number of challenges, including the role of landscapes in the context of large-scale—ultimately global—struggles among participants of unequal economic power; intense local scrutiny of environmental quality in densely populated urban settings—the quest for just landscapes; the disputed land places defined by social hierarchies such as ethnicity, class, race or age; the relationships between humans and nature—and the costs of separating humans from nature; and the strongly differing points of view among those who conceptualize visually, contrasting with those whose thoughts turn to theory and any underlying or unseen ills.[19]

Dwelling on the complexity of these assorted disciplinary groups and trends risks obscuring three principal purposes of this study: to identify key land-related fields of endeavor that are closely tied to cycling history; to examine the writing of a number of authors and theorists who have made important contributions to those fields, thus calling attention to their exclusion of cycling history; and to offer samples of cyclists' writing, illustration, and photography as beginning points for continued investigation by those who are well versed in these disciplines. Both the past and present value of cycling's ties to landscape-related studies are material, especially in the context of relationships between pace of travel and awareness of our surroundings. The need to confront *placelessness*—the dreary voids that pervade our environments – can provide a bond among all of these disciplines, but only an interdisciplinary approach can hope to address that challenge in meaningful ways. Unfortunately, such interdisciplinary alliances remain elusive. Historical interpretation of cultural landscapes—both urban and rural—remains relevant to such efforts at alliance, and the writing, illustration, and photography related to nineteenth- and early twentieth-century cycling can assist that difficult undertaking. Undeniably, much of cyclists' writing can be interpreted as journeys to discover and chart precisely those land places that reveal harmony between nature and culture.

For their part, today's cyclists who follow J. B. Jackson's counsel and learn to read the books that are our cultural landscapes can go far toward confronting forgotten environments by offering imaginative ways to connect cultural and natural resources, prospects that are visible to cycling's landseeërs. Such connectivity will add to the individuality of sense of place sought by both Jackson and Carl Sauer. By engaging in interdisciplinary wheeling, cyclists will find common ground among those who confront a moral imperative—namely, the changeful and often destructive relationships between humanity and its environments.[20]

Bicycle Touring: A Starting Point

Historians of tourism in America also have overlooked the role of bicycles in exciting public interest in travel and have neglected to draw from the large body of touring literature assembled by cyclists. Adding irony to those omissions, the genesis of bicycle touring borrowed greatly from the growing popularity of travel in this country during the second half of the nineteenth century. In turn, those unfolding trends depended entirely on the technological advances in bicycle and tricycle design that made touring possible. Initially confined to limited segments of the population, cycling attracted multitudes of enthusiasts by the 1890s, enthusiasts who propelled themselves on safety bicycles with mechanical features that are still functional today: two wheels of equal size, a diamond frame with a bottom bracket and crank hanger, a chain-driven rear wheel, pneumatic tires, and varying gear ratios. Resourceful inventors have improved each feature and added others, but the fundamental design has changed very little for more than a century. Both the advances in bicycle technology and the emerging popularity of bicycle travel can be credited to progress in Europe, especially in France and England.

The historical context for bicycle touring in America and its relationship to the history of travel and tourism in this country is multifaceted. A brief summary of those developments—advances in bicycle design, trends in Europe, emerging interest in travel among Americans, and the corresponding ties to bicycle touring—provides a useful backdrop for the chapters that follow. Although no one in this country has written a history of bicycle touring or a comprehensive history of travel and tourism (one that includes the important contributions by bicycles), neither is essential for the purposes of this study, which seeks greater utilization of the body of writing, illustration, photography, and cartography produced by cyclists in the larger context of landscape-related studies. Those who are engaged in the disciplines of travel or tourism are part of that context and are allied in efforts to confront placelessness. Most too will recognize the potential economic benefit of securing safe and viable corridors for bicyclists.

Evolution of the Bicycle

In 1869, Richard Lesclide, editor of the French journal, *Le Vélocipède Illustre*, authored a series of articles using the pseudonym L. G. (Le Grand) Jacques. His stories, titled "Le Tour du Monde en Vélocipède," are fictitious accounts of an American, Jonathan Schopp, and his travels throughout the world on a velocipede. Lesclide subsequently assembled the series into a book of the same title published in Paris in 1872 and 1876, and the work provides a useful beginning point for summarizing the important advances in bicycle design that made touring possible.[21]

The bicycle that Schopp rode utilized a key improvement over an older version of the velocipede. Introduced in 1817 as the "laufmaschine" (running machine), this older device resembled a hobbyhorse on two wheels and was later called the "draisine" after its inventor, Karl von Drais, a German baron who sought an easier means to traverse the forest he managed in the Grand Duchy of Baden. With the addition of a leg-driven, rotating mechanical crank with pedals, mounted on the hub of the front wheel, Schopp could maintain balance on only two points of support as long as forward motion continued. Absent of the need to push one's legs against the ground (the means of propulsion for the draisine), velocipedists could average speeds of eight or ten miles per hour. By 1868, France had become the center of a velocipede craze, and devotees established riding schools, formed clubs, engaged in day trips or longer excursions, and competed in races. The invention also sparked the imagination of writers such as Lesclide, who envisioned independent journeys to distant lands. Bicycle touring had arrived.[22]

Velocipedes reached America following the appearance of Pierre Lallement, who in 1865 had embarked on a voyage to this country with the components of a machine that he assembled and then demonstrated on a trial run near Ansonia, Connecticut. In 1866, Lallement secured an American patent for his design, but he returned to France in 1868 with little to show for his efforts. By then, however, carriage makers and entrepreneurs in this country already had begun borrowing the design. These early bicycles enjoyed a similarly captivated following in America, but for a very brief period. No longer pedestrians but not yet vehicular travelers, velocipedists incurred the enmity of city officials, who barred them from both sidewalks and streets, leading to calls for separate velocipede paths in places such as Central Park as early as 1869.[23]

FIGURE 1.8

Boulevard Saint Martin (Paris), in 1863. A wood engraving by H. E. Sylvester for *The Wheelman* (October 1883), after an earlier, 1868 drawing or painting by John W. Dunsmore. Although barely roadworthy, velocipedes such as that being ridden by Pierre Lallement in the foreground, marked the origins of bicycle touring.

Made heavy by an iron bar frame and forks that joined closely spaced wooden wheels held together in compression by large wooden spokes and iron straps—the front wheel slightly larger than its companion to improve the ratio of crank to wheel—velocipedes proved to be both difficult to propel and uncomfortable. Although riders sat upright, the seat rested well behind the front wheel's hub and pedals, forcing riders to extend their legs outward in an awkward, inefficient thrusting motion. The weight of the front wheel hindered both steering and forward progress, each essential to maintaining balance. Improvements to the front wheel soon followed—initially a rubber tire to fit over the iron band, followed by metal spokes joined to the rim in tension, thus eliminating the need for an iron strap—but these advances could not overcome the machine's inherent flaws, and the poor condition of American roads aggravated those shortcomings. Dubbed "boneshakers," a term initially assigned to models without rubber tires but eventually applied collectively, velocipedes quickly fell out of fashion in America.[24]

All the while, English machinists had been studying velocipedes with careful interest. There, as in France, clubs had engaged in touring and racing, creating incentives to improve the design. In 1869, for instance, two members of the Liverpool Velocipede Club traveled between that city and London via Oxford and Henley, a journey of more than 200 miles. By that time, inventors in both England and France had begun enlarging the front wheel and reducing the size of the rear wheel, employing the latter principally for stability and to facilitate mounting and dismounting. Wheels with light metal spokes in tension, described as spider wheels, suspended the weight of the rider and frame from the uppermost portion of the rim to the hub, reducing weight of the wheel considerably and making enlargement possible. With increased size, the gearing ratio between hub and wheel improved, increasing potential speed substantially. With increased speed, riders also gained the innate benefit of momentum. In addition, the seat could be moved forward on the backbone, placing the rider more directly above the crank and pedals, thus improving thrust and the control of the front wheel's side-to-side motion, which corresponded to pressure on the pedals.[25]

Although designers in both countries understood these advances, the Franco-Prussian War of 1870 and its aftermath paralyzed France's economy, and the manufacturing of velocipedes shifted to England. Advances in the design of spokes, the application of tubular steel for frames, steel wheel rims, a mounting step on the backbone, and the use of solid rubber tires led in 1871 to the manufacture of the first of the English high-wheel bicycles: the Ariel, designed by James Starley and William Hillman. Other inventors experimented with various designs, and two years later members of England's Middlesex Bicycle Club demonstrated the reliability of high-wheel machines by journeying from London to John O'Groats in northern Scotland, covering the distance of more than 680 miles in fifteen days. By then, numerous other clubs had formed, and members ventured forth on century rides—cyclists' hundred-mile tests of resolve. Companies continued to introduce refinements during the next several years, including improved bearings in the axles and steering head, leading eventually to the use of ball bearings throughout the bicycle by the late 1870s.[26]

By 1875, the high-wheel had been accepted as the archetype for human-propelled machines, and these grand bicycles were fast and quiet. Front wheels approached sixty inches in diameter for tall men, with rear wheels reduced to eighteen inches or less; weight dropped to the range of thirty or forty pounds, depending on the type of wheel; and average speeds eventually surpassed seventeen miles per hour over extended travel and could exceed twenty miles per hour during a sprint. By 1878, industry watchers estimated that 50,000 high-wheel bicycles had rolled across English soil. In that year, American firms joined the English vanguard, led by Boston importer-turned-bicycle-manufacturer, Albert Pope.[27]

High-wheels were challenging to mount, limiting their marketability mostly to men athletic enough to master the machines and daring enough to risk injury. To appeal to women, encourage sociable wheeling, and serve the interests of

FIGURE 1.9

What the Cricket Saw. A wood engraving by H. E. Sylvester after a drawing by Henry "Hy" Sandham for *Outing and The Wheelman* (January 1884). Skilled engravers applied this method of illustration imaginatively to capture the glint of reflected light and to suggest the speed of high-wheel bicycles.

businesses or delivery services, manufacturers marketed numerous designs for both single and tandem tricycles, all of which benefited from the improvements in technology inspired by the high-wheel. In America, however, poor roads limited the reach of these distinctive machines.[28]

Despite the apparent perfection of bicycle design during the high-wheel era, the noble appearance of these bicycles concealed a perilous defect. Riders sat high near the crown of the revolving wheel, with nothing to restrain forward motion should the wheel itself encounter obstacles (rocks or sand, for instance) that abruptly slowed the wheel's rotation. When that occurred, wheelmen tumbled head first over the handlebars, which also prevented riders from using their legs to break the fall. These *headers* or *croppers* often caused serious injury, and manufacturers in both England and America began altering the bicycle's design to minimize this hazard. Modifications varied considerably, but two of the more successful English examples decreased the size of the front wheel to reduce the height of falls. One, called the Facile and introduced in 1879, also increased the size of the rear wheel

A C.T.C. HOTEL

FIGURE 1.10

Joseph Pennell's sketch of a Cyclists' Touring Club Hotel in England, near the grey stone towers of Canterbury's West Gate. Pennell developed a distinctive, very light line for both pen-and-ink drawings and etchings, and that technique is visible here. The illustration accompanied *Cycling*, an 1887 English book by George Lacy Hillier and Viscount Bury, the Earl of Albemarle. Pennell had sketched the same view for his first book with Elizabeth Pennell, *A Canterbury Pilgrimage*, but without the tandem tricyclists. Great Britain's CTC, established in 1878 as the Bicycle Touring Club, influenced the founding of America's League of American Wheelmen.

to improve stability and used lever extensions on the pedals, allowing riders to sit lower on the frame. The second model, the 1884 Kangaroo, added a front-wheel sprocket and chain drive to improve the gear ratio. Two American versions placed the small wheel in front of the large wheel. In the process, bicycles devolved into two broad classifications: the safety and the high-wheel ordinary, the latter term distinguishing the traditional design from all others.[29]

Loyalty to the elegant high-wheel bicycles remained strong among some manufacturers during the 1880s, but when the Kangaroo demonstrated the possibilities for smaller-wheeled, chain-driven safeties by setting speed records during a one-hundred-mile road race in 1884, other firms took notice. John Starley, the nephew of James Starley, was one of those who paid close attention to the development of small-wheeled safeties, and in 1884 he introduced an awkward-looking machine called the Rover, which was promptly dismissed by skeptics. By 1885, he had improved the design to offer what became a prototype for the modern wheel: two small wheels (the front wheel still slightly larger than its companion);

an easily mounted saddle centered between the two wheels directly above the pedals; rear-wheel drive with endless chain; sprockets for gearing; and solid rubber tires. Despite its oddly fashioned framing and indirect steering, Starley's Rover soon demonstrated its superiority in races, forcing other manufacturers to adopt rear-wheel chain drive and encouraging continued refinements. By the time John Dunlop introduced the pneumatic tire in 1889, talk of obsolescence for high-wheel bicycles had begun to circulate. With the steady shift to diamond frames after 1890, high-wheels soon disappeared from company catalogs altogether. By the mid-1890s, the safety bicycle not only dominated the industry but also had transformed cycling into an activity that penetrated nearly every sector of society, blurring class boundaries in the process.[30]

Travel and Tourism History

Advances in the technology of bicycle design meshed easily with emerging interest in travel among broad sectors of the population, both in Europe and North America, and the two evolved together to mutual advantage. Those who investigate the history of travel and tourism in America will encounter curiously familiar terrain when reviewing cyclists' nineteenth-century travel accounts. For instance, many of the long-distance cyclists of that era used familiar tourist circuits, such as that linking New York City, fashionable Saratoga Springs, and Niagara Falls, probably relying on one or more of the many guidebooks then available to travelers. The author of the earliest of these American publications, Gideon Davison, described a sixty-nine-mile segment of the Erie Canal between Frankfort (about forty miles west of Fonda) and Syracuse as "the long level," setting reasonable expectations for many cyclists who traveled that corridor.[31]

By the time of bicycle travel, the tourism and printing trades had established an advantageous alliance, much to cycling's eventual benefit. From the outset, authors of travel guidebooks developed carefully devised strategies to attract varying clientele. Davison's inexpensive pocket guides, published in numerous editions between 1822 and 1840, were aimed at a growing, popular tourist market whose members had only limited leisure time but who nevertheless aspired to newly stylish travel. Other guides—for instance, that compiled in 1825 by Theodore Dwight, the nephew of Timothy Dwight—appealed to educated travelers of means, offering a literary standard and quality of print intended to reassure class-conscious readers. Still other writers, such as Henry Gilpin, refined that approach, indulging the European quest for pictorial scenery, an activity that required an advanced understanding of aesthetic doctrines concerning the picturesque or the sublime, as interpreted by art, poetry, and literature.[32]

Authors of these travel publications also adopted varying formats. Many guides served as transitory, almanac-like gazetteers, providing short descriptions of important places or historical events in addition to route maps and carrier timetables. Others added a measure of authenticity by adopting travel narratives, allowing readers to accompany the author's journey. By mid-nineteenth century, guidebooks steadily nourished the public's budding enthusiasm for travel and tourism, as did more sophisticated literary and artistic works that drew from travel experience and adventure—for instance, the stories of Washington Irving and James Fenimore Cooper or the artistry of the Hudson River School painters. After midcentury, public interest in travel also sustained popular literature, such as *Harper's Monthly*, *Scribner's Monthly*, and *The Century*, but eventually other journals devoted full attention to the travel trade.[33]

Apart from sundry railroad publications, which sometimes resembled serials, cycling periodicals such as *The Wheelman* were among the first American examples to pursue the enterprise of travel. From cycling's origins, the promotion of touring is evident in the chartered missions for both the Cyclists' Touring Club (the CTC was England's national cycling organization founded in 1878 as the Bicycling Touring Club and it subsequently formed an American branch), and the American association of clubs it influenced, the League of American Wheelmen. The composite body of cycling's written and illustrated work borrowed from all of the developments related to public interest in travel, but modified, expanded, and refined both format and content, in the process becoming an important category of travel writing.[34]

For example, road books published by state divisions of the League of American Wheelmen, travel companions that probably evolved from the first tourist guidebooks, reveal two very important distinctions from ordinary tourist guides. First, they were purposely compiled to allow cyclists to find their own way across otherwise unmarked, unmapped terrain, independent of conventional transportation and its undeviating routes. To achieve essential accuracy, league editors collaborated, pooling data from members and assembling exceptionally detailed information about roads, road surfaces, landmarks, and hotels. League members were typically well-educated, trained in various professions, and often politically influential. Editors thus tapped a broad range of skills, an aspect reflected in the quality of these guides.[35]

Second, the challenge of finding one's way created an entirely different travel experience, changing the relationship between the traveler and his or her surroundings. A self-powered cyclist charting an unknown course is forced to observe land features that other travelers, those reliant upon shared, route-bound transportation, are unlikely to notice. Moreover, attaining a sense of escape did not depend upon traveling over great distances, and a day's round-trip of fifty or sixty miles, common in 1885, could place a cyclist in territory fully as unfamiliar as far-off destinations—and just as adventuresome. These cyclists understood what today's urban explorers have learned while crawling about the abandoned, forgotten structures and tunnels of large cities: genuine discovery is possible in the nearby unknown.

When cyclists chose to translate their journeys into travel narratives, as many often did, their written accounts also differed from the travel logs of earlier periods. In particular, cyclists' stories invite readers to participate in that same clear

FIGURES 1.11 AND 1.12

Members of the Cincinnati Bicycle Club resting at the Chambers House in Miamitown, circa. 1890. High-wheel ordinary bicycles dominate, but two hard-tire safety bicycles are visible. Wheelmen on the fifteen-mile excursion from Cincinnati traveled through rolling, beautiful country along Harrison Pike, described as hilly but in generally good condition by editors of the 1886 *Hand-Book* by the Ohio Division of the LAW. The 1892 *Hand-Book* listed the Chambers House as an official league hotel, with dinner priced at $1.50. Although much altered, the building still stands on Main Street. Courtesy Cincinnati Historical Society Library.

sense of exploring the unfamiliar—of finding one's way—that can be difficult for other travel narratives to simulate. Part of the explanation concerns the characteristic pace of travel by bicycle, which contributes to a similarly distinctive sense of progress in travel stories: at times trudging—as through wheel-deep mud—but at other times coasting easily amid picturesque countryside, an experience untarnished by any prescribed, overused itineraries.

Historians who have studied the role of travel and tourism in shaping modern American culture have generated debate on a number of points, and much of the writing and illustration produced by nineteenth-century cyclists can add to those dialogues. Yet almost without exception, these historians have overlooked cyclists' contributions. A notable example concerns the distinction some historians have drawn between travel and tourism and whether, as other scholars contend, such conclusions are valid. Travel, according to the former, evolved from the Continental Grand Tour, practiced by the sons of English aristocracy as early as the sixteenth and seventeenth centuries and by the sons of the professional middle class by the late eighteenth century. Such journeys represented the completion of formal education and embodied an authenticity of experience essential to literacy, one requiring active inquiry on the part of travelers, albeit unhurriedly. However, the rise of a diverse middle class during the nineteenth century, with time for leisure and access to efficient public rail transportation, created opportunities for an emerging tourist industry to package travel experiences for a broad range of guide-toting clientele. The resulting tourism for the masses, historians argue, changed both the demeanor of travelers (from active explorers to passive amusement-seekers) and the experience itself (from a quest for authenticity to a commodity for sale)—trends that haven't abated.[36]

More recently, historians have challenged those stereotypes and contend that tourists remain active seekers of knowledge and beneficial experience, passionate observers who are engaged consistently in discovery of the authentic. Further obscuring distinctions between travel and tourism, historians argue, are the inextricable ties to complex social and cultural conventions, including vacations, consumerism, nationalism, and modern modes of transportation—especially the automobile.[37]

Although the two-decade period of cycling's nineteenth-century travel writing and illustration is short, that very brevity underscores a striking shift that occurs, germane to the debate about distinctions between travel and tourism. The high-wheel bicycles of the 1880s were expensive machines, vehicles for the wealthy, and the price of membership in most bicycle clubs was similarly limiting. Articles promoting travel by bicycle or tricycle appealed directly to that class of traveler. However, many men and women of more modest means who accepted that initial cost discovered a facile means to wheel past social boundaries.

During the 1890s, the safety bicycle rapidly transformed cycling. Annual production rose dramatically, and prices began to drop in equally precipitous fashion. By the mid-1890s, the bicycle had become a liberating mode of travel for everyman and everywoman, useful to wage laborers and members of the leisure class alike. Clubs remained a central part of cycling activities, but their extent and social makeup changed. In or near Philadelphia, for example, clubs grew from fewer than ten in 1887 to seventy-five in 1896.[38]

However, the content of travel writing published in cycling's many journals remained constant, implying the editorial opinion that much broader segments of the population could engage in the same type of independent travel activities once reserved for upper echelons of society. Part of the reason for this continued focus on travel writing is that cycling manufacturers subsidized the costs of many serials and benefited when alluring articles about travel convinced readers to buy bicycles. In addition, the speed with which change occurred made it difficult for editors to anticipate the interests of so many new readers. Yet the egalitarian nature of bicycles, a novel and very exhilarating means of travel at the time, is certainly one of the most important factors, establishing at least a semblance of common ground among people of different education, experience, and social standing.

Explanations aside, large and very diverse segments of the country's population thus were exposed to sophisticated travel writing that emphasized all the trappings of upper-class touring: independence and self-reliance, experiential authenticity, active observation, education, and a pilgrimage to picturesque scenery. For many people, the bicycle offered a means to steer around social barriers in pursuit of precisely those goals; this was surely part of cycling's broad appeal. Such circumstances lend credence to historians who argue that travel and tourism are culturally complex and that stereotypes weaken under close scrutiny.

Historians have offered many other illustrations of travel's cultural influences, but without considering the influence of bicycles. In *The Railway Journey*, for example, author Wolfgang Schivelbusch explains how the development of railroads compressed our concepts of spatial distance and time, altering our relationships with landscapes in the process. A passenger in a speeding, enclosed railroad car, he explains, snatches only momentary glimpses of framed panoramas, becoming less a traveler than a parcel moving between two points—a common sentiment expressed by nineteenth-century rail travelers. Schivelbusch also proclaims that railroads ended the intensity that once characterized eighteenth-century travel and the genre of literature it sustained: the travel novel. Astutely, he describes the true experiential quality of travel as an emotion created by a continuous sequence of impressions formed during the traverse of space.[39]

Curiously, Schivelbusch could not have crafted more lucid prose to explain what nineteenth-century cyclists both understood and valued—sentiments that Karl Kron expressed just as clearly and emphatically almost a century earlier. In truth, the strength of those impressions helped to define the cycling experience of that era. Those same qualities have not vanished, as Schivelbusch asserts, but are within easy reach today and never more valuable as we confront change and contemplate choices that may alter our perceptions of time, distance, space, or landscape—and the public memory interwoven into each.

Venturing forth by automobile rather than railroad in his groundbreaking book, *Americans on the Road*, Warren Belasco describes how automobile touring liberated travelers from the confines of railroad cars and schedules; broke the railroad's monopolistic hold over American geographical consciousness; offered unprecedented experiences of time, space, and movement; promised a sense of novelty and adventure; released long-suppressed desires of vagabondage; encouraged new trends in leisure patterns and class structure; engendered a variety of services catering specifically to tourist needs; fostered nostalgia for picturesque villages; facilitated informality in a variety of guises; dispersed summer vacations to distant agricultural domains; and allowed Americans to see the country. Although he is careful to assign those trends to the years between 1910 and 1945, he could have posited, with equal accuracy, that cyclists had opened the way for each of those culture shifts thirty years before.[40]

One can point to many other similar omissions. For example, in an intriguing essay tracking the growth of urban tourism between 1890 and 1915, Catherine Cocks points to the rise of city festivals and carnivals organized by urban business associations as a means to attract tourists and to reverse at least part of travel's steady flow from cities to country resorts. Yet she fails to mention the annual conventions of the League of American Wheelmen, certainly part of that context. Between 1880 and the early years of the twentieth century, American cities competed vigorously to secure these national meets, often at the behest of local business and industry leaders, and thousands upon thousands of people watched. Events often lasted a full week, and participants from every part of the country enjoyed parades, both day and night—the latter with lamplights and especially fashionable. Century rides, bicycle tours, several days of racing, and various other festivities dazzled the civic-minded.[41]

League conventions were not the only urban tourist draws related to cycling. City businessmen and promoters collaborated with local bicycle clubs to organize meets for amateur and professional racing, one of the country's most popular sporting competitions of that era and very profitable to promoters and winning cyclists alike. A well-established professional racing circuit crossed the country, and champion cyclists joined America's highest-paid professional athletes. Races lasted several days, were preceded for weeks by newspaper fanfare, and began with parades through city streets. The public riveted its attention to key matches between the best cyclists of the day.

Elsewhere, Lynne Withey's history of leisure travel points to the significance of Jules Verne's 1872 novel *Around the World in Eighty Days* as an inspiration for global adventure—notably, that in 1889 of a young, New York journalist, Elizabeth Cochrane, who used the pen name Nelly Bly in travel diaries prepared for the *New York World*. Cochrane's journey, an attempt to circle the globe in seventy-five days (she succeeded in seventy-two), is closely tied to Verne's story, and Withey uses that voyage to illustrate the significance of such adventures in awakening public enthusiasm for travel.[42]

However, public interest in global adventure grew from many sources during the late nineteenth century, including cycling. Although Withey might easily overlook Richard Lesclide's fictional stories of world travel by vélocipède, published contemporaneously with Verne's influential book, the solo bicycle journey around the world by Englishman Thomas Stevens between 1884 and 1887 (which was also the first crossing of the North American continent by bicycle) generated enormous public acclaim. So too did the ill-fated attempt by American Frank Lenz; begun in 1892, it ended with his murder in Turkey in 1894. The three-year global journey commencing in 1890 by two Americans, William Sachtleben and Thomas Allen Jr., partially recounted in a book published in 1894 (*Across Asia on a Bicycle*), greatly excited American interest in world travel as well. Neither published an account of the duo's American experiences, but Sachtleben added to the country's intense interest in bicycle adventure when he traveled to Turkey to solve the mystery of Lenz's death.

At least four American cyclists (George Thayer, Frederick Van Merebeke, George Nellis, and Charles Gray) successfully journeyed coast to coast on high-wheel bicycles in 1886 and 1887, contributing to public fascination with long-distance touring. With the arrival of safety bicycles, cross-country treks became almost commonplace during the 1890s, and riders such as Tom Winder left well-written accounts of their wanderings. Others, including George Loher, kept diaries inherited by grandchildren. Englishman John Foster Fraser, later knighted, and his two friends, Edward Lunn and Francis H. Lowe, crossed the North American continent in 1898 on the last leg of a twenty-six month around-the-world tour, and Mrs. Hattie McIlrath, riding with her husband, Darwin McIlrath, traveled across America as part of a world tour between 1895 and 1898. A cyclist from Nova Scotia, Karl Creelman, overcame an astounding array of hardships during his two-year, globe-girdling expedition, launched in 1899. And, in 1904, two young Americans, Clarence Darling and Claude Murphey, traveled through all forty-five states and four territories on a wager.[43]

Not all of these travelers left a legacy of observation about American places. Rather than offering keenly felt impressions of American scenes, many of these wheelmen were more concerned with adventure, with reaching their distant destinations without unnecessary delay, or with the public tributes that were sure to follow, and thus their travel accounts sometimes seem more dutiful than enlightening. The writings of those who were perceptive—for instance, George Thayer and Tom Winder—become especially valuable for that capacity. Yet all received publicity that captured the attention of other would-be explorers, inviting and encouraging ventures of a similar kind—perhaps not as lengthy, but imaginative nonetheless. Accounts of their accomplishments, and the public applause that accompanied their journeys, belong in any complete history of travel or tourism. The chapters that follow study principally those wheelmen and wheelwomen who became American landseeërs and path builders.

FIGURE 2.1
F. Childe Hassam's illustration for *The Wheelman*, commissioned for an article by Charles Pratt, *Echoes and Shadows* (February 1883). Dated 1882, the original drawing may be an etching or a pen and ink sketch and is among Hassam's earliest works as an illustrator.

CHAPTER TWO
Wheeling Large

An October day in 1877 marks the beginning of an important category of American geographical writing: the richly descriptive narratives found in the periodical literature of bicycle touring. The authoring cyclist is Alfred D. Chandler, a lawyer from Brookline, who embarks on a forty-mile trip in Massachusetts from Leominster to Boston, riding a fifty-two-inch Special Challenge manufactured by Singer and Company in Coventry, England. Having made a careful "topographical study of the towns, villages, hills, valleys, watersheds, river basins, nature of the soil," and other features along his route, Chandler envisions a pleasurable "day off" in the country, planning to limit his speed but also hoping for a back wind, to "approach the nearer to flying."[1]

Dismounting occasionally to gaze across fields, admire views at bridge crossings, or observe the changing foliage, he journeys through the Nashua River valley that morning, passing into North Lancaster, Bolton Centre, and Stow, where he joins two companions for dinner, prearranged at a wayside inn of colonial origins. Resuming the journey that afternoon, he travels near the small but thriving manufacturing center of Maynard, followed by uninspiring scenery in North Sudbury, but then on toward thrifty farms in Concord and the great meadows of the Sudbury River valley.

There Chandler pauses, recalling a series of court cases and legislative acts precipitated by disputes over mill and riparian rights between two corporations, the Proprietors of Sudbury Meadows and the Proprietors of the Middlesex Canal. An enlarged dam erected by the latter on the Concord River in Billerica in 1828 had flooded one thousand acres of meadowland along the tributary Sudbury River. From the time of Sudbury's earliest settlement, these broad plains—in some places one mile wide—had yielded unusually rich meadow grass and cranberries, but the rising river had made the lands practically worthless, capable of growing only coarse sedge used as bedding.[2]

Years before, in 1816, Sudbury landowners had formed a legislatively chartered corporation with authority to keep the river free from obstructions—and to counter the rise of encroaching industry. The two sides quarreled for many decades, but the meadows that Chandler views on that fall day in 1877 are again productive, because the Massachusetts Supreme Court had sustained an 1860 law that required canal proprietors to reduce the height of their dam. Although that law caused loss of profits to mill owners reliant on water power and to the canal owners who carefully measured and sold that power, legislators reasoned that the time had come for industry to turn from water power to steam.[3]

Chandler only briefly refers to the cases, and, although he clearly understands the symbolic importance of those meadows, we can only guess his thoughts as he surveys the river valley. Yet beyond Sudbury, as he crosses into the Charles River watershed at Lincoln and then pedals through Weston, Waltham, and Watertown before the final run home, perhaps he contemplates the continuing tension between industrial progress and agricultural inheritance. Surely, too, he notices the evidence of that struggle on the land, a contest that by then had already reshaped American attitudes about visual qualities in the environment. Undoubtedly, he realizes that his perceptions have been sharpened by a greater awareness of place: insights gained from travel by bicycle.

Later that fall, Chandler conferred with a fellow cyclist, Englishman Frank W. Weston, an architect who with several partners had just established a bicycle importing firm in Boston: Cunningham, Heath, and Company. In December, Weston began publishing *American Bicycling Journal*, and Chandler contributed the story of his October trip, "Forty Miles in Four Hours," to that inaugural issue. Both Weston and Chandler hoped to introduce the public to high-wheel bicycles and to the many beneficial qualities of a machine much improved from awkward velocipedes. Weston also included articles about bicycle touring in England, where already it had become popular, and Chandler observed that rides of sixty, eighty, or one hundred miles were then routine in that country. Both men also grasped what America's very small constituency of riders had begun to discover in 1877: a complete freedom to move beyond all-too-confining city blocks and to wheel through unfamiliar suburbs and open countryside, along routes of one's own choosing, and with little concern for schedules. Today, inured to automobile travel, we take such freedom for granted, but to the cyclists of the 1870s, 1880s, and 1890s such experiences were fresh and exhilarating, an outlook that vividly colored their observations.[4]

Touring to Worthy Purpose

Among the many categories of cyclists' geographical explorations, journal articles such as that by Chandler develop into the richest source of writing for today's historians. Narratives are infused with a spirit of adventure and discovery—"wheeling large," as Karl Kron describes it—and whether tours last a single day, become overnight excursions, or continue for longer periods, nearly all the accounts and illustrations convey a sense of possibility to readers. These are writers who relish their adventures, who are alert, who notice their surroundings, who venture off principal roads to satisfy curiosity, and who record their outings with a vivid sense of accomplishment. Time and distance are less important than experience and observation.[5]

The literature of bicycle touring originates in an impressive collection of journals, which are a vital part of cycling history. Articles needed to stir readers' interest in travel, and descriptive accounts are both compelling and informative. The story of these journals includes frequent changes in ownership, sharp editorial turns, unremitting economic challenges, and competition among bicycle company owners, who paid for advertising. There is still much to learn about the cryptic process of editorial policy making, the selection of writers and illustrators (many of whom remain obscure), and the methods of assessing ever-shifting winds of reader interest. Such factors unavoidably influenced trends such as editorial favor toward bicycle touring.

However, that contextual complexity should not obscure several key points. One is that the owners and editors of cycling journals created a dependable forum for the literature of bicycle touring. Another is that authors and illustrators present recurring themes: independence and self-reliance; a fresh appreciation for scenery, but one often free from established aesthetic doctrines—evidence of shifting attitudes about the visual quality of landscapes; inclusion of the old and the historic as worthy of notice; a concern for natural resources; and an awareness of opportunities for women cyclists. Most importantly, the substance of bicycle touring's literature represents one of cycling's significant legacies: perceptive descriptions of American places.

The Wheelman, Outing and the Wheelman, *and* Outing

During his brief tenure as publisher and editor of the *American Bicycling Journal*, Frank Weston continued to popularize bicycle touring. However, he sold the magazine in 1879 to Boston cyclists Edward Hodges and Charles Pratt, who renamed it *Bicycling World* and who shared editorial duties. Pratt was a capable writer and became a pivotal figure in organizing a two-day excursion by about thirty-five cyclists through the suburbs of Boston in September 1879, an idea conceived by Alexander Drake, director of the art department at *Scribner's Monthly*. Pratt's article describing the adventure, "A Wheel Around the Hub," appeared in the February 1880 issue of *Scribner's* and marked a formal introduction of cycling and cycle touring to the American public through popular literature.[6]

The wheelmen engaged in purposeful exploration of natural settings and places of historic interest, tarrying that first morning at Brook Farm in West Roxbury, the transcendentalist community founded by Unitarian minister George Ripley and commended by many of America's important reformists and literary figures, including Ralph Waldo Emerson, Margaret Fuller, Amos Bronson Alcott, and Henry David Thoreau. By the fall of 1879, only the Fuller cottage remained from a utopian experiment that had foundered in 1846. Still, the group relished the commanding views from the bluff on which the Eyrie and Phalanstery once stood, the latter used for common living. From there, the cavalcade traveled on, pausing at the ancient, clapboard and shingle-clad Fairbanks House in Dedham, and then pedaling to Blue Hill and nearby Ponkapog Village before stopping for the evening at Massapoag House in Canton.[7]

The Wheel Around the Hub tour also contributed to the publication of another journal two years later, *The Wheelman Illustrated*, which set a high standard for cycling literature, illustration, and bicycle touring. Approximately one year after the suburban Boston tour, Pratt began working for the Pope Manufacturing Company, concentrating on the firm's many patent imbroglios. A Quaker by birth and an attorney by profession, he also contributed to a publishing business that Colonel Albert Pope created primarily to promote the sale of bicycles but also to counter adverse publicity Pope had begun to receive due to his demands for patent royalties.[8]

FIGURE 2.2
Halt to Catch Up, a wood engraving after a drawing by Allen C.
Redwood for the article "A Wheel Around the Hub," first published in *Scribner's Monthly* (February 1880) and republished in
the inaugural issue of *The Wheelman* (October 1882).

Pope launched his journalistic venture with a reprint of Pratt's "Wheel Around
the Hub," which appeared in the first issue of *The Wheelman*, October 1882. He
announced his ambitious literary objectives in that issue and clung to that ideal
for several years, compiling a large collection of well-illustrated articles about bicycle touring (and also considerable red ink). Pope assigned chief editorial responsibilities to Samuel S. McClure, recently graduated from Knox College in Illinois
but inexperienced as a cyclist, and asked Pratt to be a contributing editor on matters requiring cycling expertise. McClure later acknowledged that he found the
accounts of long trips made through interesting parts of the country to be especially
entertaining, observing that "town men, who followed sedentary occupations, discovered the country on the bicycle." Pope also hired one of McClure's classmates,
John Phillips, who had edited the college newspaper, and McClure's younger
brother, John F. McClure, who received travel assignments. Although the fledgling editorial talents of the elder McClure, who later established his own monthly

magazine, should not be discounted, Pope and Pratt (the latter comparing his role to that of a midwife) deserve most of the credit for steering the journal in the direction of touring, likely influenced by English cycling journals. Pope also paid for literary contributions to the magazine or subsidized the travel expenses of cyclists and illustrators retained to prepare articles.[9]

Outing and the Wheelman   Editorial roles blurred a year later, in November 1883, when Pope incorporated the Wheelman Company, assigning nominal shares to Pratt, McClure, and two other men, William B. Howland and John B. Drury. In May 1882, Howland and Drury, the latter a financial backer, had begun publishing a sporting periodical, *Outing*, from offices in Albany, New York. Pope absorbed their magazine, changing his journal title to *Outing and the Wheelman* and asking Howland, McClure, and Pratt to juggle editorial duties. However, McClure departed, leaving Pratt and Howland to run the magazine. Eventually, they had the help of journalist Sylvester Baxter, who had joined cyclists in Newport for the founding of the LAW in 1880.[10]

Baxter, a resident of suburban Malden, Massachusetts, championed land conservation and progressive urban planning in the Boston area, and he encouraged state legislation to create the Massachusetts Trustees of Public Reservations, chartered in 1890 to hold title to scenic or historic public lands and guided by influential figures, including landscape architect Charles Eliot and George Mann, president of the Appalachian Mountain Club. Several years later, Baxter also became secretary of the Metropolitan Park Commission at a time when wheelmen requested separate bicycle paths in the regional park system surrounding Boston, thus playing several important roles that linked the cycling community to broader conservation and planning initiatives.[11]

Outing   Pope abandoned his costly *Outing and the Wheelman* publication in 1885, selling it to Howland and others, and its new owners renamed it *Outing*. Although this new journal retreated from an emphasis on cycling, its editors continued to offer articles about bicycle touring until the early years of the twentieth century, when automobiles began to satisfy American wanderlust. Many of the articles published during the mid-1890s at the height of bicycle popularity were among the journal's best, and *Wheelman, Outing and the Wheelman*, and *Outing* thus established a consistent forum for bicycle touring literature over a twenty-year period.[12]

Granted, Pope supported writing and illustrations that enticed the public to buy bicycles, and his economic incentives for articles about touring are transparent. He also used touring to dispel concerns about cycling sometimes voiced by physicians and clergy, the latter objecting to Sabbath rides that lowered church attendance. He even sponsored contests for the best articles about bicycling and for the best sketches suitable for wood engravings, inviting clergy and physicians to participate and offering nickel-plated Columbia bicycles as prizes. Yet if such pecuniary interests tainted cyclists' motivations, then neither the experiential quality of the touring nor the descriptive value of their writing seems to have suffered.[13]

George Blackman, a physician from Dunkirk, New York, cleverly managed to extol the healthful benefits of cycling—and also to dismiss the specter of sacrilege—in an 1882 article about a Sunday excursion to visit patients, a trip he titled "An October Ramble." Blackman's narrative begins at the edge of town, where he turns onto a county road graded originally by the New York and Erie Railroad; completed in1853 and the country's first long-distance rail corridor, it linked Piermont on the Hudson River with Lake Erie at Dunkirk. The railroad's tortuous route made it a marvel of engineering but also proved to be its undoing, because travel along Cornelius Vanderbilt's New York Central road near the Erie Canal corridor was faster and more profitable. Yet in Blackman's day, residents of communities along the old New York and Erie route knew its history well, and he quite naturally refers to a remnant of that corridor already vanishing by 1882; he also marks its location for today's historians.[14]

Blackman's observations that cloudless day illustrate cyclists' ability to view both panoramic vistas—the fleeting snapshots gathered during fast-paced rail travel—and minute details usually visible only to pedestrians. Wheeling past a crossroads settlement, Roberts Corners, he follows a graveled ridge that marks the former edge of Lake Erie, by then a blue-green expanse three miles distant and well below his elevated route. All around him is evidence of New York's agricultural empire: well-tilled farmland, white farm houses, red barns, yellow stubble fields with ranks of sheaved corn stalks, and new fields of green winter wheat. To his right, the Arkwright Hills remain forested, completing the broad vista. Stopping at leisure or to push his bicycle up a soft, sandy hill, he picks a bloom from a group of bur marigolds; he also observes a microscopic struggle between wasp and spider.[15]

As Blackman's article suggests, a sense of unfolding survey coupled with views of constantly shifting scenes—all at a pace controlled by the rider—distinguish cycling and its travel literature, and these qualities define cyclists' writing through two decades. Today, the journal literature still conveys cyclists' unmistakably keen awareness of their surroundings. Charles Pratt argued as much in "Echoes and Shadows," a gracefully-written article appearing in the February 1883 issue of The Wheelman, in which he chides the uninitiated. Pratt's winter muse is a reposeful one, and he recalls the early explorations beyond Boston by Alfred Chandler (cycling's Columbus). He also explains that discovery encompasses not only direction, grade, topography, and country roads, but also old houses, the inimitable shades of spring green, and memorable circuits on moonlit nights—when roads are empty of other travelers.[16]

Pratt's emphasis on the key relationship between cycling and exploration set a bearing that other editors adopted, and it also confirmed his role in guiding that course. Editors of The Wheelman and its two successor journals hoped to sell their magazine to readers across the country, and thus exploratory thrusts entered remote regions, including parts of Canada. Yet the sense of discovery that Pratt and others valued so highly often depended on an ability to balance views of natural and cultural features, and cyclists were at their exploratory best when traveling from the familiar to the unfamiliar—and back. Years later, Abbott Bassett, the enduring secretary–editor of the LAW, explained that the perfect tour is "one where a person goes on a roving journey and comes back to the place of starting." Trips often occurred in eastern parts of the country, radiating from major cities, such as Philadelphia, New York, Boston, or Washington, D.C., where urbanites tested manageable distances—and purchased both magazines and bicycles.[17]

Jay Howe Adams, a LAW representative, investigated routes extending to the west and south of Philadelphia. In "On and Off the Lancaster Pike," published in *Outing and The Wheelman* in 1884, Adams observes that within city limits the turnpike, by then almost a century old, amounts to no more than a roughly paved street filled with trolley tracks and traversing an unpleasant part of town. Instead, he prefers to skirt Fairmount Park, but he also complains that the Centennial Exposition's Memorial Building, built less than a decade before, stands neglected and dilapidated, and he ponders how quickly the visage of such an important American building could be wiped away.[18]

Although much of Adams's article is devoted to the history of his route—the turnpike, its Conestoga freight wagons, taverns with huge barns and great water troughs, and several colleges—he grants equal favor to both old and new. The brightly colored suburban stations of the Pennsylvania Railroad, bordered by planted flower beds (a practice soon abandoned as unsafe), catch his eye, as do a small stone church in Radnor, St. David's, and the picturesque ruins of Dove's Mills, located beyond Haverford on a macadamized side road leading to Paoli—a village he considers notable for its inn but little else. As do most cyclists, Adams and his group pay close attention to toll houses, "usually low, frame buildings, sometimes painted but often whitewashed," and he alerts readers to the foibles of sentries at Ardmore, Overbrook, and Wynnewood. Yet Adams also finds the broad, smooth, rolling turnpike to be a little monotonous, and he is tempted to turn onto obscure branch roads bordered by "overhanging trees and mossy boulders worthy of an artist's pencil."[19]

By contrast, Adams finds the city's mysterious nether regions to the south to be unique—in his words, "an opportunity to discover something new." His 1885 article for *Outing*, "Through 'The Neck' on a Bicycle," describes an expansive point of lowland at which the Schuylkill and Delaware rivers meet, the region's name concealing the idiosyncratic character of its inhabitants—mostly poor market farmers and squatters eking out an existence. Far from being dismissive, however, Adams instead admires the seclusion achieved by these "Neckers," a privacy that outsiders seem willing to concede. He follows Passyunk Road past the barren ground of Lebanon Cemetery (the burial site for the city's African Americans), and points to the government naval station on League Island in the distance (see figure 3.15), before turning southwesterly toward Penrose Ferry

FIGURE 2.3
Old House on the "Neck," a pen and ink drawing or etching by
John Arthur Fraser, reproduced for *Outing* (September 1885).

Bridge (which rendered the ferry redundant). Other than a few old stone houses, average buildings are low, rambling accretions built close to the road and bearing weather-beaten coats of whitewash. Scattered everywhere are small signs advertising products and services for sale, barely decipherable due to poor spelling. Yet Adams is accepting of the scanty houses, stagnant marshes, and illiteracy—circumstances in which residents seem to thrive. Nor is he bothered by industrial intrusions visible in the distance: coal docks on the Delaware and tall grain elevators, oil tanks, refineries, and gas works on the Schuylkill.[20]

Adams clearly sympathizes with the region's distinctive qualities, and he quotes at length from a short story written fifty years earlier by a Philadelphia physician, Silas Weir Mitchell, in which a young married couple escape the "tyranny of Philadelphia's right-angled streets and poor suburbs" to walk the crooked roads across the Neck on a summer afternoon. The hidden lowland they discover, "the only landscape near [them] which has in it something quite its own," is protected by dikes and penetrated by canals that divide the grassy meadows more agreeably than fences, leaving views open to grazing cattle, cottages, stands of willow trees, and white sails moving slowly in the distance, the hulls of their ships unseen below the rise of dikes.[21]

Adams's account is remarkable for its objective focus on the heterogeneous settlements that develop at the outskirts of large cities, clandestine places that he finds appealing. He points to the disappearance of New York's Squatter Town, which succumbed to surveyors and real estate investors moving north after construction of the city's elevated railroads, but he also believes that the Neck will avoid a similar fate, because its marshes and meandering creeks will serve as natural barriers to interference. That prediction proved to be unrealistic, but the value of Adams's writing rests with his appreciation for a landscape ignored by the aesthetic doctrines of his day. His emphasis on exploring such common places is again evidence of changing attitudes toward the visual quality of landscapes, a trend propelled by bicycle travel and sustained by humanity's natural impulse to seek new and unfamiliar places.

As the safety bicycle and pneumatic tire made long-distance travel much easier, the geographical reach of touring expanded. In response, editors often published articles in a series, giving readers a chance to pause before continuing on their way and creating a more dynamic sense of journey. Among many such articles published in *Outing* during the mid-1890s, several by cyclist John B. Carrington illustrate this trend. Carrington travels with a companion, Philip Bruce, and the pair wander away the summer months of what is probably 1896, "through Virginia Awheel," beginning in Richmond and rolling into the Tidewater region en route to Washington, D.C., before eventually turning westward to pedal "across the Alleghanies [sic] Awheel." Although his travel narratives, published in the magazine's summer issues of 1896 and 1897, lack the studious quality that characterizes Adams's explorations, they are nevertheless descriptive of both a land and a culture in which the scars of the Civil War remain visible.[22]

Carrington is also far less tolerant of urban peripheries than Adams, complaining of city beer wagons, suburban trolley rails, and dust as the pair roll beyond Washington's interior and through "a wretched district that is neither city nor country." Although his view of suburbs contrasts with the observations of many other cyclists, Carrington's writing may nevertheless represent the genre more fully than Adams in several respects: a sense of carefree adventure, an appreciation for the bucolic and its many sensory stimuli, the pursuit of scenic vistas, an awareness of American antiquities (in Carrington's case, Tidewater manor houses and Fredericksburg's old town), or hints of romance upon chance encounters with strangers.[23]

As with most travel writing by cyclists, Carrington's observations can inform today's historians and geographers. For instance, the vine-covered porches he casually notes are evidence of a common, inexpensive practice (now largely forgotten) intended to cool homes in summer and give way to light during winter months. Elsewhere, on the hard-surfaced Valley Pike linking Winchester with Staunton, built between 1838 and 1840, the cyclists encounter a repair gang

FIGURE 2.4

Cabin John Bridge, a wood engraving by H. E. Sylvester after a drawing or painting by Francis D. Noyes for *The Wheelman* (November 1883). Designed by engineers Montgomery Meigs and Alfred Rives and constructed by the Army Corps of Engi- neers to carry the Washington Aqueduct, the masonry arch structure spans Cabin John Creek in Maryland. Completed in 1864, the site became a favored destination for cyclists during both the high-wheel and safety eras.

and their foreman, who live on the road in two vans, moving about as required and breaking rock by hand. Highway historians have studied the construction of many nineteenth-century turnpikes, but information about the methods of maintaining those roads is difficult to find.[24]

Carrington's articles are typical in another manner, for they contain an under-tone of condescension that sometimes intrudes during cyclists' interaction with rural citizenry. However, not all touring wheelmen succumb to that shortcoming. A. H. Godfrey, the author of two 1898 articles for *Outing* about trips along the Hudson River's westerly shore in New Jersey and New York, rebukes his colleagues for failing to linger in rural agricultural communities, thus forsaking the chance to gain new acquaintances to mutual benefit. Only through such intercourse, he cautions, does the cyclist historian discover the truly old settlements sequestered from principal thoroughfares. Another of *Outing*'s writers, Ernest Ingersoll, had explored the same realm a few years before, pointing to Colonial-era artifacts, including the "ancient Dutch four-corners of Schraalenburg," New Jersey, a country village seeming to appear exactly as it did a century before.[25]

Bicycling World

By no means did *Outing* and its predecessor titles dominate the journalism of bicycle touring. Although not every cycling publication consistently emphasized bicycle travel, articles similar to those by Adams, Carrington, and Godfrey surfaced in most magazines during one editorial reign or another. The news weekly *Bicycling World*, significant for its longevity, developed into a chronicle of cycling's growth, and under the direction of numerous successive editors it emphasized club events, races, and corporate news. The journal also catered to the activities of the LAW, becoming *Bicycling World and the LAW Bulletin* in 1888, but eventually severing that tie and later becoming *Bicycling World and Motocycle Review* (subsequently replacing "Motocycle" with "Motorcycle"). Along the way, its owners absorbed several other cycling journals.[26]

If the journal's emphasis on cycling news and trade during the 1880s left the touring cyclist disappointed, editorial judgment had shifted enough by the mid-1890s for the magazine to offer many worthy travel articles, lengthy serials among them. W. S. Beekman, a member of the Massachusetts and Waban bicycle clubs, authored several articles and also a small book (*Cycle Gleanings: or, Wheels and Wheeling for Business and Pleasure, and the Study of Nature*), and he sometimes traveled with his wife, charting rides for cyclists who could devote only a few days to travel.[27]

As his narratives reveal, Beekman is a scientist and geologist for whom the bicycle is a vehicle to explore better what he calls the "open laboratory of nature." To Beekman, land*marks* are literally the glacial grooves, scratches, and grindings visible on bedrock laid bare, and the landscapes that he considers exquisite are sand plains, gravel ridges, clay beds, moraines, eskers, kames, and drumlins. Rather than seeking pastoral countryside, he explores former glacial river beds turned into city streets; nearby slate quarries revealing folds, faults, and compressions caused by volcanic upheaval; and the protruding traces of glacial dykes. At an old powder house in North Somerville, he notices workmen dismantling the remnants of one such dyke to create a small common, but he opines that the site would hold greater interest and educational value if the dyke's surface were left exposed. He also assesses New England's stone-filled farms with unusual objectivity, observing that rock absorbs the sun's warmth during the day and disperses it gradually to the soil at night; screens the soil from heat in times of drought, thus diminishing evaporating surfaces; and offers shade without removing moisture.[28]

Beekman is an observer, and in a thoughtful nine-part series for *Bicycling World* in June and July 1895—aptly titled "Nature, From the Standpoint of the Observant Cyclist"—he studies immense glacial boulders called erratics in North Saugus, Peabody, and Lynn; a serpentine quarry in Lynnfield; massive granite beds in

Quincy turned into deep voids punctuated by jutting derricks; and, on Cooper's Island in Cohasset, giant potholes called kettles, drilled by glacial streams. He also provides architectural critique, observing that the new and costly houses he encounters lack the dignity, to his eye, evident in time-honored landmarks; many of today's cycling landseeërs may share such sentiments. Offering advice as useful now as then, he urges cyclists to "use the wheel to see what there is around," to scan "the peculiarities of each town," and then to note and compare extreme differences as the best way to become practiced observers.[29]

As do women of that era, Beekman regards the bicycle as a great emancipator, but from dogma rather than from dependence on men. To him, bicycles offer a unique combination of mental and physical stimulation, which in turn unlocks freedom of thought, thus dispelling "the cloud of mysticism that has clung so tenaciously to the multitudes." The sparks of realization that flow from this mental awakening originate in the "record of nature's effects," a form of public property "all out-door" and available for everyone to observe. Thus, the bicycle's principal value is as an educator, a vehicle to prompt "meditations on our beautiful surroundings and our conceptions of things not temporal" that are inspired largely by nature.[30]

Beekman adds more weight to his bicycle by suggesting its value as a means to find spiritual rejuvenation free from the myth and superstition of religion and ultimately as a way for humanity to attain a higher and purer intelligence. He regards as absurd the practice of having a single day or place for exaltation, and not surprisingly many of his trips take place on Sunday mornings. Arguments aside, Beekman's writings and tours join those of other cyclists who propel the bicycle into an emerging era of secularization, trends influenced by many factors, including greater opportunities for travel. The principal thrust of his thought-clearing explorations is to instill greater awareness among readers about the role of modern science in establishing natural truths through "observation and experiment." The Great Blue Hill and its surrounding Blue Hills Reservation in Milton and Quincy, a large and very scenic land area acquired in 1894 by Boston's Metropolitan Park Commission, are the settings for one of his exploratory trips. Although Beekman's views of nature are from the vantage point of a bicycle, his writing could just as easily have contributed to any of that era's conservation journals, and he links cycling with the region's nascent environmentalism. His emphasis on practiced observation of one's surroundings also establishes a common ground with landscape historians.[31]

LAW Periodicals

The League of American Wheelmen also played a central role in advancing the literature of bicycle touring, but historians of American travel writing must sort through a complex series of titles to find articles. Between 1881 and 1883, the LAW maintained an informal agreement with the publishers of *Bicycling World*, which served as the organization's official journal and circulated league news. In May

1883, the league shifted allegiance to *The Wheel,* a New York journal established in 1880 and managed principally by Frederick Jenkins. In the following year, 1884, the league again changed course, choosing as its official paper *Amateur Athlete,* also published in New York and first printed in 1883 by Jenkins and a partner, Edwin Oliver. Format and control of that paper suffered a series of complicated changes, and in January 1885 the journal's title became *Cyclist and Athlete.* Editorial control of league news submitted to the paper during this period fell to Eugene Aaron in Philadelphia, but that arrangement also proved unsatisfactory. In July 1885, the league agreed with Aaron to publish a journal under its own masthead, *LAW Bulletin,* which remained in debt-burdened circulation until March 1888, when it became *Bicycling World and the LAW Bulletin.* By then, editorial control and publication already had shifted from Aaron to Abbot Bassett, who became the league's secretary–editor in January 1887 and who worked from Boston.[32]

Bassett played a pivotal role in cycling journalism, shaping it into a spirited venue for bicycle touring. He had joined the staff of *Bicycling World* in 1881, eventually sharing editorial duties with Josiah S. Dean before becoming principal editor. However, he grew weary of the journalistic smudges inserted by the magazine's owner, Edward Hodges, who had invested in the Overman Wheel Company. That concern had challenged the patents royalties demanded by the dominant Pope firm, and the two manufacturers became contentious litigants. Bassett quietly resigned in 1886 to establish his own Boston journal, *The Cycle,* which remained in publication until he transferred attention to *LAW Bulletin* in 1887.[33]

From its inception, the LAW promoted bicycle touring as one of its principal missions, and the evolving methods by which the league or its state divisions organized and managed the logistics of bicycle touring contribute to the broader history of packaged travel experiences by promoters such as Englishman Thomas Cook or his many competitors. Informally organized excursions, such as the Wheel Around the Hub in 1879, grew in size and complexity. In 1885, tourmaster Burley Ayers of Chicago supervised the Big Four Tour through New York and Canada, purposely dividing the 109 participants into four divisions (Chicago, Buffalo, New York, and Boston) and staggering each division on the road to facilitate pace of travel, prompt dining service, efficient baggage handling, pleasant company, and private accommodation—all without sacrificing social standing or the economy available to large groups.[34]

The following year, the league formally established a touring board and divided the country into four administrative regions, adding Europe as a fifth under the supervision of Joseph Pennell. Another league member, Frank A. Elwell from Portland, Maine, earlier had planned tours of Maine and Bermuda, and in 1889 he began organizing lengthy annual tours in Europe, which became popular enough to add a separate tour for ladies in 1892. Clergy also organized their own long-distance tours, pausing briefly to attend Sunday morning services as a group. Accounts of the league's many tours provided newsworthy content for its various journalistic outlets, and presumably the touring board influenced editorial staff in various ways. The league's devotion to publishing road books also reinforced this emphasis on touring.[35]

Fledgling journals—such as *Bicycling World*, *The Wheel*, *Amateur Athlete*, *Cyclist and Athlete*, and *The Cycle*—depended on news snippets as much as on travel literature, and publishers' efforts to secure contracts for reporting league affairs encouraged that trend. Among these LAW suitors and affiliates, *The Cycle* is especially important, because it introduced a column titled "From a Feminine Point of View," written under the pseudonym Daisie, who is Helen Drew Bassett, Abbot Bassett's wife. That column jumped from *The Cycle* to the *LAW Bulletin* as soon as Bassett began publishing the bulletin from his offices in Boston, and it continued for several years. Daisie's columns are often insightful, especially when she explains cycling's exploratory impulses: "I think we all keep to the good roads too much. We don't strike out into new territory, explore new fields of observation, try unfamiliar paths. I seldom go upon the road that I do not seek to find some new way to reach this or that point, and I have to thank this disposition for much that is rich in my experience."[36]

North Shore Tricyclists Daisie and Abbot Bassett participated in a series of annual tricycle tours organized by women, who initially planned to exclude men. The fall trips took place along the northerly shore of Massachusetts, and descriptions appeared in *The Cycle*, *LAW Bulletin*, *Outing*, *The Wheelwoman*, and *The Wheel and Cycling Trade Review*, as well as in local newspapers. Minna Caroline Smith, a staff writer for *Outing* who was just beginning a career as an author of books for young people, planned the first tour, inviting women from Boston and its suburbs to join her at Malden Square on a Thursday morning in October 1885. The group planned to travel by tricycle to Kettle Cove, a picturesque seventeenth-century fishing village in Gloucester that had been renamed Magnolia nine years before. Smith may have selected the destination after consulting an 1885 handbook published for touring cyclists, *In and Around Cape Ann* by John Webber Jr., an American consul to Britain's Cyclists' Touring Club. Webber devoted a chapter to Kettle Cove, titled "Saunterings at Magnolia," and concluded the work with a long list of the wheel*men* who had ventured to Gloucester and Cape Ann. Smith hoped to show female independence in an original manner: an exclusive procession of women-propelled machines wheeling through suburban and rural communities to the astonishment of the uninitiated.[37]

Although the women who replied were "wild to go," most agreed to the trip only if accompanied by husbands, brothers, or friends. Relenting, Smith and her cohorts decreed that only men who escorted a lady might participate, paying for the privilege by serving as mechanics or by "arranging all the details and liquidating the bills." Eight women and nine men began that year's thirty-three-mile tour, christened the "North Shore Tricycle Run." Traveling via an impressive display of tricycle and bicycle machinery, the travelers reached Salem by midday, posing on the common for a photograph after dinner. Although a few riders returned to

Boston that afternoon, including the Bassetts, most continued to Manchester-by-the-Sea to spend the night. The riders reached Kettle Cove by mid-morning on Friday, stopping at Willow Cottage (an inn frequented by artists)—only to find it closed. Gloucester and its seafood beckoned, five miles distant, and there the riders recovered at the Pavilion Hotel before returning to Boston by afternoon train or evening steamship.[38]

The North Shore tricyclists soon ventured over greater distances, lengthening their trips to four days and traveling beyond Gloucester into Rockport and Pigeon Cove, around Cape Ann, and as far north as Newburyport, roughly forty miles from Boston. Trip narratives by Smith and Daisie are valuable today as records of artfully conceived demonstrations about the utility of bicycles or tricycles as vehicles for women's independence, long before the safety-bicycle era, when that value became more widely recognized. The writings are also poignant stories of female companionship forged by zeal, stamina, and distance. Instructive for their descriptive content, the articles express recurring themes: reverence for panoramas of meadow-winding roads and distant sea, or the miles of uninterrupted, sundappled shade created by arching trees above a path through Essex Woods, all garnished by autumn foliage. Daisie proclaims the advantages of the wheel over rail, boat, and carriage, proffering: "To experience is to know. The half cannot be told." Readers also glimpse once-ordinary land features, including frequent roadside wells with pumps (as important to horses as to people), small market-farm plots of cabbages and rutabagas, a stone barn at Beaver Dam, and granite quarries in Rockport, which yielded stone for many of that era's architectural landmarks.[39]

The selection of Kettle Cove as the original destination is also significant, its modest historic name less appropriate to the residents of 1885 than the Magnolia plants that grow wild along that shore. Smith uses the old name possibly to appease her friend and companion cyclist, Mirah, to whom the village and its history are well known. Through Mirah, readers glimpse changes occurring as old and new societies overlap and chafe, the latter represented by summer residents drawn to the edges of Gloucester's artist communities. Mirah explains that she had studied with artist William Morris Hunt, who had maintained a studio at Kettle Cove before his death in 1879, and her desire to return to familiar places may have been an instrumental part of the tour's origins.[40]

Another aspect of the North Shore tours is especially important. On that first day in 1885, the cyclists who convened at Malden Square began the trip by wheeling through a portion of Middlesex Fells, a primeval region of broken-rock hills and woodlands. Decades before, as early as 1850, local citizens who roamed the Fells had begun seeking ways to protect the area, eventually forming the Middlesex Fells Association. Sylvester Baxter actively had encouraged preservation of the Fells, and by 1894 (the year that the Metropolitan Park Commission finally acquired the land), the public already owned large tracts. The cyclists also traveled through Lynn, where members of one of the region's early hiking clubs, The Exploring Circle, had begun rambling through what is now Lynn Woods, documenting its flora and natural history at about the same time that residents of Medford, Malden, and Stoneham were discovering Middlesex Fells.[41]

Minna Smith begins her story of the excursion with a plea to preserve Middlesex Fells, and by doing so she underscores the critical relationship between awareness of place, the strong sentiment of moral wrong at the possibility of losing a valued resource, and the means by which awareness of place becomes possible. Smith and her companions thus joined a growing body of men and women who roamed New England's woods and mountains during the late nineteenth and early twentieth centuries and who formed the roots of a conservation ethic that continues to shape outlook in the region today. The significant distinction is that Smith and Daisie are better able to extend that awareness of place to built and cultural environments because they ride tricycles or bicycles. Baxter is also part of that nexus, and in 1892 he penned an essay titled "Social and Economic Influence of the Bicycle," echoing thoughts expressed by Daisie, Pratt, Bassett, Beekman, and others:

The educational influence [of the bicycle] is very great upon physical and mental development. It quickens the perceptive faculties of young people and makes them more alert. They see more of the world and are broadened by the contact. While otherwise they would seldom go beyond strolling distance from their homes, on the bicycle they are constantly roaming throughout many surrounding towns, beholding fresh and varied scenes, becoming familiar with whole counties, and in vacation time not infrequently exploring several states. Such experiences produce growth in energy, self-reliance, and independence in character, and make a more complete individuality. The moral effect is no less marked.[42]

New Orleans to Boston Readers of *LAW Bulletin* during its autonomous years from 1885 to 1888 found a mix of news about the league's principal activities: wheelmen's rights, advocacy for good roads, clubs, racing events, and touring. Articles in this last category are sometimes cursory travel summaries that lack the sense of discovery that distinguishes much of cycling's best touring literature. Yet the journal published a few notable articles, including a serialized account of long-distance travel by bicycle, in four parts during October and November of 1886. The essays describe a thirty-day, 1,788-mile journey by three league members— C. M. Fairchild, Harry Fairfax, and A. M. Hill, the author—from New Orleans to Boston to attend the league meet in late May 1886. By then, Thomas Stevens already had crossed the country and had begun his trip around the world, but the bulletin's editors distinguished Stevens from the New Orleans cyclists, calling them ordinary businessmen riding for recreation rather than records and selflessly intent upon introducing cycling to the extreme South.[43]

In the genre of travel literature by cyclists, the series is exceptional for its candid record of travail: dismal swamps; drenching rains; floods; wind; physical and mental fatigue; hunger; chafed, blistered, and swollen feet; headers; cramps, fainting spells, and injuries; railroad trestles of dizzying height with cross-ties spaced eighteen inches apart; mechanical failures; and tortuous hills and roads requiring lengthy walks. If visions of sightseeing initially color the cyclists' expectations, then the first three days of travel soon change that outlook. Even the romantic point of departure, Elysian Fields Street, seems to darken as the three riders turn onto the tracks of the Louisville and Nashville Railroad and disappear into the gloomy swamps, sea-marshes, and bayous between New Orleans and Mobile, Alabama. Self-doubts gather during those first three days, and more than once the riders question whether they will reach their objective.[44]

Yet adversity has a way of hardening cyclists to overland travel, and the riders are driven forward by the promise of good roads in the Shenandoah Valley. Even before they reach that Eden, however, the "grand, wild, and picturesque" scenery of the Blue Ridge Mountains dispels any lingering agony, and their mood lightens. Hill (who at thirty-eight years of age is much older than his twenty-one- and nineteen-year-old companions) offers detailed descriptions of both hardships and heartening events, including celebratory receptions and brass-band serenades in small towns where residents had learned of the trip. Hill is also genuinely moved by the generosity of a poor farming family in Georgia's pine woods, who possess neither combs nor candles but who willingly sleep on bare boards so that the travelers might enjoy the family's one luxury: a feather bed. To Hill's great credit, no trace of condescension sullies his narratives.[45]

Historians seeking perspective on American places also will find mention of land features such as shell roads; Swiss-style cottages near Mount Airy, South Carolina; the ruined dams and broken locks of the James River and Kanawha Canal, which give its valley a "deserted and mournful appearance"; the magnificent hundred-mile straightaway of the Winchester Pike in Virginia, manageable for its entire length without dismount, a decade before John Carrington and Philip Bruce traveled the same road; and prosperous farms beyond Gettysburg where Hill declares it "difficult to find a ten-acre tract of waste land."[46]

Good Roads   The LAW again changed journalistic course in January 1892, four years after resuming its affiliation with *Bicycling World*, and began publishing a separate monthly, *Good Roads*, via the league's Road Improvement Bureau established the year before. Edited initially by Isaac Potter from offices in New York and underwritten in part by donations from Albert Pope, the journal advanced the broader strategy of seeking state legislation for highway improvement programs. Previous efforts had come to naught, because rural farmers declined to pay for better roads to aid urban cyclists or to relinquish control over local highways to state governments with similarly taxing results. In response, the league revised its strategy and launched an educational campaign, concealing its role by paying for circulars distributed through the Department of Agriculture and by editorial orchestration of *Good Roads*. Bicycle touring literature is generally absent from that inadequately funded magazine, although articles touting the value of side-paths encouraged travel indirectly.[47]

LAW Bulletin and Good Roads   By 1894, various difficulties, including the league's swelling membership, had placed strains on the agreement with *Bicycling World*, and the two again severed ties, with the league assigning publication of the weekly *LAW Bulletin* to the Bearings Publishing Company in Chicago in March of that year, under the editorial management of George K. Barrett. That arrangement also proved troublesome, and in 1895 the league merged its two journals under one weekly title, *LAW Bulletin and Good Roads*, placing it under the editorial control of Sterling Elliott and Abbot Bassett in Boston. Nixon Waterman from Chicago joined as an associate editor later that year.[48]

The league's journalistic somersaults reflected internal struggles encompassing an array of political, regional, social, racial, and economic concerns unrelated to bicycle touring, which remained central to league activities. Although the influence of the league's touring committee over editorial policy during that period is unclear, the safety bicycle's astonishing rise to popularity by 1895 had presented editors with a clear directive. Accounts of bicycle travel thus became a mainstay for *LAW Bulletin and Good Roads* between 1894 and 1899, when the league again changed course and its journalistic efforts began to splinter.

Articles are descriptive and present consistent themes, but they are also succinct: many recount short day trips—for example, "A Decoration Day Run to Babylon, Long Island" in 1896. In this category of half-holiday touring, a concise 1898 article both written and illustrated by W. E. Miles, "Ten Times across the Charles River," is exemplary. Miles uses bridge crossings to chart a thematic course through Boston's westerly suburbs and to offer opportunities for views of the river corridor. His descriptive narrative and sketches—shipyard wharves, boat houses, the Watertown arsenal, an aging paper mill with ivy-covered granite walls, and the rubble-stone tower standing in Newton's Norumbega Park—entice exploration even today. He also offers aesthetic critique, suggesting that the utilitarian character of bridges falls far short of Boston's architectural standards, and he alludes to an emerging debate among engineers about that very topic. As well, he foresees that the river will become the soul of an extensive park system, and he proposes a cycle path for each bank.[49]

Elliott's Magazine Miles's article appeared in the spring of 1898, the year that membership in the LAW peaked at 103,000 and began a steep decline (almost 98 percent by 1905). Such a drastic change forced reassessment of core concerns, and the league's bulletin ceased circulation briefly during July 1899, succumbing to the challenges of producing a weekly magazine. In August, Sterling Elliot seized the upper hand and, disregarding his contract with the LAW to publish a weekly, launched his own short-lived monthly, *Elliott's Magazine*. Elliott formatted the journal primarily as a travel geographic, but he also incorporated *LAW Bulletin and Good Roads* into its pages as a separate department, numbered identically and with continued editorial management by Elliott and Waterman, with Bassett's assistance regarding league news.[50]

Elliott thus joined Bassett as an influential figure in guiding the direction of cycling's travel literature. Versatile and imaginative, Elliott became a skilled machinist who manufactured his own inventions, and he established the Elliott Hickory Cycle Company, with a factory behind his home on the Charles River in Watertown. He also served as the league president in 1896, and his magazine likely represented an effort to pursue his own journalistic leanings, free from interference by the league's executive committee. For the first time in league publications, Elliott drew a clear line of demarcation between touring and league news, giving emphasis to the former in a polished format at least approaching that established by Pope and McClure in *The Wheelman*.[51]

LAW Magazine *Elliott's Magazine* remained in circulation for less than a year, and in June 1900 the league resumed publication of its own monthly, *LAW Magazine*, awarding the publishing contract to Cleveland's Emil Grossman, publisher of the *Cycling Gazette*. Charles W. Mears, chief consul for the league's Ohio Division, became editor (with assistance by Bassett), and the subtitle "Good Roads" appeared only on the editorial masthead. Mears reintroduced serialized accounts of extended bicycle tours, including a lengthy, two-part series by Louis Geyler, "Summer Vacations Awheel." Geyler travels throughout eastern states, but is especially at home on Long Island, a cyclist's paradise rich in maritime history and by then traversed by an extensive network of bicycle sidepaths. Geyler's advice is to avoid schedules that rob trips of pleasure, stopping instead to explore wherever curiosity beckons.[52]

Good Roads Magazine Emphasis on road improvements steadily guided editorial direction, pushing travel and touring aside, and in June 1901 the journal's name changed to *Good Roads Magazine,* a new series distinguished only slightly in title from the league's earlier monthly, *Good Roads.* One month later, publication shifted to New York, and Hrolf Wisby replaced Mears as managing editor in August. Although token articles about bicycle travel continued, Wisby sought to unite the various organizations concerned about highway improvement and to solidify the journal's role as the principal organ representing those interests.[53]

By that time, columns about motorcycles and automobiles had announced the arrival of a new era in touring journalism. Elliott began publishing articles about automobiles in September 1899, and Wisby created the "Automobile Touring Department" for the journal's November issue of 1901. By January 1902, Bassett conceded that "a frost has come upon all things cycling," and a decade later he acknowledged that "touring awheel has in a large measure gone out," made easier by automobiles in a society "more inclined to ease than to exercise."[54]

Bassett's Scrap Book Although *Good Roads Magazine* remained in circulation until the end of 1907, the league officially shifted its allegiance to *Bassett's Scrap Book* in 1903, a "magazine for riders of the wheel" edited by Bassett and produced by the LAW Publishing Company, also owned and managed by Bassett. By then, the league had lost nearly all its once-considerable sway, and membership continued to dwindle, eventually coalescing into a coterie of veterans: the Old Guard. In January 1914, the title changed slightly to *Official Bulletin and Scrap Book of the League of American Wheelmen,* and each October Bassett recounted the yearly Wheel Around the Hub tour, repeated in 1883 and 1884, and then resumed in 1890, eventually becoming the "Wheel About the Hub" when the Boston Bicycle Club changed the original route. In a 1911 recollection, Bassett believed those early expeditions captured the essence of bicycle touring: "In the old days we used to urge riding with a purpose; and a worthy purpose used to be exploring new territory, visiting places of historic interest, investigating nature's wonders and secrets."[55]

The LAW's complicated journalistic forays and internal woes should not obscure one of the league's key contributions: the consistent record of articles about bicycle travel. Although the inspirational quality of that writing and its illustration fluctuates, criticism by editors of *Bicycling World* that the league should have done more to promote touring during cycling's surging years—thus

FIGURES 2.6 AND 2.7

Country Head-Quarters (Cobb's Tavern), a wood engraving by H. E. Sylvester after a painting or drawing by Edmund Garrett for *The Wheelman* (March 1883). Garrett and Hassam were colleagues, and with Sylvester they established a high standard for illustration in Pope's journal. Cobb's Tavern is located in East Sharon, Massachusetts, on the ancient Bay Road linking Boston with Narragansett Bay. The inn became a regular stopping point for the Wheel Around the Hub, and later for the Wheel About the Hub after the original route changed. Long after the tavern ceased to be open to the public, its owners generously greeted travelers, each of whom signed a registry. The building survives today as shown, and it has been documented by the Historic American Building Survey.

giving the industry greater stability—is unjustified. Even during the first years of the twentieth century, when *LAW Magazine* and *Good Roads Magazine* began emphasizing highway improvements, readers found enticements to country riding in some of that era's best writing about the sidepath campaign, even as Bassett lamented cycling's demise.[56]

During cycling's waning years, articles about bicycle touring also mark a brief period of transition during which automobile and motorcycle touring increased. Ultimately, those methods of mobility redefined travel literature, but articles about both bicycle and motor travel coincided, providing opportunity for comparison by those who study motor travel and the roots of its influence on culture, literature, and landscape.

The Wheel, The Wheel and Recreation, *and* The Wheel and Cycling Trade Review

Another journal of long duration, New York's *Wheel and Cycling Trade Review*, rivaled Boston's *Bicycling World* and offered an abundance of well-written and illustrated articles about travel by bicycle, most of them the legacy of editor and publisher Frances P. Prial. Frederick Jenkins, Prial's predecessor, introduced the fortnightly paper *The Wheel* in September 1880, and during the following spring and summer he published several articles about touring, mostly short day trips by club members but also a ten-day sojourn in the Catskill Mountains by Jenkins and a companion from the Manhattan Bicycle Club. During the summer and fall of 1881, the paper also carried a seven-part series tracking the progress of two wheelmen, Charles E. Campbell and R. W. Parmenter, who had traveled more than one thousand miles in August and September of the preceding year— from Lima in northwestern Ohio to Boston. Campbell, who authors the series using the pseudonym Old Exodus and who compares himself to Don Quixote, approaches the journey with a spirit of adventure and, christening his wheel Rosinante, is content to roll casually along. Other than occasional headers, an axle damaged during a fall into a thistle patch, cloudbursts, and abominable roads, the two proclaim good fortune, and Campbell satisfies himself about the practicality of his Columbia bicycle—a reliable machine that survives the "rough and tumble trip" in good condition.[57]

Campbell's articles, among the country's first long-distance tours chronicled by a cycling journal, carefully trace the pair's route from town to town and provide careful descriptions of roads, but he focuses more on people than on cultural landmarks, and the two wheelmen are confronted by public astonishment at nearly every crossroads. Very few people living in rural America in 1880 knew of bicycles—fewer still had seen one—and Campbell revisits that theme throughout the journey. He also discovers what other cyclists who followed would soon encounter, namely the poor surface of the Erie Canal's towpath. However, in 1880 cyclists had not yet incurred the wrath of canal society, and Campbell answers question after question from barge owners and their families. At Little Falls, New

York, Campbell is mesmerized by the vertical rock walls and closely spaced tracks of four railroad corridors, feeling emotions similar to what another cross-country explorer, George Thayer, would experience six years later.

In 1882, the American division of England's Bicycle Touring Club gave *The Wheel* a boost by naming it the club's official organ, but momentum at the journal may have slowed during a complicated period between 1882 and 1886, when the magazine changed course several times. With editorial assistance from Charles Pratt, the journal shifted to weekly publication in October 1882, and by the end of that year Jenkins had established a partnership with Edwin Oliver, a business manager. Circulation probably increased during 1883, when *The Wheel* became the LAW's official journal, but Jenkins and Oliver dissolved their agreement at about the time of their break with the league in 1884. Jenkins then handed the management reins to Prial during the spring of 1885. Prial guided the acquisition of another journal, *Recreation*, leading to publication under the combined title *Wheel and Recreation* by December 1886. Continuing disputes about ownership of the parent company led to litigation, leaving Prial with no opportunity to purchase clear title when his lease expired, and he severed his connections with the concern, launching the first issue of *Wheel and Cycling Trade Review* from offices on Park Row in lower Manhattan in March 1888. The New York Division of the LAW promptly designated the journal as its official organ, and by 1892 Prial had established a western office in Chicago.[58]

Among cycling's many journals, Prial's publication is commendable for the quality and variety of its content, and from December 1886 to September 1900 (when *Bicycling World and Motorcycle Review* purchased *The Wheel* and moved to New York) Prial guided his paper capably, balancing club events, racing, trade news, editorial opinion, and touring. Emphasis on touring literature as a means to attract readers became evident soon after the paper's new start as *Wheel and Recreation*, when, in the spring of 1887, he negotiated an agreement to publish letters from George Nellis, tracking Nellis's attempt to break the cross-country record of Thomas Stevens.[59]

Whether heading from coast to coast, from city to city, or to other distant places, wheelmen who traveled long distances bolstered the subscription revenue of cycling magazines. Yet Prial wisely offered a blend of articles about places of local or regional interest, and metropolitan New York provided nearly endless opportunities for exploration. Stories recount trips by cyclists who rediscover forgotten fishing villages on Long Island Sound, who aspire to scenic century or half-century day excursions through the Hudson River Valley, or who embark on week-long vacation tours with destinations beyond immediate horizons—the Wallkill or Ramapo hills in northern New Jersey and southern New York. Much of the touring literature in *The Wheel* is valuable as evidence of cyclists' exploratory zeal and propensity for travel and also as a record of once-colorful places that either have vanished altogether—cognitively as well as physically—or are unrecognizable beneath layers of generational change.[60]

In the spring of 1888, an anonymous author (possibly Prial) and his artist companion departed on a four-hour ride through Mount Vernon and Port Chester into Greenwich, Connecticut, on their way—via Mianus village—to a tiny, land-locked harbor known to locals as Tomac-on-the-Sound. Even then, the lobster and eel pots, piles of oyster shells, clam rakes, old wharves, and general debris could not conceal a declining shore industry, and the village's "old tars" had become more farmer–fishermen than sailors. Yet pride of craftsmanship in their sound-going fisher boats remained apparent to both author and artist. Diminutive sketches accompany the narrative, titled "A-Wheel to Tomac," and enhance the article's contribution to travel literature. Although illustrations and photographs in *The Wheel* were limited in both quality and frequency during the high-wheel era, Prial later employed Arthur Merrick as a staff artist (luring him from *The Bearings* in Chicago), and the journal's visual appeal improved measurably.[61]

Keeping pace with *Bicycling World*, *The Cycle*, and *LAW Bulletin*, Prial offered a women's column, "For the Ladies," and Psyche became New York's best-known pseudonymous cycling journalist, joining Marguerite, Daisie, and Merrie Wheeler, who write from the Boston area. Marguerite was Maggie Kirkwood, an accomplished century rider from Maplewood, a community in the Boston suburb of Malden, and Merrie Wheeler was Mary Sargent Hopkins, but the identity of Psyche, the goddess of the soul in Greek mythology, remained a mystery in human form. Both Marguerite and Psyche were frequent contributors to *The Wheel*, often engaging in polite responses to each other's columns and discussing a range of topics, including proper riding posture (sit up straight, elbows in), dress guards, brakes, crank length, and the virtues or shortcomings of specific types of tricycles and bicycles. Responses to some of Daisie's columns also surfaced, and exchanges of letters also chronicled the shift from tricycles to safety bicycles for ladies, beginning in 1889.[62]

Following the arrival of safety bicycles, Prial introduced a greater regimen to his journal's travel department. One compilation of tours recalls the favored routes of "old time wheelmen," who lacked the advantage of good roads. The series matter-of-factly identifies day trips by number—for instance, "Route No. 5. Red Bank and Long Branch, New Jersey"—and provides very specific directions, including schedules and fares for ferries, steamships, and trains; mileage; road surfaces; and various points of interest. New Yorkers heading for the ocean at Long Branch in 1892 travel through Monmouth County, where fruit and truck farms prosper; ride along scenic Rumson Neck Road to Penny Bridge at Sea Bright; and pass through small seaside villages, including Galilee and Low Moor. Returning by a different route, cyclists veer away from Rumson Road and ride toward the village of Oceanic, there crossing a bridge leading to Navesink, and climbing to Navesink Heights to view the lower bay of New York and Staten Island. Below that overlook, at Atlantic Highlands, cyclists could sail home aboard the steamer Sandy Hook and dock at the foot of Rector Street on Manhattan's Lower West Side.[63]

By the 1895 season, Prial had modified the day-trip format into a more expansive and polished version of touring literature. Authors of these articles focused on well-defined regions and suggested that cyclists would need an entire season to explore such areas thoroughly. They also contrived titles—for example, "Beautiful Westchester County," "Rambling through the Ramapo," "In the Saw Mill River Valley," and "Owed to Jersey"—intended to entice hesitant travelers beyond the margins of day trips. Other tours are organized with specific themes in mind and stay close to home—for example, the Claremont Hotel and Inwood Hills on the northern stretches of Riverside Drive, or rural Bronx and its villages of Kingsbridge, South Mount Vernon, West Farms, and East Chester, where historic St. Paul's Church and its ancient churchyard predate the Revolutionary War. Maps and photographs supplement Merrick's sketches of landmarks, and narratives extol the historic as well as the picturesque: village gates, roadside inns, churches and rectories, colonial-period houses, park-like estates, stonewalls or ramshackle fences, bridges, ferry slips, and unusual natural features, such as split-rocks.[64]

Among many such examples, an anonymous 1896 article titled simply "Staten Island" is noteworthy, because it exemplifies this enhanced format and also underscores another theme central to much of Prial's touring literature: encouraging cyclists not to overlook the familiar or the nearby. The tour begins with a voyage from South Ferry in Manhattan to St. George on the island's northerly tip. Wheeling along the Richmond Terrace Road, travelers soon reach Sailor's Snug Harbor on the North Shore Road, a home for aging sailors that today is a National Historic Landmark District overlooking the Kill Van Kull. A row of five Greek Revival buildings that date from the 1830s, including a masterpiece by one of America's very influential architects, Minard Lafever, continue to anchor the district. The tour route then returns to St. George and continues along the Shore Road past the Marine Hospital and Fort Wadsworth, offering views of Lower New York Bay and the Narrows before reaching a spur leading to the Richmond and Amboy roads. Those highways traverse the island north to south and offer frequent roadside stopping points, including the mysterious Black Horse Tavern at New Dorp.

At the island's southerly tip in Tottenville, about fifteen miles from St. George, the tour reaches the water's edge at Ward's Point, site of the Billopp House, a seventeenth-century stone manor house that sheltered peace negotiations during the Revolutionary War, giving the building its current name: Conference House. From that point, cyclists could turn northerly again along Fresh Kills Road to Rossville, and from there continue toward the old hamlets of Green Ridge, Springville, and Bull's Head, crossing Fresh Kills Bridge on the way and passing near an abandoned tidal mill, picturesque in its decrepitude. Alternatively, cyclists could board a ferry at Tottenville, cross Staten Island Sound within sight of its ship graveyard, and dock at Perth Amboy in New Jersey, where tour routes continued—including the ride to Red Bank.[65]

Prial also publicized touring in Europe, and he befriended Frank Elwell, who with partner H. Stephen Higgens had become an accomplished tourmaster.

Elwell's travels through Ireland, England, and France in 1889 garnered extensive coverage, and in 1892 Elwell collaborated with fellow Portland cyclist and friend John Calvin Stevens, a regionally accomplished architect, to organize a fifty-day tour through France for architects and architectural students. The travelers began their voyage late in July 1892, eager to sketch France's cathedral monuments, villages of low stone houses with tile roofs, vineyards, or occasional windmills, and their excursions are described in a five-part series that started in September and ended in October of that year.[66]

Other Journals

The literature of bicycle touring is not confined to four stems of cycling periodicals or their branches: *The Wheelmen, Outing and The Wheelman,* and *Outing; American Bicycling Journal* and *Bicycling World; LAW Bulletin,* with its various roots and offshoots; and *The Wheel, Wheel and Recreation,* and *The Wheel and Cycling Trade Review.* Rather, these are but a few of the numerous publications that catered to a field of enormous popular and economic interest. Many journals, such as the *Lake Shore Wheelman,* a semimonthly published in Erie, Pennsylvania, were short-lived; a few, including *The Wheelwoman,* published by Mary Sargent Hopkins, are scarce. Mergers, acquisitions, and changes in title also add complexity, and the titles or stated editorial intentions are not always reliable indicators of the inclusion of travel writing or its locale.[67]

Some publishers represented the LAW's state divisions, and editors emulated the format for league journals. The monthly *Cleveland Mercury* belongs in this category, first published in 1884 by the Cleveland Bicycle Club as the official organ of the league's Ohio Division. Its editors gathered news about league events, club activities, race results, passable travel routes, the condition of Ohio's roads, and occasional articles about travel.[68]

Other journals grew from local interest in cycling and expanded to regional or national circulation as publishers pursued subscribers and advertisers or promoted extravaganzas. In Massachusetts, the monthly *Springfield Wheelmen's Gazette* is notable. The gazette was first published in 1883 by the Springfield Bicycle Club and one of its founders, Henry Ducker, to advertise the club's fall tournament at Hampden Park. *Springfield Wheelmen's Gazette* briefly became the country's most widely disseminated cycling journal, with circulation exceeding that of *LAW Bulletin,* and many issues offered well-written articles about bicycle travel, including several by Karl Kron.[69]

Although much more limited in reach, the monthly *American Wheelman* illustrates the ties between cycling journalism and enthusiasm for cycling in specific cities, but also the challenges of tracing ownership and editorial control. The journal originated in St. Louis in 1885, with emphasis on racing and touring—more a country newspaper than a trade circular. By 1891, the title had shifted to Buffalo, an axis for clubs, racing, and manufacturing, where a local cycling enthusiast, Dai H. Lewis, served as editor. By 1897, *The American Wheelman Annual* had found a home in New York City, circulated by the American Wheelman Publishing Company and managed by Henry L. Saltonstall.[70]

Still other publishers invested in the bicycle trade, appealing to manufacturers and retailers, who sought information about the rapidly changing technology of bicycles. Journals such as *The Cyclist* (later *American Cyclist)* and *The Bearings* (which merged with *Cycling Life* and *The Referee* to become *Cycle Age and Trade Review*) are part of this group, and among owners of these periodicals the emphasis on bicycle touring fluctuated.[71]

Editors of *The Bearings*, published in Chicago, tried to achieve broad appeal and employed illustrator Charles Cox to enliven articles about travel. Cox and Edward Elwell Jr. collaborated to provide more detailed accounts of the architectural tour in France organized by Frank Elwell and John Calvin Stevens in 1892, published as a series in July 1893, with photographs accompanying Cox's sketches. Nor did *Bearings'* editors neglect women riders. During the spring of 1894, the journal tracked the progress of two sisters-in-law, Mrs. Louis Lesure and Mrs. G. H. Chase, who pedaled more than four hundred miles from Philadelphia to Boston, stopping to sightsee along the way.[72]

Cyclists' travel writing is also found in unlikely places. For instance, a young architect, Francis H. Bent, embarked on a solo, six-month trip through Italy, France, and England during the spring and summer of 1895, principally for architectural study. However, he also sought to show how cheaply one could travel once railroad fares had been eliminated. His twelve-part series appeared in *Engineering Record* and prompted a faculty member at MIT, Professor E. B. Homer, to conduct architectural summer school in a similar manner the following year.[73]

Nor did the journalism of bicycle touring end with arrival of the automobile. The editors of *Bicycling World and Motorcycle Review* continued to offer travel writing by cyclists on occasion, and a new monthly circular, *Bicycle News*, began distribution in 1915 from the offices of the ICL Publishing Company in Newark. Although the paper represented the Cycle Dealers Association and thus catered to merchants, editors hoped to spark a renaissance in cycling. The association's traveling representative, Fred St. Onge, headed a campaign to sell one million bicycles during national bicycle week.[74]

During the early years of the twentieth century, the Century Road Club of America and its sibling, the Century Road Club Association, maintained the tradition of long-distance travel by bicycle, but without the exploratory spirit and sense of discovery that had defined overland bicycle touring before motor travel. One of the club's Traveling Centurions, Fred I. Perrault, penned a short article for *Bicycle News* that described a six-hundred-mile vacation trip in New Jersey, Pennsylvania, and Maryland. Although Perrault pauses long enough to describe some of what he sees, and although his commitment to the bicycle as an important means of travel is clear, mileage and destination are the dominant objectives, not the journey itself.[75]

CHAPTER THREE

Imagining Place

The imagery and cartography that depicts, interprets, and locates the places of cyclists' peregrinations is integral to the experience of travel by bicycle and to cyclists' role as late nineteenth-century explorers of cultural and natural geography. That imagery takes numerous forms, including illustrations (through any of several means of graphic reproduction), photography, and maps, particularly those contained in LAW road books and annotated by carefully described routes and landmarks.

Cycling's pictorial and cartographical record of travel becomes significant in many interrelated ways: stimulating public interest and instilling greater awareness of the relationships between travel and place; furthering and enlarging Americans' changing perceptions of visual qualities in landscapes; strengthening ethical ties between cycling and the country's conservationists; extending that ethic to cultural as well as natural resources; contributing to the rise of amateur photography; participating in the rapidly changing technology that was then occurring for transposing visual image to printed form for mass distribution; inviting qualitative comparisons of alternative pictorial mediums in the context of landscape and place and, in that same context, offering occasion to consider illustrator as artist; creating opportunities for the introduction or continued study of the many artists who were also cyclists; and inviting similar study of cycling's capable mapmakers.

Cycling's Wood-Engraved Illustrations

Among the varying pictorial modes employed to portray cyclists' impressions of American places, the journalistic illustrations reproduced from wood-block engravings are especially successful at transporting cycling's readers to imagined places. Wood engraving is a line medium, and cuts produce a white line on a black background. The engraver's resources are black and white: the black line and white line and the black dot and white pick. That such complex visual images can be created from those devices is one of the medium's most fascinating aspects. Ultimately, the success of imagery depended heavily on the union of artist, engraver, and printer, each with an appreciation for the skill of drawing, an instinct for composition, a sense of line, a feel for contrast—especially light and shadow, and the ability to vary intermediate tones or grays. Especially skilled wood engravers also could achieve spontaneity through the use of very fine lines.[1]

During the late 1870s and early 1880s, when cycling journals first circulated, American popular literature was already in the midst of dynamic expansion, stimulated by industry and an increasingly literate middle class. Illustration began to play a central role in that journalistic expansion. Although these developments occurred first in Europe, Englishman Frank Leslie, an engraver who headed the pictorial department of the *London Illustrated News*, immigrated to America, and in December 1855 launched *Frank Leslie's Illustrated Newspaper*, a New York weekly that transformed America's budding popular press. In January

1857, the Harper family, whose initial 1850 serial, *Harper's New Monthly Magazine*, solicited a more cosmopolitan constituency, established *Harper's Weekly Journal of Civilization* to compete for Leslie's middle-class clientele. By necessity, later journals incorporated pictorial content into editorial strategy. Among these journals was *Scribner's Monthly Illustrated Magazine*, first issued in November 1870 but succeeded in 1881 by *The Century Illustrated Monthly Magazine* under new ownership and distinguished from *Scribner's Magazine*, a separate monthly that began circulation in January 1887. In addition, New York's heavily illustrated *Daily Graphic*, founded in 1872 but short-lived, turned to photoengraving as an inexpensive way to extend pictorial news to daily circulation.[2]

The advent of cycling periodicals coincided precisely with the peak of American wood-engraved illustration, a success gained by refinements introduced to achieve faithful interpretation of important works of art into black and white equivalents. The earliest advances included the use of end grains in hardwoods, such as boxwood; sophisticated cutting tools that produced delicate lines; the protection of wood blocks by molds with thin copper surfaces—a process called electroplating; and improved paper quality. Photoengraving, the method of transferring an image of original art (whether a pen and ink drawing or a painting) directly onto a wood block through a photographic negative, expanded the medium, and a special union of artist and engraver ensued, comprising America's New School of wood engraving. Artists who formerly produced their art on blocks of wood in preparation for the engraver no longer faced the prospect of losing that art during the engraving process, and both artist and engraver could, upon completion of the illustration, turn to the original work to assess the engraver's interpretation. Thus, skilled artists began to look more favorably upon illustration, creating opportunities for artist, engraver, and publisher alike.[3]

Periodicals such as *The Wheelman*, the editors of which hoped to capture the experience of travel by bicycle, benefited directly from the acclaim surrounding the collaborative process required for wood engraving. In addition to employing staff artists, engravers, and printers, publishing firms hired special artists, a title for illustrators who also served as field journalists, recording events accurately with both sketches and notes and then preparing written reports. In many cases, the writing abilities of these special artists also strengthened their powers of observation. Staff artists or draftsmen subsequently transferred the sketches of special artists onto wood blocks in reverse, usually with the aid of a mirror, and completed the drawings in the process. Engravers then added their artistry before delivering blocks to printers, who controlled print quality by adjusting the force of impression required to achieve varying tones, by properly applying ink, and by the quality of the paper. The published images often included the signature or initials of both the original artist and the engraver.[4]

Engravers and artists jointly proclaimed the value of art through the popular press, particularly the Harper and Scribner publishing houses. For *Harper's*, Charles Parsons headed an art department that included Winslow Homer,

Howard Pyle, Frederick Remington, and William Allen Rogers, among others. At *Scribner's*, Alexander Drake assembled a similarly talented staff of artists. A coterie of exceptionally skilled wood engravers formed, leading to the founding of the American Society of Wood Engravers, the members of which included Timothy Cole, J. Friedrich Jungling, and Gustav Kruell. Capitalizing on the recognition being given to America's engravers, *Scribner's* and *The Century* sponsored competitions for students of the wood engraver's art in 1880 and 1881 and then published the winning entries with editorial critique. Thus, when *The Wheelman Illustrated* began circulation in 1882 it was perfectly timed to take advantage of those events.[5]

Yet graphic reproduction rapidly evolved during the decade of the 1880s, entering a transitional phase that culminated with conversion to photographic halftones, which largely had superseded wood engraving by the early 1890s. Cycling publications remained in circulation throughout the period of transition and the eventual conversion to photography, and in turn contributed to this period by providing a forum in which alternative methods of graphic reproduction could be displayed, often simultaneously in a single issue. Today, those illustrations provide an ideal opportunity to compare and contrast the visual qualities of each method of reproduction, illuminating the ability of wood-engraved pictorials to convey cyclists' sense of awareness for their surroundings, to capture the spirit of travel by bicycle, and to transport viewers into cyclists' exploratory realms, particularly when measured against weak halftone reproductions.

As mechanical methods began to dominate illustration, the distinctive and fragile quality of wood-engraved images suffered in several ways. With increasing competition among publishers, emphasis on reducing costs forced all concerned to work in haste against time, creating sharp divisions of labor. Staff artists became redundant, forcing special artists to furnish completed drawings and further eroding collaborative spirit. Although artists could now produce their work in larger scale—relying on photoengravers to reduce the size—the middle tints, obscure grays, and pale grays merged during that reduction, and the bold clearness and brightness that distinguished the best wood-engraved illustrations disappeared. The smoothly surfaced paper required for photographic halftones also eroded the inherent quality of wood engravings.[6]

As a consequence, wood-engraved images represented only a small portion of the illustrations appearing in cycling's journals. Instead, other less-expensive line mediums, such as etching and drypoint, became far more common. In contrast to wood engraving, these other line mediums produce black lines on a white background, achieved by any of several incising processes that use metal plates. Photoengraving also facilitated the transposition of drawings onto metal plates, and artists skilled in pen and ink or etching techniques sparked readers' imagination as well. Although Joseph Pennell marveled at the skills of wood engravers, he conceded that photoengraving reproduced an artist's etching more accurately than a wood engraving.[7]

Awareness of the overlapping methods of illustration employed during cycling's ascendancy adds to our understanding of cycling's contributions to landscape-related studies and illuminates the murky domain between artist and illustrator. Many of the artists who contributed to cycling imagery established mastery in several techniques, improving their understanding of the subtleties inherent in each.

Two of cycling's most important illustrators and authors, Frank Hamilton Taylor and Joseph Pennell, invite comparison. Taylor, born in Rochester, New York, in 1846, established a career as a special artist in Philadelphia following the Civil War. Especially skilled with pen and ink and watercolor, Taylor gained similar proficiency with lithography before establishing a printing and publishing business in 1873 with engraver Ferdinand Smith. Taylor also began working for New York's *Daily Graphic*, heading the art department of that newspaper's Philadelphia bureau, and in 1876, the firm of Taylor & Smith demonstrated photolithography at the Philadelphia Centennial Exposition. Taylor and Pennell first met at that exposition, at which Pennell, then a student, tried to bluff his way among other special artists and was rescued from embarrassment by Taylor.[8]

Following the demise of the *Daily Graphic*, Taylor continued freelance work for various journals and newspapers, including *Frank Leslie's, Harper's Weekly, Harper's Monthly*, and the *Philadelphia Public Ledger*, where he served as art director. He traveled extensively, gaining the respect of the very gifted coterie of artists at *Harper's*. A capable writer and reporter as well as illustrator, Taylor established a reputation as one of the country's most successful special artists, and his travels led to the publication of tourist guide books. When travel became a burden, he turned to writing and illustrating historical works, many of them about Philadelphia and its important institutions and architecture, and he often expressed concern about changes to the city's cultural foundations. In 1920, members of The Philadelphia Sketch Club elected Taylor, then seventy-eight years of age, as their president, a testament to his artistic skills. Pennell also became a member and eventually its president.[9]

Taylor's biographer, Nancy Gustke, notes that despite being well-known during his lifetime Taylor suffered from the same after-death obscurity that shadowed many of the country's special artists. Thus, little is known about his interest in cycling. As a special artist much in demand, Taylor accumulated moderate wealth, and he invested in a summer cottage and studio on Round Island Park in New York's Thousand Islands. There, he entertained many of his artist friends, including William Rogers, but he also hosted large gatherings of bicyclists, including one of the treks by the Big Four Tour Association, probably in 1885. That year, roving cyclists spent three days on the island, where winding paths were carefully rolled for the riders.[10]

Taylor's single most important work in cycling is a short book identifying bicycle routes in his city and its environs: *Cyclers' and Drivers' Best Routes in and around Philadelphia*, published in 1896. Superbly illustrated and mapped, the work is valuable simply for its depictions of once-familiar buildings and bridges—especially turnpike tollhouses. Taylor's guide also provides an opportunity to compare and contrast the different methods of illustration he employed in a single publication, including pen and ink, watercolor, and photographic halftones, and to focus on those images that express the wheelman's exploratory experience most spontaneously.

The best of these images probably originate as pen and ink drawings, in which Taylor displays sharp contrast between light and shadow, revealing the vitality of this line medium. Drawings of the tollhouse at Merionville on the Montgomery Pike and the city line tollgate on the Lancaster Pike are exemplary, but his sketches of numerous inns and old houses are also captivating. Among these, a few that depict winter light are especially absorbing. Although the few photographs to which Taylor resorts capture detail and information in ways that sketches cannot, those very still images are weakly reproduced and lack sharp contrast.[11]

As did Taylor, Joseph Pennell keenly felt the changes taking place in Philadelphia, his place of birth. By nature plain-spoken (to the point of contentiousness), he often railed about architectural vandalism in Philadelphia, and his dismay at the loss of pictorial antiquities probably added to his preference for Europe, where he lived most of his adult life—much of it in London. There, he rediscovered the English houses, narrow lanes, and hidden inn yards that were vanishing from Penn's city.

Unlike Taylor, however, Pennell left a sizable chronicle of his life's labors, including an autobiography, and his fame as a gifted illustrator–author originated as much in Europe as in America. Among his many works, a collection of travel books exploring Italy, France, and Great Britain—collaborative ventures begun in 1884 with his wife, Elizabeth Robins Pennell—achieved critical success at the time; today, they are hallmarks of illustrated touring by wheel. Tracing historic pilgrimages, the Pennells traveled by tandem tricycle (and later by separate bicycles): she the author and architectural critic, he the illustrator ever in search of the picturesque. *A Canterbury Pilgrimage*, published in 1884, and *Two Pilgrims' Progress*, published in 1886, became the first of the Pennells' many memorable journeys together, the latter a trip from Florence to Rome commissioned by *The Century*. Studies of European cathedrals ensued, ventures originating with a commission from art critic Mariana Van Rensselaer to illustrate her book *English Cathedrals*. However, the Pennells adapted the idea and subsequently published *French Cathedrals: Monasteries and Abbeys, and Sacred Sites of France*.[12]

Pennell's prominent role in American cycling also sets him apart from Taylor. Pennell and his wife must be counted with that era's accomplished long-distance riders and, among this intrepid group, probably the most practiced observers of their cultural surroundings. However, Pennell's involvement with cycling precedes his European travels. In 1876, he experimented with high-wheel bicycles

FIGURES 3.2 AND 3.3

Frank Hamilton Taylor's illustrations of tollhouses on the Montgomery Pike and Lancaster Pike in his 1896 book, *Cyclers' and Drivers' Best Routes in and around Philadelphia.* The original drawings are probably in pen and ink and may have been reproduced through photoengraving. Courtesy Lower Merion Historical Society, Bala Cynwyd, PA.

FIGURE 3.4
Colonial-era taverns such as the General Wayne on Montgomery Pike became popular places for exploring cyclists, and innkeepers who offered discounts for lodging gained official listing in LAW road books. During an era when photographic halftones had begun to dominate graphic reproduction, Taylor's image illustrates the ability of line mediums such as pen and ink or etching to stir the imagination of would-be travelers. Courtesy Lower Merion Historical Society, Bala Cynwyd, PA.

at the Philadelphia exposition, purchased a used bicycle two years later, became a founder of the Germantown Cycling Club in 1879, and with club companions wheeled great distances, including a trip from Philadelphia to Albany. Representing the Germantown club in 1880, he traveled to Newport, Rhode Island, to help establish the League of American Wheelmen, and he reported on the league's first meet in Boston the following year for *Harper's Weekly*. By 1886, the year the league created formal touring divisions, Pennell had moved to London, where he joined both the Cyclists' Touring Club and London's famed bicycling society, the Pickwick Club.[13]

Important differences in their careers as illustrators also distinguish the two men. Pennell, a birthright member of the Philadelphia Friends' Meeting and almost a generation younger than Taylor, seemed destined at an early age to become an illustrator. Unlike Taylor, who was largely self-taught, Pennell received formal training at the Philadelphia School of Industrial Art and the Pennsylvania Academy of Fine Arts. Artists who taught at the academy, including Thomas Eakins, noticed his abilities and strongly influenced his work. Those connections led to an important commission from Alexander Drake for *Scribner's Monthly* and to an association with editors of that journal's successor, *The Century*, with which Pennell was well positioned to advance Drake's interest in cycling. By contrast, Taylor often worked for *Scribner's* principal competitor, *Harper's*, which remained a lap or two behind the former in exploiting public fascination with bicycles.[14]

Yet the two illustrators became well acquainted and friendly toward one another, possibly explaining at least part of Taylor's acquaintance with cycling. Their art reveals important commonalities, suggesting that they respected each other's work. Both, for example, were skilled in a variety of mediums, particularly pen and ink, and each developed individualistic styles for that artistic mode. Taylor's drawings are light and fluid, conveying an impression of spontaneity. Pennell, by contrast, created expressive pictorial effect with very delicate, staccato lines, and his work is especially distinctive (see figure 1.10). Both were deeply appreciative of engravers' art, although Pennell felt that the astounding energy devoted to engraving was misdirected, and both remained committed to showing subjects in a faithful light, allowing scenes to tell a story free from subjective interpretation or temperament. Both also held strong views about pictorial quality and the need to elevate the public's awareness of aesthetic values inherent in ordinary surroundings, hoping to awaken public sentiment. That both artists turned to bicycles to advance those themes underscores the important relationship between cycling and trends in art and illustration.

Pennell looked to industrial settings to emphasize that point, and his fascination with gritty shipyards, wharves, mines, coal breakers, refineries, and iron and steel works began at an early age, when he accompanied his father on travels through the oil and coal regions of Pennsylvania. The drawings he accumulated during a lifetime of curiosity about such places belong to his "Wonder of Work" series, culminating with World War I and the loathing he felt for that conflict. Yet he was also captivated by the extent of industrial energy generated by the war, creating picturesque spectacles that he felt compelled to record, often darkly so. That he chose the word "picturesque" to describe such places is far from incidental and is clear evidence of shifting perceptions concerning the visual quality of the environment—and of the role of illustrators in shaping those changes by translating scenery in terms of human interest.[15]

The careers of both Taylor and Pennell thus shed light on the shadowy realm between art and illustration and confirm the relevance of the latter in any dialogue about realism in American art. Pennell uses the criteria of commercialism, rather than realism, to distinguish illustration from art, and for both men illustration attains humanistic purpose through imagination. This is true whether that purpose is to capture and explain the visual characteristics hidden among derelict

FIGURE 3.5
Wood-engraving titled *Oil Refinery* by J. Friedrich Jungling after a drawing by Joseph Pennell for *Scribner's Monthly* (July 1881). Pennell explored much of the Philadelphia region on a high-wheel bicycle, and his selection of subjects worthy of illustration marks a clear departure from accepted academic standards of his day. Courtesy University of Vermont libraries.

antiquities and sequestered factories, or to draw attention to ordinary places by conveying the sensations that particular subjects create in the artist—"the feeling of a place," as Pennell explained, adding: "If that sensation is strong enough, others will feel it." For Pennell, an understanding of line, tone, light, and shadow influences the overall quality of the image and dictates whether an illustrator is able to demonstrate skills that extend beyond the simple, accurate recording of a scene. Imagination becomes key for any attempt to present an idea in ways that appeal to mass readership, and the effective illustrator becomes a "spontaneous linear interpreter that achieves pictorial effect," adding "emotion and artistry to illustration."[16]

Cycling journalism and illustration are tied directly to these concerns. The commission that Alexander Drake offered Pennell in 1880 marked the beginning of

Pennell's career as an illustrator and signified acceptance of an article that Pennell had proposed about Philadelphia's lowland peninsula, called the Neck. Pennell had learned of a story to appear in *Scribner's Monthly* that would be sympathetic to the squatters of New York's Shantytown, where the city's laboring classes had created their own Bohemia near the westerly fringes of Central Park. Pennell resolved to explore Philadelphia's version, and during the summer of 1880 he discovered "old canal boats, huts, causeways, barns, and oil works that made me mad to draw them." Pennell then traveled to New York to show Drake his work, the first meeting of the two men, and Drake enthusiastically accepted the drawings.[17]

Scribner's Monthly carried the article, "A Day in the Ma'sh," in its June 1881 issue, replacing the author Pennell recommended with Maurice Egan, a Philadelphia journalist. Egan wandered into the secluded sectors of that land point, identifying the Ma'sh, its single community called Martinsville (known colloquially as Frogtown), and a style of haphazardly assembled, whitewashed dwellings as belonging to the easterly part of the region along the Delaware, below the brinks of its dikes. Pennell's drawings of reed marshes, wharves, fishing shanties, and an oil refinery reproduced from a wood engraving by Friedrich Jungling joined illustrations by Thomas Eakins and Henry R. Poore. When Jay Howe Adams ventured into the same region by bicycle four or five years later, Pennell and Egan already had offered a progressive view of the region's visual qualities, interpretations that Adams and his illustrators revisited for fellow cyclists and readers of *Outing*.[18]

The Wheelman's *Illustrators: Hassam, Garrett, and Sylvester*

Scribner's Monthly and its successor, *The Century Magazine*, are linked to cycling in several other important ways. Alexander Drake's proposal for an article about cycling, published in *Scribner's* in 1880 as Charles Pratt's "A Wheel Around the Hub," is significant because it introduces bicycle touring to the American public and because it inaugurates *The Wheelman* in October 1882, but also because it marks the beginning of an informal understanding among editors of the *The Century* and *The Wheelman*. When editors of *The Century* sold the reprinting rights for that article to Albert Pope, they probably didn't anticipate that Samuel McClure would also borrow the magazine's typography and format. Yet editorial tolerance of these circumstances seems to have prevailed, a tacit acceptance by *The Century* of what amounted to an ancillary journal aimed at a narrow group of readers, subscribers who in turn would find the pages of *The Century* to be very familiar in appearance, much to the advantage of both journals, and possibly to the disadvantage of *Harper's*.[19]

Whether that understanding was ever expressed in writing or correspondence is not known, but what becomes important in the context of cycling illustration is that *The Wheelman* and its successors, *Outing and the Wheelman* and *Outing*, also sought to emulate the standard of art and engraving established by *Scribner's* and *The Century* (and by implication *Harper's*). All three cycling periodicals thus participated in a flourishing but short-lived era of journalistic imagery during which American wood engraving excelled. That brief period became significant to cycling, because artists and engravers tried to capture the experience of bicycle travel through a distinctive art form, and the views depicted express the important relationships between travel by bicycle and awareness of place.

If Samuel McClure's editorial contributions to bicycle touring must be shared with others, then he probably deserves most of the credit for establishing this informal association with *The Century*. Although the issues of *The Wheelman* during the closing months of 1882 are dominated by text, with only weak illustrations, the issues of February and March 1883 signal McClure's quick success at identifying skilled artists. In March, an article titled "Our First Bicycle Club," which traces the history of the Boston Bicycle Club, includes exemplary illustrations by Edmund H. Garrett and Frank Myrick, with engravings by H. E. Sylvester, who may have worked for Rockwell and Churchill, the Boston press that printed Pope's journal. Sylvester's role eventually expanded, and he furnished a number of illustrations for later issues. He also became the art manager of *Outing* before it was sold to New York publishers. Notable in "Our First Bicycle Club" is Garrett's painting of Cobb's Tavern, the club's informal country headquarters, engraved by Sylvester (see figure 2.6).[20]

Whether through serendipity or inspiration, McClure also invited F. Childe Hassam, a young associate of Garrett, to furnish illustrations for *The Wheelman*. Hassam would later become one of the country's most celebrated Impressionist painters and a member of The Ten, an exhibition society the ranks of which included William Merritt Chase and Hassam's close friend, Julian Alden Weir. Hassam was a gifted and exceptionally diligent artist, who worked principally in watercolor and oil, but he began his career in the shop of a Boston wood engraver (George E. Johnson), as had Sylvester. He also learned etching and drypoint techniques early in his career, possibly with the assistance of Garrett, and returned to graphic printing late in life. During those early years, he pursued formal training in art and embraced French modernism and its American proponents, including William Morris Hunt, a distant relative. At a very early age, Hassam observed Boston artist and illustrator Frank Myrick painting outdoors, and Hassam would work from nature throughout his life.[21]

In 1882, Hassam opened a studio on School Street and that fall exhibited a collection of watercolors at Boston's reputable Williams and Everett Gallery, a few doors away from the building where McClure worked. Although Hassam's career as an artist had taken shape by this time, he supplemented his income by working as an illustrator. An 1882 sketch of a cyclist, possibly Charles Pratt, pedaling through a Boston suburb is among Hassam's earliest dated illustrations (see figure 2.1). That sketch and another drawing vaguely resembling Pratt accompanied the latter's article "Echoes and Shadows" in the February 1883 issue of *The Wheelman*, with several engravings by Sylvester. McClure and Pope seemed to have

FIGURE 3.6
The Run in Fairmount Park, Bi-Centennial Meet, H. E. Sylvester's
wood engraving of a bicycle meet in Philadelphia's after a drawing or painting by F. Childe Hassam for *The Wheelman* (July 1883).

recognized the quality of those illustrations and made announcements in the
cycling press about forthcoming work by both Hassam and Sylvester.[22]

The relationships among McClure, Hassam, Garrett, and Sylvester represent
another of the intriguing but neglected intersections between cycling history
and other disciplines. One can easily imagine McClure in the fall of 1882: he
becomes a twenty-five-year-old editor of a magazine with national circulation
overnight, is inexperienced and in immediate need of able illustrators, and discovers twenty-three-year-old Hassam at the latter's exhibition a block or two
away. Or perhaps Garrett—who at thirty-one years of age was the more established illustrator—pointed McClure in Hassam's direction. Or possibly Pratt and
McClure collaborated in the editorial selection of Hassam for that important

FIGURE 3.7

A Night Run on Commonwealth Avenue, wood engraving by Kimball C. Atwood, after a drawing by H. E. Sylvester for *Outing* (March 1885). Although skilled wood engravers could create soft tones as well as sharp contrasts between black and white, photography began to dominate graphic reproduction during the 1880s and early 1890s, rendering wood engraving obsolete. Some engravers, such as Sylvester, turned to illustration in response, but in this image he and Atwood demonstrate one of the strengths of wood engraving (depicting night views) that the camera could not yet equal.

article. In any case, McClure consistently relied on these artists, who quickly elevated the quality of imagery in *The Wheelman* and who interpreted cyclists' exploratory spirit with clarity. Hassam's work is especially fluid and spontaneous (see figure 1.1).

McClure and Hassam shared youth, energy, and ambition, traits that provided a foundation for a successful working relationship with Albert Pope. Hassam's illustrations appear in every issue of *The Wheelman* between March and September of 1883, including a painting (probably a watercolor) of Pope's residence in Newton, engraved by Sylvester. Although many of Hassam's assignments are in New England, some of his commissions may have required travel to cities such as Philadelphia, and he continued to sketch for McClure in Europe during 1883. However, by late December 1883 McClure had left Boston for New York, and

although Hassam continued to illustrate for *Outing* during 1884 and 1885 his work appeared more sporadically.[23]

Other illustrators, including Garrett, Charles W. Reed (a member of the Boston Bicycle Club), Charles Copeland, Henry "Hy" Sandham, John Arthur Fraser, and Augustus B. Shute, contributed to issues during 1883, 1884, and 1885. During those years, the number, quality, and purposes of illustrations fluctuated, but the issues of 1883, before *The Wheelman* and *Outing* merged, offer images that are expressive of cycling's exploratory possibilities. In the September issue of that year, an article titled "A Day in Andover" and illustrated by Hassam, Sylvester, Copeland, and a woman artist, E. A. Means, with engravings also by Sylvester, may represent the peak of McClure's and Pope's contribution to cycling's travel imagery during the era of wood engraving. The anonymous author ventures from

Boston on country roads, seeking the town's broad, shaded streets, educational landmarks, and ancient houses before returning home that evening.[24]

As *Outing* expanded to encompass many other forms of outdoor recreation after 1885, its editors sought contributions from well-known illustrators, including Pennell, Thomas Moran, Howard Pyle, and William A. Rogers, as well as engravers Timothy Cole, William Tenney, and Kimball C. Atwood. However, many of their illustrations are unrelated to cycling. In addition, the methods used for graphic printing rapidly shifted to mechanical processes during this period. In an 1894 retrospective, engraving already becoming a lost art, Sylvester explained the differences between wood engravings and halftones, with sentiments similar to the thoughts Joseph Pennell had expressed regarding sense of place: "The halftone only tells obscurely how a thing looks; it gives 'no color,' as the term is used in engraving, nor any texture. It does not allow the direct impact of the mind of the artist upon the mind of the observer that makes the charm of art." Sylvester might have added that photographers had not yet mastered nighttime views, and could have cited his own "A Night Run on Commonwealth Avenue," engraved by Atwood, as one type of illustration for which wood engraving remained well-suited.[25]

Joseph Pennell, Frank Hamilton Taylor, F. Childe Hassam, and Edmund Garrett are but four of many illustrators and artists who engaged the cyclists of their day. Pennell is unique because of his active involvement in cycling from its American inception and because of his prominence as an illustrator; Taylor because of his skills as an author and illustrator of touring guides; and Hassam because of his distinction as one of America's eminent Impressionists, who contributed to the important, early years of *The Wheelman* and whose first work as an illustrator is rooted in cycling. That earliest work may have prompted the editors of the renewed *Scribner's Magazine* to invite Hassam to illustrate an 1895 article titled "The Bicycle. The Wheel of Today." Hassam's sketches of New York bicyclists on Riverside Drive and at the entrance to Central Park on Columbus Circle (see figure 8.2) capture both the bicycle at the height of its nineteenth-century popularity and the influence of Impressionism on his work.[26]

If less direct, the connections between cycling and other literary illustrators are nevertheless worthy of continued study. The illustrations of William A. Rogers for Thomas Stevens's book *Around the World on a Bicycle* are noteworthy because of Rogers's long and successful years with the art department at *Harper's*; some of those illustrations may have been based on Stevens's own sketches. Rogers also illustrated for journalist Kirk Munroe, editor of *Harper's Young People*, a founding member of the LAW, and later associated with Florida's Audubon Society, contributing to the many ties between cycling and conservation.[27]

Another of cycling's important illustrators, Arthur Merrick, transferred his talents from *Bearings* to *Wheel and Cycling Trade Review* in New York and there produced sharply delineated illustrations for many touring articles after 1893. Merrick's drawings are as spontaneous as those of Taylor, and his prolific artistry

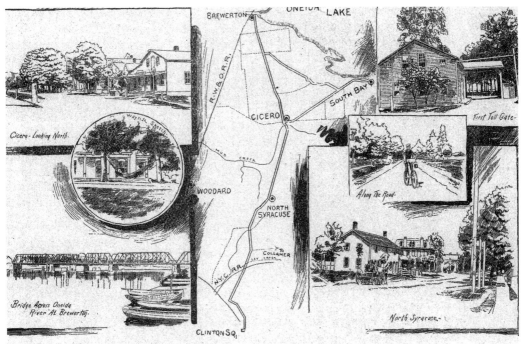

THE PLANK ROAD TO BREWERTON.

FIGURE 3.9

Special artists employed by newspapers also contributed to the popularity of bicycle travel, reaching a broad spectrum of readers and contributing to changing perceptions of American landscapes. The *Syracuse Herald* was one of many American news companies to sponsor bicycle races, and in 1897 the company also published a *Road Route Book for Central New York*. Courtesy Onondaga Historical Association, Syracuse, New York.

is more directly beneficial to cycling's legacy of geographic exploration than the work of better-known illustrators, such as Rogers. Both Merrick and his counterpart at *Bearings*, Charles Cox, deserve continued study.[28]

Other examples are also noteworthy. Although the illustrator of George Thayer's story of transcontinental travel, *Pedal and Path*, remains anonymous, the Moss Engraving Company published the book. That firm represented the successor to two companies founded by an inventor, John C. Moss, who in 1863 developed the first commercially viable photoengraving process, the innovation that ultimately made wood engraving obsolete.[29]

Newspaper Routes

Newspaper publishers also capitalized on cycling's popularity and the advances in mechanical reproduction of images. In 1897, the sporting editor of the *Syracuse Herald* compiled that newspaper's *Road Route Book for Central New York*. In

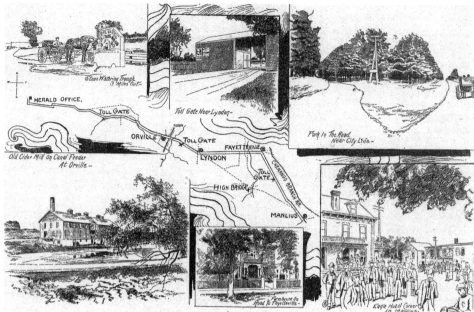

OVER THE HERALD ROAD RACE ROUTE.

FIGURES 3.10 AND 3.11
The *Syracuse Herald's* race followed a plank road for part of the course, a very common nineteenth-century land feature, but one seldom visible in landscape imagery. Courtesy Onondaga Historical Association, Syracuse, New York.

FIGURE 3.12

The Sea Breeze sidepath led north from Rochester's easterly environs, beginning at the intersection of East Avenue and Culver Street and leading to Irondequoit Bay and Forest Lawn on Lake Ontario. Photograph by Cline Rogers in an album titled *Sidepaths: Monroe County (1899)*. Courtesy Rochester (N.Y.) Public Library, Local History and Genealogy Division.

format, the well-illustrated guide is similar to Frank Taylor's book, with images that accompany maps and route descriptions. Sketches, most of which probably originate as pen and ink drawings, are presumably by the *Herald's* special artist or artists, and the importance of that imagery lies principally in the subject matter: land features that the artist suggests would appeal to the exploring cyclist. These include bridges of all types, turnpike tollgates, shaded village streets, porches with hammocks, watering troughs, an old cider mill on a feeder canal, and agricultural prosperity evident in architecturally stylish farm houses.

Editors of the *Philadelphia Inquirer* also dabbled in cycling, and in June 1896 the paper launched a column titled "Trips Awheel. Where to Go and How to Get There," which offered maps and lengthy narratives for each of the routes recommended. The column may have originated with a French émigré, Alphonse Estoclet, who translated several works by Jules Verne in addition to providing editorial services for the *Inquirer*. Estoclet assured readers that his descriptions were based on personal observations, and by the end of November he had compiled a large collection of outings, the fiftieth of which charted a twenty-seven mile ramble

FIGURE 3.13
Unusual buildings, such as octagon houses, provided important landmarks for cyclists trying to find their way along unmarked roads. This brick building (today concealed by trees) is just west of the village of Monroeville, Ohio, on current Route 20 near Norwalk, but in 1892 it marked an important turn on a route between Monroeville and Milan to the north, charted by the *Road Book* published by the Ohio Division of the LAW.

through parts of Montgomery and Delaware counties. The column resumed in 1897 with a new numbering system. Although the articles are not illustrated, Estoclet's composite body of descriptive writing is substantial, placing him in the front ranks of cycling's landseeër literates and justifying continued study.[30]

Photography

In addition to the application of photography to graphic reproduction, cycling journals also promoted the use of photography by touring wheelmen and wheelwomen. The increasing facility of cameras permitted expansive compositional studies, and these collections become valuable to geographical investigation when photographs are in some manner tied thematically to aspects of the built or cultural environment. A few such collections exist, and one of the best is an 1899 portfolio of sixty photographs taken by professional photographer Cline Rogers of Rochester, New York, showing sidepaths built by the Monroe County Sidepath Commission and extending outward from Rochester. Very little is known about the genesis of that project or about Rogers and his interest in cycling. Whether conceived by the sidepath commission in preparation for the fall sidepath convention, by one or more of the city's bicycle clubs, or by a generous benefactor, the compilation is unique.[31]

From one vantage point, Rogers's photographs are valuable as an exceptionally rare, comprehensive collection of views showing a regional system of sidepaths, and the professional quality of the images adds to the collection's contribution to cycling history. In addition, the photographs simultaneously show two transportation networks, roads as well as sidepaths, and those roads are principal arteries extending outward from one of the country's major cities. Considered as a panoramic body of work, the images provide an extensive tableau of those highways and their suburban and rural settings during a pivotal period of Rochester's growth, just before the advent of motorized transportation. Rogers almost certainly took the photographs over a very brief period, the summer and fall of 1899, and thus the snapshot of the city's advancing corridors and development is a highly focused one, making it especially valuable to those who explore urban history and landscape studies.

Most images show narrow dirt roads bordered by farmhouses, open fields, and fences. Only occasionally does a shaded residential street, plank sidewalk, electrical line, or set of trolley tracks hint at the nearby city. Yet many of those same places today edge the center of a dense metropolis, barely recognizable as one-time suburbs. These exceptional photographs thus offer an unusual opportunity to document, then and now, what has become an omitted landscape—places often ignored by image makers as neither stimulatingly urban nor soothingly rural.

Elsewhere, an amateur photographer from Philadelphia, William H. Doering, assembled a superb collection of lantern-slide images depicting numerous bicycle tours with his wife, Catherine Rupp Doering, and their relatives or friends. Many of the trips took place in the Philadelphia area, but they also traveled to Long Island for vacations, and Doering's photographs display a shared, familial interest in open countryside.

LAW Road Books

The road books published by state divisions of the LAW contain no wood engravings, etchings, or photographic halftones. Instead, the only examples of graphic art are skillfully drawn maps, and those crafted by Philadelphia engineer and cartographer Carl Hering are exceptional. Despite the absence of illustration, these road books (pocket-sized if one considers the spacious pouches of cyclists' uniforms or apparel) are vividly descriptive and can spark imagined journey.

For historians interested in remote rural America, cyclists' road books offer especially valuable information and in detail that is probably unmatched by any other type of published work. Readers of county chapters contained in the 1892 handbook published by the Ohio Division of the LAW—a volume promoted as a tourist guide—will find descriptions of cultural features as varied as octagon houses, fairgrounds with kite-shaped tracks, Shaker settlements, oil and gas wells, mines, blast furnaces, or quarries. Readers also will encounter numerous terms used to describe roads: dirt, sand, mud, clay, plank, stone, gravel, pike, trace, toll, macadamized, brick and firebrick, or simply *country road*. Today, distinctions among some of these highway surfaces may seem unimportant, but to the rural traveler of the 1890s those words held crucial meaning, particularly during poor weather when some surfaces, such as clay, became impassable.[32]

Especially helpful to historians are the references to features along identified routes: bridges or ferries, tollgates, landmark buildings, railroad tracks, telegraph poles, official league hotels that offered discounts to members, blacksmith shops where repairs might be obtained, and places for refreshment. Compilers of these valuable guides also note opportunities for scenery or mark the locations of bordering woods—possibly with caution in mind.

The quest for adequate roads also led cyclists to rediscover America's extensive network of late eighteenth- and early nineteenth-century turnpikes. Dependence on those highways had declined following the advent of canals and railroads, and most remained vivid only in local lore. Just as narratives by many bicyclists fill a void in the story of America's declining canals, cyclists' descriptions of turnpikes occur during a forgotten period of toll road history. Advocates who today try to safeguard surviving remnants of the National Road can add wheelmen's accounts to the annals of that corridor.[33]

Authors of a few early touring guides for American cyclists, including the 1884 *Wheelman's Hand-Book of Essex County* by George Chinn and Fred E. Smith and John Webber's handbook, *In and Around Cape Ann*, organized the books in narrative form and borrowed from earlier, similarly formatted tourist guides. League divisions in some states, such as New Hampshire and Ohio, continued to use similar formats, but most of the road books represent a distinctly American approach to finding one's way across unmarked countryside on a bicycle. Shortly before the league formed, Charles Pratt set a course with his 1879 manual, *The American Bicycler*, which offered thirty-nine carefully delineated routes in Massachusetts. Soon after, league officials began distributing blank route cards to local consuls, who then furnished descriptions of their riding districts and returned the data to national headquarters, where staff placed the cards on file for any member who inquired. However, circulation of that information remained difficult until the national organization established state divisions, which then began collecting, sorting, and publishing the material in book form.[34]

In Philadelphia, league consul Henry S. Wood devised the method of organizing the best factual information available about decent roads into tabulated routes, and in 1885 he published the *Pennsylvania-New Jersey Road Book*, the first to use that format. He anticipated that each state division would adopt a similar system, facilitating the exchange of stereotype printing plates for routes in bordering states, and by 1887 league divisions had compiled books for New York,

Hotel or Restaurant.	POINTS ON ROUTE 60	Total Distance from Start. Miles.	Distance Between Points.	Material of Road.	Grade of Road.	Condition of Road at its best.	Turns, Forks, General Instructions. T. L.=turn to left. L. F.=left fork. T. R.=turn to right. R. F.=right fork. T. P.=telegraph poles. X R =cross roads. ☞See also "System of Abbreviation" facing Route (1).
Wyoming Valley H.	WILKESBARRE	0.00		clay path or pike	1	A2	
ˮ	KINGSTON	2.00	2.00	clay path or pike	3	A2	About 2½ m. to walk in going to the Lake.
	MILL HOLLOW	4.00	2.00	clay path or pike	3	A2	
Ice Cave H.	ICE CAVE	6.00	2.00	clay path or pike	3	A2	Stop at Ice Cave.
	TRUCKSVILLE	9.00	3.00	clay path or pike	3	A2	Chicken and waffles at Raub's.
Raub's	DALLAS	14.00	5.00	clay path or pike	3	A2	Good bass fishing at Lake.
Rhodes'	HARVEY'S LAKE	18.00	4.00				Fine coasting on the return.
	Also Short Trip						Wilkesbarre to White Haven 18 m. direct, via Laurel Run 3½ m and Bear Creek 9¼ m.
Wyoming Valley H.	WILKESBARRE	0.00	2.00	clay	1	A2	Cross Susquehanna.
	KINGSTON	2.00	5.00	clay	1	A2	North along river.
Leacock's	WYOMING	7.00	5.00	sidepath	2	A3	From Wyoming House northwest to Drake's Mill P. O. T. R. to Camp.
Boarding H	M. E. CONFERENCE CAMP-MEETING	12.00	74				Fine view of Wyoming and Lackawanna Valleys from Lookout Point near Camp.

FIGURE 3.14

Two of more than 175 charted routes identified in the *Road Book of Pennsylvania, New Jersey, Maryland, and Delaware*, compiled by the Pennsylvania Division of the LAW and published in 1893 in its seventh edition, based on the original work compiled by Henry S. Wood, who devised the system of tabulated routes. The 1885 bicycle path linking Wilkes-Barre, Kingston, and Wyoming is noted.

Massachusetts, and Long Island using Wood's method. The year before, Wood already had demonstrated how easily the road books could be expanded by adding Maryland to the Pennsylvania-New Jersey book, and the 1887 edition of the New York book, compiled and edited by Albert Barkman (president of the Brooklyn Bicycle Club) included principal through routes in Maine (to Mt. Desert Island), New Hampshire, Vermont, Massachusetts, Rhode Island, Connecticut, New Jersey, Pennsylvania, Delaware, Maryland, Virginia (as far south as the Natural Bridge), and Ohio (to Cleveland). The New York book also included carefully drawn maps, small in scale and size, showing riding districts near New York City, Buffalo, and Philadelphia. Barkman sketched most of those maps, but Henry Wood contributed the drawings for Staten Island and Philadelphia.[35]

Although the format of tabulated routes distinguishes these LAW touring publications, as does the title "Road Book," some guides also include the subtitle "Hand Book," revealing the influence of earlier touring publications that provided a broad range of gazetteer-like information generally useful to travelers. The 1884 *Hand-Book of Massachusetts* compiled by H. W. Hayes from Cambridge makes that relationship clear, as does the 1886 *Hand-Book of the Ohio Division*, compiled by Thomas J. Kirkpatrick from Springfield. The latter included no tabulated routes but instead organized the state into county road reports in narrative form. For each edition of the Ohio guide, the committee included a copy of a state map, and Kirkpatrick described the document as a "revelation in hand-books," but one intended for reference rather than field use. Later editions of most road books, with or without the subtitle, reinforce ties to earlier travel guides, and almost always include brief introductory narratives that describe general topography and the idiosyncrasies of various locales.[36]

An innovative emphasis on specialized maps also sets these American versions of bicycle touring guides apart from earlier guide books, and state committees charged with compiling and publishing information for league members continued to expand, modify, and refine all three categories (tabulated routes, narratives or compendiums, and maps) during the 1890s, a decade during which committees republished most of the books in multiple editions. Many of those later editions reveal a merger of all three characteristics. At least part of the credit for this innovative cartography belongs to Charles G. Huntington, who began compiling the *LAW Road Book of Connecticut* in 1886, relying on Wood's system of tabulated routes. Huntington labored toward publication for two years before realizing that each principal route required notations for numerous spurs, creating a jumbled collection of more than three hundred disconnected short trips, potentially confusing to readers. Huntington suspended publication temporarily and decided to revise Wood's tabulated format by purchasing the rights to use the J. B. Beers Company road map of Connecticut and dividing the state into county sections. He reprinted every cycling road in red tint, with accompanying figures and numbers linking those roads to descriptions contained in reference tables. He then folded and bound those large maps (awkwardly, because of their size) into an 1888 publication that included standard material, such as route narratives and applicable laws.[37]

Some cyclists judged the Connecticut work to be the first truly practical road book, one depicting every road open to public travel in the state, supplemented by a special delineation of the best cycling routes and expanded by information contained in the tables: all the essential features contained in the Wood system, but in a visually comprehensive format. Other state divisions soon adopted Huntington's approach and began including specialized maps that delineated bicycle routes very clearly with red tint but also depicted networks of public roads. The 1894 seventh edition of the *Massachusetts Road Book*, which Huntington grudgingly had commended as a model for the Wood system, included a series of small-scaled maps prepared by the George H. Walker Company in Boston, encompassing the entire state by section, but showing mostly principal roads. By contrast, the 1893 edition of the *Road Book of the Pennsylvania Division* offered a combination of large-scale maps (on small pages) for key districts such as Philadelphia or Fairmount Park (see figure 8.6), with much smaller-scale maps showing entire states or large regions. Committee members for both state divisions reduced the maps to a size capable of being folded once or twice and then

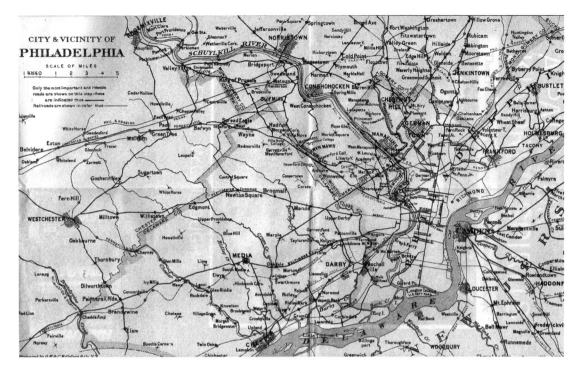

FIGURE 3.15

Map of Philadelphia and its environs, from the *Road Book of Pennsylvania, New Jersey, Maryland, and Delaware* (1893). Railroads are shown in red, and Montgomery Pike and Lancaster Pike lead westerly from the city. The region explored by Joseph Pennell and Jay Howe Adams, the Ma'sh, is located in the vicinity of League Island, near the confluence of the Schuylkill and Delaware Rivers.

bound them into the backs of the books. However, the 1896 edition of *Road Book of the New Jersey Division* included much larger-scale sectional maps prepared by the J. B. Beers Company that show the entire state and its many roads in exacting detail. Those maps have numerous folds and were placed unbound in a separate pouch accompanying the book.[38]

When he first proposed using maps rather than tabulated routes, Huntington faced resistance from league officials, probably because of concerns about the road-worthiness of large folded maps that would eventually tear. Vexed by that opposition, he harshly criticized the Wood system, bluntly calling those publications route books rather than road books and saying that they were useful only to those touring cyclists who sought destinations accessible via selected corridors—a tiny percentage of existing roads. Yet the Wood system's small, easily turned pages containing precise, detailed information about road surfaces, grades, and adjacent landmarks, all of which are linked to corresponding mile markers, were (and still are) ingeniously suited for use in the field, and the books represent precursors to modern TripTiks. Huntington may not have given adequate

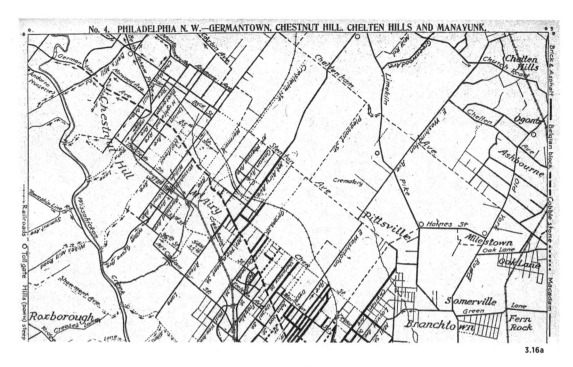

3.16a

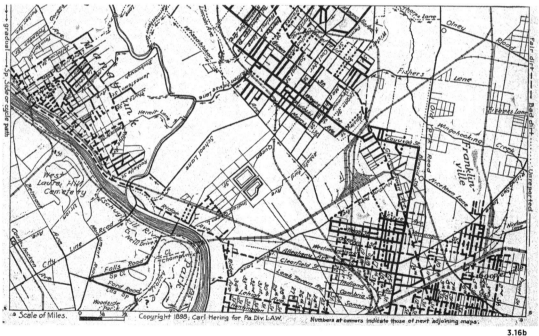

3.16b

FIGURE 3.16a, b

In contrast to the first LAW road books, which provided tabulated routes, engineer Carl Hering from Philadelphia compiled detailed map books at a time when no current map of the state's roads existed. Pennsylvania's two 1898 guides cover the eastern and western halves of the state, showing each road, town, and village. The locations of sidepaths are marked by "sp" and tollgates by "o." The books are only slightly larger than pocket-sized, with page divisions that form match lines.

consideration to those benefits, nor to the ease with which supplemental routes could be added to the Wood system. Historians, too, can be generous toward Wood, because his method of assigning specific information by precise mile markers invites the retracing of routes today.[39]

Nevertheless, Huntington's maps added a valuable travel tool, and eventually road book committees began revising formats to include the best of both methods, producing compilations only slightly larger than the earlier road books. For example, Maine's committee demonstrated that approach in a 1900 edition by mounting easily-folded maps of specific districts onto pages adjoining the tabulated routes, modifying Wood's system by providing supplemental directions for both principal corridors and side excursions. Bates Torrey, who also authored instructional books about shorthand and typewriting, had compiled earlier editions that circulated in 1891 and 1895, and he drafted maps that appeared in the 1900 edition; draughtsman F. L. Norris also crafted several of the maps included in the 1900 edition.[40]

In 1896, the New York division experimented with a new form of guide titled *Fifty Miles around New York*, with the subtitle *A Handbook of Cycling Roads and Routes*, seemingly coined to appease the league's opposing factions. Editor Walter M. Meserole placed small-scale maps showing large districts together with larger-scale maps of Manhattan, Brooklyn, and Queens at the front of the book, but then devoted remaining pages to the depiction of route skeletons that isolate just the route and key intersections, accompanied by mile markers measured along dotted lines that extend to page margins. Long routes were continued on sectional maps, with match lines overlapping. Similar to earlier books using the Wood format, corridors could be added by preparing new plates.[41]

In 1897, Pennsylvania's road book displayed a similar skeleton format, but the following year the committee, chaired by engineer and cartographer Carl Hering and with assistance from Leon Fay, improved that design by mapping all roads, an especially challenging task, because no up-to-date road map of the whole state existed. Dividing the state into a checkerboard grid, the committee identified every road, town, and village, and Carl Hering devised a method for distinguishing the condition of each road (good, fair, or bad) by solid or dotted lines of different print, without resort to color. Features such as hills, grade, tollgates, sidepaths, and road surfaces (whether clay, gravel, sand, cinders, shale, loam, slate, plank, or dirt) appear as symbols with keys in the narrow margins. The maps are reduced in size to fit across two opened pages, each page not much larger than pages in the state's earlier road books; very useful, larger-scale maps of sizable cities appear on concluding pages, as do brief notations in narrative form. The guides divided the state into two sections, eastern and western, thus making each publication easier to use. With a nod to Wood, they also included tabulated routes to locations in other states.[42]

Private mapping companies noticed the LAW road books, which state divisions often distributed at a financial loss, and printing houses led by the National

Publishing Company in Boston compiled a series of guides titled *Standard Road Books*, with the subtitle *Good Roads*. In 1897, the firm produced an eight-part series for New York State, aiming the guides directly at cyclists. The first book in the series encompassed the entire state, and the remaining seven depicted specific sections, such as the Albany-Troy region. Formatting in the series is very similar to that developed by Carl Hering, although the meticulous presentation of informative details that distinguishes Hering's work is lacking, and some of the books are slightly smaller. The quality of roads (good, fair, or ordinary) is made clear by differences in the printed lines.[43]

CHAPTER FOUR

Straightaway

Not quite a decade after Alfred Chandler's forty-mile journey from Leominster to Boston, another of cycling's landseeërs, George B. Thayer of Vernon, Connecticut, began a much longer journey to explore the country. The year is 1886, and Thayer departs from Hartford in April, traveling on a forty-six-inch Expert Columbia. He heads southerly to New Haven and then turns toward the Hudson River valley, visiting Tarrytown and its Old Dutch Church of 1699, Washington Irving's Sleepy Hollow, shafts being constructed for New York City's New Croton Aqueduct, cheap workers' shanties nearby, and by contrast the well-kept hamlets and splendid houses in the foothills of the Catskills, where he finds the climbing arduous. At Albany, he reaches the towpath of the celebrated Erie Canal, an avenue that he envisions as a bicycler's Arcadia, "perfectly level for forty, fifty, and sixty miles on a stretch."[1]

Considering its contributions to commerce, industry, labor, urban and village growth, engineering, art, literature, social strata, and politics, the Erie Canal is one of America's most important nineteenth-century transportation corridors, justifiably acclaimed and not lacking in written account or illustrated description. Yet the great canal that Thayer encounters is in decline, and the public's fascination has long since turned to railroads and the energy and speed of steam power. His account thus adds to our understanding of the canal at a forgotten moment in its history.

Whether due to seasonal closure, difficulties with water flow, or ruthless competition from railroads, no barge traffic moves through the easterly counties that Thayer navigates, and he sees mostly an empty canal bed of mud and slack water. The towpath that he had so eagerly anticipated turns out to be no path at all, but a heavily traveled common highway with a surface of ruts filled with rough, loose stones and coarse gravel unsuitable for riding. Cobbles protect the inside edge of the bank from erosion, ten feet above the canal bed, and narrow ditches cross the outside edge, making riding at either side of the towpath too dangerous. Bridges provide the only shade, and no adjacent springs supply essential drinking water, obtainable mostly at lock houses—and there usually from wells sunk in nearby swamps.[2]

The canal follows the southerly banks of the Mohawk River, passing through very few villages, and Thayer's determination to remain on the towpath weakens as he observes communities on the opposite side of the river with what he imagines are smoothly surfaced roads that promise pleasant riding. Exasperated, he leaves the canal for good at Fonda, roughly twenty-five discouraging miles west of Schenectady, and charts a different line toward Syracuse. He crosses the canal often on the way, but never finds sufficient reason to change his opinion about the towpath.[3]

Fortunately, Thayer's encounters with other cultural and natural features in central New York are less discouraging. As had Charles Campbell at Little Falls, he finds the convergence of travel corridors fascinating: highway, canal, Mohawk River, double tracks of the West Shore Railroad on the south bank, and four tracks

FIGURE 4.2

In his written accounts of travel across America by bicycle, George Thayer made special mention of unusual cobblestone houses he discovered in central New York State. Thayer may have passed not far from this 1848 school, located on the Scottsville Road in Chili, a short distance south of Rochester.

of the New York Central Railroad opposite, all squeezed together by the valley's vertical rock ledges. Watching four trains overlapping one another on the New York Central lines, Thayer muses: "Nothing dull about a trip up the Mohawk valley, even alone on a bicycle!"[4]

A little farther west, beyond towns with recognizable names, such as New Hartford and Vernon, he also notices unusual cobblestone houses faced with rounded stones not much larger than an ordinary egg and set in precise rows of mortar, some with arches over doors and windows. Thayer pedals on, but had he stopped to inquire he would have discovered that these exquisite structures exemplified folk architecture common to counties in central and western New York, where the Erie Canal had created agricultural prosperity. As farmers cleared fields, countless small stones deposited as glacial till interfered; some had been rounded by ceaseless abrasion, others smoothed by wave action in an immense glacial lake. From necessity and emulation grew a distinctive art form that proudly flourished until the Civil War, and although the artisans who crafted these buildings remain anonymous, substantial evidence of their mastery survives.[5]

Thayer, a grocer-turned-traveling correspondent, described his wanderings in occasional letters to the *Hartford Evening Post* and then assembled them into a book, *Pedal and Path: Across the Continent Awheel and Afoot*, published by the *Post* in 1887. Two years before, Englishman Thomas Stevens had departed from San Francisco, marking the start of his adventurous, record-setting global journey. However, Stevens did not publish the first volume of his two-volume work, *Around the World on a Bicycle*, until 1887, and that same year Karl Kron finally circulated his long-awaited opus, *Ten Thousand Miles on a Bicycle*, thus giving cycling's bystanders a chance to ponder three very different examples of long-distance touring during the high-wheel era. Kron favored the term "straightaway" to describe such continuous travel, contrasting with Abbott Bassett's idea of perfect tours as roving journeys with a return to the place of starting.[6]

Unlike Stevens, Thayer wheeled for pleasure, traveling from east to west and back, setting high hopes to see Yosemite National Park. He also took numerous side excursions along the way and remained indifferent to records—from the journey's inception to its end. In all, Thayer traveled more than eleven thousand circuitous miles by wheel, rail, and steamship (4,300 miles by wheel), taking time to explore California and Oregon before returning home. If Stevens hoped to tell a good tale, a saga of the Wild West to excite adventure-seekers, Thayer instead remained true to his observant objectives, and his descriptions penetrate the culture of places that he visits in ways that Stevens's narratives do not.[7]

Some of Thayer's descriptions portray significant features of cultural landscapes; others focus on more subtle conventions. He is delighted by the acres and acres of vineyards in western New York bordering Lake Eire, on low lands too poor for grains, and he wistfully envisions the fall harvest and cool wine cellars. Today, those vineyards remain the region's dominant agriculture. Although Stevens and Thayer probably traveled the same road, and although Stevens is impressed by the productivity of farms, he mentions neither the ripening grapes nor, surprisingly, their unforgettable fragrance. Later, upon arriving on Euclid Avenue in Cleveland, and by then weary of poor suburban plank roads, Thayer adopts a lighter tone when he learns from a fellow cyclist that riding on the sidewalk, called the "bob" side of the street, is prohibited, and he obediently shifts to the opposite, or "nabob," edge.[8]

Thayer veers from Stevens's route at Cleveland and instead travels southwesterly to Columbus. North and west of that city, he observes numerous log houses, and although some had been abandoned, the buildings lined both sides of the road for many miles. Far from being the inventions of pioneers, such houses represented the early period of westward settlement by Europeans, who adopted a traditional building type introduced to America by the Swedes. He also discovers easy riding on what Ohioans called "double-track roads," coarse gravel on one side, used in winter and spring, and natural clay on the other, preferable in dry summer months.[9]

At Columbus, he turns west along the National Road, the country's inaugural federally funded interstate highway built to link the Eastern Seaboard with America's rapidly expanding West. Construction of the road had begun in 1808 in Cumberland, Maryland, and by 1818 had reached the Ohio River at Wheeling, West Virginia. Eventually the road stretched across Ohio, Indiana, and Illinois, where federal funding trickled to an end at Vandalia, about seventy miles east of St. Louis. West of the Ohio River, the road advanced in halting, staggered segments, beset by political bickering, inadequate federal appropriations, and the rise of other, more efficient means of transportation—first canals and then railroads. By 1831, the government had begun transferring completed sections to states, but travelers failed to generate sufficient tolls, and some segments of the road had declined into sorry circumstances during the post–Civil War era.[10]

Yet historians who have studied the National Road have overlooked itinerant cyclists such as Thayer, who finds the section between Columbus and Indianapolis to be in superb condition, all 180 miles of it: broad, level, raised fifteen feet in low lands, and very straight—without the slightest rise or depression for distances of up to 12 miles. He calls the pike a high watermark of the roads he travels, better than the corridor between Buffalo and Cleveland. Although Ohio's charitable toll keepers may have colored that perception by allowing him free passage, his descriptions are reliable and eventually are confirmed by other cyclists. Such accounts suggest that historians' very broad generalizations about the road's poor condition during this period may not be accurate.[11]

Karl Kron's Odyssey

Among cycling's many roving explorers, Karl Kron dominates a realm between the touring literature of cycling's many periodicals, to which he often contributed, and the narratives of cyclists whose cross-continental quests best symbolize travel adventure. Unlike many other solitary adventurers during the early period of bicycle travel, Karl Kron professes no desire to rival overland time or distance feats, portrays himself as nonathletic and having only average physique, and considers his journey of ten thousand miles during a five-year period to be commonplace. He is a self-described "slow-going and observant traveler," and the legacy that he leaves for today's historians and historical geographers is more valuable for that modest assessment.[12]

Kron, born Lyman Hotchkiss Bagg in West Springfield, Massachusetts, in 1846, graduated from Yale College in 1869. During his years in New Haven, he became editor of the Yale Literary Magazine, and by 1871 he had completed his first book, *Four Years at Yale*, a study of the Yale experience, including its class societies. During the autumn of 1876, he established residence in the Gothic, white-marble New York University Building, built in 1834 at then-secluded Washington Square,

and began a six-year stint writing a Monday column for the *New York World*, called "College Chronicle." Correspondents occasionally addressed their letters to Kron using a shortened version of the column's title, "Coll Chron," and he modified the abbreviation slightly, first to Kol Kron and then, following the column's demise, to Karl Kron, his adopted pseudonym.[13]

Kron's introduction to cycling and to cycling journalism began in 1869, during his final term at Yale, when he joined the brief mania for velocipedes. His out-of-doors odyssey on a forty-six-inch Columbia ordinary, Number 234, started a decade later, in the spring of 1879, and by the end of that sweltering summer Kron had explored most of the roads in the New York metropolis, predicting that a great future awaited bicycling in the city. He stabled his wheel at a hotel on Broadway at 104th Street, then opposite the advancing terminus of New York's elevated railroad and a twenty-minute trip from Washington Square. The two transportation modes, bicycle and elevated railroad, would continue to change New Yorkers' perceptions of distance and mobility. He also began submitting stories to magazines such as *Bicycling World* and the *Springfield Wheelmen's Gazette*.[14]

Kron's ties to Yale College, his literary abilities (which are considerable), and his devotion to travel prompt inquiry about the influence of Timothy Dwight on Kron's writing and peregrinations. Kron knew of Dwight's accomplishment, and it is unlikely that he could have spent four years at Yale during the 1860s without being apprised of the historical significance of Dwight's travels. Curiously, the only reference to Dwight in Kron's cycling encyclopedia is an extract from *King's Handbook of Springfield, Massachusetts*, which Kron reviews in his description of Springfield's environs. Both Moses King and Kron found Dwight's 1803 report of pleasurable traveling in the Connecticut River Valley to be convincing.[15]

Important differences exist between Dwight and Kron, including motive, objective, method, format, and scope. For Dwight, what began in 1796 as travel during months of vacation from his presidency at Yale, principally to improve his health, sprouted into curiosity about the appearance of New England a century before and to realization that such information was mostly unattainable due to the lack of any existing records and to the rapid changes taking place. He also gained awareness about the American experiment and its significance, in his words "a novelty in the history of man." Anticipating that the country's transformation would not abate and realizing that others, one hundred years hence, would be similarly curious about the rapidly changing appearance of the region during his own era, Dwight resolved to draw a picture of that emerging society and its communities through the written word. The result is a comprehensive depiction of an entire region—a very large one, at that.[16]

Dwight also objected to the inaccurate and unflattering accounts by European travelers, especially those published in Great Britain, and his desire to correct such errors provided additional motivation. Dwight thus couches his descriptions in the form of letters to an English gentleman, at the same time making it clear that they are written for Americans. Today, Dwight's foresight has proved beneficial, and his letters are key sources for environmental and cultural historians who trace the influence of human activity on our environments.[17]

By contrast, Kron writes in the present for his fellow cyclists and for those he would convert, thoroughly convinced about the "permanence and potentiality of cycling" as an "instrument to set the world on wheels." Although his financial and physical investment in such idealism is considerable, and although he proclaims the healthful benefits of travel by bicycle, Kron is candid about the practical aspects of his business proposition—a book project that will generate income by encouraging others to engage in cycling. As he explains, "praise not sought for, but money." The three thousand subscribers who promised in advance to purchase copies for one dollar (not everyone honored those promises) are a testament to the accuracy of his predictions, even though various journals previously had published many of his accounts in shortened form. Yet Kron's initial spark of interest in travel remains a mystery, all the more puzzling because he leaves such an important travel legacy.[18]

The differing motivations and objectives held by Kron and Dwight yield diverging results. For Kron, the quality of overland routes and road surfaces are a principal concern (for the benefit of other would-be adventurers), and he often vacillates between a mile-by-mile travel diary and an awakened awareness of surroundings. By contrast, Dwight is intent on documenting the character and progress of American society, and thus his readers profit from a breadth and depth of investigation that is lacking in Kron's book. Logically, Dwight adopts a near-formulaic approach that assures inclusion of the important features of any given town: topography and natural resources; types of agriculture; street layout and overall plan (whether linear or grid like); populations; dwelling houses (indifferent, ordinary, decent, neat, handsome, or splendid); public buildings; churches and their denominations; profitable commercial or industrial ventures; and engineered structures, such as bridges.

Interspersed among Dwight's descriptions are sometimes-lengthy historical accounts of important people or events associated with the towns he visits, and many of those stories recount conflict with Native Americans or with the British. He also acknowledges the popular interest in picturesque scenery but turns to that device sparingly, cautioning against the overzealous attention paid to landscapes by European tourists at the expense of more enlightening subjects. When he relents, Dwight's descriptions of landscapes are lucid.[19]

Kron's book, by contrast, is organized into chapters but without the thematic consistency that characterizes Dwight's volumes. Kron's chapters include travel logs, essays, statistical collections of encyclopedic depth, interludes of poetry, autobiographical digressions, and a few other surprises added to the medley. Both Kron and Dwight acknowledge that the minuteness of their accounts will be disagreeable to some readers, but Kron truly puts that admission to the test, cautioning that he has considered "no fact too trivial for record" if it could help the traveling wheelman. Thus, today's historical geographers hoping to use Kron's book must be prepared to wade through extraneous detail.[20]

Nevertheless, many of Kron's chapters offer expressive narratives, fully as valuable to current study as those written by Dwight. If Kron is not as all-encompassing as Dwight in his descriptive approach, he is equally capable of observation and assessment—for example, the fundamental relationship between soil quality and prosperity. Such an aspect would have been elementary to Dwight in 1796, but possibly less so to the urban dweller of 1883, and probably overlooked altogether in 2014. In such instances, Kron shows an ability to translate the philosophical into reflective narratives, not just of the obvious—people, habitations, and roads—but also prospects that acquire allegorical meaning, as where seasonal progression, evident in falling leaves and bare branches, symbolically accompanied his travel from garden to poor barren land in southern Ontario.[21]

Explanation for the current value of both books, at least in part, may be that for Dwight and Kron the experience and not the destination dictates the pace of travel. Consider, for example, the following two passages:

> Litchfield is a handsome town; situated on an easy, beautiful slope, scarcely declining from North to South, and descending a little more rapidly to the East and to the West. It is chiefly built on two streets, crossing each other in the centre at right angles. The houses are well-built; and the Court House is handsomer than any other

in the State....The aspect of the country around Litchfield, as seen from the town, or, as it is frequently called, the Hill, is uncommonly handsome; consisting of open extensive vallies [sic], hills gracefully arched, rich hollows, and groves formed of lofty trees, interspersed every where at the most pleasing distances....Below Litchfield, the forests are universally oak, hickory, &c. In Goshen (to the north), they are composed of maple, beach, hemlock &c. The first white pines which we saw on this road, were in Goshen.[22]

Litchfield quite won my heart as a type of the quiet, old-fashioned and eminently-respectable New England town at its best estate. It is well worth visiting, if only for the sake of convincing one's self that such placid villages really do exist, undisturbed by the rush and roar of the railways, and unruffled by the fret and bustle of "fashionable summer-resort people." All the residences seem to shelter well-to-do owners, and almost none of the residences seem constructed for the purpose of proclaiming the owner's wealth. Many of the houses exhibit above the central doorway a date that indicates a century or more of history; and it soothes the nerves of the sentimental tourist to find such kindred spirits who are able thus to take pride in living within the same wooden walls that afforded comfortable and dignified shelter to the worthies of Washington's time.[23]

Both accounts of a Connecticut town reveal the considerable abilities of each traveler to observe surroundings and to translate those observations into thoughtful prose. Were it not for references to railways or summer resorts, the second passage might not be ascribed so easily to Kron. The edited excerpt from Dwight's journey, which took place in the fall of 1798, is here fragmentary, because several very long paragraphs describing a local academy and one of the town's prominent residents (interruptions that are typical) have been deleted. The unedited excerpt from Kron's book, recalling a trip taken in the summer of 1883, is atypical, because his accounts are almost always heavily punctuated with left or right turns, mounts and dismounts, cautious descents, and mention of road surfaces, all given at precise mile marks. Although Kron describes the features of a cultural landscape extensively and in careful detail, his reader must envision travel by bicycle and patiently wait for those places to appear.

The similarities of these passages illustrate that Dwight and Kron share both literary proficiency and commitment to travel, and thus both descriptions also confirm an important point: historians or historical geographers who consider Dwight's work to be useful for its descriptive content, as a means to measure change (and valuable too as one of very few such compilations during the early nineteenth century), must also recognize that Dwight writes for the benefit of other travelers. His book thus belongs to the extensive body of literature about travel and tourism in this country, which underscores the mobility that surely defines a key part of the American experience. Conversely, those few historians who are familiar with Kron's book and who regard it primarily as a curious travel diary have misjudged the substantive value of his narratives, equally descriptive of certain aspects of American countryside as those of Dwight during a much later but no-less-changeful era. In addition, Kron's bicycle opens new avenues of exploration that previously had been inaccessible to travel literature.

Yet there is more to consider. In the context of travel and tourism writing, Kron is probably superior to Dwight in his ability to capture the moment or spirit of travel and, most importantly, to compare and contrast distant places seen along the way but drawn more closely together by a novel mode of transport: the bicycle. Kron's reader sits astride a tall wheel as it rolls quietly along city streets or in open countryside, and even familiar objects—fences, bridges, hills, trolley tracks, sand, Belgian blocks, and street children—are all seen in a slightly different manner.

Kron calls this experience of travel "walking large with the wheel" or just "wheeling large," a self-perpetuating, insatiable love of outdoor adventure intensified by a vehicle that accentuates the "vivid and instructive contrasts of weather and soil and scenery, and of their relations to men and manners and houses." As Kron explains, no other mode of travel—neither foot, nor train, nor horse, nor carriage—offers the sense of exhilaration that "accompanies the noiseless rush of the man who has hitched the winged wheels to his feet." This analogy to flight is a popular one for the period and explains part of the public's fascination with cycling. The LAW specifically selected an insignia—wings attached to a wheel—that captures this feeling of imagined flight.[24]

Thus, compare the two earlier passages to the following lengthy and unedited account from Kron, who is traveling through Pennsylvania on a trip he titled "Straightaway for Forty Days," which began in Windsor, Ontario, in October 1883 and concluded in the Shenandoah Valley of Virginia, at Staunton:

> Beyond Tamaqua, I got a glimpse of a mining region, where the mountain-sides, adorned with the reddish leaves of scrub-oaks interspersed with the bright green of the pine, made quite a brilliant compensation for the unsightly heaps of coal-dust. A few hours later, my environment was again strictly agricultural, for I was gazed at by a gang of not less than twenty men who were simultaneously pulling turnips in a half-acre lot. The next day, Reading was reached, and the region of the Cumberland valley, where there were broad stretches of country enlivened by green wheat-fields, and mountain ridges looming up on the distant horizon. Red barns and whitewashed fences added to the general appearance of neatness and thrift and prosperity. The mile-posts along the pike were inscribed with the distances not only to Philadelphia and Harrisburg, its terminal towns, but also with those to Reading and Lebanon, intermediate. The villages were all made of red-brick houses, having solid wooden shutters painted white, and these shutters were invariably kept closed, so as to religiously exclude the healthful light of the sun and produce a deadly autumn chill inside. Beyond Harrisburg, where I walked about a mile along the double-bridge which spans the Susquehanna, the country seemed somewhat less thickly-settled and productive. The mountain ridges

on my left made a level line against the horizon, while those on my right were broken into peaks and spurs. Then came Carlisle, the first county-town of the strictly Southern type, whose central feature is a sort of magnified cross-roads, or open square, from which start four thoroughfares into the country, north, south, east and west. The public buildings and others—usually of brick and two or three stories high—front upon this square; and the effect is sometimes rather pleasing. Chambersburg, Greencastle, Martinsburg, Hagerstown and Gettysburg are among those towns which I recall as built in just this fashion.[25]

Dwight's writing is also redolent with the sense of progress so important to touring literature, although he admittedly finds the routine of mere travel, without opportunity to view the trappings of cultural advances available to tourists in Europe, to be dull. Presumably, Dwight could not have sustained such a prolonged period of journey without an appreciation for the activity itself. Nevertheless, his readers tend to remain in one place for a long time. Perhaps the anchor of lengthy historical accounts is the cause, or the weight of disciplined, careful description (which, to the historian, is also one of Dwight's strengths), or the slow pace of forward motion: by horse or carriage.[26]

For both Kron and Dwight, the pursuit of travel seems to acquire a dimension that surpasses each man's stated objectives at the outset of their respective journeys, or in Dwight's case at least had achieved equilibrium in a challenge of nearly unlimited scope. Kron continued to tour long after his book project had closed, and he abandoned neither his nickel-plated Columbia high-wheel nor his white flannel shirt and velveteen jacket. By the time he arrived in Burlington, Vermont, in the fall of 1903, at age fifty-seven, Kron's odometer registered more than twenty-nine thousand miles. Leaving Burlington, he crossed Lake Champlain at Rouses Point and, once in New York, headed toward Malone, Canton, and Ogdensburg, where he paused late in November. He had begun that expedition in Springfield, Massachusetts, with the intention of retracing a leg of his trip from Ontario to Virginia twenty years before, and in Ogdensburg he revisited the Seymour Hotel, the place of his overnight accommodations on that earlier adventure. However, four snow squalls in six days had slowed his progress toward Ogdensburg, and there he turned his bicycle around and headed back toward Washington Square, vowing to ride until deep snow blocked the way.[27]

Kron managed to reach Canada the following summer and, en route to Toronto, paused long enough in Belleville, Ontario, to speak with an astonished reporter at the Hotel Quinte. Asked why he continued to ride an obsolete machine, Kron may have answered more thoughtfully than the reporter surmised. Admitting to using a regulation wheel when in a hurry at home, Kron confided that he toured for the sake of fresh air and scenery, and his high-wheel provided a better perch from which to view the countryside, especially "on a level above the hedges."[28]

The overland treks by Kron and Thayer are noteworthy, because both men traveled for the sake of recreation rather than record, intent upon observing their ever-changing surroundings and on becoming landseeërs. In addition, impressions of their surroundings are formed over greater distances and during extended periods of time, very different from suburban explorations.

For many other wheelmen who traveled coast to coast or who conquered similarly daunting distances, an ultimate destination is usually in mind, albeit far in the distance, and that outlook often influences travel writing by pushing cultural milieu far into the background. Instead, stories become daily measurements of progress toward those destinations, for reader as well as cyclist, with possibilities for adventure looming at every mile. Not surprisingly, the narratives of these wheelmen are discernibly different from those who tour lands closer to home, and in many cases are less valuable to those who engage in landscape-related study. Yet such limitations should not detract from the extraordinary accomplishments of cycling's straightaway adventure seekers, who make important contributions to travel history: recounting impressions of far-off places for the benefit of urban readers, inciting public interest in the possibilities of travel by bicycle, and compiling a substantial body of written work. At times, these travelers awaken to their surroundings and summon insightful observations about cultural or natural land features, rendering their accounts more valuable to historians.

Thomas Stevens

In the category of travel adventure, whether by bicycle or any other means of transport, Thomas Stevens deserves a prominent place. Stevens began his journey in San Francisco in April 1884 on a fifty-inch Standard Columbia and crossed the continent in 105 calendar days, arriving in Boston, roughly 3,700 cycling miles distant, on August 4. He spent the winter of 1884 to 1885 in New York, translating his diary into the beginnings of a book, which from the trip's outset he had hoped to sell to finance his global expedition. After reaching an agreement with Albert Pope to serve as a correspondent for *Outing*, an arrangement that included a new nickel-plated Columbia Expert as well as stipends for articles, Stevens resumed his journey in the spring of 1885, circling the world and returning to San Francisco in January 1887.[29]

His book, published in two volumes (the second in 1888) by Charles Scribner's Sons, is less a story of geographic exploration than one of human resolve. The book's popularity helped Stevens embark on a career as an adventure writer (no small achievement given his very modest education in England), and Stevens's self-determined proficiency at descriptive writing is an intriguing part of his success. Yet his adventuresome exploits give the book its cardinal direction, and Stevens's contributions to travel history rest principally on his bold objective, daring, athleticism, stamina, and perseverance—and on the machine that made his record continental and global journey possible.[30]

Although Stevens offers views of his surroundings to readers, his principal focus is the challenge of overcoming obstacles in his path, particularly in western territories, and he measures progress daily in forty-mile quotas. His accounts thus lack the frequent and casual pauses that distinguish the writing of other wheeled travelers—for instance, the North Shore women tricyclists who found exquisite delight in the tree bowers of Essex Woods.[31]

Nevertheless, Stevens's book should not be discounted as lacking insightful commentary. When Stevens chooses to add descriptive prose, he does so competently, creating imagery that engages the reader. Among the most interesting aspects of Stevens's book, at least to historical geographers, may be the subtle shift in outlook that becomes apparent in his writing, when rugged, dominant nature gives way to less stern landscapes shaped by culture. For Stevens, travel over the western half of the country is largely a struggle between nature and man—the trials of mountains, icy streams, desert, heat, hunger, thirst, and fatigue. By the time he reaches Ogallala in western Nebraska, homesteads marked by dugouts, sod houses, groves of young cottonwood trees planted to affirm timber claims, and eventually framed buildings denote the advancing picket line of agriculture and signal his reentrance to civilization. At Fremont in eastern Nebraska, he can finally stray from the corridors of the Union Pacific Railroad and Platte River to mark a course along a military road. From that point eastward, the pace of his travel writing quickens, the outcome of his quest no longer in doubt.[32]

Equally important, although Stevens doesn't linger philosophically at this point of divide (he's too intent on reaching his destination), his intuitive grasp of the changes taking place around him expresses the fundamental tension between nature and culture in shaping land, a factor that continues to explain important regional differences in America—and one that is often obscured by the conflict that often grows from those elemental differences.

During most of his travels in western territories, Stevens's reliance on the corridors of the Central Pacific and Union Pacific railroads is another aspect that makes his journey less exploratory than adventurous. Following the railroad became essential for several reasons: a means to avoid becoming lost, which added both time and distance to his trip; a dry grade to replace soggy roads or floods; passage through mountain gaps or across canyons and wide rivers; opportunities for food and overnight shelter provided by frequent section houses; and essential water—if in no other form, then from tanks that leaked just enough to quench the thirst of occasional travelers passing through. Thus, Stevens's horizons are in many ways similar to those experienced by the builders of railroads.[33]

At the same time, his vantage points remain very different from those framed by the window of a moving rail car, and he views much that is unseen by railway passengers: track sidepaths; forty miles of dreary, icy, dripping snow sheds—the distinctive structures built over tracks, buildings, and water tanks belonging to the Central Pacific in the Sierra Nevada Mountains as protection from snow and rock slides; the primitive visages of section houses, gang bunkhouses, and their occupants; the inventive, self-governing windmills at water stations, a uniquely American contribution to the technology of wind power; railroad coal mines; and flumes by which poles, ties, and cordwood are floated from mountains to railway tracks. At Kelton, Utah, Stevens also observes corrals crammed with abandoned prairie freight wagons, graveyards that foretell modern automobile junkyards.[34]

Stevens's impressions of other cultural landscapes offer geographers and historians much to consider: California's lush farms, fruit and almond orchards, or meticulous vineyards tended by Chinese laborers, or its verdant sheep farm pastures dotted with clusters of oak trees, recalling to Stevens the wooded groves and open understory characteristic of English parks, and one of the most memorable parts of his trip; patent medicine advertisements painted on the sheer rock walls above the Humboldt River valley at Palisade, a railroad stop in northeastern Nevada—paintings that are ruinous to Stevens's aesthetic sensibilities; in Utah, a Mormon community (Willard City) hidden in the midst of an orchard forest; the meticulous communal lands of Iowa's Amana Society; corduroy roads and shaded city streets in Indiana; and the magnificent farms and farm buildings bordering Lake Erie in Ohio, studied contrasts to the sod houses of Nebraska's homesteaders.[35]

Stevens's narratives also warrant study in the context of nature writing, both for what he sees and for his impressions of those land features. On his first day, for example, he must navigate the tidal marshes bordering northern California's Suisun Bay, swamps that are dense with dry tule grass, a thickly growing rush reaching a height of nearly ten feet. As dusk gathers at the end of that difficult day, obscuring troublesome mud holes in the road, a wind rises and fans small grass fires, which miraculously light his way.[36]

Several days later, as he begins to cross the Sierra Nevada Mountains, he is aware that hillsides gaily decorated by white chaparral blossoms have disappeared, replaced by gloomy pine forests and the thunderous echoing of distant snow avalanches. Spring has returned to winter, and the face and voice of nature reign supreme, reminding him that he is alone and trivial. Yet at Laramie in Wyoming Territory, before he descends into the vast prairie, Stevens looks back to what he calls a great wonderland, acknowledging that written descriptions are inadequate to convey human impressions of the sublime. As the emptiness of the prairie begins to envelop him, perhaps he is reassured by his bicycle's mobility—heartened enough at least to turn his attention to the wealth of surrounding wildflowers.[37]

The enormous publicity accompanying Stevens's travels and book contributed to several important developments: people realized that bicycles were durable enough to offer an exciting and inexpensive means for self-propelled, long-distance travel; cycling's adventurers found inspiration in similarly challenging quests, attempting to surpass Stevens's record in time and distance; and transcontinental passages evolved into America's most celebrated bicycle treks.

FIGURE 4.4
Thomas Stevens amid California's tule grass marshes
at dusk, a wood engraving by H. E. Sylvester after a
drawing by William A. Rogers for *Outing* (April 1885).

Hugh High and George Nellis

The records of many other journeys differ greatly as to routes, distances ridden, purpose, and written chronicle. Long-distance cyclists often kept diaries that represent legacies for travel historians, yet many remain unpublished. A year after Stevens had crossed the continent, a music teacher and orchestra leader from Pottstown, Pennsylvania, Hugh High, traveled from that city to Seward, Nebraska, and back to visit fellow musicians. High, who also served as captain of the Pottstown Bicycle Club, spent three months in the Midwest and then returned by a different route, amassing more than three thousand miles over a five-month period: May to October of 1885. As did Stevens, High took note of prairie sod houses, but he lingered long enough to describe them in greater detail. He also observed that many Kansas homesteaders had replaced sod houses with brick dwellings, retaining the former as reminders of poorer days.[38]

Journalists enthusiastically tracked the progress of these often-feted travelers, and newspaper articles thus add to cyclists' legacy of writing. A number of newsmen embarked on tours of their own, translating writing ability to great advantage. In the spring in 1887, another newspaper correspondent, George Nellis from Herkimer, New York, decided to break Stevens's cross-country record. As did Thayer, Nellis traveled from east to west on a nickel-plated Columbia Expert, although he started at Herkimer and crossed into Canada at Niagara Falls, traveling north of Lake Erie to Detroit. Upon reaching San Francisco seventy-two days and 3,369 miles later, he returned to New York City by steamship, taking three more days to pedal from there to Albany and finally Herkimer. Arriving home, he rode directly to the county fair, already in progress, and accepted applause as a hometown hero.[39]

Similar to Thayer, Nellis funded his venture by writing articles for local newspapers (the *Herkimer Citizen* and *Herkimer Democrat*), but he also made arrangements with Frances Prial to publish accounts in *Wheel and Recreation*. As a capable writer and budding journalist, Nellis probably understood the important distinction between stories of travel adventure with broad appeal and the very detailed accounts compiled for the benefit of other cyclists, so typical of Kron's writing; he chose the former.[40]

Two historians separately have traced Nellis's journey from numerous newspaper articles and have contrasted or compared Nellis, Stevens, and other straightaway cyclists. Bicycle historian Charles Meinert notes that although Nellis's cycling adventure unfolds in daily regimen, the cyclist occasionally ties segments together thematically by comparing East to West, particularly New York's by then mature agricultural empire with California's young and flourishing orchards.[41]

By contrast, Keven Hayes (whose field of study is early American literature and whose book *An American Cycling Odyssey* tells the cyclist's story) observes that Nellis adopted different writing styles for two different categories of readers. For general audiences, Nellis's narratives offer vicarious adventure, but for fellow cyclists his accounts are more descriptive of travel conditions and roads; he also succumbs to condescension toward rural citizenry. Nevertheless, Hayes credits Nellis with writing a chronicle of people and places, and one that also offers adventuresome reading.[42]

Subtle differences in analysis aside, Meinert and Hayes each regard Nellis and Stevens as writers of adventure stories, tales that are centered on transcontinental journey by bicycle. Hayes, in particular, separates that genre of writing from the often-tedious statistical narratives compiled by Kron. Hayes also gives short shrift to Thayer, principally because the latter didn't travel across the entire continent by bicycle. Yet neither Meinert nor Hayes seizes the opportunity for comparison between Stevens and Nellis or their ilk, on the one hand, and straightaway cyclists such as Thayer, on the other, in the context of geographical exploration rather than adventure. Kron also clearly belongs in such comparisons, once the abundance of extraneous detail has been pared.

Despite his hurry, Nellis does take time to visit important sites, and he offers valuable observations for those who explore cultural and built environments. For example, he is impressed by the mountainous salt yards at Syracuse and especially by the extensive landscape nurseries in Geneva, New York. He also marvels at the well-appointed clubhouse interiors furnished by bicycle clubs, the members of which entertained him along the way.[43]

Bart Johnson with Irving and Arthur Woods

Both Meinert's essays and Hayes's book illustrate the potential for similar studies about the many long-distance cyclists whose travel accounts or diaries have yet to be compiled and studied. As safety bicycles gained popularity, overtaking high-wheels, the number of straightaway travelers multiplied dramatically. In 1889, Irving and Arthur Woods, brothers aged eighteen and sixteen years, respectively, and a friend, Bart Johnson, straddled this transition during a trip from Jacksonville, Illinois, to Washington, D.C., and back (approximately 2,500 miles). The Woods brothers relied on high-wheels (Irving rode a fifty-two-inch American Light Champion manufactured by the Gormully & Jeffrey firm in Chicago), but Johnson rode a safety bicycle with hard tires. The trio traveled easterly from Jacksonville through Springfield and Decatur en route to Indianapolis, where they reached the National Road and followed that corridor for much of the remaining distance, recording very detailed descriptions for the *Jacksonville Journal* and for their parents.[44]

Through Indiana and western Ohio, their narratives conform to those of Thayer and High, but east of Zanesville road conditions deteriorated. Gravel had eroded, exposing layers of rock, and east of Wheeling sizable stone bridges were in ruins. In the hill regions of southwestern Pennsylvania, the highway became practically unusable. Eventually, at Confluence, the riders chose an alternate route to Cumberland, Maryland, where they shifted to the towpath of the Chesapeake and Ohio Canal. However, that corridor was also in shambles, and the riders soon returned to the National Road, but not before contemplating the engineering significance of the Paw Paw Tunnel in western Maryland, so named for the pawpaw trees that grow nearby. In Maryland, floods also had destroyed the pike's bridges, and the route seemed unused—overgrown with weeds and recognizable only by its telegraph wires.[45]

In addition to their descriptions of the National Road and the canal, the riders observed other cultural and natural features. To three mid-westerners who had never seen an oil well, the town of Washington, Pennsylvania, appeared to be a wilderness of oil derricks, one in practically every backyard and each accompanied by steam engine and boiler. Not far to the east, they befriended Uniontown mill workers, who instructed the trio about the manufacture of steel. Much to the riders' delight, abundant blackberries lined the corridors of both road and canal.[46]

Frank Lenz

Among cycling's many adventure seekers inspired by Thomas Stevens, Pittsburgh resident Frank Lenz occupies a singular place in cycling history. From the outset, Lenz conceived his plan to circle the world by bicycle as a means to a specific end: public acclaim and, if not fortune, at least destiny. As did Stevens, Lenz negotiated an agreement with *Outing* magazine to publish accounts of his travels and to provide stipends for expenses. Unlike Stevens, Lenz contrived a strategy to establish his qualifications for that undertaking, embarking on a long-distance ride to New Orleans and also becoming adept at photography. Remarkably, he lugged a cumbersome camera box on his back throughout his world journey. That he succeeded in traversing some of the most rugged and dangerous parts of Asia before losing his life, almost within reach of Constantinople—the city that promised safe passage beyond—is a poignant part of his story.[47]

In addition, his ride completed the transition from high-wheel to safety bicycles among straightaway travelers, and he selected a Victor model with pneumatic tires, manufactured by the Overman Wheel Company. The bicycle and its tires served him well, although he exercised great care along the cinder path between the tracks of the New York Central and Hudson River Railroads, avoiding the litter of broken glass.[48]

Lenz began his journey in Pittsburgh during the spring of 1892. After reaching the National Road, he turned east. Aware that in Maryland the old pike remained in poor condition, he shifted to the Chesapeake and Ohio Canal, en route to Washington, D.C., and found the canal towpath in better repair than had Johnson and his companions three years before. Without access to towns, though, he had trouble finding water and food along the sixty-mile stretch between Cumberland and Hancock, the latter near Hagerstown, and he complained about the poor provisions at lock stores; curiously, he found the endless pedaling along the flat canal corridor to be monotonous.[49]

From the nation's capital, his route turned north to New York City, then Albany, and from there westerly along the Erie Canal corridor toward Niagara

Falls, where he crossed into Canada, detouring to Toronto before resuming his westerly course toward Detroit and Chicago. In contrast to Stevens, Lenz chose to travel across the country's northern tier through Minnesota, South Dakota, North Dakota, Montana, Idaho, and Washington before reaching Portland, Oregon, late in September and San Francisco on October 20, 107 riding days and 5,412 miles from Pittsburgh. By necessity, he followed the route of the Northern Pacific Railroad for much of the way.[50]

Understandably, the twelve articles in *Outing* that describe Lenz's progression across America compress a great detail of information into narratives, part of the reason why those accounts are more summaries of progress toward a distant objective than they are impressions of American settings. To his credit, Lenz—or his editor—successfully balances several different themes in each article: travel and route log, gazetteer-like descriptions of important cities, the hospitality provided by members of local bicycle clubs, agricultural and industrial productivity, and noteworthy land features. As did Stevens, Lenz manages at times to overcome this mechanical format and offers insightful comment, as in Yellowstone National Park, where he willingly forfeits five valuable days to explore most of the region and extols the government's decision to preserve the land as a park.[51]

Elsewhere, he finds pleasure in the many fragrant miles of Wisconsin strawberry fields ripening under the July sun; notices unexplained rings of dark grass, much longer than surrounding prairie grass, near Odessa, Minnesota; discovers a Dutch windmill near Millbank, South Dakota—odd because American wind-powered pumping engines had superseded those mills decades before; and is moved by the differences between the eastern and western slopes of the Rocky Mountains, the former magnificent in primitive grandeur as well as somber and the latter's forests more park like and inviting. Although Lenz grows tired of the dreary prairie, he also acquires a horror for section houses as he continues on a westward course through the mountains, at last arriving in Spokane, where he discovers that city's very advanced use of hydroelectric power for water works, lighting, and transportation. At Celilo Falls along the spellbinding Columbia River between Washington and Oregon, he watches as fish wheels, powered by the water's current, transfer salmon directly from river to factory. Among the many peaks he views, he reserves special praise for Mt. Shasta in northern California.[52]

Lenz's camera also distinguished the *Outing* series, which is titled "Around the World with Wheel and Camera." Yet more often than not, at least for those images reproduced for the articles, the camera documents his journey, addressing authenticity as much as recording his impressions of American places, a subtle but important distinction. Toward that end, he devised a long trip cord attached to the camera shutter, and also a timer, and Lenz stepped or rode into almost every composition. The relationship between photographer and setting thus becomes difficult to interpret, even in Yellowstone, where the monthly installment includes images of only natural features, but the photographs are not by Lenz. A few exceptions are notable, and his interest in the Paw Paw Tunnel is

FIGURE 4.5
"Going Straight Through the Mountain." Frank Lenz at the
entrance to the Paw Paw Tunnel on the Chesapeake and Ohio
Canal, a wood engraving by Robert Hoskin after a photograph
by Lenz for *Outing* (August 1892).

apparent, even though a standing Lenz dominates the image's foreground. Illustrations also accompany the articles, and some of those images are paintings by Albert Hencke, a staff artist for *Outing*, who may have drawn from Lenz's photographs. If so, he occasionally omits features such as railroads tracks.[53]

Tom Winder

By the mid-1890s, the lure of distance had become a siren, and American adventurers on safety bicycles were exploring practically every corner of the country, seeking new records to break and writing about their experiences. Among many such exploits, the extraordinary travels of reporter Tom Winder charted new territory and, according to a report in the *New York Times*, struck even wheelmen as a little odd. Winder's journey began in New Orleans on March 14, 1895, the consequence of a wager challenging him to ride many thousands of miles around the United States, following coastal lines and international boundaries as closely as possible and in no more than 300 consecutive days, arriving in New Orleans before January 6, 1896.[54]

Winder chose to follow warm weather and headed west as a traveling correspondent for the *Illustrated Buffalo Express*, sending its editors weekly letters and establishing more than seventy-five points of registration at cities along the route. In New Mexico, he endured thirty-six hours without food, and he walked for twenty-seven miles in Washington following a mechanical breakdown. As had Lenz, Winder wisely fashioned an umbrella for his bicycle to provide protection from sun and rain. Opinions of New York City wheelmen notwithstanding, much of Buffalo turned to out to greet Winder when he arrived in that city on August 9. From there, he wheeled into New England before following the Eastern Seaboard as far south as Jacksonville, Florida. In that city, he turned west again, advancing into the Deep South and returning to New Orleans on December 10, 224 days and thirty-three states later.[55]

Although pursuing a record and averaging impressive daily mileage, Winder seems confident that the difficulty of his objective requires little emphasis, and he develops narratives that are as informative as they are adventurous, a skillful balance of challenge, storytelling, and observation. His writing touches a broad range of topics, such as industry, agriculture, natural resources, and architecture, and he develops these subjects in depth. He is filled with wonder in Oregon's forest wilderness, and he is captivated by the wild swans that feed on wapato root in that state's inland waters. Yet he also regards the dense stands of pine, fir, and hemlock to be gloomy walls of darkness, blocking all sunlight.[56]

A continent away, he finds the long-needle pine forests of South Carolina and Georgia to be similarly foreboding, the sound of wind in the tall branches inexpressibly sad and inducing melancholia. However, he prepares a thorough discourse about the industries dependent upon those forests: lampblack, dyes, charcoal, creosote, alcohol, and naval stores from the sap (pitch, rosin, and turpentine). Winder is a keen observer, recognizing that railroad beds that appeared unused and overgrown with wire grass are designed in that manner to prevent sandy soil from being lifted by the vacuum of passing trains. He also discusses social issues, including Southern attitudes toward African Americans, seeming to be objective but also betraying his own cultural bias in the process.[57]

George Loher

Winder is far from alone during this period, and numerous wheelmen who became continental or global travelers also added to the growing body of travel writing by cyclists. George Loher, a member of Oakland's Acme Cycling Club and a butcher by trade, embarked on a transcontinental journey in 1895, using a route very similar to that selected by Lenz between Chicago and San Francisco, but traveling west to east. Similar to the account by Stevens, the story of Loher's journey through western states becomes a trial that pits man and machine against nature; east of Madison, Wisconsin, the trip is almost anticlimactic, because telegraph poles connect all large cities on the main roads. Although Loher proved to be equal to nature's challenges, his bicycle, a Stearns Yellow Fellow (so named after its bright yellow paint), did not. Loher also started late in the year, in August, and the most astonishing aspect of his trip may have been his ability to complete the journey before the onset of winter, given the frequent mechanical problems with his bicycle.[58]

Loher's story is recounted in a book by his granddaughter, *The Wonderful Ride: Being the True Journal of Mr. George T. Loher, Who in 1895 Cycled from Coast to Coast on His Yellow Fellow Wheel*, based on a diary and manuscript that survived. The reader's point of view is that of relentless forward progress—similar to the narratives by Stevens and Lenz, but Loher loses his way several times in Montana and North Dakota, adding suspense. Wryly, he observes that Americans could wheel through Europe without ever leaving the North American continent, thanks to the many small German towns in North Dakota and Norwegian and Swedish communities in Minnesota. He also inspects the disassembled ruins of Chicago's Columbian Exposition, a view usually omitted from accounts of that fair. He finds the cider mills in Indiana's farming country tempting, and discovers that Ohio residents east of Bryan observe two different times: sun time and standard time, the former twenty-five minutes slower than the latter and observed mostly by workers. He travels along an eighteen-mile bicycle path between Oberlin and Elyria in Ohio and in New York discovers paths between New Hartford and Utica and between Schenectady and Albany; he also applauds the state's temperance towns, such as Fredonia. Loher's diary offers quick, cross-sectional snapshots of America's ever-changing places and people, far less structured than the accounts by Lenz or Stevens and perhaps more valuable for that quality. He arrived in Manhattan on October 30, after sixty-three days of riding and 4,354 miles of nearly straightaway travel.

John Fraser, Edward Lunn, and Francis H. Lowe

In July of the following year, 1896, three Englishmen—John Foster Fraser, Samuel Edward Lunn, and Francis Herbert Lowe—left London, intending to the circle the world, but seeking casual travel rather than adventure. They returned to London quietly in August 1898, 774 days later, and in 1899 Fraser compiled their stories into a lighthearted book, *Round the World on a Wheel*. Fraser's portraits of the American West, particularly the sheds of the Central Pacific Railroad in the Sierra Nevada Mountains, are often more descriptive than those by Stevens, and although Fraser offers unflattering accounts of American society, he nevertheless finds America's emerging heartland appealing: "The towns we slipped through were neat and clean; the houses were of the bungalow style, of wood, usually painted two shades of green, standing under shady trees on rich, well-cared-for plats of grass, and there were always hammocks...happiness and plenty were the two words stamped over Iowa."[59]

CHAPTER FIVE

Country Riding

The paradise of open country beckoned to cyclists irresistibly, but the torment of poor roads lurked relentlessly—just out of sight around every bend and beyond the rise of every hill. From its inception, the LAW voiced increasingly focused appeals for better rural roads, and the promotional, administrative, journalistic, and legislative efforts that comprised the Good Roads movement represent one of cycling's important legacies. However, that campaign made slow progress in provincial America, and restless wheelmen instead turned their energies to more satisfying endeavors: the building of suburban and rural bicycle paths.

Contexts for the conception, planning, construction, and use of these paths began during the high-wheel era, at least as early as 1885, and quickly became multifaceted. Initiatives developed locally, grounded in an ever-present urge among wheelmen to take full advantage of the mobility offered by bicycles. When sparks of enthusiasm encountered opportunity, plans for bicycle paths took shape spontaneously and advanced with persistent efforts by influential wheelmen. Cycling's many journals circulated accounts of these local successes, as did those who attended gatherings of the LAW and its state divisions.

Various other factors contributed to the historical contexts for bicycle paths that eventually stretched across the countryside. Wheelmen sometimes turned to sidepaths, narrow traces adjacent to roads and foot-worn by pedestrians, who sought to avoid the mud, hardened wheel ruts, and broken-rock surfaces of country highways. When communities adopted ordinances prohibiting the use of bicycles on principal streets, sidepaths provided the best alternatives; similar corridors sometimes extended along railroad tracks as well. Wheelmen soon began building their own versions, and during the 1890s the sidepath movement influenced bicycle path building in many regions. Apart from Long Island, where wheelmen pedaled along an extensive network of sidepaths in place before the high-wheel era, the campaign to build sidepaths originated in western and central New York.

Still other cyclists converted a variety of existing corridors to bicycle use, and some, such as abandoned trolley lines or canal towpaths, related only tangentially to highways. With permission from landowners in some locales, cyclists also constructed overland paths that linked origins and destinations by direct routes. By the mid-1890s, the sheer number of bicycle riders had greatly enlarged the contexts for path building in most of its facets, and cyclists believed they had found the means to experience country riding.

High-Wheel Era Origins

Nineteenth-century bicycle paths originated in scattered localities, where irrepressible enthusiasm for cycling propelled initiative. Success of initial efforts often led to the extension of existing paths or to the building of new corridors, creating far-reaching networks of paths.

Wilkes-Barre, Kingston, and Wyoming

During the high-wheel era, clubs in several clustered communities in Pennsylvania's Luzerne County planned one of the country's very early path systems, linking Wilkes-Barre, Kingston, Wyoming, and Pittston. Work on the first of these cinder paths may have begun during the spring of 1885, and for much of its length the path followed the road leading northeasterly from Kingston to Forty-Fort, Wyoming, Exeter, and West Pittston on the western side of the Susquehanna River. By the following year, a second path extended from Kingston to the bridge at Wilkes-Barre, joining those two towns and creating a continuous route about ten miles in length. In 1886, cyclists constructed a path along the eastern side of Main Street in Kingston and built a third corridor, linking Wilkes-Barre with Pittston on the river's opposite side at a cost of nearly $800, funds generated by subscriptions. During ensuing years, wheelmen may have extended these paths to the southwest as far as Nanticoke and Dorrance, and a separate network of paths eventually encircled Harvey's Lake to the northwest.[1]

Members of five bicycle clubs, all formed between 1880 and 1886, financed and built these paths: the Wilkes-Barre Bicycle Club, the Pittston Bicycle Club, the Wilkes-Barre Ramblers, the Kingston Bicycle Club, and the Wyoming Wheelmen. A third Wilkes-Barre club, the West End Wheelmen, was organized in 1889 and participated as well. Members of the large Scranton Bicycle Club also wheeled south to Wilkes-Barre, a round trip of about forty miles, adding to cycling activity in the region.[2]

Spirited clubs in these nearby communities influenced the expansion of paths into adjoining communities, but much of the credit for initiating the first paths between Kingston and Wyoming and between Kingston and Wilkes-Barre belongs to a prominent figure in Kingston, Stephen B. Vaughn. Older than most of his fellow wheelmen, Vaughn became a founding member and captain of the Kingston club at age fifty-three and later served as an elected representative to the Pennsylvania Division of the LAW. His respected standing as a director of several local businesses and institutions may have placed him in the role of peacemaker among cyclists and other users of local streets and roads.[3]

In the spring of 1885, Vaughn served on a committee charged with keeping the road between Kingston and West Pittston in good condition. After conferences with citizens, and to discourage ordinances unfavorable to wheelmen, the group asked cyclists to abstain from riding on Sundays at hours when interference with churchgoers could occur and to ride courteously at all times. Plans for a separate path may have sprouted from those discussions as a form of compromise, and that summer wheelmen began pedaling their high-wheels along a cinder trace between Kingston and West Pittston. Vaughn possibly used his influence as a director of the Wilkes-Barre and West Side Railway Company to obtain construction materials, but he also may have contributed his own resources, because two of the Wilkes-Barre clubs elected him an honorary member, as did the Scranton club.[4]

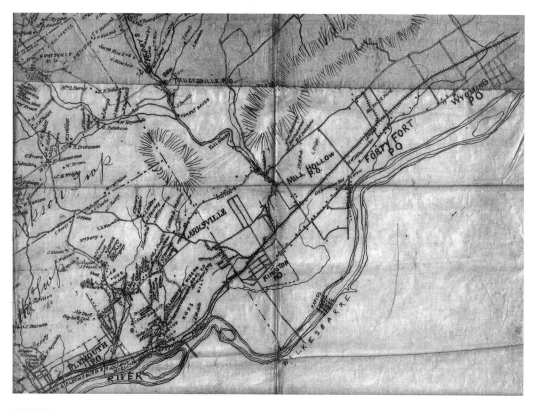

FIGURE 5.2

Map of the west side of the Susquehanna River, circa 1880. In 1885, members of several bicycle clubs in Luzerne County, Pennsylvania, built one of the country's very early networks of cinder-surfaced bicycle paths, linking Wilkes-Barre, Kingston, Forty Fort, and Wyoming, about eight miles apart. Courtesy Luzerne County Historical Society, Wilkes-Barre.

Frequent club excursions, races, parades, and a favored network of paths—all publicized by local newspapers—helped to make the region a hub of cycling activity, attracting wheelmen from nearby cities, including Hazleton and Bloomsburg. Delegates from both cities journeyed to Wilkes-Barre in the summer of 1887, the year the Pennsylvania Division of the LAW convened its annual meet in that city, culminating with a festive parade and races on July 4. On a Sunday morning, with participants arriving from cities as distant as Philadelphia, Harrisburg, Williamsport, and Binghamton, more than one hundred wheelmen embarked on a run to Wyoming along the cinder path, and Abbott Bassett reported the event in the *LAW Bulletin*. Five years later, Scranton wheelmen took a turn at entertaining the state meet, and they repeated the journey on the by then famous cinder path through Wyoming Valley, pausing at Vaughn's home.[5]

During these early years, Wilkes-Barre wheelmen learned an important lesson about rural bicycle paths: they had a never-ending need for maintenance, whether caused by vegetation, heavy rain, livestock, or by drivers of wheeled vehicles who found the paths easier to navigate than the adjoining roads—a practice that aggravated the often fractious relationships among cyclists and rural citizenry.[6]

Despite these difficulties, the Wilkes-Barre and Pittston paths remained in good condition for many years, suggesting a regimen of care. In 1893, the LAW's Pennsylvania Division published the seventh edition of that state's road books, awarding its highest rating, A1, to the paths. However, constant use or damage from other sources must have taken a steady toll, and in 1898, when a new committee issued a revised edition, editors cautioned cyclists not to use the paths. At least some of the region's wheelmen continued to favor separate corridors, and the new edition included a route for a proposed cycle path from Scranton to Hawley, about forty miles to the northeast. The corridor probably followed the Pennsylvania Coal Co. Gravity Railroad, which also stretched into Pittston, and at Hawley cyclists could transfer to the Delaware and Hudson Canal towpath.[7]

Binghamton Bicycle Club

During both high-wheel and safety bicycle eras, the network of paths in the Wilkes-Barre region influenced projects in several cities. Members of the Binghamton Bicycle Club, chartered in 1882, traveled to the LAW meet in July 1887 and returned to their city with reports of the cinder path. Later that month, other cyclists formed the Binghamton Wheel Club, and in August they voted to construct a path to Union, nine miles west. A committee solicited subscriptions from all the city's wheelmen, quickly raised $400, obtained permission from road commissioners and adjoining property owners, and employed a local contractor, John Shultz, to begin work.

That fall, Shultz removed sod, graded the surface for drainage, and erected small bridges over swales too wide to fill with gravel. The following spring, in 1888, he surfaced the path with three inches of coal ashes (more easily obtained in Binghamton than cinders) and rolled the composition into a smooth surface. During the winter months, the committee continued to raise funds, and the club's three-foot path with five bridges eventually cost about $800.[8]

Holyoke, Northampton, and Springfield Wheelmen

Enthusiasm for cycling fostered communication among wheelmen from region to region, and word of the path between Binghamton and Union soon reached Massachusetts, where in January 1888 members of the Holyoke Bicycle Club established a committee to raise money and build a path to Northampton, about nine miles away. Wheelmen in Northampton and Springfield added to Holyoke's subscriptions, and the towns also consulted Shultz about building their path. The corridor began at the base of Quarry Hill in Holyoke and for much of its distance clung within three feet of boundary fences, far enough from the highway to prevent teams from destroying it. Where the road remained usable, the two corridors merged. By the end of July, wheelmen had completed portions of the path along sections of the road too sandy for their high-wheels, but difficulties in gaining permission from town officials may have hampered the effort .[9]

Two months earlier, cyclists had opened a short path between Springfield and Chicopee, but interest in completing a path for the entire distance between Springfield and Holyoke soon waned, and club members abandoned the idea. Nevertheless, project promoters envisioned unions of wheelmen constructing sidepaths throughout the Connecticut River Valley and venturing far north into the White Mountains. That summer, a New Haven cyclist named Alvah G. Fisher began a subscription list for a seventy-mile path from his city to New York, urging clubs to form an association to undertake the work. Rival manufacturers Albert Overman and Albert Pope both added their names to the tally, but Fisher's job responsibilities intervened; by October, he had forsaken the project. Editors of *Bicycling World* continued to support the scheme and encouraged clubs to plan extensive path networks, suggesting that dealers and manufacturers also should take notice.[10]

Sidepaths in LAW Road Books

Although Binghamton's wheelmen likely borrowed inspiration from Wilkes-Barre's path, they just as easily might have found motivation from the many sidepaths noted in the first edition of the *New York Road Book*, published that same year (1887). In contrast to the road books circulated during the high-wheel era by the LAW's Pennsylvania Division, which identify only a few sidepaths, New York's book points to numerous examples in several parts of the state, including the Binghamton area, where Karl Kron had found the sidepaths from Port Dickinson to Binghamton (three miles south) to be very serviceable in 1883. In the Hudson River valley, wheelmen compared the sidepath surface between Valatie and Kinderhook to a racing track.[11]

Although evidence is probably buried in local news accounts, wheelmen improved or extended local sidepaths already in place during the high-wheel era, particularly where clubs became active. At a minimum, the mere compacting of soil caused by wheelmen's repeated use amounted to a simple form of extension or maintenance. Both the Pennsylvania and New York road books provided routes and maps for wheeling in other states, and each advises the use of sidepaths in various regions. The *Connecticut Road Book* of 1888 recommends both roads and sidepaths in towns stretching along the Connecticut shore from New York City to the Rhode Island border and also favors a route from New London to Worcester through the valleys of the Thames and Quinnebaug rivers, where cyclists could find sidepaths in the vicinity of manufacturing districts.[12]

In New Jersey, where both the Pennsylvania and New York editions identified routes, the New York road book plotted the locations of sidepaths scattered among the towns of South Orange, Rahway, Springfield, Scotch Plains, Plainfield, Summit, Morristown, Montclair, and several other towns, part of a large riding district within easy reach of clubs in many nearby cities. Wheelmen could travel easily between at least two of these towns, Scotch Plains and Plainfield, along a very good, three-mile sidepath marred only by a few bad roots. Cyclists from New York City also ventured into those regions, and Kron found sidepaths in the vicinity of Wayne and Pompton Plains to be preferable to the roads during his excursions through the Jersey hills.[13]

Existing sidepaths in New Jersey probably led to thoughts about opening new paths across that state. In 1886, the Hudson County Wheelmen from Jersey City and the Bellerophon Wheelmen from Westfield proposed building a long-distance cinder path linking Jersey City with Philadelphia, adjacent to the tracks of the Pennsylvania Railroad, but the project may have ended in the discussion stage. Nevertheless, ideas for such long-distance routes lingered, and early in 1895 wheelmen proposed a path from Philadelphia to Atlantic City and from Trenton to Asbury Park; the latter advanced at least as far as route planning for the forty-five mile corridor. Jersey City cyclists also sought a much shorter path to Newark at about the same time.[14]

Far to the west, the LAW's Ohio Division published editions of its handbook in 1886 and 1892, straddling the period when high-wheel machines fell behind the rapidly advancing safety bicycles. The few references to sidepaths occur mostly in northeastern counties, along a principal corridor connecting Buffalo with Cleveland and continuing westerly toward Elyria, reinforcing a supposition that sidepaths often evolved along heavily traveled routes and existed long before the arrival of bicycles.[15]

Wheelway Leagues and Safety Bicycles

As wheelmen sped headlong into the era of safety bicycles, clubs continued to furnish the stimuli needed to propel ambitious path-building projects, as did the resolve of individual cyclists. Those circumstances remained true whether local paths originated spontaneously or were influenced by successful projects elsewhere. However, the principal challenges of planning, funding, and building paths led to the formation of more inclusive wheelmen's associations, varying in composition but often representing unions among several clubs or communities of riders. Ironically, associations formed as part of the Good Roads movement also led to plans for several bicycle paths. Cycling's fantastic growth in popularity following the invention of the safety bicycle generated a corresponding boost in the number of both riders and clubs, whose swelling membership rosters embodied a much broader cross-section of American society by the mid-1890s. Path building became a broadly based campaign, bolstered by legislative support that also helped to advance interest in bicycle paths beyond club doors.

In New York State, the zeal for country riding seemed unbounded in many cities during both the high-wheel and safety bicycle eras. Albany, Utica, Rome, Syracuse, Rochester, and Buffalo all became regional centers of cycling activity and all were well represented by bicycle clubs. Syracuse and Buffalo became two of the country's

FIGURE 5.3
Edward DeGraff's 1893 path in Amsterdam, New York, marked the early stages of what would become a nearly continuous system of sidepaths from Albany to Buffalo, carefully planned from town to town and largely complete by 1901. From *Good Roads* (February 4, 1898), courtesy of the Center for Research Libraries, Chicago.

major centers for bicycle manufacturing. However, the beginnings of the state's sidepath movement in Niagara County straddle the high-wheel and safety bicycle eras; thus, segregating the impetus for bicycle paths elsewhere in the state from the influence of that campaign can be difficult. Although that larger movement soon dominated path building the following important initiatives begun before county sidepath commissions attained authority.

DeGraff Path
On Labor Day in 1893, Edward T. DeGraff, a bank teller, toiled with fellow wheelmen to build a short path over one of the town's imposing hills near his family's home in Amsterdam, New York, located in Montgomery County, roughly seventeen miles west of Schenectady. During the next several years, DeGraff continued to invest his own funds and energies to enlarge that project, aided by private contributions from an appreciative community. By 1898, Amsterdam's bicycle paths had lengthened to fifteen miles, extending westerly toward Aikin and easterly to

FIGURES 5.4

For centuries, New York's Mohawk River Valley has served as a vital, long-distance transportation corridor, evident in its many layers of travel history: Native American trails, the Erie Canal, the New York Central Railroad, the New York Barge Canal, and the New York State Thruway. Late nineteenth-century bicycle paths added another layer to that historic corridor. Although the precise location of the 1893 path depicted here is not known, it may be near St. Johnsville in Montgomery County. Courtesy Fulton-Montgomery Photographic Archives, Margaret Reaney Memorial Library and Museum, St. Johnsville.

Cranesville and Hoffman's Ferry, the latter just beyond the Schenectady County border.[16]

Following passage of the state's uniform sidepath law, the Montgomery County Sidepath Commission continued the work begun by DeGraff, eventually completing a sidepath to the county's western border beyond St. Johnsville. DeGraff, who became captain of the local cycling club (the Amsterdam Wheelmen) and who embarked on long-distance rides with another Amsterdam cyclist, racer Adelbert Payne, thus played a key role in Amsterdam's cycling history. However, the lasting significance of his contribution is that it signals the beginning stages of nearly an unbroken corridor of sidepaths stretching across the entire state between Albany and Buffalo, lengthy parts of which followed the Mohawk River valley. Although other New York cyclists were thinking and working in similar fashion during the early 1890s and although scant evidence of DeGraff's path survives, it nevertheless should be counted among the first tangible indicators of the direction that path building would soon take in New York.[17]

Montauk Wheelmen

During the summer of 1893, the same year that DeGraff began building the Amsterdam path, cyclists in Easthampton, Long Island, joined forces as the Montauk Wheelmen and began improving an existing three-mile path, probably as far as Bridgehampton. The new organization asked its members either to contribute work on the path or to bestow an equivalent value to the club treasury. Although occupying a seemingly remote place in the larger context of path building, the Montauk wheelmen illustrate a subtle shift in club makeup that had begun to occur with the arrival of safety bicycles. Although social agendas remained a visible aspect of many clubs, projects such as path building offered a different type of cohesion to bind members. In many rural towns and small cities, both in New York and beyond its borders, path building became a principal reason for clubs to exist, a worthy substitute for impressive (and expensive) clubhouses, and an effective means to boost membership.[18]

Crescent Cycling Club

Titusville, located in Pennsylvania's far northwest corner and straddling Crawford and Venango counties (the origins of the country's commercial oil production), illustrates that trend. Wheelmen organized the Crescent Cycling Club during the early months of 1893, but riders remained confined to local streets because roads leading away from the town were impassable. When some cyclists, who professed little interest in organizing social events, began to doubt the club's usefulness, practical members devised a path project adjacent to the road leading north through the valley of Oil Creek to Hydetown, three miles away. After clearing the corridor, workers added a surface of cinders but also experimented with acidic slag obtained from the Titusville Chemical Works, which extracted sulfur from iron pyrites. Club members completed the project by the fall of 1893, and the slag proved adequate for controlling vegetation.[19]

The success of that first venture created a central purpose for the club and led to plans that same fall and winter to extend the path eighteen miles to Lake Canadohta, which gave the wheelway its name. Work resumed during the spring of 1894 after members obtained permission to use the abandoned grade of the Union and Titusville Railroad, adjacent to Oil Creek. By the fall of 1894, the path had lengthened to eight miles, reaching as far as Tryonville Station. There, residents of Centreville joined the project, pushing the corridor forward an additional two miles to their village by year's end. Work resumed the following spring, and by the fall the path had reached Riceville, fourteen miles from the start. From there, a decent road carried cyclists to Lake Canadohta.[20]

Associated Wheelmen of Hazleton

Cyclists in some Pennsylvania communities engaged in path building before establishing formal associations, which then added a measure of permanence. Hazleton cyclists, who were probably familiar with cinder paths in nearby

Wilkes-Barre, began building short bicycle paths during the mid-1890s on the city's south side, the first of which connected Audenreid to Jeansville, about 1.5 miles apart. The second connected Audenreid to Hazleton, three miles distant. Success of these first projects led to the formation of the Associated Wheelmen of Hazleton and Vicinity, incorporated solely for the purpose of opening, constructing, and maintaining roads for bicyclists. Their corporate charter, granted in September 1897, provided an easy method for issuing shares to supporters, including at least one Wilkes-Barre resident, and the corporation successfully negotiated for rights of way from several of the region's coal mining companies.[21]

Led by mining engineer Louis O. Emmerich, the association completed the north side path the following year, possibly one of the country's most enduring nineteenth-century bicycle corridors. The path began in Hazleton along Diamond Road but then climbed to a mountain ridge above the hamlet of Ebervale and followed its rocky spine to the mining village of Eckley, seven miles away (today, a historic site managed by the Pennsylvania Historical and Museum Commission). Construction began in the early spring, and by mid-May workers had crossed the road to No. 7 Stockton mine. At its juncture with that corridor, the path descended in a gradual loop and then continued along a level course, reaching Eckley and its coal breaker by mid-June. Any sections of the corridor that may have survived for more than a century are a tribute to Emmerich and his crew foreman, Anthony Payne, who supervised a large force of laborers paid to cut, dig, chip, and blast through brush and rock, surfacing the six-foot wide opening with clay and gravel and then compacting it with a three-ton roller. Strip mining in the region eventually erased some sections of the corridor, but an abundance of rock and gravel on the mountain surely contributed to the path's longevity. Complementing its careful construction, the route's high elevation offered commanding scenery. The ride became a local favorite, particularly on warm summer evenings, when cyclists navigated the route by lamplight.[22]

Although Emmerich's original survey of the corridor is lost, the path is marked on an important series of mining lease surveys from 1904, encompassing Eckley, Buck Mountain, Stockton, and Beaver Meadows. Maps show the intersections of the path with lease boundaries and also mark the distances from corner monuments to those junctures, providing a means to compare the location of an existing path with the survey coordinates. However, the maps also show boundary intersections with what may be logging roads, which in a few locations are near the path. In addition, above the mining village of Hazlebrook, more than halfway from Hazleton to Eckley, the survey also shows the path in close proximity to the bed of an old switchback railroad, constructed at midcentury as a temporary line by the Lehigh and Luzerne Railroad and then abandoned when its tunnel beneath Council Ridge had been completed. Whether Emmerich used a portion of that corridor is not known, but written accounts from 1898 verify that approximately three thousand feet of the path did not require clearing.[23]

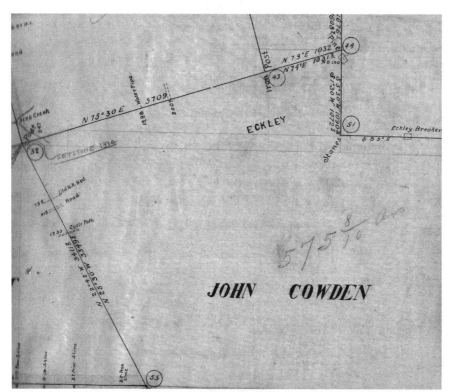

FIGURES 5.5 AND 5.6

In 1898, the Associated Wheelmen of Hazleton and Vicinity constructed a bicycle path along a mountain ridge between the coal mining communities of Hazleton and Eckley in eastern Pennsylvania. The path's location is shown on 1904 mining lease surveys titled "Hayhurst and Hartwell Surveys. Map Showing Eckley, Buck Mountain, Stockton and part of Beaver Meadow Leases" by I. E. Hartwell. A path along the mountain ridge exists today and leads to the former site of the Eckley coal breaker. Both that structure and the bicycle path are identified on the survey, but a study is needed to determine whether the two coincide. Courtesy of Butler Enterprises, successor to Tench Coxe Holdings, Drifton, Pennsylvania.

Today, a well-worn path courses through a high, wind-blown forest of stunted hardwoods on that ridge, with mountain laurel and rhododendron scattered throughout. Unfortunately, traces of those other corridors on the mining surveys create uncertainty about the origins of the current path, and a survey is needed. The path's location along the mountain ridge is consistent with published descriptions of the route by John Sharpless, the attorney for the association who secured the corporate charter in 1897, and current residents of Hazleton who have lived much of their lives in that city recall using the existing path as long ago as the 1950s. Surveys also show what may be traces of spur corridors, indicating that a network of bicycle paths once existed. For example, at Jeddo (about two miles east of Ebervale) wheelmen organized an auxiliary association and opened a link to the north side path. About two miles north of Jeddo, the Associated Wheelmen of Freeland, a small city, incorporated in 1898 with identical path-building objectives for their city.[24]

During the years when wheelmen in Hazleton and Freeland formed corporations to build bicycle paths, cyclists in other locales throughout the Northeast created associations with similar objectives. Although some cities and towns may have been isolated geographically, few cycling communities remained unaware of the rapidly growing campaigns to build bicycle paths. At the same time, long-standing local enthusiasm for cycling required little stimulus from afar, and credit for inspirational projects, such as the Eckley path, often belongs more to local initiative than it does to the influence of cycling's pace setters. After all, poor roads everywhere jolted cyclists into thoughts about blissful rides on smooth surfaces.

Cycle Path League of Springfield

Events in Springfield, Massachusetts, illustrate this mix of local and regional influence in the formation of bicycle path associations. In 1898, a decade after following the example of Binghamton cyclists, wheelmen in Holyoke and Northampton joined with the much larger cycling city of Springfield, a few miles to the south and home to several bicycle clubs. Together, they formed the Cycle Path League of Springfield, and that organization improved and extended a cinder path along the Connecticut River, leading south from the city roughly four miles to Agawam and its amusement park. During ensuing years, the league continued the passage as far south as Suffield, Connecticut, and members also pondered the challenge of building a path ascending Mt. Tom, between Holyoke and Northampton. Several years earlier, wheelmen in Pittsfield in the western part of the state secured public funding and, with supervision from the public works department, built paths from Pittsfield Junction to Glenn House Corner and also a path linking the city to Lenox Highway.[25]

Keene's Five-Mile Drive

New England towns often pursue independent courses, and bicycle path projects offered no exception. In Keene, the New Hampshire Good Roads Association and its president, Francis C. Faulkner, jointly advocated bicycle paths at a time when many promoters of good roads believed that building sidepaths would divert funding from their cause. Thus, when Faulkner addressed the annual banquet of the Monadnock Cycle Club in February 1898 with a talk titled "Cycle Paths," wheelmen and LAW officials had good reason to listen. Faulkner observed that bicycles served a then new order of travelers, whose numbers had grown to exceed those of earlier categories. Just as pedestrians justifiably demanded separate and safer travelways when vehicular congestion became oppressive and dangerous, so did cyclists deserve corridors free from interference. In remarks as relevant today as then, Faulkner declared: "I believe it is practicable and proper to have a part of the highway in every road in this country set apart for the use of wheelmen."[26]

Faulkner's words may not have carried very far beyond Keene's environs, but the city's mayor and aldermen authorized a path adjoining Five-Mile Drive, supplementing an earlier path along Court Street en route to Four Corners. Subsequent newspaper accounts also describe a cycle path along Main Street. Today, Maple Avenue occupies a segment of what had been Five-Mile Drive, and the road is still bordered by pathways.[27]

Middletown-Meriden Path

In Connecticut, a bicycle path built in 1896 between Middletown and Meriden (via Westfield and Highland House) illustrates the type of initiatives that fostered public support for bicycle paths during this period. Early in June, wheelmen in Middletown launched a subscription campaign and raised $400 by month's end, aided by the *Penny Press*, a local newspaper that offered to collect pledge letters. Wheelmen began using the completed path early in August, gaining access to an earlier, nine-mile path to New Haven built by the Meriden Wheel Club and also funded by subscriptions, including donations from Albert Pope and Albert Overman. Although heavy rains washed away sections of the Middletown-Meriden path the following summer, excursions toward New Haven and Hartford continued. Aided by another financial contribution from Albert Pope in 1898, Hartford cyclists constructed a path most of the way to New Britain.[28]

The previous year (1897), cyclists in New London and Norwich had collaborated in the building of a path between those two cities. In addition, work on a path leading west from New Haven may have reached the vicinity of Bridgeport during the summer of 1900, possibly boosted by renewed interest in Fisher's decade-old proposal to link New Haven and New York with a bicycle corridor.[29]

Vineland and Southampton Cycle Path Associations

In the sandy plains of southern New Jersey, wheelmen's confederations also built bicycle paths after 1896. The Vineland Cycle Path Association cleared a short, three-mile corridor to South Vineland and then began a similar route leading west from the town. Not far away, the Southampton Bicycle Road Association took advantage of a rail line belonging to the Evansville and Vincentown Branch of the Pennsylvania Railroad, opening a path adjoining that right-of-way from Vincentown to its depot at Smalley's Corner. The path also linked two important stone roads, the first between Mount Holly and Pemberton and the second between Vincentown and Camden. On opposite sides of the state, a three-mile corridor linked Paulsboro and Gibbstown near the Delaware River south of Camden, and another path joined Pleasantville with Atlantic City.[30]

As in other remote locales, these associations provided a means for cyclists from scattered communities to join in common purpose. Both groups formed after enactment of an 1896 law allowing New Jersey townships to raise money for the construction of bicycle paths along public roads and implicitly encouraging the formation of such associations. Passage of this law, early in March 1896, corresponded almost to the day with passage of New York's first law to create a county sidepath commission, although the latter bill had been drafted almost two years before. A year later, in 1897, New York's legislature passed a law allowing clubs, corporations, or associations in Chautauqua County to build bicycle paths. The timing of these bills points to the growing influence of regional as well as local impetus in the origins of specific bicycle paths, and the provisions in New Jersey's law that encouraged the formation of collaborative associations to build paths reinforces that trend. Although local enthusiasm remains very important, separation of the two influences becomes increasingly difficult.[31]

Wheelway League of Oneida County

Similar developments in New York State confirm the trend toward regional influence and the continuing role of local wheelmen as catalysts for path-building associations and projects. By the early 1890s, residents in the Oneida County cities of Rome and Utica, about eighteen miles apart along the Erie Canal, had grown devoted to cycling. During the summer of 1893, Rome wheelmen followed the example set by Niagara County cyclists and established the Rome Sidepath League. The following summer, they began building a path to nearby Ridge Mills, but remained only loosely organized until the spring of 1897, when members finally drafted a constitution and bylaws. During the spring of 1894, State Assemblyman Joseph Porter, a lawyer from Rome, had introduced legislation authorizing county highway commissioners to approve the construction of bicycle paths along highways when requested to do so by any town. The bill's authors presumed that corporations similar to those created for the construction of turnpikes would physically build the paths and permitted those corporations to erect gates and to collect tolls.[32]

Whether that unsuccessful initiative originated from activities in Rome or Utica, or both, is not known, but by the fall of 1895 Utica cyclists had formed the Wheelway League of Oneida County, probably encouraging the wait-and-see approach apparently adopted by Rome cyclists, who eventually focused their energies on building paths north or west of Rome and entrusted the remaining county to their sibling. In any case, origins of both organizations sprouted from

South Street, New Hartford, N. Y.

FIGURE 5.7

Bicycle paths rarely appear in landscape imagery from the late nineteenth century. The photographer who recorded this scene along South Street in New Hartford, New York, a few miles west of Utica, may not have intended to document the narrow sidepath between sidewalk and street; those few image makers who did usually placed a bicyclist or bicycle in the scene. Nevertheless, the seemingly innocuous trace is actually a carefully patrolled toll corridor, eligible only to those riders whose bicycles displayed sidepath tags purchased from county sidepath commissions.

frustration with the poor condition of county roads. Historical accounts concerning the genesis of each entity suggest a spontaneous call to action, but one borrowing directly from the organizational structure developed at Lockport.[33]

Utica's wheelmen solicited subscriptions for funds rather than memberships, and generated revenue from bicycle shows and exhibitions, reasoning that the popularity of initial ventures would lead naturally to a substantial corps of members. That strategy proved workable, and that same fall the league raised enough money to build a path from the Genesee Street crossing of the West Shore Railroad to New Hartford village, followed by a second, much longer path from New Hartford to Kirkland (approximately five miles), with loops linking Clinton, New York Mills, and Yorkville—in all, about twenty-four miles. Paths from New Hartford south to Washington Mills, Clayville, and Cassville soon followed, as did an extension of the Kirkland path to Oneida Castle near the county's western boundary.[34]

By the close of 1897, nearly 3,900 county residents had become members of the wheelway league; sidepath building had continued to increase each year;

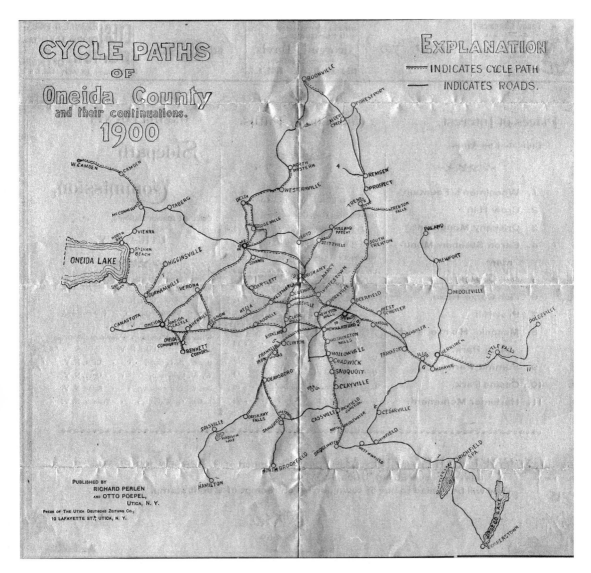

FIGURE 5.8

Beginning in 1893, cyclists from Rome and Utica established wheelway and sidepath leagues to raise money for path building. By 1899, the year state lawmakers adopted the Ellsworth Sidepath Law, county wheelmen had constructed more than 130 miles of paths. A year later, when Richard Perlen and Otto Poepel of Utica published this map, that figure had lengthened to about 170 miles and eventually reached almost two hundred miles. Long after the public's interest in cycling had waned, Oneida County cyclists traveled the region's sidepaths; during the 1907 season, these cyclists purchased more than 1,700 sidepath tags. Reproduction by permission of the Buffalo and Erie County Public Library, Buffalo, New York.

the league had adopted standard specifications for path design and construction; and two other towns, Lee (1896) and Verona (1897), also had formed sidepath leagues to connect with paths originating from Rome and Utica. By the time New York adopted its uniform sidepath bill, in 1899, Oneida County could report more than 130 miles of sidepaths to delegates at the state's convention of sidepath commissions, held in Rochester that fall. Debate about sidepath routes soon developed, and cyclists in Kirkland and Vernon formed their own Seneca Turnpike Cyclers' Association to assure construction of a path linking their communities. County sidepaths continued to lengthen for several more years, eventually reaching about two hundred miles, and the sidepath commission divided the county into four districts to facilitate the selection of routes, assigning the management of paths to commissioners in each district.[35]

Country Riding Transition

The accomplishments of Oneida County wheelmen marked an evolving transition between earlier path building during both the high-wheel and safety bicycle era and the rise of New York's sidepath era. That earlier period was rooted in local initiatives, bound by club organization, propelled by energetic individuals, and aided by a far-reaching web of communication strung with the camaraderie of country riding. Transition began when wheelmen's associations formed for the express purpose of building bicycle paths. As these organizations steadily gained influence, bolstered by state enabling laws such as that in New Jersey and New York and also by laws protecting sidepaths from damage by unauthorized users, the type of broad interest in bicycle paths demonstrated in Oneida County gathered momentum. Between 1896 and 1899, when New York legislation shifted from enabling laws applicable to specific counties to a statewide sidepath law, initiatives showed characteristics from both periods. Events in Oneida County revealed that type of overlap, as did similar developments in Chemung and Onandaga counties, where, respectively, Elmira and Syracuse cyclists established sidepath leagues, and in Steuben County, where wheelmen formed the Corning Sidepath Association. Growing enthusiasm for sidepaths in New York also extended to women's associations, and in Ontario County the Ladies' Cycling Club in Canandaigua raised money to build a path to Victor.[36]

Very similar advances also occurred in Monroe and Albany counties during that same period, and these counties might just as easily be used to illustrate this transitional phase but for the existence of state laws authorizing each county's governing body, called a board of supervisors, to appoint a county board of sidepath commissioners. Each law gave commissioners the power to issue licenses to cyclists, to build sidepaths with funds generated from the sale of licenses, and to enforce rules for the use of sidepaths through constabulary authority. Violations of these rules became misdemeanors, circumstances that also increased public attention to sidepaths, but sometimes in a contentious light. This formal structure—backed by government authority, sustained by fall conventions for county sidepath commissions held annually between 1898 and 1903, and nudged forward by a small but growing industry catering to sidepath construction—all distinguished the mature phase of New York's sidepath movement.

Towpath Riding

In the midst of this mounting enthusiasm for paths reserved principally for bicycles, wheelmen began looking more closely at canal towpaths. In general, cyclists risked becoming trespassers along canals; if they were not considered so by government or company officials, then they were by the boatmen, whose mules startled easily. Not surprisingly, LAW road books cite canal towpaths sparingly. However, many sections of the vast canal system traversing New Jersey, New York, Pennsylvania, Maryland, Ohio, Indiana, and part of New England had been in an advanced stage of decline by the time that cyclists arrived.[37]

Erie Canal

Where towpaths still offered a potentially decent surface, where railroad companies had not converted those corridors to rail transport, or where the owners of electric interurban lines were not yet maneuvering in similar fashion, cyclists saw advantage—if not year round, then at least at times when barge traffic had temporarily ceased. Along the Erie Canal, which remained in use during the safety bicycle era, New York wheelmen may have ignored the high-wheel hardships encountered by Thomas Stevens and George Thayer and remained sanguine about opportunities to use the towpath as a direct route between Albany and Tonawanda. In June 1896, George Aldridge, the New York State Superintendent of Public Works, raised those hopes by authorizing repairs for towpaths along the canal's entire length and by opening the path's blue-line side, owned by the state, to cyclists.[38]

Aldridge, an avid wheelmen with political ambitions and eager to secure the influential LAW lobby, had broached the idea a year before, intending to encourage cyclists in cities along the route to make repairs to the towpath; in many places, this was a less costly alternative to the construction of new sidepaths and thus beneficial to cyclists, barge owners, and taxpayers alike. That same year (1895), another prominent wheelman, Frank W. Hawley, had made similar overtures about the towpath's value to cross-state travel. Hawley had secured the rights to operate electric traction along the canal on behalf of the Cataract General Electric Company at Niagara Falls, and he predicted that the path would see little use once electrified rail had been installed.[39]

Scottsville Sidepath

Whether wheelmen traveled along canals by permission, prescription, or pluck, such passageways became familiar to cyclists in a number of locales, and remnants of at least two important examples survive. In New York, the Scottsville

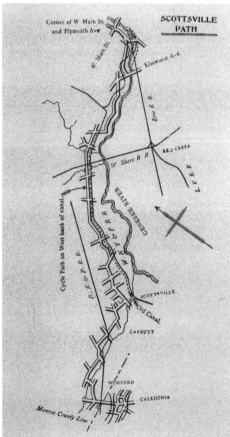

FIGURES 5.9 AND 5.10

The sidepath linking Rochester with Scottsville to the south became especially popular in Monroe County. For much of its length, the nine-mile trace followed the berm bank of the Genesee Valley Canal. Map courtesy of New York State Library, Manuscripts and Special Collections, Albany. Photograph by Cline Rogers in an album titled *Sidepaths: Monroe County (1899)*. Courtesy Rochester (N.Y.) Public Library, Local History and Genealogy Division.

FIGURE 5.11
Beyond Scottsville, the path veered southwesterly toward Mumford, and although the canal's berm side is heavily overgrown in many sections, the old towpath survives as part of an extensive greenway system that continues far beyond Scottsville.

Sidepath between that village and Rochester, roughly nine miles to the northeast, followed the berm side of the Genesee Valley Canal most of the way. That canal had been closed for decades, but on a perfect Saturday afternoon in September 1896, more than 1,500 riders celebrated the path's opening, possibly sharing that waterway with trains of the Western New York and Pennsylvania Railroad on the canal's opposite, or eastern, bank. Scottsville resident and miller Isaac W. Salyerds, also the town's deputy sheriff and later its representative to the New York State Assembly, is credited with conceiving the path and, with the help of village volunteers, constructing a large portion of its length. Salyerds thus joins a long list of local cycling enthusiasts whose energy and commitment to bicycle path projects have yielded timeless benefits for their communities.[40]

Sunday rides to Scottsville, followed by dinner at the Cargill Hotel, soon became so fashionable for Rochester's wheelmen and wheelwomen that editors of the Monroe County Atlas added the route in 1902. Today, the hotel is gone, but the Scottsville path reveals that canals are not erased as easily as sidepaths adjoining highways. Although traces of the Genesee Valley Canal are faint today, lengthy segments of its bed and towpath remain, and bicyclists have reclaimed the latter as part of a lengthy greenway.[41]

Broad Ripple Cycle Path and Millersville Cycle Path

Far to the west, cyclists in Indianapolis secured the LAW's national meet in August 1898 by offering a number of inducements, including an extravagant quarter-mile racing track called the Newby Oval and two scenic bicycle paths. One of these paths, the newly built Millersville path, opened just in time for tours by visiting cyclists and included an impressive suspension bridge. The path began near the intersection of Thirtieth Street and College Avenue and followed a corridor formed by Fall Creek and Millersville Road, also called Miller's Pike, to a small settlement located about seven miles northeast of the city's center. Scant remnants of that mill village survive and nothing of the path, but in 1909 Hartford architect George Keller designed a greenway along that water course, and in 1937 park commissioners opened a bicycle path along Fall Creek Parkway, which borders the creek's northwestern bank. Today, bicycle paths still exist along this corridor and may date from that later period.[42]

The Broad Ripple path adapted the towpath of the ill-fated Indiana Central Canal, which bordered the White River between Indianapolis and Broad Ripple village located north of the city. Construction of that canal ended in bankruptcy in 1839, with only eight miles of its nearly 300-mile planned length completed. Roughly half a century later, cyclists began wheeling along those same eight miles with permission from the Indianapolis Water Company, which had acquired control of the canal and used it as a source of water to power the city's waterworks. Enthusiasm for towpath touring must have increased after 1889, when the Citizens Street Railway Company began developing Fairview Park, a pastoral setting along the river about midway between the city's center and Broad Ripple. The company built a boathouse and eventually introduced amusements, including a carousel, to compete with similar enticements at Broad Ripple Park, located near the canal terminus and owned by a different streetcar concern. However, the path's surface remained ragged until the spring of 1896, when the city's cyclists chartered the Wheelway League of Indianapolis. Members raised funds through stock subscriptions, carefully graded and improved the path, and also installed rustic benches.[43]

By 1898, the Broad Ripple path had become a favorite circuit, and that year the city acquired lands bordering both the canal and the White River, creating Riverside Park. On Wednesday morning of the meet, with tourists still arriving, wheelwomen rode the path to Broad Ripple during a carefully organized outing that included a luncheon. Newspaper accounts proclaimed the excursion delightful for one and all, and the following day a large contingent of more than fifty women wheeled to Millersville, with equal acclaim for scenery and sustenance. The success of the LAW meet, coupled with praise for the city's bicycle paths from visitors, must have encouraged park commissioners, because the following year they approved construction of another bicycle path to Riverside Park along Crawfordsville Road.[44]

During ensuing years, the availability of both Fairview Park and Riverside Park undoubtedly encouraged steady use of the canal towpath by bicyclists. Women

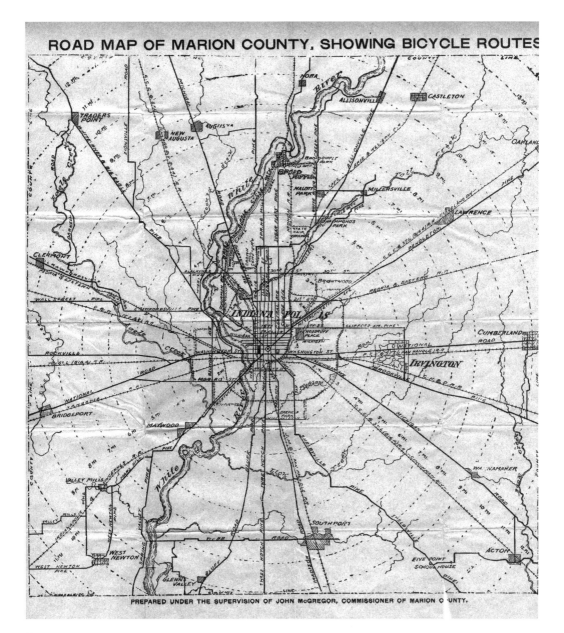

ROAD MAP OF MARION COUNTY, SHOWING BICYCLE ROUTES

PREPARED UNDER THE SUPERVISION OF JOHN McGREGOR, COMMISSIONER OF MARION COUNTY.

FIGURES 5.12
Indianapolis cyclists completed two bicycle paths in time for the
League of American Wheelmen's national meet in 1898. Both the
Millersville Path and the Broad Ripple Path extend to the north of
the city and are depicted on this 1911 road map of Marion County.
Courtesy Manuscript Section, Indiana State Library.

CANAL AND CYCLE PATH AT FAIR VIEW PARK,
INDIANAPOLIS, IND.

FIGURES 5.13 AND 5.14
The Broad Ripple Path, opened on the former towpath of the
Indiana Central Canal, survives and today adjoins land owned
by Butler University.

riders actively supported the league and kept pace with local cycling activities by reading the column "Wheel Whirls" in the journal *Indiana Woman*. A year before the LAW meet, that journal had published a special "Bicycle Number," and its cover illustrated couples riding along the towpath. The county commissioner also added both the Broad Ripple and Millersville paths to a road map printed in 1911, confirming the importance of these paths even as interest in cycling had begun to wane. Although the Millersville path is gone, continued ownership of the canal by the water company probably contributed to the Broad Ripple path's longevity, as did purchase of Fairview Park by Butler University in 1922. Today, a botanical garden has replaced the boathouse as a public attraction, but the towpath on the canal's opposite side continues to offer an afternoon's excursion for the city's cyclists.[45]

Waterside Wheelways

By no means did the decline of canals occur uniformly from region to region or even from place to place along specific waterways, and towpaths offered tempting prospects for wheelmen in many other parts of the country. True, the frequent edicts published by canal companies declaring towpaths off limits to cyclists, coupled with occasional newspaper notices citing the arrest of riders, confirm the general status of cyclists along many canals. Yet those same notices also reveal that wheelmen often used these corridors as de facto bicycle paths, particularly where they provided direct routes to popular destinations or opportunities for scenic excursions. In 1883, Karl Kron ventured along the Delaware and Hudson Canal between Honesdale and Port Jervis, describing it as especially picturesque. About a decade later, during a period of drought, he returned to explore the canal's lower half between Port Jervis and Kingston, finding it equally scenic and with numerous villages located at convenient intervals, many with comfortable hotels. The proprietor of one such inn, at Cuddebackville, also owned a secluded island where guests could swim or bathe, as Kron put it, "without the encumbrance of clothes." Formal abandonment of that canal in 1899 may have changed the patterns of cyclists' wanderings only marginally. Elsewhere, cycling's journalists in New Jersey mention both the Morris Canal and the Delaware and Raritan Canal, and remnants of all three corridors survive, with towpaths today used as recreational trails for both pedestrians and cyclists.[46]

The Chesapeake and Ohio Canal towpath tempted many cyclists, and rules about its use seem to have been applied inconsistently. In 1892, Frank Lenz rode the path without incident, but two years later members of Baltimore's Thirteen Cyclers found regulations strictly enforced in the vicinity of Great Falls, and they were compelled to abandon their wheels and walk to view the falls, vowing pointedly to visit an alternative attraction, Cabin John Bridge, on their next run to Washington.[47]

CHAPTER SIX

Good Roads and *Good Sidepaths*

Apart from the value of the Broad Ripple Cycle Path in Indianapolis and the Scottsville Sidepath in Rochester as two very successful, enduring examples of canal corridors converted to bicycle use, the two paths can be compared in another important respect: the expanding influence of New York's sidepath campaign. In the spring of 1898, months before the League of American Wheelmen meet, John H. Furnas (an Indianapolis wheelman) visited Rochester and found his city's twin sibling, very similar in population and with beautiful parks, well-paved streets, and avid cycling. Probably thinking of the Broad Ripple and Millersville cycle paths, Furnas also applauded Rochester's sidepaths, observing that the idea was catching on in his hometown. However, he may not have considered the subtle difference in nomenclature employed by Rochester's wheelmen, a distinction that becomes important when tracing the origins, development, and influence of New York's sidepath campaign.[1]

In September 1896, when the *Rochester Herald* and the *Rochester Democrat and Chronicle* both reported the celebratory dedication of the Scottsville corridor, editors specifically used the term *sidepath*, doing so more than a year before Monroe County wheelmen drafted legislation authorizing a county sidepath commission and two years before that bill became law. Rochester subsequently became one of New York's influential centers of sidepath planning and construction and helped to popularize the word "sidepath." However, that city's wheelmen borrowed the term from Niagara County, where sidepath building had begun in Lockport about four years before the Scottsville path opened.[2]

Niagara County's Sidepath League and Sidepath Commission

Lockport's leading role in the origins of New York's sidepath campaign is the legacy of Charles T. Raymond, a graduate of Rensselaer Polytechnic Institute in Troy and a successful business manager. A founding member of the Lockport Wheelmen in 1885, Raymond often ventured along the old sidepath bordering well-traveled Ridge Road, joining Rochester with Lewiston on the Niagara River, roughly seventy miles apart. After assessing the dim prospects for good roads in his locale, Raymond concluded that cyclists needed separate wheelways more than good roads and could build them much faster. From the outset, he envisioned a regional system of paths, with gaps between existing sidepaths closed and new spurs created. In the fall of 1890, he persuaded like-minded wheelmen to establish the Niagara County Sidepath League, and by the following March that body had achieved formal organization, with Raymond as president. As had path builders before him, Raymond sought funding through membership dues and public subscriptions, the latter buoyed by donations from rival manufacturers Albert Pope and Albert Overman.[3]

Funds accumulated slowly and a year elapsed, but Raymond and his colleagues soon focused on the twelve-mile stretch of road between Lockport and Olcott on Lake Ontario to the north, passing through Wright's Corners, where the highway

FIGURE 6.2
New York's sidepath campaign began in Lockport in 1890, when Charles Raymond and fellow members of the Lockport Wheelmen organized the Niagara County Sidepath League to raise money for building bicycle paths. From the journal *Sidepaths* (September 1901). Courtesy National Transportation Library, Washington, D.C.

intersected Ridge Road. In Lockport, the route followed Lake Avenue to the city limits, but there the corridor changed to a two-mile toll road operated by the Lockport-Wright's Corners Plank Road Company. Loose stones interspersed with deep ruts concealed any surviving planks, making the road impassable for bicycles; even worse, sand loomed beyond the toll road.[4]

Despite those challenges and with only limited financial backing, league members began work on a section of the path during the spring of 1892. With earth from a ditch dug between path and road (to provide a drainage channel but also to keep farm vehicles from straying onto the path), workmen created an elevated foundation, placing tile drainage pipes beneath the path at soggy locations. Where streams crossed the path's route, two twelve-inch pipes faced with loose stone served as small culverts. At elevated locations, a second ditch channeled water from slopes above the corridor into small pipes placed every twenty or thirty feet along the path. Workmen then graded and rolled the path to a width of six feet before surfacing it, and although Raymond acknowledged his inexperience with surface materials or their thickness and taper he vowed to test various coverings, including ground anthracite cinders, gravel, crushed stone, and shale. Those experiments ultimately favored crushed sandstone siftings.[5]

FIGURES 6.3 AND 6.4
The Niagara County Sidepath League's path between
Lockport and Olcott, begun in 1892, adjoined Lake
Avenue (today Route 78) and passed in front of
the Independent Order of Odd Fellows Home and
Orphanage. From Isaac Potter, *Cycle Paths* (Boston:
LAW, 1898).

Good Sidepaths

Although the details of Raymond's project may seem mundane, they underscore several important connections between New York's sidepath campaign and the larger Good Roads movement. Raymond intentionally relied on highway contract specifications published in *Good Roads* magazine, part of that campaign's efforts to introduce scientific methods of road construction. Raymond described the events at Lockport in an article for that journal in 1894, and the builders of New York sidepaths would continue to emphasize construction techniques, borrowing from practices developed for good roads.

In addition, lobbying efforts by the LAW for state-funded highway improvements had failed, forcing a change in strategy that led to an educational campaign begun by the league's Road Improvement Bureau (created in 1891 for that express purpose), followed by publication of *Good Roads* magazine in 1892; the National League for Good Roads also formed in 1892. Thus, construction of the Lockport-Olcott bicycle path by the Niagara County Sidepath League that same year established a symbolic link between the two important campaigns. Financial contributions by Albert Pope to all three bodies reinforced that relationship, as did Raymond's continuing activity for the LAW and the county league (as well as the latter's successor, the Niagara County Sidepath Commission). Raymond's résumé soon included legislative lobbying as well.

Raymond's belief that wheelmen needed separate wheelways more than good roads also marks the origins of what would become a contentious debate in the LAW, initially causing the league to withdraw support for a uniform sidepath law in New York. However, that dissension gradually abated as sidepaths gained favor, carried in part by arguments that sidepaths cost less to build and maintain than roads and could serve as demonstrations to farmers about the value of proper road construction. The campaign for sidepaths thus became a form of protest against bad roads, and what originated as separate corridors promoted by discrete campaigns instead overlapped, creating an impromptu alliance in the dual quests for good roads and sidepaths—better still, "Good Sidepaths." That merger becomes a notable characteristic of New York's sidepath era, distinguishing it from earlier local or regional path networks. That the Lockport-Olcott corridor marks the origins of those developments also adds to that path's historic significance.[6]

Bicycle Tax Bill

Raymond's legislative proposal to fund sidepath construction is by far the most significant outcome of the Lockport-Olcott project, reflecting his conviction that all who used the paths should pay for the privilege. Late in 1894, and by then very frustrated with the trickle of funds from public subscriptions or occasional cake sales, Raymond drafted a bill that allowed the county's governing body (its board of supervisors) to tax all bicycles and to apply the proceeds to sidepath building. Introduced during the early months of 1895 and passed promptly by both legislative chambers in Albany, the bill then moved to the city councils and mayors in Lockport and Niagara Falls for concurrence before returning to Albany for the governor's signature. Through oversight, that approval did not occur until after the state legislature had adjourned, preventing the governor from signing the bill. Undeterred, Raymond successfully reintroduced the legislation the following year, and it became effective on March 4, 1896.[7]

As adopted, the law included several amendments to Raymond's initial draft, but it retained the crucial provision permitting the board of supervisors in Niagara County to establish a yearly tax for each bicycle owned by county residents. The measure established minimum and maximum fees (fifty cents and one dollar, respectively), and required payment to local tax collectors or city treasurers. Wheelmen who bought new bicycles paid a portion of the tax soon after the date of purchase. Collectors then transferred the money to the county treasurer, who deposited receipts into a special sidepath fund. Unpaid taxes became a lien on bicycles, and the law gave officials the authority to enforce liens by seizing bicycles and selling them at public auction.[8]

The law also established a county board of sidepath commissioners, giving them authority to draw from the sidepath fund, oversee construction of sidepaths along county highways and streets, repair existing sidepaths, and exercise the power of eminent domain when acquiring rights-of-way. Commissioners (who served without pay) also could adopt rules governing use of the paths, the violation of which became misdemeanors with fines not to exceed five dollars. The law prohibited the driving of other vehicles or animals along sidepaths, but expressly precluded interference with county and local officials who had jurisdiction over highways and streets, skirting an area of potential conflict. Raymond and his colleagues may have been sanguine about their ability to dispel any friction, but disputes eventually occurred, requiring amendment to the law.[9]

Concerns about the tax provision also developed—and for a number of different reasons. Although Raymond's original 1894 bill encountered little or no opposition in either legislative chamber that spring, Francis Prial penned a scathing editorial in a March issue of *Wheel and Cycling Trade Review*, accusing the bill's author of plotting a devious scheme to create toll paths across the state. He also complained that wheelmen who chose not to use paths still would be taxed and that cyclists would be better off if public funds paid for road improvements. Other opponents argued that the law gave all cyclists the privilege of using paths, but county supervisors held authority to tax only wheelmen from Niagara County.[10]

Niagara County Sidepaths
Justifiably buoyed by their legislative accomplishment, Raymond and his fellow wheelmen pushed forward, prompting county supervisors to appoint a board of sidepath commissioners in the fall of 1896, chaired by Raymond, and to adopt a fifty-cent tax, making that tariff effective beginning January 1, 1897. Meanwhile,

the county sidepath league (which remained in existence until disbanded in 1897) turned its attention beyond the Lockport-Olcott corridor and voted early in May 1896 to build a three-mile path between Lockport and Lockport Junction to connect with a path to be built from Buffalo (in Erie County) via Tonawanda, thus joining Lake Erie with Lake Ontario at Olcott by way of Lockport. Buffalo and Niagara Falls cyclists also focused on long-standing plans for a path along the Niagara River between North Tonawanda and Niagara Falls, delayed by a particularly poor section of road. Throughout the 1897 season, Niagara County wheelmen successfully implemented the new law, and by the 1898 season they had constructed about thirty miles of paths, reducing the average cost of construction from $1,200 to between $200 and $300 per mile. Confirming the predictions of some cyclists, farmers saw advantage in decent paths available for foot travel, and they began assisting in path building, drawing the sidepath campaign still closer to that for good roads.[11]

Legislative Labor

Although Niagara County became the testing ground for New York's inaugural sidepath legislation, wheelmen in other counties watched closely and soon followed Raymond's lead, creating a flurry of legislative activity during the next several years. In the state's southern tier, Elmira wheelmen needed funds to improve their cinder path to Corning, which opened in the spring of 1895, and during the early months of 1896 the city's Kanaweola Bicycle Club prepared sidepath legislation for Chemung County at almost the precise date that Raymond's bill became law. The legislation passed both the house and senate chambers in Albany without delay, but to the surprise of local wheelmen it failed to win approval from Elmira's common council, the members of which considered it a county bill and beyond the city's jurisdiction. Monroe County cyclists sought passage of a comparable bill that same session, specifying a one-dollar tax. However, Rochester's mayor and common council also withheld their approval, because the bill included city streets and because a sufficient number of wheelmen opposed the tax. A measure presented by Oneida County cyclists suffered a similar fate that same year.[12]

Other counties explicitly sought Raymond's assistance in drafting a uniform law, and in the fall of 1897 Raymond acquiesced. Conceding that a county tax presented issues of fairness for cyclists who didn't use the paths, offered no authority over wheelmen from other counties, and aroused the type of resentment typically reserved for taxes, Raymond removed the provision in favor of more equitable licensing, to be administered by sidepath commissions that would arrange for the sale of sidepath tags for display on bicycles. This approach also eliminated the prospect of forfeiture sales when cyclists failed to pay the tax. He also gave commissioners the authority to plant shade trees between paths and highways, a practical and effective strategy to keep farm wagons off the paths.[13]

LAW Road Blocks

With strong support, Raymond's bill arrived in Albany in January 1898, only to be met by vehement opposition from an unanticipated sector: the state arm of the LAW. The league's New York division had been busy preparing Good Roads legislation, which it also intended to present in the January session, and late in December 1897 division officials arbitrarily adopted a resolution denouncing the sidepath proposition as contrary to wheelmen's best interests. Fearing that passage of the sidepath law would hinder the prospects for improving rural roads, the division's chief consul, Walter S. Jenkins, traveled to Albany and successfully lobbied against Raymond's bill.[14]

To be fair, the well-intentioned promoters of the Good Roads bill faced enormous political challenges presented by the state's wretched rural roads and by farmers who opposed taxes for highway improvements that benefited bicyclists. Albany's legislators had rejected a Good Roads bill earlier that year, and the road improvement lobby understandably would have loathed the prospect of facing yet another setback in their Sisyphean task. One of the bill's sponsors, Senator William W. Armstrong from Rochester, also had been a friend to cyclists, securing an 1897 law that barred all vehicles and interlopers from using wheelways constructed for bicycles. He and his cosponsor in the Senate, Richard Higbie, may have believed that the 1898 legislative session offered bright prospects for the state's first comprehensive program to improve rural highways.[15]

Nevertheless, the resolutions adopted by the New York division sparked intense disagreement among New York cyclists and added to the league's already long list of internal woes. The controversy also pulled the rural sidepath campaign into the larger arena of conflict created when Brooklyn's park commissioners sought to restrict cyclists to the Coney Island bicycle paths, prohibiting them from using Ocean Parkway. Although concerns differed, quarreling had spilled over into other states where proposals for bicycle paths were being considered or where lawmakers were pondering legislation similar to that in New York.

In that larger debate, rather than apprehension about bicycle paths leading to cyclists' exclusion from carriage roads, those who opposed sidepaths argued that with separate corridors available wheelmen would lose interest in promoting good highways, to the detriment of the greater cycling community. Moreover, once proper highway construction occurred sidepaths would become unnecessary. Others expressed concern that exclusive paths would nullify cyclists' hard-fought gains in public opinion concerning both the need for better roads and the rights of cyclists to travel on common highways without concern for recrimination. Cycling journals contributed to the fray, and Francis Prial continued to use his journal to oppose separate bicycle paths, predicting that special laws favoring wheelmen would mean more trouble than satisfaction. Albert Parsons, the LAW's founding secretary and a figure of considerable standing, wrote: "I fear, even now, that the result of obtaining special paths will be a strong feeling by drivers of horses that we do not belong *with them* on the good roads we have done so much to create." Even during the high-wheel era, cyclists had tempered backing for bicycle paths with reminders that good roads would be even better.[16]

Less patient cyclists countered by pointing out that appropriations for highway projects were far too stingy, that projects were too slow in developing, and that the process often succumbed to political squabbling that diverted funds away from the highways of greatest value to cyclists. Other riders argued that good sidepaths would inevitably lead to good roads. Still others observed that the need for better roads had become so universally understood that improvement would be bound to occur with or without the bicycle. The problem, to these wheelmen, was that only later generations of cyclists would enjoy those roads. As one proponent proclaimed: "Don't wait for good roads. They'll soon be spoiled again, and we've waited long enough anyway." W. B. Heck, a member of the Warren Sidepath Association in northwestern Pennsylvania, eventually stated the argument as cogently as anyone: "A cycle path is the only solution to country riding, during the lives of the present generation."[17]

An Object Lesson

Respective merits of those arguments aside, Jenkins, Armstrong, and the promoters of New York's Good Roads bill miscalculated. Perhaps they had been focusing too intently on their own immediate legislative objectives, were still suffering from the defeat of a Good Roads bill the previous year, or were simply unaware of the rapid awakening to the promise of country riding in counties where sidepaths existed. In any case, they failed to anticipate both the depth of outrage created by their opposition to the uniform law and the adamant refusal among cyclists to accept the league's weakly reasoned position. In Niagara County, members of the Lockport Wheelmen expressed their vexation by withdrawing from the league, concluding that the club's annual fee of $175 could be spent more effectively by building sidepaths.[18]

The league's stance against sidepath legislation caused several important developments. Ironically, it helped to galvanize support for the state's sidepaths, pushing lingering concern about a tax on bicycles into the background. Counties scrambled to prepare their own laws to meet legislative deadlines for review of local matters, and Monroe and Albany counties crafted bills modeled after Raymond's uniform legislation, using licenses as a means to generate revenue. Columbia and Cattaraugus counties offered bills that allowed individuals or associations to construct sidepaths within public highways, leaving the matter of raising money to those organizations. Each of these laws became effective in either March or April of 1898.[19]

Two of the sidepath commissioners appointed in Monroe County later that year, Frank J. Amsden and Charles U. Bastable, issued a statewide circular calling for a conference to consider strategies for securing a uniform state sidepath law. At that pivotal meeting, held in the Monroe County Court House in Rochester on November 12, the group formed a lobbying committee comprised of Raymond,

Bastable, Jenkins, John D. Chism Jr., and William S. Mackie (the last three representing Buffalo, Albany, and Utica, respectively). In his role as the state's chief consul, Jenkins may have been an obligatory member of the committee, at least initially. In any case, as framed and distributed to wheelmen in each county for review, the committee's bill borrowed heavily from the Niagara County law, absent any tax, and gave sidepath commissions leeway in assessing license fees, from twenty-five cents to one-dollar. Although Armstrong also attended that meeting and again voiced objections to the uniform law, the committee politely listened to his comments and then enlisted the backing of Timothy E. Ellsworth, a lawyer and state senator from Lockport. Ellsworth, who had served on the Judiciary Committee before being elected temporary president of the Senate during the 1899 session, willingly offered to sponsor the bill.[20]

On another front, LAW president and Brooklyn resident Isaac Potter offered a strong proclamation that favored separate corridors for wheelmen, doing so in a concise booklet titled *Cycle Paths*, a timely publication from the LAW in 1898. The book also clarifies his earlier ambivalence toward separate bicycle paths in cities. Potter, who had studied engineering before turning to law, emerged as a leading figure in the league's campaign for Good Roads, compiling an 1891 bulletin, *The Gospel of Good Roads*, before becoming the inaugural editor of the league's *Good Roads* journal in 1892. As president of the Brooklyn Bicycle Club and as New York State's elected chief consul in 1894, Potter also played a key role in convincing Brooklyn's park commissioners to construct the 1895 Coney Island Bicycle Path.[21]

As president of the LAW in 1897 and 1898, Potter may have been chagrined by his chief consul's determined opposition to New York's sidepath legislation, and his book is a strong rebuttal of Jenkins' policy. Hinting that urban cyclists with access to paved surfaces were often unaware of the difficulties encountered by country riders, Potter adopted a conciliatory tone and acknowledged that bicycle paths offered only intermediate steps in the quest for highway improvements—not a substitute for the wheelman's agitation for better roads but an auxiliary to the greater cause. However, his strong record as an advocate for Good Roads gave considerable weight to his principal argument that bicycle paths were very effective demonstrations of the benefits of properly built highways and the strongest possible protests against bad roads. In sum, wheelmen could move easily from town to town, and no farmer stuck in the middle of a road would ever forget watching cyclists gliding by on a well-constructed sidepath.[22]

Potter's book reinforces that theme with images of successful bicycle paths throughout the country, including those in Monroe County, but he reserves special praise for the pioneering work of Charles Raymond at Lockport. Potter's declaration thus gave official sanction to the informal Good Sidepaths campaign that Raymond initiated. Although the argument that sidepaths served as object lessons for good roads may have been an expedient for quelling the league's internal dissension, Chism's firsthand experiences eventually confirmed that sidepath construction caused an awakening of interest in road improvement. Although Prial continued to oppose sidepath legislation, by October 1898 his editorials had acknowledged the bicycle path to be an established institution in America and "a good-roads missionary in its way."[23]

LAW State Committee on Sidepaths

Potter's book changed the tone of New York's debate about sidepath legislation, and it probably convinced Potter's successor, Conway W. Sams from Maryland, to establish the LAW's National Sidepath Committee early in 1900. Sams appointed a physician from Minneapolis, Dr. Charles Hunter, to head that body, with the goal of codifying all laws and court decisions relating to sidepaths and becoming a bureau of information capable of advising states about various strategies. By then, Sams also viewed the national committee as an opportunity to boost the LAW's declining influence.[24]

However, other factors led more directly to adoption of the Ellsworth bill in the spring of 1899. By December 1898, Milo M. Belding Jr. had replaced Jenkins as chief consul, and Belding promptly appointed John Chism to head the LAW State Committee on Sidepaths, presumably a formal successor to the lobbying committee created the previous month. On December 17, 1898, at the annual meeting of the LAW's New York State Division, its new board of officers (led by Belding) unanimously adopted a resolution authorizing the sidepath committee to present a uniform bill to the legislature. Nodding to their fellow cyclists, the board also adopted a resolution requesting that newly elected Governor Theodore Roosevelt acknowledge the need for good roads in his annual message to the legislature and recommending an appropriation of $1 million dollars for highway improvements. In February 1899, the sidepath discussion also reached a much larger audience; at the LAW's national assembly in Providence, Potter addressed the gathering and described cycle paths as good roads for bicyclists.[25]

Despite the careful maneuvering by Raymond, Belding, and other supporters of the uniform law, Chism, who also served as president of the Albany Bicycle League, remained wary of opposition, and he advised all interested counties to prepare local sidepath bills for quick submission to the legislature in the event that the general bill remained mired in debate. Chism may have been guileless, but his advice proved to be astute. Whether tiring of county bills and legislative bickering, or yielding to the prodding of Ellsworth, the Judiciary Committee appointed a subcommittee, to which all local sidepath bills were referred, and instructed it to draft a single state law. With all such bills stalled in committee, everyone's attention turned to the Ellsworth law.[26]

As Chism had feared, opposition to the bill developed. Although the legislature had finally passed the Higbee-Armstrong Good Roads law in 1898 and although he didn't actively oppose the bill, Senator Armstrong continued to view the bill as a tax on a special class of vehicles to improve highways, establishing a bad precedent. He also grumbled weakly about the law's failure to address conditions that varied from county to county, mentioning uncertainty about the rights of wheelmen and pedestrians on sidepaths already in existence. Other opponents made similar claims, adding that the subcommittee's control of the county bills prevented wheelmen from having their say about local concerns. Despite Chism's pleas, New York City's association of cycling clubs lobbied against the bill, fearing that passage of the law would damage the prospects for appropriations under the Good Roads law (probably Armstrong's true concerns). Instead, they asked for the $1 million dollar allocation to improve highways. Still other wheelmen believed the bill didn't go far enough, because it didn't give wheelmen specific rights-of-way over paths they built, as Albany County's law provided.[27]

Nevertheless, in addition to overwhelming support for the measure from wheelmen in New York's upstate counties, opponents now faced endorsement of the bill by the LAW, and legislators gave considerable weight to both factors. While journalists in cities throughout New York tracked the bill's progress, Raymond, Chism, and Belding reminded all concerned that sidepath laws already were working well in Niagara, Monroe, and Albany counties and noted that the proposed law also permitted touring cyclists to travel from one county to another with the purchase of just one county's license. The measure quickly moved through both the Senate and Assembly with only a few amendments, and on March 27, 1899, Roosevelt signed the bill's first version into law, remarking, "I would have signed this bill even though there had been opposition."[28]

The Ellsworth Sidepath Law

As adopted, the Ellsworth law deserves recognition as landmark legislation, and it remains among the country's most important laws related to cycling. Less than a month after Roosevelt's signature, more than half of New York's counties had established sidepath commissions, confirming the strong local roots of path building that spread from Raymond's exploratory diggings at Lockport almost a decade before—earlier if one considers similar efforts during the era of high-wheel bicycles in places such as Wilkes-Barre or Binghamton. That same force of local interest remains at the core of efforts to create path networks today.[29]

The Ellsworth law is also significant because it marked a surge in the building of sidepaths in New York and other states during the next several years, continuing the work begun in Niagara, Monroe, Albany, Oneida, and other counties, even as the bicycle craze had begun to fade after 1900. Historically, the years between 1894 (the year of Raymond's first legislative draft) and 1904 (when a New York law required counties to transfer the duties of sidepath commissions to county engineers) represent one of the country's most active and important periods of path building for bicycles. Nor did path construction end uniformly during the early period of decline in cycling, further evidence of the law's significance—as well as proof of the value of local support for bicycles.[30]

Moreover, in any current dialogue about establishing a proper place for bicycle transportation (an issue that remains sorely unresolved today) the methods of administrative oversight, licensing, financing, construction, maintenance, and enforcement established by the Ellsworth law deserve recognition. Although Armstrong was at least partially correct in believing that sidepaths would become redundant when road surfaces improved, he failed to see far enough into the future to anticipate the incompatibility between bicycles and motor vehicles. Today, looking toward a very distant future, one might imagine legislatively enabled local commissions charged with the task of identifying and managing roads to be closed to all but nonmotorized transport during specified hours. If that occurs, then we may recall that those administrative bodies closely resemble New York's nineteenth-century sidepath commissions.

Apart from its licensing provisions that replaced a bicycle tax with a sidepath tag, the Ellsworth law is based largely on the concepts tested by Raymond's original 1894 draft, adding historic significance to the Niagara County legislation adopted early in 1896. In general, the modifications contained in the 1899 legislation either refine or amplify provisions of the earlier law. County judges, rather than boards of supervisors, are authorized to appoint sidepath commissions upon petition by fifty resident wheelmen. The law also gave counties flexibility in determining the size of commissions, either five or seven members, and in establishing licensing fees, from fifty cents to one dollar.

However, the Ellsworth law as adopted is narrower in one important respect: it limited the authority of commissioners to build sidepaths along only those public roads located outside the limits of incorporated cities and villages, subject to written consent from the county commissioner of highways or from town supervisors. No such restriction existed in the Niagara County law or in the original draft of the Ellsworth bill. Both sidepaths and sidewalks are more carefully defined, the former between three- and six-feet wide and the latter reserved by custom for the use of pedestrians. Although construction of sidepaths on sidewalks was prohibited, except by consent of persons owning abutting lands, footpaths worn only by travel were excluded from that ban.[31]

With passage of the uniform law, Niagara County wheelmen acceded to the repeal of their 1896 legislation. Monroe and Albany counties amended their laws in 1899, but each county successfully sought exclusion from the Ellsworth law, preferring instead to manage sidepaths under separate legislation. The Monroe County law, which remained in effect for one more year before merging with the Ellsworth law, retained its lower license fee of twenty-five cents; replaced a clause giving bicycle riders exclusive use of sidepaths (subject to rights of pedestrians when necessary) with one prohibiting all vehicles except bicycles; and forbade the driving of animals on sidepaths. The Albany County law limited the locations of sidepaths to roads exceeding two rods in width and did not define sidewalks as precisely as the Ellsworth law. The Albany measure also tried to clarify cyclists' rights-of-way on corridors open to both bicyclists and pedestrians, giving the former preference "on the beaten track worn by bicycles," and gave sidepath commissioners authority to appoint sidepath police, who served without compensation.[32]

Sidepaths for Country Riding

Late in September 1899 (while still enjoying their legislative success), sidepath commissioners from twenty-nine counties traveled to Rochester for a second convention. Charles Raymond ceded the office of chairperson to Charles Bastable but then offered a congratulatory address to the gathering, applauding the efforts of wheelmen in Monroe, Albany, and Oneida counties, chiding the narrow-minded opposition of Good Roads proponents and the cold indifference of wheelmen who declined to support the law, and reminding his audience that the sidepath movement had grown spontaneously, a natural outgrowth of the desire to make country riding easier and more pleasant. Raymond also recommended a key amendment to the Ellsworth law, giving commissioners the power to construct sidepaths along the streets of cities and towns, and delegates approved the appointment of a committee comprised of Raymond, Bastable, and several others to codify any proposed amendments.[33]

Members of the Rochester convention committee already had worked closely with John Chism, who late in January 1900 issued a report summarizing sidepath progress during the period following passage of the Ellsworth law. By the time of Chism's report, forty-eight counties had established sidepath commissions, raising more than $100,000 from the sale of sidepath tags and supervising work on hundreds of miles of paths. Affirming Raymond's advice at the Rochester convention, Chism cautioned that wheelmen should seek as few changes to the law as possible, but he also acknowledged the need for the commission's authority to build sidepaths along streets in cities and towns. At approximately the same time that Chism presented his report, Monroe County Assemblyman Richard Gardiner introduced legislation to secure that and other revisions.[34]

Earlier that fall, two members of the Central Wheelmen Club in Brooklyn, Charles C. Enderle and Harry Hawxhurst, had journeyed to Niagara Falls and back, reporting that the many good miles of sidepaths they encountered already were a credit to the Ellsworth law. Among the first wheelmen to field-test New York's new sidepath program straightaway, and offering a very different perspective from that of George Thayer thirteen years before, the pair counted forty-eight miles of sidepaths just between Albany and Fonda and continued to add to that total throughout the Mohawk River valley, confirming what Edward DeGraff had envisioned six years earlier. After reaching Syracuse along another stretch of more than twenty sidepath miles, the two continued to Rochester and from there traveled along Monroe County's trunk lines before crossing Orleans and Niagara counties, probably via Ridge Road and its ancient paths.[35]

Gardiner Amendment

With so many county sidepath commissions already at work building or repairing sidepaths, Gardiner's bill generated negligible debate. Even Albert Pope's praise for New York's sidepath campaign, an endorsement that circulated in Rochester newspapers in March 1900, probably attracted little attention. Pope, by then hoping to dominate a nascent automobile industry just as he had bicycle manufacturing, pointed to the different road surfaces required by bicycles and automobiles and, as did Isaac Potter, viewed sidepaths as a means to demonstrate good roads. Yet by acknowledging that separate corridors offered a good solution for bicyclists—"let each look after his own vehicle"—and by calling for sidepaths everywhere throughout the country, he also hints at the potential incompatibility of bicycles and automobiles, the two means of conveyance that he believed would revolutionize society. Pecuniary incentives aside, Pope may have been better positioned than anyone of his day to glimpse that future conflict.[36]

Gardiner's bill moved easily through the Senate and Assembly and became law in April 1900 as an expanded restatement of the Ellsworth Law. In addition to giving commissioners authority to construct sidepaths along streets in incorporated villages and cities, subject to permission from trustees or common councils (or abutting owners when sidepaths adjoined sidewalks), the law also permitted commissioners to acquire land beyond the boundaries of highways, either by lease or by outright purchase. Amendments also required commissioners to issue annual financial reports to county judges, maintained the range of license fees from fifty cents to one dollar (except in Monroe County, where the cost remained at twenty-five cents), and made fines for violations of the law compulsory (varying from five to twenty-five dollars). A concluding clause repealed Monroe County's separate law, and only Albany County's sidepath administration continued to function apart from the state act.[37]

A few months after the legislature adopted the Gardiner amendments, the state's highest court added its sanction to the sidepath campaign. The owners of an estate in Bay Shore on Long Island had objected to the construction of a sidepath in front of their property adjoining South Country Road and had challenged the constitutionality of the Ellsworth law, claiming that it appropriated a portion of public highways for the exclusive use of bicyclists. They also pointed to the provision specifically limiting the right of commissioners to build sidepaths along existing sidewalks without the consent of abutting property owners. However, in a much-publicized decision reflecting the broad public attention being given to sidepaths, the New York Supreme Court rejected the claim, observing that sidewalks already were well-established corridors in public rights-of-way reserved for pedestrians and that sidepaths simply provided a similar type of corridor for cyclists. In sum, the Ellsworth law represented a form of regulation in furtherance of public safety and convenience. In addition, the court interpreted the word "along" to mean that the legislature had intended only to prevent sidepath commissions from building within the existing lines of sidewalks, an action that would interfere with the rights of pedestrians.[38]

The Ellsworth law survived other legal challenges from time to time, most by disgruntled property owners or by angry cyclists who faced arrest and fines. In 1902, the legislature amended the law once again to give county sheriffs and deputy sheriffs the same powers held by local constables to enforce the law. By that time, residents of New York communities had grown accustomed to the cinder-surfaced toll corridors reserved for bicyclists, narrow passages that stretched in every direction as visible land features. For those who needed reminders about the law's stiff penalties, local newspapers faithfully—and at times almost gleefully—reported the apprehension of those who risked riding on sidepaths without license tags. Some constables employed by sidepath commissions gained regional notoriety, their reputations magnified by stories of wayward cyclists being apprehended after relentless pursuit and then taken to local magistrates. In Monroe and Oswego counties, the sagas of sidepath deputies Frank McKeon and Ira Palmer, respectively, must have enthused newspaper reporters and readers alike. The drivers of farm wagons or other vehicles who dared to trespass on sidepaths faced a similar fate. Even the United States Post Office felt the sting of arrest when one of Onandaga County's sidepath agents detained a postal service messenger, leading to a test case over state and federal authority. Nor were clergy en route to church services immune to magisterial rebuke.[39]

FIGURE 7.1
A sidepath in an unidentified Long Island community, circa 1900. Photograph by William H. Doering. Courtesy Library Company of Philadelphia.

CHAPTER SEVEN
Sidepath

By the time New York's legislature and courts had sanctioned the Ellsworth Sidepath Law and its 1900 amendments, the state's campaign already had a substantial head start. From county to county, cyclists representing out-of-the-way towns joined ranks to select the best routes, a collaborative process that united rural communities and one that often generated debate; plans to build sidepaths became front-page news, even for major newspapers; commissions perfected the technology of sidepath construction, aided by specially designed machinery; the periodical *Sidepaths* sustained the campaign; annual conventions solidified advances across the state; and more cyclists engaged in country riding, contributing to cycling's legacy of geographic exploration. Sidepaths also inspired stories that exploited themes of cycling and romance, exemplified by "A Dangerous Sidepath," an article published in *Outing*, in which the protagonist is a disciple of the tour who "loves not his bike less but nature more" and succumbs to the witchery of moonlit rides with a newly found companion. Optimistically, New York wheelmen predicted that the sidepath movement would make their state a tourist mecca, ending the envy of Great Britain.[1]

Building Sidepaths

Charles Raymond's 1892 path in Lockport encouraged emphasis on proper sidepath construction, linking sidepaths to the Good Roads movement. Monroe County's commission followed with a number of innovations, placing their progress on display in September 1899. The convention began with a lamplight parade accompanied by fireworks at Seneca Park, but the next morning delegates examined sod cutters, scrapers, rollers, trimmers, and other devices. Attendees also watched a display of sidepath building near the entrance to the Scottsville path, where superintendent A. P. Dean oversaw completion of more than one hundred feet of path in less than half an hour, including application of cinders and surface rolling. Frank McKeon demonstrated the ability of a modified bean cutter to remove sod and pare encroaching grass, and participants tested the county's sidepaths during a tour of the East Henrietta and Scottsville paths.[2]

Before adjourning, commissioners adopted the semimonthly journal *Sidepaths* as the convention's official circular, published in Rochester by William S. Harrison and Percy F. Megargle, the latter appointed to the LAW's national sidepath committee in 1900. The journal bolstered ties to the Good Roads movement, becoming a counterpart to the monthly *Good Roads* and offering opportunities for comparison on various topics: advocacy; technical information about construction techniques; illustration of successful projects across the country; news reports; trade advertisements; and articles about good roads and sidepaths, which appeared in each. However, the Social Age Publishing Company purchased *Sidepaths* in 1900, and the magazine's circulation soon ceased.[3]

FIGURES 7.2 AND 7.3

Sidepath commissioners from twenty-nine counties attended the 1899 convention, held in Rochester, and watched as the Monroe County Sidepath Commission demonstrated sidepath construction. Photographs by Cline Rogers in an album titled *Sidepaths: Monroe County (1899)*. Courtesy Rochester (N.Y.) Public Library, Local History and Genealogy Division.

FIGURES 7.4

Sidepath commissioners experimented with a variety of mechanical equipment fashioned to construct and maintain sidepaths. The device depicted here on the East Henrietta path is probably a modified bean harvester, used to remove sod from path surfaces and to pare encroaching grass, a never-ending task. The LeRoy Plow Company, located southwest of Rochester, manufactured several implements employed by county sidepath commissions. Photograph by Cline Rogers in an album titled *Sidepaths: Monroe County (1899)*. Courtesy Rochester (N.Y.) Public Library, Local History and Genealogy Division.

Sidepath Machinery

Local interest energized New York's sidepath era, and between 1900 and 1903 the organizers of fall sidepath conventions held in Utica, Buffalo, Patchoque, and Cortland adopted formats similar to that used for the 1899 meeting in Rochester, emphasizing machinery exhibits, construction, presentations addressing a variety of topics (such as maintenance and weed control), and tours of local sidepaths. Machinery consistently attracted attention, and many commissioners invested in equipment and hired day labor rather than engaging individual contractors. Some farm implements, such as side-hill plows and harrows, proved useful, but enterprising manufacturers also modified road construction machinery. Those companies often contributed to sidepath projects, experimenting with designs and giving commissions opportunities to test machinery and to circulate evaluations in newspapers, in yearly reports, or at annual conventions. Despite wide dissemination of that information, familiarity with equipment remained with local workers and soon passed from collective memory when the sidepath era ended.[4]

FIGURES 7.5 AND 7.6

In Churchville, George Turner manufactured farm implements and other machinery, including this sidepath roller, advertised in *Sidepaths* (November 1900) and used on the Monroe Avenue path. Advertisement courtesy of the National Transportation Library, Washington, D.C. Photograph by Cline Rogers in an album titled *Sidepaths: Monroe County (1899)*. Courtesy Rochester (N.Y.) Public Library, Local History and Genealogy Division.

Sidepaths sometimes linked communities in which companies fabricated equipment. Cyclists who traveled to Scottsville could continue on a path to Mumford and from there westerly along another path to the town of LeRoy in Genesee County, where the LeRoy Plow Company manufactured the patented bean cutter adapted by Frank McKeon. The company also produced a specially designed sidepath machine, which removed weeds efficiently, especially in wet weather. Another of Monroe County's very popular paths linked Rochester with Churchville to the southwest, where shop owner George Turner assembled sidepath rollers.[5]

Equipment ranged from very primitive devices to patented machines that performed multiple functions. A contraption called a *loot* resembled an old sled with a blade below it that removed loose sticks and stones. In Unadilla, Rufus K. Teller, president of the Tie Company, invented a more sophisticated machine that employed a cross rake and scraper, allowing a laborer to cut a thirty-inch path with one passing. Another unnamed opportunist designed a more elaborate path-smoothing machine with six-foot iron runners and a steel knife aligned in

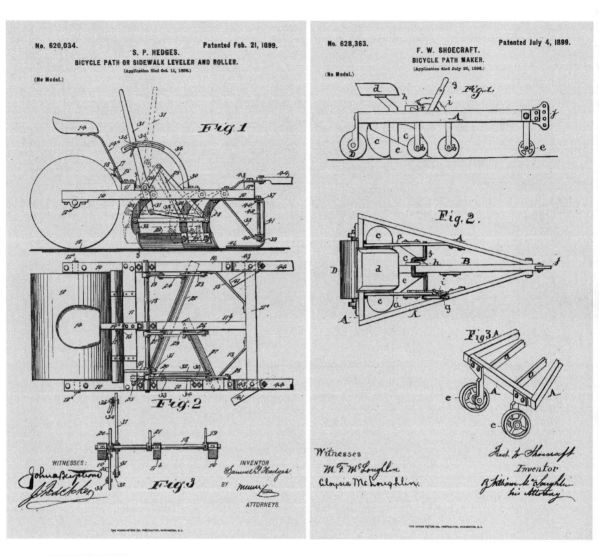

FIGURES 7.7 AND 7.8

Samuel Hedges from Greenport, New York, obtained an 1899 patent for a device that scraped, leveled, and rolled the surfaces of sidepaths. That same year, Michigan resident Fred Shoecraft patented a slightly larger bicycle path maker that utilized cutting discs, a plow, and a scraper for leveling and rolling. Courtesy University of Vermont libraries.

front of a v-shaped plow, to be drawn by a team of horses or mules. Sod and earth cut by the blade fell back onto the path, where the plow pushed it aside to create bordering ridges.[6]

Samuel Hedges from Greenport, New York, secured an 1899 patent for a horse-drawn mechanism that combined scraping, leveling, and rolling, and Fred Shoe-craft from Sturgis, Michigan, patented a similar machine that added cutting discs and a plow, describing his invention as a bicycle path maker. The Erie County Sidepath Commission may have fashioned its own, much enlarged version of Shoecraft's design and used it to construct sidepaths around the perimeter of Grand Island. Their machine required two men: one to drive a team of horses or mules and one to guide the plow and scraper.[7]

Weed Control

Other than repairing damage to sidepaths caused by weather, livestock, or farm wagons, controlling weeds remained the most stubborn challenge. Cyclists aggravated the problem by staying on the narrow traces worn by continuous use, about two feet wide, and avoiding the outer edges of sidepaths originally built to widths of five or six feet; grass and weeds quickly obscured those verges. In Albany County, sidepath commissioners used a Griffen sidepath machine designed to slice off thin layers of old paths and restore original borders. Commissions experimented with a variety of surface materials, but the application of well-compacted furnace cinders became standard. Cinders drained well, residual acid from the coal impeded weed growth, and cyclists could obtain coal ash from practically unlimited sources: water works, gas works, electrical power stations, or local businesses. Some bicycle clubs began collection drives in their communities.[8]

However, not all commissions found cinders satisfactory, because the sharp edges of clinkers (small consolidations of coal waste) sometimes punctured tires and ash residue clung to wheels. Gravel or crushed stone, especially shale and sandstone, often worked as well as any material and resembled asphalt if carefully compacted with a stone dust binder. Rome's commission successfully used quarry screenings, but other towns resorted to salt, cement, various chemicals, and even odious lime residue from gas works, usually with only limited success; hand labor with scythes, hoes, and mowers typically became necessary. Neither commissioners nor Good Roads proponents expressed much concern about the ecological effects of chemicals used on sidepath and highway surfaces, and some commissions recommended saving costs by using oil as a surface binder. However, at least one city forester cautioned cyclists against the application of furnace cinders near the roots of shade trees.[9]

Costs per Mile

Commissions consistently promoted the sale of tags by placing notices in newspapers, and they carefully monitored costs, halting construction when revenue

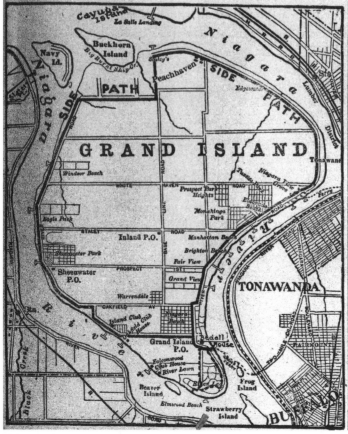

FIGURES 7.9 AND 7.10
The Erie County Sidepath Commission built a twenty-three-mile circumferential path on Grand Island and invested in machinery to complete the project. From *Buffalo Illustrated Express* (June 10, 1900). Courtesy New York State Library, Manuscript and Special Collections.

dwindled. Counties also competed, and this latent rivalry surfaced at annual conventions when commissions announced the number of licenses sold and miles of paths opened. As mileage increased, however, commissioners devoted ever-larger shares of revenue to maintenance, a quandary that builders of highways continue to face. When the sale of licenses declined with fading interest in cycling, even maintenance ended.[10]

Charles Raymond's estimates based on his work near Lockport proved to be reasonably accurate, and counties could expect an average cost per mile of $325. He also observed that large-scale construction equipment might reduce costs to $200 per mile, depending on grading, terrain, type and transportation of surface materials, or drainage required. As county commissions gained experience, more information about construction methods and costs became available, and commissions anticipated expenses ranging between $150 and $600 per mile, with maintenance averaging about fifty dollars per mile. When compared to the building of today's bicycle paths, sidepath construction was uncomplicated, rapid, and inexpensive.[11]

Sidepath Traces

Although the sidepath era occurred more than a century ago, lasted only briefly, and left little physical evidence of its extensive reach, the traces of that era remain important. As the authors of Monroe County's *Sidepath Guide* proclaimed, sidepaths in some New York counties extended into most villages and towns, traversed principal roads and crossroads, transformed communication between urban and rural communities, and allowed children living in the country to attend school in the city. In many places, the ability of cyclists to move easily about the countryside depended on sidepaths. Yet despite being once ever present in that state, sidepaths are seldom mentioned in historical accounts of its rural countryside and rarely included in visual depictions of those landscapes.[12]

In New York counties where wheelmen left careful documentation of sidepaths and in those few regions such as Oneida, Monroe, Suffolk, and Albany counties where that chronicle includes comprehensive photographs or maps, we can visualize what cyclists experienced during their late nineteenth- and early-twentieth-century peregrinations. Keeping those perceptions and impressions in our outlook today can aid efforts to make thoughtful choices about our lands and places. The following accounts of sidepaths underscore the expansive reach of those corridors, emphasize the role they once played as very visible features of cultural landscapes, and mark the many locales worthy of continued study.

Monroe County
Monroe County and its principal city, Rochester, demonstrate the expansive scope of New York's sidepath campaign, evident from the exceptional written,

cartographical, and photographic record left by wheelmen and from the creative initiatives, policies, and publications they introduced.

Sidepath Associations Rochester's wheelmen began a fundraising campaign for bicycle paths during the late 1880s, about the same time as Holyoke cyclists' campaign began, and a few years later began watching events in Lockport. The city's cyclists had only limited tolerance for a five-mile path leading northerly from Ridge Road to Charlotte and the amusements at Ontario Beach, Rochester's version of Coney Island. The Rochester, Charlotte, and Turnpike Toll Company had financed the path, probably in 1888 after cyclists' attempts to raise money had fallen short, but failed to keep it in good repair and also required a five-cent toll—a charge that eventually led to unsuccessful litigation by the city's wheelmen (see figure 1.7). By 1892, cyclists had grown dissatisfied and had formed their own organization, the Rochester Wheelmen's League, to promote good roads by securing legislation and constructing sidepaths. Early in 1893, they began soliciting subscriptions for a twenty-five mile path encircling the city, but contributions languished. During the winter of 1895–1896, the league petitioned the state legislature to enact a law similar to that introduced by Niagara County, taxing each Monroe County bicycle one dollar. When that controversial tax failed to win local approval, wheelmen began creating separate sidepath organizations.[13]

Early in May 1896, the Southeast Sidepath Association formed and immediately began constructing a short path along Elmwood Avenue between Mt. Hope Avenue and Genesee Valley Park. That path became part of the Highland and Elmwood Avenue path, which eventually linked several corridors leading outward from the city in different directions, including the Scottsville path, the Monroe Avenue path, and the East and West Henrietta paths, the last becoming popular after cyclists discovered breakfast at the Bartholomay Cottage Hotel.[14]

Two other groups organized that month, one each for the city's northeastern and southwestern quadrants, and they promptly began raising funds and building paths, including two by the Northeast Sidepath Association: one along East Avenue and one flanking Culver Road. Both sidepaths soon linked important diverging routes, including one to Sea Breeze on Lake Ontario and another southeasterly to Brighton Village and then Fairport (about seven miles from Rochester's center, known as "Four Corners"), with a spur to Pittsford. Wheelmen representing eastern, western, and northwestern sectors of the city also considered forming associations, with plans for specific paths in mind.[15]

Strategic Fundraising Enthusiasm for sidepath building gained momentum during the late spring and summer of 1896, spurred by a sequence of key developments. One of the city's newspapers, the *Post-Express*, renewed the campaign to build a belt-line path encircling the city, resulting in the appointment of a special wheelman's committee and garnering support from the city's surveyor, James Young McClintock, known to his colleagues and constituents as J.Y. The city's park commissioners also began constructing a path along the westerly side of the

7.11a   7.11b

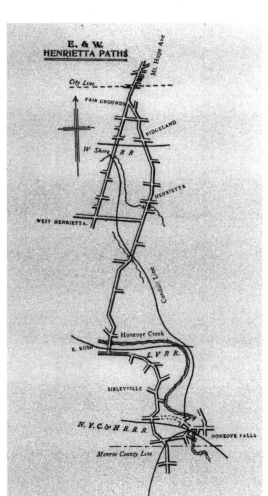

FIGURES 7.11a, b, AND 7.12

During an era when country roads often did not have names and route markers were scarce, the Monroe County Sidepath Commission diligently identified its paths with signs; here, the West Henrietta Path extending southerly from Rochester to the county line is shown. Cycler's rests, such as Bartholomay's LAW Park Hotel, became popular stopping points for touring wheelmen. Although electricity had reached this far south of Rochester in 1899, the Aermotor windmill continued to provide power to pump water. Map courtesy of New York State Library, Manuscripts and Special Collections. Photograph by Cline Rogers in an album titled *Sidepaths: Monroe County (1899)*. Courtesy Rochester (N.Y.) Public Library and Local History and Genealogy Division. Sidepath tag from the journal *Sidepaths* (December 1900), courtesy National Transportation Library.

FIGURE 7.13

Similar to other transportation networks, sidepaths required bridges such as that depicted here on the Scottsville path, crossing the Genesee Valley Canal. Photograph by Cline Rogers in an album titled *Sidepaths: Monroe County (1899)*. Courtesy Rochester (N.Y.) Public Library, Local History and Genealogy Division.

Genesee River, providing another link to the Scottsville Path when it opened late that summer.[16]

Consolidation of these efforts became inevitable, hastened by the city's efforts to exclude wheelmen from sidewalks, and on June 20 thousands of cyclists gathered at the city's driving park for what authors of the county's 1899 *Sidepath Guide* would recall as "callithumpian exercises" to voice support for wheelmen's rights and to raise funds. McClintock chaired the organizing committee for the grand event, which netted sufficient revenue ($2,500) from its twenty-five-cent admission charge to pay for sidepaths under construction that season. Taking advantage of momentum that lasted into the fall, the city's cyclists formed the Rochester Association of the LAW, a local division of the national league. Several members of the new organization—notably, Armstrong and Bastable—also belonged to another body, the Monroe County Wheelman's Association. However, the extent to which those two groups functioned separately is unclear. The much-publicized, celebratory opening of the Scottsville path on September

FIGURES 7.14

Sidepath laws authorized the planting of trees to separate roads and paths, but in village centers such as Churchville's, sidepaths and sidewalks competed for limited space, and conflict with property owners occasionally occurred. Photograph by Cline Rogers in an album titled *Sidepaths: Monroe County (1899)*. Courtesy Rochester (N.Y.) Public Library, Local History and Genealogy Division.

12 quickly added stature to these embryonic organizations, as did the gala inaugurations of the popular paths to Sea Breeze and Fairport, each a few weeks later. Memories of these successful fetes lingered long enough for wheelmen to plan a second, similarly profitable carnival the following year.[17]

Although Monroe County's sidepath campaign evolved amid the context of sidepath initiatives occurring in Niagara, Albany, Oneida, and other New York counties, Rochester's campaign also became linked to events in Brooklyn. There, the second of the paths between Coney Island and Prospect Park had opened late in June 1896, and McClintock had acted as a consultant for that project. Rochester newspapers touted his role, and those accolades probably encouraged him to champion the city's sidepaths. Fundraising and path building advanced, and by the close of 1898—the year in which the county's law authorizing a sidepath commission won approval from Rochester's mayor and common council—Monroe County wheelmen already had opened more than 130 miles of paths from private contributions.[18]

Success of those efforts explains the county's decision in 1899 to retain a license fee of twenty-five cents and to remain apart from the state's uniform sidepath law until the 1900 amendments. From the outset, Rochester's wheelmen had sought broad support for sidepaths—from businesses and farmers as well as cyclists—and they emphasized the ability of paths to improve communication with rural communities. Toward that end, wheelmen's associations built sidepaths quickly, rendering once-formidable distances manageable for county residents—and at a reasonable outlay. When administration shifted to a county sidepath commission after 1898, license revenue could be used to improve paths already built. The very reasonable price also helped sales to accumulate early in the spring, facilitating plans for work during the summer. Judging from the sale of nearly 31,000 sidepath tags between April and December 1898, those strategies worked well, and Monroe County's commission pointed to the higher prices charged in other counties as explanation for the low number of tags sold in some parts of the state.[19]

Well before appointment of the county's sidepath commission and circulation of its detailed reports, accounts by wheelmen's associations provided informative descriptions of selected routes, revealing a rural landscape on the verge of urban discovery. In June 1896, for instance, a committee appointed to inspect existing sidepaths identified a romantic preserve, Palmer's Glen, at the head of Irondequoit Bay near Brighton. No more than three miles from Four Corners, the scene offered "an impression of absolute wildness" and, apart from the musical cascades of rivulets, a "silence unbroken." McClintock, a member of that committee, convinced the group that a mile-long spur from the Brighton path would provide access to an ideal cycler's rest.[20]

County Sidepath Commission   Once established, the county sidepath commission promptly advanced the campaign, adding roughly twenty miles of new corridors during 1898. Although accounts conflict, by the end of the 1901 season the total extent of county sidepaths may have increased to about 193 miles. The commission's comprehensive *Sidepath Guide* contained detailed maps, descriptions of paths, and a restatement of its enabling law, and the booklet is the most comprehensive publication by any of New York's many sidepath commissions.[21]

Maps in the *Sidepath Guide* also disclose the important efforts by Monroe County's commission to link their network of paths to those being built in adjoining counties, probably encouraging other counties to establish cross-country routes. For instance, the Little Ridge Road Path led westerly, connecting Rochester with sidepaths leading to Lockport and Niagara Falls, a seventy-mile journey, and wheelmen may have used the route in 1901 to reach the Pan-American Exposition in Buffalo.[22]

Many of the resourceful initiatives credited to Monroe County took place in 1899 and herald a campaign in its peak stages of development. These undertakings included an amendment strengthening the county's enabling law, the highly successful fall convention, publication of the commission's *Sidepath Guide*, the compilation of photographs by Cline Rogers, steady improvement of the county's network of paths, and even the sponsorship of a twenty-five mile road race on Decoration Day by publishers of the magazine *Sidepaths*. Passage of the state's uniform law that same year turned public attention toward the county's accomplishments.[23]

Albany County

Wheelmen in Albany, both a city and a county, also joined the vanguard of sidepath building that originated in Lockport and achieved success in cities such as Utica, Rome, Rochester, and Syracuse. As in Monroe, Oneida, Onandaga, and Clinton counties, Albany's ambitious network of sidepaths merged with routes in neighboring counties. These corridors became part of an expansive regional system of sidepaths that connected communities along the Hudson River to the south, popular tourist destinations in Saratoga Springs and Glens Falls to the north, and towns situated in the Mohawk River valley.

The total mileage of sidepaths in Albany County probably never exceeded half that in Monroe County, a factor shaped partly by topography and partly by the pattern of sidepaths radiating outward from the city but confined by the Hudson River to the east. Nevertheless, Albany County's role as a pivotal hub in this regional network distinguishes its sidepath campaign, as does the preference of its sidepath commissioners for remaining apart from the state's uniform sidepath law. That detachment also becomes apparent in decisions by its commissioners not to attend state sidepath conventions.

Albany County sidepath builders adopted familiar strategies, beginning with collaborative efforts by local clubs, succeeded by a confederation of concerned wheelmen called the Albany Bicycle League, and then followed by passage of a law enabling the appointment of a county sidepath commission in 1898. Albany County's commission eventually issued a guide with an accompanying map, and the efforts of John D. Chism helped to place Albany County at the fore of New York's sidepath campaign. Chism initially served as president of the Albany Bicycle League, then president of the Albany County Sidepath Commission, then as a member of the special committee formed in Rochester in 1898 to prepare a uniform state sidepath law, and subsequently as chair of the LAW's New York State Committee on Sidepaths, charged with securing passage of that law.[24]

Among the county's first sidepaths, that between Albany and Schenectady along the Schenectady Turnpike is notable. Opened during the summer of 1895, the fourteen-mile corridor originated as a joint project by clubs from each city and became one of the county's principal bicycle arteries, serving as a connector for sidepaths leading to more distant places, such as Ballston Spa and Saratoga Springs in Saratoga County; numerous spur sidepaths also linked nearby locales. Used by as many as 1,500 wheelmen on some days, the path also became the focus of litigation when the Schenectady Railway Company began building its electric road over sections of the sidepath in 1900.[25]

As did Monroe County's 1898 and 1899 enabling laws, those enacted for Albany County during the same two years required licenses. However, the legislation for Albany County authorized a fee between fifty cents and one dollar, and its commissioners opted for the latter. Although the number of licenses sold in the two counties during 1898 and 1899 may have been influenced by a number of factors, the respective costs of those licenses likely caused Albany County to fall behind in sales and revenue.[26]

Lacking the many miles of sidepaths already in place in Monroe County by 1898, Albany County commissioners were free to allocate funds for building new sidepaths along strategic routes and connecting them with spurs that created a complex web of paths. They wasted no time in starting, and two weeks after the county's enabling law became effective the newly appointed commissioners (led by Chism and Charles H. Van Allen) began inspecting existing paths, breaking ground for new paths, and surveying future routes; sidepath police commenced patrols as well. One of the new paths, with construction underway on April 25, extended northerly from Albany to Watervliet and then to Cohoes on the Saratoga County boundary (the Cohoes and Albany path). By the end of April, commissioners had sold more than one thousand tags, and that figure tripled during the next two months. By summer of the following year, commissioners had opened approximately seventy-five miles of paths.[27]

Other than the county's comparatively limited sidepath mileage, its commissioners made no concessions to Monroe or other counties in terms of vigorous commitment to sidepath building and maintenance—in every respect a substantial undertaking. The county developed a number of creative solutions to the construction, use, and maintenance of its sidepaths: a portable house where workers remained at night, eliminating time spent traveling to and from work sites; large hollow wooden rollers that could be transported to sites easily and there filled with water; stone flagging across street intersections; and section signs placed at one-half-mile intervals to measure distances and locate damage to paths.[28]

Despite common interests and objectives, and for reasons not entirely clear, a split developed between Albany County's commission and their counterparts in western New York, and that friction influenced the outcome of initiatives for the uniform sidepath bills of 1899 and 1900. Some of the dissension may have originated in the early months of 1899 during that year's legislative session, when Albany County objected to several provisions of the Ellsworth law and declined to abandon its own enabling act. Resentment probably mounted that summer with the vote to hold the 1899 fall convention in Rochester despite complaints from Albany wheelmen that the previous year's gathering also had convened there.[29]

Although Chism initially had planned to attend the 1899 convention and to present a paper—an argument that sidepaths represented object lessons for good roads—organizers asked Albany County to defray conference costs with money raised by the sale of sidepath licenses, an expenditure not authorized by the county's law. The Albany delegation declined, elected not to attend, and left the task of reading Chism's paper to Charles Raymond and to the convention's secretary–treasurer, William W. Canfield of Utica. With no one from Albany County there to object, voters selected Utica for the following year's conference, probably deepening the rift.[30]

Disagreements continued during the 1900 legislative session, when the legislature considered various amendments to the Ellsworth law, measures introduced principally to make that law consistent throughout the state by creating a single sidepath tag and license fee and by pulling Monroe and Albany counties into the fold. Those issues had surfaced during the 1899 Rochester convention and had joined the list of topics given to the convention's legislative committee. Raymond added a related proposal to create a state sidepath fund and commission with authority to transfer money from one county to another, to help sparsely populated regions contribute to a continuous network of paths for the benefit of all touring cyclists.[31]

Satisfied with its own sidepaths, the Albany commission lobbied against consolidation, rankling many wheelmen, including Charles Bastable, who had been elected chair of the legislative committee and president of the Utica convention to be held later that year. Albany wheelmen also objected to Raymond's proposal, but William Mackie and a number of other influential commissioners agreed with Albany's position, fearing that politics would quickly govern distribution of the funds. Although Raymond's plan languished, it reappeared on the agenda for the fall convention in Utica, giving Albany's commissioners another excuse for not attending. Their absence may have been noted when, at the close of that gathering, officials selected Buffalo to host the 1901 convention—offering attendees a chance to visit the Pan-American Exposition. Quibbling aside, those events explain key aspects of the legislative structure that fostered the planning and construction of sidepaths in New York between 1898 and 1904.[32]

Long Island: Suffolk and Nassau Counties

By contrast to Niagara, Monroe, Oneida, and Albany counties, the Long Island counties of Nassau and Suffolk played only supporting roles in framing the legislative and administrative structure that guided New York's sidepath era. Only the two important test cases in which New York's courts sustained the constitutionality of the Ellsworth law gave Long Island a voice in the shaping of that structure. Yet the region's wheelmen and the Suffolk County Sidepath Commission (led by Henry Preston from Shelter Island Heights, Ansel B. Gildersleeve from Huntington, and several other energetic figures) pursued a single objective very well: they built or improved (and then maintained) hundreds and hundreds of miles of sidepaths—substantially more than other counties.[33]

Long Island's topography and patterns of settlement caused distinctive configurations in its sidepath system. Rather than corridors radiating outward from the center of a major city, paths forming an intricate web, or links creating an extended county-to-county corridor, Long Island's sidepaths evolved as two principal trunk lines, one each along the South and North Shores. Those paths formed an elongated loop around the island, providing access to numerous spur sidepaths that meandered into communities along the region's many bays, inlets, and harbors or that led to railroad stations. Paths also heightened the appeal of bicycle touring on Long Island as an alternate route to New England, and wheelmen could board ferries to Connecticut and Rhode Island or explore remote havens, such as Block Island.[34]

Several important connectors joined these two trunk lines, including the fourteen-mile Cross County path that linked Patchogue to Port Jefferson and its harbor on Long Island Sound, a route popular enough to support refreshment stands. Another cross-island path, one promoted by the Riverhead Bicycle Club early in 1894, connected Riverhead on the North Shore with Eastport and Westhampton on the South Shore and included a branch to Quogue, also on the South Shore. At the island's far easterly reaches, cyclists could travel from the South Shore at Bridgehampton along a path bordering Bull's Head Turnpike en route to Sag Harbor; from there, cross by ferry to North Haven; pedal across that island on a path to South Ferry; and cross to Shelter Island. From Shelter Island, scenic paths led to North Ferry, linking Shelter Island Heights with Greenport on the North Shore.[35]

New York's formal sidepath campaign arrived on Long Island just as the region's political boundaries changed. In 1898, a large portion of Queens County joined New York City as the Borough of Queens, and a year later what remained of Hempstead, North Hempstead, and Oyster Bay in Queens County became instead Nassau County. From Jamaica, today part of Queens, wheelmen rambled along the Jericho Turnpike or its old sidepath across nearly the entire length of what is now Nassau County. At Jericho (roughly midway between the North Shore and the South Shore), cyclists could continue northeasterly toward Huntington or veer southeasterly toward Amityville. From Jamaica, cyclists also could reach the South Shore via Springfield Road and Merrick Road. Whether because wheelmen had long used those heavily traveled routes and found them adequate, or because those corridors provided passage to more enticing destinations beyond, or because borough and county officials paved many roads with macadam surfaces, Nassau County never established a sidepath commission. Only a few bicycle paths constructed in that county during the late 1890s are notable, including a six-mile circuit in Westbury through a neighborhood of country estates planned by wealthy New Yorkers, including Benjamin Hicks and William C. Whitney.[36]

Tag Sales   With sidepath licenses unnecessary in Nassau County, club wheelmen from Manhattan, Brooklyn, and Queens filled Suffolk County's coffers, burnishing Long Island's reputation as a cycler's paradise. During 1899 and 1900, the commission collected about $18,000 from the sale of fifty-cent tags, slightly more than the revenue generated by Monroe County's commission during its first two years of existence (1898 and 1899). During the 1900 season, the commission circulated

East Main St., Bay Shore, L. I., N. Y.

Made in Germany.   C. W. Race, Importer & Publisher, Bay Shore, L. I., N. Y.

FIGURE 7.15

A postcard showing the Bayshore sidepath. The card is postmarked October 1907, the year that legislation sponsored by Assemblyman John Lumpton appointed town highway commissioners in Suffolk County to serve as sidepath commissioners, with the goal of removing fees and making the paths available to everyone.

a sidepath map prepared by architect Henry C. Wintringham, and cartographer Robert Delano Servoss crafted a second map at about the same time, depicting roads as well as bicycle paths. By the fall of that year the South Shore paths extended continuously to Amagansett village. Among the North Shore paths, the path between Riverhead and Greenport (twenty-two miles apart) gained a reputation as one of the district's most appealing. To accommodate cyclists, New York newspapers regularly reported the condition of Long Island's roads and sidepaths, and during 1902 (when cycling had begun to decline in many regions) Suffolk County's sidepath commission increased license sales from the year before.[37]

Reports summarizing overall activity and mileage differ, ranging from three hundred to as many as five hundred miles, and various circumstances may explain those discrepancies. Trustees in a few towns constructed their own sidepaths, and at least one community, Southampton, purchased a sidepath machine. The county's highway commissioners also built paths, creating occasional conflict with sidepath commissioners concerning the proximity of highways and paths. In addition, administrative organization gave commissioners in specific districts substantial autonomy once funds had been distributed by the commission at large. Nevertheless, evidence concerning the beginning and ending points for many paths is adequate to conclude that Suffolk County's network of side-paths surpassed three hundred miles—and probably by a considerable margin.[38]

Regional Sidepath Networks

By early 1900, New York counties had created regional provinces for wheelmen who relished simple country riding, or alternatively who sought opportunities for more venturesome, cross-country touring. In many sectors, sidepaths also provided a convenient means for workers to reach places of employment. Many of the patterns of sidepath development visible in Niagara, Oneida, Monroe, Albany, and Suffolk counties were repeated elsewhere in the state, including radial webs extending outward from large cities; trunk lines or arterial paths bordering well-traveled turnpikes; links in long-distance routes joining several counties; connectors; and spurs or circuits to especially scenic, fashionable, or recreational destinations.

Sidepaths in Syracuse and surrounding Onandaga County illustrated all of these categories and also contributed to corridors that crossed the state. Prior to passage of the Ellsworth law, Syracuse cyclists had formed one of the state's many wheelway leagues and had begun building paths that the county's sidepath commission soon lengthened to create two principal trunk lines: one leading across the county from east to west and a second pointing south through the valley of Onandaga Creek to Cortland County, where that county's commission built a network of paths leading to Ithaca in Thompkins County. Lured by Onandaga County's many lakes, members of the wheelway league also built a circuit northerly to South Bay on Oneida Lake (see figure 3.9), and commissioners later opened a radial path heading northwesterly from Syracuse along Onondaga Lake to Baldwinsville, with connections to Oswego County paths bordering the Oswego Canal. Those paths led to Fulton, Oswego on Lake Ontario, and Fruit Valley along the shores of that immense water body.[39]

The success of the trunk lines in Onandaga County led to numerous spurs, including one funded by anglers: a five-mile path from Jordan Station to the Riverside Hotel on the Seneca River, near the outlet of Cross Lake. Cyclists in Skaneateles at the northerly tip of scenic Skaneateles Lake also raised money to build a path to Skaneateles Junction, creating links to paths in Cayuga County and from there into the great web of sidepaths connecting towns in the Finger Lakes region. Commissions in many other scenic parts of New York aspired to regional networks, albeit on a smaller scale than that stretching outward from Onandaga County. For example, the Seneca County commission contributed to the state's east–west sidepath corridor through the Finger Lakes region by constructing paths linking Seneca Falls near Cayuga Lake with Geneva on Seneca Lake to the west.[40]

In several regions, commissions in neighboring counties collaborated in the planning of routes, whether to scenic locales or between distant cities. Although the Oswego River offered a well-established travel corridor between Oswego, Fulton, and Syracuse, Oswego County's sidepath commissioners also turned their attention to Lake Ontario and to Jefferson County to the north. There, paths along a north–south highway linked Adams with Adams Center and Watertown to the north and Brewerton to the south near the outlet of Oneida Lake near South Bay, almost sixty miles from Watertown and within easy distance of Syracuse paths.[41]

Sidepath commissions throughout the state focused on routes to popular scenic destinations, adjusting plans as needed to take advantage of projects underway in neighboring counties or to establish junctions with principal through corridors. East of Utica in Fulton County, for example, commissioners constructed a sidepath leading northeasterly from Gloversville to Sacandaga Park and Northville on the Sacandaga River. In the state's far southwest corner, the Chautauqua County commission opened or improved a sidepath leading northwesterly from Jamestown, also a center for bicycle manufacturing, to Bemis Point on Chautauqua Lake.[42]

Southern Tier Trunk Sidepath

Efforts to construct a continuous trunk line across New York State's southern-tier counties represent one of the most ambitious collaborations among the state's sidepath commissions. At least part of the southern-tier route originated from a proposal by the LAW's state division to accommodate New York City wheelmen who hoped to attend the 1901 Pan-American Exposition in Buffalo. That scheme may have been bolstered by ongoing efforts (never quite completed) to build a nearly continuous corridor through Broome, Tioga, Chemung, Steuben, Allegany, and Cattaraugus counties, east to west. Despite enthusiasm for the LAW scheme in many sectors, the project succumbed to lengthy gaps between the Hudson River valley and Binghamton. The route's arduous terrain in several regions presented challenges, but the course also ventured into territory with few population centers to pay for sidepaths.[43]

Overgrowth

The preceding descriptions of New York's sidepaths and the places they joined are only samples of the state's far-reaching traces of country riding, little more than fragments in both pattern and extent. In many communities, sidepath commissions obtained authorization from village or city officials to build short paths along broad boulevards or to reach local parks, railroad depots, cemeteries, factories, and scenic vantage points. Commissions thus created subsidiary webs of bicycle paths within the larger, regional or statewide networks. Detailed accounts of those and other sidepaths help to underscore the extraordinary extent of the sidepath campaign and to enlarge our understanding of that period of history and its bicyclists. No less remarkable is the speed with which commissions and wheelmen energetically completed path projects. Those aspects—local enthusiasm, efficient administration, the rapid opening of cycling corridors, and the network's quickly expanding reach—are all important considerations for today's builders of bicycle paths.

Sidepath Decline

Equally remarkable is the sidepath era's similarly swift decline, and from its peak in 1900 or 1901, the campaign quickly began to crumble. In 1904, Charles Raymond's principal adversary, state Senator William Armstrong, stepped into the sidepath spotlight once again to reiterate his opinion that good roads would make sidepaths unnecessary. That year, Armstrong successfully introduced legislation transferring the responsibilities of sidepath commissions to county engineers, who governed highway construction and maintenance. His bill became law that spring, and in any county that already had an engineer the statute required sidepath commissioners to transfer all of their records to that official by June 1, 1904; thereafter, those commissions ceased to exist. In counties yet to appoint an engineer, commissions remained in place, with a requirement to complete the transfer of records within ten days of the appointment of an engineer and then to dissolve. A year later, the *Rochester Democrat and Chronicle* reported that "the sale of tags has practically ceased in every community" and opined that "no fad ever died out more rapidly than the bicycle sidepath craze." Although not quite accurate about tag sales, the report nevertheless identified a clear trend.[44]

Explanation for the sidepath campaign's sudden collapse rests largely with the correspondingly abrupt decline of cycling as a recreational activity. With fading enthusiasm among cyclists, the willpower to surmount ever-present obstacles— a vital force that had characterized the grassroots campaign for sidepaths from its outset—also dissolved. Frank Amsden, who chaired Monroe County's commission from its time of inception to its accounting in 1904, supported Armstrong's bill, likely because his commission lacked adequate revenue from license sales and could neither build new sidepaths nor adequately maintain those already in place. Without maintenance, sidepaths quickly became overgrown or washed away during heavy rains, and roads soon provided better surfaces. In response, even earnest cyclists stopped purchasing licenses, and enforcement of the law—troublesome from the start—became futile. Most of the ten thousand tags that Monroe County's commission had ordered for 1905 remained unsold, and in August of that year commissioners ended Constable Frank McKeon's employment.[45]

Wheelmen continued to use sidepaths in some counties, and staunch supporters of the campaign viewed Armstrong's bill chiefly as an effort to increase the authority of county highway departments, providing opportunities to repay political patronage. Those same cyclists pointed to the sidepath movement's admirable record of volunteer work by commissioners, untarnished by political influence, and lamented the emerging trend. Undeniably, that commitment to public service joins the extraordinary reach of sidepaths as two of the campaign's important legacies.[46]

Despite dire reports, sidepath use, construction, and maintenance did not decline uniformly in New York—either in location or period—and a chronicle of those developments adds to our understanding of an important period in cycling history, when the bicycle loses luster as an adult activity and does so for reasons that remain partially clouded. A key part of that record concerns the manner in which some sidepath commissions divided counties into districts and assigned oversight of those sectors to individual commissioners, who then kept careful records of licenses sold to justify expenditures in specific communities. As a result, commissioners could identify those locales where cycling activity remained strong, and they could also monitor demographic factors influencing those trends. Commissioners in a number of counties observed that workers continued to rely on bicycles for travel to factories, businesses, farms, or other places of employment, and sidepaths serving those wheelmen often remained open. Although fashionable riding waned among the wealthy, some wheelmen clung to the practice simply for exercise. As one wheelman explained: "Automobiles are still the toys of wealthy people, but the cycle is the vehicle of the workingman, of the factory laborer, and of the clerk," the only means of traveling into the countryside during evenings. School children also continued to use the paths.[47]

That chronicle also establishes important connections between the emerging popularity of automobiles or motorcycles and the disappearance of sidepaths. That cause-and-effect relationship becomes clear as the automobile industry adds its weight to the quest for good roads, with two very direct consequences for sidepaths: First, as Armstrong had often reminded his wheelmen friends, improved highway surfaces made sidepaths unnecessary. Second, and with considerable finality, the physical process of creating good roads destroyed abutting sidepaths. Highway crews improving the old turnpike between Albany and Schenectady in December 1904 demonstrated that trend, erasing Albany County's landmark sidepath and marking a symbolic conclusion to the year that Armstrong's bill became law.[48]

Those same connections also confirm a corresponding relationship between the rise of automobiles or motorcycles and the decline of cycling itself. True, some cycling historians have argued convincingly that automobiles were not the cause of cycling's ebbing popularity at the turn of the century and that other factors may have played more important roles, including the physical difficulty of riding over uncharitable terrain. As one cyclist remarked, "It took the wind out of a rider to pedal any distance at all." Discussions during annual sidepath conventions also hint at some of those factors, including the lure of interurban trolleys and their expanding networks. Yet many sidepath commissioners (who observed trends closely and who held a fiscal stake in assessing those developments accurately) attributed dwindling revenues to the growing popularity of automobiles. Granted, in locales where sidepaths remained in use after 1904 that relationship probably became more obvious as automobile and motorcycle travel increased. Yet accounts by many sidepath commissioners over a period of years substantiate that the two modes of travel—bicycles and automobiles—competed for public favor, much to the detriment of the former.[49]

If Senator Armstrong had secretly harbored resentment toward Charles Raymond, Charles Bastable, John Chism, or others following the 1899 invitation to Timothy Ellsworth to sponsor the state's uniform sidepath law, then he may have enjoyed a sense of satisfaction in knowing that his predictions concerning the eventual redundancy of sidepaths were becoming true, at least during that era. Yet in response to queries about the 1904 legislative proposal, he graciously credited Amsden and his sidepath commission for performing a very useful public service and for creating countless opportunities for pleasurable travel. He also remarked that with many highway improvement projects then underway, a single administrative system for both roads and sidepaths would be more efficient.[50]

Charles Raymond's Crucible

Charles Raymond doggedly continued to confront the campaign's principal challenge: the need for consistent revenue to build and maintain sidepaths. During the summer of 1899 (following passage of the Ellsworth law), Raymond tried to solve a specific concern of sidepath commissioners, who had difficulty selling licenses during the months before cycling began. Without available funds, commissioners could not engage maintenance or construction workers or plan new sidepaths. To solve that problem, he proposed legislation authorizing counties to issue bonds for sidepath building, to be repaid through the sale of licenses. Early drafts of the Gardiner amendments of 1900 included a weak version of that proposal, authorizing commissioners to enter into contracts for up to one-half of the revenue collected from license sales during the preceding year. However, the final bill removed that provision and continued to limit expenditures to the amount of funds actually on deposit in sidepath accounts. Later that year, at the Utica convention in the fall of 1900, Raymond lobbied for the special state sidepath commission authorized to disperse funds broadly. Unfortunately, those efforts also came to naught.[51]

Undeterred, Raymond addressed the sidepath convention in Buffalo a year later and proposed sidepaths beside every new highway funded by the state's Good Roads law, reasoning that the paths benefited pedestrians as well as wheelmen and that the latter should not bear all the costs. Although Raymond may have been motivated by his personal attachment to a resourceful state program that had originated at Lockport, the proposal underscores his persistent focus on the costs of building and maintaining sidepaths. Raymond's idea also countered Armstrong's contention that good roads would make sidepaths redundant and suggests an intuitive awareness on Raymond's part that bicycles and other modes of transportation were—and would remain—incompatible, an insight that clearly eluded Armstrong. Perhaps Raymond and Albert Pope were the two men of that era who glimpsed the magnitude of future incompatibility between the bicycle and the automobile.[52]

By the fall of 1902, the trickling revenue and uncertain pace of sidepath building had become obvious. At the Patchogue convention, Raymond proposed state legislation to enable county boards of supervisors to levy general taxes on real or personal property for the construction of sidepaths, not to exceed $5,000 annually. The measure allocated costs among entire county populations and acknowledged the bicycle to be a "vehicle of the people." Raymond's plan did not obligate county boards to impose any tax, but left the matter to public sentiment, with the hope that a successful network of sidepaths would stabilize revenue from the sale of licenses and eventually make any tax unnecessary. Raymond initially planned to retain license requirements for cyclists who continued to use the paths, but the convention's legislative committee probably modified the proposal, opening sidepaths to the public in those counties that adopted such a levy and eliminating sidepath tags. In any case, Raymond and the committee found a sponsor for the bill in Senator Irving L'Hommedieu, a lawyer whose district included Orleans, Niagara, and Genesee counties. With only minor opposition, the bill became law in May 1903.[53]

In addition to his various official appointments at annual sidepath conventions, Raymond also chaired the Niagara County Sidepath Commission, and during the 1903 season he supervised improvements to paths between Niagara Falls and Lewiston, between Lewiston and Youngstown on Lake Ontario, and in the village of Mapleton about midway between Lockport and Tonawanda. Raymond remained optimistic in the face of mounting scorn for sidepaths, particularly in Niagara Falls, where paths had been poorly maintained. In 1904, editors of the *Niagara Falls Gazette* harshly criticized the city's decaying sidepaths, proclaiming them useless and bemoaning the loss of funds that could have been spent instead on permanent improvements to country roads. A year later, in response to news reports from Niagara Falls that bicycle tags and sidepaths were "a dead issue," he vowed to enforce license requirements, adding naively that sidepaths would regain favor as motorcycle touring became popular.[54]

Resilient Sidepaths

By no means did the type of sidepath erosion evident in cities such as Niagara Falls occur consistently across the state after 1904. In Monroe County, engineer James Young McClintock reassured concerned wheelmen and agreed to maintain the county's principal paths, which by 1906 had dwindled to about forty miles. In other counties, commissions dutifully remained solvent and pleaded with cyclists to purchase licenses. When that strategy faltered, some commissions petitioned county boards of supervisors for special appropriations. That tactic worked briefly in Chemung County, where the sale of tags had decreased steadily from 4,648 in 1901, to 3,409 in 1902, to 2,307 in 1903, to 1,562 in 1904, to 899 in 1905, and to 817 in 1906. Following the 1906 season, commissioners convened a special meeting to decide the fate of the county's modest sidepath network (chiefly, the paths from Elmira westerly to Corning and easterly toward Binghamton). Grudgingly, they agreed to keep the paths open for another year and, dipping into last of their reserves, ordered one thousand tags for the 1907 season.[55]

Commissions in many other counties adopted a similarly practical approach and continued to repair sidepaths only when funds became available. Inevitably, that strategy led to maintenance only for favored paths and to the abandonment of others. In 1906, commissioners in Cortland County voted to maintain two paths used by workers in local factories but to discontinue all others. That same year, and at the opposite end of the economic spectrum, commissioners in Suffolk County agreed to fund repairs for the sidepath to Westhampton Beach. Several commissions experimented by reducing the costs of licenses with the hope of increasing sales. In Warren County, the commission lowered the price of licenses by half for the 1904 season, with the stipulation that unless sales doubled from the year before the price would return to one dollar. When such tactics failed (and as revenue continued to decline), even favored sidepaths became overgrown, and commissions were left with neither work nor purpose; many quietly dissolved. Yet the absence of commissions did not always extinguish efforts to maintain paths, and Chautauqua County cyclists who enjoyed riding close to home began subscription lists in 1907 to repair sidepaths along village streets in Fredonia.[56]

Cyclists used sidepaths tenaciously in several regions during declining years, including Onandaga, Seneca, Oswego, Suffolk, and Oneida counties. In Syracuse, the steady paving of local streets rejuvenated interest in cycling, and newspaper articles during the 1904 season proclaimed a revival of the bicycle craze. The commission built several new paths that year and the next, and on a hot day in June 1904 the owners of the *Syracuse Journal* sponsored a successful parade to Onandaga along the Valley Path, a celebration commending the commission's work. In adjoining Oswego County, the commission continued to sell licenses during the 1907 season and remained in existence at least through the early months of 1908. In Seneca County, the commission generated enough revenue to maintain a few paths during the 1906 and 1907 seasons.[57]

On Long Island, cyclists in the towns of Southampton, Southold, and Babylon purchased enough licenses during the 1906 season to pay for repairs to sidepaths in those communities, but in January 1907 the Suffolk County Commission convened in Sag Harbor for their final accounting, at last yielding to the abandonment of wheeling by its former votaries. However, state assemblyman John M. Lupton successfully introduced legislation that year naming town highway commissioners in Suffolk County as sidepath commissioners and giving control over all existing or newly built sidepaths to towns. County boards of supervisors retained the authority to order licenses and set fees, but commissioners issued those licenses, and in most respects the law copied the Ellsworth law. Cyclists generally favored the bill and anticipated an end to license fees, but highway commissioners in some towns destroyed paths in the process of widening roads.[58]

Remarkably, a corps of wheelmen and wheelwomen in Oneida County continued to travel the region's sidepaths and during the 1907 season purchased more than 1,700 plates; however, three years before that figure had been 6,557, down slightly from the previous year. Rome cyclists, in particular, contributed a hefty share of those receipts, and the commission's report late in December of 1907 showed a modest balance on hand for repairs during the coming 1908 season.[59]

Nevertheless, in the early spring of 1908, a reporter for the *Otsego Farmer* in Cooperstown characterized the status of New York's sidepath era quite well: "With the passing of the bicycle craze has gone the sidepath commission, and every now and again we read in our exchanges of their ceasing to exist in localities where formerly they were in a flourishing condition." By the time automobiles began to dominate overland travel during the 1920s, scant evidence of sidepaths remained. Those paths that had not been erased completely by road widening or usurped by electric railways typically had disappeared beneath a growth of vegetation. In a retrospective frame of mind in 1921, Abbott Bassett penned an editorial concerning Rhode Island's decision that year to repeal its sidepath statute, but his column offered a glimpse of the future when he suggested that the excision would "remind old timers of the days when they sat upon their lofty perch and looked eagerly for narrow smooth sidings where the perils of wheeling were not so great as on the rough highways."[60]

Traces of a few paths managed to remain visible for many years. The Patchogue-Port Jefferson Cross-County path on Long Island continued to provide a shortcut for hikers crossing Bald Hill, even though Brookhaven's town board officially closed a portion of the path in 1932. In some locales today, where rural roads remain narrow and unimproved, workers may discover subsurface layers of cinders that were once part of New York's vast network of country bicycle paths.[61]

Other sidepaths probably survive today as sidewalks, particularly in quiet villages that have escaped development. The *Otsego Farmer* reporter may not have known that in 1904 a few Monroe County residents had begun a quiet campaign to preserve sidepaths as sidewalks for pedestrians after disputes had developed concerning a newly constructed road between Brockport and Hamlin. When (due to inadequate funds for maintenance) sidepath commissioners elected to abandon the path, abutting property owners voiced alarm. They had found the path convenient for walking and, pointing to a 1902 law that authorized the use of highway labor to build sidewalks, argued that the town highway commissioner should assume responsibility for maintenance, a much less expensive undertaking than building new sidewalks.

In October 1904, at the inaugural convention of the Monroe County Good Roads Association, A. P. Dean addressed members of that newly formed organization in a speech titled "The Utility of Sidepaths in Connection with Improved Highways." Summarizing the decline of the sidepath era and the inability of sidepath commissioners to maintain paths, Dean cited the conflict in Brockport and Hamlin, observing: "The sidepath was the forerunner of good roads, as the bicycle was the forerunner of sidepaths; and their building in this county was a powerful factor in the good roads movement. Their utility has been so demonstrated that they are now used quite as much by pedestrians as by wheelmen. And the public demand for their preservation warrants the appropriation of sufficient money to keep them in repair."[62]

Between 1899 and 1901, a number of New England, Mid-Atlantic, and Midwestern states adopted sidepath legislation modeled after the landmark Ellsworth Sidepath Law of 1899 (or its predecessors), and the campaign also reached into parts of Canada. In many instances, both the phrasing of those laws and the use of the term "sidepath" make the influence of New York's law explicit. Those legislative initiatives affirmed the broad appeal of sidepaths as a means for wheelmen and wheelwomen to venture beyond the confines of city streets and to experience country riding, and they pay tribute both to New York's far-reaching network of paths and to the originator of those paths, Charles Raymond. Reinforcing Raymond's legacy, several of those state laws included provisions he had proposed for New York, including the authority to impose a tax rather than a license fee and the creation of a state sidepath commission with authority to transfer license revenue from one county to another. Concurrence with those strategies by state legislatures validated Raymond's emphasis on creative ways to finance sidepath construction.[63]

In New England, three states adopted bicycle path laws during the years between 1898 and 1901, and legislatures in two of those states, Rhode Island and Connecticut, borrowed directly from the Ellsworth Law. Rhode Island's 1900 bill required its governor to appoint a statewide sidepath commission and authorized that commission to construct sidepaths along public highways (subject to approval from towns) and along private lands (with approval from landowners). The yearly sale of licenses paid for construction, and the commission could set fees between fifty cents and one dollar. Connecticut's legislature also resorted to license fees in that same range after debate about a registration tax, but the 1901 law allowed county commissioners in any county to appoint a single county sidepath commissioner, giving that commissioner the authority to build paths along public roads outside the limits of cities, subject to approval from selectmen for each town.[64]

Among New York's five bordering states, three did not pass legislation modeled after the Ellsworth Law: Vermont, Massachusetts, and New Jersey. However, each state either considered adopting a similar law or enacted legislation that created a means to finance and build bicycle paths. In Massachusetts, an 1898 law made no reference to sidepaths, but it did enable towns to build bicycle paths and to appropriate public funds for that purpose, a fairly efficient way to accommodate cycling. New Jersey wheelmen remained content with the state's 1896 law that allowed local organizations to build bicycle paths through private subscription.[65]

Vermont's 1900 bill, practically identical to the Ellsworth law, passed the House of Representatives but stalled in the Senate. Although Maine and New Hampshire did not adopt legislation, cyclists in those states developed various sidepath projects. In New Hampshire, a path linked Dover with Somersworth in the state's southeasterly corner, and another led from Nashua to the Massachusetts border. The Maine Division of the LAW orchestrated the building of a path between Portland and a nearby summer resort.[66]

Laws enacted in Pennsylvania in 1899 and in both Maryland and Ohio in 1900 borrowed very directly from the Ellsworth Law—and even expanded it. Pennsylvania's law authorized county courts to appoint sidepath commissions and then gave those commissions the power to levy an annual tax on each bicycle, not to exceed one dollar. Strategically, the law also specified that sidepaths were intended for pedestrians as well as bicycles but placed no financial burden on the former. Curiously, the legislation contained no provision for verifying payment of the tax, such as bicycle tags, and thus sidepaths constructed under the law may have been open to the public.[67]

Among the commissions appointed in scattered locales across the state, that in Bradford County took full advantage of New York's sidepaths and developed plans for a path linking Towanda with Athens to the north. From there, cyclists could cross the border into New York at Waverly and turn westerly toward Elmira or easterly toward Binghamton. Nearby, Lackawanna County commissioners received an allotment of $12,000 for paths in the vicinity of Scranton. Unfortunately, Pennsylvania courts declared the law invalid in 1900, reasoning that county sidepath commissions, in exercising authority over path construction, interfered with functions granted to municipalities under the state's constitution.[68]

Ohio's sidepath law authorized the appointment of county commissions by county probate judges and permitted those commissions to build sidepaths along public roads outside the limits of incorporated cities and villages. The bill assessed yearly license fees of one dollar, and cyclists residing in counties without a commission could purchase a tag from any commission. Ohio's legislation copied all of the state sidepath laws enacted during this period by including a provision that required sidepath commissioners to work without compensation.[69]

Poor roads and long distances prompted Ohio's impatient wheelmen to view the Good Roads movement with increasing skepticism and to shift their focus to building sidepaths. Those efforts were well underway in a few northern counties long before passage of the 1900 law, and Ohio's experiments resemble local campaigns in New York in several respects. Warren County cyclists established the Good Roads Wheel League, solicited yearly membership subscriptions for one dollar, purchased a secondhand planer, and opened a five-mile path between Warren and Niles, not far from Youngstown. Members also discovered through practice that by keeping the path narrow—eighteen inches where travel remained light, but no more than three or four feet on primary roads—drivers resisted the temptation to use the paths.[70]

Path from Baltimore to Washington, D.C.
Maryland created a state board of sidepath commissioners with the authority to appoint county sidepath commissions rather than a single administrator. State

FIGURE 7.16
In Ohio, proponents of good roads and good sidepaths found common ground. The Good Roads League of Warren County formed a subsidiary association, the Good Roads Wheel League, and constructed a path between Niles and Warren. From Isaac Pottter, *Cycle Paths* (Boston: LAW, 1898), 29.

commissioners sold yearly licenses and then allocated funds to the counties from which fees had been collected. The law also permitted the state board to transfer fees collected from Baltimore City or from any county to any other county by mutual agreement, thus providing a means to distribute funds equitably among counties with few cyclists, much as Raymond had envisioned for New York.[71]

Impetus for the passage of Maryland's law may have grown from enthusiasm in Baltimore and Washington, D.C., for a long-sought, thirty-seven-mile path joining the two cities. Among the many schemes for paths developed during this period, the Baltimore–Washington path deserves recognition for the importance of the corridor on the Eastern seaboard, for the imaginative scope of the plan, for the complexity of its development (with costs ranging from $12,000 to $50,000), and for a curious alliance that formed. However, the project is also noteworthy for the more dubious distinction of having come to naught in three identifiable phases.

Proposals for the path began circulating in 1896 or earlier. During its first phase, H. L. Millner of Baltimore tried to form a private company to oversee construction and management, including the building of a clubhouse at the midway point, subsidiary clubhouses at intermediate points in Relay and Hyattsville, and an adjacent fence to preserve the path exclusively for cyclists. Millner envisioned tolls of varying amounts, explaining the need for a fence. Two years passed before Washington wheelmen formed a committee to study Millner's plan, and almost another year elapsed before the Century Cycling Club of Maryland established its own study committee in January 1899. During the interim, the idea of a private toll road lost ground, Millner seemed to vanish from the scene, and the project's first phase closed.[72]

However, late in January 1899 the LAW began supporting the Century Cycling Club committee, which then became known as the Intercity Cycle Path Committee of the LAW Maryland Division, and its members organized a conference with their counterparts in the District of Columbia. From those deliberations, plans emerged to incorporate a number of separate associations that represented, respectively, Baltimore, Washington, D.C., and towns along the route. Shareowners would be entitled to use the path upon payment of an annual membership fee of one dollar. With Conway Sams as counsel, the Maryland Cycle Path Association (MCPA) formed in March 1899; residents of Laurel organized the Laurel Branch of the MCPA that same month; and the Washington Cycle Path Association received its corporate charter the following month, with John Frazee as president. Enthused by the response, proponents of the path hoped to connect with Philadelphia and there join long-standing plans for a Philadelphia–New York path.[73]

During much of 1899, prospects for the path seemed bright. All concerned agreed to a route that, with a few exceptions, followed the Baltimore Pike and linked (from south to north) Bladensburg, Hyattsville (passing near the Agricultural College), Beltsville, Contee, Laurel, Waterloo, Savage, Elk Ridge Landing, Relay, and Druid Hill Park. Baltimore city engineer Frank Sloan surveyed and mapped the corridor, showing grades and distances; cost estimates settled into the range of $18,000 to $20,000; and Washington cyclists agreed to pay half that cost, with Baltimore and other towns contributing the balance. Even real estate developers began advertising the proximity of the proposed path to suburban lots for sale. In Washington, D.C., surveyors marked a starting point at the intersection of Bladensburg Road and the District of Columbia line. In Baltimore, the route followed Washington Road from the terminus of Columbia Avenue and led directly to Laurel, about 18.5 miles away, bypassing Catonsville and Ellicott City to reduce the path's length.[74]

Optimism mounted when the LAW elected Conway Sams to be its new president. Sams had been instrumental in drafting Maryland's sidepath legislation, had drafted a bill to protect sidepaths from trespassers—also modeled after New York's law—and then early in 1900 had created the LAW's National Committee on Sidepaths. Following the appointment of the Maryland State Sidepath

Commission later that spring, chaired by Baltimore resident and park commissioner Henry Casey, cyclists continued to contemplate strategies for connecting Washington with Baltimore. In August, Frank Sloan traveled through New York State to study sidepaths in Rochester, Buffalo, Elmira, and Albany. He also stopped in Brooklyn, presumably to inspect the Coney Island paths, and then explored Long Island. Once back in Baltimore, he helped to stake out a mile-long section of roadbed in Elkridge that fall, an object lesson for the full path. Work on the Elkridge segment probably started in late October of that year, resulting in possibly the only length of the route ever built.[75]

By the close of 1899, the thousands of subscribers anticipated by promoters unfortunately had turned out only to be hundreds, and in December a reporter queried Casey about the project's status. Although Casey vowed to continue the effort, he confided: "Matters pertaining to the cycle path are now in a state of quiet." Without adequate funding to build the path, aware of dwindling membership in the LAW, and vaguely confident that road surfaces inevitably would improve between the two cities in the not-too-distant future, Casey may have unintentionally signaled the end of the path's second phase.[76]

Baltimore wheelmen could point to one more source of funding: a potentially lucrative alliance with the well-heeled owners of racing horses who had sought a speedway for harness racing. During 1899, the two groups had begun working together and had focused on proposals for a new boulevard that would expand Park Heights Avenue, leading northwesterly from the north gate of Druid Hill Park. For some time, members of the Pimlico Boulevard Improvement Association had been lobbying for a speedway in that vicinity, and park commissioners had opened a bicycle path along a portion of Pimlico Road near the park. Whether cyclists or horse owners were the first to gauge political strength in collaboration is unclear, but during the early months of 1899 the two groups enlisted the support of Frank Sloan, who developed plans for the project. Sloan placed the improvements on the boulevard's west side and assigned (east to west) a five-foot sidewalk, a five-foot planting strip, a twenty-foot cycle path, another five-foot planting strip, and a forty-eight-foot speedway.[77]

In the spring of that year, the coalition presented three ordinances to the city council. The first changed the name of Park Heights Avenue to Pimlico Boulevard, the second authorized the use of eminent domain to acquire the land needed, and the all-important third called for public appropriation of $40,000 to build the project. Initially, the corridor would extend only as far as the Baltimore city line, but eventually it would lead into surrounding Baltimore County, and a special commission appointed by the mayor would oversee use of the corridor. With a visibly successful bicycle corridor in place, promoters may have anticipated that financing the Baltimore–Washington path would fall easily into place. Unfortunately, the alliance failed to muster adequate support for its public funding linchpin, and the measure failed. So did the alliance, and the bold plan to link two of the country's most important cities, within easy reach of one another by bicycle, advanced very little beyond that point. On a more positive note, cyclists in other Maryland towns or cities may have found at least partial success through collaboration. For example, wheelmen in Chambersburg, Greencastle, and Hagerstown opened a path linking those three communities and did the work themselves for the reasonable sum of $1,500.[78]

Regional Contexts

Despite the influence of the Ellsworth Law, evident in the similar structure and phrasing of enactments in other states, other factors are part of the contexts for those initiatives and share in the role of shaping legislative campaigns. Some paths may have grown spontaneously from cycling's enormous popularity, others from cyclists' frustration with the Good Roads movement and its universally slow progress, and still others from individual inspiration or determination.

Adding to the increasingly multifaceted context for legislative campaigns, the work of the LAW National Committee on Sidepaths and the league's state divisions prompted the introduction of bills in some parts of the country (particularly in Midwestern and Western states) and the planning of specific paths. Granted, the origins of the LAW National Committee on Sidepaths in 1900 can be traced directly to events in New York and to the conflict within the LAW over the Ellsworth law. However, league president Isaac Potter boldly used his national office to promote cycle paths as object lessons for good roads, probably encouraging his successor, Conway Sams, to create that committee. Although members represented principally Eastern states, the committee chairperson, Dr. Charles H. Hunter, lived in Minneapolis, where an extensive network of bicycle paths already connected the city's many scenic lakes.[79]

The LAW also began a wildly ambitious (and equally unrealistic) campaign to build "Great Trunk Lines" of bicycle paths from New York to Chicago, via Buffalo and Cleveland; from Chicago to St. Paul and Minneapolis; from Minneapolis to Denver; and from Denver to the Golden Gate. Editors of *Wheel and Cycling Trade Review* broached the idea for a cross-country corridor between New York and Chicago as a way to give impetus to the sidepath movement and, in the process, to revive the LAW's declining membership and waning influence following the league's decision to drop control of racing. Cyclists had circulated similar schemes several years before, and substantial portions of the route already existed across much of New York State and across a few sections of northern Ohio, but proponents argued that international publicity for the corridor would be a boon to American cycling. Predictably, financial resources failed to materialize, and efforts never really progressed much beyond mapping and planning stages. Nevertheless, the idea generated considerable attention, and communities along selected routes took notice, probably leading to the building of individual paths.[80]

Despite such constraints in evaluating the influence of the Ellsworth law, one important aspect becomes clear. In New York, the law represented the culmination of a well-established sidepath campaign begun almost a decade earlier, and the bill benefited from substantial sidepath networks already widely used by 1899. In states that lacked similar programs, sidepath laws became a means to set new programs into motion rather than to define a financial structure for programs already underway. Unfortunately, cycling's waning years gave wheelmen in most of those states neither sufficient time nor adequate opportunities to develop successful path systems supported by adequate constituencies, which in turn could have provided a foundation for continued path building. As a consequence, New York stands alone in both the depth and reach of its sidepath campaign.

Separate Paths

Apart from matters concerning the influence of the Ellsworth law, the country's nineteenth- and early twentieth-century bicycle paths—whether in New York or in other parts of the country and whether described as sidepaths, cycle paths, or wheelways—are historically significant as particularly American phenomena. This is true in terms of enabling legislation, financial structure, administrative planning and oversight, construction equipment and techniques, patterns of development and location, extent, supporting literature, and overall comprehensive scope of the campaign. Explanation for that distinction is found along America's poor rural roads and across its great distances. Many European countries where cycling had gained popularity had little need for separate bicycle paths in 1899, because roads were adequate. Although exceptions exist (for instance, paths in parts of Belgium), the relegation of bicycles to separate lanes in those countries did not begin in earnest until conflict with automobiles arrived.[81]

Similar to the Good Roads campaign, the sidepath movement generated debate about taxation to advance objectives that benefit limited members of the public and about whether such projects represent a public good for which taxes are justified. In a thoughtful analysis of policy, historian James Longhurst has pondered whether, had public funding been authorized more consistently for the construction and maintenance of sidepaths, a more permanent structure for separating bicycles from highways would have evolved and would be available today. Although the debate about taxes surrounding New York's sidepath legislation differs from the Good Roads campaign in subtle ways, the question is a valid one. Yet even if such a structure had been supported by taxes before Charles Raymond's 1903 law authorized public funding, sidepath commissions would not have continued to receive appropriations once cyclists stopped using the paths. The few counties that did authorize such funding after 1903 made the inevitability of that outcome clear. Nor would paths vulnerable to the elements have survived much more than a year or two after road improvements offered preferable travel surfaces.[82]

From several vantage points, America's short-lived quest to build bicycle paths might be viewed as one of uncertain distinction or value and at considerable cost for such a limited future. The sidepath era was short-lived, often beset by conflict, and is long forgotten. It is also true that cyclists expended considerable sums in order to build paths that would disappear within a decade. Yet for a modest cost—from twenty-five cents to one dollar each year—cyclists purchased opportunities for country riding. Manifestly, the campaign's voluntary financial structure was sturdy enough to pay for the construction of more than two thousand miles of bicycle paths during a short span of time. Rather than a failure, one might view it as a shining example of a grassroots program and a valuable legacy. Passage of the 1903 legislation also suggests that the program's champions, aided by a steady show of newspaper headlines, persuaded many people in rural New York that cycling served a worthy public purpose—a success of sorts. Ultimately, when viewed in the harshest possible light, the sidepath campaign simply stumbled upon circumstances that many people in today's society continue to disregard, to our economic peril: as transportation systems expand, maintenance costs increase.

Surprisingly, although possibly not so to many cyclists, recollection of that campaign surfaced less than a decade after the last of New York's sidepath commissions quietly dissolved. By the end of World War I, conflict between bicycles and automobiles had developed, and fears for the safety of cyclists (particularly children) had grown into a principal concern. Calls for a revival of bicycle paths appeared in journals such as *Bicycle News* as early as 1917, making the country's overgrown sidepath system relevant once again, but applicable on a much broader scale and with no foreseeable ending or geographic boundaries. Contrary to Senator Armstrong's claims in 1899, highway improvements did not render sidepaths redundant; rather, they hastened the need for separate paths or, better still, wheelways for bicycles. Perhaps a few wheelmen belonging to Charles Raymond's generation sensed that rising conflict.[83]

CHAPTER EIGHT

Park Privileges

The high-wheel cyclists of 1880 rolled pell-mell into the midst of America's romantic era of picturesque park planning, which (apart from a number of garden cemeteries designed during the 1830s) had begun with the 1857 plan for New York City's Central Park, Greensward, designed by an unlikely pair: an English architect, Calvert Vaux, and a Connecticut-born, Staten Island scientific farmer, nurseryman, and writer, Frederick Law Olmsted. The celebrated plan for Central Park captured the country's imagination, creating a public enchantment with pleasure grounds that offered quiet, democratic respite for weary urban populations. Following the Civil War, many American cities established similarly romantic preserves, which beckoned to cyclists irresistibly.

For Olmsted and Vaux, the success of Central Park led to other commissions, thrusting the partners into new careers as the country's foremost park planners. In turn, they produced more sophisticated park designs and also augmented their plans with parkways that transformed sequestered pleasure grounds into networks of connected parks. Those efforts first took root in Brooklyn in 1868, but later that same year Olmsted also began working in Buffalo, where he fashioned plans for parks and parkways into a fully integrated park system. Olmsted soon championed plans for expansive linear parks after framing his own landscape architecture firm and moving to Brookline, Massachusetts, in 1881. Park commissioners in many American cities embraced similar projects, and cyclists found those settings appealing as well.

American parks are important to cycling history as settings in which wheelmen fought—famously so in Central Park—to define the bicycle as a form of carriage, entitled to the same rights as other types of vehicles. Cycling historians have long recognized the significance of those contests. Yet wheelmen's organizations also shaped the features of those parks and thus contributed to park planning, a role that both park and cycling historians have overlooked. Although that shaping is sometimes subtle, it is clearly visible in paths reserved for bicycles, both in pleasure grounds and along the broad travel corridors that became parkways or park-like boulevards.

Historically, another battle involving bicycles took shape in parks and other urban settings. This second conflict involved the proper place for bicycles, whether confined to separate paths when available or entitled to use roads and carriage drives as well. Although these two important contests—the classification of bicycles as a type of vehicle and the proper place for bicycles where separate paths exist—occurred in small towns as well as large cities, the debate became sharply focused in urban settings and especially in parks.

The two landscape types—parks and parkways—are distinguishable in the context of cycling history. Although the drives of each invite cycling as a form of recreation, parkways conceived as linear corridors connecting one distant place to another also encourage the use of bicycles as a means of transportation. When creatively designed to accommodate the different modes of transportation that can safely coexist—bicycles, trolleys or light rail, and foot travel—such park-like corridors acquire a valuable dimension.

The design of Central Park and the story of cyclists' efforts to gain access to park drives are subjects that park and cycling historians have studied exhaustively. Yet a brief revisiting of both topics is essential as part of the context for the topics newly explored by this study: cyclists' efforts to create separate bicycle paths in parks, similar but potentially more valuable proposals for bicycle paths along parkways and park-like boulevards, the consistent opposition to proposals for separate bicycle paths in parks and along certain parkways by the Olmsted firm, and the histories of park and parkway bicycle paths planned or built during the nineteenth century. Summarizing the theories of landscape design fundamental to Olmsted parks is essential both to explaining the firm's opposition to separate bicycle paths and to assessing whether that resistance hindered opportunities for creatively designed wheelways.

Gated Central Park

In June 1881, three wheelmen pedaled boldly but unlawfully into Central Park, intending to challenge a city park ordinance that prohibited all bicycles and tricycles. Almost two years before, in the fall of 1879, members of several bicycle clubs had sought permission from park commissioners to ride along Central Park drives. Those unsuccessful pleas resumed during the following spring, but in June 1880 commissioners instead voted to exclude bicycles altogether. That decision rankled among members of the fledgling LAW (then barely a week old) and in particular with Kirk Munroe, captain of the New York Bicycle Club.[1]

Early the following spring, the league petitioned the park board to repeal the law, but that bid also failed, setting the stage for more drastic devices. Park police obligingly arrested the three volunteering wheelmen, William Wright, Henry Walker, and S. Conant Foster, who each received the option of paying a five-dollar fine or spending five days in jail. However, Charles Pratt, president of the LAW, already had retained a New York lawyer, Edmund Wetmore, who promptly secured the wheelmen's release pending a trial before the combined city and county court of New York. Standing in the background, Albert Pope agreeably financed the undertaking.[2]

At that lengthy and expensive proceeding, which began early in July and continued through much of the summer, the presiding referee listened to prolonged but conflicting testimony regarding the hazards created by cycling, especially for the occupants of horse-drawn carriages. By mid-December, he had completed his copious summary of that testimony, but the court's ruling judge was equally painstaking, weighing the matter until the following July and then issuing an opinion upholding the ordinance. An appeal to the New York State Supreme Court followed, and in April 1883, the justices of that lofty body declined to overturn the lower court's ruling, reasoning that the appeals court had no jurisdiction to retry questions of fact already decided by the lower court. Not quite two years after the original trial had begun, New York City's wheelmen still faced gates at Central Park entrances, barriers that would remain until 1887.[3]

Despite the unfavorable rulings, the Central Park case advanced the cause of cycling in several ways. At a minimum, the trial demonstrated the league's resolve as well as its ample financial, legal, and political resources. In addition, the hearings became a public forum that helped to elevate awareness of bicycles and to sway sentiment in wheelmen's favor. The ordeal also encouraged some New York park commissioners to consider cycling in a less arbitrary, more reasoned manner. Evidence of that shifting outlook surfaced even before the final court ruling when, late in March, commissioners granted the league permission to hold a parade along West Drive and along Riverside Drive in Riverside Park on Decoration Day, 1883.[4]

That same spring, park commissioners accepted a proposal from the Citizens Bicycle Club on behalf of the LAW and opened the full length of West Drive, with permission to enter or leave from either the Eighth Avenue gate at Fifty-Ninth Street or the Seventh Avenue entrance at 110th Street—during the hours before nine o'clock in the morning. Although the resolution was not explicit, it implied that riders could begin riding after midnight, and many did. As a writer for *Harper's Weekly* explained, that "privilege was not, as might be inferred, accorded by the commissioners in a spirit of gentle irony. It was granted in all seriousness, and joyously accepted by the riders." As proof, the article offered a fascinating description of moonlit, noiseless apparitions, with wheels lost in shadow and riders seeming to float "like frightened ghosts along the leafy drive in the small hours of any pleasant, July night."[5]

Liberty Bill

Wheelmen persistently sought greater latitude, soon gaining permission to ride along Riverside Drive during specific hours and subject to strict regulations. Intense bias against bicycles ebbed, and by the end of 1884 New York cyclists had achieved an uneasy accord that would continue for two more seasons. All the while, the LAW had been maneuvering adroitly in the political background to secure a more durable place in Central Park and elsewhere. Late in June 1887, the league's chief consul, George Bidwell, proclaimed the success of those travails shortly after New York Governor David Hill signed state legislation called the Liberty Bill, so christened by wheelmen. The concisely worded law classified bicycles as a type a carriage, entitled to the same rights and subject to the same restrictions as vehicles drawn by horses. The law also prohibited all commissioners who had authority over public streets, drives, or parkways from excluding bicycles along those public places, subject to continuing powers of regulation.[6]

In a gracious letter to New York's park board on June 28, 1887, Bidwell sought a conference to discuss implementation of the new law, observing with polite understatement that the matter "seemed to have excited a special local interest in that section of the state." By July, the city attorney had issued an opinion recommending that bicycles be given all the privileges accorded to carriages, and the board accepted that advice, marking a truce in the contentious and widely publicized period of debate about the use of Central Park drives. The following year, New Jersey legislators followed New York's lead and adopted a matching Liberty Bill, eliminating any question about wheelmen's use of carriage drives in Newark, Trenton, or other New Jersey cities.[7]

Bicycles in Urban Parks

In Central Park, the years between 1880 and 1887 marked an important phase during which bicycles attained recognition as legitimate vehicles entitled to traverse the same public travel corridors as other vehicles. In addition, the highly focused skirmishes in New York gave sharp definition to the visible role of urban parks as stages on which those dramas took place. Nevertheless, this important phase did not develop uniformly from place to place, and park commissioners in many other cities reached amicable agreements with cyclists well before 1887—and without the need for legislative admonition.

With thinly veiled ridicule of their brethren across the East River in Manhattan, Brooklyn's park commissioners resolved in 1885 to give wheelmen full access at all times to West Drive in Prospect Park and to Ocean Parkway, Eastern Parkway, and the Coney Island Concourse. They also allowed use of all pathways in Prospect Park from November through April inclusive, imposing restrictions only during certain hours for the remaining months. In a reasonably worded caveat, the regulations required cyclists to "avoid as far as possible all cause for complaint." However, the matter of riding on pathways continued to generate debate, and many wheelmen emphasized the incompatibility of bicycles and pedestrians, pointing to the need for separate paths.[8]

Philadelphia's park commissioners calmly obliged cyclists. Fairmount Park, established in 1867, is substantially larger than Central Park and Prospect Park combined, extends over more varied and scenic terrain, is more distant from the city proper, and is divided by the Schuylkill River with its scenic drives. The park also includes an elongated corridor adjoining Wissahickon Creek, reaching northerly into the city's suburbs and providing a natural parkway—a lengthy riparian version of the linear park connectors that Olmsted and Vaux conceived in Brooklyn and Buffalo. In addition, Ford Hill in West Fairmount Park became a famous site for hill-climbing contests during the high-wheel era, vying with Eagle Rock in Orange, New Jersey, and with Corey Hill in Brookline, Massachusetts. Many of those aspects appealed to wheelmen and also may have influenced the park board's temperate attitude toward bicycles.[9]

During the spring of 1879, wheelmen began circulating petitions to use Fairmount Park between midnight and the early morning hours. That fall, park staff granted temporary licenses to cyclists during restricted hours and in restricted locations in order "to report intelligently to the board on the subject." By

FIGURE 8.2
A drawing or painting titled "Entrance to Central Park at Fifty-Ninth Street and Eighth Avenue, New York—the Grand Circle," by F. Childe Hassam, reproduced for illustration in *Scribner's Magazine* (June 1895).

March 1880, that body had found no appearance of danger, and its members recommended that privileges be accorded to bicycles, subject to regulation. A year of study elapsed, and in November 1881 the board adopted a resolution that removed all restrictions against bicycle riding in the park, other than on sidewalks, and imposed the same rules and regulations governing other vehicles—thereby reaching a state of accord that would elude their counterparts in New York for another six years.[10]

Baltimore's park commissioners also avoided acrimony with cyclists and even served as landlords for the Park Bicycle Association, which rented the Stone House in Druid Hill Park, the city's picturesque pleasure ground established in 1860. Commissioners admitted cyclists into that park in April 1883 and eventually attempted to count entrants during the mid-1880s as more wheelmen on high-wheel bicycles began venturing past park gates; however, the traffic counts lasted only two years. During the fall of 1890, after briefly decreeing that cyclists should yield rights-of-way to horse-drawn vehicles, commissioners quietly revoked that rule and imposed uniform regulations for all vehicles, but also restricted cyclists from using bridle paths and footways.[11]

Park Paths for Bicycles

The period in which wheelmen successfully achieved vehicular status for high-wheel bicycles merged easily into a second, closely related phase concerning the planning of separate bicycle paths. That phase also started during the high-wheel era but expanded greatly following the arrival of the safety bicycle and the hordes of cyclists who whirled into urban parks. In one direction, wheelmen and wheel-women faced dangerous congestion on park drives; in the other, they confronted an inherent incompatibility with pedestrians; and in both directions, they encountered hostility from other park users. Not surprisingly, such circumstances led to thoughts about separate cycling corridors, and Karl Kron mused that on the day in Central Park when wheelmen outnumbered horseback riders, perhaps the former would demand equal justice and have roads built exclusively for bicycles.[12]

The impetus for establishing bicycle paths in parks and other scenic urban settings originated among cyclists as a means to improve the wheeling experience by avoiding conflict with both vehicles and pedestrians, but also as a response to frustrations with poorly maintained roads. Two debates ensued: The first grew from subtle concerns by landscape architects and park officials that separate bicycle paths would be inconsistent with the goals of picturesque park design, especially the slow pace essential for quiet contemplation of scenery. The second pitted cyclists against one another over fear that the hard-won license to use public roads would be for naught, because park officials would force cyclists to use separate paths. That quarrel erupted with intensity on the Coney Island bicycle paths in 1896, but occurred elsewhere at about the same time; it also overlapped with the squabble about whether sidepath construction undermined the quest for good roads.

Olmstedian Barriers

During the 1890s, the Olmsted firm played a visible role in the first debate and persuaded park officials in several cities to reject proposals for bicycle paths, arguing that the cost of removing land from the private sector, in which it generated tax revenue, could be justified best by scenery that soothed public souls—that is, the greatest good for the greatest number of people, principally on foot. Features such as bicycle paths that did not augment the aesthetic qualities of scenery—or interfered with contemplation of that scenery—thus represented unwarranted costs. Addressing the matter more bluntly in correspondence with Boston's park board, the firm regarded drives as unsightly blemishes on park landscapes, to be minimized to the extent possible.[13]

Given the seemingly benign and visually unobtrusive character of narrow bicycle paths as features of today's parks, the concerns expressed by the Olmsted firm require explanation. Olmsted and Vaux intended pleasure grounds such as Central Park and Prospect Park to offer a chance for restful contemplation of scenery, the means by which park users could draw from nature's restorative powers to lighten the heavy burdens of urban living. The partners' park designs orchestrated four principal landscape types into a single, integrated work of art: meadow or glade, with sylvan backdrop; park, implying arboreal effect but with open understory; woodlands, evincing a more rugged quality; and water courses, to add sound to sensory perceptions. Park users quietly meandered through slowly unfolding sequences of those landscapes, taking advantage of winding corridors that carefully separated carriages, pedestrians, and equestrians, allowing each to experience an illusion of rural freedom. Vistas of these ever-varying landscapes opened from carefully placed vantage points.[14]

At least two aspects of these objectives are relevant to the activity of cycling: One concerns the original plans for carriage drives, intended to accommodate restful, continuous passage through a series of landscapes, with carefully placed occasions for pause. The second is more directly related to bicycle paths and acknowledges that parks require places for activities other than just quiet observation of picturesque scenery.

With regard to the first, East Drive and West Drive in Central Park created a winding passage through the park, but one that in its original form established a very strong north–south orientation. Olmsted and Vaux emphasized the continuity of that circulation corridor by placing transverse roads below grade to funnel cross-town traffic, unseen from the bridges that carried both drives and footpaths above. They also reinforced the full lure of that north–south journey by avoiding park perimeters and by offering only a limited number of entrance gates.

The desire to reinforce that tranquil passage is at least part of the context in which Central Park commissioners made decisions about use of the park by cyclists. When commissioners gave wheelmen permission to pedal along West Drive in 1883 and to enter or leave the park only at the far north and south gates, the board may have envisioned cyclists merging with that flow of travel without disruption. Unfortunately, visualizing that sense of progression is difficult today, because the drives have been weakened severely by changes to the original design and in particular by numerous cross-corridors and new entrances.

Subsequent correspondence by the Olmsted firm makes it almost certain that the senior Olmsted regarded cycling as an interference with the quiet enjoyment of scenery by pedestrians and by the occupants of slowly moving carriages. Granted, Olmsted had ended his long and trying tenure with New York's difficult park board in 1878, and whether some park commissioners still shared his outlook years later is unclear. Kron, in proclaiming the need for more modern commissioners, at least hints at that possibility by complaining in 1887 that the board still included "objectors of the old red-sandstone period." However, concern for the safety of park users offered a more expedient reason to prohibit wheelmen, and the speed and silence with which cyclists could roll along carriage drives probably remained at the core of those misgivings.[15]

In addition, Colonel Egbert Viele, whose uninspired plan for Central Park had been rejected in favor of Greensward but who remained convinced that Olmsted and Vaux had plagiarized his design, had managed to secure a seat on the park board during the early 1880s. Perhaps it is coincidence, but Viele became the commissioner who introduced resolutions that authorized cyclists to use West Drive and Riverside Drive in 1883. Viele may have been politically motivated, seeking support from the LAW, and the strategy worked, because wheelmen in the Central Park parade that spring greeted him with rousing cheers. However, one cannot help but wonder whether he also welcomed an opportunity to flout Olmsted and Vaux's persistent efforts to protect the park's tranquility. In any case, both his role and the ideals of park design are part of the broader context for the cycling debate.[16]

With regard to the second concern—namely, the need to accommodate more active forms of recreation—the senior Olmsted devised a method for protecting pleasure grounds from the pressures of heavy public use, segregating active forms of recreation into separate, smaller parks. Borrowing from European cities, he then joined these smaller parks with linear parkways to create a far-reaching park system. In the process, Olmsted and other landscape architects created ideal places for bicycle paths—or at least wheelmen viewed it that way in a number of cities, including Cleveland, Brooklyn, Buffalo, Boston, Louisville, Rochester, and East Orange, New Jersey.[17]

The role of the Olmsted firm in the debate about bicycle paths in parks also requires clarification. By 1895, Olmsted's health had declined substantially, and active management of the Brookline firm, then called Olmsted, Olmsted, and Eliot, had devolved to Olmsted's nephew and later stepson, John Charles Olmsted, and to Charles Eliot, who had studied agriculture and horticulture at Harvard and whose father served as president of Harvard University. Olmsted's own son, Frederick Law Olmsted Jr., began assisting the firm during this period, but he did not become a partner until Eliot's sudden death in 1897; the pair then changed the firm's name to Olmsted Brothers. Thus, most of the correspondence with park commissioners that explains the firm's objections to bicycle paths originated during a time when the senior Olmsted was no longer actively engaged in his practice.[18]

Bicycle Path Proposals for Olmsted Parks and Parkways

The Olmsted firm's correspondence with park commissioners in Boston, Buffalo, Louisville, and Essex County, New Jersey, substantiates their view of cycling as inconsistent with the ideals of picturesque park planning—and in three principal ways: the pace of travel by wheelmen, the potential interference with other park users seeking tranquility, and the unjustifiable costs of building bicycle paths that detracted from the overall quality of scenery. That park commissioners in two of those cities, Buffalo and Louisville, persuaded the Olmsted firm to design bicycle paths illustrates the force of cycling's influence on park planning. Bicycle paths in a fourth Olmsted pleasure ground, Genesee Valley Park in Rochester, achieved success without intervention from the Olmsteds.

Boston's Beacon Street and Emerald Necklace

In Boston, as in other cities, cyclists had called for special bicycle ways in both parks and along parkways or principal streets. In 1886, the Olmsted firm had designed a cycleway as part of plans to widen and improve Beacon Street between Boston's Back Bay and Brookline, creating a 200-foot avenue for commercial as well as pleasure vehicles. The plan offered several alternatives, one of which placed a single path for bicycles flanked on one side by a centrally located corridor for trolley cars and on the other by a bridle way. A narrow planting strip separated the cycle and bridle paths, but bicycle and trolley ways abutted; a wide lawn flanked the railway's opposite side, and roadways bordered both bridle path and lawn. An alternative, symmetrical design employed two cycle paths, one each flanking the central railway, with planting strips separating bicycle paths from adjoining bridle paths. A third design placed a single cycleway between railway and road, with a planting strip separating bicycles and trolley cars, but with no division between road and path (see figure 0.3a, b).[19]

Unfortunately, city officials reduced the street width to 160 feet, sacrificing the cycle and bridle paths. Nevertheless, the project joins Ernest Bowditch's 1886 design for a combined parkway and bicycle path in Cleveland as among the country's first plans for bicycle paths during the high-wheel era. Moreover, by placing the bicycle path adjacent to the trolley line, the firm seems to have recognized the potential compatibility of bicycles and trolleys long before conflict between wheelmen and other vehicles on city streets had become acute. Whether credit for that observation belongs to John Olmsted or to his stepfather is not known, but one can speculate that Albert Pope, a resident of Brookline, offered a guiding hand.[20]

By the mid-1890s, Boston's park commissioners and their landscape architects nearly had completed a continuous series of parks and parkways—the Fens and Riverway, Leverett Park, Jamaicaway and Jamaica Park, and Arborway—joining Boston Common with Franklin Park and forming an Emerald Necklace about seven miles in length. Earlier that fall, commissioners had authorized a count of the three principal classes of pleasure travel—carriages, bicycles, and saddle horses—in order to assess the public's use of its linear parks that joined town to country. Although carriages dominated the poll that October afternoon and early evening, and by a large margin, bicyclists nevertheless established a consistent presence, averaging more than 1,200 riders in most of the park's segments.[21]

Confronted by the rising popularity of bicycles during this period, the city's park commissioners considered the matter of bicycle paths, including whether bridle paths should be transferred to bicyclists, and then sought an opinion from their landscape architects. In a lengthy letter dated May 21, 1896, and addressed to the park commission's chairman, Edward C. Hodges, the Olmsted firm advised against such paths, restating their regard for large country parks as places for the public to enjoy inspiring scenery, in sharp contrast to the ordinary outlook along city streets. The removal of such large land areas from the city's tax rolls could not be justified, they opined, if used for activities that smaller or less costly spaces could satisfy equally well. Such proposals would defeat the primary and only justifying purpose for country parks, where "the general landscape is of first importance."[22]

Just how well the Olmsteds knew Edward "Ned" Hodges isn't clear, but presumably they must have gathered at least hints of his family's venerable Boston roots and, more importantly, of his station as one of cycling's old guard of the high-wheel era. In addition to giving financial footing to *Bicycling World*, Hodges had been a member and president of the Boston Bicycle Club, a founding member of the League of American Wheelmen, and in general supported cycling financially in Boston until his death in 1903. He also served as chairman of Boston's park board from 1895 until August 1897, and thus the communication between Hodges and the Olmsted firm represents an articulate dialogue between two opposing points of view at the peak of cycling's nineteenth-century popularity.[23]

The typeset of that 1896 letter to Hodges must be credited to the Olmsted firm—still Olmsted, Olmsted, and Eliot at the time—and John Olmsted may have borne the brunt of bicyclists' entreaties. However, the views and the thoughts behind those words almost certainly belonged to the elder Olmsted, by then incapacitated. Equally important, that letter explains with considerable depth the firm's concerns about bicycles in parks and consequently has value beyond Boston, illuminating factors that indirectly may have influenced decisions by park commissioners in New York City to exclude bicycles from Central Park years before. At the core of that clash, as the letter explains, is the inherent conflict between rapid pace of travel and enjoyment of scenery.[24]

After affirming the primary importance of parks as landscape preserves, the letter continues by observing that only people who ventured into parks on foot moved slowly enough to contemplate scenery fully, adding that the most charming settings are accessible only to walkers. Although the public's demand for driving through parks made carriage roads unavoidable, the writer makes it clear that thronged drives are objectionable, because they interfere with the use of parks by pedestrians. Only by limiting the number of junctures (or by separating the two corridors by grade, as in Central Park) could people on foot gain the entire benefit of country landscapes. Bridle paths caused considerably greater interferences, becoming even more objectionable.[25]

The letter's author then explains that separate bicycle ways would be still more intolerable than carriage drives or bridle paths, because bicycles move so rapidly and so quietly that separation from all other corridors would be essential. However, that same separation also would enable cyclists to traverse the park much more quickly than would be possible on drives used by slower carriages, which were already moving as rapidly as possible without losing the their occupants' ability to contemplate scenery. Any faster pace, for carriages or for bicycles, would cause the park to be used in ways inconsistent with its main purpose, and the costs of creating separate paths thus would be unjustified.

During their tenure at Central Park, Olmsted and Vaux had faced unrelenting efforts to build a speedway for harness racing. In a retrospective pamphlet circulated in 1882, following his move to Brookline a year earlier, Olmsted recounted the political corruption and ignorance the pair had constantly faced in their work with the city's park board. Among the numerous examples he cites, an especially vexing episode with an influential proponent of the speedway seems to have stayed with Olmsted, possibly explaining one of the more forceful statements in the 1896 letter to Hodges: "In other words, a park is a preserve of scenery, and as such it is no place for the driver's speedway, the rider's race-course, or the bicycler's scorching track."[26]

That declaration underscores comparative speed as the root of cycling's incompatibility (as viewed by the Olmsteds) with both carriages and foot travel in park settings, and the tone of antipathy toward bicycles is evident elsewhere in the communication. Still, the letter concludes in a more conciliatory manner, noting that miles and miles of roads fit for bicycling already existed near Boston. Although the city's cyclists may have been able to offer a more informed assessment about the challenges encountered along those routes, the writer judged that no special hardship would occur if cyclists did not have separate paths in parks or if regulations governed the speed of cycling on parkway drives. Implicit in that observation is the belief that carriage drives were adequate for bicyclists intent upon pleasure travel.[27]

By the time of that letter, the plan that Olmsted and Vaux had offered to Brooklyn in 1868 already had been adapted to a successful bicycle path along Ocean Parkway, joining Prospect Park with Coney Island; construction of a second, return path advanced toward completion, even as that letter was being written. Undoubtedly, John Olmsted and Charles Eliot knew of those developments in Brooklyn, if not from Hodges or other cyclists eager to follow Brooklyn's example then from the wide publicity given to those popular corridors. Whether either John Olmsted or Eliot actually had inspected the paths or had assessed any visual or functional intrusion on the original design is not known. However, simple awareness of those paths gives the 1896 letter greater emphasis, a pointed effort to respond to what the firm may have perceived as a growing trend.

Conceivably, the firm may have injected that emphasis because their designs for connective parkways had evolved from the broad boulevard used in Brooklyn into a series of complex, linear parks. Rather than a wide carriage drive flanked by green strips and shaded by tree canopy, intended to improve prospects for residential development and to augment property values along access roads, Boston's Emerald Necklace represented an unfolding sequence of landscapes of varying depth and composition, but with scenery an integral part of each contiguous segment. Thus, concern about the pace of travel remained paramount.

The question of whether the Olmsteds' deeply seeded concern for the speed with which cyclists traveled prevented the firm from considering whether designs for separate bicycle paths could be incorporated successfully into those linear parkways (much as landscape architect Ernest Bowditch had proposed in Cleveland a decade before) remains unanswered. That same outlook also may have hindered any inclination to consider whether the pace of travel by bicycle and the contemplation of scenery are inherently inconsistent. Indisputably, cycling's travel literature establishes that the exploration of scenic landscapes remained fundamental to the cycling experience for many wheelmen and wheelwomen. Indeed, one might ponder the outcome of a dialogue between Olmsted and the women riders who explored the North Shore in Massachusetts, and Daisie's remarks about the sun-dappled, autumnal shade of Essex Woods are worth repeating here: "To experience is to know. The half cannot be told."[28]

Buffalo's Delaware Park

Similar debates developed in Buffalo, where wheelmen had become distressed about the dangers of riding on crowded park drives, and during the closing months of 1894, the city's cyclists began a carefully orchestrated campaign. Early in February 1895, at a hearing conducted by the park board's influential Committee on Roads and Grounds, wheelmen presented a petition with eighteen thousand signatures, calling for a twelve-foot-wide path through the city's large country preserve called The Park. Although receptive to the plan in principle, park commissioners developed doubts about path locations and potential damage to the park's design, leading to strained discussions and ultimately to an uninspired compromise.[29]

Frederick Law Olmsted had designed The Park in 1868 with assistance from John Bogart. Renamed Delaware Park in 1896, the site encompassed about 350 acres located roughly four miles north of the city's hub. A vast open field (Meadow Park) with an adjoining lake to the west (Water Park) dominated Olmsted's design, but he also considered The Park as just one part of a much larger park system to be developed according to a master plan.[30]

At that February gathering, park committee members listened to pleas for safe passage but also to an argument from a district attorney, who observed that commissioners had unjustly favored some classes of park users, such as boaters, equestrians, and cricket players. Cycle Path Committee chairman Frederick W. Minton boldly encouraged construction of the path and began working with several wheelmen to plot the path's route. League cyclists Thomas Welch and George Guthrie played principal roles in that task, and the group offered its joint proposal to the board later that year. Unwisely, Minton and his collaborators placed the path through the central meadow in order to follow a favorable grade, and commissioners rejected the plan, ruling the meadow out of bounds to all encroachment.[31]

A year elapsed before the committee successfully guided the proposal into another board hearing, and in April 1896 the group presented a revised route for consideration. The path followed Lincoln Parkway, Water Park's principal approach from the south, and then circled both the lake and meadow near park perimeters, eventually reaching Aggasiz Place and Humboldt Parkway—Meadow Park's formal axial approach from the south. That parkway joined Delaware Park with a separate Olmsted park, The Parade, today called Martin Luther King Jr. Park.[32]

8.3a

8.3b

FIGURE 8.3a, b

A plan for Delaware Park in Buffalo by John Charles Olmsted in 1899, showing the location of a short bicycle path completed in 1896. Concealed near border plantings for Meadow Park, the path bypassed overcrowded Meadow Drive. Courtesy National Park Service, Frederick Law Olmsted National Historic Site.

Although impressed by the group's diligence, commissioner John Graves noted that the path's route would disrupt the park's carefully designed and planted boundary screens, suggesting that a path through the meadow adjoining the present drive would be a wiser choice. Another commissioner reminded Graves that the wheelmen's earlier proposal had been rejected because it crossed the open meadow, and Welch diplomatically offered maps to show that the path could wind among and around the trees without damage to any. Affably seeking a solution, participants elected to enjoy the spring day and walk the route, agreeing at the conclusion of that outing to build the path at the location recommended by the park's landscape architects, Olmsted, Olmsted, and Eliot. Soon after, cyclists also secured a commitment from the city's Common Council to appropriate $5,000 for the project.[33]

The sunny promise of that afternoon clouded visibly about three weeks later, when John Olmsted, who had traveled to Buffalo during the interim, prepared a letter strongly opposing the path. However, unlike the firm's report to Boston's park commissioners, which rejected separate bicycle paths as fundamentally inconsistent with park design, Olmsted instead challenged the proposal on very specific points. Sympathizing with the cyclist's concerns, Olmsted nevertheless regarded the park as too small, the boundary areas too narrow, and the plantations and rambles too well established to warrant the extensive revisions needed to accommodate a path near the park perimeter. Moreover, placing the path inside the circuit drive would force the destruction of trees planted to shade that drive, and moving it farther into the park would spoil the breadth and simplicity of Meadow Park, the preserve's most important landscape feature. The Water Park's narrow, sloping margins presented even greater challenges, with plantings carefully placed for walkers alone. With finality, he recommended that drives be proved inadequate for cyclists before the board sanctioned encroachment on the greensward.[34]

The city's wheelmen felt betrayed and abruptly demanded a public hearing. In particular, they suspected that park superintendent William McMillan, who had opposed the project, may have presented a one-sided version of the proposal in his letter to the firm requesting advice and also may have steered Olmsted away from conversations with Welch during the former's visit. Yet Graves graciously complied with the request and a week later convened a meeting, promptly soothing tensions by announcing that he favored construction of the path, provided it did not interfere with the park's design and approaches. Welch and other LAW members then outlined their responses to Olmsted's concerns, offering several options for locating a new path or for adapting underutilized pedestrian or bridle paths. After a reminder by Welch that the bicycling season was fast approaching, all agreed to meet the following week at the boathouse and study possible sites.[35]

Fortuitously, Olmsted had left a small opportunity for compromise in his report, offering no objection to a path concealed in the border plantations of Meadow Park, where trees and shrubs of value could remain undisturbed. By the end of May, Graves and his colleagues had focused on that area and decided to usurp a bridle path that offered a way to address cyclists' complaints about the crowded conditions along the park's principal thoroughfare (called simply The Drive) at the juncture of Water and Meadow Parks. With that same goal in mind, they also agreed to build a short segment of road that would allow cyclists to reach South Meadow Drive from the bicycle path without venturing onto either Delaware Avenue or the main road.

The path began at Delaware Avenue near the stone arch bridge that carried the main road between the two parks. Just beyond, the road separated into South and North Meadow Drives, where traffic became less troublesome. From its point of beginning, the path continued along the park's southern boundary not far from South Meadow Drive, ending at the park's entrance at Agassiz Place. Workers began by widening the bridle path to twenty feet, but unanticipated excavation doubled the path's estimated cost and reduced its length to about 2,600 feet. In their annual report for 1896, the board sought to appease cyclists by calling the project an experiment, adding that few riders used the path because of its proximity to South Meadow Drive, which was rarely crowded. Nevertheless, the path remained in place during the coming years, and the Olmsted firm carefully marked its location on their 1899 plan for Delaware Park. Buffalo cyclists also gained a measure of compensation from paths added to several of the city's parkways.[36]

Lamentably, little evidence of Buffalo's early period of bicycle path building survives. During the 1960s, the Scajaquada Expressway obliterated any traces of the experimental path in Delaware Park and damaged other park features extensively. Although John Olmsted's direct involvement with the path design remains noteworthy, particularly for his stated willingness to consider separate bicycle paths (circumstances permitting), the firm's emphasis on a measured pace of travel in country parks continued to pose challenges, and a lingering bias against bicycles probably shaped the firm's relationships with its clients. In turn, those undercurrents hindered collaborative, thoughtful study about the best approaches to path design. In Buffalo, as in Boston and East Orange, the firm foreclosed opportunities to craft a carefully integrated system of bicycle paths as part of the city's park or parkway plans.

To their credit, John Graves and Buffalo's other park commissioners resisted pressures to alter the design of Delaware Park, fearing that the landscape's visual quality would be damaged. Commendably, they turned to their landscape architects for advice, placing the onus of finding design solutions precisely where it belonged. Had Olmsted been inspired, he might have matched Graves' sincerity toward cyclists by placing narrow sidepaths or lanes on either side of some park drives without compromising visual quality or spatial relationships, much as Ernest Bowditch had suggested for Doan Brookway in Cleveland in 1886. To some extent, well-established shade trees along those drives presented obstacles, but Welch and his colleagues apparently found ways to avoid those concerns.

Louisville's Iroquois Park

Elsewhere, cyclists politely managed to dent the Olmsted firm's resolve. Soon after his 1896 letter to Buffalo's park commission, John Olmsted also became involved with similar proposals in Louisville's Iroquois Park, one of the firm's few projects in which a circuit bicycle path was an integral part of a park design. As he had in Buffalo, the senior Olmsted developed plans for three principal parks in Louisville, but they are located in the city's outlying western, southern, and eastern sectors and are called Shawnee, Iroquois, and Cherokee Parks, respectively. Each site provided separate opportunities for distinctive natural scenery: meadow, sylvan woodland, and park, in that same order. Several years before

Olmsted's involvement, members of a literary and conservation society called the Salmagundi Club, led by businessman Andrew Cowan, had circulated proposals for a network of rural preserves, identifying three geographically balanced reservations simply as West, South, and East Parks and connecting them with a series of broad boulevards.[37]

In 1889, the city purchased Burnt Knob, a portion of the site described as South Park and located about four miles south of the city limits, with more than three hundred rugged acres, encompassing heavy woods, deep ravines, and a great hill providing views of the surrounding countryside. A year later, the newly created park board obtained jurisdiction of the property, by then called Jacob Park, and began acquiring additional parcels, including a restful grove of oak, beech, and poplar trees known as Fenley Woods, thus increasing the park's overall size to slightly more than 550 acres. Cowan, who admired Olmsted's work, invited him to Louisville in the spring of 1891 to address supporters of the city's fledgling parks program, and Olmsted extolled the grandeur of the site's forest depths, which offered opportunity for one to "wander musingly" in secluded hours. The contract followed, and by August of that same year the park board had renamed the preserve Iroquois Park.[38]

Enthusiasm for path-building among Louisville's cyclists swelled during the mid-1890s, with a strong focus on the system of parkways being developed to connect the three parks. The earliest paths are related to Fontaine Ferry Park, colloquially known as "Fountain Ferry" and located on the Ohio River near Shawnee Park, where it developed into an amusement area. In 1894, the year the LAW held its annual meet in Louisville, Fountain Ferry became the site of one of the country's famed bicycle racing tracks. In December 1895, the president of the Fountain Ferry Cycle and Athletic Association, William W. Watts, offered to build a cinder path from the entrance of Shawnee Park to Fountain Ferry, at no cost to the city. The park board quickly approved, and the following year wheelmen formed the '96 Meet Club Association with the goal of constructing paths in and around Louisville. However, the organization languished for want of funds, and early in 1898 a second group (called the Highwaymen) organized for the same purpose. Pointing to the wheelway league in Indianapolis, members began a subscription campaign to construct paths linking Iroquois Park with Shawnee and Cherokee Parks, making those corridors available to cyclists who purchased plates, similar to New York's sidepath tags. The path between Iroquois and Shawnee Parks officially opened in July 1898 but remained unfinished due to conflict with adjoining property owners and inadequate funding.[39]

Olmsted Plan for Iroquois Park The park commission took notice of path-building efforts by cyclists and opened a bicycle path along Southern Parkway, connecting the city's hub with Iroquois Park at the latter's northeasterly corner, where Olmsted placed a formal entrance called Southern Concourse. When combined with the bicycle paths proposed in Olmsted's plan, the parkway path created a lengthy circuit, the former sheltered by a forest canopy and the latter by regimental rows of linden, ash, elm, oak, sweet gum, red maple, and Kentucky coffee trees.[40]

As shown on the plan, the park's principal circuit drive, Rundill Road, immediately diverges from Southern Concourse in opposite directions, but a second drive, Uppill Road, soon climbs circuitously toward a broad summit field, the park's only broad expanse of open meadow and where the drive becomes Toppill Road. From Southern Concourse, cyclists could turn immediately onto the bicycle path, which twists and turns along the park's perimeter, sometimes hidden among tree-lined borders, sometimes moving closer to the circuit drive to create occasional junctures, occasionally offering glimpses of secluded glades, and even penetrating the park's interior a little more boldly in one or two locations—but always between the principal carriage drive and park boundaries, discreetly removed from the park's principal features.[41]

Olmsted's plan is a masterwork in the context of bicycle paths designed for urban parks—ironically so. Undoubtedly, concerns about cycling remained, and the plan was a confirmation of his statement to Buffalo's park board the year before that bicycle paths concealed in border plantations would be acceptable, provided they could be built without damage to contributing vegetation. The dense forest at Iroquois Park offered Olmsted the perfect chance to demonstrate the feasibility of that strategy—and also to prove his sincerity, but without that wooded cover, he likely would not have recommended the circuit path. In May 1896, at almost the same time that he responded to queries from Buffalo's commissioners, Olmsted wrote to Louisville's park board, cautioning them about the constant tendency among drivers or bicyclists to demand facilities for driving or riding to almost every park sector of interest. In one especially emphatic passage, he remonstrated: "Most parks are created for visitors on foot. Drives are in themselves ugly blots on the landscape." Perhaps cowed, the park board included no bicycle paths in either Shawnee or Cherokee Park.[42]

Yet once Olmsted began to explore beyond those barriers, he produced a design that offered creative responses to the concerns that cyclists presented: pace of travel, purposeful use of parks, and justifiable public expenditure. The winding course, with occasional sharp turns and changes in grade, provided a natural restraint for wheelmen intent upon swift whirls through the park. In addition, the arboreal setting and canopy may have encouraged cyclists to observe their surroundings and to engage the muse of wheeling. The decision to include the path also forced Olmsted to draw from his design abilities to serve a new class of park users, whose needs, necessities, and rights were little understood at the time. General John B. Castleman, president of the park board in 1897, framed that task quite well, adding that the park system unavoidably would be affected but that park accommodations for wheelmen and wheelwomen should occur as a matter of course. Olmsted's 1897 plan thus marks a dramatic change in outlook from the park privileges accorded to Central Park cyclists by the Liberty Bill in 1887.[43]

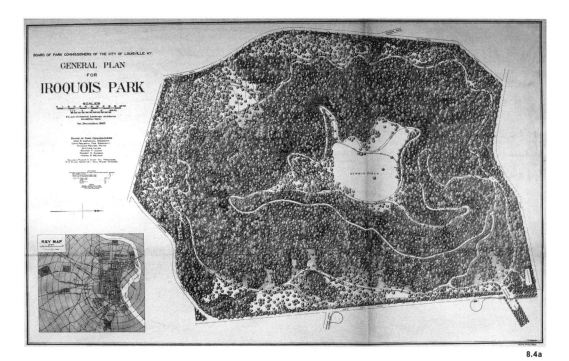

FIGURE 8.4a, b
Enthusiasm for cycling in Louisville led to an inspired plan for a
bicycle path in Iroquois Park, designed by John Charles Olmsted
in 1897. Credit for the path belongs to General John B. Castleman,
president of the park board, who insisted that the city's park system accommodate bicyclists, and in 1897 the board built a bicycle
path along Southern Parkway, leading to the park. From the
parkway's concourse at the park's northeastern corner, cyclists
could turn immediately onto the park path, which winds along the
park's perimeter, sheltered by woodland cover that also screened
the path from view. Courtesy National Park Service, Frederick
Law Olmsted National Historic Site.

8.4b

Unfortunately, development of Louisville's parks occurred only gradually, hampered by lack of funding, and the drives and paths in Iroquois Park were not completed until well after cycling's popularity had declined. Although some paths
today may exist in the general location of the bicycle paths that Olmsted proposed,
at least in a few sections of the park, there is little evidence that any of the paths
eventually constructed were designated specifically for use by bicyclists.[44]

Rochester's Genesee Valley Park
About seventy miles east of Buffalo, Rochester's park commission also embarked
on ambitious plans for several parks and retained Frederick Law Olmsted to prepare designs. However, land acquisition did not begin until 1888, the year the

park commission formed, and thus development of the parks occurred much later than in Buffalo. As in Louisville, the city's limited budget also constrained improvements, and the parks took shape only gradually, limiting the senior Olmsted's involvement with planning.[45]

For two of those preserves, Genesee Valley Park south of the city and Seneca Park to the north, Olmsted focused principally on protecting natural features bordering the Genesee River. In Genesee Valley Park, Olmsted created three distinct domains, two of which occupied the river's eastern banks: a broad meadow with a circuit drive similar to Buffalo's Meadow Park, and an adjoining sylvan preserve to add pastoral effect. By 1898, commissioners had opened several bicycle paths in the latter area. Hampered by railroad tracks assigned to a portion of the river's western shelf, he proposed athletic fields for that division, and it became the site for numerous activities related to cycling, including a racing track with banked curves and grandstand, and a strategically placed bicycle path constructed in 1896. The path began at the entrance to the athletic grounds and followed the river's edge to the park's southern boundary, also providing access to the Scottsville sidepath and creating a continuous cycling corridor stretching from Four Corners to Scottsville.[46]

Commissioners built two paths in the park's easterly division during 1897, one nearly a mile long and offering views along Red Creek, which separated that park's two principal landscape realms, and the second a one-half-mile path that reached the Genesee River near the old General Jackson hickory tree. A third path opened in 1898 and led cyclists to a small deer park and a scenic grove of cedar trees before descending a steep hill near an ice house. Rochester's cycling population justified the city's nickname, "cycle town," and although the inevitable squabbles over the proper place for bicycles occurred in Rochester, arguments generally concerned efforts by officials to exclude cyclists from sidewalks. Cycling coalitions emerged, in turn prompting a search for solutions that undoubtedly influenced the park board's decisions to build paths. By contrast to their colleagues in other major cities, Rochester's park commissioners located those paths without difficulty of any kind and with little or no involvement or reproach from the Olmsted firm.[47]

The city's park superintendent, Calvin C. Laney, probably deserves much of the credit. Although park ordinances forbade cyclists from riding on walks without permission, Laney regarded river walks as the best places to view autumn foliage, and he recommended that cyclists be granted permission liberally. The board also adopted a resolution that excluded all driving or horseback riding from the park's newly created bicycle paths. Moreover, by the time Genesee Valley Park gained popularity Rochester already had become a hub of activity for the state's growing sidepath campaign, and cyclists had set their sights on more ambitious opportunities for country riding. Thus, the conflict that often occurred in large cities, caused by overcrowding on park drives and by the different modes of travel, remained manageable in Rochester. Only during the beginning years of cycling's decline did disputes emerge concerning the responsibility for repairs to paths built by the county commission but located in parks.[48]

Instead, Rochester's pivotal role in the state's sidepath campaign established a rare nexus involving an Olmsted-designed park system and two governing bodies with the authority to build bicycle paths. Shortly after the Southeast Sidepath Association formed in the spring of 1896, Laney and park commissioners attended one of the group's meetings and offered maps showing the locations of proposed paths in Genesee Valley Park, to be built jointly by the park board and the sidepath association. Notably, two park commissioners in attendance personally contributed to a fund created to pay for construction. Those efforts marked the beginning of an informal alliance among park commissioners and the city's sidepath associations, an aspect that distinguishes Rochester's park planning for bicycles from the planning in Buffalo, Louisville, Brooklyn, and other cities.[49]

Rochester's sidepaths also strengthened that collaborative outlook. Rather than destinations where large numbers of cyclists steadily accumulated, Rochester's parks became places for cyclists to pause along a vast path network leading to outlying communities. As the successor to the first sidepath associations, the county sidepath commission seemed to recognize that distinction and assisted the park board in 1899 by constructing a path along the west side of Genesee Valley Park, intended as a bypass to create a direct route from Genesee Street to the Scottsville path without intruding on park activities.[50]

Today, although much of Genesee Valley Park's easterly division is a golf course, the impressive Genesee Riverway Trail system includes trails along both sides of the river through other sections of the park, and a separate trail also follows Red Creek within the park's boundaries. The entrance portal to the Scottsville path that once stood near the park is gone, but the city's parks department has created spur paths to the Genesee Valley Greenway trail system leading to Scottsville. In addition, the Erie Canal Heritage Trail intersects both trails in the park. Some of these passages—notably, those following the river's western edge and that along Red Creek—may overlap segments of the former bicycle paths, offering opportunities to interpret the city's inspiring history of bicycle travel.

Metropolitan Boston's Charles River Speedway and Bicycle Track

All the while, the Metropolitan Park Commission had been working with the Olmsted firm to acquire large reservations of land in Boston's suburbs for public parks. Charles Eliot had helped to establish the commission, and as part of its study the firm proposed a system of radial boulevards and parkways to connect those outlying pleasure grounds with Boston proper. Whether motivated by constant prodding, by a determination to demonstrate the proper place for speed in parks, by a desire to appease their clients and the Massachusetts legislature during a troubling year for the firm, or by all three, Frederick Law Olmsted Jr. and John Olmsted designed an elaborate course for harness racing as part of the Charles River Reservation, and they also included an adjoining bicycle track. The plan is dated December 1, 1897, identical to the date of the plan for Iroquois Park and only eight months after the unexpected death of Charles Eliot.

The commission directed its landscape architects to design the speedway, which required an unbroken stretch of land at least one-mile long with no interference from cross streets. An opportunity emerged in Brighton when marshlands bordering the south bank of the Charles River near Western Avenue required stabilization. By consigning cyclists to a specific area adjacent to a speedway for trotters, the firm also may have expressed its views about the speed of travel by cyclists, and in their report to the commission the Olmsteds acknowledged this fact: "If there is to be any provision for speeding horses in connection with the public park system, this is the place to have it."[51]

The speedway, fifty-feet wide and located across the river from Mt. Auburn Cemetery in Cambridge, consumed a portion of Soldiers' Field and Longfellow Meadow, both owned by Harvard University, and its course generally followed the river's gradual curve. The adjoining bicycle track, twenty-feet wide and placed between the speedway and the river, could be reached via underpasses to avoid conflict with horses. At each end, the track looped in a graceful curve to form a continuous 2.25-mile course, with the two twenty-foot paths running parallel with one another for much of their length. The speedway opened in September 1899 and remained in use for many years. However, the commission postponed construction of the bicycle track in the fall of 1899, and, although photographs from that period seem to show the track, the history of its use is unclear.[52]

As a place for bicycle racing, the plan borrows imaginatively from the oval- or kite-shaped driving tracks for harness racing, long popular at county fairgrounds, and the plan may be an elegant, Olmstedian response to the earthy, clamorous examples of bicycle tracks then in use. Charles River Park, little more than a stone's throw across the river in Cambridge and promoted by the Charles River Athletic Association (headed by Edward Hodges), exemplified that latter category of tracks in use. Although the Charles River Speedway includes a concourse at a mile's end, no grandstands or other observation points are provided for the bicycle paths, and the firm may have designed the track as an outlet for the racing impulse, possibly with the goal of removing that inclination from other parts of a growing park system. Whether they also hoped the track would provide a place for cyclists to circulate free from the ordinary congestion of roads isn't known. If so, the landscape architects misunderstood one of cycling's chief appeals—namely, the freedom of unrestricted travel, confined by neither schedule nor route.[53]

The plan's emphasis on racing requires consideration of the project in the context of sites, buildings, and structures related to bicycle competition, a separate topic. Whether the track was ever completed and whether cyclists ever used it for racing or training isn't clear; if so, the unusual design remained in the shadow of organized racing on the track at Charles River Park nearby. Nevertheless, the Charles River Reservation's speedway and bicycle track are related to park design, and the project represents one of the Olmsted firm's few landscape plans

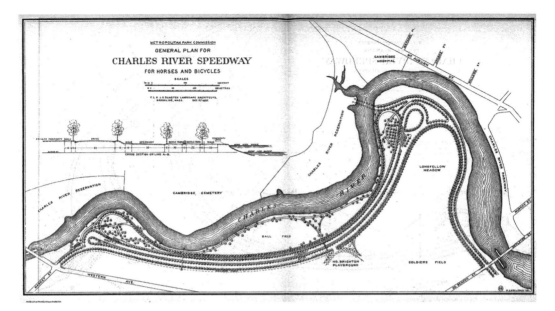

FIGURE 8.5

The 1897 Charles River Speedway is a rare concession to cyclists in park plans by the Olmsted firm. In addition to the track for harness racing, the plan provided a 2¼-mile bicycle course, with the two twenty-foot tracks aligned parallel with one another for most of their length but gracefully looping at each end. Courtesy Massachusetts Department of Conservation and Recreation Archives.

intended specifically for bicycles. The unusual plan also offers a unique interpretation of the cycling experience, and it may have influenced the metropolitan commission's willingness to consider other bicycle tracks—for example, one at Nantasket Beach Reservation. In addition, the project may have encouraged the firm to experiment with other designs for precisely measured bicycle tracks, including a kite-shaped, one-third-mile loop at the Lake Weequahic Reservation for the Essex County Park Commission in New Jersey.[54]

Bicycle Paths in Other Urban Parks

In Philadelphia, the foundation of accord established by cyclists and commissioners during the high-wheel era in Fairmount Park eventually led to a very practical method for constructing bicycle paths with surfaces of vitrified brick that served doubly well as drainage corridors for adjacent park drives. The idea may have originated in 1897 with the construction of a brick-surfaced bicycle path along Mount Prospect Drive in West Fairmount Park. However, by 1899 park appropriations had dwindled, and commissioners decided to make the most of available materials by extending the path system with a slightly narrower corridor along East River Drive in the form of gutters, two-feet wide and slightly concave but adequate as dual bicycles lanes and drainage channels. The strips also formed clearly defined paths that alleviated congestion along the drive. Cyclists seemed to approve, and the improvisational solution offered the added advantage of permitting work on the drives without disrupting travel along the bicycle lanes. Furthermore, as cycling's popularity began to wane commissioners could remain confident that public funds had been spent prudently.[55]

Roughly a century ride to the south, park roads in Baltimore's Druid Hill Park had become congested by the time of cycling's greatest popularity, and commissioners responded in 1896 by creating a separate bicycle path along the carriage course in the vicinity of Sea Lion Pond. That same year, they also converted an unused trolley car bed known as the Dummy Line into another path, not quite one-half-mile long and leading to Seven Oaks. The following year, commissioners confidently opened a pedestrian corridor, the Clipper Path, to cyclists during evening hours, noting that a decline in the number of wheels made that decision a safe one.[56]

Although the examples in both Philadelphia and Baltimore are not ideal corridors for bicyclists, the simplicity of the solution at Fairmount Park at least points toward park drives and parkways designed to separate bicycles from other types of vehicles—the bike lanes of today.

Cycling Rests

Wheelmen and wheelwomen gained park privileges in forms other than exclusive bicycle paths, adding to the influence of cycling on park design. Cycling rests are among the most visible of these privileges, often serving as both refreshment stands and comfort stations but also in simpler form as benches, water fountains, or just shade.

Louisville's Ruff Memorial

Along Southern Parkway in Louisville, Kentucky's LAW division erected a bench and fountain in memory of Alexander "Pap" Ruff, one of the state's venerable cyclists and bicycle inventors, who bequeathed $1,000 to the league in 1896. Members commissioned Louisville sculptor Enid Yandell to design the monument, and although the fountain has not survived Yandell's recently restored wall and bench remain in Wayside Park, a small triangular patch of land near the parkway's northern terminus.

Yandell spent much of her youth in Louisville before enrolling at the Cincinnati Art Academy, where she excelled. Following completion of her studies at that institution in 1889, she began assisting sculptors Loredo Taft and Karl Bitter, contributing to their art at the World's Columbian Exposition in Chicago. After the fair, she traveled to Paris, where she worked with Frederick MacMonnies and Auguste Rodin, later establishing a studio in that city and often exhibiting there. In 1898, members of America's National Sculpture Society elected her a member.[57]

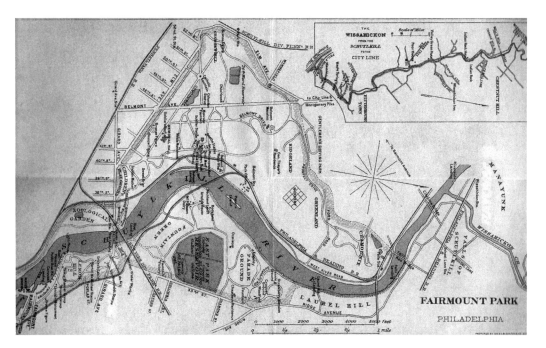

FIGURE 8.6

A map of Philadelphia's Fairmount Park, from *Road Book of Pennsylvania, New Jersey, Maryland, and Delaware*, 7th ed. (1893), by the Pennsylvania Division, LAW. The map was drawn by G. W. and C. B. Colton & Co., New York. In 1897, park com-missioners established a bicycle path along the edge of Prospect Drive, paving it with vitrified brick and also using it as a drainage corridor.

Yandell's 1897 design for the Ruff Memorial is both elegant in its simplicity and superbly functional, consisting of a stone seat and back set in a semicircular, quarry-faced stone wall roughly four-feet in height, with a radius of fifteen feet and a total length of approximately fifty feet, concluding with two slightly raised end walls. The wall is limestone, but both the bench and its back are a smoothly surfaced Ohio sandstone. Four elaborate, wrought iron standards mounted on wall pedestals of stone support globe lanterns, and a three-sided, marble drinking fountain guarded by bronze, griffon-head spouts stands at the center of the circle. Stone brackets at the base of the wall's outside perimeter serve as bicycle racks. Park commissioners submitted Yandell's drawings to John Olmsted, who approved the project and suggested designs for walks and plantings for the small park called Wilder Triangle.[58]

Unfortunately, the monument endured decades of neglect and vandalism, causing park officials to dismantle and rebuild the deteriorated structure during the early 1980s, but without close attention to what remained of Yandell's original design. Members of the Louisville Bicycle Club took up the cause in 1984 and began the long process of reclaiming the monument's former stature,

FIGURES 8.7 AND 8.8

At about the same time that Louisville's park commission opened a bicycle path along Southern Parkway, the Kentucky Division of the LAW commissioned Louisville sculptor Enid Yandell to design a fountain and bench honoring one of their members, Alexander "Pap" Ruff. Although the drawing is part of the Olmsted firm's collections and although some of the writing on the plan may be in Olmsted's hand, the drawings of the fountain and bench are by Yandell. Courtesy National Park Service, Frederick Law Olmsted National Historic Site.

completing the restoration in 1987 and, in a dedication that year, adding the name of one of the club's former presidents, Wallace "Sprad" Spradling, to its commemorative inscription.[59]

Central Park's Swedish Schoolhouse

Soon after the Philadelphia Centennial Exposition in 1876, Sweden's government donated its Swedish Schoolhouse, the country's national exhibit at that fair, to New York City, where it stood for many years in Central Park at Seventy-Ninth Street near West Drive. In 1900, officials repaired and repainted the building, installed plumbing, adapted the largest of its three rooms to the sale of refreshments, and converted the cottage to a place of rest for park cyclists. Following the decline of cycling, the building evolved into a comfort station and continued in that capacity until 1912, when (because of protests by Swedish-American citizens) it became an entomology laboratory. Many years later, in 1973, the park board transformed the building into a marionette theater.[60]

Pope Park and Memorial Fountain, Hartford

When the country's foremost bicycle manufacturer, Albert Pope, donated land to the city of Hartford for a park, located within easy reach of his sprawling factory complexes, John Charles Olmsted and Frederick Law Olmsted Jr. prepared the design. The two landscape architects remained true to the elder Olmsted's dictates for parks as places for quiet contemplation of scenery, and despite the park's modest size they skillfully integrated a range of landscapes similar to those that Olmsted and Vaux had introduced in much larger pleasure grounds.

The 1898 plan is exemplary for the diversity of its modestly scaled features and the park is an important landscape directly related to cycling history. An open meadow called Hollowmead dominates the ninety-three acre tract, with irregular edges defined by a sylvan backdrop that screens the park from the surrounding city and also shelters a perimeter pathway. A lakelet, Hollowmead Pool, extends into the meadow, and a pergola placed adjacent to the park's single formal element—the High Mall, with fountain, music pavilion, and semicircular flower garden—frames views toward the meadow and its pool but also toward a more rugged outcropping, the Hillside Ramble. In the park's northern sector, separated from Hollowmead by tree-lined Park Street, a park-like landscape with an open understory shelters winding paths through Bank Side Grove bordering Park River. Scattered throughout the park are more intimate glades as well—Nethermead, Hithermead, and Thithermead. Alas, nary a reference to bicycles: no symbolic path and no cycler's rest.[61]

In 1913, the Hartford Board of Trade rectified that omission by retaining Hartford architect George Keller to design a granite monument and fountain commemorating Albert Pope's inventive, industrious, and philanthropic contributions to the city and to bicycling history. The crown of the cylindrical monument is a large granite globe with a belt of smaller spheres that symbolize the

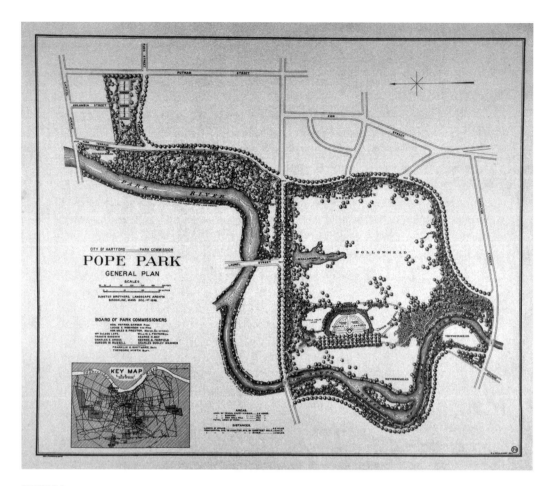

FIGURE 8.9

A plan for Pope Park in Hartford by Frederick Law Olmsted Jr. and John Charles Olmsted, 1898. The design compactly arranges a variety of landscapes on a modestly sized parcel of land, about ninety-three acres. Courtesy National Park Service, Frederick Law Olmsted National Historic Site.

ball bearings that led to Pope's successful enterprise, and the bronze portrait of Pope in bas-relief is by sculptor Lee Lawrie. The monument once stood at the entrance to the park near his Capitol Avenue complex. However, officials moved the monument into the park in the early 1960s, because it stood in the way of highway construction. Although not in its original location and today sadly marred by graffiti, the fountain marks a resting place on a grassy hillside near the park's southwestern edge.[62]

CHAPTER NINE

Park Way

During the decade following passage of the Liberty Bill in 1887, cyclists steadily expanded park privileges, ultimately achieving the exclusive paths envisioned by Karl Kron in 1885. If that progress occurred haltingly within the boundaries of urban parks, then it advanced more rapidly along parkways and boulevards connecting one park to another in urban park systems. While providing access to parks, those routes also joined remote urban sectors, thus serving as functional transportation corridors. Where paths for wheeling were added along those corridors, the bicycle became an alternative means of transportation, as well as a form of recreation.

Olmsted and Vaux's 1868 plan for a Park Way in Brooklyn became a prototype for parkway designs, and Olmsted explicitly separated the two words to make clear the corridor's function as a pleasing access to country parks. Ocean Parkway, which had joined Prospect Park with Coney Island by 1876, demonstrated the design's merits, and almost twenty years later, in 1895, Brooklyn's park commissioners modified the plan and opened the landmark Coney Island bicycle path. One year later, they added its younger sibling on the parkway's eastern side for cyclists returning to Prospect Park. In 1868, Olmsted also began working in Buffalo, developing a comprehensive plan for parks and parkways by 1876, and Buffalo's park commissioners later modified the same Park Way design to accommodate bicycle paths. Elsewhere, a few park boards recognized the appeal of cycling (or at least the strength of its political lobby) and took initiative without prodding.

Despite cycling's popularity during the 1890s, few landscape architects designed bicycle paths as integral units of park or parkway plans from inception, and those who did—Ernest Bowditch, John Bogart and Nathan Barrett, or John Olmsted—are noteworthy. The 1886 plan for Cleveland's Doan Brookway path by Bowditch and the 1897 East Orange Parkway paths by Bogart and Barrett are both important, but for different reasons; unfortunately, neither was ever completed. Both are overshadowed by the very successful Coney Island paths, and although Bogart and Barrett proposed the East Orange paths as part of a regional transportation system, making them more advanced in concept than the Coney Island paths, the two landscape designers probably drew inspiration from the latter.

Cleveland's Doan Brookway Bicycle Path Plan

Olmsted and Vaux's Park Way design for Brooklyn and the plan crafted between 1868 and 1876 for Buffalo's connective park system influenced the designs for parkways and boulevards in many American cities. However, one of the country's earliest plans for a connective parkway that incorporated a bicycle path from inception can be traced to other sources. Cleveland's East Side Park Way, later called Doan Brookway, is the contribution of Ernest Bowditch, a capable engineer and landscape gardener from Brookline, Massachusetts, who studied at MIT and who, early in his career, worked with park planner and landscape gardener Robert Morris Copeland. Prior to that affiliation, he had worked in a variety of capacities before returning to New England, where in the fall of 1870 he began working for a Boston engineering firm, Shedd and Sawyer, and his assignments for that concern led him to Mt. Auburn Cemetery in Cambridge and its influential landscape design. In 1871, he established his own consulting office near that of Copeland, and the two men collaborated on a number of projects prior to Copeland's death in 1874.[1]

Copeland's demise gave Bowditch an opportunity to acquire the former's practice and to expand beyond surveying and engineering. By then well-schooled in plans favoring numerous small parks joined by broad boulevards (rather than a single large pleasure ground), Bowditch continued to work on Copeland's projects for the Boston region. In 1874 and 1875, he circulated plans that enlarged Copeland's 1872 proposals into a metropolitan scheme. Consulting assignments for influential architects and clients followed, and during the 1880s he collaborated with Frederick Law Olmsted and John Charles Olmsted, but their influence on his work is unclear. His engineering and landscape gardening practice steadily flourished, leading to commissions for wealthy patrons in Cleveland, including Warren H. Corning, William Gordon, and Jeptha Homer Wade.[2]

Park Plans in Cleveland

Wade, a financier and philanthropist, founded a group of companies that became part of the Western Union Telegraph conglomerate in 1856, the year he settled in Cleveland. Although serving briefly as president of Western Union, he began devoting most of his energies to civic activities, including plans for public parks in the city's eastern sector, and in 1882 he gave the city roughly sixty-three acres along Doan Brook, creating what would become Wade Park.[3]

Doan Brook is a riparian corridor roughly seven miles in length that flows northerly from Shaker Lakes in the city's southeastern heights into Lake Erie. Near that outlet, another Cleveland industrialist, William J. Gordon, developed landscape plans for his private estate along the lake and periodically opened those pleasure grounds to the public. By the spring of 1883, park commissioners had begun calling the preserve Gordon Park, and by bequest it became city property following Gordon's death in 1892. At that time, the land stretched for almost a mile along the lake and contained about 122 acres.[4]

In 1883, the park board recommended acquiring a rugged, unimproved ravine along Doan Brook between the Gordon and Wade estates, linking the two parks. In 1890, while in Cleveland on another project, Bowditch met Gordon and discussed ideas for improving the intervening lands. Local park committees had formed by this time, and Bowditch suggested a comprehensive park system in the shape of a horseshoe, with each arm terminating at the lake on the city's western and eastern edges. Gordon favored the idea and conditioned his bequest on development of such a plan, specifying that the park commission retain Bowditch. Efforts to

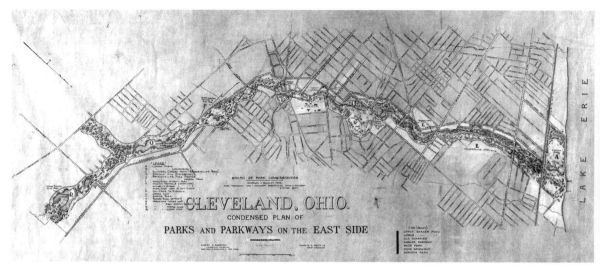

FIGURE 9.2

In 1894, Boston landscape gardener and engineer Ernest Bowditch and his resident engineer, Charles W. Pratt Jr., prepared this plan for Cleveland's East Side Parkway, also called Doan Brookway or Doan Brook Parkway. In 1886, Bowditch and Jeptha Homer Wade, a city benefactor and member of the park commission, collaborated in the planning of a bicycle path along a segment of the parkway linking Wade Park and Gordon Park to the north. Courtesy Cleveland Public Library Digital Gallery.

purchase lands along Doan Brook valley in its entirety continued during the coming years, culminating with the donation of 279 acres by the Shaker Heights Land Company in 1895 and 270 acres by John D. Rockefeller shortly after, thus giving the city ownership of the valley between Gordon Park and Shaker Lakes.[5]

Anticipating those donations, Bowditch and his resident engineer, Charles W. Pratt Jr., prepared a detailed plan titled "Condensed Plan of Parks and Parkways on the East Side," dated December 31, 1894. Their meticulous study shows the entire Doan Brook valley between Lake Erie and Shaker Lakes, encompassing lands totaling about 740 acres and with twenty-three miles of drives. By that time, the park board had begun describing the area as Doan Brookway or Doan Brook Parkway, and improvements to the portion between Gordon and Wade Parks, a little more than two miles apart, began late in 1894. Today, Martin Luther King Jr. Drive winds along much of that corridor.[6]

Bicycle Path Design

Although not identified on the Bowditch-Pratt plan, a separate bicycle path borders the western edge of the drive along the valley floor. On an earlier 1886 plan by Bowditch, titled "East Side Park Way," a short segment of the bicycle path is shown in plan and profile near Superior Street, a short distance north of Wade Park. The path merges with the drive beneath the overpass, but extends both north and south of that crossing. The path's dimensions are not provided, but it appears to be half the width of the drive, or about eighteen feet; the park board's report from 1894 narrows it to fifteen feet.[7]

The 1886 plan is one of a series of drawings by Bowditch for the parkway. However, three 1897 plans for planting, grading, and paving establish the bicycle corridor between St. Clair Street and Superior Street, passing through an area of Rockefeller Park called the Cultural Gardens and concluding near Doan Street in Wade Park. A fourth 1897 plan shows the corridor as a continuous wheelway that narrows slightly as it passes beneath the Superior Street Bridge, rather than merging with the drive, as depicted on the 1886 plan. Presumably, the wheelway continued north of St. Clair Street and entered Gordon Park, evident from the narrowing of the path beneath the St. Clair Street Bridge.[8]

Credit for the conception of Cleveland's unusual, high-wheel era bicycle path designed as part of a park system likely belongs to Jeptha H. Wade, a member of the park commission, and his grandson, Jeptha H. Wade Jr., a member of the Cleveland Bicycle Club, the wheelmen of which actively participated in the city's park planning. Following the untimely death of his father in 1876, the younger Wade developed a close relationship with his grandfather, who groomed his grandson to become a civic-minded benefactor. One can easily imagine the elder Wade encouraging his colleagues to adopt a benevolent attitude toward wheelmen and to provide a bicycle path on or near land he had donated to the city for a park. That aspect distinguishes both the city and its park commissioners, who creditably accommodated cyclists without any of the bother that developed in Central Park. Gordon may have approved of the sympathetic outlook toward wheelmen as well.[9]

Bowditch also deserves recognition. He acknowledged that Wade, who died in 1890, had consulted him from time to time regarding the designs for Wade Park. As a consulting landscape gardener experienced in picturesque park designs and connective parkways, he could have recommended confining wheelmen to carriage drives, as did the Olmsteds. Instead, he found a practical solution by combining drive and bicycle path into a single corridor along the valley floor, separated for purposes of travel but unified visually and thus minimizing any interference with the parkway's scenic qualities. Perhaps coincidentally, Bowditch separated the words "park" and "way," just as Olmsted and Vaux had done in Brooklyn eighteen years before.[10]

Interlude

During the years that separated the early planning stages of the Doan Brookway bicycle path and the 1894 Bowditch-Pratt plan that hastened completion of the parkway, the spirit of accord that created the wheelway dissolved as plans for the city's park system evolved. New generations of cyclists on safety bicycles instead turned their attention to the city's proposals for broad boulevards linking different parts of the city, which would be designed to serve streetcars as well as other modes of transportation.

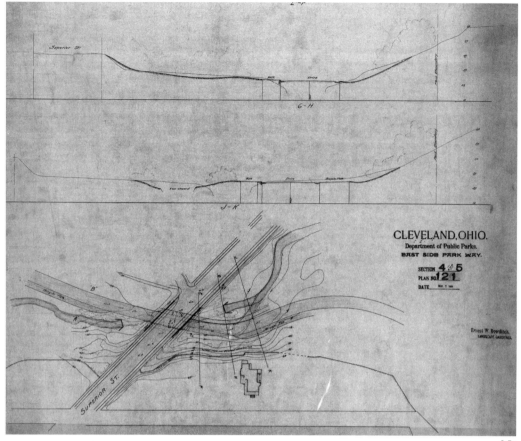

CLEVELAND, OHIO.
Department of Public Parks.
EAST SIDE PARK WAY.

SECTION 4 & 5
PLAN NO. 121
DATE DEC. 7 1896

Ernest W. Bowditch,
LANDSCAPE GARDENER.

9.3a

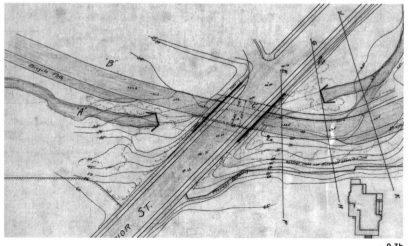

9.3b

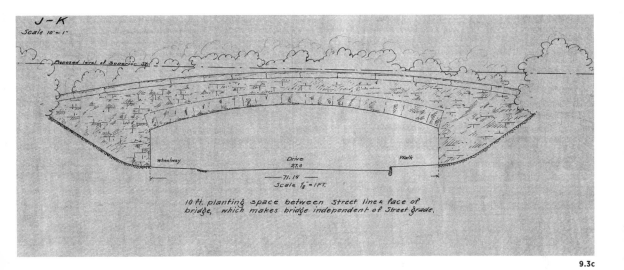

J-K
Scale 10'-1"

Proposed level of Superior St.

Wheelway   Drive   Walk
27.0

71.14
Scale ⅛"=1FT.

10 ft. planting space between street line & face of
bridge, which makes bridge independent of street grade.

9.3c

FIGURE 9.3a, b, c

A plan for Cleveland's East Side Park Way by Ernest Bowditch, dated December 7, 1886, shows a bicycle path adjoining the western side of the parkway's central drive, separated by Superior Street and leading toward Gordon Park on Lake Erie to the north, or left side, of the plan (a and b). When the city finally prepared bids for construction of the path during 1896, cyclists opted to use the park drives instead, and the project ended. Curiously, Bowditch or Pratt continued to show an enlarged path extending beneath the bridge on a later plan dated 1897 (c). Courtesy Cleveland Public Library Digital Gallery.

Remarkably, the park board did not forget its promise to the city's wheelmen—or perhaps to the elder Wade. On their own initiative, and apparently without cyclists' knowledge, the board continued to refine plans for the Doan Brookway bicycle path between Wade and Gordon Parks. Sometime between the early months of 1895 and spring or early summer of 1896, commissioners modified the plan, moving the path from the valley floor to the east high-level drive along the eastern limits of the parkway between the two parks; the board also expanded the path's width to sixteen feet. Intending to complete the path during the 1896 construction season, the board approved the plans and then prepared bid advertisements.

At that point, cyclists recalled the project and objected, expressing fear that once the path had been completed commissioners would exclude bicycles from East Drive. Debates about the proper place for cycling had been developing for some time in Cleveland while the city's plans for connective boulevards progressed, and concern probably grew spontaneously from that dialogue, begun in 1894; alternatively, they may have learned of a similar conflict in Brooklyn in 1896. Cleveland's astonished park commissioners gave up trying to please the wheelmen and eventually abandoned the project, although Bowditch or Pratt continued to show the wheelway on plans prepared in 1897.[11]

Brooklyn's Sidepaths to the Sea: The Coney Island Bicycle Paths

In June 1895, the Brooklyn Good Roads Association began organizing a festive parade to mark the official opening of the Coney Island Bicycle Path. Committee members hoped to give Brooklyn and Long Island clubs the privilege of leading the cavalcade, in recognition of their persistent support and financial backing for the project. However, those plans yielded to constabulary authority, and on that spring Saturday an escort of blue-coated police on copper-rimmed wheels set the pace, followed in turn by a second escort of three hundred soldiers riding in regimental columns of four, also in uniform and with broad-brimmed, slouch campaign hats.[12]

Once those regiments had rolled by, crowds of spectators began cheering for the ninety-two members of the Brooklyn Bicycle Club, heading the parade's first division in a display of meticulous discipline. Each member wore dark blue uniforms, coats buttoned to the neck, with white gloves and starched white collars. The Kings County Wheelmen and Long Island Wheelmen pedaled next in line, trailed in turn by the Prospect Wheelmen, Brooklyn Ramblers, South Brooklyn Wheelmen, Amity Wheelmen, Bushwick Wheelmen, New Utrecht Wheelmen, and various other Brooklyn clubs, including the Ocean Parkway Wheelmen, all in near perfect alignment, four abreast.[13]

Amiably upstaged, New York City's clubs settled for a leading role in the second division, beginning with the Harlem Wheelmen in mouse-colored knickerbockers and white sweaters adorned with racemes of violets. The Riverside Wheelmen, the Gramercy Wheelmen, the New York Wheelmen, and other city and metropolitan clubs followed, many of them from New Jersey, in all numbering about three thousand cyclists. A third division trailed behind, far less orderly and much more boisterous, but with almost as many citizen riders. For seventy-five minutes, cyclists rolled past the reviewing stand at Parkville, midway between Prospect Park and Coney Island, accompanied by a military band playing a rousing new composition, the "Cycle Path March and Two Step." The procession halted at the just-completed Manhattan Beach track, where the annual meet of the LAW's New York State Division convened that weekend. Adding spectators to the total, ten thousand people may have gathered in Brooklyn on that spring day to celebrate cycling, culminating a decade-long quest for a bicycle path joining the city proper with the ocean beach at Coney Island.[14]

Park Way

Brooklyn's bicycle path owes much of its success to the strength of the 1868 Park Way design by Olmsted and Vaux, and the corridor's story begins long before the arrival of bicycles. Olmsted and Vaux's report to the city's park commission that year contained a lengthy essay about the growth of great towns, emphasizing that current expansion represented merely a premonition of the vastly greater enlargement to come. As suburbs spread outward, no longer could one stroll

FIGURE 9.4
In June 1895, reporters estimated that ten thousand cyclists
and spectators gathered for a parade to open the five-mile
route to Coney Island along Ocean Parkway. Courtesy New
York City Parks Photo Archive.

easily into the countryside in search of tranquility. Hence, country parks accessible to all dwellings became crucial for modern town life. However, the chaos
and dangers of ordinary streets rendered such parks no more accessible than
suburbs, and thus a series of ways were needed for walking, horseback riding, and
the driving of carriages en route to restful pleasure grounds. Those travelways or
boulevards augmented park advantages, providing a continuous parkway neighborhood of open, desirable residences and gardens—a means to guide the development of a community growing ever larger.[15]

Anticipating public needs far into the future, Olmsted and Vaux gave their
Park Way very generous spatial qualities. Creditably, Brooklyn's park commissioners retained most of the plan's dimensions for Ocean Parkway, 210 feet overall, to create a seventy-foot central drive, two thirty-foot dividing strips (each
with two rows of trees sheltering a central walk), two twenty-five-foot access
roads, and two fifteen-foot sidewalks. More than twenty years later, those ample
spaces made the melding of parkway and bicycle path nearly flawless—by most
appearances, a carefully integrated design.[16]

Engineers had completed construction plans for Ocean Parkway by the fall
of 1872, and by the close of the following year work had reached as far as King's

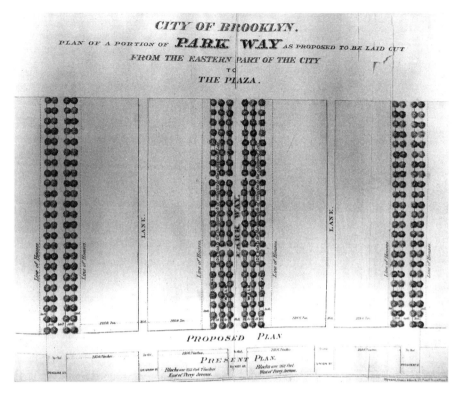

FIGURE 9.5

A plan for a Park Way for the City of Brooklyn by Frederick Law Olmsted and Calvert Vaux, 1868, which was also offered to Buffalo that same year. The design for a central drive flanked on each side by open malls, service roads, and pedestrian walks became widely copied by park planners throughout the country and eventually led to bicycle paths in a number of cities. Courtesy New York City Parks Photo Archive.

Highway in Gravesend, slightly more than three miles from Prospect Park. Commissioners sporadically pushed construction forward, reaching the seashore by November 1876 and building an oceanfront promenade, the Coney Island Concourse. With an improved parkway, greater numbers of visitors reached Coney Island and its beach, calling public attention to the area's bawdy character and encouraging efforts to improve its reputation. As the seaside resort grew, the volume of traffic along Ocean Parkway escalated; by 1880, when wheelmen began arriving, park commissioners already had reported the need for substantial repairs.[17]

Sidepath

Cyclists' use of Ocean Parkway increased during the mid-1880s and included races, some of them organized by the Brooklyn Bicycle Club but others impromptu events. Complaints about the road surface multiplied, and calls for a separate bicycle path began to circulate. Journal and newspaper articles vary as to the idea's genesis, but at least partial credit belongs to Colonel John Y. Culyer, chief engineer and park superintendent, who in 1885 offered the suggestion to Albert H. Angell of the Long Island Wheelmen. Others, including Albert Pope, may have broached the topic several years before as a logical outgrowth of Long Island explorations, in which cyclists plied a network of existing sidepaths.[18]

The influence of sidepaths in the origins of the Coney Island paths becomes evident at several points. During this period, poor roads between Brooklyn and Jamaica had prompted calls for sidepaths in that vicinity, and similar proposals for Ocean Parkway logically would have followed. In addition, many of the articles promoting a parkway path describe the project as one for a sidepath. In 1889, Charles H. Luscomb (who served as park commissioner and as president of the LAW that year) gave cyclists the exclusive use of a ragged pedestrian way between the carriage drive and the western service road. Thus, the first Coney Island bicycle path originated during the high-wheel era as a sidepath, at least along some portions of its length.[19]

Good Roads and a Good Sidepath in Brooklyn

The beginnings of Brooklyn's celebrated path overlapped with New York State's sidepath network in another important respect: the Good Roads movement. By 1892, the boulevard's sorry condition had extended to the sidepath, prompting renewed calls for a proper path, and park commissioners requested an appropriation of $10,000 to complete the project. Unfortunately, the city's governing body bestowed far less, $1,000, and cyclists responded by founding the Brooklyn Good Roads Association with the express goal of building a wheelman's highway from Prospect Park to Coney Island. The association's president, George T. Stebbins, guided a group of influential figures who championed the project, including Angell, Luscomb, Isaac Potter, Charles Schwalbach, and William O. Tate, the last three men representing the Brooklyn, Kings County, and Montauk clubs, respectively. By that time, Potter already had become a central figure in the LAW's crusade for good roads.[20]

In April 1893, an association committee met with Park Commissioner George V. Brower, who agreed to build a sample half-mile section to test surface materials, verify cost estimates, and provide an object lesson—all strategies borrowed from the Good Roads campaign. Potter and Culyer developed plans, and the experiment began south of Eighteenth Avenue near Parkville. The design specified a corridor twelve feet wide and a crowned, compacted surface of screened stone called Roa Hook gravel, available at a site along the Hudson River. That small start must have prompted optimism among park commissioners, who secured sufficient funds to excavate, grade, and surface portions of a two-mile stretch that year.[21]

The appointment of Frank Squier as Park Commissioner hastened the project toward completion the following year. Squier vowed to build the path as far as public resources allowed, and at a joint meeting in mid-August 1894 the

Brooklyn Good Roads Association pledged up to $3,500 toward the cost, provided commissioners finished the path that season and promised to maintain the corridor for the exclusive use of cycling in the future. As chairman of the association's subscription committee, Isaac Potter promptly launched a fundraising campaign, issuing an appeal to Brooklyn cyclists to contribute one dollar each.[22]

Subscription ledgers began filling before month's end, and in early November the account surpassed the $3,000 mark. By that time, workers had graded the path's entire length to Coney Island, with a bed of gravel stretching about half that distance. Late in December, the *Brooklyn Eagle* donated fifty dollars, tipping the balance in cyclists' favor, and laborers added the last of the gravel. Cyclists turned their attention to plans for the June parade, but long before that event thousands of Brooklyn residents watched an even larger number of cyclists spontaneously parade along their popular new path one Sunday in April, riding from early morning until long after sunset.[23]

Return to Prospect Park

As early as 1887, some Brooklyn cyclists had questioned the value of a sidepath along Ocean Parkway, reasoning that it would not be wide enough for travel in two directions and arguing that one of the parkway's access roads would provide a better highway for wheeling if given a macadam surface. Such worries proved accurate, and hardly had the spring riding reason begun in 1895 when talk of a return path to Prospect Park on the parkway's eastern mall began to circulate.[24]

An opportunity arose after Frank Squier guided passage of state legislation in 1895, placing the care of many Brooklyn streets under the commission's control and substantially adding to the city's parkways. He then watched with tacit approval as tenacious cyclists quietly secured an amendment to the law during the early months of 1896, authorizing funding for specific street improvements, including sidewalks along the access roads bordering Ocean Parkway—a fair recompense to pedestrians—and a second bicycle path. The law took effect early in April, Squier promptly funded a contract for construction of a path eighteen-feet wide, and sixty days later—almost before Squier's successor, Timothy L. Woodruff, had time to ponder his assignments and approve the work—the new path stretched far into the distance, ready for travel. Simultaneously, Squier authorized much-needed repairs to the surface of the original path, by then called the "old path," and moderately increased its width. Combined, the two Prospect Park–Coney Island paths gave Brooklyn's cyclists a convenient, eleven-mile jaunt. On June 27, Woodruff as Grand Marshal led thousands upon thousands of cyclists past the intersection of Bedford Avenue and Eastern Parkway to begin a second parade, no less spectacular than that from the year before.[25]

Wheelmen Warned Off

If the celebratory flow of cyclists joining in the 1896 parade contained an undercurrent of dissent, few participants noticed. Yet not quite two months before,

Woodruff (a member of the Brooklyn Bicycle Club, but also an aspiring state politician) astounded his fellow wheelmen by announcing that cyclists no longer would be allowed to ride along Ocean Parkway's central carriage drive and would face arrest for violating that rule. Woodruff likely bowed to pressure from horse owners, who enjoyed pacing their trotters unhindered by cyclists, and he may have reasoned that wheelmen would be satisfied with two exclusive paths—built and maintained partly at public expense—or at least would hesitate to complain.[26]

Calculations notwithstanding, Woodruff probably overlooked the dramatic implications of his proclamation, which reawakened the contentious debate about the rights of cyclists to use public thoroughfares. Editor Francis Prial immediately reminded readers of *Wheel and Cycling Trade Review* that his journal consistently had opposed separate wheelways, calling them a selfish institution and expressing fear that a vast civic resentment would awaken if, at public expense, cyclists acquired roads of their own, forbidden to all others, yet remained free to use public ways; for comment, he turned to Isaac Potter, by that time the LAW's chief consul in New York State and also politically mindful. A few days after Woodruff's order, Potter had challenged its legality as a violation of New York's Liberty Bill, and he issued an open letter to wheelmen urging them to ignore the regulation, promising legal and financial support from the LAW in the event of arrest.[27]

Potter and the LAW may have been caught off guard by Woodruff's bold decision, but Woodruff also seemed to have been surprised by Potter's response, and the dispute between two members of the Brooklyn Bicycle Club is a notable one in the long history of conflict surrounding bicycles. However, factors other than thoughtful policy about the proper role and place for bicycles shaped the outcome. Instead, political reckoning, the convenience of Brooklyn's two popular bicycle paths, and a shrewd interpretation of the Liberty Bill produced a stalemate tolerable to cyclists and face-saving to park commissioners.[28]

About a week after Woodruff's order, the two men consented to a friendly test case. Although the prohibition remained in effect during the pendency of that challenge, Woodruff temporarily agreed that park police would not arrest cyclists. Each man also stated his case publicly. In his interview with Prial, Potter declined to be an advocate for paths but softened Prial's stern opposition, pointing to the value of paths in places where poorly-maintained roadways remained unfit for bicycles, and cyclists clearly faced that problem on Ocean Parkway. Potter also contended that Brooklyn wheelmen had afforded the park board an inexpensive alternative to repairing the road, which because of its condition had become an embarrassment to the city, and after generously contributing money had received an unjust penalty in return.[29]

Woodruff claimed that the restriction had become necessary as a means to suppress speeding cyclists, but Potter dismissed that claim, reasoning that enforcing speed limits through arrests made far more sense and adding that scorchers on the paths would be much more difficult to apprehend than on the carriage drive; moreover, speeding cyclists posed greater danger on paths, especially to women and children. With justification, cyclists also took aim at the unequal treatment given to equestrians, who enjoyed separate paths as well as carriage drives in Prospect Park. By this time, cyclists could truthfully claim that the bicycle had become a vehicle of the people, whereas horsemen continued to represent the wealthy.[30]

Gambit

Relying on advice from the city's attorneys, Woodruff sidestepped Potter's arguments by explaining that Ocean Parkway included not just the carriage drive but also the adjoining green belts with bicycle paths, access roads, and sidewalks. Consequently, his order did not exclude cyclists from Ocean Parkway, as thus defined, but instead assigned them to specific parts of the corridor, a form of regulation expressly permitted by the Liberty Bill. Pressing further, Woodruff warned that if cyclists challenged the rule successfully, then a court might decide that the park board had no authority to exclude any vehicles from the parkway's various divisions, thus opening the bicycle paths to use by other forms of transport, including horses.[31]

Potter called Woodruff's tactic an official bluff and described it as an ungraceful attempt to discriminate against cyclists. As the state's chief representative for the LAW, he rejected any attempt to trade the rights of wheelmen for two bicycle paths, promising to take the matter to the state legislature if necessary. However, the threat seemed plausible enough to worry Brooklyn's cyclists, and Woodruff decided to enforce the rule, seeking allegiance from a newly appointed corps of cycle-mounted park patrolmen, most of whom were members of local bicycle clubs as well as the LAW.[32]

At a pivotal ceremony in mid-May, Woodruff administered the oath of office to his patrolmen and specifically asked whether all were willing to enforce the ordinance prohibiting cyclists from using the carriage drive. Only bicycle dealer Alex Schwalbach voiced dissent and declared the rule illegal, declining his appointment and inviting arrest for the purposes of a test case. During the debate that followed, Woodruff steered the discussion toward the crucial question: Would cyclists give up the bicycle paths in order to maintain the privilege of using the drive? Schwalbach remained adamant, but his colleagues strongly disagreed, thus exposing a critical division among Brooklyn's wheelmen and undermining the league's influence.[33]

In the battle of political wills that developed between Woodruff and Potter, Woodruff held the upper hand on practical grounds. In general, cyclists were overjoyed with the two paths, and the comparatively few wheelmen who still used the carriage drive lacked sufficient voice to sustain Potter's stand on principle. Although Prial continued to send editorial salvos toward the city's park board, Woodruff managed to obtain the backing of the Brooklyn Good Roads Association, the members of which expressed gratitude for Woodruff's role in

FIGURE 9.6
Park Commissioner Frank Squier prepared the groundwork for
a return path to Prospect Park on the eastern mall, and his successor, Timothy L. Woodruff, completed the project in 1896 and
led a similarly well-attended parade that year. Courtesy New
York City Parks Photo Archive.

supporting the second bicycle path, thus further weakening Potter's stance. With
options dwindling, the league's state division (acting through its Committee on
Rights and Privileges) issued a strongly worded condemnation of Woodruff's ordinance at their yearly meeting early in June.[34]

By then, enthusiasm for a test case had waned, and by the time parading
cyclists had rolled past the reviewing stand later that month thoughts of challenge mostly had vanished. Ultimately, the two sides reached a guarded accord.
The league continued to maintain that cyclists could not be deprived of their legal
privilege to use the central drive, and park commissioners eventually acknowledged that right. However, wheelmen courteously accepted the rule imposed by
Woodruff, and if Potter and the league suffered a minor setback, then the Liberty
Bill nevertheless remained intact beyond the confines of Ocean Parkway.

Any lingering ill will between Potter and Woodruff probably dissolved in September, when Potter received an invitation to be the grand marshal in a timely
bicycle parade honoring the park commissioner, who had become the Republican
candidate for lieutenant governor. In his letter of reply to the parade's organizers,
Potter graciously acknowledged Woodruff's energy and ability as commissioner,

omitting any reference to the parkway controversy. At the same time, he accepted the honor with the understanding that the parade would be free from political significance, cautioning that cyclists could ill afford to take part in public demonstrations concerning candidates for public office.[35]

Potter's initial ambivalence toward separate bicycle paths, as explained to Prial at the conflict's outset, soon shifted to support, and this sharp turn in policy requires explanation. When (as president of the LAW two years later) Potter authored the league's most important publication on the topic, *Cycle Paths*, he became a champion of separate paths, especially in rural settings where paths became essential for country riding and served as object lessons for good roads. In urban areas, the fear that by promoting separate paths wheelmen would lose the right to use city streets or boulevards forced Potter to act cautiously. True, the two contexts overlapped in some places, and both also touched on the broader topic of bicycles as a form of transportation, but Potter's principal concern in both settings may have been that of resolving internal conflict among members of the LAW.[36]

Cycle Path Handicap

During the coming years, Brooklyn cyclists settled into familiar patterns of travel along Ocean Parkway's two famous bicycle paths. Occasional closures, lapses in maintenance, encroachments by horses and wagons, or spotty patrols by bicycle-mounted police caused periodic consternation, but enthusiasm for the corridors remained strong. Coney Island steadily grew into a boisterous amusement center during this period, adding to the paths' popularity.[37]

A Labor Day race called the Cycle Path Handicap also turned public attention toward Ocean Parkway at summer's end. Race organizers had added ceremony (and prizes) to the competitions begun during the mid-1880s, forging a rivalry with New Jersey's Memorial Day races at Irvington and Millburn. In 1900, the Associated Cycling Clubs of Long Island enticed more than 150 entries, and event referee Francis Prial estimated that more than thirty-five thousand spectators watched the twenty-five-mile chase. However, repairs near Parkville in 1904 forced cancellation of the race, and in 1905 officials postponed the contest until Thanksgiving Day. Yet the estimated ten thousand observers who withstood the cold and wind on that blustery, sunny day are a testament to the important role of bicycle racing during a long period of dormancy for recreational cycling, by then in its early stages. Traditional races on New Year's Day may have attracted far fewer spectators, but the event also bolstered the parkway's renown.[38]

Save the Path

Racers and throngs of spectators damaged the paths' surfaces, as did opportunistic equestrians and motorcyclists, the latter banned from Ocean Parkway. In addition, growing numbers of pedestrians gained influence with park commissioners, and during the fall of 1903 workers ominously placed curbstones across the paths at the gateways to Prospect Park, requiring cyclists to dismount and fueling rumors that commissioners intended to convert the paths to walkways. By the spring of 1904, editors of *Bicycling World* opined that the paths had never been in worse condition, but absent a concerted voice of complaint from cyclists park commissioners were able to escape with promises of better maintenance.[39]

Conflict finally erupted in 1911 after park commissioners, yielding to the demands of horsemen, sequestered more than a mile of the central drive as a speedway for harness racing. At two intersections, automobiles and other pleasure vehicles veered from the drive and crossed the bicycle paths to reach access roads, creating dangerous conditions for cyclists and causing numerous accidents. Adding insult to injury, races occurred only one afternoon each week, but the traffic regulations remained fixed each day.[40]

In 1911, commissioners considered removing the traffic hazard by partitioning the central drive: one two-lane corridor for automobiles and a single lane for trotters. Sulky drivers returning to the starting point would be given the adjoining bicycle path. Cyclists rebelled and late in August roused support for an organization to preserve the threatened path. Calling themselves the Greater New York Cyclists Association, the group elected veteran path-keeper Alex Schwalbach president and then planned a protest parade. On September 4, multitudes of incensed New York cyclists began arriving in Brooklyn. The parade's Manhattan contingent mustered at Columbus Circle before departing for Brooklyn, and by midafternoon an estimated fifteen thousand wheelmen, wheelwomen, motorcyclists, and spectators had congregated at Bedford Rest on Eastern Parkway. Once in formation, the parade column stretched for more than three miles and included more than 4,500 bicycles and brightly polished motorcycles. After pausing midway for inspection and prizes, the column continued toward Coney Island and Luna Park.[41]

In headlines proclaiming "Cyclists Save Coney Island Bicycle Path," New York's newspapers called the event a huge success. Surprised by the bicycle's continuing popularity, Brooklyn's borough president, Alfred Steers, vowed to abolish the speedway from Ocean Parkway if elected mayor of New York, and he proposed a similar parade each year. He also applauded the growing use of bicycles for transportation, as they were far less expensive than automobiles. The parade may have temporarily reawakened enthusiasm for the paths, but pointed reminders that cyclists had paid for most of the first path hopefully lingered in public memory a little longer.[42]

Motor Era

For the next decade, motorcyclists continued to use the paths, justly so after having helped to vanquish the opposition. However, as the speed and weight of motorcycles increased, so did the dangers to cyclists and pedestrians. Prompted by a 1921 editorial in the *Brooklyn Daily Eagle* titled "Make the World Safe for Cyclists," a heading as apt today as then, a special committee appointed by the

LAW's New York Division agitated to preserve existing bicycle paths by excluding all vehicles other than those propelled by muscle power. Committee members asked Park Commissioner John Harman to issue an order prohibiting motorcycles from the Coney Island paths, reminding him that the western path had been built with funds provided by wheelmen and that the state legislature had passed a law prohibiting vehicles other than bicycles from using sidepaths or wheelways specifically constructed for bicycles.[43]

Surprised by the request, and uncertain whether cyclists used the paths enough to justify such an injunction, Harman agreed to conduct a travel census. In his subsequent report, Harman observed that most cyclists chose the access roads and central drive rather than the paths, presumably favoring the better road surfaces, and an order prohibiting motorcycles from the paths thus could not be justified. He also revived the hated prospect of restricting cyclists to the paths, which was only fair if motorcycles could not venture onto those strips. Yet less than a month later he reversed his decision, reasoning that by confining motorcyclists to the drives the dangers to pedestrians would be alleviated.[44]

Applauding Park Commissioner Harman's order limiting the paths to bicycle use, Abbott Bassett also placed the Coney Island corridors into a meaningful context twenty-six years after the 1895 inaugural parade. Recalling that during the ensuing years the Lincoln Highway had opened, and that concrete-surfaced roads had reached into the country's most remote regions, Bassett observed that none of those events stirred the depth of interest present among cyclists at the opening of the first Coney Island path. In his words: "The bicycle trail that was to establish quick connection between Brooklyn and Coney Island was no mere local affair. It furnished one of the favorite topics clipped by editors of sporting pages in other cities. In those days, the tourist could check his wheel as baggage…and travel the day coach in cycling togs."[45]

All the while, Ocean Parkway had been stimulating neighborhood expansion, much as Olmsted and Vaux had envisioned. Additional streets became necessary, creating an increasing number of parkway intersections; for cyclists, those crossings posed dangers as automobiles multiplied. Counting cars turning from both the central drive and access roads, cyclists at each cross street could anticipate vehicles approaching from numerous directions. The repeated pausing at cross streets also disrupted the cycling experience, contributing to the paths' decline in popularity. As neighborhood populations increased, the wide bicycle corridors eventually became pedestrian promenades. Today, both corridors are paved, and cyclists and pedestrians share the original, western path, which is partitioned by railings. To their credit, Brooklyn cyclists continue to use that path for trips to the beach at Coney Island.

Influence

The Coney Island bicycle paths are historically significant for several reasons. The corridor in use today is one of the country's few nineteenth-century bicycle paths to survive—possibly the only one traceable to the high-wheel era. More than a century ago, such paths were common symbols of an important period in the country's history following the introduction of bicycles. In our modern era, when solutions to transportation quandaries are elusive, resources ever more scarce, and auto commuting a great vacuum of unproductive time, Americans increasingly are turning to bicycles as viable means of conveyance. As that trend evolves, the places of cycling history will gain influence as points of reference.

In addition, Brooklyn's cyclists, park commissioners, and engineers demonstrated a successful way to adapt Olmsted and Vaux's 1868 Park Way plan to bicycle use without unduly disrupting the corridor's original design. That reworking confirms the viability of separate bicycle paths as components of linear parks and parkways and gives the Coney Island paths an important place in the history of parkway planning. The path's substantial width, in particular, is one of its most important characteristics, pointing toward wheelways that resemble old roads rather than paths and toward travel corridors that are scenic, economically efficient, multifaceted, and healthful for people as well as the environment.

The ties to Ocean Parkway also add to the path's historic significance. In 1975, the New York City Landmarks Preservation Commission designated Ocean Parkway a scenic landmark, crediting Olmsted and Vaux's design with establishing a new concept in road building for the country. Although the surviving bicycle path did not receive separate consideration, amending the commission's designation remains possible, and an acknowledgment of Brooklyn's landmark bicycle path is long overdue.[46]

The Coney Island paths are also historically important as influential models of path-building. Faced with entreaties by bicyclists, park commissioners elsewhere took notice of the popular corridors in Brooklyn and built paths in parks or along parkways in their own cities. Evidence of that influence is explicit in some locales and circumstantial in others. For example, the plan for East Orange Parkway by Bogart and Barrett likely borrows from Brooklyn, although there is little proof.

Yet caution is needed when measuring the role of Brooklyn's sidepaths to the sea in the context of park and parkway planning that included bicycle paths. That context unfolded so expansively during the closing years of the nineteenth century, and the popularity of bicycles became so universal during that period, that plans for many bicycle paths likely sprouted spontaneously from dialogue among cyclists and park planners. Many cities, such as Buffalo, established their own regional sphere of influence by creating successful parks, and various methods for accommodating bicycles along those corridors probably developed as a natural outgrowth of the planning process and the great popularity of bicycles, with little need to draw from examples elsewhere.

Beyond the overlapping urban contexts of parks, parkways, and campaigns for civic improvements, assessing the influence of the Coney Island paths becomes much more difficult. Fairly stated, Brooklyn's paths were well designed, carefully constructed, popular, and widely publicized, and they contributed to the broad enthusiasm for bicycle paths that developed during that period. However, New York's sidepath campaign was well underway when celebration of Brooklyn's paths began, and that movement chartered its own independent course, guided by a legislative framework for financing path construction. Programs similarly reliant on legislatively enforced licenses, rather than the subscription model used in Brooklyn, were widely copied—often without involvement from urban park commissions. Ultimately, cycling's cresting popularity and the search for a method to finance construction guided the origins of many local paths throughout the safety bicycle era.[47]

East Orange Parkway Paths

Plans for urban or regional parkways took shape in many other metropolitan locales, and some illustrate the grand possibilities for parkway designs that incorporate bicycle paths from inception. One such example—the 1897 proposal for Essex County, New Jersey, by engineer John Bogart and landscape architect Nathan Barrett in partnership—is exceptional. Retained by the Essex County Park Commission in 1896, the two designers confronted the challenge of planning a comprehensive park system to serve Newark (the county's principal city), the Oranges (an entire urban district with a large population), and many smaller towns (widely dispersed but adding to citizenry counts). Most of the county had been developing within easy reach of New York City, and from Eagle Rock in Orange (a supreme test for hill climbing during the high-wheel era) views encompassed a vast metropolitan area. The plan by Bogart and Barrett designated eight discrete parkway corridors, most with potential for extensions, and formed a complete chain of communication throughout the county. The two designers also furnished a sample parkway plan for East Orange, assigning carriages, pedestrians, and bicycles to separate corridors.

The Essex County Park Commission organized following legislative charter in 1896 and soon retained Bogart and Barrett, both of whom had forged accomplished careers at a time when landscape architecture and park planning remained embryonic professions. Barrett, born on Staten Island in 1845, gained experience with plant materials as a nurseryman and then studied landscape design on his own initiative. Early commissions for railroad station grounds in New Jersey led to a long association with George Pullman, who in 1880 hired Barrett to design the streets and parks of Pullman, Illinois. Other park and municipal projects followed, adding to Barrett's résumé, and he became a founding member of the American Society of Landscape Architects and eventually its president. In 1893, he assisted Frederick Law Olmsted in the landscape plan for the World's Columbian Exposition, and, soon after his selection in Essex County, the Palisades Interstate Park Commission retained him as its principal landscape architect.[48]

Bogart, Barrett's senior by eleven years, graduated from Rutgers College and gained experience in park design early in his career by assisting Olmsted and Vaux in both Central Park and Prospect Park, eventually becoming chief engineer for the latter. As would Barrett, Bogart journeyed to Chicago, where he joined well-known engineers William LeBaron Jenney and Louis Schemerhorn in work on that city's fledgling park system. Through that association, he aided Olmsted and Vaux in the suburban development of Riverside, Illinois. By 1872, he had returned to the East, where he became chief engineer of the New York City Department of Public Parks and later state engineer and surveyor, before forming the partnership with Barrett.[49]

Path Design

Although Barrett and Bogart commanded considerable expertise in parkway planning, probably neither man held any special interest in cycling. Instead, urging from the well-established wheeling community in Newark and the Oranges surely explains the park commission's willingness to oblige cyclists. Yet the two men deserve credit for the expansive scope of their countywide proposal and for their inclusion of bicycle paths in the spacious parkway they proposed for East Orange.

Although recommendations for that plan could have originated with its designers, with cyclists, or even with the park commission, no one had very far to look for a successful model. From Eagle Rock, one could see Brooklyn and its many church spires and could visualize cyclists pedaling along the two paths adjoining Ocean Parkway. If prior familiarity with Prospect Park by Barrett and Bogart (especially the latter) was not enough, then news of the grand parades crossed New York Harbor immediately with participating cyclists, including the East Orange Cyclers Club. The nearness in years also suggests the influence of Brooklyn's paths.[50]

The parkway plan that Barrett and Bogart prepared for East Orange in 1897 is practically identical to Olmsted and Vaux's 1868 Park Way, as later modified for bicycle paths. Each design employs a broad central carriage drive flanked on both sides by ample swaths of green space that separate the drive from bordering service roads, in turn skirted by pedestrian walks. The principal difference is that Barrett and Bogart offered a design for a curvilinear section, which contrasts with the undeviating alignment of Ocean Parkway. The partners proposed two separate bicycle paths, one on each side of the central carriage drive, and where the central drive bends the paths follow a slightly different curve, skirting the carriage drive at one point and the service roads at another. That election suggests that the designers expected heavy use of the paths and anticipated the need for one-way travel by cyclists, similar to Brooklyn's paths. Whether Barrett and Bogart intended to employ an identical design for all Essex County parkways isn't clear; if so, the plans are unique in combined design and scope.[51]

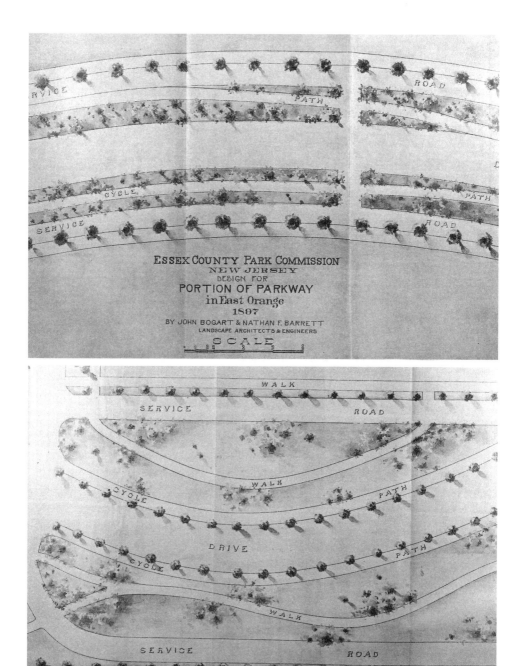

FIGURES 9.7 AND 9.8

A plan for a parkway and bicycle paths in East Orange, New Jersey, by engineer John Bogart and landscape architect Nathan Barrett in 1897, part of a larger plan the two partners proposed for Essex County, serving Newark, the Oranges, and outlying communities. The Olmsted firm recommended against the bicycle path, and the final plan adopted a broad central lawn flanked by access roads. Courtesy Loeb Library, Harvard University.

Plan Revisions

Bogart and Barrett submitted their proposals in December 1897, and the park commission voted to build the East Orange Parkway, extending from Central Avenue to Springdale Avenue. However, in August 1898 commissioners decided to retain the Olmsted firm to design that parkway. The firm's December 1899 report expressed concerns about costs, likely reflecting similar fears among park commissioners, and recommended eliminating both the wide central carriage drive and the two adjoining green swaths with their bicycle paths. Although they regarded the Bogart-Barrett parkway plan as suitable for pleasure driving between large parks and reservations, they believed that greater benefits would accrue to adjoining properties if the central drive and its bordering strips became a broad grass lawn forty-six feet wide and with rows of trees accented by ornamental shrubbery. They also widened the side roadways, converting them to residential streets.[52]

The Olmsteds' politely phrased observation about benefits attaching to adjoining properties was simply a reminder that improved property values along the parkway would increase property taxes and pay for the project. The firm thus converted a connective travel corridor for different modes of transportation into open space envisioned as neighborhood playgrounds for children or as restful areas of retreat, similar to city squares. That type of linear open space has successfully sustained residential character in some neighborhoods, but in others that expanse has succumbed to visual and functional erosion. The Olmsteds also pushed consideration of the bicycle as a means of transportation far into the background, and the project thus becomes noteworthy as further evidence of the firm's policies toward bicycles.

During their discussions with Bogart and Barrett, park commissioners pointed to the work of the Metropolitan Park Commission in Massachusetts, suggesting that the challenges facing that body were similar to those in Essex County. The two designers disagreed, noting that the metropolitan organization had been entrusted only with rural and suburban projects beyond the boundaries of Boston, which had been developing its own park system, overseen by a separate, much older commission. By contrast, Newark, the Oranges, and the county's outlying towns challenged planners to design a park system that served both densely populated urban centers and more remote, lightly populated regions. The two men addressed that concern in their 1897 report by calling for a study and general scheme for park and parkway improvements for the entire county. One wonders too whether the two landscape architects farsightedly viewed the bicycle as an efficient way to draw the county's remote regions more closely together.[53]

Whether continued disagreement on that point caused park commissioners to consult with the Olmsteds is unclear. Nevertheless, the firm's 1896 letter to Edward Hodges in Boston, cautioning against separate bicycle paths, sheds light on the decision by Essex County's park commissioners to eliminate the bicycle paths.

Cycling's Corridors of Collaboration

The bicycle corridors that originate from the adaptation of park or parkway plans represent important contributions by cyclists to park planning history. The origins and locations of those paths are diverse, and in addition to revealing the country's sweeping enthusiasm for cycling they also illustrate the attentive outlook of many park commissioners toward the public's use of parks. Although park boards sometimes eroded the integrity of park designs by accommodating certain activities, historians can gain insight about those difficult choices by assessing that decision-making process in a single context: bicycle paths. Still other examples reveal the thread of influence tying the Olmsted firm ineluctably to plans for bicycle paths, principally from the sweeping extent of their many park plans and secondarily from the firm's continuing objections to paths devoted exclusively to bicycles.

Manhattan's Riverside Drive

Lacking a proper passage to the sea such as that in Brooklyn, Manhattan cyclists settled for spectacular views across the Hudson River from Riverside Drive. By resolution adopted in December 1897, New York's park board officially designated a portion of that thoroughfare as a bicycle path, giving the drive a crown of distinction long sought by the city's wheelmen and wheelwomen. Although Brooklyn's Coney Island paths must have planted a seed of envy among Manhattan cyclists, Riverside Drive held its own honorable lineage, having played a principle role in wheelmen's efforts to secure park privileges during the high-wheel era.

Riverside Park is a steep hillside reserve that by 1898 stretched more than three miles from Seventy-Second Street to 129th Street. To Frederick Law Olmsted, who had devised conceptual plans for the park by 1873, the value of the site as a place for public recreation existed wholly in the higher elevations near the park's eastern boundary, a place of commanding views over the river valley—unobstructed by the docks, buildings, and railroad tracks below. Hoping to extend the park's original eastern edge to secure those views for pedestrians and carriage travelers, he proposed a one-hundred-foot-wide avenue placed on a broad shelf, ample for driving, riding, or walking and shaded by trees strategically placed to preserve views.[54]

Olmsted's role in the park's development soon ended, but other designers, including Calvert Vaux, remained true to his vision for a picturesque setting, pulling the romantic Hudson River valley into the city itself. After 1887, when the Liberty Bill gave cyclists the freedom to use all park roads, New York's park commissioners grudgingly turned their attention to rules for cyclists, and those regulations evolved as the conversion from high-wheel to safety bicycles became universal. Yet the most carefully crafted rules did little to abate overcrowding, especially along the asphalt surfaces of Riverside Drive, where multitudes of cyclists congregated in the shadow of fashionable residences or noble architectural monuments such as Grant's Tomb. Many artists, F. Childe Hassam among them, found the scene delightful (figure 3.8).[55]

At the start of the 1897 season, park commissioners capitulated and established an experimental bicycle path along the western edge of Riverside Drive between 104th Street and 120th Street. The public voiced its approval throughout that season, and with little fanfare the board converted the trial path to a permanent one, making no effort to exclude cyclists from the drive. Consequently, the concerns about separate bicycle paths voiced in Brooklyn the year before did not materialize in Manhattan, and the path became an alternative corridor for those cyclists who preferred it.[56]

Humboldt, Chapin, Bidwell, Lincoln, and Scadjaquada Parkway Paths

Buffalo's cyclists probably expressed exasperation with the park board's bicycle path in Delaware Park in 1896, but the campaign they had begun in 1894 soon yielded better results. During the summer of 1897, the board constructed three separate bicycle paths, totaling nearly four miles along Humboldt, Chapin, and Bidwell Parkways, the latter two converging at a grand circle (Soldiers Place), where Lincoln Parkway and its path began an axial approach to Water Park. Earlier that year, commissioners had revealed more ambitious plans for a bicycle path along Scajaquada Parkway leading to park land south of Scajaquada Creek, and that path opened during 1898.[57]

Today, the approach parkways have been extensively altered, and although swaths of green space still divide some sections of parkways, formal bicycle paths are not in use. Yet Buffalo's bicycle corridors invite comparison to Brooklyn's Coney Island paths in several ways. Both illustrate the vigorous dialogue among cyclists and park commissioners that produced successful bicycle corridors; both represent well-organized campaigns in cities with large populations of cyclists; each concerns important park plans intended as parts of large metropolitan park systems; each employs scenic parkway connectors joining remote sectors of their respective cities; and both involve creative, slightly different adaptations of park and parkway designs for bicycles.

Along Buffalo's parkway paths, commissioners used just one of the malls flanking the central drives, creating two corridors of modest, eight-foot widths to accommodate cyclists traveling in opposite directions; the mall on the drive's opposite side became a bridle path. The magnetic draw of Coney Island's amusements and ocean beaches as a destination also distinguishes the Ocean Parkway paths from those in Buffalo.

In addition, Buffalo's parkway paths illustrate the difficulty in assessing the influence of Brooklyn's two very popular paths, which could easily have served as models for Buffalo's park board. However, the city's enthusiastic cyclists or its commissioners may have reached decisions spontaneously, possibly from the dialogue begun in 1894 or earlier. Although the board adapted several of the city's parkways to bicycle use during the summer of 1897, two years after the first Coney Island path opened, the similarity in design might not be the result of one borrowing from the other but of both borrowing from Frederick Law Olmsted's 1868 design for a Park Way. Olmsted's plan for Buffalo also created a more comprehensive park system than that in Brooklyn, and progress toward that objective advanced more rapidly in Buffalo. For many years, Buffalo cyclists also had been watching closely as Charles Raymond encouraged sidepath building near Lockport, thirty miles away, and the idea of placing paths in the malls adjoining Buffalo's parkway drives may have originated with the sidepath model, as it did in Brooklyn.

Louisville's Southern Parkway Path
If Buffalo's parkway paths demonstrate the difficulty of assessing the influence of the Coney Island paths, then Louisville's Southern Parkway path illustrates the great reach of Brooklyn's landmark corridors, especially the parades that generated such publicity. The plan for Southern Parkway, initially called Grand Boulevard, already existed when the city retained Frederick Law Olmsted in 1891, but the corridor's overall width—initially 150 feet—was considerably less than that in Brooklyn, forcing the firm to narrow both the central carriage drive and adjoining medians. Olmsted managed to increase the width to 170 feet by recommending that adjoining property owners cede ten feet for sidewalks, but the forty-foot-wide central drive is substantially narrower than its seventy-foot counterpart in Brooklyn, and the flanking median strips are twenty-eight rather than thirty feet wide. When Southern Parkway opened to the public in 1893, cyclists leaving the center of Louisville on Third Street enjoyed a continuous six-mile excursion to the entrance of Iroquois Park, and in the fall of 1894 they celebrated the achievement with a carnival and parade.[58]

The popular parkway fueled enthusiasm for cycling in Louisville, as did the LAW's 1896 national meet at Fountain Ferry Park with its famous racetrack. When droves of cyclists created crowded conditions on the parkway, the park board purchased four bicycles that same year, requiring its superintendent and guards to learn how to ride. The board also sought assistance from John Olmsted, who visited the city in 1897 with Warren Manning and prepared designs for two fourteen-foot bicycle paths, identical to the revised width of the first path along Ocean Parkway and separated from the central drive by seven-foot planting strips. Commissioners subsequently confined the bicycle path to the parkway's eastern median and then graded and surfaced the corridor in 1897. However, difficulties with drainage developed, and work continued into the following year. The decision to build the path also led directly to John Olmsted's important design for a circumferential bicycle path in Iroquois Park.[59]

As in Brooklyn and Buffalo, the initiative to add bicycle paths to the city's parkways originated with cyclists, but Louisville's park commissioners (headed by General John B. Castleman) were amenable, and cyclists had good reason to applaud the board's efforts with another parade and show of cycling's popularity, visible to all who harbored political ambitions. The October event in 1897 began during the early evening hours, with bicycles adorned by Japanese lanterns, and concluded with a public meeting and a resolution thanking park commissioners for the park privileges granted to cyclists.[60]

Unfortunately, sections of the path became soggy, the cinder surface did not harden, and cyclists used the central drive instead. Subsequent repairs improved the path only marginally, and cyclists continued to use the drive. Today, although a median strip separates the central drive from the eastern access road, that strip has been narrowed in some sections, the parkway's design has been modified for use by automobiles, and nothing remains of the path.[61]

Boulevard Bicycling

Legislation giving powers to park boards usually authorized those bodies to take control of public roads, not just in parks but also beyond park boundaries when part of a park system. In many cities, those travelways soon extended over considerable distances and in some cities merged with city beautification campaigns, inspired by the World's Columbian Exposition in Chicago in 1893. Cyclists sometimes participated in the planning of those projects, and a few intriguing designs evolved from those efforts. In addition, park boards periodically faced voters who opposed spending money for parks and fashionable thoroughfares. In response, commissioners sometimes sought favor from cyclists as a group in order to gain political leverage; at least a few bicycle paths originated from those negotiations.

Cleveland's Euclid Avenue and Edgewater Boulevard

Cleveland's acquisition of park lands occurred sporadically during the 1880s, but prospects improved in 1893 when, supported by bond issues, park commissioners prepared a master plan calling for principal parks in each of the city's seven districts and for a series of wide boulevards encircling the city and connecting the parks. The board retained Ernest Bowditch to develop park plans, and land acquisition began in 1894.[62]

The Cleveland Wheel Club promptly formed a committee to explore the possibility of adding bicycle paths to the proposed boulevards and began assembling information about the costs, materials, and anticipated use. In 1894, those talks produced at least one proposal for a bicycle path along Euclid Avenue—a broad travelway with a central corridor for double trolley tracks, planting strips, drives for carriages or other vehicles, and bordering grass plots wide enough for three-foot bicycle paths. The plan attracted the attention of wheelmen as far away as Louisville and Indianapolis, but by the spring of 1895 many of Cleveland's cyclists reasoned that road surfaces paved with vitrified brick would be adequate for wheeling. They also feared that the paths would be too narrow for legions of riders and may have decided to forego the paths in return for sufficiently wide boulevards. Such sentiments lingered, and when Ohio adopted legislation in

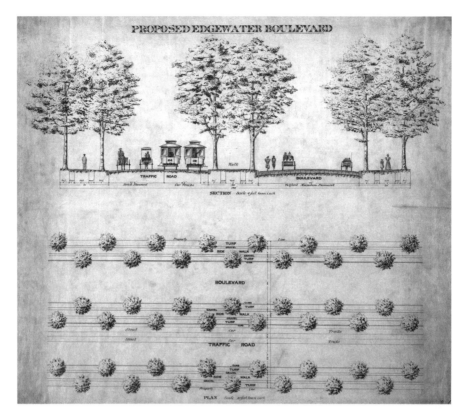

FIGURE 9.9

Cleveland's Department of Public Works collaborated with cyclists to develop plans for boulevards that accommodated different modes of transportation moving at different speeds, and its engineers produced this plan for Edgewater Boulevard, undated but circa 1900. Cyclists, light carriages, and a new type of vehicle—the horseless carriage—are placed in one drive; trolleys and commercial traffic are placed in a second, with pedestrian passages between and bordering the two drives. Courtesy Cleveland Public Library Digital Gallery.

1898 authorizing county commissioners to tax cyclists and use the funds to build bicycle paths, many of the city's wheelmen objected and emphasized the need for better roads rather than separate paths.[63]

Not all of Cleveland's bicyclists shared that concern, and park commissioners created a separate path in South Side Park (today Lincoln Park), with connections to adjacent streets. Having barred wheels from sidewalks, village officials in East Cleveland also decided to build a path exclusively for bicycles, and placed the path along heavily traveled Euclid Avenue adjacent to an electric railway line.[64]

At least one plan—that for Edgewater Boulevard—confirms that designers specifically sought ways to accommodate different modes of transportation moving at varied speeds, bicycles included. The corridor provided an approach to Edgewater Park, which occupies bluffs and beaches along Lake Erie in the city's western reaches. The park commission began acquiring land for Edgewater Park in 1894, and park plans probably came from Bowditch's office, at least initially. Although undated and unsigned, one of those plans includes a parkway that descends from the area's upper terrain to the lake. However, during the late 1890s disputes developed regarding the park board's accountability to Cleveland's working citizens and the accessibility of parks to residents of the city's core neighborhoods. Those skirmishes led to the dissolution of the park commission in 1900 and to the transfer of its authority to the Department of Public Works, which produced the plan for Edgewater Boulevard.[65]

The plan divides the boulevard into two principal roads: one paved for ordinary traffic and streetcars and the second for recreational vehicles, including horseless carriages and bicycles. The two roads are separated by a broad mall with a sidewalk and are flanked on each side by similar malls with walks, all of which are bordered by gravel drainage strips. The plan is intriguing for its arrangement of streetcars and recreational traffic, clearly and efficiently separated but also in close proximity, and for an apparent compromise growing from discussions with wheelmen. Intentionally or not, the plan's designers offered an alternative to Olmsted's original design for a Park Way, as modified for bicycle use in Brooklyn and Buffalo, but it also hints at the influence of Frederick Law Olmsted's 1886 plan for widening Beacon Street in Boston.

Toledo's Riverside Alliance

American antecedents for Cleveland's 1893 plan to encircle the city with parks connected by wide boulevards can be found in several places, including the 1872 plan for Boston by Robert Morris Copeland. At about that time, Chicago embarked on a similar scheme that had begun to take shape by the mid-1880s. The Chicago exposition followed in 1893, offering a vision of urban planning on a grand scale, with broad axial corridors connecting civic plazas and formal parks. In turn, Cleveland's park system influenced planning in smaller Ohio cities, such as Toledo at the western tip of Lake Erie. Yet Toledo's progressive citizens orchestrated the growth of their parks a little differently than their counterparts in Cleveland, promoting boulevards strategically to advance their cause. Thus, the role of Toledo's cyclists who participated in that campaign was also different, and they became part of a loosely bound coalition supporting city parks.

Strategic proposals to include bicycle paths in plans for the city's boulevards may have originated not with cyclists but with a local businessman, Sylvanus Pierson Jermain, who became a principal figure in Toledo's park movement. Jermain began promoting parks for Toledo at least as early as 1889, the year in which a wealthy resident bequeathed thirty-five acres of land for a park in the city's eastern sector subject to a condition that the city obtain an equal area of adjoining land within three years. A successful legislative initiative followed in 1891, enabling the city to issue bonds to purchase additional lands. Despite progress, disagreements surfaced about the proper locations for parks, and in 1892 the

Toledo Blade conducted an informal survey among its readers, isolating several opposing points of view. Some residents foresaw a growing city and urged a series of large, outlying parks accessible to residents via connecting drives, similar to plans in Cleveland. However, other citizens demanded small neighborhood parks that benefited taxpayers immediately, providing breathing spots in the heart of town for workers and eliminating the need for travel. As one taxpayer candidly replied: "The rich people can go to the country when they want to, and don't need a park purchased by the city for them."[66]

Park commissioners sharpened that debate after secretly inviting landscape architect Horace W. S. Cleveland from Minneapolis and landscape gardener Maximilian G. Kern from St. Louis to inspect potential sites. Cleveland recommended a 280-acre farm well beyond the city limits, and in July 1892 commissioners announced the purchase of that property, later named Ottawa Park. However, rumors of the decision already had found their way into newspapers, and a flurry of angry responses ensued, calling the decision a cruel one for the workers of the city and an insult to the demand for neighborhood parks. That dissension also placed future bond votes in jeopardy. A similar conflict would eventually occur in Cleveland, resulting in bitter political battles, but Toledo managed to avoid that outcome, and Jermain, boulevards, and bicycles deserve at least partial credit.[67]

During the period between 1889 and the bond vote in 1891, Jermain had taken initiative along several fronts, including studying parks in New York, Philadelphia, Baltimore, Chicago, and Cleveland. He also sketched proposed improvements to city-owned property overlooking the Maumee River in a district called Lower Town or Riverside (a narrow strip of land with sheltering trees that had become a restful site for neighborhood residents), and he contributed benches and flower beds. Kern transformed those ideas into a formal plan after being hired by the park board late in 1892, and the board then improved the site by creating terraces leading to the river, constructing a boat house, and adding ponds, fountains, and walks. Equally important, Riverside offered the type of small, accessible park sought by many of Toledo's voters, probably placating some of the public anger over acquisition of the Ottawa Park property.[68]

Jermain recognized the value of large pleasure grounds as places of egalitarian retreat, great social equalizers giving health and hope to citizens compelled to live in cities. Yet he also recognized the economic benefits that accrued for cities when park systems improved the value of property, and he correctly judged that adjoining property owners would be willing to donate strips of land fronting existing roads to create park-like boulevards. Toledo's park board agreed, and in June 1892 the board revealed plans for a string of boulevards around the city. That decision accomplished several objectives: the boulevards would become a type of linear park that could extend easily into many parts of the city, thus satisfying demands for neighborhood parks for working people; the boulevards could be established cheaply and quickly, demonstrating the commissioner's resolve to use bond funds equitably and to meet the needs of the city's present population; and the corridors would eventually link the larger outlying parks, creating a park system accessible from all parts of the growing city. In the grand scheme of park planning, those incremental benefits created solid footing for future bond votes.[69]

At some point, Jermain, park commissioners, and cyclists discovered common ground. In return for supporting the park board's campaign, cyclists gained a promise from commissioners to include bicycle paths in the boulevards. In addition to securing support from an influential group of voters, the park board profited by pointing to the bicycle as a convenient, healthful, and independent means of transportation to outlying parks, further justifying their decision to acquire remote tracts of land; by the mid-1890s, commissioners could supplement that list of practicalities, noting that bicycles had become affordable. If simply logical, then that alliance nevertheless distinguished Toledo's park projects from planning in many other cities, where cyclists and park commissioners battled one another; it also adds to the list of contributions by bicyclists to park planning history.

Despite those mutual benefits, park commissioners probably never completed any bicycle paths on city drives. By the summer of 1895, the park board had clarified plans for boulevards, each to be from one- to two-hundred-feet wide with room for a carriage drive, bridle path, bicycle path, and walks for pedestrians. However, commissioners had exhausted available funds by then, and political winds also shifted when the city's mayor, Samuel Jones, announced his opposition to boulevards, describing them as expensive luxuries used only by the wealthy who owned carriages. Jermain disagreed, arguing that the corridors would be available for vehicles of working citizens, bicycles among them, making the city's parks accessible to all classes; by 1899, Jones had acquiesced. In that year, he participated in a groundbreaking ceremony that marked the start of a lengthy period of boulevard construction that would continue sporadically for decades, as funds permitted. Initially, plans to include bicycle paths along specific corridors moved forward, but work progressed slowly after 1900, just as cyclists began dwindling in number, and paths likely succumbed to cost cutting.[70]

Riverside Park and its adjoining Summit Street may be the one area in Toledo where the alliance crafted by Jermain and cyclists became evident: a short bicycle path and a resting pavilion. Kern completed plans for Riverside sometime between 1893 and 1895, and he divided the park into The Terrace and The Mall. The former is dominated by a large central drive flanked by corridors of varying widths and shaded by rows of trees. One of those corridors is a lawn, which in turn is bordered by pedestrian walks along a terrace, with another walk bordering the river below. The Mall is similar to the type of linear parkway developed by Bowditch in Cleveland, with shaded, curvilinear drives, small meadows, and pedestrian walks. Neither the plans nor the park board's reports explain these various corridors, and distinguishing bridle paths from bicycle paths is not possible.

Yet cyclists used this narrow commons, and photographs show well-surfaced corridors of moderate width and entrance bollards. The city's successful bicycle manufacturers also donated funds to build a bicyclists' pavilion in 1896, using it later to post advertisements—to the chagrin of park commissioners, who ordered the bills removed. Attaching an accurate date to that bicycle path becomes difficult, but the period during which Kern prepared plans, followed by the construction of improvements, is a reasonable estimate, sometime during the cycling seasons of 1893 or 1894.[71]

CHAPTER TEN

Wheelways

During the 1890s, cyclists developed a variety of plans for separate bicycle corridors that enlarge the three principal contexts for path building discussed in the preceding chapters: club or wheelway-league sponsored projects, legislatively governed sidepath campaigns, and park or parkway paths authorized and maintained by municipal or metropolitan park boards. Wheelmen and wheelwomen also sought to improve cycling's lexicon, wishfully hoping to secure well-recognized places for riding. These cyclists regarded the term "bicycle path" as both clumsy syllabically and much too suggestive of a footpath. Instead, they favored the more euphonic "wheelway," which provided clarity, because the term "way" implied the use of an entire corridor or road. However, regional nomenclature often reigned, and in some parts of the country wheelmen traveled from place to place along "cycle ways."[1]

A number of proposals for wheelways originated spontaneously when opportunities to convert existing passageways to bicycle riding occurred, foretelling cycling's adaptation of abandoned railroads after World War II. With support from newspaper editors, cyclists in several cities launched efforts to use aqueduct corridors, which were scenic as well as perfectly level. Then, as now, objections by adjoining property owners sometimes thwarted cyclists' spirited efforts.

Other plans grew from attempts to address the inherent incompatibility of vehicles and bicycles on crowded city streets or bridges, and these projects ranged from very practical asphalt strips to fanciful schemes for elevated paths. In the process, city public works and engineering departments joined wheelmen's organizations, county sidepath commissions, and park boards as sources of public funding. Then, as now, solutions proved elusive.

Still other proposals, such as travel ways combining separate corridors for bicycles and trolleys, remain intriguing today, encouraging creative designs that employ berms, separate grades, landscaping, or other devices to establish clearly defined corridors for each; ideally, such designs also add visual quality to the travel experience. Increasingly, plans in urban settings considered the bicycle as a form of transportation, and that distinction gained importance as the popularity of recreational bicycling by adults declined after 1900. At least one venture—a bicycle railroad built to transport workers from Mount Holly, New Jersey, to the H. B. Smith Machine Company in nearby Smithville—qualifies as unique.

Brick and Asphalt Bicycle Lanes

Today's ubiquitous bicycle lanes, often designated by painted lines on hard-surfaced roads, owe their origins to nineteenth-century versions that utilized several techniques to divide cycling corridors from streets or highways. Sidepath commissions in New York and other states sometimes left only small ridges of earth dividing the two thoroughfares, relying on legislated sanctions to keep horse-drawn vehicles off bicycle surfaces. Although wheelmen seldom wrote about "bicycle lanes" during that period, distinguishing such paths from modern bicycle lanes becomes difficult, at least in terms of location in relation to roads. Yet establishing some form of physical division from adjacent streets and highways remained a priority for cyclists, both to preserve riding surfaces and to protect cyclists from traffic. Those concerns prompted experiments with various partitions, including grass strips, curbs, elevated grades with retaining walls, berms, or shade trees; such features became characteristic of paths, rather than bicycle lanes, from that era.[2]

Along crowded city streets, however, cyclists had no opportunity to build separate paths and instead opted for well-defined, smoothly paved strips that became the true precursors to modern bicycle lanes. Public works departments usually placed those passages adjacent to curbs and conspicuously delineated them by lasting means, typically via one of two paving materials that gained widespread use during the closing decades of the nineteenth century: vitrified brick or sheet asphalt. By the late 1890s, concrete sufficed as a durable substitute.[3]

Although cyclists complained that the campaign to build good roads seemed to move at glacial speed, engineers made important advances in the science of highway construction before century's end. By then, road builders understood that the surfaces of the broken-rock roads developed by John Loudon McAdam or Thomas Telford succumbed to heavy traffic, and the need for better paving materials had become obvious. By the early 1890s, manufacturers in several states (including Pennsylvania and Ohio) had begun producing large quantities of vitrified paving brick, and when Philadelphia's park commissioners decided to use that material for combined drainage channels and bicycle paths in Fairmount Park in 1897 the city already had used it to pave numerous streets. As brick manufacturing centers multiplied, improving its availability and reducing transportation costs, more cities began using the material. The town of Catskill, New York, on the Hudson River (not far from Albany) became one such center; in 1897, when Albany officials recommended that some streets be paved with brick near the gutters to create paths for bicycles, the city didn't have far to look.[4]

Elsewhere, sheet asphalt became widely used during the 1880s and 1890s. Asphalt rock contains varying amounts of mineral tar or bitumen and is refined by pulverizing, heating, and softening with a petroleum-based flux before being transported to the site still hot, where the mixture is spread on a clean base of cobblestones, brick, or cement. Natural asphalt mined from a great pitch lake in the British West Indies colony of Trinidad fueled the early years of America's paving industry, as did large alluviums of sand-rock in California and Kentucky. Production became concentrated in New York and in other large cities, and the industry's fortunes boomed during this period.[5]

New York's Asphalt Ribbons

In 1895, wheelmen mapped Manhattan's sixty-five miles of asphalt-surfaced streets, hoping that paving would continue northerly to the Harlem River and southerly along Hudson Street to Canal Street. Cyclists reasoned that when the paving had been completed, such smoothly surfaced corridors surely would

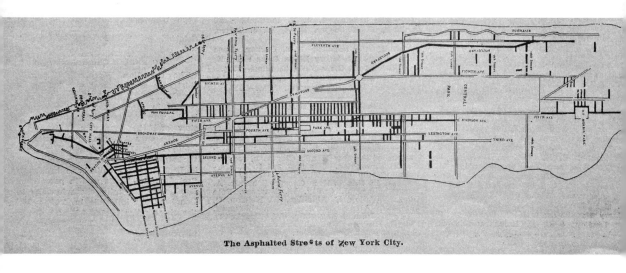

The Asphalted Streets of New York City.

FIGURE 10.2

A map from *Wheel and Cycling Trade Review* (July 5, 1895) showing roughly sixty-five miles of asphalt-surfaced streets in Manhattan in 1895, about the time cyclists began demanding curbside

strips of asphalt on the heavily congested streets in Manhattan's Lower West Side along Hudson Street and as far as its intersection with Canal Street. Courtesy Smithsonian Institution.

encourage thousands of clerks to ride to work rather than rely on the elevated trains or cable trolleys, thus alleviating the city's heavily burdened transit system. By the time of that map's creation, the city's public works departments had installed asphalt strips in scattered locations, in order to facilitate street cleaning, test the material, or to cover recently installed underground utilities. Cyclists quickly recognized the strips' potential as bicycle corridors and believed that the narrow ribbons also would lead to something better: good roads.[6]

During the next half decade, New York wheelmen orchestrated a network of asphalt lanes, focusing on the selection of streets and also plotting the best ways to keep other traffic off. Frustrated by the latter challenge, cyclists debated whether to place the paving strips adjacent to curbs or in street centers, but soon turned instead to promoting legislative controls—with little success. Unfortunately, those same concerns remain unresolved more than a century later, and a column in one Midwestern newspaper, written in 1896 about events in New York, could just as easily have appeared today: "On paved streets a strip at either side set apart for the use of the wheel is to be the rule of the future, and ought to be the rule of the present." Despite such disappointing results, the record of that asphalt strip campaign provides a useful map that shows cyclists' patterns of travel for both commuting and touring and confirms the collaborative efforts by wheelmen and the city's public works department.[7]

Manhattan and Brooklyn bicyclists probably began requesting asphalt strips in 1894 or 1895, but signs of progress may not have emerged until the spring of 1896, when Charles H. Collis, commissioner of public works in Manhattan, announced plans for ribbons of pavement three or four feet wide along the curbs of all streets surfaced with granite blocks. Collis hoped to distribute cycling's routes broadly to alleviate traffic congestion and to provide access to the city's numerous ferries. By early September, laborers had added strips to Hudson Street, beginning at Thirteenth Street and extending southerly on Manhattan's Lower West Side to Chambers Street. Yet by the end of that month, cyclists described the corridors as useless, particularly on weekdays. In addition to the long lines of delivery wagons blocking the strips, street sweepers pushed refuse toward the curbs, and then sprinkling carts made the asphalt slippery.[8]

Optimistically, Collis offered a novel solution for some streets, such as Western Boulevard in lower Manhattan, where trolley tracks had established a central partition. He proposed dividing the roadways on each side of the tracks in half and paving with different colors of asphalt: black adjacent to curbs and assigned to trucks and white next to rails, to be used by light vehicles and bicycles.[9]

City officials probably never experimented with Collis' plan to "stripe the Boulevard," as one reporter pictured it, but cyclists did secure a through corridor to South Ferry, charting a route that eventually coursed along Greenwich, Dey, and Whitehall Streets and concluded with a separate path leading from the ferry to Battery Park. From that point, cyclists could gaze longingly across the harbor and view the Shangri-La of bicycle paths encircling Governor's Island: shaded by trees, cooled by ocean breezes, meticulously built and maintained by military prisoners held at Castle William, and available only to government personnel stationed there—or to their fortunate companions on evening rides.[10]

As the asphalt era unfolded, cyclists and public works officials focused on strategic locations for strips in Manhattan, including 153rd Street leading toward the Harlem River bridge at McComb's Dam and along cross-streets linking principal paved arteries with ferries across both the Hudson and East Rivers. Similar plans developed in Brooklyn, where efforts to connect Bedford Avenue with ferries docking at Broadway resulted in a network of asphalt strips in the vicinity of Division Avenue and Leonard and Berry Streets. Alert to opportunity, owners of the New York and Brooklyn Ferry Company donated $1,000 toward construction of paved lanes from the fountain in Bedford Avenue to the ferry dock. A circuitous route of asphalt strips led cyclists from the Greenpoint district of Brooklyn, linked to Manhattan by the Twenty-Third Street ferry, to Eastern Parkway, which offered easy passage to Prospect Park and the Coney Island paths.[11]

Both the Brooklyn Good Roads Association and the Associated Cycling Clubs of New York joined the campaign, recommending that nine- or ten-foot strips be placed in the middle of streets located in business districts or at other key locations. A few such strips were placed, including segments of both Westchester Avenue and 138th Street in the Bronx, the latter street leading to the Madison Avenue bridge over the Harlem River. On both roads, the paths abutted trolley car tracks, and the experiment proved satisfactory, leading to proposals that strips be placed adjacent to tracks rather than curbs whenever possible. Yet skeptical cyclists predicted that vehicles quickly would usurp those corridors too and suggested that paving selected roads in their entirety would be wiser. Eventually, vehicles also dominated those streets, leaving little room for bicycles.[12]

Van Wyck's Wheelmen

Following consolidation of the city's boroughs on January 1, 1898, newly elected mayor Robert Van Wyck (a wheelman who favored bicycle paths) had captured cycling's votes with promises to construct ribbons of asphalt through Long Island City in Queens, providing easy passage from the upper East River ferries to distant points on Long Island's North and South Shores. He honored those promises after the election by promoting a substantial appropriation to complete the work, but political rivalries and concerns about the asphalt industry's monopoly intervened, and the project stalled after excessive bids for the project prompted Van Wyck to consider opening a city-owned asphalt plant.[13]

However, by January 1899 Van Wyck may have feared criticism from his fellow wheelmen, and that month the city announced a contract for three-foot asphalt strips beginning at the Queens entrance to the Thirty-Fourth Street ferry and extending along each side of Borden and Jackson Avenues to Thomson Avenue; from there, the route connected with macadam-surfaced Hoffman Boulevard (today Queens Boulevard) leading to Newtown, about 2.5 miles in all. Notably, the contract specified placing the strips eight feet from curbstones, and work began in May.[14]

Whether that curb distance proved advantageous remains unclear, as does the precise location of the strips when completed, and legislative efforts to prohibit the drivers of wagons and other vehicles from using the strips were not effective. By December of 1900, dispirited Brooklyn cyclists had all but given up trying to coerce rights-of-way. In addition, heavy use of the strips by industrial vehicles with narrow wheels quickly damaged asphalt surfaces, leading to the use of concrete. Ironically, although the paving of entire streets continued (improved after 1900 by bitulithic pavement that combined crushed rock with asphalt), cycling as a recreational activity steadily declined. By 1904, reporters observed that cyclists rarely used Westchester Avenue in the Bronx, once a heavily traveled route, and the asphalt strips that remained had become footpaths instead.[15]

The miles of asphalt ribbons placed throughout the city boroughs stretched much farther than the examples cited here. In addition, the influence of New York's campaign reached well beyond the city's borders, extending into suburbs such as Mount Vernon and across the Hudson River to Hoboken and Jersey City. Cyclists in major cities such as Philadelphia, Buffalo, Cleveland, and Hartford encouraged similar projects. In preparation for the national meet in 1897, for example, Philadelphia officials added asphalt strips to each side of Broad Street between Vine and Spring Garden Streets. That same year in Cleveland, merchants along poorly paved Woodland Avenue proposed asphalt strips on both sides of

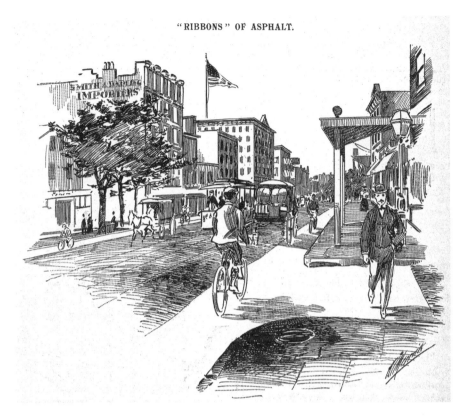

"RIBBONS" OF ASPHALT.

FIGURE 10.3
Arthur Merrick's 1896 sketch of asphalt strips for bicycles, precursors to modern bicycle lanes. New York City cyclists orchestrated a well-planned network of bicycle lanes paved with sheet asphalt during the early years of that industry. *Wheel and Cycling Trade Review* (September 18, 1896). Courtesy Smithsonian Institution.

the street, anticipating that their businesses would benefit if cyclists could be lured from other parts of the city. Wheelmen in smaller cities also petitioned for asphalt path projects, and the campaign reached many other states, including Virginia and Minnesota.[16]

New York's Croton Aqueduct Cycle Path Plan

Among a number of inspired proposals during this period, that for a bicycle path along the crest of the Old Croton Aqueduct in New York City and Westchester County generated immediate enthusiasm among Manhattan wheelmen, promising to eclipse rival Brooklyn's Ocean Parkway paths by almost thirty miles. Brooklyn resident George E. Stackhouse, a sporting editor for the *New York Tribune*, suggested the idea in an article published late in March 1895. Although pedestrians and cyclists had used segments of the corridor informally for many years,

Stackhouse envisioned a serpentine passage through picturesque countryside or along elevated terraces with views of the Hudson River. Best of all, the readymade corridor deviated only forty-three feet in grade over its entire length, averaging an imperceptible thirteen and one-quarter inches per mile. Cyclists needed only to raise modest subscriptions for surface patching or fence removal, and the path could be ready in a matter of days. Calling the passageway a wheelman's paradise, the *Tribune* promised to throw its support behind the project.[17]

Engineered by David Bates Douglass and his successor, John B. Jervis, and built between 1836 and 1842, the Old Croton Aqueduct tapped water from the Croton River watershed, located primarily in New York's Dutchess, Putnam, and West-chester counties. Douglass surveyed a route capable of carrying the city's water by gravity, and Jervis designed both a dam and the brick and masonry arched aqueduct, the latter an enclosed, mostly underground chamber. The aqueduct's meandering course followed the Croton River from the dam to the Hudson River and then continued southerly through Sleepy Hollow, Tarrytown, Irvington, Dobb's Ferry, and Yonkers before turning sharply east to cross the ridge separating the Hudson and East Rivers. Not far north of what is today Van Cortlandt Park, the aqueduct turned south again, and crossed the Harlem River on the High Bridge, a landmark masonry arch structure designed by Jervis and completed in 1848. From there, the aqueduct carried its water to a receiving reservoir at Central Park, enlarged in 1862, and to a distribution reservoir at Murray Hill, where the New York Public Library stands today in Midtown Manhattan. Over the decades, water supply failed to keep pace with the city's population, and engineering of the much larger New Croton Aqueduct began in 1885 via a deep tunnel the entire distance.[18]

Stackhouse's timely article gained endorsements from New York's mayor and from the aqueduct board; even publisher Francis Prial urged wheelmen not to let the proposal smolder. Isaac Potter called the plan a grand idea, wondering why no one had thought of it before, and on the Wednesday following the article's publication he crafted legislation authorizing the grading and paving of the aqueduct's surface for pedestrians and cyclists. His bill gave regulatory authority to the Department of Public Works, but specified that no appropriations of additional land could occur and also stipulated that title to the land would revert to abutting land owners if the aqueduct ceased to be used for water. On Friday of that same week, Assemblyman William Halpin and Senator Jacob Cantor each introduced the bill to the state's Assembly and Senate chambers, respectively.[19]

Ominously, on the Monday following introduction of the legislation, an editorial in the *New York Times* explained the bill's legal and political vulnerability but also offered cyclists hope by identifying sections of the aqueduct bordering city lands where legislation would be unnecessary. Cyclists soon acknowledged the challenges and by mid-April had pared the plan to an eight-mile stretch extending from High Bridge through Yonkers. Potter consoled the city's wheelmen, noting that even that distance exceeded Ocean Parkway's path by 2.5 miles, and with the city's end of the aqueduct secure, cyclists could plot a strategy for completing the remaining distance to Croton Dam. However, Senator Cantor informed supporters on April 29 that property owners in Westchester County strongly opposed the legislation. He recommended amending the bill in order to restrict the path to unimproved or public property and to avoid all private residences.[20]

A committee of wheelmen complied, and both Cantor and Halpin remained optimistic during the coming weeks. They continued to negotiate with property owners, making additional concessions, and early in May the bill passed the Senate and the Assembly. Rebuffing complaints from Westchester County residents, who descended on City Hall to express fears that cyclists would injure children or damage lawns or steal from orchards, New York Mayor William L. Strong approved the legislation on May 21 and sent it to Governor Levi P. Morton for signature. Several weeks elapsed, and on June 14—the day before bicycle clubs in the metropolitan region began gathering for the celebratory parade to Coney Island—telegrams arrived from Albany warning cyclists that the governor had misgivings about the law. Despite a flurry of cables from prominent wheelmen, Morton vetoed the measure the following week, citing concerns about its constitutionality.[21]

During the short span of three months, an imaginative and energetically orchestrated plan for a superb recreational corridor very nearly had succeeded. But for the narrow outlook of politically influential landowners in Westchester County, wheelmen would have established a path to rival the trails being established in the Northeast by cycling's counterparts in the hiking community—one traversing a cultural landscape and the other a mountainous antiquity explored by members of the Appalachian Mountain Club. Equally important, the path would have followed one of the country's most important engineering landmarks. Instead, private interests shattered the plan, resulting in cyclists' furtive use of the aqueduct corridor along certain sections where fences did not bar the way. Although wheelmen revived the proposal several times during the coming years, energy for lobbying gradually waned, and the aqueduct corridor remained a ragged, de facto path for a determined few.[22]

Yet seventy years later, cyclists and hikers ultimately prevailed, and those portions of the aqueduct beyond New York's city limits became part of Old Croton Aqueduct State Historic Park, created in 1968 after the aqueduct ceased supplying water (first to New Yorkers in 1955 and then to several Westchester communities a decade later). Today, the trail park extends for twenty-six miles along the aqueduct, which is now a National Historic Landmark and a National Historic Engineering Landmark.[23]

Although attempts to convert the corridor to bicycle use during the spring of 1895 lasted for such a short period, the episode remains valuable to cycling history as a prologue to countless well-intentioned plans for other trails developed after World War II, many of which faced barriers similarly rooted in self-interest.

Lamentably, such conflicts endure, and in any story of those struggles (whether successes or failures) the Croton Aqueduct Cycle Path remains important.

Trolley Trails

About a month after Morton's 1895 veto, Stackhouse's idea led to another short-lived plan for an aqueduct bicycle path, one that would extend twenty-three miles from Brooklyn's Ridgewood Reservoir (located near the boundary of Brooklyn and Queens) east to Massapequa Reservoir in Nassau County. To reach the open country of South Shore Long Island, Brooklyn's cyclists often traveled along well-surfaced Merrick Road, but before reaching that highway wheelmen negotiated a maze of crowded city streets, and the aqueduct offered an enticing alternative. However, Albert Angell opposed the scheme as a costly and unnecessary venture because of the aqueduct's general proximity to Merrick Road. Angell believed that limited funds could be spent more productively along other corridors, and the idea never gained momentum among Brooklyn's cyclists.[24]

Brooklyn Aqueduct Trolley-Bicycle Plan

All the while, owners of Brooklyn's trolley companies had been observing the city's aqueduct debates. In January 1896, financial backers of a proposed electric line along Brooklyn's aqueduct as far as Wantagh (a few miles west of Massapequa) offered to build and maintain twenty-foot bicycle paths on each side of its tracks at no cost to cyclists, in return for cycling's endorsement of the project. Although the venture never advanced much beyond discussion, the proposal addressed the potential conflict created when the two modes of transportation competed on crowded city streets. Cyclists suffered the most, but in all fairness to the streetcar companies, wheelmen who used the cars for drafting or pacing or who rode along the smooth surfaces between two sets of tracks became interlopers and fostered conflict. Companies also viewed bicycles as a source of lost revenue, and thus each side had reasons to distrust the other. Yet the Brooklyn proposition signaled a shifting outlook and seems to have encouraged some trolley companies to favor rather than oppose cycling.[25]

Greenville and Coxsackie Path

In the Hudson River valley, the Western Engineering & Construction Company won a contract to build an electric line between Greenville and Coxsackie and took notice of New York's sidepath campaign. The firm advertised its officers as wheelmen and proved it in 1900 by building a bicycle path adjoining the Coxsackie route at no cost to cyclists, also offering to carry the luggage of travelers who arrived from New York by boat and then wheeled to towns along the trolley line. The experiment led to an offer to build paths along all electric lines for which the company obtained future contracts, and the company's officers asked bicycle dealers and riders to alert the firm about potential projects, in order to draw their "company to the favorable attention of the proper authorities."[26]

Akron and Barbarton Path
Still other trolley companies reasoned that cyclists traveling far enough in one direction might prefer returning to the point of origin by trolley. The Northern Ohio Traction Company, which operated an extensive system of interurban lines in the vicinity of Cleveland and Akron, tested that theory and agreed to construct a substantial, one-hundred-foot-wide boulevard between Akron and Barbarton, with double trolley tracks in the center, flanked on each side by rows of trees, drives, sidewalks, and bicycle paths.[27]

Electrified Parkways
By collaborating, the two sides also set the stage for thoughtful discussion about the best ways to design corridors that combined bicycles and trolleys. When the Metropolitan Park Commission retained the Olmsted firm to assist with the planning of large reservations of land for public parks in Boston's sub-urbs, the firm proposed a system of parkways to connect those areas with the city proper. Laudably, they designed the corridors not just with footpaths and drives for carriages but also with separate passageways for trolleys, making the outlying parks accessible to the city's wage earners. The design for Blue Hills Parkway is illustrative, accommodating two roadways separated by an ample grass median for the exclusive use of electric cars; sidewalks flanked the outer edges of each roadway, and the wider of the two roads served principally carriages (figure 0.4).[28]

By recognizing the need for separate passageways for trolleys, the firm transformed parkway designs that emphasized the relationships between scenery and pleasure travel exclusively into corridors that accommodated different modes of transportation moving at different speeds. John Olmsted acknowledged as much in 1915 by asserting that the pleasure of traveling along scenic corridors ought to be made available to people who used streetcars, whether for business or pleasure, and he offered designs for electrified parkways that retained scenic quality, relying on depressions or overpasses to eliminate grade crossings; reduced the rise of slopes adjacent to the railroad as a way to introduce attractive plantings; and added vine-clad fences to screen the tracks in key locations. He also recognized the need to provide for bicycles, but left designs unfinished.[29]

Successfully integrating separate corridors for electrified rail, bicycles, and pedestrians into scenic passageways remains a challenging topic for today's urban designers. Those three methods of travel are not inherently incompatible and if carefully separated can be placed compactly into a single, linear park that is also a transportation corridor, with only moderate sacrifice to the scenic quality available to each mode of travel. At the height of cycling's popularity more than a century ago, landscape architects nearly succeeded in offering such a plan, and the challenge today is to complete the task by learning how to design expansive transportation corridors that exclude automobiles.

Great Falls Bicycle Paths

By contrast to their counterparts in New York City, cyclists in Washington, D.C., encountered neither private factions, nor petty fears, nor political faltering during their campaign to build several short bicycle paths on War Department lands traversed by the Washington Aqueduct. Built between 1853 and 1863 and designed chiefly by engineer Montgomery Meigs, the subsurface engineering landmark still carries water from a dam at the Potomac River's Great Falls, about seventeen miles northwest of the city, to the Dalecarlia Reservoir, a receiving basin straddling the Maryland and District of Columbia border, and from there to a distributing reservoir in Georgetown. The government also built Conduit Road adjacent to the aqueduct to aid inspection, but the corridor soon became a popular carriage and cycling drive bordered by private clubs and inns. A particularly steep grade just beyond the Angler's Clubhouse proved challenging, and ideas for a bicycle path began to circulate in 1895, centering on a two-mile shortcut to the falls along the aqueduct itself, a route that crossed rugged but level and scenic terrain. Cyclists presumed that the government would own and maintain the path, which would also benefit waterworks employees.[30]

Times-Wheelman Path

With support from the *Washington Times* (whose editors claimed credit for suggesting the plan and called the project the Times-Wheelmen Path), an obliging government engineer, Captain David D. Gaillard, studied the route during the summer of 1896, pronounced the plan practicable, and estimated costs. As conceived, the nine-foot-wide path would diverge from Conduit Road at the clubhouse and follow the aqueduct for more than a mile, reaching a point overlooking the river near Lock 16 on the Chesapeake and Ohio Canal, roughly a half mile downriver from the falls. There, rocky bluffs stood in the path's way, and Gaillard suggested a forty-foot tunnel along one section of the course—a novelty for path building of that era. Unfortunately, the *Times'* estimates of $3,000 had been too optimistic, and Gaillard's tabulations reached a staggering $10,000.[31]

Unfazed by the estimates and dismissive of doubting editorials by rival *Washington Star*, *Times* editors argued that the path's benefits to Washingtonians would far surpass its costs. The paper launched a subscription list, and by early August the LAW had endorsed the campaign, established a finance committee, and proffered fifty dollars to the cause. Local bicycle dealers created a lamp oil fund, encouraging cyclists to deposit a nickel when filling lanterns with fuel; shop owners donated bicycles as prizes; and promoters discussed plans for a great bicycle carnival. Pursuing a tangent strategy, cyclists commissioned by the War Department assisted Captain Gaillard in apprehending speeding wheelmen on

Conduit Road—a federal offense. Sensibly, the *Times* reasoned that if ten thousand of the city's forty thousand cyclists each contributed one dollar, then the path could be completed by October. Yet despite near-unanimity among cyclists, favorable outlook toward the path did not translate into a sizable treasury; by summer's end, cyclists had begun exploring other options. A bold scheme to lobby Congress for a matching appropriation of $5,000 temporarily boosted spirits, but club delegates soon turned to more realistic plans to erect gates and charge tolls.[32]

Great Falls Cycle Path Association

Whether from hesitancy by the War Department or due to the considerable costs, the project stalled for two years. Eventually, new promoters formed the Great Falls Cycle Path Association, appointing a special committee that included Alphonse Girouard, Charles Wood, and Dr. Walter W. Alleger. Efforts to build the path revived, funding increased, and during the early spring of 1899 the project at last moved forward. At a meeting late in June, Girouard reported that work had begun earlier that month and that the six-foot-wide corridor marked a continuation of Conduit Road, beginning at the Angler's Club and extending for three miles. Cyclists embarked on a celebratory tour on July 4, halting at marshes near Lock 16, and construction continued into the fall. Late in October, two important contributors toured the completed path and extolled its scenery: George Putnam (the librarian of Congress) and Kirk Munroe.[33]

Adding to that year's acclaim, the Great Falls Cycle Path Association built a second bicycle path bypassing the Conduit Road's climb over Stoney and Dalecarlia hills near the Dalecarlia Reservoir. Early in August 1899, the association had organized a fundraising excursion aboard the paddlewheel steamer Charles Macalester, voyaging upriver to Marshall Hall, the site of an early eighteenth-century plantation that entrepreneurs had converted to an amusement park. With proceeds from that clamorous event in hand, association members acquired the necessary rights-of-way and began work early in October, anticipating a Thanksgiving Day tour to Great Falls.[34]

Bicycle Bridges

Proposals for combining trolleys and bicycles along a single thoroughfare addressed two important concerns: safety and riding surfaces. Unfortunately, such schemes did little to alleviate crowded and dangerous conditions on city streets, where designating separate passageways for bicycles became difficult. Those perilous conditions were especially acute on major bridges, where hordes of commuters converged.

The epic quest for a bicycle path on the landmark Brooklyn Bridge is especially important and is comparable to the Old Croton Aqueduct path proposal in many ways: city newspapers championed both projects; various bicycle clubs and associations joined forces to present strong political fronts; success appeared to be within grasp and the outcome certain; and for each, cyclists countered initial setbacks with persistence during a period lasting several years. Both also ended in failure, but for different reasons. Unlike the Croton project, the Brooklyn Bridge proposal faced little public opposition; instead, the bridge's engineers decreed that a path could not be designed to avoid crowding at the New York approach.

The Battle of Brooklyn Bridge

For a number of years, New York and Brooklyn cyclists had suffered the bridge's dangerous conditions during the rush of early morning and late afternoon traffic. However, plans during the mid-1890s to add trolleys to the roadways triggered special alarm. In February 1896, editors of the *New York World* demanded a path, suggesting two possible designs: the first supported by a superstructure over the roadway from one end of the bridge to the other and the second resting on an existing trestle-like framework above the cable car tracks. The *Brooklyn Eagle* joined the *World*'s cause, and in the spring of 1897 four of the metropolitan region's cycling organizations (the Brooklyn Good Roads Association; the League of American Wheelmen, New York Division; the Associated Cycling Clubs of New York; and the Associated Cycling Clubs of Long Island) formed a joint committee to negotiate with William Berri, president of the bridge's board of trustees, and Charles C. Martin, its chief engineer.[35]

Both Berri and Martin agreed that a separate bicycle path would be necessary once trolleys began using the bridge. The project quickly generated enthusiasm from the cycling community, leading to a variety of design proposals submitted that spring, including one using elevators. During a conference with cyclists late in May, Berri and Martin agreed to build a path, favoring a platform above the existing cable car trestle that avoided the cost of building a new superstructure, and the *World* proclaimed victory. From the Brooklyn side, the path would begin at High Street and climb on a trestle above the approach plaza, joining the existing trestle above the cable car tracks. From there, cyclists would travel on a plank surface (twelve-feet wide with railings) to the Manhattan side (where the path veered to the south on another trestle), down a gradual grade to City Hall Park, and very nearly to the *World's* doorstep on Park Row. After professing support for bicycles, both Berri and Martin invited wheelmen to suggest creative alternatives to the difficult problem of crowded approaches, particularly in Manhattan.[36]

La Manna Plan By November 1897, the joint committee had accepted assistance from an engineer and wheelman, Eugene La Manna. Addressing concerns about the Manhattan approach, he placed the path on a light trestle above Park Row, well beyond the bridge, where cyclists would descend gradually to Mail Street at the base of City Hall Park. He also widened the path at the approaches and reduced the path's overall grade as much as possible. Late that month at a special hearing, committee members offered La Manna's schematic drawings to the

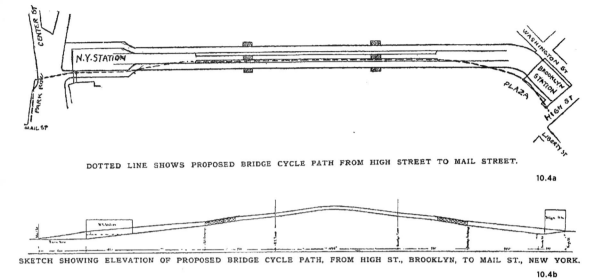

DOTTED LINE SHOWS PROPOSED BRIDGE CYCLE PATH FROM HIGH STREET TO MAIL STREET.

10.4a

SKETCH SHOWING ELEVATION OF PROPOSED BRIDGE CYCLE PATH, FROM HIGH ST., BROOKLYN, TO MAIL ST., NEW YORK.

10.4b

FIGURE 10.4a, b
Engineer Eugene La Manna's plan for a bicycle path across the
Brooklyn Bridge in 1897. From *Brooklyn Daily Eagle* (November
10, 1897). Courtesy Brooklyn Public Library, Brooklyn Collection.

bridge trustees, strategically emphasizing that the trustees needed only to construct that part of the path physically occupying the bridge and that cyclists would build the approach corridors above the streets in lower Manhattan. As an alternative, cyclists also suggested modifications to the pedestrian promenade. The hearing concluded amicably, with the understanding that the proposal would be referred to the chief engineer for a report on its feasibility.[37]

Hazardous Approach Unfortunately, the strategy misfired, and La Manna's plan presented Martin with an avenue of escape. Although the plan seemed practicable, Martin explained that the board had no jurisdiction over any structures beyond the bridge and thus would be foolish to approve a path on the crossing until permission from city authorities had been obtained. Still, cyclists continued to voice optimism, and in January 1898 the committee met with Berri's successor, Commissioner of Bridges John L. Shea, who also professed strong support for the project, even to the point of recommending elevators. During the months following that meeting, Shea and Martin undoubtedly discussed the matter, because hints of conflict between the two men surfaced. Martin ultimately issued a terse report to Shea in December of 1898, stating simply that his engineers had found no satisfactory solution for the New York approach.[38]

If cyclists' optimism for the bridge path had dimmed by the close of 1898, their determination hardly wavered, and agitation renewed during the spring of the following year, buoyed by a resolution from the city's board of aldermen in early May calling for an ordinance requiring a path. A few weeks before, a cyclist had suffered ghastly injuries when he fell beneath a trolley, and the accident may have influenced that vote. Later that month, Shea once again agreed to meet with members of the joint committee, hoping to narrow discussion to two choices: either obtaining city authority to build over Park Row and into City Hall Park, as recommended by La Manna, or installing elevators. In a letter to the Brooklyn Good Roads Association that month, Shea acknowledged that the problem had "overpowered the engineers"—hardly flattering to his engineering staff. Cyclists replied by urging Shea to hire outside talent. Discussions that May also led to separate schemes for access to the bridge in Manhattan via stairways, but in a report that summer containing a tone of stubborn finality, Martin rejected those proposals, characterizing the obstacles to the path as insurmountable. Before summer's end, two cyclists would die following accidents involving trolley cars.[39]

Committee of One Hundred Wheelmen responded to Martin's assessment with anger, and the joint committee passed a harshly worded resolution that called Martin and the bridge's engineering staff incompetent and requested their resignations. The committee also voted to seek state legislation requiring the path, and by November those efforts had resulted in a newly formed organization, the Committee of One Hundred.[40]

Meanwhile, another problem had developed. Sometime between their May meeting with Shea and the subsequent report by Martin, some members of the joint committee had consulted two other experienced engineers and had agreed to abide by Martin's final report. A series of blunt communications between the committee's two factions aired in the *Brooklyn Eagle*, weakening the campaign's momentum. Still, the Committee of One Hundred pressed on, gaining a temporary boost in December 1899, when the Brooklyn Good Roads Association elected James D. Bell as president. In April of that year, New York's mayor fortuitously had appointed Bell as a commissioner for the Williamsburg Bridge, the second of the East River's landmark crossings and by then under construction. Bell urged his Brooklyn confederates to continue their fight for a path on the Brooklyn Bridge, but he cautioned that other improvements needed attention as well. Legislative initiatives eventually stalled, however, and the broader campaign succumbed to the weight of inertia.[41]

Engineering Initiative Today, without the ability to stand on the bridge and observe traffic conditions and bridge features exactly as they existed in 1899, evaluating details of the various path proposals and their true practicality is difficult. Without doubt, congestion on the bridge and its approaches—especially in Manhattan—posed problems that directly affected the safety of people who used the crossing.

La Manna's plan best addressed the bridge's crowded conditions but also raised issues about the visual effect of an elevated corridor near Park Row and City Hall Park. La Manna did not ignore those concerns but argued that public safety became paramount. In addition, he contended that the lightly structured path with a sweeping curve onto the bridge would be much more appealing than the city's existing elevated railroads. Moreover, the New York approach already had become a teeming warren of trolley tracks, ramps, stairs, elevated tracks and platforms, and a large, enclosed elevated terminal—all within a stone's throw of City Hall and a number of other architectural landmarks. Whether adding another structure to that vibrant medley of human ingenuity would have caused special alarm is doubtful. More likely, it would have fit quite easily, at least in terms of aesthetic quality.[42]

Reconciling Charles Martin's avowed support for wheelmen's interests with his inability or reluctance to find a solution becomes especially challenging. On the one hand, cyclists' claims of incompetence can be dismissed as exasperated venting. Martin had been one of the lead engineers in the building of Prospect Park and had worked on the Brooklyn Bridge almost from its inception, first as an assistant to John Roebling and, following his death, as second-in-command under Washington Roebling, responsible initially for materials and labor. He remained loyal to the younger Roebling during a period late in the building of the bridge during which several trustees doubted Roebling's competence to remain as chief engineer. From Washington Roebling, Martin also may have learned to distrust the meddling by politicians in matters of bridge engineering and to trust his own judgment. He became chief engineer in 1883, following Roebling's formal resignation once the bridge opened.[43]

Yet Martin's reasons for rejecting cyclists' proposals warrant closer scrutiny. From one point of view, Martin may have been a guardian of the bridge's structural and functional integrity, and if he and his engineering staff believed that by the mid-1890s the bridge had reached or exceeded its full capacity at the busiest times of day, then they were probably close to the truth. However, whether a stubborn concern for protecting his engineering office from outside interference also became a factor, causing Martin to turn his back on potential solutions, must also be considered. One proposal in particular—that from the *Brooklyn Eagle*— casts doubt on Martin's objectivity. The *Eagle*'s editors reasoned that the promenade could be divided among cyclists and pedestrians for short distances at each end of the bridge before cyclists switched to a separate path above the cable cars. During that approach, cyclists would walk their bicycles along a narrowly defined portion of the promenade.

With regard to the concerns about increased congestion at the New York approach, Martin had two choices: work with city authorities and cyclists to resolve what amounted to a problem of traffic control or retreat behind the boundaries of his office's jurisdiction and proclaim an inability to find solutions. By choosing the latter, he failed to convince cyclists either that he truly supported their cause or that the obstacles were unsolvable.

One more comparison is needed regarding the proposals for bicycle paths across the Brooklyn Bridge and along the Croton Aqueduct. Both are historic landmarks that today are also well-traveled cycling corridors. In September 1970, almost seventy-five years after the *New York World* had rashly declared victory for cycling's path builders, Mayor John Lindsay began urging New Yorkers to look more closely at the bicycle as an alternative means of transportation, and he joined nearly one thousand cyclists who pedaled down Fifth Avenue to demonstrate the need for special bicycle lanes on city streets. In the spring of the following year, he approved an experimental bicycle path on the Brooklyn Bridge, and workers installed ramps on the promenade, dividing the deck with stripes of white paint and paying tribute to the wheelmen of 1896 who had believed in the path's feasibility.[44]

Williamsburg Bridge

Cyclists did not fight the battle of Brooklyn Bridge in vain. When the Williamsburg Bridge opened in 1903, linking the Lower East Side at Delancey Street with the Williamsburg neighborhood of Brooklyn, the crossing became one of the world's most important bridges to include a bicycle path as part of its final design. The origins of that path owe much to the campaign waged on the Brooklyn Bridge and probably also to bridge commissioner James Bell and his Brooklyn Good Roads Association.[45]

Designed principally by engineer Leffert L. Buck, with minor ornamental modifications by New York Commissioner of Bridges Gustav Lindenthal and architect Henry Hornbostel after 1902, the crossing helped to alleviate the intolerable congestion on the Brooklyn Bridge, and it also provided a means for immigrants living in the shabby tenements of Manhattan to escape to Brooklyn and its burgeoning industries. When completed, the bridge became the world's longest suspension bridge, exceeding the span of the Brooklyn Bridge by fewer than five feet.

Construction of the tower footings began in 1896, and the corridors for various modes of transportation evolved as work progressed. Although special paths for bicycles surfaced during early stages of planning, their locations kept changing, alternately arousing either cheer or anxiety among skeptical wheelmen. By the summer of 1896, plans included two carriage ways, six railroad tracks (two for the city's elevated railroads), two pedestrian walks, and two bicycle paths. Two years later, commissioners reassured wary members of the Associated Cycling Clubs of Long Island that the bridge would include a path, located either above the trolley tracks or as part of the roadways on each side of the bridge. However, by summer's end the path's location had moved to become part of a single central promenade, reducing the portion for pedestrians from twenty-feet to twelve feet. By October of 1899, plans and specifications had changed again, calling for two seven-foot paths, one each for cyclists traveling in opposite directions.[46]

In May 1900, Buck offered the public its first glimpse of plans, but newspaper illustrations amounted to incomplete sketches. At the New York entrance, a

FIGURE 10.5

When the Williamsburg Bridge opened in 1903, the crossing became the world's longest suspension bridge and possibly the first major bridge to include a bicycle path as part of its final design. Credit for the path belongs to New York and Brooklyn cyclists who fought valiantly but unsuccessfully for a bicycle path across the Brooklyn Bridge. The two-tiered approach decks shown in this illustration from *Scientific American* (July 18, 1903), one for bicycles and one for pedestrians, may not have been completed as designed, and bicycles and pedestrians may have shared a single deck, as they do today from the Manhattan side. Courtesy University of Vermont libraries.

three-story superstructure dominated the bridge's central corridor, flanked on each side by sets of trolley tracks and by vehicular drives for automobiles as well as carriages, thus adding to the bridge's significance as one of the first to be engineered for both cars and bicycles. The central frame divided traffic moving in opposite directions, both within and without its structure. At the bridge approaches, a foot walk occupied the lowest level of that frame, with the bicycle path above it as the two rose and approached the elevated railroad on the third level. An accompanying description explained that the bicycle path would be accessible via steps and an inclined plane and that both pedestrian and bicycle paths climbed steadily, but at slightly different grades. Before the three travel ways passed through the towers, the foot and bicycle paths would achieve the same level as the elevated railroad, and there the paths would diverge, with westbound cyclists and pedestrians moving to the north of the railroad along a divided platform and eastbound cyclists and pedestrians to the south. At that point, the cycling path would narrow to seven feet.[47]

Drawings published during the summer of 1903, about five months before city officials formally opened the bridge's southern roadway to travel, were more complete. Those illustrations depicted the New York side and showed a similar central superstructure for the elevated railroad, but a sloping deck used by cyclists sheltered the four sets of trolley tracks flanking that framework (two on each side), at a height sufficient to clear the trolley car roofs. The pedestrian path was in the identical location shown on the 1900 drawings, and after reaching the same level as the bicycle path near the anchorage piers it merged with that latter path and occupied the deck's inner lanes on both sides of the elevated railroad's superstructure; bicyclists and pedestrians were to be separated by an iron rail. Before reaching the anchorage, roughly to the point where the sectional drawing of the elevated railroad superstructure begins, the width of the deck for bicycles corresponded to the width of that central structure, and the trolley lines were not sheltered by a platform. However, the drawings failed to show the entire approaches or the means by which cyclists gained access to the path.[48]

The text accompanying the illustration is only partially helpful, explaining that surface cars, street vehicle traffic, heavy and light automobiles, bicycles, and pedestrians would enter the bridge approach at street grade, but bicycles would approach the anchorage piers on a central platform located beneath the elevated structure and above the footpath. Although the height of the elevated cars was substantially greater than that of the trolley deck near the anchorage piers, the steep grade of the bridge would force the trolley tracks and elevated railroad (with its separate structure) to reach nearly a common level between the towers, because the elevated railroad climbed less steeply. Thus, at mid-span the platform for bicyclists and pedestrians would be considerably higher than the deck of the elevated road.

An accurate description of the bicycle path's original 1903 plan becomes important for several reasons. Although the design for the crucial approaches

FIGURE 10.6
Stereoview of the Williamsburg Bridge, 1905.

is not shown, and although the path entrances may not have been completed according to the final plans, at the very least the design provides a vantage point from which the battle over the Brooklyn Bridge path can be assessed with greater clarity. By creating spacious plazas at each approach for the Williamsburg Bridge, especially on the Brooklyn side, engineers alleviated many of the entanglements occurring at the entrances to the Brooklyn Bridge, and the importance of those locations for both bicycles and pedestrians becomes very clear on major bridge projects. In addition, the methods by which engineers separated pedestrians and bicyclists at those entrances and along the corridors flanking the elevated road establish a valuable starting point in the history of bridges designed to accommodate bicycles.

The Williamsburg Bridge also illustrates how easily plans for bicycle paths can be pushed aside. Several months before the bridge opened, bridge officials conceded that they were considering fanciful plans to build a moving sidewalk across the bridge for the city's rapid transit system. In October 1903, Chief Engineer William Parsons alarmed cyclists by acknowledging that such a platform would be feasible and that the bicycle path offered the only available space on the bridge. The Associated Cycling Clubs of New York responded with a resolution of protest and began enlisting support from the New York Motorcycle Club, the Century Road Club, former bridge commissioner James Bell, and the United Cycle Clubs of Greater New York. Suspecting that city officials viewed bicycles as out of fashion, cyclists also urged a demonstration at the bridge opening later that year, but they may have been mollified by a report from Lindenthal, which recommended that a pair of tracks on the bridge's southern side be used for the sidewalk instead. Yet when the bridge's southern roadway opened on December 21, the bicycle path remained unfinished, and when the pedestrian path opened without ceremony on April 23, 1904, newspaper accounts made little mention of bicycles.[49]

Worse still, less than a week later the engineering firm hired to design the moving sidewalk submitted their report and placed the structure almost entirely on the bicycle path. Cyclists began drawing battle lines, enlisted political backing to "Block the Path Grab," and demanded a hearing before the transit commission. In a series of publicized exchanges that followed (eerily reminiscent of the Brooklyn Bridge skirmishes), bridge officials reassured cyclists. This time, however, those promises proved to be more reliable, and the Williamsburg Bridge bicycle path survived the episode, most likely because engineers viewed the sidewalk scheme as impractical.[50]

Yet as workers slowly completed the bridge and as cyclists declined in numbers, interest in the bicycle path faded. Photographs of the bridge during its first decades seldom show bicycles, and when commissioners first opened the bridge to pedestrians in 1904 the platform may not have included a rail dividing the two travel ways. The captions for photographs from 1916 describe that platform as a recreation deck, and no dividing rail is visible. Yet if the bicycle path remained dormant for several decades, then the strength of its forgotten design did not lessen; as cycling regained popularity, bridge officials rediscovered the plan's latent value and reestablished the path.[51]

After many years of use by bicyclists and pedestrians, the city decided to rehabilitate the decks used by both pedestrians and bicyclists, and work continued between 2000 and 2005. Today, cyclists travel the north corridor and pedestrians stay to the south, although wider travel lanes for automobiles have reduced the width of approaches. On the New York side, bicycles and pedestrians share a single, divided corridor that gradually climbs to the point of the anchor piers, where the bicycle path moves to the north side. On the Brooklyn side, both pedestrian and bicycle corridors flank the roadways.[52]

Elevating the Bicycle

Eugene La Manna's thwarted plans for an elevated bicycle path on the Brooklyn Bridge and Leffert Buck's design for an elevated cycle corridor across the Williamsburg Bridge were not the only proposals for placing the bicycle at a comfortably safe height above street traffic. In 1901, for example, financial backers of the Pan-American Exposition in Buffalo envisioned an elevated bicycle path encircling the fair, accessible via elevators and giving wheelmen and wheelwomen a chance to view the entire grounds. New York had its fair share of such schemes, and that city's elevated railroads gave cyclists a clear vision of how an equally lofty bicycle network might appear, blessedly free from obstruction. The same can be said for cyclists in other major cities, and once cycling's many journals began publicizing these tantalizing ideas, wheelmen elsewhere embarked on similar daydreams.[53]

Bicycle "L"

New York wheelmen began talking about an elevated path at least as early as the summer of 1895, when Manhattan cyclist Thomas J. Burton suggested a route from Chambers Street to Fifty-Ninth Street, using Hudson Street and then Eighth Avenue to reach Central Park. If that experiment proved successful, then the corridor could be extended along the full length of Manhattan. Burton placed the twelve-foot-high path between the tracks of Eighth Avenue streetcars, and he used single stilts to support a twelve-foot-wide wooden deck. Although everskeptical Frances Prial soon added elevated paths to his list of cycling's misguided exuberances, by the spring of 1896 the Associated Cycling Clubs of New York had endorsed the scheme enthusiastically, calling it a necessity.[54]

Triple "L"

The association also considered a second, more daring plan to create a threetiered transit corridor. During the early 1890s, Jay Gould—controlling owner of the Manhattan Railway Company and its profitable elevated railroads—had introduced a double-deck design, with express trains running on the upper level. Although Gould died in 1892, his son George succeeded him and continued efforts to build two-tiered lines, aided by financier Russell Sage and by a prominent citizen of Washington Heights, Lawson N. Fuller. During this period, Fuller had been promoting an extension of the elevated line north along Tenth Avenue, and when wheelmen began discussing an elevated road built exclusively for bicycles, he sensed a golden opportunity. Fuller proposed that Gould modify the design for a double-deck line by adding a third tier for bicycles that would be wide enough for two nine- or ten-foot paths separated by a railing with openings every quarter mile, surfaced with pine floor boards (as smooth as a dance floor), and protected by a five-foot rail in case cyclists fell (or became dizzy from the height). Elevators at one-mile intervals would provide access, and the line would extend from the Battery to Yonkers. The one-way, three-cent fare would pay for the additional costs of construction and would add considerably to the company's coffers; cyclists on a round-trip would pay five cents.[55]

In one masterful stroke, Fuller had erased cyclists' two principal concerns—the cost of construction and opposition from the railroad's owners; identified a new and potentially lucrative source of company revenue—quite literally out of thin air; harnessed whatever political weight cyclists might throw behind the company's quest for longer routes; reduced crowding on the elevated lines by shifting some passengers to bicycles; improved the health of those riders; and practically solved the city's rapid transit problem, at least in theory. Rolling high in the air above streets, cyclists could add delightful views of the city to their traveling experiences.

Not even Frank Prial could resist giving his imagination lighter rein. Although he called the scheme an air castle and believed its prospects amounted to naught, his account of Fuller's scheme nevertheless gave journal readers just enough leeway to indulge in wishful thinking—before he pulled them down to earth with concerns about cyclists being roasted by steam engines or blinded by cinders.[56]

To Fuller's likely dismay, and for reasons that remain unclear, Gould and Sage declined to forge an alliance with cyclists. Concern for the well-being of riders may have been a factor, at least among wheelmen. The hot steam, smoke, sparks, and cinders rising around cyclists and fanned by moving air would have been dangerous, especially for women in skirts, with soot merely an added annoyance. Once the elevated railroads became electrified, those problems would have been replaced by concerns about power transmission. More likely, the financial risks of expanding the company's elevated lines were too great during a period when city officials were considering a publicly owned subway system. A similar scheme for only a two-tiered elevated line in Brooklyn—touted as a way for scorchers to elude that city's bicycle police and prompting visions of high-speed chases above city streets—quietly disappeared as well.[57]

Buckley Bikeway

Similar to the proposals for bicycle paths along the Croton Aqueduct and across the Brooklyn Bridge, interest in a Manhattan bicycle "L" resurfaced after 1960, albeit from a surprising source. During the 1965 mayoral contest, which led to the election of John Lindsay and to bicycle lanes on the Brooklyn Bridge, the city's transportation system became an important issue for voters. Lindsay, a Republican, captured enough of the liberal votes from Democratic constituencies represented by Abraham Beame to defeat both Beame and Conservative Party candidate William F. Buckley Jr., who offered a comprehensive, multifaceted program for addressing the city's traffic concerns; reviving and expanding the nineteenth-century schemes for elevated bicycle toll paths was part of his imaginative strategy.

Buckley's Bikeway, as it became known, stood twenty-feet high and twenty-feet wide on Manhattan's East Side, stretching up and down both sides of Second Avenue for almost the entire length of that corridor, from 125th Street at the Triborough Bridge to First Street. Not stopping there, Buckley also proposed cross-town spurs at 125th, Ninety-First, Fifty-Sixth, Thirty-Fifth, Twelfth, and Sixth streets. Ramps at every block would provide a means of access and egress, and turnouts would give cyclists enough space to park and lock their bicycles. Adding to convenience, cyclists could shift to crossways built at subway stops. Buckley predicted that a fifteen-cent toll would retire the $14 million cost over a period of ten years, a reasonable outlay. Yet he may have overlooked a matter of vital

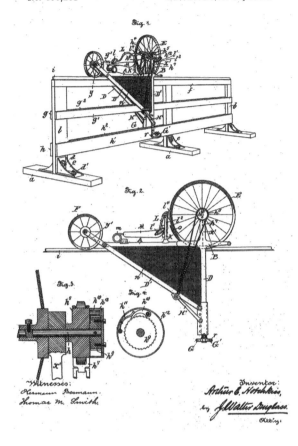

A. E. HOTCHKISS.
VEHICLE.

No. 488,201   Patented Dec. 20, 1892.

FIGURE 10.7
Inventor Arthur Hotckiss patented this wheeled apparatus—part bridge, part bicycle, and part railroad—and developed an experimental commuter corridor between Mount Holly and Smithville, New Jersey. Patent drawing courtesy United States Patent Office and the University of Vermont libraries.

concern: Would cyclists have feared the loss of their rights to use city streets and have pointed to the Liberty Bill of 1887?[58]

Hotchkiss Bicycle Railroads

New Yorkers wheeling to Philadelphia in 1893 could take an eighteen-mile detour at Trenton, traveling south toward Mount Holly and Smithville to inspect one of the era's novel bicycle roads, newly built. Part elevated bicycle path, part bicycle bridge, and part railroad, the Mount Holly and Smithville Bicycle Railway carried workers back and forth between the two communities on a monorail track. However, commuters provided the power, propelling themselves by sitting astride mechanized, wheeled frames that straddled an inverted T rail and its supporting structure, which resembled a post-and-plank fence.

Riders engaged elongated pedals to drive a fixed, grooved front wheel connected to the pedal shaft by two nearly vertical chains, one for each pedal. The pedals functioned as treadles, requiring a pumping motion, and the smaller rear wheel (also grooved) provided traction; a set of small guide wheels at the base of the frame turned horizontally along a flange, preventing derailments. Handlebars provided stability but did not control the wheels in any way, and riders braked by pushing the handlebars against the wheels; to reverse direction, riders could pedal onto turntables at each end of the line.[59]

Inventor Arthur Hotchkiss from Cheshire, Connecticut, patented this unusual apparatus in December 1892, but by then he had constructed a successful prototype in partnership with the H. B. Smith Machine Company in Smithville, the manufacturer of Star high-wheel bicycles. A number of the company's shop workers lived in Mount Holly, an inconvenient two miles away by foot and longer by trolley. However, undeveloped lowlands bordering Rancocas Creek provided a direct route between the two towns and offered Hotchkiss the perfect chance to display his invention. In January 1892, he and several associates formed the company and began a demonstration project. Construction of the nearly two-mile track advanced haltingly during the spring and summer of 1892, but the railroad began operating early in September of that year, just in time for Burlington County's Great Mount Holly Fair.[60]

Thousands of fairgoers who paid a ten-cent toll made the enterprise an overnight financial success. Double tracks extended for about a half mile from the Mount Holly depot, and riders could travel the remaining distance to Smithville on a single track. Buoyed by the railroad's profits and envisioning a nationwide industry of bicycle railroads, Hotchkiss erected an exhibit at Chicago's Columbian Exposition the following year, at which the company displayed two designs. The first demonstrated the system used at Smithville, but the second employed overhead steel rails with bicycles suspended by pulleys. Initial interest in both inventions as amusements soon faded, however, and Hotchkiss scrapped plans to build several railways in New Jersey and Pennsylvania amusement parks.[61]

As one of the country's early examples of a bicycle commuter corridor, the Mount Holly-Smithville railroad attained slightly better success. Initially, workers used the railroad consistently and paid monthly fees of two dollars, allowing the company to show a modest profit during its first years and leading to discussions about completing the second track and extending the route to nearby towns. Initially, the machines worked well, and strong riders could reach adequate speeds, benefiting from a ratchet device that increased thrust (similar to the mechanism used on Star bicycles). Pleased workers discovered they could reduce commuting time to six or seven minutes and travel through a scenic valley to boot.[62]

However, construction costs had been substantial. The machines functioned best along a straight line, and thus the route crossed the meandering creek at numerous locations, requiring costly bridges and hindering prospects for a second track. In addition, farmers demanded that gates be installed to allow access to

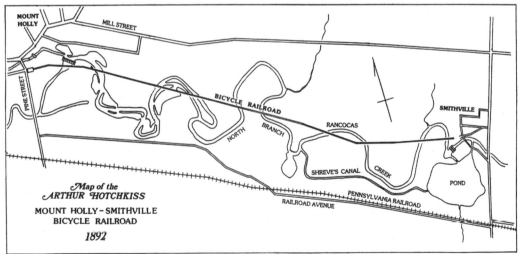

Map of the
ARTHUR HOTCHKISS
MOUNT HOLLY – SMITHVILLE
BICYCLE RAILROAD
1892

FIGURES 10.8 AND 10.9

For a small monthly fee, employees of the H. B. Smith Machine Company could propel themselves to work along scenic Rancocas Creek. Image and map are courtesy of Wayne and Kim Batten.

fields, increasing expenses. The single track also created difficulties, and although the company added sidings, riders meeting from opposite directions had to stop and remove one of the heavy machines to pass; slow riders hindered the pace of trailing commuters, as well. Compounding those problems, Hotchkiss turned his energies toward other projects and neglected his company. From the outset, the metal machines operated poorly in a headwind and needed greater refinement in design; with lack of maintenance, they also began to rust. All the while, bicycles had been gaining popularity, rendering the bicycle railroad redundant, and by the mid-1890s the company had begun an irreversible decline. Abandoned, the railway structure steadily deteriorated and eventually vanished.[63]

Cycle Ways in Other Regions

Elevated wheelways represent very minor contributions to bicycle history, yet even these novel corridors illustrate the importance of compiling a geographically complete history of American bicycle paths that assesses the extent to which projects in one part of the country influenced historical contexts in other regions. For example, a Southern California businessman, Horace M. Dobbins, in 1897 began planning one of the very few elevated bicycle paths ever built. Called the Great California Cycleway, but little more than a mile long, the proposed scheme nevertheless captured the imagination of many cyclists. Dobbins conceived the path for horseless carriages as well as bicycles and hoped to avoid the steep hills between Los Angeles and Pasadena, nine miles apart. He also backed the project with his own resources, tackling an array of daunting obstacles. These included forming a corporation and securing financial support; introducing state legislation authorizing counties, cities, and towns to grant franchises for bicycle paths; countering legislative opposition over concern that the path would become an elevated railroad; surveying a route; purchasing rights-of-way without resort to eminent domain; successfully obtaining franchises; and designing the road carefully enough to assure its popularity among cyclists. That he succeeded at most of those tasks well enough to build a path of any length is a remarkable feat.[64]

Inevitably, many of the paths built in regions beyond the boundaries of this study will add to the historical contexts and thematic patterns traced here. In some cases, the origins of those paths will seem familiar; others may establish subtle departures or display the mark of originality in addressing the many obstacles facing path builders. In addition, tracing the gradual shift from private to public funding for path construction strengthens those contexts, as do the increasingly important roles of park commissions and public works officials.

Examples deserving much closer study abound. In Minnesota, wheelmen in the adjoining cities of St. Paul and Minneapolis established separate cycle path associations in 1896 and began building substantial networks of sidepaths, which by the end of two cycling seasons extended nearly fifty miles. Both organizations also used the term "sidepath," suggesting the influence of New York's campaign. In general, the St. Paul paths followed principal streets leading away from the city to recreational sites (such as Lake Como and Minnehaha Falls), skirting the terraces overlooking the Mississippi River, or pointing toward suburban communities (such as White Bear Lake).[65]

The Minneapolis organization began to build paths linking the city's many lakes and exquisite parks, but members encountered a series of problems, including insufficient subscriptions, objections by property owners, and opposition from members of a local cycling club, who sounded the refrain that bicycle paths hindered efforts to build good roads. Progress slowed, and the initial organization dissolved, transferring its mission and modest bank balance to a new association with an identical name.[66]

Park commissions elsewhere also contributed to the historically important ties between cycling and parks. By 1900, for example, one of Seattle's city engineers, George Cotterill, had developed a plan for a twenty-five-mile network of bicycle paths around the city. When park commissioners retained the Olmsted firm in 1902 to expand the city's park system, John Charles Olmsted acknowledged the value of Cotterill's proposal and included bicycle paths in several of his park plans. Little more than a decade later, in his report for a parkway system in Essex County, New Jersey, Olmsted unequivocally recommended bicycle paths as integral parts of parkways and boulevards, clarifying some of the firm's earlier ambivalence. He also circulated relevant portions of that report nationally in an article published in the journal *Landscape Architecture* in 1915. As in Minneapolis and St. Paul, the original locations for the paths in Seattle's parks warrant study.[67]

In Oregon, the state division of the LAW secured passage of sidepath legislation in 1899, authorizing county assessors to tax bicycles as personal property. County highway officials constructed roughly sixty miles of paths in Multnomah County during the 1899 season, beginning on the outskirts of Portland and leading to surrounding communities.[68]

Cyclists in Benton Harbor, Michigan, didn't wait for state legislators to pass a sidepath law but instead obtained permission from their city council to occupy a portion of the city's sand-filled streets. They enlisted the support of the city surveyor, who established a grade for the path eight inches higher than the street and added plank curbing to retain the fill. The design worked well enough to convince city officials to build similar paths with public funding. Michigan's state division of the LAW continued to push for sidepath legislation, however, and toward that end organized a "Side-Path Building Day," July 4, 1900, when wheelmen were asked to assemble and construct five hundred continuous miles of paths across the state.[69]

In neighboring Wisconsin, members of the Eau Claire Cycle Club established the Eau Claire and Chippewa Falls Cycle Path on private lands in 1897, marking its entrance with a pointed-arch portal, slightly more formal than the

Adirondack-style portals at the termini of the Scottsville sidepath in New York. By contrast, cyclists in Cedar Rapids, Iowa, roamed a twenty-mile path constructed at public expense in 1899 or 1900.[70]

Farther to the west, in Colorado, the Globe Bicycle Path Company obtained a corporate charter in 1897 to manufacture materials used in the building and repairing of bicycle paths. Two years later, the Denver-Palmer Lake Cycle Path Association obtained legislative appropriations sufficient to complete a path between those two points; the following year, the Arapahoe County Good Roads Association mustered support for legislation that improved roads for bicycle travel as a means to promote tourism.[71]

The few examples cited here reinforce the importance of strengthening the historical contexts for American bicycle paths and will hopefully encourage others to pursue that goal. Possibly, explorations also will identify bicycle paths that survive from early periods, offering cyclists a chance to preserve and interpret those resources for continued public benefit.[72]

FIGURE 11.1
Robert Moses launched his 1938 plan for bicycle paths in New York City by adapting a portion of the former Long Island Motor Parkway, constructed by William K. Vanderbilt in 1908 as a racecourse for automobiles but later converted to a toll road for pleasure travel. Located in Queens, the Long Island Motor Parkway bicycle path leads to Alley Pond Park and is now more than seventy-five years old. Traces of the original parkway's width survive, as do some of the concrete posts for cable guard rails.

AFTERWORD

Revival

Throughout much of the country, the first several decades of the twentieth century were a time of dormancy for adult recreational cycling. Yet characterizing that era as an idle one for bicycles in America unfairly ignores the men and women who continued to use the wheel as a convenient and economical mode of transportation or as a healthful manner of recreation. Rather than vanishing during those decades, these adult cyclists continued to roll along city streets or country roads, but they remained almost invisible to a public spellbound by automobiles and motorcycles. In 1911, editors of *Bicycling World and Motorcycle Review* may have unintentionally divulged their share of cycling's decline with the sketch of a ghostly wheelman from the high-wheel era, stylishly attired, observing a youth touring the countryside by motorcycle. Musing enviously, the wheelman remarks: "To see what I missed by being born too soon!"[1]

Despite that dormancy, an apparatus of support for cycling endured. Buoyed by annual rides and banquets, many bicycle clubs survived tenaciously; numerous others formed anew. Cyclists in major cities such as Boston and Cleveland organized revival runs, and more than twenty-five hundred participants from Boston gathered at Chestnut Hill Reservoir in May 1904; a somewhat smaller but no less enthusiastic crowd assembled at Cleveland's Gordon Park the following month. Several cycling periodicals circulated during different periods between 1910 and 1935: *Bicycling World and Motorcycle Review*; its successors, *Motorcycle and Bicycle Illustrated* and *American Motorcyclist and Bicyclist*; and the trade journal *Bicycle News*, published by Cycle Trades of America after 1915. In addition, Abbott Bassett continued to publish the *Official Bulletin and Scrap Book of the League of American Wheelmen* until 1922, even though the league had surrendered its influence twenty years before. In 1920, Bassett pointed to a growing trend among young people who, frustrated by increasing trolley fares and enticed by smoothly paved roads, had turned to bicycles as convenient vehicles for the country's expanding suburbs, whether for ordinary errands or to reach newly relocated industrial plants.[2]

Both the Century Road Club of America (organized in Chicago during the summer of 1891) and its eastern-states progeny of 1899, the Century Road Club Association, filled at least part of the void left by the LAW, creating numerous divisions and promoting touring, century rides, and road racing. The latter flourished during the 1920s, advanced by both the National Cycling Association and a splinter group, the Amateur Bicycling League of America, which formed late in 1920. Both organizations helped to keep bicycles in public sight.[3]

Ironically, just as the Great Depression began to pull bicycle racing into decline, cycling as a form of adult recreation began to regain popularity. During the early 1930s, trendsetters on the West Coast turned again to bicycles, and interest soon spread to other parts of the country, boosted by the trade's successful strategy of marketing to women. By this time, road surfaces invited travel by bicycle, but the stimulus for those improvements—the automobile—posed dire threats. The menace became acute in urban centers, where cyclists of all ages interacted with ever-greater numbers of cars, and the revival of bicycle paths developed most vigorously in principal cities, such as New York and Chicago.[4]

Robert Moses's Bicycle Path Plan

New Yorkers in particular sought ambitious destinations. Having won support from Park Commissioner Robert Moses, city cyclists dusted off their latent talents at path planning and encouraged the parks department to develop a system of bicycle paths throughout city parks. In August 1938, Moses presented Mayor Fiorello LaGuardia with a plan titled "Program of Proposed Facilities for Bicycling," which included an introductory letter by Moses that imparted his view of cycling as a rapidly reviving sport. The letter is brightly optimistic on behalf of cyclists, setting a goal of creating more than fifty miles of park paths throughout the city's five boroughs, and not even his blunt declaration that "bicycles have no place on public highways" alters that tone.

Unfortunately, the plan succumbed to inadequate funding, which caused delays in achieving that mileage goal and also resulted in the concentration of mileage at a few widely dispersed sites. In addition, the paths that eventually opened in Central Park and Prospect Park were much less extensive than those delineated on the plan's map. Nor, regrettably, did the plan offer anything to those who regarded bicycles as a means of transportation. Yet even with considerable shortcomings, the document is a prelude to the modern era of path building following World War II.[5]

Two years before, the city had returned park privileges to cyclists in Central Park, albeit symbolically and limited only to Center Drive from Sixty-Sixth to Seventy-Second Streets on Saturday mornings. Grateful even for that modest offering, wheelmen and wheelwomen once again assembled for a celebratory parade, with silver cups for best costumes bestowed by the fashion director of the newly revived League of American Wheelmen. Award recipients included actress Fifi D'Orsay and ten-year-old twins in trendy Minnie and Mickey Mouse attire. More than one thousand spectators viewed the procession from a grandstand on the Mall, as velocipedes, high-wheels, safety bicycles, tandems, unicycles, and modern bicycles rolled by.[6]

Possibly taking a cue from that parade, Moses recommended more than five miles of bicycle paths or lanes in both Central and Prospect parks, achieved by utilizing portions of unnecessarily wide drives and by constructing spur paths at many park entrances. The plan also rearranged short sections of pedestrian walks to reduce intersections and designated the Mineral Spring House in Central Park as a cycler's rest. As proposed, the Central Park paths established a circuitous route, beginning at the Fifty-Ninth Street entrance on Fifth Avenue and continuing northerly on a looping course until returning to Fifth Avenue at 102nd Street.[7]

Although the Central Park paths did not develop according to plan, several paths originating from the Moses report survive and are historically significant

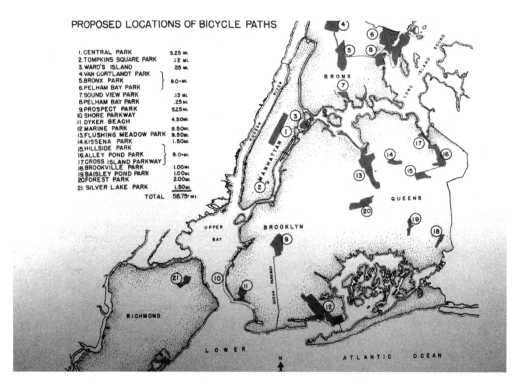

PROPOSED LOCATIONS OF BICYCLE PATHS

I. CENTRAL PARK	5.25 MI.
2. TOMPKINS SQUARE PARK	.12 MI.
3. WARD'S ISLAND	.25 MI.
4. VAN CORTLANDT PARK	
5. BRONX PARK	9.0+MI.
6. PELHAM BAY PARK	
7. SOUND VIEW PARK	.13 MI.
8. PELHAM BAY PARK	.25 MI.
9. PROSPECT PARK	5.25 MI.
10. SHORE PARKWAY	
II. DYKER BEACH	4.50 MI.
12. MARINE PARK	9.50 MI.
13. FLUSHING MEADOW PARK	9.50 MI.
14. KISSENA PARK	1.50 MI.
15. HILLSIDE PARK	
16. ALLEY POND PARK	8.0+MI.
17. CROSS ISLAND PARKWAY	
18. BROOKVILLE PARK	1.00 MI.
19. BAISLEY POND PARK	1.00 MI.
20. FOREST PARK	2.00 MI.
21. SILVER LAKE PARK	1.50 MI.
TOTAL	58.75 MI.

FIGURE 11.2
The plan for bicycle paths in New York proposed by Robert
Moses in 1938. Courtesy New York City Hall Library.

in the context of modern bicycle path planning. The first opened in 1938 along
a two-and-a-half-mile section of William K. Vanderbilt's abandoned Long Island
Motor Parkway in Queens, stretching between Horace Harding Boulevard and
Alley Pond Park. Three years later, several path segments—twelve miles in all—
opened along portions of the newly built Shore Parkway in Brooklyn. In his
report, Moses had described the first of those paths, a wheelway then under construction along a portion of Shore Parkway to link Owl's Head Park with Dyker
Beach Park. As eventually completed, that segment reached as far as Bensonhurst
Park, extending the length to about five miles.[8]

Shore Parkway and portions of its related Belt Parkway thus join the Williamsburg Bridge as major transportation projects designed to accommodate bicycles
from inception, and both deserve designation as landmarks in cycling history. In
Brooklyn, the Moses plan prompted cyclists to reclaim a portion of the Coney
Island path, and by the summer of 1939 park workers had divided the original
path on the western mall into two corridors: one for bicycles and one for pedestrians, with the two separated by a railing. Those changes also signaled the beginning of the modern era for that historic wheelway.[9]

Long Island Motor Parkway Bicycle Path

On a Saturday morning in July 1938, Robert Moses addressed a gathering of several hundred children and adults delighted with a chance to pedal along the new path to Alley Pond Park. He called the project a practical experiment, declaring: "The way to make progress, sometimes, is to go backward." Moses also spoke of irony, pointing to the parkway that William K. Vanderbilt had conceived as a race course for speeding automobiles in pursuit of the Vanderbilt Cup, but a corridor that modern traffic conditions had rendered obsolete. Instead, riders on bicycles and tricycles had become the parkway's pacesetters.[10]

Yet as the son of park engineer William Latham snipped a ceremonial ribbon to open the path, a few of those present may have pondered a larger irony surrounding the event. For more than a decade, Moses had been engaged in the planning and construction of parkways and expressways to serve metropolitan New York, a transportation system that boldly championed automobiles. That campaign shaped the region's development for the remainder of the twentieth century, irreversibly altering cultural and natural environments and contributing greatly to many of the city's continuing problems. If any of the participants at that gathering were farsighted enough to sense the difficulties that were already emerging from those policies, then they likely viewed the abandoned parkway in a different light: not simply as a corridor for recreation, but as a transportation alternative to the automobile.

Adding subtlety to that irony, Vanderbilt had intended the parkway to function as a racecourse and as a corridor for pleasure travel. When races ended in 1910, the route became a private, forty-five mile toll road for commuters traveling between New York City and their Long Island retreats—a corridor tantalizingly free from police patrols. However, the difficulties of managing a private highway steadily mounted, and Vanderbilt eventually appealed to Moses to acquire the right-of-way. Moses declined, reasoning that the costs of improving the circuitous course to meet then-current highway standards were too high. Instead, he constructed the toll-free Northern State Parkway nearby and forced Vanderbilt out of business. Vanderbilt eventually conveyed the right-of-way to county governments for taxes owed, and the dedication of the Queens section as a bicycle path followed. As Moses watched children on tricycles pedal along the newly created path that Saturday, he may have contemplated Vanderbilt's involuntary contribution to recreational cycling.[11]

Today, another layer of irony cloaks the historic bicycle path. For all its folly, Vanderbilt's highway remains important to the history of parkway design in America. Chartered as a corporation in 1906, followed by groundbreaking at Levittown in 1908, the Long Island Motor Parkway became one of the country's first automobile highways engineered for pleasure travel, employing features such as controlled access, a reinforced concrete surface, banked curves, separation from cross streets via overpasses, architecturally stylish toll houses, and aesthetically pleasing bridges. Almost overnight, similar features became common on a celebrated class of American roads that soon added scenic landscapes to the traveling experience. Although commuters quickly overtook pleasure travelers along most of the country's metropolitan parkways, the Long Island Motor Parkway (or LIMP, as it is known today by its guardians) deserves recognition for its contribution to the history of American highway engineering.

Whether or not we credit Vanderbilt's parkway for its contribution to the vast network of commuter parkways that followed, few would deny the significance of those highways in shaping American culture, for good or bad, or the importance of those highways in helping us comprehend our current transportation predicaments. By offering an alternative to automobile travel, the Long Island Motor Parkway bicycle path presents a clear juxtaposition of contrasting points of view, cognizable in a single place rich in memory—and unique in American cycling history. If from that place we are better able to visualize expansive, fully integrated designs for parkways as commuter corridors for bicycles and other alternative methods of transportation, then the historic value of both parkway and path will become apparent.

Plan Features

That sunny summer's day in Queens belonged to bicycle riders, young and old, whose numbers included Charles "Mile-a-Minute" Murphy and six-day racer Norman Hill. Moses viewed the path to Alley Pond Park as a chance to assemble the data needed to meet bicyclists' demands, and the results of that test path are worth noting. During the year following the corridor's opening, roughly thirty-eight thousand cyclists traveled the former parkway. Regular Sunday morning buses departing from West Forty-Second Street in Manhattan delivered enthusiasts to the site, and more than twelve thousand riders rented bicycles during that period, most often on weekends. In a report to Moses in July 1939, parks superintendent Allyn R. Jennings summarized the results of that first year, observing blandly that the experiment had been worthwhile. Perhaps explaining that ambivalence, William Latham later acknowledged that although bicycle concessions had paid for police to patrol the path, the contracts had been a headache.[12]

In his opening speech the year before, Moses had promised a bright future for the city's cyclists, vowing to turn the calendar back forty years by planning a comprehensive network of paths exclusively for bicycles throughout the city's parks. Publicly circulated less than a month later, the report outlined the results of a study begun six months before by park executives, who identified locations where paths could be created without delay or substantial construction costs. Thus, from the outset the plan's scope was a limited one—impelled by the quest for immediate results, constrained by financial resources, and cast by regard for the bicycle as a form of recreation.

Bronx and Queens Paths Among the city's five boroughs, the Bronx offered the most promising locales for a series of paths linking several sizable parks. The plan's

FIGURE 11.3

Among various proposals for bicycle paths included in New York's 1938 plan, those in the Bronx offered the greatest potential for a continuous route that connected parks in different parts of the borough, attaining considerable length in the process. Courtesy New York City Hall Library.

continuous nine-mile route, twice that long if one counts spurs and loops, began at the Westchester County boundary and followed the Croton Aqueduct corridor south through Van Cortlandt Park to Mosholu Parkway, which in turn led southerly to Bronx Park. After skirting the edge of that latter park, the course turned east along the Bronx-Pelham Parkway to Pelham Bay Park, and then through that expansive reserve, joining the projected Hutchinson River Parkway extension en route northerly to the Westchester County border. Paths along the perimeter of Pelham Bay Park also connected with a spur leading to Orchard Beach.[13]

The plan proffered a similar strategy for Queens, focusing on extending the western terminus of the Motor Parkway path into Hillside Park and lengthening the eastern end by heading north into Alley Pond Park to connect with Cross Island Parkway. That latter corridor continued north along Little Neck Bay and Little Bay into, respectively, the Bayside and Whitestone sections of Queens. In Flushing Meadow Park, where work for the 1938 World's Fair already was underway, Moses added a bicycle path adjacent to the outer circulation system used by pedestrians, separating the two with planting strips but consigning both to pedestrian use during the fair.

Belt Parkway Paths   By far, the most intriguing aspects of the Moses plan concern bicycle paths along a series of parkways being fashioned into a circumferential highway system called the Belt Parkway in Brooklyn and Queens, some of it still in the conceptual stages of planning in 1938. Shore Parkway became the first to include paths, but the plan also anticipated similar designs along Shore Parkway Extension to Marine Park, where perimeter loops added nine miles to the city's grand total of paths. From Marine Park, the proposed beltway skirted Jamaica Bay on a northeastern course to Queens, there becoming Southern Parkway and continuing easterly, eventually turning abruptly north on Laurelton Parkway to join Cross Island Parkway, which offered easy connections to Alley Pond Park.[14]

Park planners and engineers regarded these parkway paths as recreational opportunities, and thus their potential as circumferential transportation corridors for bicycles is limited. As compensation, authors of the plan pointed encouragingly to the views of expansive water bodies along most of the Belt Parkway, and by 1941 cyclists could agree. That year, twelve miles of paths opened along Brooklyn's share of the corridor, with continuity broken only by the parkway's elevated sections beginning at Bensonhurst Park. The segmented route reached as far as the boundary with Queens County at Spring Creek Basin and there joined a four-mile path already in use, leading to Cross Bay Boulevard in Queens.[15]

Plan Assessment

Objective evaluation of the Moses plan for bicycle paths presents challenges on several fronts, among them a strong temptation to measure the document solely by Moses's promise of a comprehensive approach or alternatively by what Jennings dutifully described as his commissioner's foresightedness.

Moses's regard for the bicycle as a means of recreation rather than transportation clearly weakens the plan, and had he thoroughly investigated cycling from forty years before or had he studied trends in many European cities or had he listened more closely to what some of New York's cyclists were telling him, then that omission would have become apparent. The plan also must be considered against the backdrop of a relentless crusade for urban and regional parkways that were built with the knowledge that they promptly would become commuter corridors and not just a means of access to parks, thus accelerating suburban growth and draining the city's resources. By 1938, many of the undesirable consequences of that campaign were plainly visible, including traffic congestion and destruction of built environments, and reform groups (including the Regional Plan Association) had called for the improvement of mass transit systems to address growing traffic congestion. Strictly stated, the plan for bicycle paths was neither comprehensive nor conceived in true foresight.[16]

Moreover, the plan's origins belonged mostly to the city's cyclists, who by Moses's own admission had persistently clamored for better opportunities, including exclusive lanes on parkways and arterial highways or the expressly permitted use of roads during assigned hours. Thus, the Moses plan is largely a reaction to prodding rather than a careful look into the future, no matter how thorough the study of potential sites by park staff may have been.[17]

The city's archives are full of letters to Moses from cycling advocates who pointed to the need for better places to ride. Replies from Moses are typically blunt defenses of his plan, with little evidence of his having grasped the potential value of bicycles as a form of transportation. Clifton Fadiman, book review editor of *The New Yorker* and a radio personality, wrote in January 1941 to complain that West Drive in Central Park had been taken away from cyclists and given to automobile drivers. Offering his own share of foresight, Fadiman protested: "Everything, it seems to me, is being done today for motorists, although statistics show that from two-thirds to four-fifths of their car space is always vacant and therefore an economic waste." Moses replied that a longer path (about a mile long between Seventy-Second and Eightieth Streets) replacing West Drive was then under construction, but dismissed Fadiman's statistics regarding empty car space as meaningless, concluding tersely: "Take the chip off your shoulder. We are with you."[18]

One can also challenge Moses for his conviction that bicycles had no place on public highways, an outlook that created impediments for those who continued to use bicycles for transportation. The industry's trade association (Cycle Trades of America) had distributed bulletins to park executives, focusing principally on safety and emphasizing proper riding skills but also reminding readers that bicycles had as much right to the streets as automobiles.[19]

Granted, even the most ardent cyclists acknowledged having been pushed off the roads by automobiles—despite being there first—and understood the mortal nature of their standing. Yet much of their writing during this period urges the planning of inclusive systems designed to achieve harmony among bicycles and cars. For instance, Charles Merz (chief editorial writer for the *New York Times*, who lived in an apartment building next door to that of Moses and who often conversed with the commissioner) penned a thoughtful column in 1939 titled "Highways and Byways." Conceding that a truly good system of bicycle paths linking cities and towns could not be realized overnight, he argued that such a plan should be something to "think about and look ahead to." Moses made a point of replying, but he failed to respond to the thrust of Merz's argument, doing little more than chiding Merz for not acknowledging the park department's 1938 plan.[20]

Not all of Moses's letters are so obdurate, and some even hint at a shifting outlook toward bicycles. The onset of World War II may have been a factor, and when the secretary of the College Cycle Club wrote to Moses in the spring of 1942 to suggest that all sidepaths adjacent to parkways be opened to cyclists at all times and to ask for the opening of at least one parkway in each borough on Sundays, the reply from Moses is far more restrained. Declining to devote one lane of the narrow Bronx River Parkway to cyclists, he explained that traffic had not yet dropped to the point of safety. Yet he conceded that as cars on the city's parkways decreased in number due to rationing the use of bicycles would probably increase, adding that when the preponderance of use shifted, regulations governing parkways would be adjusted to meet demands. Although he declined to open the boardwalk at Jones Beach to cyclists, his reasons for doing so are curious: "We believe that a person riding a bicycle to Jones Beach is using the bicycle first as a means of transportation" and thus upon arriving is interested in other recreational activities.[21]

Despite its considerable shortcomings, Moses's plan must also be judged from another point of view, one that considers the context of American cycling in 1938. Although Moses viewed the experimental Long Island Motor Parkway bicycle path as a chance to count the number of riders that first year and thus gauge overall demand on city parks, the experiment is telling for another, more significant reason. Both Jennings and landscape architect Francis Cormier tempered their evaluation of the path's success by pointing to the path's location, remote from densely populated neighborhoods and convenient only by car or bus. Subsequent counts revealed that only moderate numbers of cyclists' used the path, and those tallies supported the assessment by Jennings and Cormier. Offering further confirmation of that tepid interest, one of Moses's assistants, George Spargo, acknowledged lack of demand for the 1938 bulletin and recommended against reprinting in 1940. However, the inconvenience of distance was due neither to the lack of roads nor to the distance itself (at least for adults), but instead to the dominance of automobiles on those roads. Forty years before, cyclists would have regarded that distance as an opportunity rather than an impediment. Turning the calendar back, unfortunately, had become impossible.[22]

During the intervening years, cycling had become a recreational activity primarily for children, and although adults began returning to bicycles during the early 1930s, concern for children's safety remained paramount. Laudably, the plan moved children off the streets and into parks, and in terms of scale the paths proposed by Moses were well-suited for children. Consequently, the challenge for Moses was to design two path systems: one for children and one for adults. Adding to those difficulties, American bicycle manufacturers had not kept pace with European designs for adult bicycles thus limiting the distances that some adult cyclists were willing to travel and creating another dimension to path planning. Consequently, Moses and his park staff are probably entitled to a certain amount of leeway.[23]

Moses's plan also must be evaluated in the context of other developments. When Moses became commissioner of the city's consolidated department of parks following the election of Mayor LaGuardia in 1934, his transformation of the city's park system was nothing short of miraculous. LaGaurdia's campaign had promised reform, and the new mayor quickly swept the corrupt Tammany political machine out of city government. Using labor funded through the Civil

Works Administration, Moses immediately began reversing the deplorable condition of the few parks that did exist and managed, against staggering economic odds, to snatch control of overlooked parcels of land in some of the city's most densely populated areas—neighborhoods that desperately needed sunlight and open space. Between 1934 and 1937, he established more than 250 new parks and playgrounds, and the public response to these successes (guided by a steady flow of glowing press reports) could not have been more favorable.[24]

Moses sought to maximize the use of the city's parks by people, and his team of architects and engineers designed permanent spaces for active recreation, such as tennis, baseball, and basketball; quiet contemplation of nature all but vanished. At the outset of this period of park transformation in New York, cycling may not have regained sufficient popularity to capture the attention of either Moses or his park planners, and thus bicycles may not have been adequately considered in the astonishingly rapid changes then taking place. In parks large enough to accommodate cycling, the potential for conflict among cyclists and pedestrians had always existed, and Moses would not have wanted that conflict to tarnish the public's perception of his considerable efforts. Once cyclists began pedaling in greater numbers, the task became one of finding places where bicycles would not hinder the activities of other park users.

Whether park planners might have responded differently to the needs of cyclists had the timing been different is a fair question. However, at the time when Moses became the city's park commissioner he also controlled six other government agencies, and his attention to the design of improvements for the city's parks became increasingly standardized and superficial, with much of the design work delegated to subordinates. Demands on his time thus were stretched to extraordinary limits, and he had little incentive to solve the thorny matter of incompatibility between cars and bicycles.[25]

Plan in Progress

Implementation of the plan was similarly contradictory, adding to the challenge of objectively assessing its significance. Especially troubling are the discrepancies that developed between the paths proposed by the 1938 report and those actually opened during the next decade, particularly in Central and Prospect Parks. Moses made slow progress in fulfilling his promises to wheelmen, and his truculent declarations of effort on cycling's behalf are contradicted by very limited opportunities for car-free cycling by either children or adults for many years to come. In the spring of 1939, for instance, William Latham anticipated that only the Coney Island path would be available during the coming year.[26]

By the end of that season, opportunities were only slightly better than Latham had predicted. Excluding the Coney Island and Motor Parkway paths, cyclists in Brooklyn and Queens had access to a quarter-mile path on Well House Drive in Prospect Park; a three-quarter-mile path in Marine Park; and slightly more than two miles of boardwalk at Coney Island during very limited hours. Bronx

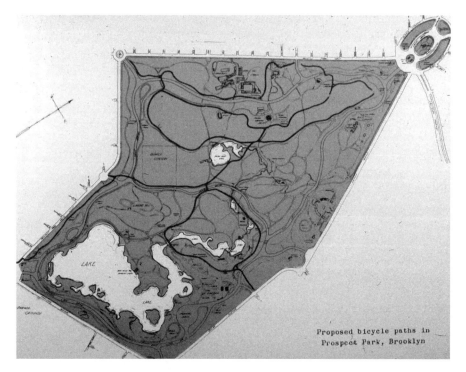

Proposed bicycle paths in
Prospect Park, Brooklyn

FIGURE 11.4

New York City's 1938 bicycle path proposals promised lengthy routes for cyclists in both Central Park and Prospect Park, accomplished in plan by appropriating portions of unnecessarily wide drives and by constructing new paths. However, work progressed very slowly, and years later the results bore little resemblance to the routes marked on the plan's maps. In Prospect Park, for example, cyclists attained only a token, quarter-mile path along Well House Drive, not the sub- stantial loops depicted near the lake and around Long Meadow. In Central Park especially, rather than assign portions of drives to cyclists and thus constrict motorized traffic, Moses instead widened the drives for automobiles, reducing sharp curves and transforming the drives into extensions of city streets, leaving neither room nor appeal for cyclists or pedestrians. Courtesy New York City Hall Library.

cyclists fared slightly better, with access to closed roads in Crotona, Pelham Bay, and Claremount parks; the Croton Aqueduct path in Van Cortlandt Park; and seasonal privileges on the roads and parking areas at Orchard Beach.

In Manhattan, cyclists could use very short paths in Central Park and a newly opened but similarly limited sixteen-block path along the Henry Hudson Parkway, ending at 116th Street. Motor vehicles continued to dominate the principal drives in both Central and Prospect Parks, the most obvious locations to experiment with designs that achieved the equilibrium among cars and bicycles that Charles Merz had sought. Debate about the proper place for automobiles in parks already had begun, but Moses ignored the opportunity that cyclists had given him to curtail the volume and speed of motor traffic. Rather, he did just the opposite and encouraged the use of drives as extensions of the city's street system.

His engineers redesigned park drives to facilitate higher speeds, removing impediments such as sharp curves and adding new vehicular entrances. Instead of corridors for pleasure travel, the drives become one-way shortcuts for taxi drivers. Unfortunately, those circumstances would not change for many decades. Tallying overall mileage of paths at the end of 1939 is difficult without more information about the closed roads in the Bronx parks, but designated paths totaled no more than fourteen miles, with eight of those miles credited to the combined lengths of the Motor Parkway and Coney Island paths.[27]

During the summer of 1940, possibly to stem the flood of complaints, Moses opened running tracks to bicycle use during limited hours in specified parks, a boon to children, and by then a few more short paths had opened in Queens, including three separate mile-long corridors: one connecting the World's Fair Boat Basin with Jackson Creek Boat Basin near LaGuardia Airport, another in Brookville Park, and a third in Baisley Pond Park. Elsewhere, a newly opened path circled the Silver Lake Park reservoir on Staten Island. That same summer, landscape architect Francis Cormier inspected portions of Southern and Cross Island Parkways, concluding that construction of bicycle paths would be feasible despite inadequate clearance beneath bridges.[28]

Yet by the end of the cycling season that year, overall mileage of paths (excluding running tracks) had reached only about twenty-nine miles, with many of the paths less than a mile in length; boardwalks that were available only during limited hours comprised about seven miles of that total. Cormier attributed the delays to construction financing by the Works Progress Administration, which eventually provided funding for the paths along the Belt Parkway. War in Europe also added difficulties.[29]

When the twelve-mile Belt Parkway paths finally opened in 1941, at a cost of almost $587,000, the city could claim the metropolitan region's longest bicycle path, and Moses may have been justifiably pleased with one of the country's most important bicycle paths of that era. Still, the experience offered little of the sense of freedom that had characterized cycling forty years before. When Manhattan cyclist Margaret Keating requested directions to Shore Parkway from her home on West 183rd Street, William Latham prepared a helpful reply. He advised her to take the Fourth Avenue local of the BMT (Brooklyn-Manhattan Transit) to the Bay Ridge Avenue station, about four blocks from the parkway, and there rent a bicycle from any of several shops. Once on the path, she would find a twelve-foot wide corridor that skirted the water's edge along Upper New York Bay, the Narrows, and Graves End Bay for a distance of about five miles before reaching Bensonhurst Park. There, the path ended and she would need to follow a circuitous, three-mile route with turns onto Bay Parkway, Cropsey, Neptune, and Emmons Avenues and then Shell Road before reaching the path again at Plum Beach in the Sheepshead Bay district.[30]

The following season, several more paths lifted the total, including corridors in Riverside Park and a path on the Hutchinson River Parkway in the Bronx. In Queens, the Belt Parkway paths had been lengthened by a stretch along the Cross Island Parkway from Northern Boulevard in Alley Pond Park to Utopia Parkway near Little Bay. The Central Park Loop opened that year as well, beginning at Seventy-Second Street and West Drive and leading southerly to Fifty-Ninth Street, easterly to East Drive, and then northerly near East Drive back to Seventy-Second Street. Although an improvement, the route toured far less of the park than the route proposed in 1938. More than a decade later, a cyclist frustrated with the city's indulgence toward automobiles described that route as a short, erratic oval of·very limited reach, frequently usurped by pedestrians who also sought refuge from motorcars.[31]

By the spring of 1942, total path length had inched forward to about forty-five miles, not far short of the goal set by the 1938 plan. Correspondence from Moses and other park department staff claiming more than fifty miles of paths during previous years probably included running tracks in the total. About twenty-eight miles of that overall distance remained concentrated in the Belt Parkway paths, the Coney Island path, the Motor Parkway path, and the restricted use of boardwalks at both Coney Island and Rockaway Beach. Other paths were very short and offered limited usefulness, at least to the cyclists who sought more than just quick, quarter-mile loops. Such minor paths, coupled with the department's emphasis on available running tracks during restricted hours, intimate that Moses was more concerned about keeping cyclists at bay with statistics than with innovative, comprehensive solutions to the serious conflict between cars and bicycles. Those circumstances also suggest that publicity given to the proposed system of bicycle paths in 1938 was aimed more at shaping public opinion than at developing a comprehensive, farsighted plan.[32]

Only the Belt Parkway paths suggest otherwise, but even the promise of those paths as potential transportation corridors soon dimmed during the postwar era. John Heaslip, who managed park operations and maintenance, replied discouragingly to a woman cyclist who inquired about extensions to parkway paths, calling continuations of the existing bicycle paths along the Belt and other Long Island parkways as "out of the question" due to the poor topography, costs, and dangers to cyclists.[33]

Influence

Public awareness of the Moses plan extended well beyond New York City's boroughs, reaching major cities such as Detroit and Chicago, where park officials were grappling with similar demands by cyclists. Even the National Park Service sought advice about bicycle paths from Moses, whose reputation for public works projects had been polished by a dazzled New York press and by the editors of journals with national circulation. Whether or not other cities specifically borrowed from New York's plan, Gotham nevertheless played a significant role in the early stages of modern planning for bicycle paths.

New York's park engineers and landscape architects often answered queries from park managers in other cities. Francis Cormier supplied Detroit with specifications for the construction of new paths like those along the Belt Parkway. Similarly, Elbert Cox, superintendent of Colonial National Historical Park in Yorktown, Virginia, wrote to New York's park department in 1942, describing plans for a parkway linking Williamsburg to Jamestown Island and asking for information about construction costs and maintenance requirements for an adjoining path. James Dawson, a park designer, supplied Cox with much of the information that Cormier had given to Detroit.[34]

Specifications for revised designs eventually arrived in Chicago via exchanges of correspondence occurring over a period of years. In 1940, possibly uncertain about headway in his own parks, Allyn Jennings wrote to Victor K. Brown, director of recreation in Chicago's Park District, to inquire about bicycling activities. Brown replied that in small parks with circular drives the city closed gates on Sunday mornings to allow racing or other special events, and he noted that gates had been shut in some parks to eliminate automobile traffic entirely. Brown conceded that New York seemed to be far ahead of Chicago in designating paths in major parks, explaining that Robert Dunham, President of the Chicago Park District, favored pointing cyclists toward the city's hinterlands and forest preserves, where country roads presented fewer dangers than the major highways along lakefront parks. With a hint of apology, Brown summarized the city's policy: "Bicycle riding itself is minimized in our parks, if not actually discouraged, on grounds of safety."[35]

Brown was far more optimistic in his discussion of the growing number of bicycle clubs and the emerging popularity of hosteling. The department had begun offering workshops to help touring cyclists prepare for rides into open country, whether traveling in groups or independently, and his letter identified a future trend that would develop following World War II.[36]

Foresight

A 1956 letter to Moses in his role as chairman of the State Council of Parks is among the most forward-looking of bicycle-related inquiries to arrive on his desk during the postwar era. Josephine Young Case, the wife of Colgate University president Everett Case, composed the letter—full of optimism—to ask Moses to apply his fertile mind to a problem. Mrs. Case's eleven-year old son and two companions had planned a camping trip by bicycle, but she had denied permission because there were no safe roads to travel. Having considered the problem, she observed that small railroads throughout the state had gone out of use or, with regard to the New York, Ontario, and Western Railroad, which served Hamilton, were about to do so. Why not, she wondered, fill in the center of the railroads with asphalt and make bicycle paths? The gradients were perfect and the scenery lovely in many places. In conclusion, she posed a question: "Both our children and we adults need more air and exercise; here is a big recreational possibility. How can we go about it?"[37]

Moses's reply to Mrs. Case must be weighed in the context of his ability to surmount the insurmountable, as his biographer, Robert Caro, concedes. The staggering register of parks, parkways, bridges, urban renewal projects, and other public works ventures completed by Moses is matched only by the equally astonishing methods he used to remove nearly every barrier in his path, whether natural or human.

In his letter to Mrs. Case, Moses begins "Your suggestion to use abandoned railroad rights of way for bicycle paths is interesting," and then accurately adds "but problems of acquisition of title, which in many cases reverts on abandonment to adjacent owners, franchising, regulation and policing, construction funds etc., are extremely involved."[38]

Moses declined to confront those challenges or to pursue a comprehensive program to develop what Mrs. Case obviously believed he could achieve. Although many factors may have contributed to that decision, his unwillingness to do so is best explained by his inability to view cycling as anything more than a pleasing recreational activity, and especially one with a limited public voice. Instead, his focus on the importance of automobiles becomes clear in his letter of reply: "In light of the present-day traffic needs and the competition for limited funds for urgent public improvements, I doubt very much if anything could be accomplished on a state-wide basis along the lines you suggest. I know of no practical expedients to accomplish what you have in mind on a state-wide or regional basis. It is something which must be done on municipal levels."[39]

Far more than any of Moses's promotional bulletins and correspondence regarding the 1938 plan, the exchange of letters with Mrs. Case in 1956 illuminates Moses's initiatives on behalf of cyclists and whether they can be judged as either comprehensive or farsighted. Clearly, her letter, not his, looks to the future, and the conversion of abandoned railroad corridors to bicycle paths would become one of the most important contexts for path building during the modern post-World War II era.

Twenty years after Mrs. Case's letter, Congress passed the Railroad Revitalization and Regulatory Reform Act, asserting public control over abandoned railroad corridors—a strategy described as "railbanking"—and authorizing the use of those corridors for public trails or for the eventual return of rail service. Ten years later, in 1986, the Rails-to-Trails Conservancy in Washington, DC, became the country's principal organization promoting a nationwide network of bicycle trails, and today those corridors continue to extend in ever-greater lengths across the countryside.[40]

Whether one views the Moses plan for bicycle paths to be a well-intentioned but limited effort (given the context for bicycling in 1938) or alternatively a makeshift device intended to appease a small but vocal group of enthusiasts, we might reasonably ask whether the Robert Moses era represented an opportunity lost for cyclists. Robert Caro compares Moses to a force of nature, and whether we are horrified by his flawed character and abuse of power or mesmerized by the products of his energy and genius, the temptation to consider whether, had he turned those forces toward building a system of public roads for bicycles, he might have propelled us in the right direction, is nearly irresistible.

Acknowledgments

Travel has dominated this study during the past twelve years: exhausting, exhilarating, dispiriting, encouraging, disorienting, enlightening, expensive, and richly rewarding travel. Invariably, the people I have encountered along the way have steered me in one or more of those directions. Fortunately, the episodes that linger longest in memory are the gratifying ones, and five are representative.

Lost once again, and with time quickly running out for limited evening hours offered by a local archive one day each week, I managed to reach Ted Goldsborough at the Lower Merion Historical Society in Bala Cynwyd, Pennsylvania. Ted calmly guided me by phone to the society's building, where I found a rare copy of Frank Hamilton Taylor's *Cyclers' and Drivers' Best Routes in and around Philadelphia*, which opened the door to more thorough investigation of the role of special artists as illustrators in nineteenth-century periodicals. Both Ted and Max Buten were especially helpful in providing images from that publication.

Similar scheduling difficulties developed in Rochester in 2007, where City Historian Ruth Rosenberg Naparsteck went out of her way to help during a very difficult period of city budget cuts and retrieved from her office the album of photographs by Cline Rogers for the Monroe County Sidepath Commission. At the time, that portfolio was not included in the catalog of the Rochester and Monroe County Library, and without her assistance I would not have discovered that invaluable collection.

At the Cleveland Public Library, Michael Ruffing and Ann Olszewski were especially helpful in tracking down a collection of plans transferred to the library by the Cleveland Parks Department but never cataloged. Ann played a principal role on the committee organized to review and conserve the plans, and she invited me to attend the group's first meeting, which led to the discovery of the plans for a bicycle path by Ernest Bowditch in 1886. Alicia Naab has been similarly helpful in notifying me when more of the Bowditch plans were discovered.

After fielding my routine inquiries about old bicycle paths, Robert Skulsky, director of the Greater Hazleton Area Civic Partnership, organized an impromptu gathering in his offices and encouraged Thomas Ogorzalek from Butler Enterprises to search for mining surveys that might show the location of the 1897 path to Eckley. Those surveys pinpoint the path and may eventually aid the community's efforts to establish trails systems throughout that mountainous region. Robert and I also enjoyed a memorable afternoon walk with Libby along the existing trail, which hopefully corresponds to the old bicycle path for at least some portions of its length.

In Vincentown, New Jersey, Kim and Wayne Batten opened their farmhouse to me, and together we spent several hours at their kitchen table poring over photographs and newspaper records of the Mount Holly-Smithville Bicycle Railroad. I enjoyed that evening immensely—a rewarding conclusion to a difficult week of travel.

Others who have graciously aided this project are numerous and include James Amemasor, Newark; Dona Brown, Underhill; Michele Clark, Brookline; Bruce Epperson, Davie; Larry Finison, Needham; Amanda Fontenova, Wilkes-Barre; James Glass, Indianapolis; Lisa Hite, Louisville; Tony Huffman, Dayton; Margaret Humberston, Springfield; Amy Johnson, Reading; Tom Jones, Wilkes-Barre; Benjamin Krall, Toledo; Jeffrey Monseau, Springfield; Sarah Mycroft, Providence; Michele Plourde-Barker, Springfield; John Swintosky, Louisville; and Luis Vivanco, Burlington.

Over the years, Sean Fisher, archivist for the Massachusetts Department of Conservation and Recreation, has steadfastly fielded questions and searched for images. Similarly, historians James Garvin and Donna-Belle Garvin in New Hampshire have been unfailingly generous in offering assistance on a broad range of topics. In the University of Vermont's Interlibrary Loan Department, Barbara Lamonda and Lisa Brooks never flinch from my unending requests for obscure materials. Graduate students who assisted with the unenviable task of reading newspapers on microfilm include Michael Plummer, Matthew Preedom, and Laura Sadowsky.

I am sincerely grateful to the University of Vermont for its Lattie Coor awards and for the funding made available by the university's Department of History. It has been a genuine pleasure to work with manuscript editors Melinda Rankin (who is also a century rider) and Kathleen Caruso; designer Molly Seamans, who did superb work with the text, images, cover design, and appendix table; and assistant acquisitions editor Justin Kehoe. I also owe special thanks to editor Roger Conover and to readers David Herlihy, Charles Meinert, John Weiss, and John Stilgoe—to whom I am particularly indebted. And finally, to Ruth, my straightaway companion.

Appendix: New York State Sidepaths

The following inventory of New York State sidepaths serves two principal purposes. First, the list supports conclusions about the length and reach of that state's sidepath campaign. During the period that starts in 1892 (the year that Charles Raymond began building a path between Lockport and Olcott on Lake Ontario) and draws to a close by 1904, sidepath associations and commissions constructed or improved more than two thousand miles of sidepaths. Newspaper accounts proclaimed that during just a twelve-month period following adoption of the landmark Ellsworth Sidepath Law, from September 1899 to September 1900, county commissions opened approximately thirteen hundred miles of new paths. Yet those who focus on the many miles traversed by these sidepaths should not overlook the equally remarkable register of cities, towns, villages, and places connected by those wheelways, and the catalog is equally useful as a record of bicycle travel across New York's late nineteenth-century countryside.

Second, the paths and the newspaper articles cited here are offered as beginning points for continued inquiry about the former locations of New York's paths and are not intended to be a complete catalog. Granted, many of these wheelways have been lost to road widening. However, in communities where development and road building have not been overwhelming, some sidepaths may survive as sidewalks in village centers or remain as layers of cinders beneath the edges of still-narrow country roads. For towns engaged in modern path building, reclaiming the physical history of nineteenth-century bicycle paths may prove valuable. Toward that end, the United States Geological Survey maps are useful, because surveyors mapped many regions of New York at about the same time that sidepath commissioners were building paths. However, these maps cannot replace knowledge of local terrain or landmarks, and opportunities to correct and expand the information contained here will undoubtedly occur.

The calculations and estimates for total miles of sidepaths are conservative and probably underestimate the total mileage of New York's sidepaths—the result of several factors. Newspaper accounts often refer to sidepaths that connect two communities, but estimating the lengths of those paths is not as simple as measuring the distance between two town centers. Initially, the Ellsworth law did not authorize commissions to build paths within city or village limits without the authority of local officials. Yet many towns and cities allowed cyclists to build sidepaths along local streets, and amendments to the Ellsworth law later expanded commission authority. In either case, pinpointing the locations of those beginning and ending points remains difficult. In addition, many newspaper accounts refer to paths by name but without providing either beginning or ending points. When mileage estimates become too speculative, because information is lacking, the paths are listed and if commission expenditures are sufficient (assuming an average cost of $250 per mile), then the paths are assigned a nominal length of one mile. When neither origin nor destination is known, or when the possibility of overlap exists, the paths are listed but assigned no mileage. I have identified more than a hundred paths to which no mileage is assigned, and many others contribute only nominal mileage. Most individual estimates are rounded down to the nearest half mile, but subtotal estimates have been rounded in the customary manner. For three counties (Monroe, Oneida, and Suffolk), reports of mileage conflict, and I have not been able to resolve those discrepancies; thus, I have cited the conflicting reports.

This inventory also should be regarded as a supplement to the 1901 *Progress Map Showing Side Path Construction* prepared by the New York State Division of the LAW, and the two should be reviewed together. In Saratoga, Monroe, Orleans, and a few other counties, paths are noted on that map but are not identified in the inventory, because I was unable to verify them through newspaper accounts. In addition, the inventory does not include preexisting sidepaths unless county commissions assumed authority for those paths. Thus, only small portions of the continuous sidepath route along Ridge Road in Niagara, Orleans, and Wayne counties, visible on the map, are added to the inventory. Suffolk County poses special challenges, because some of that county's sidepaths existed prior to the arrival of cyclists and because commissioners opened spur sidepaths leading into village centers or toward shore points. Estimates in the inventory are thus substantially less than those offered in several newspaper accounts, which also vary considerably.

The map of Oneida County sidepaths prepared by Richard Perlen and Otto Poepel also supplements data included in the inventory. Another map, that of Long Island roads and bicycle paths prepared by Robert Delano Servoss, circa 1900, is useful because it shows roads and adjoining bicycle paths separately; the map is available at the Brooklyn Historical Society. Unfortunately, two important maps have eluded discovery. In the spring of 1900, the Albany County Sidepath Commission published a map and sidepath guide identifying the names and locations of each of the county's eighteen paths. During the fall of that same year, the Matthews-Northrup Company published a road and sidepath map of Erie and Niagara counties. Both maps hopefully will add to the information contained in this inventory.

Citations to more than one newspaper account or journal article are offered to establish the start or completion of construction for specific paths, to clarify location, or to provide other useful information, such as nearby landmarks. Many of the newspaper articles have been gathered from Thomas Tryniski's website, Old Fulton Post Cards (http://fultonhistory.com), and from the Library of Congress website Chronicling America: Historic American Newspapers (chroniclingamerica.loc.gov). As more local newspapers are scanned, additional information will become available.

In January 1900, the *Otsego Farmer* (published in Cooperstown) reported that forty-eight New York counties had established sidepath commissions, also naming the counties without commissions: Clinton, Delaware, Essex, Hamilton, Kings, New York, Putnam, Queens, Richmond, Schohaire, Sullivan, and Wyoming. That report may have overlooked then recently established Nassau County, which never did establish a commission but is included in this catalog because cyclists opened several paths, totaling about six miles. Cyclists also can claim credit for building at least one sidepath in Queens County, and the paths in both Nassau and Queens Counties are added to the total. I have been unable

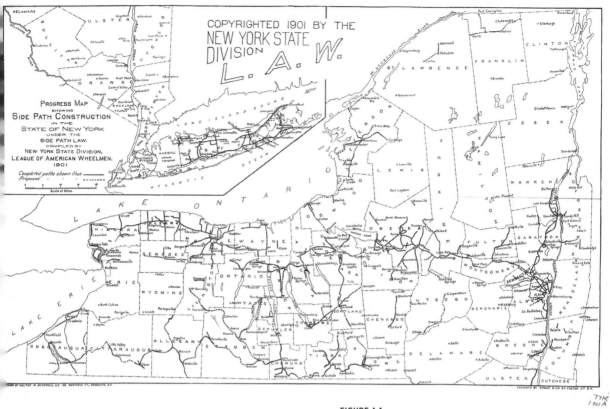

FIGURE A.1

Progress Map Showing Side Path Construction, prepared in 1901 by the New York State Division, LAW. Courtesy Yale University.

to find any reference to a sidepath commission in Lewis County, but Oneida County's commission identifies two paths with the names of two Lewis County towns, Turin and Lowville, and thus I have listed that county but have not assigned any mileage to paths. Including Lewis County, but excluding Nassau and Queens Counties, this inventory identifies forty-seven counties with sidepath commissions, leaving Rockland County as the lone discrepancy with the 1900 report. In 1901, shortly before the annual sidepath commission convention held in Buffalo that year, *Cycle Age and Trade Review* reported forty-three counties with commissions, but the report provided no list. Separately, I was able to locate newspaper articles with individual county reports showing the total miles of sidepaths in eighteen respective counties, for a cumulative total of 1,239 miles, leaving the other thirty counties to account for the additional mileage.

The following abbreviations are used in the column headings: REP.CSM for Reported County Sidepath Miles; REP.SM for Reported Sidepath Miles; and EST.SM for Estimated Sidepath Miles. The totals for some counties are the sum of reported and estimated sidepath miles; for others, reports of total county miles are used, unless newspaper articles established that new sidepaths were completed after the dates of those reports. For each county, subtotals are provided for each column (Reported County Sidepath Miles, Reported Sidepath Miles, and Estimated Sidepath Miles), and a separate subtotal column shows the total mileage tallied for each county.

All of the citations are to newspaper or journal articles, with four exceptions. One is the 1901 map prepared by the New York State Division of the LAW (NYLAW), which I have used to verify the locations of a few sidepaths that are cited in newspaper accounts but not located with clarity. The second is the map of Oneida County sidepaths prepared by Richard Perlen and Otto Poepel. The third is an unpublished, undated volume (circa 1997) titled *The History of Bicycling in the Hudson-Mohawk Region of New York State. 1880–1900*, authored by a knowledgeable bicycle historian, Charles W. Meinert of Delmar, New York. A copy is available at the Rensselaer County Historical Society in Troy. Meinert is a frequent contributor to *The Wheelmen* magazine, and his list of sidepaths in the region was assembled from newspaper accounts on microfilm. Meinert's research is meticulous and reliable. The fourth is Isaac Potter's 1898 book, *Cycle Paths*.

| --- | --- | --- | --- | --- | --- | --- | --- | --- | --- | --- |

1. Albany County

Albany

Partridge Street from Central Avenue to Western Avenue (St. Mary's Park)			0.5		Albany Evening Journal	27 May 1899	6			
Allen Street Path to New Scotland Plank Road			1		Albany Evening Journal	2 Jul 1898	7			
Western Avenue Path to Whitbecks Hotel at McKownville			3		Albany Evening Journal	23 Apr 1898	7	Albany Evening Journal	30 Apr 1898	7
Whitehall Road Path—Delaware Avenue to New Scotland Plank Road			2		Albany Evening Journal	2 Jul 1898	7			
Country Club to Whitbecks Hotel at McKownville			0		Albany Evening Journal	23 Apr 1898	7			
South Pearl Street to Kenwood			1		Albany Evening Journal	27 May 1899	6			
Hurstville Path (New Scotland Road from Allen Street to Whitehall Road)			1		Albany Evening Journal	23 Jul 1898	7	Albany Evening Journal	15 Jun 1900	12
Madison Avenue to Ridgewood along Partridge			0		Meinert, Bicycling Hudson-Mohawk Region	c. 1997	36			
Albany to Schenectady (Schenectady County) via Schenectady Turnpike			14		LAW Bulletin and Good Roads, vol. 22	29 Nov 1895	21	Albany Evening Journal	2 Jul 1898	7
Albany to Cohoes via Watervliet (West Side of Second Avenue)			10		Albany Evening Journal	23 Apr 1898	7	Albany Evening Journal	30 Apr 1898	7
Watervliet to intersection of Sand Creek and Wolf Road			0		Meinert, Bicycling Hudson-Mohawk Region	c. 1997	36			
Cohoes to Schenectady via Latham's Corners (Upper Cohoes Path)			15		Albany Evening Journal	23 Apr 1898	7	Utica Sunday Tribune	2 Jun 1901	13
Rensselaer Lake Path—Schenectady Path to McKownville			2		Albany Evening Journal	2 Jul 1898	7			
Karner Path—Schenectady Path at Halfway House (HH) to Karner Station			1		Albany Evening Journal	2 Jul 1898	7			
Shaker Cross Path—Schenectady Path at HH to Shaker Road			1		Albany Evening Journal	2 Jul 1898	7			
Loudonville to Newtonville			1		Albany Evening Journal	2 Jul 1898	7	Albany Evening Journal	26 Jan 1899	6
Albany to Delmar and Slingerlands via Normansville/Delaware Avenue			7		Albany Evening Journal	28 Jun 1898	7	Utica Sunday Tribune	2 Jun 1901	13
Slingerlands to Indian Fields via Voorheesville			4.5		Albany Evening Journal	7 Jan 1899	7			
Kenwood to Cedar Hill, Selkirk, and Coeymans, via River Road			11		Albany Evening Journal	7 Jan 1899	7			
Selkirk to Becker Corners			2		Utica Sunday Tribune	2 Jun 1901	13			
South Bethlemen to Ravena			5.5		Albany Evening Journal	25 Jun 1898	7	Albany Evening Journal	28 Jun 1898	7
Bethlehem Path (Albany to Bethlehem Center, presumably)			0		Utica Sunday Tribune	2 Jun 1901	13			
Altamont to Guilderland at Great Western Turnpike			0		Meinert, Bicycling Hudson-Mohawk Region	c. 1997	36			
County sidepath miles reported	80				Utica Sunday Tribune	2 Jun 1901	13			
Subtotals—Albany County:	**80**	**0**	**83**	**80**						

2. Allegany County

Wellsville to Alfred			17		Ithaca Daily News	26 Apr 1902	7	Tioga County Record	1 May 1902	3
Cuba to Hornellsville (Steuben County)			35		Ithaca Daily News	26 Apr 1902	7	Tioga County Record	1 May 1902	3
Subtotals—Allegany County:	**0**	**0**	**52**	**52**						

3. Broome County

Binghamton to Union (Binghamton Wheel Club—High Wheel Era)			0		LAW Bulletin, vol. 5	23 Dec 1887	351			
Binghamton (Lestershire Hill) to Union			9		Tioga County Record	27 Jul 1899	5	Broome Republican	29 Jul 1899	3
Binghamton North Path			2		Broome Republican	27 Jan 1900	3			
Binghamton to Chenango Bridge—along Fifth Avenue Chanango River			6		Tioga County Record	21 Apr 1898	3	Broome Republican	18 May 1901	6

SIDEPATH LOCATIONS: COUNTY AND TOWNS	REP. CSM	REP. SM	EST. SM	SUB TOT.	SOURCE CITED (A)	DATE OF SOURCE	PG	SOURCE CITED (B)	DATE OF SOURCE	PG
Binghamton to Conklin, near sugar beet factory		8			*Broome Republican*	24 May 1902	5	*Broome Republican*	30 Aug 1903	5
Binghamton to Apalachin (as far as Tioga County line)			14		*Tioga County Record*	28 Apr 1898	3			
Subtotals—Broome County:	0	19	20	**39**						

4. Cattaraugus County

Salamanca to Little Valley			9		*Randolph Register*	7 Jun 1899	1			
Little Valley to Napoli, Randolph, and Chautauqua County line			0		*Randolph Register*	7 Jun 1899	1			
Olean to Hinsdale and Allegany County line at Cuba			6.5		*Randolph Register*	7 Jun 1899	1			
Olean to Allegany			4		*Randolph Register*	7 Jun 1899	1			
Elko Path		3.5			*Randolph Register*	7 Jun 1899	1			
Subtotals—Cattaraugus County:	0	4	20	**24**						

5. Cayuga County

Port Byron to Weedsport			3.5		*Auburn Democrat-Argus*	7 Apr 1903	5	*Auburn Democrat-Argus*	5 May 1905	5
Weedsport to Jordan (Onondaga County)		1			*Auburn Democrat-Argus*	7 Apr 1903	5			
Auburn to Port Byron			8.5		*Auburn Democrat-Argus*	15 Mar 1901	8			
Auburn Owasco Street Path to Swartout Corners			3		*Auburn Bulletin*	6 Sep 1899	6	*Auburn Democrat-Argus*	15 Mar 1901	8
Auburn South Street Path to Fleming		1.5			*Auburn Democrat-Argus*	7 Apr 1903	5	*Auburn Democrat-Argus*	5 May 1905	5
Auburn East Genesee Street Path			0.5		*Auburn Democrat-Argus*	3 May 1904	8			
Half Acre (Aurelius) to Lehigh Valley Railroad (Half Acre Station)		1			*Auburn Democrat-Argus*	15 Mar 1901	8			
Owasco Lake paths			0		*Auburn Democrat-Argus*	15 Mar 1901	8	*Auburn Semiweekly Journal*	24 Apr 1906	5
Cayuga Path			8		*Auburn Democrat-Argus*	5 May 1905	5			
Moravia West Cayuga Steet to Owasco Inlet			0.5		*Moravia Republican*	16 Jun 1899	5			
Moravia (from Owasco Inlet) to Cascade			4		*Moravia Republican*	18 May 1900	5	*Auburn Democrat-Argus*	5 May 1905	5
Cascade to Wyckoff (WyckoffPath)			8.5		*Auburn Democrat-Argus*	3 May 1904	8			
County sidepath miles reported	38				*Auburn Democrat-Argus*	3 May 1904	8			
Subtotals—Cayuga County:	38	4	37	**38**						

6. Chautauqua County

Dunkirk										
Roberts Road to Main Road		1			*Fredonia Censor*	9 Apr 1902	5			
Dunkirk to Hickoryhurst	1				*Buffalo Courier*	28 Jan 1901	9			
Dunkirk to Silver Creek—Lake Road Path	9				*Buffalo Courier*	28 Jan 1901	9			
Silver Creek to Irving	3				*Buffalo Courier*	28 Jan 1901	9			
Fredonia										
East Main Street	1				*Fredonia Censor*	17 Jun 1903	8			
Temple Street		0			*Buffalo Courier*	28 Jan 1901	9	*Fredonia Censor*	31 Jul 1907	5
Eagle Street		0			*Buffalo Courier*	28 Jan 1901	9	*Fredonia Censor*	31 Jul 1907	5
Liberty Street		0			*Buffalo Courier*	28 Jan 1901	9	*Fredonia Censor*	31 Jul 1907	5
Fredonia to Brockton	5				*Buffalo Courier*	28 Jan 1901	9			
Sheridan Path	6				*Buffalo Courier*	28 Jan 1901	9	*Fredonia Censor*	15 May 1901	4

SIDEPATH LOCATIONS: COUNTY AND TOWNS	REP. CSM	REP. SM	EST. SM	SUB TOT.	SOURCE CITED (A)	DATE OF SOURCE	PG	SOURCE CITED (B)	DATE OF SOURCE	PG
Jamestown to Bemis Point on Chautauqua Lake			9		*Buffalo Courier*	28 Jan 1901	9	*Holly Standard*	5 May 1901	1
Jamestown to Celeron along Jones Avenue and Gifford Avenue		1			*Buffalo Courier*	28 Jan 1901	9			
Mayville to Chautauqua Assembly		3			*Buffalo Courier*	28 Jan 1901	9			
Hartfield Path		1			*Buffalo Courier*	28 Jan 1901	9			
Kennedy Path			0		*Buffalo Courier*	28 Jan 1901	9			
County sidepath miles reported	40				*Buffalo Courier*	28 Jan 1901	9			
Subtotals—Chautauqua County:	**40**	**30**	**10**	**40**						

7. Chemung County

SIDEPATH LOCATIONS: COUNTY AND TOWNS	REP. CSM	REP. SM	EST. SM	SUB TOT.	SOURCE CITED (A)	DATE OF SOURCE	PG	SOURCE CITED (B)	DATE OF SOURCE	PG
Waverly (Tioga County) to Hurlburt Crossing in Chemung		1.5			*Elmira Daily Gazette & Free Press*	15 Mar 1902	3	*Elmira Daily Gazette & Free Press*	14 Mar 1904	8
Chemung to Lowmanville		9			*Elmira Daily Gazette & Free Press*	14 Mar 1904	8			
Lowmanville to Wellsburg (Wellsburg Spur)		1			*Elmira Daily Gazette & Free Press*	2 Jul 1899	4	*Elmira Daily Gazette & Free Press*	14 Mar 1904	8
Wellsburg to Elmira (Chemung to Elmira via Wellsburg)		7			*Elmira Daily Gazette & Free Press*	14 Mar 1904	8	*Elmira Daily Gazette & Free Press*	8 Jul 1901	5
Elmira										
West Water Street Path		2			*Elmira Daily Gazette & Free Press*	2 Jul 1899	4	*Elmira Daily Gazette & Free Press*	29 May 1901	3
Polly Path across Fitch's Bridge			0		*Elmira Daily Gazette & Free Press*	2 Jul 1899	4	*Elmira Daily Gazette & Free Press*	14 May 1900	4
West Church Street Path		2			*Elmira Daily Gazette & Free Press*	14 Mar 1904	8			
Maple Avenue Path to Maple Avenue Park			0		*Elmira Daily Gazette & Free Press*	2 Apr 1904	8	*Elmira Daily Gazette & Free Press*	30 Jun 1903	5
Grand Central Avenue			0		*Elmira Daily Gazette & Free Press*	14 Apr 1903	7			
Elmira-Horseheads-Corning Path (Steuben County line)		14			*Elmira Daily Gazette & Free Press*	18 Apr 1895	7	*Elmira Daily Gazette & Free Press*	14 Mar 1904	8
Section: Elmira to Horseheads			0		*Elmira Daily Gazette & Free Press*	5 Oct 1895	8	*Elmira Daily Gazette & Free Press*	9 Apr 1896	4
Section: Horseheads to Big Flats			0		*Elmira Daily Gazette & Free Press*	2 Apr 1907	7	*Elmira Daily Gazette & Free Press*	9 Apr 1896	4
Section: Big Flats to Steuben County line			0		*Elmira Daily Gazette & Free Press*	2 Jul 1899	4	*Elmira Daily Gazette & Free Press*	22 May 1907	2
Section: Eldridge Park to Gibsons (Steuben County)			0		*Elmira Daily Gazette & Free Press*	28 Apr 1895	16			
Elmira to Pine City			5.5		*Elmira Daily Gazette & Free Press*	2 Jul 1899	4			
Horseheads to Breesport			5.5		*Elmira Daily Gazette & Free Press*	28 Jan 1902	5			
Horseheads to Millport		5			*Elmira Daily Gazette & Free Press*	2 Jul 1899	4	*Elmira Daily Gazette & Free Press*	24 Jul 1899	8
County sidepath miles reported	35				*Elmira Daily Gazette & Free Press*	14 Mar 1904	8			
Subtotals—Chemung County:	**35**	**42**	**11**	**53**						

8. Chenango County

SIDEPATH LOCATIONS: COUNTY AND TOWNS	REP. CSM	REP. SM	EST. SM	SUB TOT.	SOURCE CITED (A)	DATE OF SOURCE	PG	SOURCE CITED (B)	DATE OF SOURCE	PG
Norwich to Oxford			8		*Cooperstown Otsego Farmer*	21 Jul 1899	1			
South Otselic Path			1		*DeKuyter Gleaner*	21 Jun 1900	1			
Subtotals—Chenango County:	**0**	**0**	**9**	**9**						

9. Columbia County

SIDEPATH LOCATIONS: COUNTY AND TOWNS	REP. CSM	REP. SM	EST. SM	SUB TOT.	SOURCE CITED (A)	DATE OF SOURCE	PG	SOURCE CITED (B)	DATE OF SOURCE	PG
Hudson to Claverack			4		*Hudson Register*	20 Jul 1900	4	*Hudson Register*	9 Apr 1901	1
Hudson to Stottville			4.5		*Hudson Register*	9 Apr 1901	1			
Hudson to Blue Store on the Albany Post Road			12		*Hudson Register*	9 Apr 1901	1			
Valatie to Chatham			5.5		*Hudson Register*	9 Apr 1901	1			
Valatie to Niverville			2		*Hudson Register*	9 Apr 1901	1			

SIDEPATH LOCATIONS: COUNTY AND TOWNS	REP. CSM	REP. SM	EST. SM	SUB TOT.	SOURCE CITED (A)	DATE OF SOURCE	PG	SOURCE CITED (B)	DATE OF SOURCE	PG
New Lebanon Path			1		*Hudson Register*	9 Apr 1901	1			
Subtotals—Columbia County:	0	0	29	**29**						

10. Cortland County

SIDEPATH LOCATIONS: COUNTY AND TOWNS	REP. CSM	REP. SM	EST. SM	SUB TOT.	SOURCE CITED (A)	DATE OF SOURCE	PG	SOURCE CITED (B)	DATE OF SOURCE	PG
Cortland: Groton Avenue Path, city limits to brick schoolhouse			0.5		*Cortland Evening Standard*	3 Aug 1900	6			
Cortland to Little York (via Homer)			7		*Cooperstown Otsego Farmer*	21 Jul 1899	1	*Syracuse Post Standard*	14 May 1906	9
Little York to Tully (Onondaga County)			6		*Syracuse Evening Herald*	27 Apr 1900	8	NYLAW, *Map of Sidepath Construction*	1901	
Homer										
Copeland Avenue			0		*Cortland Standard*	22 Apr 1898	5			
North Main Street			0		*Cortland Standard*	22 Apr 1898	5			
Town Line at gas house to Homer Village			0.5		*Syracuse Evening Herald*	12 Sep 1901	3			
Cortland to McGrawville			4		*Oswego Daily Times*	3 May 1901	7	*Syracuse Herald*	14 May 1906	3
Cortland to South Cortland			4		*Syracuse Post Standard*	14 May 1906	9			
McLean Path and Gilette Loop to the Ithaca Path (Tompkins County)			2		*Syracuse Evening Herald*	31 Mar 1901	15	*Syracuse Post Standard*	1 Jul 1902	10
Cortland to Scott (via Homer)			8		*Syracuse Post Standard*	14 May 1906	9			
Scott to Glen Haven (Cayuga County)			5		*Syracuse Journal*	8 Jul 1902	7	*Syracuse Journal*	2 Aug 1902	5
Cortland to Truxten			11		*Syracuse Post Standard*	14 May 1906	9	*Syracuse Herald*	14 May 1906	3
County sidepath miles reported	40				*Syracuse Evening Herald*	31 Jan 1901	5			
Subtotals—Cortland County:	40	0	48	**48**						

11. Dutchess County

SIDEPATH LOCATIONS: COUNTY AND TOWNS	REP. CSM	REP. SM	EST. SM	SUB TOT.	SOURCE CITED (A)	DATE OF SOURCE	PG	SOURCE CITED (B)	DATE OF SOURCE	PG
Poughkeepsie to Washington Hollow—Post Road & Dutchess Turnpike			1		*Amenia Times*	15 Jul 1899	5	*Millbrook Round Table*	12 Jul 1951	7
Poughkeepsie and vicinity			1		*Amenia Times*	14 Oct 1899	4			
Poughkeepsie: Southeast Avenue			0		*Millbrook Round Table*	4 Nov 1899	6			
Poughkeepsie to Millbrook			1		*Poughkeepsie Daily Eagle*	14 Feb 1896	5	*Millbrook Round Table*	12 Apr 1951	6
Subtotals—Dutchess County:	0	0	3	**3**						

12. Erie County

SIDEPATH LOCATIONS: COUNTY AND TOWNS	REP. CSM	REP. SM	EST. SM	SUB TOT.	SOURCE CITED (A)	DATE OF SOURCE	PG	SOURCE CITED (B)	DATE OF SOURCE	PG
Buffalo										
Main Street to Williamsville			4		*Buffalo Morning Express*	15 Jul 1899	9	*North Tonawanda Evening News*	28 May 1900	3
Niagara Street (westerly side) from Cornelius Creek to Riverside Park			1		*Illustrated Buffalo Express*	11 Feb 1900	14			
Buffalo to Niagara Falls (not completed)			0		*Buffalo Express*	21 Nov 1895	9	*Buffalo Express*	17 Dec 1895	12
Grand Island		23			*Illustrated Buffalo Express*	10 Jun 1900	3	*North Tonawanda Evening News*	23 Jul 1900	3
Blasdell to Hamburg via White Corners Road		1			*Buffalo Express*	20 Jan 1900	9			
Akron Path		2			*Buffalo Morning Express*	24 May 1903	20			
County sidepath miles reported	20				*Buffalo Morning Express*	24 May 1903	20			
Subtotals—Erie County:	20	26	5	**26**						

13. Franklin County

SIDEPATH LOCATIONS: COUNTY AND TOWNS	REP. CSM	REP. SM	EST. SM	SUB TOT.	SOURCE CITED (A)	DATE OF SOURCE	PG	SOURCE CITED (B)	DATE OF SOURCE	PG
Malone to North Bangor (Bicknell Hill)			6		*St. Regis Falls Adirondack News*	27 May 1899	1			
Subtotals—Franklin County:	0	0	6	**6**						

SIDEPATH LOCATIONS: COUNTY AND TOWNS	REP. CSM	REP. SM	EST. SM	SUB TOT.	SOURCE CITED (A)	DATE OF SOURCE	PG	SOURCE CITED (B)	DATE OF SOURCE	PG

14. Fulton County

SIDEPATH LOCATIONS: COUNTY AND TOWNS	REP. CSM	REP. SM	EST. SM	SUB TOT.	SOURCE CITED (A)	DATE OF SOURCE	PG	SOURCE CITED (B)	DATE OF SOURCE	PG
Gloversville to Mayfield and Northville (Sacandaga Park)			15		*Gloversville Daily Leader*	4 Jun 1900	7	*Gloversville Daily Leader*	20 Aug 1901	8
Cranberry Creek segment of Northville Path			0		*Gloversville Daily Leader*	11 Mar 1902	7			
Gloversville to Broadalbin			8.5		*Gloversville Daily Leader*	23 Apr 1900	7	*Gloversville Daily Leader*	17 Jan 1901	5
Gloversville (South Main Street Path along trolley line)			0.5		*Gloversville Daily Leader*	23 Apr 1900	7	*Gloversville Daily Leader*	7 Jun 1901	7
Gloversville to Johnstown			4		*Gloversville Daily Leader*	7 Jun 1901	7			
Johnstown-North Perry Street Path (fair grounds to Fern Dale Cemetery)			0.5		*Gloversville Daily Leader*	7 Jun 1901	7	*Gloversville Daily Leader*	17 Jan 1901	5
Johnstown to Quackenbush's Road House near Montgomery County line			1		*Fulton County Republican*	1 Jun 1899	6	*Amsterdam Evening Recorder*	24 Jun 1903	4
Quackenbush's Road House to Fonda toll gate			0		*Gloversville Daily Leader*	9 Aug 1899	5			
County sidepath miles reported	23				*Gloversville Daily Leader*	9 Aug 1899	5	*Gloversville Daily Leader*	22 Sep 1900	7
Subtotals—Fulton County:	**23**	**0**	**30**	**30**						

15. Genesee County

SIDEPATH LOCATIONS: COUNTY AND TOWNS	REP. CSM	REP. SM	EST. SM	SUB TOT.	SOURCE CITED (A)	DATE OF SOURCE	PG	SOURCE CITED (B)	DATE OF SOURCE	PG
Batavia to LeRoy via Stafford			18		*Batavia Daily News*	16 Jun 1898	4	*Batavia Daily News*	18 Jun 1898	1
LeRoy to Caledonia (Livingston County)			1		*Rochester Democrat & Chronicle*	19 Apr 1897	15	*Batavia Daily News*	12 Mar 1900	4
Batavia to East Pembroke via Bushville			6.5		*Batavia Daily News*	29 Nov 1899	1	*Batavia Daily News*	14 Jun 1900	1
Batavia to Elba			0		*Batavia Daily News*	14 Jun 1900	1	*Batavia Daily News*	23 Jun 1900	5
Bergen to Churchville (Monroe County)			1		*Batavia Daily News*	23 Jul 1901	5			
County sidepath miles reported	21				*Batavia Daily News*	31 Dec 1900	1			
Subtotals—Genesee County:	**21**	**0**	**27**	**27**						

16. Greene County

SIDEPATH LOCATIONS: COUNTY AND TOWNS	REP. CSM	REP. SM	EST. SM	SUB TOT.	SOURCE CITED (A)	DATE OF SOURCE	PG	SOURCE CITED (B)	DATE OF SOURCE	PG
Coeymans (Albany County) to New Baltimore and Coxsackie			0		Meinert, *Bicycling Hudson-Mohawk Region*	c. 1997	36			
Coxsackie to Athens			0		*Albany Evening Journal*	26 May 1900	11			
Athens to Catskill			4		Meinert, *Bicycling Hudson-Mohawk Region*	c. 1997	36			
Catskill to Palenville			9.5		*Brooklyn Daily Eagle*	18 Jun 1899	18	*Millbrook Round Table*	1 Jun 1901	4
County sidepath miles reported	10				*Gloversville Daily Leader*	22 Sep 1900	7			
Subtotals—Greene County:	**10**	**0**	**14**	**14**						

17. Herkimer County

SIDEPATH LOCATIONS: COUNTY AND TOWNS	REP. CSM	REP. SM	EST. SM	SUB TOT.	SOURCE CITED (A)	DATE OF SOURCE	PG	SOURCE CITED (B)	DATE OF SOURCE	PG
Frankfort to Utica (both sides of Mohawk River)			18		*Little Falls Times*	4 Aug 1899	1	*Utica Observer*	13 Oct 1900	12
Frankfort to Ilion			2.5		*Little Falls Times*	21 Jun 1899	4	*Utica Herald-Dispatch*	13 Jun 1900	3
Ilion to Mohawk			2		*Utica Observer*	4 Aug 1899	5	*Utica Herald-Dispatch*	22 Apr 1903	5
Mohawk to Herkimer (Herkimer Path)			1.5		*Little Falls Times*	21 Jun 1899	4	*Utica Herald-Dispatch*	3 May 1902	5
Schuyler Path (Mohawk to Schuyler Corners)		4.5			*Utica Observer*	12 Sep 1900	4	*Utica Observer*	13 Oct 1900	12
Herkimer to Little Falls (Little Falls Path)			3		*Little Falls Times*	21 Jun 1899	4	*Utica Observer*	13 Oct 1900	12
Herkimer: Mohawk Street Path			0		*Utica Observer*	9 Jun 1899	5			
Newport to Poland			4		*Little Falls Times*	21 Jun 1899	4	*Utica Herald-Dispatch*	31 Aug 1900	5
West Canada Creek Valley Path to Newport			0		*Utica Observer*	13 Oct 1900	12			
Poland to Cold Brook			1.5		*Little Falls Times*	23 Jul 1898	2			
Poland to Trenton Falls			0		*Utica Observer*	13 Oct 1900	12			

SIDEPATH LOCATIONS: COUNTY AND TOWNS	REP. CSM	REP. SM	EST. SM	SUB TOT.	SOURCE CITED (A)	DATE OF SOURCE	PG	SOURCE CITED (B)	DATE OF SOURCE	PG
Dolgeville to Little Falls			8		Cooperstown Otsego Farmer	21 Jul 1899	1	Little Falls Times	4 Aug 1899	1
Little Falls to East Creek			6		Cooperstown Otsego Farmer	21 Jul 1899	1	Utica Observer	13 Jun 1900	3
Subtotals—Herkimer County:	0	5	47	52						

18. Jefferson County

Adams to Adams Center			3		Watertown Daily Times	3 Jun 1899	8	Jefferson County Journal	21 May 1901	5
Adams to Henderson			9.5		Jefferson County Journal	25 Jun 1901	5			
Adams to Pierrepont Manor			5.5		Watertown Daily Times	3 Jun 1899	8	Jefferson County Journal	21 May 1901	5
Pierrepont Manor to Mannsville			1.5		Syracuse Sunday Herald	2 Jul 1899	22			
Mannsville to Lacona (Oswego County)			3		Watertown Daily Times	3 Jun 1899	8	Syracuse Sunday Herald	2 Jul 1899	22
Sackets Harbor to Watertown (Arsenal Street)			11		Watertown Daily Times	3 Jun 1899	8	Watertown Daily Times	22 Aug 1899	7
Sackets Harbor to Dexter, via Carter's Corners			0		Watertown Daily Times	17 May 1901	2			
Sackets Harbor Half-Way House Path—Bagg's Corners to Mill Creek Hill			1		Syracuse Sunday Herald	2 Jul 1899	22			
Watertown to Huntingtonville			1		Syracuse Sunday Herald	2 Jul 1899	22			
Subtotals—Jefferson County:	0	0	36	36						

19. Lewis County

Turin-Lowville Path (see Oneida County, Rome District)			0		Utica Herald-Dispatch	20 Dec 1904	4	Utica Herald-Dispatch	Dec 24 1906	9
Subtotals—Lewis County:	0	0	0	0						

20. Livingston County

Avon Path to Geneseo		1			Avon Herald	16 Jun 1899	3			
Dansville Path to Mount Morris			15		Castille Castilian	7 Jul 1899	3	Avon Herald	5 Aug 1899	3
Subtotals—Livingston County:		1	15	16						

21. Madison County

Oneida

Lenox Ave. to Wampsville and Canastota			4		Utica Daily Press	14 Jun 1901	8	Syracuse Journal	1 Jun 1907	3
Lake Street from Central Railroad to Sconondoa Street			0		Syracuse Herald	26 Apr 1906	3			
Glenwood Cemetery Path			1		Syracuse Herald	28 May 1909	5			
Oneida to South Bay			6		Madison County Times	28 May 1897	2	Utica Observer	14 Aug 1899	5
Canastota to South Bay			6		Utica Observer	14 Aug 1899	5	Chittenango Madison County Times	19 Jul 1901	2
Canastota: Peterboro Steet from Chapel Street to cinder path			0		Syracuse Evening Journal	26 Mar 1901	11			
Chittenango to Chittenango Station			3		Chittenango Madison County Times	8 Jun 1900	2			
Hamilton to Poolville			4.5		Utica Observer	20 Apr 1896	5			
Hamilton to Madison Lake										
Section: Hamilton to Pecksport			3		Utica Observer	20 Apr 1896	5			
Section: Pecksport to Bouckville			1.5		Utica Observer	20 Apr 1896	5			
Section: Bouckville to Madison Lake			2		Utica Observer	20 Apr 1896	5	Brookfield Courier	4 Jun 1902	2
Morrisville to Peterboro—Stone Road Path			5.5		Brookfield Courier	3 May 1899	3			
County sidepath miles reported	27				Brookfield Courier	18 Oct 1899	3	Utica Herald-Dispatch	21 Sep 1900	4-5
Subtotals—Madison County:	27	0	37	37						

SIDEPATH LOCATIONS: COUNTY AND TOWNS	REP. CSM	REP. SM	EST. SM	SUB TOT.	SOURCE CITED (A)	DATE OF SOURCE	PG	SOURCE CITED (B)	DATE OF SOURCE	PG
22. Monroe County										
Rochester										
Highland and Elmwood Avenue Path			4		*Monroe County Sidepath Guide*	1900	30			
Scott Road Path to Little Ridge Road		4.5			*Monroe County Sidepath Guide*	1900	36			
South Park Path			0.5		*Rochester Democrat and Chronicle*	12 May 1901	20			
Charlotte Path		5			*Monroe County Sidepath Guide*	1900	34			
Stone Road Path—West Side Boulevard Bypass along Dewey Avenue			0.5		*Rochester Democrat and Chronicle*	15 Aug 1901	5	NYLAW, *Map of Sidepath Construction*	1901	
Scottsville Path		9			*LAW Bulletin and Good Roads*, vol. 24	2 Oct 1896	465	*Monroe County Sidepath Guide*	1900	34
Scottsville to Mumford		6.5			*Monroe County Sidepath Guide*	1900	34			
Mumford to Caledonia (Livingston County)			0.5		*Monroe County Sidepath Guide*	1900	36			
East Henrietta Path to Honeoye Falls		14			*Monroe County Sidepath Guide*	1900	34			
West Henrietta Path		6			*Monroe County Sidepath Guide*	1900	34			
Buffalo and Churchville Path		12			*Monroe County Sidepath Guide*	1900	34			
Churchville to Bergen (Genesee County)			2		*Batavia Daily News*	23 Jul 1901	5	NYLAW, *Map of Sidepath Construction*	1901	
Little Ridge Road Path to Brockport		19			*Monroe County Sidepath Guide*	1900	34			
Brockport to Hamlin			6		*Rochester Democrat and Chronicle*	12 Oct 1904	14			
Manitou Beach Path			10		*Monroe County Sidepath Guide*	1900	50			
Long Pond Path			5		*Monroe County Sidepath Guide*	1900	24			
East Avenue Path to Fairport		7.5			*Monroe County Sidepath Guide*	1900	34			
Sea Breeze Path to Forest Lawn		7.5			*Rochester Democrat and Chronicle*	8 Oct 1896	8	*Monroe County Sidepath Guide*	1900	34
Monroe Avenue Path to Pittsford & Fairport		10			*Monroe County Sidepath Guide*	1900	36			
Irondequoit: Float Bridge Road			0.5		*Rochester Democrat and Chronicle*	6 Jun 1902	16			
Penfield Path		5			Isaac Potter, *Cycle Paths*	1898	43			
Webster Path to Nine Mile Point		6			*Monroe County Sidepath Guide*	1900	24			
County sidepath miles reported (excluding Brockport-Hamlin Path)	150				*Monroe County Sidepath Guide*	1900	70	*Rochester Democrat & Chronicle*	12 Oct 1904	14
County sidepath miles reported	193				*Batavia News*	11 Dec 1901	6			
County sidepath miles reported	200				*Bicycling World*, vol. 48	13 Feb 1904	566			
Subtotals—Monroe County:	193	112	29	**193**						
23. Montgomery County										
Hoffman's Ferry (Schenectady County) to Cranesville			3		*Amsterdam Evening Recorder*	29 Dec 1934	5			
Cranesville to Amsterdam			4.5		*Amsterdam Daily Democrat*	5 Apr 1899	7	*Johnstown Daily Republican*	11 May 1899	6
Amsterdam										
DeGraff Path			1.5		*LAW Bulletin and Good Roads*, vol. 27	4 Feb 1898	118	*Amsterdam Daily Democrat*	5 Apr 1899	7
Main Street (between trolley tracks)			3		*LAW Bulletin and Good Roads*, vol. 27	4 Feb 1898	118	*New York Sun*	22 Jun 1902	2
Rockton to Hagaman			1.5		*Gloversville Daily Leader*	7 Apr 1898	5			
Amsterdam to Akin and Tribes Hill			5.5		*New York Sun*	22 Jun 1902	2	*Amsterdam Evening Recorder*	29 Dec 1934	5
Tribes Hill to Fonda			5		*Johnstown Daily Republican*	11 May 1899	6	*Amsterdam Evening Recorder*	27 May 1902	2
Fonda to Nelliston and Fort Plain			14		*New York Sun*	22 Jun 1902	2	*Gloversville Daily Leader*	23 May 1901	5

SIDEPATH LOCATIONS: COUNTY AND TOWNS	REP. CSM	REP. SM	EST. SM	SUB TOT.	SOURCE CITED (A)	DATE OF SOURCE	PG	SOURCE CITED (B)	DATE OF SOURCE	PG
Nelliston and Fort Plain to St. Johnsville			6		*Gloversville Daily Leader*	23 May 1901	5	*New York Sun*	22 Jun 1902	2
St. Johnsville to East Creek (Herkimer County)			2		*Little Falls Evening Times*	8 Jun 1899	4			
County sidepath miles reported	40				*Johnstown Daily Republican*	11 May 1899	6			
Subtotals—Montgomery County:	**40**	**0**	**46**	**46**						

24. Nassau County, Long Island (no sidepath commission)

Westbury Path		0			*New York Daily Tribune*	2 Sep 1899	4			
Westbury Station to Westbury Educational Hall		2			*LAW Bulletin and Good Roads,* vol. 29	3 Feb 1899	160			
Westbury Educational Hall to Hicks Estate		2.5			*LAW Bulletin and Good Roads,* vol. 29	3 Feb 1899	160			
Hicks Estate to Jericho Turnpike		1.5			*LAW Bulletin and Good Roads,* vol. 29	3 Feb 1899	160			
Subtotals—Nassau County:	**0**	**6**	**0**	**6**						

25. Niagara County

Lockport to Olcott		12			*Good Roads,* vol. 6	Nov 1894	263	Isaac Potter, *Cycle Paths*	1898	9-13
Ridge Road Path at Lake Avenue and Wright's Corners in Hartland		1			*Niagara Falls Gazette*	31 Dec 1902	1			
Lockport										
Lake Avenue (Olcott Path)		0			*Illustrated Buffalo Express*	15 May 1898	16			
First Avenue to Royalton		4			*Illustrated Buffalo Express*	15 May 1898	16			
East Avenue to Cottage Hotel (Gasport and Middleport Path)		0			*North Tonawanda Evening News*	17 Feb 1900	3	*Niagara Falls Gazette*	31 Dec 1902	1
Shawnee Road Path		0			*Niagara Falls Gazette*	25 May 1899	5			
West Avenue to Gothic Corners (Lockport Junction Path)		0			*North Tonawanda Evening News*	16 May 1896	1	*Illustrated Buffalo Express*	15 May 1898	16
Lockport to Gasport		6			*North Tonawanda Evening News*	17 Feb 1900	3			
Gasport to Middleport		5.5			*North Tonawanda Evening News*	17 Feb 1900	3			
Middleport to Ridge Road		2.5			*North Tonawanda Evening News*	17 Feb 1900	3	*Niagara Falls Gazette*	31 Dec 1902	1
Ridge Road Path: Johnson Creek to Orleans County line		3			*North Tonawanda News*	17 Feb 1900	3	*Niagara Falls Gazette*	31 Dec 1902	1
Lockport to Lockport Junction	3				*Buffalo Express*	9 May 1896	11			
Lockport to Lewiston		1			*North Tonawanda Evening News*	23 Mar 1900	3			
Lewiston to Youngstown		5			*Niagara Falls Gazette*	11 Jan 1899	1	*Niagara Falls Gazette*	27 May 1899	5
Lewiston to Niagara Falls		7			*Niagara Falls Gazette*	5 Jun 1902	1	*Niagara Falls Gazette*	14 Mar 1903	1
Niagara Falls										
North Main Street (to Lewiston)		0			*Niagara Falls Gazette*	25 Apr 1903	1			
East Avenue Path		0			*Niagara Falls Gazette*	31 Dec 1902	1			
West Avenue Path		0			*Niagara Falls Gazette*	31 Dec 1902	1			
Buffalo Avenue from Portage Road to city line		0.5			*Illustrated Buffalo Express*	8 Apr 1900	14			
Niagara Falls to North Tonawanda via LaSalle		11			*Wheel and Cycling Trade Review,* vol. 20	10 Dec 1897	36	*Niagara Falls Gazette*	31 Dec 1902	1
North Tonawanda										
Corner of Paynes Avenue and Wheatfield Street (Martinsville Path)		0			*North Tonawanda Evening News*	12 Jun 1900	1	*North Tonawanda Evening News*	11 Aug 1900	1
Transit Road to Erie County line		0			*North Tonawanda Evening News*	5 Jun 1902	1			
River Road, Felton Street to Gratwick		0			*North Tonawanda Evening News*	24 Jul 1905	1			
North Tonawanda to Martinsville		2			*North Tonawanda Evening News*	21 Jul 1900	1	*North Tonawanda Evening News*	11 Aug 1900	1

SIDEPATH LOCATIONS: COUNTY AND TOWNS	REP. CSM	REP. SM	EST. SM	SUB TOT.	SOURCE CITED (A)	DATE OF SOURCE	PG	SOURCE CITED (B)	DATE OF SOURCE	PG
Martinsville to Mapleton			0.5		*Niagara Falls Gazette*	15 Apr 1903	4			
Mapleton to Mapleton Station			0.5		*Niagara Falls Gazette*	13 Jun 1903	8			
Subtotals—Niagara County:	0	7	58	**65**						

26. Onandaga County

Syracuse

South Salina Street (Valley Path)			0		*Syracuse Post Standard*	14 Jul 1899	6			
North Salina Street			0		*Syracuse Post Standard*	14 Jul 1899	6			
Onondaga Avenue			0		*Syracuse Post Standard*	14 Jul 1899	6			
Willis Avenue			0		*Syracuse Post Standard*	14 Jul 1899	6			
Hiawatha Avenue			0		*Syracuse Post Standard*	14 Jul 1899	6			
Lakeview Avenue			0		*Syracuse Post Standard*	14 Jul 1899	6			
Boulevard Path			0		*Syracuse Post Standard*	3 May 1899	2			

Valley Path

Section: Salina Street to Onondaga Castle Hotel			7		*Syracuse Journal*	26 Jun 1900	3			
Section: East Onondaga to Cortland Avenue and Dorwin's Spring			0.5		*Syracuse Journal*	26 Jun 1900	3	*Syracuse Sunday Herald*	5 May 1901	15
Section: Cortland Avenue Path to Onondaga Valley			2		*Syracuse Journal*	26 Jun 1900	3			
Section: Onondaga Valley or Onondaga Castle to Cardiff			6.5		*Syracuse Journal*	21 Apr 1903	7			
Section: Cardiff to Tully and Cortland County line			7		*Syracuse Sunday Herald*	31 Mar 1901	15	*Syracuse Evening Herald*	6 Apr 1902	15
Cicero to Lower South Bay on Oneida Lake			2.5		*Syracuse Post Standard*	21 Jun 1897	2	*Syracuse Journal*	9 Dec 1904	4
Syracuse to Fayetteville			8		*Syracuse Post Standard*	8 Jul 1898	3	*Syracuse Journal*	12 Apr 1899	3
Fayettville to Manlius Village		2			*Syracuse Sunday Herald*	6 Apr 1902	15	*Syracuse Journal*	15 May 1902	8
Fayetteville to Madison County line		5			*Syracuse Sunday Herald*	6 Apr 1902	15	*Syracuse Journal*	15 May 1902	8
Stiles Station to Long Branch on Onondaga Lake		1			*Syracuse Post Standard*	3 May 1899	2	*Syracuse Daily Journal*	17 May 1899	3
Long Branch to Baldwinsville		5			*Syracuse Sunday Herald*	31 Mar 1901	15	*Syracuse Journal*	9 Dec 1904	4

Jordan Path

Section: Syracuse to Jordan		18			*SyracuseJournal*	31 Mar 1901	15	*Syracuse Journal*	6 Jun 1904	3
Section: Jordan to Elbridge		2.5			*Syracuse Journal*	23 May 1905	7	*Syracuse Journal*	9 Dec 1904	4
Section: Jordan to Cayuga County line		1			*Syracuse Sunday Herald*	31 Mar 1901	15	*Syracuse Sunday Herald*	5 May 1901	15
Section: Jordan Station to Riverside Hotel on Seneca River	5				*Syracuse Journal*	6 May 1904	6	*Syracuse Post Standard*	23 May 1905	12
Section: Iona to Jack's Reef on the Seneca River		0			*Syracuse Sunday Herald*	31 Mar 1901	15			
Section: Memphis Station to Jack's Reef on the Seneca River	5				*Syracuse Journal*	6 May 1904	6	*Syracuse Journal*	23 May 1905	12
Solvay to Elbridge		0			*Syracuse Post Standard*	23 May 1905	12			
Camillus to Fairmount Station		4			*Syracuse Sunday Herald*	6 Apr 1902	15			
Skaneateles to Skaneateles Junction via Mottville	5				*Marcellus Weekly Observer*	1 May 1903	4	*Syracuse Journal*	6 Jun 1904	3
Syracuse to Phoenix		0			*Cooperstown Otsego Farmer*	21 Jul 1899	1			
County sidepath miles reported	85				*Syracuse Journal*	22 Jun 1904	6			
Completed county trunk lines, east-west and north-south					*Syracuse Journal*	15 May 1902	8			
Subtotals—Onandaga County:	85	23	64	**85**						

| --- | --- | --- | --- | --- | --- | --- | --- | --- | --- | --- |

27. Oneida County

Utica to Rome

Section: Utica to Yorkville (Cross County Path)				1	Utica Saturday Globe	19 Jun 1897	8	Utica Sunday Journal	7 May 1899	2
Section: Yorkville to Whitesboro (Cross County Path)				2	Rome Citizen	25 Jul 1899	1	Utica Sunday Journal	7 May 1899	2
Section: Whitesboro to Oriskany				3	Rome Citizen	6 May 1898	1	Utica Observer	4 May 1899	5
Section: Oriskany to Rome		7			Utica Sunday Tribune	29 May 1898	5	Rome Citizen	25 Jul 1899	1

Utica District

Utica

Turner Street (Harbor Path)	0.5				Utica Observer	29 Jul 1897	5	Waterville Times	13 Oct 1899	4
Broad Street (Harbor Path)	0				Utica Observer	29 Jul 1897	5	Isaac Potter, Cycle Paths	1898	25
Frankfort Road (Harbor Path)	0				Utica Observer	29 Jul 1897	5	Isaac Potter, Cycle Paths	1898	25
Pleasant Street Loop	3.5				Utica Sunday Journal	1 Jul 1900	12	Utica Sunday Journal	22 Jul 1900	4
Tilden Avenue	0				Utica Sunday Journal	22 Jul 1900	4			
Genesee Street	0				Utica Observer	12 Jun 1899	5	Utica Observer	28 Dec 1907	4
Clinton Road	0				Utica Saturday Globe	19 Jun 1897	8			
Oriskany to Reeders Mills and Clark Mills		5			Rome Citizen	10 May 1901	1	Utica Observer	29 Dec 1902	9
Utica to New Hartford Village	4				Utica Saturday Globe	19 Jun 1897	8			
New Hartford Village (North Street and Chenango Canal towpath loop)			0.5		Utica Sunday Journal	26 May 1901	4			
New Hartford to New York Mills and Yorkville	3.5				Rome Citizen	25 Jul 1899	1	Waterville Times	13 Oct 1899	4
New Hartford to Bridgewater										
Section: New Hartford to Washington Mills (Washington Mills Path)		1.5			Utica Sunday Tribune	12 Apr 1896	7	Utica Observer	29 Jul 1897	5
Section: Washington Mills to Clayville		5.5			Utica Observer	4 May 1899	5	Utica Sunday Journal	7 May 1899	2
Section: Clayville to Cassville (Wheelmen's Fountain)		3			Utica Sunday Journal	10 Jun 1900	12	Utica Observer	13 Sep 1900	6
Section: Cassville to Bridgewater (Sauquoit Valley Path)	3				Waterville Times	13 Oct 1899	4	Utica Herald Dispatch	12 Oct 1900	4
New Hartford to Oriskany Falls										
Section: New Hartford to Clinton		5			Rome Citizen	24 Jul 1896	1	Utica Saturday Globe	19 Jun 1897	8
Section: New Path from New Hartford to Clinton (west side of road)		0			Rome Citizen	15 Oct 1901	4			
Section: Clinton to Franklin		1			Utica Observer	29 Dec 1902	9			
Section: Franklin to Oriskany Falls	8				Utica Observer	4 May 1899	5	Utica Sunday Journal	7 May 1899	2
Spur Section: Deansboro to Waterville	5				Utica Sunday Journal	21 May 1899	7	Waterville Times	26 May 1899	5
New Hartford to Kirkland		5			Utica Saturday Globe	19 Jun 1897	8			
Whitesboro to Westmoreland via Walesville (Cross-County Path)	5				Utica Sunday Journal	12 Aug 1900	12	Utica Herald Dispatch	18 Sep 1900	4
Whitesboro: Westmoreland Street		0			Utica Observer	25 May 1904	5			
Middle Settlement to Risleys (Middle Settlement Path)	4				Rome Citizen	25 Jul 1899	1	Waterville Times	13 Oct 1899	4
Utica to Trenton Falls										
Section: Utica to Deerfield (Deerfield Path)	3				Utica Sunday Journal	21 May 1899	7			
Section: Deerfield Corners to South Trenton (Trenton Plank Road)		4			Utica Daily Press	9 Jun 1899	10	Rome Citizen	27 Jun 1899	1

SIDEPATH LOCATIONS: COUNTY AND TOWNS	REP. CSM	REP. SM	EST. SM	SUB TOT.	SOURCE CITED (A)	DATE OF SOURCE	PG	SOURCE CITED (B)	DATE OF SOURCE	PG
Section: South Trenton to Trenton Falls	6				*Rome Citizen*	25 Jul 1899	1			
Spur Section: Trenton Falls to Trenton		2			*Utical Sunday Journal*	22 Jul 1900	12			
Spur Section: Prospect to Hinckley		2			*Utica Morning Herald*	9 Jun 1899	4	*Utica Sunday Journal*	22 Jul 1900	12
Rome District										
Rome										
Dominick Street			0		*Rome Citizen*	31 Aug 1897	1	*Rome Citizen*	1 Apr 1902	1
North James Street			0		*Rome Citizen*	30 Jun 1899	1	*Rome Daily Sentinel*	21 Sep 1905	9
South James Street			0		*Rome Citizen*	30 Jun 1899	1			
Verona Avenue			0		*Rome Citizen*	15 Jul 1898	1			
Floyd Avenue			0		*Rome Citizen*	30 Jun 1899	1			
Wright Settlement Road			0		*Rome Citizen*	30 Jun 1899	1			
Mill Street to City Line			0		*Rome Citizen*	1 Oct 1901	5	*Rome Citizen*	15 Oct 1901	7
Rome Cemetery Path			0		*Utica Observer*	29 Dec 1902	9			
Big Horn Path	7				*Rome Citizen*	30 Jun 1899	1	*Rome Citizen*	25 Jul 1899	1
Small Horn Path	5				*Rome Citizen*	30 Jun 1899	1	*Rome Citizen*	25 Jul 1899	1
Rome to North Western										
Section: Rome to Kimball Corners (Delta Path)			2.5		*Utica Observer*	19 May 1899	5			
Section: Kimball Corners to Delta (Delta Path)			2.5		*Utica Sunday Journal*	7 May 1899	2	*Rome Citizen*	30 Jun 1899	1
Spur Section: River Road to Hicks Mills and Black River House	3.5				*Rome Citizen*	8 Jun 1900	1	*Utica Herald Dispatch*	18 Sep 1900	4
Section: Delta to Westernville	4				*Rome Citizen*	23 Apr 1897	1	*Rome Citizen*	25 Jul 1899	1
Section: Westernville to North Western	3				*Rome Citizen*	25 Jul 1899	1	*Utica Sunday Journal*	22 Jul 1900	12
Rome to Stanwix, Bartlett, and Westmoreland	9				*Rome Citizen*	24 Jul 1896	1	*Waterville Times*	13 Oct 1899	4
Floyd to Nuth's Corners (Oriskany)		1			*Rome Citizen*	10 Jun 1898	8			
Lee Center to Lee Line Hotel			0		*Rome Citizen*	7 Aug 1896	8	*Rome Citizen*	27 Apr 1897	4
Lee Center to Stokes	2.5				*Rome Citizen*	1 Apr 1902	1			
Lee Canning Company Path			0		*Rome Citizen*	2 Jul 1901	4	*Utica Observer*	29 Dec 1902	9
Rome to Verona										
Section: Rome State Custodial Asylum to Verona (Verona Path)	7				*Rome Citizen*	7 May 1897	1	*Rome Citizen*	25 Jul 1899	1
Spur Section: Custodial Asylum to Verona Springs via Lowell		1			*Rome Citizen*	3 Jun 1902	4	*Utica Observer*	29 Dec 1902	9
Spur Section: Verona to Skenandoa			0		*Utica Observer*	29 Dec 1902	9			
Verona to Oneida (Madison County)		5			*Utica Observer*	29 Dec 1902	9	Map, *Cycle Paths of Oneida County*	1900	
Oriskany to Holland Patent via Turner's Corners and Stittville	7				*Utica Sunday Journal*	22 Jul 1900	12	*Utica Herald Dispatch*	18 Sep 1900	4
Holland Patent to Trenton		1			*Utica Daily Press*	21 Jun 1901	8	*Rome Citizen*	2 Jul 1901	4
Rome to Taberg via Coonrod		2			*Rome Citizen*	1 Apr 1902	1	*Rome Citizen*	20 Jun 1902	4
Alder Creek to Boonville	2				*Utica Sunday Journal*	22 Jul 1900	12			
Turin-Lowville Path (see Lewis County)			0		*Utica Herald-Dispatch*	20 Dec 1904	4	*Utica Herald-Dispatch*	Dec 24 1906	9

SIDEPATH LOCATIONS: COUNTY AND TOWNS	REP. CSM	REP. SM	EST. SM	SUB TOT.	SOURCE CITED (A)	DATE OF SOURCE	PG	SOURCE CITED (B)	DATE OF SOURCE	PG
Oneida Castle District										
Oneida Castle to Sylvan Beach on Oneida Lake										
Section: Oneida Castle to Oneida (Madison County)		1			Utica Morning Herald	9 Jun 1899	4			
Section: Oneida to South Bay (Madison County Path)		0			Madison County Times	28 May 1897	2	Utica Observer	14 Aug 1899	5
Spur Section: Durhamville to State Bridge and Higginsville		3			Utica Herald Dispatch	18 Sep 1900	4			
Section: South Bay to Sylvan Beach		2.5			Utica Observer	28 Jun 1899	8	Waterville Times	13 Oct 1899	4
Oneida Castle to Oneida Community and Bennett Corners		2			Utica Sunday Journal	22 Jul 1900	12			
Oneida Castle to Sherrill (Cross-County Path)		1			Utica Sunday Journal	12 Aug 1900	12			
Sherrill to Oneida Community		1			Utica Sunday Journal	22 Jul 1900	12			
Sherrill to Vernon and Westmoreland (Cross-County Path)		9			Rome Citizen	14 Jul 1899	8	Waterville Times	13 Oct 1899	4
Vernon to Lairdsville and Kirkland Hill (Seneca Turnpike Path)		8			Rome Citizen	27 Jul 1900	1	Utica Observer	30 Nov 1900	4
Kirkland Hill to Kirkland Village			0.5		Rome Citizen	10 May 1901	1			
Vernon to Verona		3			Utica Sunday Journal	19 Aug 1900	12	Utica Herald Dispatch	18 Sep 1900	4
Camden District										
Camden to West Camden		2			Utica Herald Dispatch	18 Sep 1900	4	Utica Sunday Journal	22 Jul 1900	12
Camden to McConnellsville			5.5		Utica Sunday Journal	21 May 1899	7	Rome Citizen	15 Apr 1902	5
McConnellsville to Vienna			2.5		Rome Citizen	8 Sep 1899	4			
County sidepath miles reported	132				Waterville Times	13 Oct 1899	4			
County sidepath miles reported	170				Utica Sunday Journal	22 Jul 1900	12			
County sidepath miles reported	185				Rome Citizen	10 May 1901	1			
County sidepath miles reported	200				Rome Citizen	28 Feb 1902	4			
Subtotals—Oneida County:	200	134	65	**200**						
28. Ontario County										
Geneva to Oaks Corners/Armstrong's Corners			6		Geneva Daily Times	20 Jul 1899	5	Rochester Democrat and Chronicle	11 Aug 1899	4
Oaks Corners to Phelps			3		Geneva Daily Times	20 Jul 1899	5	Geneva Daily Times	14 Jun 1900	5
Phelps to Clifton Springs			3		Geneva Daily Times	7 May 1901	5			
Clifton Springs to Shortsville			0.5		Geneva Daily Times	21 Aug 1899	4			
Shortsville to Canandaigua			0.5		Geneva Daily Times	21 Aug 1899	4			
Canandaigua to Victor (Ladies' Path)			10		Rochester Democrat and Chronicle	29 May 1897	18	NYLAW, Map of Sidepath Construction	1901	
Subtotals—Ontario County:	0	0	23	**23**						
29. Orange County										
Newburgh to Orange Lake			5		New York Sun	24 Jun 1899	4	NYLAW, Map of Sidepath Construction	1901	
Goshen to Middletown			0		New York Sun	24 Jun 1899	4			
Middletown to Port Jervis			0		New York Sun	24 Jun 1899	4			
Subtotals—Orange County	0	0	5	**5**						
30. Orleans County										
Holly to Troutburg										
Section: Holly to Ridge Road (Ladies' Path)			2.5		Holley Standard	24 Mar 1898	1	Holley Standard	26 May 1898	3

SIDEPATH LOCATIONS: COUNTY AND TOWNS	REP. CSM	REP. SM	EST. SM	SUB TOT.	SOURCE CITED (A)	DATE OF SOURCE	PG	SOURCE CITED (B)	DATE OF SOURCE	PG
Section: Ridge Road to Troutburg via Morton (County Line Path)			10		Holley Standard	22 Apr 1897	1	Oswego Times	24 Mar 1898	5
Section: County Line Path Division—Orleans and Monroe commissions			0		Holley Standard	16 Aug 1900	1			
Spur Section: Morton to Kendall Corners			2		Holley Standard	24 May 1900	1			
Spur Section: Kendall Corners to West Kendall			2.5		Holley Standard	10 May 1900	1	Holley Standard	16 Aug 1900	1
Holly to Clarendon			3		Holley Standard	12 Apr 1900	1	Holley Standard	10 May 1900	1
Medina to Ridgeway and Lyndonville			7.5		Rocheser Democrat and Chronicle	22 May 1897	15	Medina Tribune	16 Aug 1900	3
Medina—South Path			0.5		Medina Tribune	23 May 1901	3	NYLAW, Map of Sidepath Construction	1901	
Albion to Barre Center			4		Batavia Daily News	17 May 1899	1	Holley Standard	7 Sep 1899	1
Albion to Oak Orchard on Lake Ontario, via Two Bridges			9		Holley Standard	15 Apr 1897	3	Holley Standard	29 Apr 1897	3
Subtotals—Orleans County:	0	0	41	**41**						

31. Oswego County

Oswego

First Street			0		Fulton Patriot	7 Jun 1899	1			
River Road			0		Oswego Daily Palladium	7 Jun 1899	9			
Seneca Street			0		Oswego Daily Palladium	21 Feb 1901	4			
Oswego to Seneca Hill and Minetto (East River Path)			5		Fulton Patriot	7 Jun 1899	1	Oswego Daily Palladium	7 Jun 1899	9
Oswego to Minetto and Fulton (West River Path)			6		Fulton Patriot	7 Jun 1899	1	Oswego Daily Palladium	1 May 1901	8
Oswego to Fruit Valley		4			Oswego Daily Palladium	21 Feb 1901	4	Fulton Patriot	14 Aug 1901	8
Oswego toward Pleasant Point and Lake View (Lake Road Path)		1			Fulton Patriot	14 Aug 1901	8	Syracuse Telegram	23 Jul 1903	10
Fulton to Phoenix			9		Fulton Patriot	19 Jun 1901	1	Oswego Daily Palladium	15 Jul 1901	4
Phoenix to Three Rivers		3			Syracuse Evening Herald	2 Apr 1903	13			
Mexico to Texas		5			Oswego Daily Times	14 May 1900	7	Oswego Daily Palladium	1 May 1901	8
Lacona to Mannsville (Jefferson County)		2			Oswego Daily Times	29 May 1900	7			
Oneida Lake Path, Lake Road between Constantia and Cleveland		1			Oswego Daily Palladium	11 Aug 1899	8	Oswego Daily Palladium	1 May 1901	8
Brewerton to Pulaski via Central Square			0		Fulton Patriot	25 Aug 1899	3			
Orwell to Pulaski via Richland			0		Fulton Patriot	25 Aug 1899	3			
County sidepath miles reported	35				Oswego Daily Palladium	21 Dec 1904	8			
Subtotals—Oswego County:	35	11	25	**36**						

32. Otsego County

Middle Village to East Springfield			1		Richfield Springs Mercury	26 Apr 1900	1			
Cooperstown to Oneonta			4		Cooperstown Otsego Farmer	1 Jun 1900	5	NYLAW, Map of Sidepath Construction	1901	
Oneonta to Otego			6		Richfield Springs Mercury	31 Aug 1899	1	NYLAW, Map of Sidepath Construction	1901	
Oneonta-Otego Path at Otego Creek Bridge			0		Cooperstown Otsego Farmer	8 Sep 1899	5	Richfield Springs Mercury	19 May 1904	2
Subtotals—Otsego County:	0	0	11	**11**						

33. Queens County (No Sidepath Commission)

Whitestone to Willett's Point			2		New York Daily Tribune	17 Apr 1897	3			
Subtotals—Queens County:	0	0	2	**2**						

SIDEPATH LOCATIONS: COUNTY AND TOWNS	REP. CSM	REP. SM	EST. SM	SUB TOT.	SOURCE CITED (A)	DATE OF SOURCE	PG	SOURCE CITED (B)	DATE OF SOURCE	PG
34. Rensselaer County										
Rensselaer to Teller's Crossing—River Road Path			1		*Albany Evening Journal*	29 Jun 1899	3			
River Road Path to Castleton on Hudson			1		*Albany Evening Journal*	6 Jun 1900	11	*Troy Daily Times*	18 May 1899	3
North Lansingburg Path—Around the Horn			1		*Troy Daily Times*	18 May 1899	3			
Troy to Averill Park and Sand Lake			0		*Troy Daily Times*	18 May 1899	3	*Albany Evening Journal*	6 Jun 1900	11
Troy to Cohoes (Albany County)			0		*Albany Evening Journal*	25 Mar 1898	8			
Subtotals—Rensselaer County:	0	0	3	**3**						
35. St. Lawrence County										
Norwood to Potsdam		4			*St. Lawrence Plain Dealer*	21 Jun 1899	1			
Potsdam to Canton		10			*St. Lawrence Plain Dealer*	24 May 1899	4			
Subtotals—St. Lawrence County:	0	4	10	**14**						
36. Saratoga County										
Saratoga Springs to Glens Falls (Warren County)										
Section: Saratoga Springs to King's Station		6			*Glens Falls Morning Star*	8 Jun 1896	5	*Schuylerville Standard*	17 Jun 1896	5
Section: King's Station to Wiltonville		1			*Glens Falls Morning Star*	25 Apr 1896	4	*Glens Falls Morning Star*	3 Jun 1896	8
Section: Wiltonville to Glens Falls		7			*Glens Falls Morning Star*	29 Apr 1896	4	*Glens Falls Morning Star*	8 Jun 1896	5
Saratoga Springs: Geysers Loop via Broadway		5.5			*LAW Bulletin and Good Roads*, vol. 29	3 Feb 1899	160	*Saratoga Daily Saratogian*	29 Oct 1948	5
Saratoga Springs to Saratoga Lake			1		*Lockport Daily Journal*	13 May 1898	8	*Saratoga Daily Saratogian*	29 Oct 1948	5
Saratoga Springs to Ballston Spa			7		*Troy Daily Times*	1 Apr 1897	3			
Ballston Spa to Burnt Hills and Schenectady County line			7		*Troy Daily Times*	3 Aug 1900	4	*Saratoga Daily Saratogian*	8 Jun 1903	5
Saratoga Springs to Hadley (Hadley Path)										
Section: Saratoga Springs toward South Corinth			1		*Saratoga Daily Saratogian*	24 Apr 1902	6	NYLAW, *Map of Sidepath Construction*	1901	
Section: South Corinth to Corinth			4		*Corinth Corinthian*	2 Oct 1896	4	*Saratoga Daily Saratogian*	10 Jun 1903	6
Section: Corinth to Hadley and Luzerne (Warren County)		4.5			*Saratoga Daily Saratogian*	10 Jun 1903	6	NYLAW, *Map of Sidepath Construction*	1901	
Charlton to Schenectady County line			2		*Troy Daily Times*	24 Apr 1902	3	*Amsterdam Evening Recorder*	27 May 1903	4
Waterford to Mechanicville—vicinity of Pratt's Hotel			1		*Troy Daily Times*	26 May 1896	2	*Troy Daily Times*	17 Aug 1896	3
Subtotals—Saratoga County:	0	20	28	**48**						
37. Schenectady County										
Schenectady										
Schenectady Turnpike to Albany County line (Albany Path)			2		*LAW Bulletin and Good Roads*, vol. 22	29 Nov 1895	21			
Upper State Street			0		*Wheel and Cycling Trade Review*, vol. 21	28 Apr 1898	32			
Washington Street			0		*Wheel and Cycling Trade Review*, vol. 21	28 Apr 1898	32			
College Pasture between Nott and Union streets			0		Meinert, *Bicycling Hudson-Mohawk Region*	c. 1997	36			
Freeman's Bridge Spur to Burnt Hills Path			¶		*Troy Daily Times*	14 Sep 1900	4			
Ballston Road, Stamford Corners to Union Street	3				*Troy Daily Times*	14 Sep 1900	4			
Schenectady & Troy Turnpike to Albany County line (Troy-Cohoes Path)			3		*Troy Daily Times*	9 May 1900	4	NYLAW, *Map of Sidepath Construction*	1901	
Niskayuna Spur linking Albany Path and Troy-Cohoes Path			0.5		*Troy Daily Times*	9 May 1900	4	NYLAW, *Map of Sidepath Construction*	1901	

SIDEPATH LOCATIONS: COUNTY AND TOWNS	REP. CSM	REP. SM	EST. SM	SUB TOT.	SOURCE CITED (A)	DATE OF SOURCE	PG	SOURCE CITED (B)	DATE OF SOURCE	PG
Schenectady to Saratoga County line (Burnt Hills & Ballston Spa Path)			6		Albany Evening Journal	9 Aug 1901	8	NYLAW, Map of Sidepath Construction	1901	
Charlton Spur—Burnt Hills & Ballston Spa Path to Saratoga County line			0		Amsterdam Evening Recorder	27 May 1903	4			
Schenectady to Montgomery County line (Amsterdam Path)			8		Gloversville Daily Leader	23 Jan 1900	8	NYLAW, Map of Sidepath Construction	1901	
County sidepath miles reported	42				Albany Evening Journal	26 Mar 1903	11			
Subtotals—Schenectady County:	**42**	**3**	**21**	**42**						

38. Schuyler County

Watkins: Fourth Street Path			0.5		Watkins Express	1 Jun 1899	3	Watkins Express	25 Jul 1901	3
Watkins to Montour Falls			2.5		Elmira Daily Gazette	29 Jul 1897	8	Montour Falls Free Press,	28 Apr 1898	3
Subtotals—Schuyler County:	**0**	**0**	**3**	**3**						

39. Seneca County

Seneca Falls to Bridgeport			2		Illustrated Buffalo Express	19 May 1907	17			
Seneca Falls to Cayuga Lake Park			3		Geneva Daily Times	5 Jul 1899	5	Illustrated Buffalo Express	19 May 1907	17
Cayuga Lake Park to Canoga			3		Rochester Democrat and Chronicle	7 Jun 1899	4	Geneva Daily Times	5 Jul 1899	5
Seneca Falls to Waterloo			3.5		Geneva Daily Times	5 Jul 1899	5			
Waterloo to Ontario County line along South River Road (Geneva Path)			5		Geneva Daily Times	5 Jul 1899	5	Phelps Citizen	13 Jul 1899	3
Waterloo to Romulus			11		Rochester Democrat and Chronicle	7 Jun 1899	4	Phelps Citizen	1 Feb 1900	3
Romulus to Ovid			5.5		Phelps Citizen	1 Feb 1900	3	Auburn Bulletin	30 Aug 1901	3
Ovid to Willard			2.5		Phelps Citizen	1 Feb 1900	3	Auburn Bulletin	30 Aug 1901	3
Ovid to Lodi			4		Rochester Democrat and Chronicle	26 May 1899	4			
Ovid to Hayts Corners			3		Ithaca Daily News	16 Jun 1899	3			
Subtotals—Seneca County:	**0**	**0**	**43**	**43**						

40. Steuben County

Corning to Chemung County line (Elmira Path)			5		Rochester Democrat and Chronicle	3 Apr 1895	4	Corning Journal	14 Jun 1899	5
Cohocton Valley Paths										
Section: Corning and Painted Post to Coopers Plains			1		Corning Journal	14 Jun 1899	5	Elmira Daily Gazette & Free Press	4 Nov 1899	6
Section: Campbell to Savona			4		Corning Journal	5 Jul 1899	4			
Section: Bath District										
Bath to Hammondsport			6		Corning Journal	31 May 1899	4	Elmira Daily Gazette & Free Press	26 Jun 1900	5
Bath to Lake Salubria			0.5		Rochester Democrat and Chronicle	13 Apr 1897	15			
Bath to Kanona and Avoca			1		Rochester Democrat and Chronicle	13 Apr 1897	15	NYLAW, Map of Sidepath Construction	1901	
Section: Cohocton to North Cohocton			5.5		Rochester Democrat and Chronicle	16 Jun 1900	4			
Corning and Painted Post to Addison via Gang Mills and Erwin Station			9		Elmira Star Gazette	13 Jul 1899	8	Elmira Daily Gazette & Free Press	4 Nov 1899	6
Hornellsville to Canisteo			3.5		Alfred Sun	20 Apr 1898	5	Alfred Sun	31 May 1899	1
Hornellsville to Arkport			4		Canaseraga Times	24 Sep 1897	3	NYLAW, Map of Sidepath Construction	1901	
Hornellsville to Allegany County line (Almond-Alfred Path)			4.5		Alfred Sun	5 Apr 1899	4	NYLAW, Map of Sidepath Construction	1901	
County sidepath miles reported	45				Moravia Republican	21 Sep 1900	4			
Subtotals—Steuben County:	**45**	**0**	**44**	**45**						

SIDEPATH LOCATIONS: COUNTY AND TOWNS	REP. CSM	REP. SM	EST. SM	SUB TOT.	SOURCE CITED (A)	DATE OF SOURCE	PG	SOURCE CITED (B)	DATE OF SOURCE	PG

41. Suffolk County (Long Island)

South Shore Sidepaths

Amityville to Amagansett	78				New York Evening Telegram	Aug 5 1999	7	Brooklyn Daily Eagle	13 Oct 1900	15
Section: Amityville to Babylon		5.5			Brooklyn Daily Eagle	27 Sep 1900	4	Isaac Potter, Cycle Paths	1898	47
Section: Babylon to Bay Shore		5			Brooklyn Daily Eagle	23 Nov 1899	7	Newtown Register	12 Apr 1900	2
Section: Bay Shore to Blue Point via Oakdale, Sayville, and Bayport		12			Brooklyn Daily Eagle	13 Oct 1900	15	Newtown Register	17 Jan 1901	2
Section: Islip to Oakdale		0			Sayville Suffolk County News	16 Nov 1900	3	Newtown Register	17 Jan 1901	2
Section: Oakdale-Westbrook Golf Club Path		0			Lake Shore Wheelmen	15 Mar 1899	8			
Section: Oakdale to Sayville		0			Sayville Suffolk County News	16 Nov 1900	3			
Section: Blue Point to Patchogue		2			Brooklyn Daily Eagle	3 Jul 1899	7	Huntington Long Islander	8 Jul 1899	3
Section: Patchogue to Moriches		11			New York Daily Tribune	2 Sep 1899	4	Brooklyn Daily Eagle	19 Aug 1899	4
Section: Moriche to Quogue		12			Brooklyn Daily Eagle	13 Oct 1900	15			
Spur Section: West Hampton Beach Path		1			Sag Harbor Express	25 Nov 1897	2	Isaac Potter, Cycle Paths	1898	48
Spur Section: Quogue Station Path		0.5			New York Times	29 Apr 1900	12	Sayville Suffolk County News	4 May 1900	2
Section: Quogue to Canoe Place		7.5			Brooklyn Daily Eagle	13 Oct 1900	15			
Section: Canoe Place to Southampton		7.5			Brooklyn Daily Eagle	22 Jul 1899	6			
Section: Shinnecock Hills Path from Canoe Place Bridge		0			Sag Harbor Corrector	11 Nov 1899	3	Brooklyn Daily Eagle	27 Apr 1900	4
Section: Southampton to Bridgehampton		6.5			Brooklyn Daily Eagle	13 Oct 1900	15			
Section: Bridgehampton to Easthampton		5.5			New York Sun	14 Aug 1898	5	Brooklyn Daily Eagle	22 Jul 1899	6
Section: Easthampton to Amaganset		3.5			New York Sun	14 Aug 1898	5	Brooklyn Daily Eagle	22 Jul 1899	6
Patchogue										
Bay Avenue, South Road to Manor Station		1			New York Times	29 Apr 1900	12	Sayville Suffolk County News	4 May 1900	2
Main Street		0			Newtown Register	6 Nov 1902	2			
Water Street		0			Newtown Register	6 Nov 1902	2			
Bridgehampton to Sag Harbor	4.5				Brooklyn Daily Eagle	13 Oct 1900	15			
Bull Head Corner to Wainscott		0.5			Sag Harbor Corrector	6 Oct 1900	3			
Easthampton to Sag Harbor via Hard Scrabble	6				Sag Harbor Corrector	29 Sep 1900	3	Brooklyn Daily Eagle	13 Oct 1900	15
Easthampton Village										
Easthampton Path		2			Brooklyn Daily Eagle	22 Jul 1899	6	Isaac Potter, Cycle Paths	1898	47
Main Street to beach via Pantigo		1			Sag Harbor Corrector	6 Oct 1900	3			
Sag Harbor										
Village Path		0			Brooklyn Daily Eagle	13 Oct 1900	15			
South Street between Main and Madison streets		0			Sag Harbor Corrector	21 Sep 1901	3			

Cross-Island and Central Sidepaths

Babylon to Queens County macadam road	5				Rochester Democrat and Chronicle	16 Aug 1899	11			
Islip to Central Islip	1				Brooklyn Daily Eagle	22 Jul 1899	6			
Bayshore to Smithtown via Brentwood and Hauppage	10				LAW Bulletin and Good Roads, vol. 29	28 Apr 1899	596	Brooklyn Daily Eagle	13 Oct 1900	15
Smithtown to Cold Spring Harbor via Huntington	14				Brooklyn Daily Eagle	13 Oct 1900	15			

SIDEPATH LOCATIONS: COUNTY AND TOWNS	REP. CSM	REP. SM	EST. SM	SUB TOT.	SOURCE CITED (A)	DATE OF SOURCE	PG	SOURCE CITED (B)	DATE OF SOURCE	PG
Smithtown to Port Jefferson via St. James, Stony Brook and Setauket			12		*Huntington Long Islander*	20 Apr 1900	1	*Brooklyn Daily Eagle*	13 Oct 1900	15
Spur Section: Blydenburgh Pond Path				1	*Huntington Long Islander*	20 Apr 1900	1			
Smithtown to Lake Ronkonkoma			4		*Brooklyn Daily Eagle*	13 Oct 1900	15			
Farmingdale (Nassau County) to Lake Ronkonkoma				20	*Newtown Register*	7 Dec 1899	2	*Brooklyn Daily Eagle*	13 Oct 1900	15
Lake Ronkonkoma to Patchogue-Port Jefferson Cross Island Path			7		*Brooklyn Daily Eagle*	22 Jul 1899	6	*Huntington Long Islander*	18 Nov 1899	2
Patchogue to Port Jefferson (Cross Island Path)			14		*New York Times*	17 Sep 1899	25	*Brooklyn Daily Eagle*	13 Oct 1900	15
Eastport to Riverhead			9		*Bicycling World and LAW Bulletin, vol. 30*	15 Mar 1895	713	*New York Sun*	14 Aug 1898	5
Westhampton to Riverhead			8		*New York Times*	17 Sep 1899	25	*Brooklyn Daily Eagle*	13 Oct 1900	15
Quogue to Riverhead			6		*Brooklyn Daily Eagle*	22 Jul 1899	6	*Brooklyn Daily Eagle*	13 Oct 1900	15
Sag Harbor to South Ferry via North Haven and Hog Neck			4		*Huntington Long Islander*	8 Jul 1899	3	*Brooklyn Daily Eagle*	13 Oct 1900	15
Shelter Island Paths			4		*Brooklyn Daily Eagle*	22 Jun 1907	3			
North Shore Sidepaths										
Cold Spring Harbor to Woodbury (Nassau County)			3		*Huntington Long Islander*	9 Dec 1899	2	*Newtown Register*	7 Dec 1899	2
Cold Spring Harbor to Huntington			1.5		*Brooklyn Daily Eagle*	15 Aug 1999	11	*New York Daily Tribune*	2 Sep 1999	4
Huntington										
Huntington Station Path			0		*Sayville Suffolk County News*	27 Jul 1900	1	*Huntington Long Islander*	20 Apr 1900	1
Huntington Harbor Path			1.5		*Brooklyn Daily Eagle*	3 Jul 1899	7			
Huntington Schoolhouse Path			0.5		*Huntington Long Islander*	25 Nov 1899	2			
New York Avenue Sidepath (Shell Road) to Halesite			1		*Wheel and Cycling Trade Review, vol. 25*	19 Apr 1900	24	*Huntington Long Islander*	3 Oct 1902	2
Huntington to Northport via Fort Hill and Woodhull's			5.5		*Brooklyn Daily Eagle*	27 Apr 1900	6	*Huntington Long Islander*	10 May 1901	2
Northport Village Path			0		*Brooklyn Daily Eagle*	13 Oct 1900	15			
East Northport Station Path			1		*Huntington Long Islander*	26 Jul 1901	1	*Huntington Long Islander*	30 Aug 1901	1
Port Jefferson Paths										
Main Street to Ralroad Depot and Harbor			1		*Brooklyn Daily Eagle*	6 Nov 1899	7	*Brooklyn Daily Eagle*	30 Jul 1900	8
Water Street to Hotel Square			0		*Newtown Register*	17 May 1900	2			
Jones Street			0		*Brooklyn Daily Eagle*	3 Jul 1899	7	*Huntington Long Islander*	8 Jul 1899	3
Port Jefferson to Riverhead (Plateau Path)										
Section: Port Jefferson to Wading River (Gaps)			7		*Brooklyn Daily Eagle*	22 Jul 1899	6	*Brooklyn Daily Eagle*	13 Oct 1900	15
Section: Wading River to Riverhead (Gaps)			4		*Brooklyn Daily Eagle*	22 Jul 1899	6	*Brooklyn Daily Eagle*	13 Oct 1900	15
Riverhead										
Main Street Path			0		*Newtown Register*	14 Jun 1900	2			
Roanoke Avenue Path			0.5		*New York Times*	29 Apr 1900	12			
Riverhead to Orient via Jamesport, Southold and Greenport			23		*Brooklyn Daily Eagle*	22 Jul 1899	6	*New York Evening Telegram*	Aug 5 1899	7
Jamesport to South Jamesport			1		*New York Evening Telegram*	16 Dec 1899	11			
Mattituck to Baiting Hollow			12		*Brooklyn Daily Eagle*	19 Aug 1899	4			
Greenport Paths										
Front Street			0		*Brooklyn Daily Eagle*	2 Aug 1900	3			
Main Street			0		*Brooklyn Daily Eagle*	2 Aug 1900	3			

SIDEPATH LOCATIONS: COUNTY AND TOWNS	REP. CSM	REP. SM	EST. SM	SUB TOT.	SOURCE CITED (A)	DATE OF SOURCE	PG	SOURCE CITED (B)	DATE OF SOURCE	PG
County sidepath miles reported	350				*Brooklyn Daily Eagle*	27 Jun 1899	7			
County sidepath miles reported	200				*New York Daily Tribune*	23 Sep 1900	10			
County sidepath miles reported	500				*Brooklyn Daily Eagle*	13 Oct 1900	15			
County sidepath miles reported	300				*Brooklyn Daily Eagle*	24 Jan 1906	2			
Subtotals—Suffolk County:	300	209	66	**300**						

42. Thompkins County

Ithaca—Renwick Park Path along Cayuga Street			1		*Ithaca Daily News*	4 May 1899	3	*Ithaca Daily News*	9 Jun 1899	3
Ithaca to Trumansburg			11		*Geneva Daily Times*	22 Mar 1901	4	*Brooklyn Daily Eagle*	29 May 1901	4
Ithaca to Cortland County line via Varna, Freeville and Dryden			18		*Ithaca Daily News*	4 May 1899	3	*Ithaca Daily News*	17 Jul 1902	7
Dryden to Willow Glen			1		*Ithaca Daily News*	25 May 1899	3			
Subtotals—Thompkins County:	0	0	31	**31**						

43. Tioga County

Owego Paths

Owego Bicycle Club Path—East Village		0			*Owego Tioga County Record*	12 May 1898	3			
Fifth Avenue Path		0			*Owego Tioga County Record*	21 Apr 1898	3			

Southern Tier Paths

Section: Owego to Broome County via Blue Island Ferry & Apalachin		10			*Owego Tioga County Record*	21 Sep 1899	2	NYLAW, *Map of Sidepath Construction*	1901	
Section: Ice House to Sawyer's Crossing		0			*Owego Tioga County Record*	16 Jun 1898	3	*Owego Tioga County Record*	27 Apr 1899	2
Section: Hiawatha		0			*Owego Tioga County Record*	21 Apr 1898	3	*Owego Tioga County Record*	31 Aug 1899	3
Section: Owego to Nichols		9			*Owego Tioga County Record*	21 Sep 1899	2			
Section: Tioga from Glenmary Bridge to Jones District Schoolhouse		0			*Owego Tioga County Record*	12 May 1898	3	*Owego Tioga County Record*	25 May 1899	2
Section: South Tioga Path from the cemetery to the town line		1			*Owego Tioga County Record*	10 May 1900	2			
Section: Nichols to Barton Ferry		1			*Owego Tioga County Record*	11 Sep 1902	3			
Section: Barton to Chemung County line via Ellistown and Waverly		3			*Owego Tioga County Record*	21 Sep 1899	2	*Owego Tioga County Record*	26 Jun 1902	1

Catatonk Creek Corridor

Section: Red Bridge at Newark Valley Road to Catatonk		4			*Owego Tioga County Record*	8 Jun 1899	2–3	*Owego Tioga County Record*	21 Sep 1899	2
Spur Section: Bridgeshops to Red Mill Narrows		1			*Owego Tioga County Record*	21 Sep 1899	2			
Section: Catatonk to Candor		3			*Owego Tioga County Record*	21 Sep 1899	2			
Spur Section: Candor to Spencer		2			*Owego Tioga County Record*	5 Sep 1901	1	*Owego Tioga County Record*	23 Jan 1902	2

Owego Creek and East Branch Corridor

Section: Owego to Newark Valley			10		*Owego Tioga County Record*	23 Jan 1902	2	*Owego Tioga County Record*	21 Aug 1902	3
Section: Newark Valley to Berkshire			8		*Owego Tioga County Record*	21 Sep 1899	2			
Section: Berkshire Town Path			4		*Owego Tioga County Record*	22 Jun 1899	2	*Owego Tioga County Record*	21 Sep 1899	2
Section: Berkshire to Richford			1		*Owego Tioga County Record*	21 Apr 1898	3	*Owego Tioga County Record*	10 May 1900	2
County sidepath miles reported	44				*Tioga County Record*	21 Sep 1899	2			
County sidepath miles reported	31				*Ithaca Daily News*	7 Oct 1899	3			
Subtotals—Tioga County:	44	42	15	**57**						

SIDEPATH LOCATIONS: COUNTY AND TOWNS	REP. CSM	REP. SM	EST. SM	SUB TOT.	SOURCE CITED (A)	DATE OF SOURCE	PG	SOURCE CITED (B)	DATE OF SOURCE	PG
44. Ulster County										
Kingston to Saugerties			13		*Millbrook Round Table*	5 Aug 1899	6	*Rhinebeck Gazette*	30 Jul 1901	3
Saugerties Path			0		*LAW Magazine*, vol. 31	Oct 1900	17			
Subtotals—Ulster County:	0	0	13	**13**						
45. Warren County										
Glens Falls										
Brick Yard Loop (DeLong Brick Kiln)		2			*Glens Falls Morning Star*	21 May 1900	6	*Glens Falls Morning Star*	14 Jan 1901	4
Ridge Road Path		5			*Glens Falls Morning Star*	14 Jan 1901	4	*Glens Falls Morning Star*	3 Mar 1904	6
Glens Falls to Hudson Falls and Sandy Hill (Washington County)			3		*Cato Citizen*	15 Jun 1901	1	NYLAW, *Map of Sidepath Construction*	1901	
Glens Falls to Caldwell-Lake George via French Mountain (Plank Road)			9		*Warrensburgh News*	24 Jun 1897	6	*Glens Falls Morning Star*	31 May 1899	4
Caldwell-Lake George to Bolton via Hill View			10		*Glens Falls Morning Star*	19 Apr 1901	6			
Caldwell-Lake George to Luzerne			10		*Troy Daily Times*	30 May 1899	4			
Warrensburg Path			1		*Glens Falls Morning Star*	19 Apr 1901	6	*Glens Falls Morning Star*	3 Mar 1904	6
Subtotals—Warren County:	0	7	33	**40**						
46. Washington County										
Hudson Falls-Sandy Hill to Warren County line			0.5		*Glens Falls Morning Star*	20 Jun 1899	4			
Sandy Hill toward Fort Ann			2		*Glens Falls Morning Star*	20 Jun 1899	4	NYLAW, *Map of Sidepath Construction*	1901	
Hudson Falls-Fort Edward to Fort Miller			7		*Schuylerville Standard*	18 Oct 1899	1	*Glens Falls Morning Star*	10 Apr 1899	6
Greenwich to Hudson River bridge at Schuylerville (Saratoga County)										
Section: Greenwich to Middle Falls			1		*Schuylerville Standard*	7 Jun 1899	8	*Glens Falls Morning Star*	20 Jun 1899	4
Section: Easton to Hudson River bridge			2		*Glens Falls Morning Star*	15 Sep 1899	4	*Schuylerville Standard*	12 Jul 1899	5
Cambridge toward Lauderdale			2.5		*Glens Falls Morning Star*	15 Sep 1899	4	*Salem Washington County Post*	4 May 1900	3
Subtotals—Washington County:	0	0	15	**15**						
47. Wayne County										
Lyons-Sodus Point Path										
Section: Lyons, North to Vanderbilt and VanMarter farms		5			*Arcadian Weekly Gazette*	9 Sep 1896	8	*Arcadian Weekly Gazette*	30 Sep 1896	8
Section: South Sodus—Alton			0.5		*Arcadian Weekly Gazette*	13 Jun 1897	18	*Arcadian Weekly Gazette*	28 Jul 1897	3
Section: Alton to Sodus Point			4.5		*Elmira Telegram*	13 Jun 1897	18	*Rochester Democrat and Chronicle*	3 Jun 1899	15
Setion: Lyons, South to Alloway			2		*Newark Union*	7 Oct 1899	1			
Clyde-Sodus Bay Path										
Section: Clyde toward Rose			4		*Syracuse Post Standard*	16 Jun 1899	10	NYLAW, *Map of Sidepath Construction*	1901	
Spur Section: Rose Valley to Wolcott			1		*Sodus Record*	20 Oct 1899	5	*Oswego Daily Palladium*	7 Jun 1900	6
Spur Section: Wolcott Paths										
New Hartford Street			0.5		*Oswego Daily Palladium*	7 Jun 1900	6			
West Main Street			0.5		*Oswego Daily Palladium*	7 Jun 1900	6			
Ridge Road Path										
Section: Ontario			1		*Rochester Democrat and Chronicle*	19 Apr 1897	15			
Section: Williamson			1		*Rochester Democrat and Chronicle*	19 Apr 1897	15	*Arcadian Weekly Gazette*	16 Jun 1897	5

SIDEPATH LOCATIONS: COUNTY AND TOWNS	REP. CSM	REP. SM	EST. SM	SUB TOT.	SOURCE CITED (A)	DATE OF SOURCE	PG	SOURCE CITED (B)	DATE OF SOURCE	PG
Section: Sodus			1		Rochester Democrat and Chronicle	19 Apr 1897	15			
Newark Paths										
Newark to East Newark (Union Street Path)			0.5		Arcadian Weekly Gazette	14 Jun 1899	9	Rochester Democrat and Chronicle	31 Jan 1900	13
Main Street			0.5		Newark Union	17 Jun 1899	5			
Palmyra to Monroe County line via Macedon			4		Rochester Democrat and Chronicle	2 Jun 1899	4	NYLAW, Map of Sidepath Construction	1901	
Subtotals—Wayne County:	0	5	21	**26**						

48. Westchester County

Tarrytown to Scarborough			4		New York Daily Tribune	11 Apr 1897	2	Wheel and Cycling Trade Review, vol. 25	8 Mar 1900	40
William Rockefeller Path—Tarrytown			0		LAW Bulletin and Good Roads, vol. 22	18 Nov 1895	18			
Subtotals—Westchester County:	0	0	4	**4**						

49. Yates County

Penn Yan Paths										
Fourth Street to Burdett Hill			0		Penn Yan Democrat	28 Jul 1922	4			
Lake Street Path along fairground fence			0		Penn Yan Democrat	28 Jul 1902	4			
Branchport Road			0.5		Rochester Democrat and Chronicle	20 Sep 1899	4			
Penn Yan to Willow Grove (Keuka Lake Path)			3		Rochester Democrat and Chronicle	4 Jul 1898	4	Rochester Democrat and Chronicle	5 Jul 1901	13
Trunk Line Path—Rochester to Elmira										
Section: Bellona (near Ontario County line)			0		Elmira Daily Gazette	28 Jul 1899	8	Penn Yan Democrat	4 Aug 1899	1
Section: Benton			1		Rochester Democrat and Chronicle	20 Sep 1899	4			
Section: Penn Yan and Milo			0		Rochester Democrat and Chronicle	20 Sep 1899	4	Rochester Democrat and Chronicle	30 May 1900	13
Section: Himrods			0		Elmira Daily Gazette	28 Jul 1899	8	Penn Yan Democrat	4 Aug 1899	1
Section: Dundee			1		Rochester Democrat and Chronicle	20 Sep 1899	4			
Spur Section: Starkey			0.5		Rochester Democrat and Chronicle	20 Sep 1899	4	NYLAW, Map of Sidepath Construction	1901	
Spur Section: Eddytown			0		Elmira Daily Gazette	28 Jul 1899	8	Penn Yan Democrat	4 Aug 1899	1
Section: Rock Stream (near Schuyler County line)			0		Elmira Daily Gazette	28 Jul 1899	8	Penn Yan Democrat	4 Aug 1899	1
Subtotals—Yates County:	0	2.5	3.5	**6**						

Reported state sidepath miles constructed (Sept. 1899 to Sept. 1900):	1300				New York Daily Tribune	23 Sep 1900	10			
Reported state sidepath miles constructed (1898):	1200				Worcester Daily Telegram	9 Feb 1899	4			
Total reported county sidepath miles (18 counties):	1239									
Total sidepath miles:				2062						
Total counties with sidepath commissions (1900):	48				Cooperstown Otsego Farmer	26 Jan 1900	1			
Total counties with sidepath commissions (1901):	43				Cycle Age and Trade Review, vol. 27	17 Oct 1901	n.p.			

Abbreviations

The following abbreviations are used consistently throughout the endnotes, although the sources listed here represent only a small portion of the journals and newspapers cited. Designations are typically assigned to sources used with frequency, but readers will undoubtedly find the system to be an arbitrary one. In explanation, the Internet makes it possible to gather volumes of information from newspapers and to weave that material thematically across a broad region: a marvelous innovation. However, the challenge of citing sources both thoroughly and concisely can be a daunting one. The appendix in this book demonstrates one method of addressing that challenge.

Newspapers

AEJ	Albany Evening Journal		NTEN	North Tonawanda (NY) Evening News
BE	Illustrated Buffalo Express		ODP	Oswego (NY) Daily Palladium
BDE	Brooklyn Daily Eagle		PB	Philadelphia Bulletin
BDSU	Brooklyn Daily Standard Union		PI	Philadelphia Inquirer
BS	Baltimore Sun		RDC	Rochester Democrat and Chronicle
CPD	Cleveland Plain Dealer		RC	Rome Citizen
EDGFP	Elmira Daily Gazette and Free Press		RDS	Rome Daily Sentinel
HPS	Hazleton (PA) Plain Speaker		SSCN	Sayville Suffolk County News
LCJ	Louisville Courier Journal		SJ	Syracuse Journal
MPP	Middletown (CT) Penny Press		SPS	Syracuse Post Standard
NYDT	New York Daily Tribune		TB	Toledo Blade
NYET	New York Evening Telegram		UDP	Utica Daily Press
NYEP	New York Evening Post		UHD	Utica Herald-Dispatch
NYH	New York Herald		UO	Utica Observer
NYP	New York Press		WES	Washington Evening Star
NYS	New York Sun		WP	Washington Post
NYT	New York Times		WT	Washington Times
NYW	New York World		WBR	Wilkes-Barre Record
NFG	Niagara Falls Gazette			

Journals

BSB	Bassett's Scrap Book
BSB	Official Bulletin and Scrap Book of the LAW
BW	Bicycling World
BWLAWB	Bicycling World and LAW Bulletin
BWMR	Bicycling World and Motorcycle Review
GR	Good Roads

LAWB	LAW Bulletin
LAWBGR	LAW Bulletin and Good Roods
LAWM	LAW Magazine
OW	Outing and The Wheelman
SWG	Springfield Wheelmen's Gazette
WCTR	Wheel and Cycling Trade Review

Park Commissions

BABPC	Baltimore Board of Park Commissioners
BOBPC	Board of Commissioners, Boston Department of Parks
BUBPC	Buffalo Board of Park Commissioners
BPC	Brooklyn Park Commission
FPC	Fairmount Park Commission
CBPC	Cleveland Board of Park Commissioners

LBPC	Louisville Board of Park Commissioners
MPC	Metropolitan Park Commission (Boston)
NYBPC	New York Board of Park Commissioners
NYCDP	New York City Department of Parks

Notes

Preface

1. Thirteen Cyclers Club, *Route Book*, vol. 1 (March 31, 1895): 77–75; and Thirteen Cyclers Club, *Route Book*, vol. 1 (September 15, 1895): 127–132, Maryland Historical Society, MS815.

2. *Oxford English Dictionary*, compact ed. (1971), vol. 1: 2709; and Robert Louis Stevenson, "A Gossip on Romance," *Longman's Magazine* 1 (1882): 79.

3. Charles E. Pratt, "Echoes and Shadows," *The Wheelman* 1 (February 1883): 321; and Karl Kron, *Ten Thousand Miles on a Bicycle* (New York: printed by the author, 1887), 503.

4. Abbott Bassett, "Boston Bicycle Club Dinner," *BSB* 13 (March 1915): 35–37, recalling that he had counted seventy-four publications devoted exclusively to cycling, presumably including European as well as American works.

1 Awheel

1. See, for example, Massachusetts Division, LAW, Road Book Committee, A. D. Peck, comp., *Road Book of Massachusetts*, 4th ed. (Boston: printed by the author, 1892); Ohio Division, LAW, Thomas J. Kirkpatrick, comp., *Hand Book of the Ohio Division of the League of American Wheelmen*, 1st ed. (Springfield, OH: Mast, Crowell and Kirkpatrick, 1886); and New York State Division, LAW, Albert B. Barkman, ed., *Hand-Book and Road-Book of New York*, 1st ed. (Philadelphia: Stanley Hart and Co., 1887).

2. C. E. Bristol, "The Coming Horse," *The Wheelman* 1 (October 1882): 35–37. See also "The Camera Page," *LAWBGR* 26 (August 6, 1897): 204–205; and "Photo-Cycling," *LAWBGR* 27 (June 17, 1898): 645.

3. Carl Sauer, *The Geography of the Ozark Highland of Missouri* (New York: Greenwood Press, 1960), preface, vii–ix; Sauer first presented the study in 1915 at the University of Chicago, and presumably he refers to published works by writers such as Peter Kalm,

Jeremy Belknap, and Timothy Dwight. See also Sauer, "Morphology of Landscape," *University of California Publications in Geography*, ed. Carl Sauer, 2 (1925): 19–54; and Sauer, "Forward to Historical Geography," in *Annals of the Association of American Geographers*, ed. Derwent Whittlesey, 31 (1941): 1–24.

4. Sam Bass Warner, *Streetcar Suburbs* (Cambridge, MA: Harvard University Press, 1962); John Stilgoe, *Borderland: Origins of the American Suburb* (New Haven, CT: Yale University Press, 1988); and Stilgoe, *Metropolitan Corridor: Railroads and the American Scene, 1880 to 1935* (New Haven, CT: Yale University Press, 1983).

5. "Jonah's Jersey Dottings," *Wheel and Recreation* 11 (April 15, 1887): 37–38. See also Gary Allen Tobin, "The Bicycle Boom of the 1890s: The Development of Private Transportation and the Birth of the Modern Tourist," *Journal of Popular Culture* 7 (Spring 1974): 838–849.

6. Sauer, "Forward to Historical Geography."

7. The example of Wallace Nutting is apropos. His nerves exhausted from duties as a pastor in Providence, Rhode Island, Nutting began riding a bicycle in 1897 to relax, and he discovered that taking a camera on those trips made the experience more calming. His view from the road on a bicycle soon changed, however, because he switched to a carriage to accommodate larger camera equipment and then to an automobile. Although the themes expressed in his images can be complex, he (and the bicycle) did much to establish quiet roads as universal vantage points for homogeneous views of landscapes. See Wallace Nutting, *Biography* (Framingham, MA: Old America Company, 1936), 70; and Thomas A. Denenberg, *Wallace Nutting and the Invention of Old America* (New Haven, CT: Yale University Press, 2003), 28–29, 52–56.

8. Sauer, "Forward to Historical Geography."

9. Kent Mathewson, "Carl Sauer and His Critics," in *Carl Sauer on Culture and Landscape,* ed. William M. Denevan and Kent Mathewson (Baton Rouge: Louisiana State University Press, 2009), 9–28. See also John Brinckerhoff Jackson, *A Sense of Place, A Sense of Time* (New Haven, CT: Yale University Press, 1994); "The Need of Being Versed in Country Things," *Landscape* 1 (Spring 1951): 1; and Chris Wilson and Paul Groth, *Everyday America: Cultural Landscape Studies after J. B. Jackson* (Berkeley: University of California Press, 2003).

10. Sauer, "Morphology of Landscape"; and Jackson, *Sense of Place*, 159. See also "Glint from the Spoke of a Fifty-Four Inch Wheel," *Amateur Athlete* 2 (October 16, 1884): 6. In *Ride to Modernity: The Bicycle in Canada, 1869–1900* (Toronto: University of Toronto Press, 2001), author Glen Norcliffe argues that bicycles changed the meaning of countryside and transformed it into recreational space. However, in *Inventing New England: Regional Tourism in the Nineteenth Century* (Washington, DC: Smithsonian Institution Press, 1995), historian Dona Brown makes it clear that a growing tourist industry strategically packaged and marketed intangible products such as scenic countryside during much of the nineteenth century, catering to recreational touring long before the arrival of bicycles—at least in some regions. Thus, rather than redefining the meaning of countryside as a form of recreational space, cyclists extended the reach of that transformation, identifying new places where countryside acquired added meaning. Yet to the extent that cyclists' experiences differed from those of other tourists, whether because they often had to find their way along unnamed roads, or because their perceptions of visual qualities in landscapes ignored accepted standards, or because their relationships with rural citizenry reshaped the outlook of each, or because their explorations fostered environmental awareness, the meaning of countryside as a form of recreational space may have been expanded or refined, and Norcliffe's arguments open avenues for continued study.

11. "The First American Bicycle Tour," *Bicycling World and Archery Field* 2 (March 11, 1881): 275.

12. Fred Fisk, "How the Wheelmen Helped Save a Wright Brothers Bicycle Shop," *The Wheelmen* 29 (November 1986): 3–5; and Fred Fisk, "The Six Wright Brothers Bicycle Shops," *The Wheelmen* 29 (November 1986): 7–13.

13. In *Inventing New England*, 133–134, Brown points to the marketing of nostalgia during the late nineteenth century via historical attractions such as old buildings, which offered alternatives to scenic countryside for tourists. Cyclists clearly practiced heritage tourism, and by several means including articles in journals subsidized by bicycle manufacturers. Yet cyclists also seemed determined to discover the old and historic independently, and without resorting to prescribed itineraries, thus heightening the experience and often bypassing the tourist trade. See also New York City Landmarks Preservation Commission, "Ocean Parkway, Borough of Brooklyn," LP-0871, no. 3 (January 28, 1975).

14. Kevin Lynch, *What Time Is This Place?* (Cambridge, MA: MIT Press, 1972), 65; and David Lowenthal, *The Past Is a Foreign Country* (New York: Cambridge University Press, 1985).

15. Karl Kron, *Ten Thousand Miles on a Bicycle* (New York: printed by the author, 1887), iii, iv, 303.

16. Roderick Nash, *Wilderness and the American Mind* (New Haven, CT: Yale University Press, 1967), 30, 42, 53; William Cronon, *Changes in the Land: Indians, Colonists and the Ecology of New England* (New York: Hill and Wang, 1983), 120, 122, 168–169, 210; and Laura and Guy Waterman, *Forest and Crag: A History of Hiking, Trail Blazing, and Adventure in the Northeast Mountains* (Boston: Appalachian Mountain Club, 1989).

17. Untitled notebook, Frank C. Kirkwood Collection, Maryland Historical Society MS1501, box 5; Frank C. Kirkwood, *A List of the Birds of Maryland* (Baltimore: Deutsch Lithographing and Print Co., circa 1895; and Kron, *Ten Thousand Miles*, 781.

18. J. B. Jackson, "Roads Belong in the Landscape," *A Sense of Place*, 190; and [S. C. Babb, pseud.], "A Brief Lexicon of Road Words: Together with a Selection of Topics Suitable for Meditation by the Earnest Taxpayer-Motorist," in *Landscape* 2 (Autumn 1952): 32–33.

19. Wilson and Groth, "The Polyphony of Cultural Landscape Study," in *Everyday America*, 1–22.

20. Sauer, "Forward to Historical Geography," 359.

21. Kron, *Ten Thousand Miles*, 698; Pryor Dodge, *The Bicycle* (New York: Flammarion, 1996), 48; and David Herlihy, *Bicycle. The History* (New Haven, CT: Yale University Press, 2004), 127–128.

22. Nadine Besse and Ann Henry, eds., *Le Vélocipède: Objet de Modernité, 1860–1870* (Saint Etienne, France: Musée d'Art et d'Industrie, 2008); Alex Poyer, "The Origins of Velocipede Clubs," in *Vélocipède*, 87; and Herlihy, *Bicycle*, 75. For a summary of the sources used to trace the evolution of bicycle design, see the bibliographic essay.

23. "What Is to Be Done about Velocipedes?" *NYS* (April 9, 1869): 2; and Herlihy, *Bicycle*, 102–126.

24. Dodge, *The Bicycle*, 31–55.

25. Herlihy, *Bicycle*, 159–181; and "A Journey on Bicycles from Liverpool to London…," *NYS* (April 12, 1869): 2.

26. Dodge, *The Bicycle*, 58–70; and Herlihy, *Bicycle*, 159–185.

27. Herlihy, *Bicycle*, 159–187.

28. Dodge, *The Bicycle*, 70–78.

29. Herlihy, *Bicycle*, 216–221, 228–229.

30. *Herlihy*, Bicycle, 225–250; and Luther Henry Porter, "Evolution of the Cycle," Part 15 *LAWBGR* 27 (April 1, 1898): 309.

31. Gideon M. Davison, *The Traveler's Guide through the Middle and Northern States and the Provinces of Canada*, 7th ed. (Saratoga Springs, NY: G. M. Davison and S. S. and W. Wood, 1837), 231. See also Brown, *Inventing New England*, 23–31.

32. Richard Gassan, "The First American Tourist Guidebooks: Authorship and the Print Culture of the 1820s," *Book History* 8 (2005): 51.

33. Gassan, "Tourist Guidebooks."

34. Charles E. Pratt, "What of the League?" *The Wheelman* 1 (November, 1882): 133–137; "The C.T.C.," *The Amateur Athlete* 2 (November 6, 1884): 5; and Irving A. Leonard, "The Beginnings of the L.A.W.," *The Wheelmen* 16 (May 1980): 5.

35. See, for example, *Road-Book of New York* (1887).

36. Works in the field of travel history that omit references to cycling include Dean MacCannell, *The Tourist: A New Theory of the Leisure Class* (New York: Schocken Books, 1976); Lynne Withey, *Grand Tours and Cook's Tours: A History of Travel, 1750 to 1915* (New York: William Morrow and Company, Inc., 1997); Cindy Aron, *Working at Play: A History of Vacations in the United States* (New York: Oxford University Press, 1999); Marguerite S. Shaffer, *See America First: Tourism and National Identity, 1880–1940* (Washington, DC: Smithsonian Institution Press, 2001); and Sheeley Baranowski and Ellen Furlough, eds., *Being Elsewhere: Tourism, Consumer Culture, and Identity in Modern Europe and North America* (Ann Arbor: University of Michigan Press, 2001). For distinctions between travel and tourism, see Withey, *Grand Tours*, 3–31; Daniel Boorstin, *The Image: A Guide to Pseudo-Events in America* (New York: Atheneum, 1987); and John Urry, *The Tourist Gaze: Leisure and Travel in Contemporary Societies* (London: Sage, 1999).

37. MacCannell, *The Tourist*, 17–37, 39–56; and Baranowski, *Being Elsewhere*, 1–31.

38. Frank Hamilton Taylor, *Cyclers' and Drivers' Best Routes in and around Philadelphia* (Philadelphia: printed by the author, 1896), 33.

39. Wolfgang Schivelbusch, *The Railway Journey: The Industrialization of Time and Space in the 19th Century* (Berkeley: University of California Press, 1977), 52–69. See also Boorstin, *The Image*, 86–87, for references to travel by rail and, in particular, the impressions of critic John Ruskin.

40. Warren James Belasco, *Americans on the Road: From Autocamp to Motel, 1910–1945* (Cambridge, MA: MIT Press, 1979), viii, 15–17, 20–23, 26–29, 48–63.

41. Catherine Cocks, "The Chamber of Commerce's Carnival: City Festivals and Urban Tourism in the United States (1890–1915)," in Baranowski, *Being Elsewhere*, 89–107; and "The National Cycling Meet," *TB* (August 15, 1895): 5.

42. Withey, *Grand Tours*.

43. Charles Meinert, "From Sea to Shining Sea," *The Wheelmen* 60 (May 2002): 11; John Weiss, "The First," *Adventure Cyclist* 40 (June 2013): 22; and Frank Cameron, "Transcontinental Challenge: Its History and Mystique," *The Wheelmen* 24 (May 1984): 22; and "The Longest Road to Chicago: The McIlraths' around the World Ride," *The Wheelmen* 43 (November 1993): 25–32. See also "The Female Globe-Girdler Starts," *WCTR* 13 (June 29, 1894): 35; Norcliffe, *Ride to Modernity*, 231–235; and Brian Kinsman, *Around the World Awheel: The Adventures of Karl Creelman* (Hantsport, Nova Scotia: Lancelot Press, 1993).

2 *Wheeling Large*

1. "Forty Miles in Four Hours," *American Bicycling Journal* (December 22, 1877): 12–13.

2. Alfred S. Hudson, *The History of Sudbury, Massachusetts: 1638–1889* (Sudbury, MA: Sudbury Press, 1889), 633–642.

3. *Proprietors of Sudbury Meadows v. Proprietors of the Middlesex Canal*, 40 *Massachusetts Reports* 36 (1839); and *Talbot v. Hudson*, 16 Gray 417, 82 *Massachusetts Reports* 417 (1860).

4. "Forty Miles in Four Hours," *American Bicycling Journal* 1 (December 22, 1877): 12–13; "Fathers of American Cycling," *BWLAWB* 25 (December 30, 1892): 294; S. Michael Wells, "Sunrise in America: The Wheel Around the Hub Tour," *Wheelmen* 46 (May 1995): 2; and "Death of Frank W. Weston," *BSB* 9 (March 1911): 8–12.

5. Karl Kron, *Ten Thousand Miles on a Bicycle* (New York: printed by the author, 1887), 308.

6. Wells, "Sunrise in America," 2–11.

7. Abbot Bassett, "Brook Farm," *BSB* 9 (August 1911): 87.

8. Irving Leonard, "The Father of the League of American Wheelmen," *Wheelmen* 13 (December 1978): 5–8; Kron, *Ten Thousand Miles*, 504, 656–659, 661, 664.

9. Samuel S. McClure, *My Autobiography* (Valparaiso, IN: Lewis E. Myers & Company, 1914), 149. See also Kron, *Ten Thousand Miles*, 504, 656–659, 661, and 664; and John F. McClure, "A Trip through Eastern Pennsylvania," *Wheelman* 2 (April 1883): 28. Kron calls

The Wheelman an elaborately illustrated trade circular, but it was one of the country's first magazines devoted principally to touring.

10. Kron, *Ten Thousand Miles*, 657; and McClure, *My Autobiography*, 159. The certificate of incorporation of the Wheelman Company is dated October 26, 1883, recorded November 7, 1883, in the Office of Secretary of the Commonwealth of Massachusetts. For Baxter, see Irving Leonard, "The League of American Wheelmen: The Meet at Newport," *Wheelmen* 16 (May 1980): 16.

11. Frederick Law Olmsted Jr. and John Charles Olmsted, "Landscape Architects' Report," in *Annual Report*, Board of Metropolitan Park Commissioners (January 1898); and Green Ribbon Commission, Metropolitan District Commission, *Enhancing the Future of the Metropolitan Park System* (Boston: MDC, 1996), 14.

12. Kron, *Ten Thousand Miles*, 504; "Is Outing Altogether Lost to Cycling?" *LAWB* 5 (September 9, 1887): 149; "Outing Changes Hands," *Wheel and Recreation* 12 (May 13, 1887): 462; and "William B. Howland," *BSB* 15 (April 1917): 56.

13. Kron, *Ten Thousand Miles*, 657–659 and 661; and Cressy Morrison, "The League of American Wheelmen," *Frank Leslie's Popular Monthly* 45 (April 1898): 363–372.

14. George E. Blackman, "An October Ramble," in *Wheelman* 1 (November 1882): 112.

15. Ibid.

16. Charles E. Pratt, "Echoes and Shadows," *Wheelman* 1 (February 1883): 321; and Kron, *Ten Thousand Miles*, 503.

17. W. O. Owen, "A Wheel to the Gold Mines of Cummins City," *Wheelman* 2 (April 1883): 46–51; and "A Summer Ramble among the Black Hills," *Wheelman* 2 (May 1883): 81. See also Abbot Bassett, "First Bicycle Tour," *BSB* 8 (June 1908): 51.

18. Jay Howe Adams, "On and Off the Lancaster Pike," *Outing and the Wheelman* 5 (October 1884): 3.

19. Ibid.

20. Jay Howe Adams, "Through 'The Neck' on a Bicycle," *Outing* 6 (September 1885): 682.

21. Adams, "Through "The Neck'"; and S. Weir Mitchell, *Hephzibah Guinness, Thee and You, and A Draft on the Bank of Spain* (Philadelphia: J. B. Lippincott & Co., 1880), 159–160.

22. John B. Carrington, "Through Virginia Awheel," *Outing* 28 (June 1896): 204; "Awheel Thro' the Tide-Water of Virginia," *Outing* 30 (April 1897): 65; "Across the Alleghanies [sic] Awheel," pt. 1, *Outing* 30 (May 1897): 132; ibid., pt. 2 *Outing* 30 (June 1897): 240; and ibid., pt. 3 *Outing* 30 (July 1897): 380. See also Daniel F. Gay, "Through the Shenandoah Valley Awheel," *Outing* 32 (June 1898): 232.

23. Carrington, "Through Virginia Awheel;" "Awheel Thro' the Tide-Water Virginia;" and "Across the Alleghanies [sic} Awheel."

24. Carrington, "Alleghanies Awheel"; and "The Shenandoah Valley," *LAWBGR* 24 (July 31, 1896): 167. See also "A Vine Clad Veranda," *American Agriculturalist* 64 (July 22, 1899): 77 (morning glory); and "Concerning Vines," *The Household* 17 (July 1884): 194 (Virginia creeper). In addition to its serials during the mid-1890s, *Outing* included a special column on cycle touring authored under the pseudonym The Prowler; this column often provided routes, maps, and advice about preparing for trips; see, e.g., "Cycling," *Outing* 28 (June 1896): 42.

25. A. H. Godfrey, "Up to the Tappan Zee Awheel," *Outing* 32 (July 1898): 375; and "Up to the Catskills Awheel on the West Shore," *Outing* 32 (August 1898): 458. See also Ernest Ingersoll, "Cycling on the Palisades of the Hudson," *Outing* 26 (September 1895): 442–447.

26. In 1881, *Bicycling World* became the official journal of the LAW. See Daniel J. Dwyer, *Prominent Wheelmen and Bicycle Club Directory of Massachusetts, 1894* (Boston: Garfield Publishing Co., 1894), 12–16B; and Kron, *Ten Thousand Miles*, 663–664.

27. W. S. Beekman and C. W. Willis, *Cycle Gleanings, or Wheels and Wheeling for Business and Pleasure and the Study of Nature* (Boston: Skinner, Bartlett and Co., 1894), 34–37. See also Beekman, "Through the White Mountains Awheel," pt. 1, *BW* 30 (February 15, 1895): 527–537; and ibid., pt. 2, *BW* 30 (February 22, 1895): 567–571; and Dwyer, *Prominent Wheelmen*, 87.

28. W. S. Beekman, "A Bicycle Tour: Under Sky and Clouds of Another State," 27–37; and Beekman, "A Geological Ride: Slate Quarries, Dykes, and Glacial Scratches," 38–41; both in Beekman and Willis, *Cycle Gleanings*.

29. W. S. Beekman, "Nature, From the Standpoint of the Observant Cyclist," pt. 1, *BW* 31 (June 7, 1895): 52; ibid., pt. 2, *BW* 31 (June 14, 1895): 95; ibid., pt. 3, *BW* 31 (June 21, 1895): 141; ibid., pt. 4, *BW* 31 (June 28, 1895): 187; ibid., pt. 5, *BW* 31 (July 5, 1895): 234; ibid., pt. 6, *BW* 31 (July 12, 1895): 282; ibid., pt. 7, *BW* 31 (July 19, 1895): 330; ibid., pt. 8, *BW* 31 (July 26, 1895): 374; and ibid., pt. 9, *BW* 31 (August 2, 1895): 414.

30. Beekman, "Nature," pt. 2: 95; and "Nature," pt. 6: 283.

31. Beekman, "Nature," pt. 6: 283; "Nature," pt. 5: 234. See also *Annual Report*, Metropolitan Park Commission (January 1895).

32. Dwyer, *Prominent Wheelmen*, 14–16, 34; Kron, *Ten Thousand Miles*, 654, 663–68. *Amateur Athlete* began publication on April 4, 1883; its first LAW issue was June 12, 1884; it became *Cyclist and Athlete* on January 1, 1885; and it suspended publication in October 1885.

LAW Bulletin began publication with vol. 1, no. 1 (July 2, 1885) under Aaron's editorial management. For the shift from Aaron to Bassett, see *LAW Bulletin* 4, no. 3 (January 21, 1887); and 4, no. 8 (March 4, 1887); the latter was the first issue published in Boston. See also *Bicycling World and the LAW Bulletin* 16, no. 18 (March 2, 1888) for the first issue of that journal; and "Shall the League Continue to Issue the Bulletin?" *LAWB* 6 (January 27, 1888): 39, questioning the financial merits of issuing a publication free to all league members.

33. Dwyer, *Prominent Wheelmen*, 34, and Kron, *Ten Thousand Miles*, 663–665. The first issue of *The Cycle* began in 1886 (vol. 1, no. 1, April 2, 1886), and concluded in 1887 (vol. 2, no. 16, January 14, 1887). See also "Abbot Bassett," *LAWM* 1 (July 1900): 11.

34. "The Big Four Tourists," *LAWB* 1 (July 2, 1885): 6; Burley B. Ayers, "The Big Four Tour Association," *LAWB* 1 (July 2, 1885): 12; and Burley B. Ayers, "Big Four Bicycle Tour," *LAWB* 1 (September 25, 1885): 232.

35. For the LAW Touring Committee, see Kron, *Ten Thousand Miles*, 627. During the spring of 1886, the league amended its constitution to include a touring board. See "General Meeting of the League of American Wheelmen," *LAWB* 1 (July 9, 1885): 28–29; and "Constitution LAW" *LAWB* 2 (May 21, 1886): 453–456, at 454. The Big Four Bicycle Tour Association subsequently merged with that touring board; see Burley B. Ayres, "The Big Four Disband," *LAWB* 2 (April 9, 1886): 318–319. See also Frank A. Elwell, "Come East," *Wheelman* 1 (February, 1883): 332–334; "Fifty Clerical Wheelmen on a Tour in Canada," *LAWB* 1 (July 2, 1885): 6; and "The Cycling Clergymen," *PI* (August 21, 1886): 5.

36. Daisie, "From a Feminine Point of View," *The Cycle* 1 (June 18, 1886): 214.

37. Daisie's first installment for *LAWB* appears in that journal's first issue published in Boston, vol. 4, no. 9 (March 4, 1887): 182. See also Abbot Bassett, "Historic Dates of Cycling," *BSB* 19 (May 1921): 56; ibid., *BSB* 19 (November 1921): 129; Marguerite "Around Cape Ann," *WCTR* 4 (October 18, 1889): 153; and Lisa Peek Ramos, *Magnolia* (Charleston, SC: The History Press, 2008), 15–19. For excellent biographical sketches of the North Short tricyclists, see Lorenz Finison, *Boston's Cycling Craze, 1880 to 1900* (Amherst: University of Massachusetts Press, 2014), 43–68. See also Ed Muench, "The Ladies' Eastern Tricycle Tour," *The Wheelmen* 50 (May 1997): 25–27, a reprinting of Daisie's description of the fourth tour, "From the Merrimac to Naumkeag."

38. "Bicycling and Tricycling," *Outing* 7 (December 1885): 343; Minna Caroline Smith, "The Ladies' Tour to Kettle Cove," *Outing* 7 (January 1886): 431; and "North Shore Trip," *The Cycle* 2 (October 29, 1886): 58.

39. Daisie, "From a Feminine Point of View," *The Cycle* 2 (October 29, 1886): 57; Merrie Wheeler, "Some of the Trials and Triumphs of the Tandem Tourists," *The Cycle* 2 (November 5, 1886): 79; Daisie, "From a Feminine Point of View," *LAWB* 5 (September 23, 1887): 179; Daisie, "From a Feminine Point of View," *LAWB* 6 (January 6, 1888): 4; and Daisie, "The Ladies' Eastern Tricycle Tour: From the Merrimac to Naumkeag," *Outing* 13 (December 1888): 260. See also Smith, "Tour to Kettle Cove," 431.

40. Smith, "Tour to Kettle Cove," 431.

41. Medford Historical Society, *Round about Middlesex Fells* (Medford, MA: printed by author, 1935), 5–12; Keith N. Morgan, Elizabeth H. Cushing, and Katherine Boonin, "Historic Landscape Report: Lynn Woods, Lynn, Massachusetts," unpublished report available at the Lynn Historical Society; Sylvester Baxter, "Lynn Public Forest," *Garden and Forest* 2 (October 30, 1889): 526; and Green Ribbon Commission, Metropolitan District Commission, *Metropolitan Park System*, 14.

42. Smith, "Tour to Kettle Cove." For a list of women cyclists, see Smith, "Women as Cyclers," *Outing* 6 (June 1885): 317–321. See also "Sylvester Baxter and the Bicycle," *WCTR* 10 (November 11, 1892): 16.

43. A. M. Hill, "From New Orleans to Boston," pt. 1, *LAWB* 3 (October 29, 1886): 450; ibid., pt. 2, *LAWB* 3 (November 5, 1886): 470; ibid., pt. 3, *LAWB* 3 (November 12, 1886), 490; and ibid., pt. 4, *LAWB* 3 (November 19, 1886): 510.

44. Hill, "From New Orleans to Boston," pts. 1–4.

45. Ibid.

46. Ibid.

47. *Good Roads* 1, no. 1 (January 1892); Isaac Potter, "Potter to Elliott" and Sterling Elliott, "Elliott to Potter," *LAWB* 1 (April 26, 1894): 18; Bruce Epperson, *Pedaling Bicycles to America: The Rise of an Industry* (Jefferson, NC: McFarland and Company, 2010), 93–96; and Charles T. Raymond, "Side Paths," *Good Roads* 6 (November 1894): 263.

48. Dwyer, *Prominent Wheelmen*, 15–16A, 16B. See *LAW Bulletin* (Chicago) 1, no. 1 (March 22, 1894). See also *LAW Bulletin and Good Roads* 21, no. 14 (April 5, 1895), which (despite its confusing numbering) is the first issue under the combined title. See also "Nixon Waterman," *LAWBGR* 21 (May 24, 1895): 9. For editorial perspective on the shift to the Bearings Publishing Co., see "The League's New Organ," *WCTR* 13 (March 9, 1894): 22; and "The League's Publication," *WCTR* 14 (February 8, 1895): 23.

49. George T. Morey, "A Decoration Day Run to Babylon, Long Island," *LAWBGR* (June 26, 1896): 935; W. E. Miles, "Ten Times Across the Charles River," *LAWBGR* (May 27, 1898): 559; and Henry Tyrrell, *Artistic Bridge*

Design (Chicago: The Myron C. Clark Publishing Co., 1912).

50. "Report of the Secretary-Treasurer," *BSB* 18 (October 1920): 149; "What about the L.A.W.?" *Good Roads Magazine* 2 (January 1902): 24; and "The Bulletin Change," *WCTR* 23 (July 20, 1899): 15. *Elliott's Magazine* begins with vol. 30, no. 1 (August 1899), continuing the sequence used by *LAW Bulletin and Good Roads*. As a separate department in *Elliott's Magazine*, "The Law Bulletin and Good Roads" also begins with vol. 30, no. 1 (August 1899). For league staff who required current notice of league news, Bassett and Elliott collaborated in the publication of a weekly newsletter, *LAW Bulletin and Good Roads Supplement*, beginning in August 1899.

51. Harmon P. Elliott, *The Sterling Elliott Family* (Cambridge, MA: Elliott Addressing Machine Co., circa 1945); and "Elliott Is President," *NYT* (February 12, 1896): 6.

52. *LAW Magazine* superseded *LAW Bulletin* and began as New Series, vol. 1, no. 1 (June 1900) but maintained a reference to Old Series, vol. 31, resuming the sequence concluded when Elliott's Magazine ceased publication. See Conway Sams, "A Few Words from the President," *LAWM* (June 1900): 13, in which Sams explains that publication of a weekly bulletin was financially impossible. See also Louis Geyler, "Summer Vacations Awheel," pt. 1, *LAWM* 1 (July 1900): 7; ibid., pt. 2, *LAWM* 1 (August 1900): 9.

53. "Our Observations of the Month," *LAWM* 1 (May 1901): 1. *Good Roads Magazine* begins with vol. 2, no. 1 (June 1901). The announcement of the retirement of Charles Mears, the arrival of Hrolf Wisby, and the publication's dedication to the improvement of highways is found in vol. 2, no. 3 (August 1901): 17. For a touring article, see Bertram J. Bishop, "Awheel in Old Manilla," *Good Roads Magazine* 2 (September 1901): 6–8.

54. F. F. Granby, "The Automobile in Paris," *Elliott's Magazine* 30 (September 1899): 133; "Motor Cycles: As They Come and Go," *LAWM* 1 (February 1901): 14; and Bassett, "National Assembly, L.A.W.," *BSB* 10 (October 1912): 307.

55. *Bassett's Scrapbook* begins with vol. 1, no. 1 (March, 1903). The *Official Bulletin and Scrapbook of the League of American Wheelmen* begins with vol. 12, no. 1 (January 1914). See also Bassett, "Brook Farm," *BSB* 9 (August 1911): 87; and "Wheel About the Hub," *BSB* 18 (October, 1921): 116.

56. David Herlihy, *Bicycle: The History* (New Haven, CT: Yale University Press, 2004), 343–351; Bassett, "How many more if...," *BSB* 9 (April 1911), 20; "Inter-State Side Paths," *LAWM* 1 (June 1900): 2; and "Promoting Maryland Paths," *LAWM* 1 (July 1900): 3.

57. Kron, *Ten Thousand Miles*, 488; and Fred Jenkins, "Ten Days in the Catskills," *The Wheel* 1 (July 20, 1881): 173. See also "By Bicycle to Boston," pt. 1, *The Wheel* 1 (June 22, 1881): 157; ibid., pt. 2, *The Wheel* 1 (July 6, 1881): 165; ibid., pt. 3, *The Wheel* 1 (August 3, 1881): 181; ibid., pt. 4, *The Wheel* 1 (August 17, 1881): 189; ibid., pt. 5, *The Wheel* 1 (August 31, 1881): 197; ibid., pt. 6, *The Wheel* 1 (September 14, 1881): 206; and ibid., pt. 7, *The Wheel* 2 (September 28, 1881): 5. See also "Excursions: Lima, Ohio, to Boston," *BW* 2 (December 3, 1880): 53.

58. In *The Wheel's* editorial columns, see 2 (April 26, 1882): 124; 2 (June 7, 1882): 150; 3 (October 4, 1882): 4; and 3 (December 6, 1882): 4. See also "How I Spent My Fourth," *The Wheel* 4 (July 6, 1883): 7. Also see Kron, *Ten Thousand Miles*, 667–669; and "Historical Dates of Cycling," *BSB* 18 (July 1920): 108. For Prial's accounts, see "Change of Publishers," *Wheel and Recreation* 11 (December 3, 1886): 101; and "Wheel and Cycling Trade Review," *WCTR* 1 (March 2, 1888): 5. See also "Ourselves," *WCTR* 10 (December 23, 1892): 25.

59. "Our Acquisition," *BW* 41 (September 13, 1900): 455. See also George W. Nellis, "Across the Continent," pt. 1, *The Wheel* 12 (June 3, 1887): 534; ibid., pt. 10, *The Wheel* (August 26, 1887): 771.

60. Ashton Nichols, "Delightful Trip in the Wallkill Valley on a Machine," pt. 1, *WCTR* 3 (May 10, 1889): 230; ibid., pt. 2, *WCTR* 3 (May 17, 1889): 183.

61. "A-Wheel to Tomac," *WCTR* 1 (May 25, 1888): 279; and "A Summer Tour Awheel," *WCTR* 1 (July 27, 1888): 499.

62. For accounts of the North Shore tour, see "From Boston to Cape Ann and Newburyport," *Wheel* 11 (October 15, 1896): 32; for letters by Psyche in *WCTR*, see "Cycling for Women," 3 (March 22, 1889): 66; for letters by Marguerite in *WCTR*, see "Why Ladies Should Ride Bicycles," *WCTR* 3 (March 8, 1889): 22; and for Margaret Kirkwood's century rides in *WCTR*, see "Miss Margaret Kirkwood," *WCTR* 12 (September 29, 1893): 15.

63. "Route No 5. Red Bank and Long Branch, N.J.," *WCTR* 10 (August 26, 1892): 21; "Pompton, N.J.—Route No. 4," *WCTR* 9 (August 19, 1892): 21; and "Half-Century Rides," *WCTR* 17 (March 13, 1896): 52.

64. "Beautiful Westchester," *WCTR* 15 (June 7, 1895): 27; "Rambling Through the Ramapo," *WCTR* 16 (September 20, 1895): 35 and supplement, i; "In the Saw Mill River Valley," *WCTR* 17 (April 24, 1896): 65; "Where Heroes Have Lived and Died," *WCTR* 17 (May 15, 1896): supplement, i–iii; "A Tour on Long Island," *WCTR* 17 (July 17, 1896): 57; "Owed to Jersey," *WCTR* 18 (August 29, 1896): 30; "Grandest of Drives," *WCTR* 18 (January 29, 1897), 114; and "Three-Four-Five, Over the Fourth," *WCTR* 19 (June 25, 1897): supplement, i–iii.

65. "Staten Island," *WCTR* 18 (November 20, 1896): 40; and "Staten Island: A Favorite Run," *WCTR* 25 (September 6, 1900): 14.

66. Tam O'Shanter, "Elwell's European Tourists," pt. 1, *WCTR* 3 (June 14, 1889): 381-382; ibid., part 2, *WCTR* 3 (June 21, 1889): 405-406; ibid., pt. 3, *WCTR* 3 (June 28, 1889): 445; ibid., part 4, *WCTR* 3 (July 5, 1889): 461-462; ibid., part 5 *WCTR* (July 12, 1889): 492; ibid., part 6 *WCTR* (July 19, 1889): 511; ibid., part 7 *WCTR* (July 26, 1889): 532; ibid., part 8 *WCTR* (August 2, 1889): 552; ibid., part 9 *WCTR* (August 9, 1889): 570; and ibid., part 10 *WCTR* (August 16, 1889): 599; See also Edward H. Elwell Jr., "American Cycling Architects in France," pt. 1, *WCTR* 10 (September 2, 1892): 32; ibid., pt. 2, *WCTR* 10 (September 16, 1892): 31; ibid., pt. 3, *WCTR* 10 (September 30, 1892): 26; ibid., pt. 4, *WCTR* 10 (October 21, 1892): 18; and ibid., pt. 5, *WCTR* 10 (October 28, 1892): supplement, i. See also Traveler, "An American Cyclist in Wales," *WCTR* 2 (November 30, 1888): 287.

67. For *The Wheelwoman*, see Finison, *Boston's Cycling Craze*, 55.

68. F. T. S. [probably Fred T. Sholes], "A September Vacation," *The Cleveland Mercury* 1 (April 1884): 9-11.

69. A. L. Fennessy, "The Springfield Bicycle Club," *SWG* 1 (August 1883): 9; "Hampden Park," *SWG* 3 (August 1885): 57; "The Springfield Wheelman's Gazette," *SWG* 2 (October 1884): 100; H. L. Mundy, "From Williamsport to Ithaca," *SWG* 3 (August, 1885): 65; and Kron, "Shore and Hill-Top in Connecticut," *SWG* 3 (June 1885): 32. See also Kron, *Ten Thousand Miles*, 661-662. The title later changes to *Wheelman's Gazette*.

70. Kron, *Ten Thousand Miles*, 671-672.

71. "Three In One," *WCTR* 20 (November 12, 1897): 1; and "Editorial," *The Bearings* 16 (November 18, 1897): 1234.

72. Karl Kron, *Ten Thousand Miles*, 654-672. *The Cyclist* began publication in Hartford in 1890 and merged with *Bicycling World* in 1898, with Joseph Goodman as editor. *The Bearings* began circulation in 1890 in Chicago, published by The Cycling Authority of America—N. H. Van Sicklen, president and business manager—and various editors collaborated, including George K. Barrett and L. P. Berger. *The Cycle Age and Trade Review* began publication in Chicago with vol. 1, no. 1 (November 25, 1897); the New Series began with vol. 20, no. 7 (December 16, 1897). The journal became the official publication of the National Association of Cycle Dealers, under the combined direction of Bearings, The Referee and Cycling Life publishing companies. For the Elwell-Stevens tour of France, see Edward H. Elwell Jr., "A Tour in Sunny France," pt. 1, *The Bearings* 7 (July 7, 1893): 10-11; ibid., pt. 2, *The Bearings* 7 (July 14, 1893): 14-15; and ibid., pt. 3, *The Bearings* 7 (July 21, 1893): 6-7. See also "Quakertown to the Hub," *The Bearings* 9 (June 1894): 12.

73. Francis H. Bent, "A Young Architect's Bicycle Trip in Europe," pt. 1, *The Engineering Record* 32 (October 26, 1895): 388-390; ibid., pt. 2, *The Engineering Record* 32 (November 9, 1895): 424-425; ibid., pt. 3, *The Engineering Record* 32 (November 16, 1895): 441-442; ibid., pt. 4, *The Engineering Record* 32 (November 23, 1895): 462; ibid., pt. 5, *The Engineering Record* 32 (November 30, 1895): 476; ibid., pt. 6, *The Engineering Record* 33 (December 7, 1895): 9; ibid., pt. 7, *The Engineering Record* 33 (December 14, 1895): 28; ibid., pt. 8, *The Engineering Record* 33 (December 28, 1895): 64; ibid., pt. 9, *The Engineering Record* 33 (January 11, 1896): 101; ibid., pt. 10, *The Engineering Record* 33 (January 18, 1896): 118; ibid., pt. 11, *The Engineering Record* 33 (January 25, 1896): 136; and ibid., pt. 12, *The Engineering Record* 33 (February 22, 1896): 209.

74. "National Cycle Dealers' Association Makes Progress," *Bicycle News* 3 (February 1917): 11; and Quince Kilby, "A-Wheel in New England," *BWMR* 63 (April 29, 1911): 323. See also "The Bicycle News," *BSB* 13 (April, 1915): 57.

75. Fred I. Perrault, "Six Hundred Miles Awheel in Three States," *Bicycle News* 5 (August 1916): 23; and "Just Like Old Times," *BWMR* 65 (May 4, 1912): 36.

3 Imagining Place

1. William A. Chatto, "The Practice of Wood Engraving," in *A Treatise of Wood Engraving, Historical and Practical*, ed. Henry G. Bohn (London: Henry G. Bohn, 1861), 561-652; William M. Laffan, *Engravings on Wood* (New York: Harper and Brothers, 1887), 5; Joseph Pennell, *The Adventures of an Illustrator* (Boston: Little, Brown & Co., 1925), 58; and Clare Leighton, *Wood-Engraving and Woodcuts* (London: The Studio, Ltd., 1932), 7-22.

See also "Wood-Engraving and the 'Scribner' Prizes," *Scribner's Monthly* 21 (April 1881): 937; and Mariana G. Van Rensselaer, "Wood Engraving and the Century Prizes," *Century Magazine* 24 (June 1882): 230.

2. William J. Linton, *The History of Wood Engraving in America* (Boston: Estes and Lauriat, 1882); repr. as *American Wood Engraving: A Victorian History*, with introduction by Nancy C. Schrock (Watkins Glen, NY: Athenaeum Library of Nineteenth Century America by the American Life Foundation and Study Institute, 1976). See also Richard Kenin, "Introduction," in *A Facsimile of Frank Leslie's Illustrated Historical Register of the Centennial Exposition: 1876*, ed. Frank G. Norton (New York: Frank Leslie's Publishing House, 1876); repr., New York: Paddington Press, Ltd., 1974, 1-5 unnumbered.

3. Schrock, "William James Linton and His Victorian History of Wood Engraving," in *American Wood Engraving*, 1–10 (unnumbered).

4. Theodore L. De Vinne, "The Growth of Wood-Cut Printing," pt. 1, *Scribner's Monthly* 19 (April 1880): 860; ibid., pt. 2, *Scribner's Monthly* 20 (May 1880): 34–45. See also Nancy L. Gustke, *The Special Artist in American Culture: A Biography of Frank Hamilton Taylor (1846–1927)* (New York: Peter Lang, 1995), 29–63.

5. De Vinne, "Wood-Cut Printing"; Linton, *Wood-Engraving*, 41–51; and Van Rensselaer, "Wood-Engraving and the Century Prizes."

6. Pennell, *Illustrator*, 105; and De Vinne, "Wood-Cut Printing."

7. Anthony Gross, *Etching, Engraving, and Intaglio Printing* (London: Oxford University Press, 1970), 30–53, 67–81; Mariana G. Van Rensselaer, "American Etchers," *The Century Magazine* 25 (February 1883): 483; Joseph Pennell, *Etchers and Etching*, 4th ed. (New York: Macmillan Company, 1926), 207–240, esp. 221; and Laffan, *Engravings*, 5.

8. Pennell, *Illustrator*, 69.

9. Gustke, *Special Artist*, 157–161; and Pennell, *Illustrator*, 37, 69.

10. Gustke, *Special Artist*, 113–117. See also Burley B. Ayers, "The Big Four Tour Association," *LAWB* 1 (July 2, 1885): 12; and "The Big Four Disband," *LAWB* 2 (April 9, 1886): 318–319.

11. Frank Hamilton Taylor, *Cyclers'and Drivers' Best Routes in and around Philadelphia* (Philadelphia: the author, 1896), 22–23; and "First Turnpike in United States," *PI* (February 9, 1896): 25.

12. Pennell, *Illustrator*, 176; and Irving Leonard, "Joseph Pennell, Artist: Illustrator of Early Cycle Touring," *The Wheelmen* 11 (March 1977): 2. See also, for example, Elizabeth Robins Pennell, *French Cathedrals: Monasteries and Abbeys, and Sacred Sites of France* (New York: The Century Co., 1909).

13. Pennell, *Illustrator*, 44, 58–59. See also Pennell, "England's L.A.W.," *LAWBGR* 27 (March 25, 1898): 277; Karl Kron, *Ten Thousand Miles on a Bicycle* (New York: printed by the author, 1887), 627; and Leonard, "Joseph Pennell."

14. Pennell, *Illustrator*, 1, 69.

15. Ibid., 43–44, 330.

16. Ibid., 175.

17. H. C. Bunner, "Shantytown," *Scribner's Monthly* 20 (October 1880): 855–869; and Pennell, *Illustrator*, 60–63.

18. Maurice Egan, "A Day in the Ma'sh," *Scribner's Monthly* 22 (June 1881): 343–352.

19. Samuel S. McClure, *My Autobiography* (New York: Frederick A. Stokes Co., 1914), 149–150, 159.

20. George Hawes Whittle, "Monographs on American Wood Engravers," *Printing Art* 33 (April 1919): 99. McClure employed other engravers, including William M. Tenney and K. C. Atwood.

21. Stephanie L. Herdrick, "Hassam in Boston, 1859–1886," in *Childe Hassam: American Impressionist*, ed. H. Barbara Weinberg (New Haven, CT: Yale University Press for the Metropolitan Museum of Art, 2004), 29–51; and Elizabeth E. Barker, "A Truly Learned Weaving of Light and Dark: Hassam's Prints," in Weinberg, *Hassam*, 267–284.

22. McClure, *Autobiography*, 150–151; *The Wheelman* 1 (February, 1883): 321, 328; Herdrick, "Hassam in Boston," 30–33; and "That the illustrations of the January and February *Wheelman*..." *The Wheel* 3 (December 27, 1882): 5. Garrett's studio stood at 12 West Street.

23. H. B. Hart, "The Bicycle in Philadelphia," *The Wheelman* 3 (July 1883): 257–265; and Albert S. Parsons, "The Massachusetts Bicycle Club," *The Wheelman* 3 (June 1883): 161–172. Between February and September 1883, Hassam contributed at least eighteen signed illustrations and probably several others that are not signed.

24. C. E. M., "A Day in Andover," *The Wheelman* 2 (September 1883): 401–412. See also "Charles W. Reed," *BSB* 18 (November 1920): 171.

25. "Decadence of Wood-Engraving," *Publisher's Weekly* 46 (October 6, 1894): 544. For Sylvester's illustration, see S. H. Day, "The New House of the Massachusetts Bicycle Club," *Outing* 5 (March 1885): 433.

26. Philip G. Hubert Jr., "The Bicycle: The Wheel of To-Day," *Scribner's Magazine* 17 (June 1895): 692.

27. Irving A. Leonard, "An Illustrator of Thomas Stevens' *Around the World on A Bicycle*," *The Wheelmen* 7 (Winter 1976): 2; and "Stony Hill Bicycle Path," *WES* (October 28, 1899): 9.

28. "Charming Jersey: Fort Lee," *WCTR* 13 (March 23, 1894): 38; "Beautiful Westchester," *WCTR* 15 (June 7, 1895): 27–30; and "Into a New Studio," *WCTR* 20 (December 3, 1897): 36. See also "Artist Merrick Married," *Bearings* 7 (April 28, 1893), 5; and "Stray Shots," *Bearings* 7 (May 12, 1893): 2. Harry L. Spencer of Pawtucket, Rhode Island, is another of cycling's illustrators who warrants study; see "Harry L. Spencer," *BSB* 9 (May 1911): 39.

29. Benson J. Lossing, *The History of New York City* (New York: G. E. Perine, 1884), 842–846; and "Photo-Engraving," *Scientific American* 33 (September 18, 1875): 178.

30. A. Estoclet, "You Ride a Wheel?" *PI* (June 7, 1896): 23; and "Our Cycle Route No. 50," *PI* (November 26, 1896): 7. See also "Inquirer Cycle Map No. 21," *PI* (August 29, 1897): 32.

31. "Amateur Photography," pt. 1, *WCTR* 3 (March 15, 1889): 48; ibid., pt. 2, *WCTR* 3 (March 29, 1889): supplement, n.p.; Cline Rogers, *Sidepaths: Monroe County (1899)*, unpublished album of photographs compiled for the Monroe County Sidepath Commission and available at the Rochester (N.Y.) Public Library, Local History and Genealogy Division.

32. *Road Book of Ohio* (1892), 49, 67, 81–82, 90–91, 94–95, 114–118, 143, 150, 152.

33. Adams, "On and Off the Lancaster Pike," *OW* 5 (October 1884): 3; and George Streaker, "Cycling over an Old Virginia Pike," *Outing* 35 (November 1899): 147.

34. Pratt, *American Bicycler*, 130–149; George Chinn and Fred E. Smith, *Hand-Book of Essex County* (1884); John S. Webber, *Around Cape Ann* (1885); H. J. Taggart, *Road Book of New Hampshire* (1895); and Charles G. Huntington, "The Making of a Road Book," *Cyclist* 1 (February 1890): 8.

35. "The PA, NJ, and MD Road Book," *The Wheel* 10 (April 30, 1886): 10; Huntington, "Road Book"; and "Touring Department," *LAWB* 4 (April 15, 1887): 304. See also *Road-Book of New York* (1887); "The New York Road Book," *The Wheel* 12 (May 13, 1887): 459; and "Road Books and Touring," *LAWBGR* 27 (June 24, 1898): 670. LAW state divisions in Indiana, Michigan, and California also published road books before 1890.

36. Huntington, "Road Book." See also *Road Book of Ohio* (1886); and *Road Book of Pennsylvania* (1893).

37. Huntington, "Road Book"; "Touring Department"; and *Road Book of Connecticut* (1888).

38. *Road Book of Massachusetts* (1892); *Road Book of Pennsylvania* (1893); and *Road Book of New Jersey* (1896).

39. Huntington, "Road Book."

40. Maine Division, LAW, Bates Torrey and Percy H. Richardson, eds., *A Road Book for Cycling and Carriage Driving in Maine* (n.p.: printed by the author: 1900).

41. New York State Division, LAW, Walter M. Meserole, ed., *Fifty Miles around New York* (New York: printed by the author, engraving by Bormay & Co., 1896).

42. Pennsylvania Division, LAW, Road Book Committee, Carl Hering, chair, *Road Book of Pennsylvania: Eastern Section*, 2nd ed. (Philadelphia: printed by the author, 1900), and Pennsylvania Division, LAW, Road Book Committee, W. West Randall, chair, *Road Book of Pennsylvania: Western Section*, 1st ed. (Philadelphia: printed by the author, 1898).

43. W. L. Chase & Company, *Standard Road Book of New York State* (Boston: W. L. Chase & Company, 1897); and National Publishing Company, *The Standard Road Book: Binghamton–Elmira Section* (Boston: National Publishing Company, 1897). See also "Editor of The Bicycling World," *BW* 44 (December 19, 1901): 261.

4 Straightaway

1. George Thayer, *Pedal and Path: Across the Continent Awheel and Afoot* (Hartford, CT: Evening Post Association, 1887), 8-21.

2. Ibid.

3. Ibid.

4. Ibid.

5. Thayer, *Path*, 24; and Richard and Susan Freeman, *Cobblestone Quest: Road Tours of New York's Historic Buildings* (Pine Glen Court, FL: Footprint Press, 2005).

6. Abbot Bassett, "First Bicycle Tour," *BSB* 8 (June 1908): 51; and Karl Kron, *Ten Thousand Miles on a Bicycle* (New York: printed by the author, 1887), 294.

7. Thayer, *Path*, 5; Kron, *Ten Thousand Miles*, xcvii–xcvlll; Irving A. Leonard, "A Bicycle Ramble Across America in 1886," *The Wheelmen* 14 (May 1979): 18; and Charles Meinert, "From Sea to Shining Sea," *The Wheelmen* 60 (May 2002): 11.

8. Thayer, *Path*, 37-38; and Thomas Stevens, *Around the World on a Bicycle*, vol. 1 (New York: C. Scribner's Sons, 1887), 84-85.

9. Thayer, *Path*, 41-42.

10. Thayer, *Path*, 43-44; Billy Joe Peyton, "Surveying and Building the Road," in *The National Road*, ed. Karl Raitz (Baltimore, MD: The Johns Hopkins University Press, 1996), 123-158, at 144-145; Gregory Rose, "Extending the Road West," in Raitz, *The National Road*, 159-192, at 173; and Hubert G. H. Wilhelm, "The Road as a Corridor for Ideas," in Raitz, *The National Road*, 256-284, at 265. The absence of cyclists' contributions is felt most keenly in John Jakle's chapter: "Travelers' Impressions of the National Road," in Raitz, *The National Road*, 227-255.

11. Thayer, *Path*, 43-44.

12. Kron, *Ten Thousand Miles*, iv-v.

13. Kron, *Ten Thousand Miles*, 65, 720; and letter from Ann Arbor Courier, May 4, 1882, to Coll Chron, Lyman Hotchkiss Bagg Papers, Box 5, Sterling Memorial Library, Yale University.

14. Kron, "Bone-Shaker Days" and "Four Seasons on a Forty-Six," in Kron, *Ten Thousand Miles*, 394-397, 24-26; "Bicycling in New York," *American Bicycling Journal* 1 (October 18, 1879): 6; and "Shore and Hill-Top in Connecticut," *SWG* (June 1885): 32.

15. Kron, "Environs of Springfield," in Kron, *Ten Thousand Miles*, 127.

16. Timothy Dwight, *Travels in New England and New York*, vol. 1 (New Haven, CT: printed by the author, 1821: 9–23. Later editions were edited by his nephew, Theodore Dwight Jr.

17. Dwight, *Travels*, vol. 1: 9–23; and ibid., vol. 2: 309.

18. Kron, *Ten Thousand Miles*, vi. Kron's archival papers include catalog cards for travel guides by Verlag Karl Baedeker, suggesting an interest in travel. Kron did not complete his book on schedule, many subscribers defaulted, and the book was not a financial success. See "Karl Kron Is No More," *BSB* 9 (November 1911): 135.

19. Dwight, *Travels*, vol. 1: 12, 358.

20. Kron, *Ten Thousand Miles*, iii.

21. Ibid., 301–302.

22. Dwight, *Travels*, letter 1 of "Journey to Vergennes," (Fall 1798), vol. 2: 370–371, 374.

23. Kron, *Ten Thousand Miles*, 142–143.

24. Ibid., 296, 302–303.

25. Ibid.

26. Dwight, *Travels*, vol. 1, 14.

27. "Karl Kron on Tour," *BWMR* 48 (November 28, 1903): 229.

28. "Why Kron Rides the Ordinary," *BWMR* 49 (July 9, 1904): 468.

29. Stevens, *Around the World*, vol. 1, 1887 (repr. with introduction by Thomas Pauly, Mechanicsburg, PA: Stackpole Books, 2001), iii–xv; subsequent citations are to vol. 1. See also Irving A. Leonard, "First Reviews of Thomas Stevens' *Around the World on a Bicycle*," *The Wheelmen* 22 (May 1983): 21.

30. Pauly, "Introduction," in Stevens, *Around the World*, iii–xv

31. Stevens, *Around the World*, 39.

32. Thomas Stevens, "Bicycling in the Far West," *OW* 4 (September 4, 1884): 463; and Stevens, *Around the World*, 72–75.

33. Stevens, *Around the World*, 13.

34. Stevens, *Around the World*, 13 (elevated dry grade), 17 (snow sheds), 34 (gang bunkhouses), 47 (freight-wagon graveyards), 46, 51, 72 (section houses), 57 (flume), and 59 (coal mines).

35. Stevens, *Around the World*, 4–8 (farms), 38–39 (palisades), 52–53 (Willard City), 77–78 (Amana Society), 80–82 (Indiana), and 83–84 (Ohio).

36. Stevens, *Around the World*, 5–6 (tule grass).

37. Stevens, *Around the World*, 16–17 (pine forests), 64–65 (western wonderland), and 67 (wildflowers).

38. Kron, *Ten Thousand Miles*, 484–486; see also Kathleen Wilcox, "Hugh High: Intrepid Cyclist," *The Wheelmen* 28 (May 1986): 2.

39. Kevin Hayes, *An American Cycling Odyssey* (Lincoln: University of Nebraska Press, 2002), 171–173; and Meinert, "From Sea to Shining Sea."

40. Hayes, *Cycling Odyssey*, 10–11, 14, 20. Both Hayes and Meinert agree that Nellis set out to travel coast to coast as rapidly as possible to surpass Stevens's record.

41. Meinert, "From Sea to Shining Sea."

42. Hayes, *Cycling Odyssey*, 14.

43. Hayes, *Cycling Odyssey*, 28, 35, 37.

44. Edwin G. Gerling, "The Three Prairie Pioneer Wheelmen," *The Wheelmen* 34 (May 1989): 13–17.

45. Ibid.

46. Ibid.

47. David Herlihy, *The Lost Cyclist* (New York: Houghton Mifflin Harcourt Publishing Co., 2011), 58–60, 69.

48. Frank Lenz, "Around the World with Wheel and Camera," pt. 2, *Outing* 20 (September 1892): 482.

49. Ibid., pt. 1, *Outing* 20 (August 1892): 339–346.

50. Ibid., pt. 12, *Outing* 22 (July 1893): 306.

51. Ibid., pt. 7, *Outing* 21 (February 1893): 378.

52. Ibid., pt. 4, *Outing* 21 (November 1892): 149; ibid., pt. 5, *Outing* 21 (December 1892): 205; ibid., pt. 8, *Outing* 21 (March 1893): 444; ibid., pt. 10, *Outing* 22 (May 1893): 132–135; and ibid., pt. 12.

53. Lenz, "Around the World," pt. 7 and pt. 1.

54. "Winder's Proposed Long Ride," *NYT* (December 26, 1894): 7; "Tom Winder's Progress," *BE* (August 4, 1895): 12; and "Tom Winder's Great Tour," *BE* (August 16, 1895): 6.

55. "Tom Winder's Progress," *BE* (August 4, 1895): 12; "In Michigan Sand," *BE* (August 4, 1895): 4; "Tom Winder," *BE* (August 9, 1895): 1; "Tom Winder's Great Tour," *BE* (August 16, 1895): 6; "Tom Winder's Great Tour," *BE* (August 16, 1895): 6; and "Good Bye, Tom Winder!" *BE* (December 29, 1895): 7, 10.

56. "Up the Oregon Trail," *BE* (June 16, 1895): 1.

57. "Pine and Palmetto," *BE* (November 24, 1895): 5.

58. George T. Loher, *The Wonderful Ride. Being the True Journal of Mr. George T. Loher, Who in 1895 Cycled from Coast to Coast on his Yellow Fellow Wheel*, ed. Ellen Smith (New York: Harper and Row, 1978).

59. John Foster Fraser, *Round the World on a Wheel* (London: Thomas Nelson and Sons, 1899), 529. Numerous cyclists traveled long distances during the safety bicycle era, including Frank Beedleson, Harry Libby, William A. England, John La France, Norman De Daux, and John Wiltz. Women also made global or

transcontinental passages, including Mrs. H. Darwin McIlrath, Annie Londonderry, Margaret Valentine Le Long, and Norma Belloff. See Frank Cameron, "Transcontinental Challenge: Its History and Mystique," *The Wheelmen* 24 (May 1984): 22–25.

5 Country Riding

1. "Local Affairs," *WBR* (August 8, 1885): 4; "Bicycling News," *WBR* (June 22, 1886): 1; "Wyoming Wheel Notes," *WBR* (July 22, 1886): 4; and "Kingston," *WBR* (September 18, 1886): 4. See also Harrison H. Smith, "Area Once Had Bike Clubs by the Score," *Valley Views* (September 24, 1960): 351; and "West End Wheelmen Formed Nucleus of the 65-Year Old Franklin Club," *Valley Views* (January 13, 1968): 1182.

2. "A Five-Year-Old Bicycle Club," *WBR* (June 1, 1885): 4; "Kingston," *WBR* (May 1, 1886): 4; and "Wyoming Wheel Notes," *WBR* (July 22, 1886): 4. See also "League Clubs," *LAWB* 5 (September 16, 1887): 163.

3. Oscar J. Harvey and Ernest G. Smith, *A History of Wilkes-Barre, Luzerne County Pennsylvania*, vol. 6 (Wilkes-Barre, PA: The Smith Bennett Corp., 1930): 543–544; "A Veteran Bicyclist," *WBR* (September 17, 1885): 1; and "News and Comment," *BWLAWB* 19 (July 12, 1889): 295.

4. "Notice to Bicyclists," *WBR* (May 22, 1885): 3, and "Notice to Bicyclists," *WBR* (May 22, 1885): 3 (two articles with the same title on the same page); "A Five Year Old Bicycle Club," *WBR* (June 1, 1885): 4; and "A Prosperous Bicycle Club," *WBR* (May 4, 1886): 1.

5. "State Bicycle Meet," *WBR* (July 5, 1887): 1; "The Fifth Annual Meet of the Pennsylvania Division, and the Third Annual Meet of the Wilkes-Barre Bicycle Club," *LAWB* 5 (July 15, 1887): 19; and "Wheel Gossip," *WCTR* 9 (June 10, 1892): 40.

6. "Bicycle Gossip," *WBR* (April 5, 1887): 1.

7. Pennsylvania Division, LAW, Road Book Committee, Henry S. Wood, ed., *Road Book of Pennsylvania New Jersey, Maryland and Delaware*, 7th ed. (Philadelphia: printed by the author, 1893), 75. For sidepaths, see Route 28 (pp. 35–36), Route 35 (p. 47), Route 42 (p. 53), Route 56 (p. 69), Route 64 (pp. 79–80), and Route 107 (p. 122). For Delaware and Hudson Canal towpath, see Route 27 (p. 33); and New York State Division, LAW, Albert B. Barkman, ed., *Hand-Book and Road Book of New York*, 1st ed. (Philadelphia: E. Stanley Hart and Co., 1887), Route (36)1. See also Pennsylvania Division, LAW, Road Book Committee, Carl Hering and Leon Fay, eds., *Road Book of Pennsylvania: Eastern Section*, 2nd ed. (Philadelphia: printed by the author, 1898 and 1900), Map 26 (pp. 28–29), and Map 26A (p. 98)

8. "The Binghamton Cinder Path," *LAWB* 5 (December 23, 1887): 351. Shultz (also spelled Schultz) later supervised construction of a path between Owego and Blue Island Ferry in Tioga County; see "To Start Sidepath," *Broome Republican* (May 15, 1899): 8.

9. "Another Cycle Road," *LAWB* 6 (January 20, 1888): 31. See also "Wheelmen of Western Massachusetts...," *BWLAWB* 16 (March 2, 1888): 285; "Wheelmen of Northampton...," *BWLAWB* 16 (March 16, 1888): 327; "News and Comment," *BWLAWB* 17 (June 22, 1888): 166; "Some Holyoke Parties...," *BWLAWB* 17 (July 13, 1888): 216; "When the Cinder Path...," *BWLAWB* 17 (July 20, 1888), 235; "Paths for Wheelmen," *WCTR* 1 (March 2, 1888): 12; and "The Subscription Paper...," *WCTR* 1 (May 4, 1888): 204.

10. "Cyclers Attention," *BWLAWB* 17 (May 18, 1888): 45; "Mr. A. G. Fisher...," *BWLAWB* 17 (June 22, 1888): 167; and "News and Comment," 17 (October 12, 1888): 460. See also "New Haven," *WCTR* 1 (May 25, 1888): 273; and "A Cinder Path from New York to New Haven," *WCTR* 1 (June 8, 1888): 319.

11. Karl Kron, *Ten Thousand Miles on a Bicycle* (New York: printed by the author, 1887), 338; and New York State Division, LAW, *Road Book of New York* (1887), "Local Riding Districts—The Hudson River," no page, but see near Kinderhook; Route (1B); Route (2)1; Route (2)2; Route (2)3; Route (3); Route (4); Route (6); Route (8); Route (9); Route (12); and Route (30)2, among others. See also "Long Island Notes," *LAWB* 4 (June 17, 1887): 451.

12. Harry Rambler, "Wheelmen's Side Paths," *GR* 7 (February 1895): 111; and Connecticut Division, LAW, Charles H. Huntington, comp., *Cyclists' Road-Book of Connecticut* (Hartford, CT: Case, Lockwood and Brainard Co., 1888): 7–9.

13. New York State Division, LAW, *Road Book of New York* (1887). For New Jersey towns with sidepaths, see Route (57), Route (59), Route (60), Route (62), Route (63)1 (Plainfield-Scotch Plains); and Kron, *Ten Thousand Miles*, 165. See also "League Clubs," *LAWB* (September 16, 1887): 163; and "Bicycle Club Directory," *SWG* 2 (March 1885): 178; and (April 1885): 210.

14. "Wheel Gossip," *The Wheel* 10 (August 20, 1886): 1; and "A Cinder Path from New York to Philadelphia," *The Wheel* 11 (December 3, 1886): 12. See also "A Cycle Path to Atlantic City," *WCTR* 14 (January 11, 1895): 36; "Another Cycle Path Project," *WCTR* 14 (February 1, 1895): 50; "A Cycle Path from Trenton across New Jersey to Asbury Park," *WCTR* 15 (July 26, 1895): 43; "Asbury Park-Trenton Side Path Route," *WCTR* 17 (May 8, 1896): 52 (spur to Lakewood); and "Planning a Jersey Cycle Way," *WCTR* 21 (August 4, 1898): 19 (Elizabeth to Staten Island).

15. Ohio Division, LAW, Thomas J. Kirkpatrick, comp., *Hand-Book of Ohio*, 1st ed. (Springfield, OH: Mast, Crowell & Kirkpatrick, 1886), 85, 98; and Ohio Division, LAW, State Executive Committee, comp., *Hand-Book of Ohio*, 2nd ed. (Cincinnati: Chas. H. Thomson, 1892): 38, 57, 99, 107, 128.

16. Hugh P. Donlon, *Amsterdam, NY. Annals of a Mill Town in the Mohawk Valley* (Schenectady, NY: Benchmark Printing, 1980): 181; and *Amsterdam City Directory* (1897–1898): 125. Refer also to newspaper articles cited in the appendix of this book under the heading Montgomery County.

17. "Sidepath Driven Upon," *Amsterdam Evening Recorder* (June 9, 1902): 3. Refer also to newspaper articles cited in the appendix of this book under the heading Montgomery County. The relationships of Edward DeGraff, H. A. DeGraff from Fonda (president of the county sidepath commission in 1903), and W. H. DeGraff, who assisted in compiling the *Road Book of New York* (1887), are not known. See also "From the Pacific to the Atlantic on a Bicycle," *Syracuse Standard* (June 7, 1896): 11.

18. "They Will Build a Path," *BWLAWB* 26 (July 21, 1893): 399; and "Long Island's Pioneer Path," *LAWBGR* 28 (January 27, 1899): 121.

19. Charles A. Ridgway, "A Practical Bicycle Club and Its Practical Work," *LAWBGR* 22 (November 15, 1895): 22.

20. Ibid.

21. Isaac Potter, *Cycle Paths* (Boston: LAW, 1898), 33–35; "Bicycle Riders Were Users of Primitive Wheels," in scrapbook of newspaper clippings, undated and without source, date, or page numbers, but probably the *Hazleton Plain Speaker*, at approx. page 21; available at the Hazleton Historical Society. See also "In Re Incorporation of the Associated Wheelmen of Hazleton and Vicinity," dated August 20, 1897, recorded in *Luzerne County Charter Book*, vol. 4 (September 22, 1897), 581, Luzerne County Registry of Deeds, Wilkes-Barre; and "Cycle Path Notes," *HPS* (May 7, 1898): 4.

22. Potter, *Cycle Paths,* 33–35; "Cycle Path Work Begins," *HPS* (April 28, 1898): 4; and "Associated Wheelmen Notes," *HPS* (May 21, 1898): 4. See also "Bicycle Riders Were Users of Primitive Wheels."

23. Hayhurst and Hartwell Surveys, "Map Showing Eckley, Buck Mountain, Stockton, and Part of Beaver Meadow Leases," by I. E. Hartwell, Map G-30 (September 1904) in the records of Butler Enterprises, successor to Tench Coxe Holdings, Drifton, PA.

24. Potter, *Cycle Paths*, 33–35; "Associated Wheelmen Notes," *HPS* (May 21, 1898): 4; and "Charter of Associated Wheelmen of Freeland PA," dated August 20, 1898, recorded in *Luzerne County Charter Book*, vol. 5 (August 1898), 283, Luzerne County Registry of Deeds, Wilkes-Barre. Interview with Robert Skulsky, Executive Director of the Greater Hazleton Area Civic Partnership, March 7 and 8, 2012. Skulsky grew up in Hazleton and recalls using the path during the 1950s.

25. Massasoit Cycle Club, *History of the Massasoit Cycle Club, 1892–1902* (Springfield, MA: printed by the club, circa 1902), 22, available at the Connecticut Valley Historical Museum, Springfield; "For the Wheelmen," *MPP* (April 18, 1898): 5; Harry Andrew Wright, *The Story of Western Massachusetts*, vol. 2 (New York: Lewis Historical Publishing Co., 1949): 838–839; and "Cycle Paths at Pittsfield, MA," *LAWBGR* 28 (January 20, 1899): 91.

26. "Cycle Club Banquet," *Keene Evening Sentinel* (February 26, 1898): 8; and "City News," *Keene Record Group Collection* (February 26, 1898), Cheshire County Historical Society.

27. J. G. Griffin, *A History of the Town of Keene* (Keene, NH: Sentinel Printing Co., 1904), 700–702; "A Cycle Path in the Granite State," *LAWBGR* 28 (November 25, 1898): 392; and "City News" column, *Keene Record Group Collection* (April 6, 1898), ibid. (August 2, 1899), available at the Cheshire County Historical Society.

28. For Middletown-Westfield-Meriden Path, see "To Build a Bike Path" *MPP* (June 6,1896): 5; "Bicycle Path" *MPP* (June 8, 1886): 8; "Path Fund Completed" *MPP* (June 27, 1896): 8; "The Cycle Path" *MPP* (August 5, 1896): 8; and "The Bicycle Path" *MPP* (September 4, 1897): 8. For Meriden-New Haven, see W. F. Cooper, "A Cycle Tax for Cycle Paths," *LAWBGR* 23 (January 10, 1896): 57. For New Britain, see "For the Cycle Path," *Hartford Courant* (July 26, 1898): 5.

29. "Side-Path for New Haven," *WCTR* 25 (June 7, 1900): 20; "Cycling Notes," *Monticello (NY) Republican Watchman* (August 24, 1900): 7; "Live Bicycle News," *MPP* (August 28, 1897): 4; "Cycle Path Leading From Norwich, CT" *LAWBGR* 27 (February 25, 1898): cover; "Cycle Path at Norwich, CT," *LAWBGR* 28 (January 20, 1899): 91; and "Live Bicycle News," *MPP* (August 28, 1897): 4.

30. "Cycle Path at Vineland, NJ," *LAWBGR* 29 (February 3, 1899): 160; "New Jersey Sidepaths," *LAWBGR* 29 (May 19, 1899): 688; "New Jersey Bicycle Paths," *LAWBGR* 29 (June 30, 1899): 890. See also Henry H. Bisbee, *Place Names in Burlington County* (Riverside, NJ: Burlington County Publishing Co., 1955), 97. Smalley's Corner occupied what is today the intersection of County Route 530 and New Jersey Route 206. See also "Good Roads Notes," *WES* (April 24, 1897): 23; and "Life at Atlantic City—Bicycle Path to Pleasantville," *WES* (May 10, 1897): 9.

31. *Laws of New Jersey*, chap. 62 (1896), 100–101; *Laws of New York*, vol. 2, ch. 68 (1896), 90; and *Laws of New York*, vol. 2, chap. 343 (1897), 314–315 (Chautauqua County).

32. "Sidepath League," *RC* (July 26, 1893): 1; "The Sidepath League" *RC* (April 9, 1897): 1; "Tabloid Tails of the Past," *RDS* (June 29, 1934): 3; and refer also to newspaper articles cited in the appendix of this book under the heading Oneida County. See also "A Bill for the Construction of Cycle Paths," *WCTR* 13 (March 23, 1894): 34. For Porter, see *New York Red Book*, ed. Edgar Murlin (Albany: James B. Lyon, 1897), 510–511.

33. "The Wheelway League," *Saturday Utica Globe* (June 19, 1897): 8; John J. Town, "League Wheelways," *LAWBGR* 22 (November 29, 1895): 21–23; and "The Cyclists of Utica...," *WCTR* 16 (September 27, 1895): 40.

34. Potter, *Cycle Paths*, 12; and refer also to newspaper articles cited in the appendix of this book under the heading Oneida County.

35. "The Wheelway League," *Saturday Utica Globe* (June 19, 1897): 8; Potter, *Cycle Paths*, 22–25; "Lee Center," *RC* (August 7, 1896): 8; "Verona Sidepath League," *RC* (April 23, 1897): 1; "To Build the Vernon Path," *UHD* (June 12, 1900), 5; and "Seneca Turnpike Sidepath," *UDP* (July 26, 1900): 6. For mileage, see "Cycler's Paradise," *Rome Citizen* (July 25, 1899): 1; "The County's Bicycle Paths," *Waterville Times* (October 13, 1899): 4; "Nearly 170 Miles of Path," *Utica Sunday Journal* (July 22, 1900): 12; and "Season of 1902," *RC* (February 28, 1902): 4. See also "Oneida County...," *Otsego Farmer* (May 24, 1907): 1; and "Along the Sidepath," *Waterville Times* (March 9, 1900): 5.

36. *Laws of New York*, vol. 1, ch. 267 (1897), 140; "Governor Visited," *EDGFP* (May 15, 1896): 5; and "Wheelway League in Annual Meeting," *Syracuse Post Standard* (April 12, 1899): 3. See also "An Association...," *RDC* (April 3, 1895): 4; and "Sidepaths," *RDC* (May 29, 1897): 18.

37. "Tow-Paths for Bicycles," *LAWBGR* 23 (June 12, 1896): 866.

38. "The Proposed Cycle Path along the Erie Canal," *BW* 31 (September 13, 1895): 661. "After the Wheelmen," *BE* (June 3, 1896): 1; "Tow-Paths for Bicycles," *LAWBGR* 23 (June 12, 1896): 866; and "Wheelmen to Fix the Path," *NYT* (June 30, 1896): 6.

39. "The Proposed Cycle Path along the Erie Canal," *BW* 31 (September 13, 1895): 661. "After the Wheelmen," *BE* (June 3, 1896): 1; and "Tow-Paths for Bicycles," *LAWBGR* 23 (June 12, 1896): 866.

40. "The Opening of the Scottsville Path," *RDC* (September 3, 1896): 10; "Scottsville Sidepath," *RDC* (September 14, 1896): 8; and "Sidepaths in and about Rochester," *LAWBGR* 24 (October 2, 1896): 465.

41. J. M. Lathrop and Roger H. Pidgeon, comp., *Atlas of Monroe County, New York* (Philadelphia: J. M. Lathrop & Co., 1902), plate 17 (Chili, NY) and plate 26 (Scottsville, NY); and Carl F. Schmidt, *History of the Towns of Wheatland, Scottsville, Mumford, Garbutt, Belcoda, Beulah, and Wheatland Center* (Rochester, NY: printed by the author, 1953): 116–117.

42. John McGregor, commissioner of Marion County, *Road Map of Marion County Showing Bicycle Routes* (1911), available at the Indiana State Library; Alice Taylor Reed, "When the Wheelmen Came to Town," *Indianapolis Star Magazine* (August 9, 1970): 25; and "Bicycles Only and Fans Are Happy," pt. 1, *Indianapolis Star* (June 30, 1937): 4.

43. David G. Vanderstel and Connie Zeigler, "Fairview Park," in *The Encyclopedia of Indianapolis*, ed. David J. Bodenhamer et al. (Bloomington: Indiana University Press, 1994), 559; and "Here Is a Wheelway," *WCTR* 17 (August 7, 1896): 60.

44. "The Runs for Fair Cyclers," *Indianapolis Journal* (August 9, 1898): 3; "A Run for Sleepy Eyes," *Indianapolis Journal* (August 12, 1898): 3; and "Bicycle Path to Riverside," *Indianapolis Journal* (April 29, 1899): 8. See also "The Coming LAW Meet," *LAWBGR* (July 29, 1898): 99; Reed, "Wheelmen Came to Town"; and Max R. Hyman, ed., *The Journal Handbook of Indianapolis: An Outline History* (Indianapolis: The Indianapolis Journal Newspaper Co., 1902): 92–98.

45. Hester Anne Hale, "Growth and Change: Indianapolis 1820–1920," typewritten manuscript, dated circa 1982, available at the Indiana State Library, Special Collections; and "Wheel Whirls," *Indiana Woman* 3 (May 15, 1897): 14.

46. Karl Kron, "Touring along the D. & H. Canal Tow-Path," *WCTR* 145 (September 21, 1894): supplement, iii; "An Order Has Been Issued...," *WCTR* 13 (June 22, 1894): 48. "Wheelmen Are Agitating...," 17 *WCTR* (February 21, 1896): 84; and "News of the Wheelmen," *NYS* (March 14, 1899): 5.

47. Frank G. Lenz, "Around the World with Wheel and Camera," *Outing* 20 (August 1892): 339–346; Thirteen Cyclers Club, *Route Book*, vol. 1 (September 16, 1894): 44–48, Maryland Historical Society, MS815; and "Wylie Trying for Record," *WCTR* 14 (September 14, 1894): 23.

6 *Good Roads* and *Good Sidepaths*

1. "Rochester's Twin," *RDC* (May 30, 1898): 10.

2. "Scottsville Sidepath," *Rochester Herald* (September 14, 1896): 8; and "The Dedication of a Side-Path, *RDC* (September 13, 1896): 13.

3. "Charles T. Raymond," *Sidepaths* 4 (February 1901): 72; C. T. Raymond, "Side Paths," *Good Roads* 6 (November 1894): 263; and Isaac Potter, *Cycle Paths* (Boston: LAW, 1898), 9–12.

4. Raymond, "Side Paths," *Good Roads* 6 (November 1894): 263; and Potter, *Cycle Paths*, 9–12.

5. Raymond, "Side Paths," *Good Roads* 6 (November 1894): 263; and Potter, *Cycle Paths*, 9–12

6. Raymond, "Side Paths," *Good Roads* 6 (November 1894): 263; and Potter, *Cycle Paths*, 9–12

7. Chapter 68, *Laws of New York*, vol. 2 (1896), 90.

8. Ibid.

9. Ibid.

10. "That Wheel Path Bill," *WCTR* 13 (March 30, 1894): 22.

11. "The Sidepath," *NTEN* (November 27, 1895): 4; "Talking over the Sidepath," *NFG* (April 22, 1897): 1; refer also to the appendix of this book for further information. For farmers' changing attitudes toward sidepaths, see "Farmers and Cycle Paths," *LAWBGR* 24 (October 9, 1896): 498; "Official Cycle Path," *WCTR* 20 (December 10, 1897): 36; and "There Has Been a Remarkable Change...," *Oswego Daily Palladium* (April 21, 1898): 5.

12. For Chemung County, see "Elmira Bicyclists," *EDGFP* (February 26, 1895): 8; "Corning Wheelmen," *EDGFP* (March 16, 1895), 6; "More Funds Needed," *EDGFP* (April 18, 1895): 7; "The Bicycle Bill," *EDGFP* (April 9, 1896): 4; and "Governor Visited," *EDGFP* (May 15, 1896): 5. For Monroe County, see Monroe County Sidepath Commission, *Sidepath Guide* (Rochester, NY: Sidepath Guide Company, 1899), 19–20; and "Sidepaths in and about Rochester," *LAWBGR* 24 (October 2, 1896): 465. For Oneida County, see Charles D. White, "Side-Path Building," *LAWBGR Good Roads* 24 (October 9, 1896): 499.

13. "General Sidepath Bill," *Batavia Daily News* (December 23, 1897): 2.

14. "Charles T. Raymond," *Sidepaths* 4 (February 1901): 72.

15. "Keep Off the Path," *WCTR* 18 (January 22, 1897): 61; "Held Up by Hayseeds," *WCTR* 19 (March 5, 1897): 48; New York Division, LAW, *The Highbie-Armstrong Good Roads Law* (New York: New York Division, LAW, 1898); and *Laws of New York*, vol. 1, chap. 115 (1898), 218.

16. "While That Special Cycle Path Scheme...," *BWLAWB* 16 (March 23, 1888): 345; "Dangerous Path Propositions," *WCTR* 22 (December 8, 1898), 44; "Paths of Pleasure," *LAWBGR* 23 (February 21, 1896): 275; "Roads and Sidepaths," 23 (June 12, 1896): 864 (concerning Parsons); and "This Is Our Anniversary Month...," *BSB* 11 (May 1913): 36 (concerning Parsons).

17. "Sidepaths," *LAWBGR* 23 (May 29, 1896): 777; A.T. Cook, "Side Paths vs. Roads," *LAWBGR* 24 (July 31, 1896): 167; and "For Side Paths," *Lake Shore Wheelman* 2 (March 15, 1899): 9 (concerning W. B. Heck).

18. "Wheelmen May Withdraw," *BE* (April 3, 1898), 19; and "The Lockport Wheelmen...," *Elmira Morning Telegram* (October 23, 1898): 7.

19. Chapter 45, *Laws of New York*, vol. 1 (1898), 95–96 (Cattaraugus County); Chapter 71, *Laws of New York*, vol. 1 (1898), 131–132 (Monroe County); Chapter 224, *Laws of New York*, vol. 1 (1898), 597–600 (Albany County); "Bicycle Legislation," *AEJ* (March 31, 1898), 8 (Albany County); and Chapter 277, *Laws of New York*, vol. 1 (1898), 860–862 (Columbia County).

20. "A Universal Sidepath Law," *Elmira Star Gazette* (October 29, 1898): 9; "The Sidepath Convention," *EDGFP* (November 15, 1898): 8; "Ellsworth's New Bill," *NFG* (January 21, 1899): 1; "In the Interests of the Sidepaths," *RDC* (November 13, 1898): 18; and Edgar J. Murlin, *New York Red Book* (Albany, NY: James B. Lyon, 1901), 54–55 (concerning Ellsworth).

21. Potter, *Cycle Paths*; and "Chief Consul Favored," *NYT* (December 27, 1895): 7.

22. Potter, *Cycle Paths*, 4–8; and "A Few Words from the President," *LAWM* 31 (June 1900): 13–15.

23. "Cycle Paths," *WCTR* 22 (October 6, 1898): 7; "Dangerous Path Proposition," *WCTR* 22 (December 8, 1898): 44; and John D. Chism, "Cycle Paths in New York," *WCTR* 29 (January 13, 1899): 52.

24. "Cycle Path Movement," *BS* (June 9, 1900): 6.

25. "Some Popular Misstatements," *EDGFP* (March 8, 1899): 6; "New York Sidepath Bill," *LAWBGR* 29 (January 13, 1899): 52; "Amounting to $3,000," *NYT* (May 25, 1900): 8; "National Committee Leaders," *LAWM* 1 (July 1900): 3; and "League to Keep Racing Control," *Worcester Daily Telegram* (February 9, 1899): 4.

26. "Ellsworth's New Bill," *NFG* (January 21, 1899): 1; and "LAW Legislation," *Newark (NY) Arcadian Weekly Gazette* (February 15, 1899): 10.

27. "In the Interests of the Sidepaths," *RDC* (November 13, 1898): 18; "A Dog in the Manger Case," *Utica Sunday Journal* (March 12, 1899), 6; and "State Side Path Law," *Otsego Farmer* (January 26, 1900), 1.

28. Chapter 152, *Laws of New York*, vol. 1 (1899), 301–305; "Some Popular Misstatements," *EDGFP* (March 8, 1899): 6; and John D. Chism, "Cycle Paths in New York," *WCTR* 24 (January 4, 1900): 34.

29. "New and Old Laws," *BE* (April 23, 1899): 23.

30. "Explanation of Sidepath Change," *RDC* (March 27, 1904): 20.

31. Chapter 152, *Laws of New York*, vol. 1 (1899), 301–305; and "Sidepath Men Close Meeting," *EDGFP* (September 30, 1899): 5.

32. Chapter 194, *Laws of New York*, vol. 1 (1899), 357–359 (Monroe County); and Chapter 428, *Laws of New York*, vol. 2 (1899), 893–898 (Albany County). The Monroe County laws of 1898 and 1899 were repealed by Chapter 640, *Laws of New York*, vol. 2 (1900), 1393–1398.

33. "Builders of Cycle Paths," *RDC* (September 29, 1899): 14–15.

34. "A Bill of Interest to All Wheelmen in the State," *EDGFP* (January 20, 1900): 8; and "State Side Path Law," *Otsego Farmer* (January 26, 1900): 1. Also refer to the appendix for total sidepath commissions.

35. "News of the Wheelmen," *BDE* (September 28, 1899): 5.

36. "The Sidepath Movement," *RDC* (March 26, 1900): 12; and Bruce Epperson, *Peddling Bicycles to America. The Rise of an Industry* (Jefferson, NC: McFarland and Company, 2010), 101–104.

37. Chapter 640, *Laws of New York*, vol. 2 (1900), 1393–1398. The clause that gave commissioners the authority to contract in excess of available funds was removed. Charles Raymond had suggested a similar provision secured by county bonds for up to $10,000 as a means to complete sidepaths in the fall, secured by tag sales during the coming spring. See "Charles F. Raymond," *ODP* (August 21, 1899): 1. Concerning Gardiner, see Murlin, *New York Red Book*, 129.

38. *Ryan vs. Preston*, 50 App. Div. 97, 32 Misc. 92, 66 NYS 162 (1900); and "Commission Wins," *Sidepaths* 111 (December 1900): 460. The case added controversy when John Ryan deliberately destroyed a portion of the path, resulting in his arrest and prosecution; see "Side-Path Commission Won," *WCTR* 25 (June 21, 1900): 20. In *O'Donnell vs. Preston*, 74 AD 86, 77 NYS 305 (1902), the court upheld the law a second time.

39. "Stopped Sidepath Work," *BDE* (July 30, 1900): 8; "A Sidepath Suit," *BDE* (November 11, 1901): 8; "Caught on a Suffolk Side-Path," *WCTR* 25 (May 17, 1900): 21. See also Chapter 305, *Laws of New York*, vol. 1 (1902), 863; "McKeon's Double Capture," *RDC* (July 15, 1902): 10; "Sidepath Commissioners," *ODP* (May 1, 1901): 8; "A Nice Question," *Syracuse Herald* (September 1, 1904): 4; and "Special Deputy Sheriff Palmer...," *Fulton Patriot* (June 5, 1901): 3.

7 Sidepath

1. "Bicycle Sidepaths," *Batavia Daily News* (April 18, 1900): 8; and John Wood, "A Dangerous Sidepath," *Outing* 22 (April 1893): 209.

2. "Builders of Cycle Paths," *RDC* (September 29, 1899): 14; "Cyclers on Parade," *RDC* (September 30, 1899): 15; and "McKeon's Labor Saver," *RDC* (May 17, 1899): 10.

3. "Sidepath Commissioners Meet," *NYDT* (September 30, 1899), 3; Charles T. Raymond, "Side Paths," *Good Roads* 6 (November 1894): 263; "Good Roads," *Sidepaths* 111 (December 1900): 434; Monroe County Sidepath Commission, *Sidepath Guide* (Rochester, NY: The Sidepath Co., 1899), 40; "A New National Committee," *LAWM* (June 1900): 2; "Sidepaths Changes Hands," *WCTR* 25 (July 5, 1900): 17; and "Amounting to $3,000," *NYT* (May 25, 1900): 8.

4. "Cayuga Was Represented," *Auburn Daily Bulletin* (September 21, 1900), 3; "Plan a Campaign," *Utica Observer* (September 16, 1902), 4; and *Otsego Farmer* (April 6, 1900): 1.

5. "Special Sidepath Rollers," *Sidepaths* 111 (November 1900): 427; and "The Building of Sidepaths," *UHD* (September 21, 1900): 4.

6. "Makes Bicycle Path," *WCTR* 16 (December 20, 1895): 44; "The Building of Sidepaths," *UHD* (September 21, 1900): 4; "A Bicycle Path Machine," *LAWBGR* 23 (February 7, 1896): 187; and "A Bicycle Path Machine," *LAWBGR* 26 (October 22, 1897), 507.

7. Samuel P. Hedges, Bicycle-path or sidewalk leveler and roller, US Patent 620,034, filed February 21, 1899; Fred W. Shoecraft, Bicycle-path maker, US Patent 628,363, filed July 4, 1899; and "Island Sidepath," *BE* (June 10, 1900), sec.1:3.

8. "The Troutburg Sidepath," *Holley Standard* (May 6, 1897): 1; "Collect the Ashes," *LAWBGR* 23 (January 31, 1896): 167; and "Report on Side-Path Commission," *WCTR* 25 (March 15, 1900): 36.

9. "New Wrinkle in Sidepath Building," *RDC* (April 4, 1899): 4; "Tree Planting," *RDC* (March 27, 1897): 6; "Figures Show...," *WCTR* 24 (September 28, 1899): 12; "Screenings for Sidepaths," *WCTR* 25 (March 29, 1900): 26; and "R. O. Bascom...," *Schuylerville (NY) Standard* (July 4, 1900), 4. See also "The Building of Sidepaths," *UHD* (September 21, 1900): 4; and "Rome Members of the County Sidepath Commission...," *Utica Sunday Tribune* (March 18, 1900): 2.

10. "Discussing a Uniform Rate," *EDGFP* (September 28, 1899): 7.

11. Charles T. Raymond, "Sidepaths," *Good Roads* 6 (November 1894): 263; "Building Cycle Paths," *WCTR* 24 (August 31, 1899): 17; Monroe County, *Sidepath Guide*, 26; and Potter, *Cycle Paths*, 9–12.

12. Monroe County, *Sidepath Guide*, 8, 18, and 64.

13. "If Wheelmen...," *BWLAWB* 16 (March 23, 1888), 343; "The Rochester (NY) Wheelmen's League," *WCTR* 10 (December 9, 1892): 32; "Rochester's New Association," *WCTR* 11 (April 11, 1893): 34; "Some Rochester Peculiarities," *WCTR* 13 (June 15, 1894): 30; "Must Continue to Pay Toll," *WCTR* 14 (September 21, 1894): 28; "Wheelmen Fail to Win," *WCTR* 23 (June 8, 1899):

9; "The Cycle League Heard from Again," *RDC* (June 25, 1896), 10; and "Sidepaths of Monroe County," *RDC* (March 28, 1898): 9. See also "Another Scheme Is Being Pushed in Rochester…," *BWLAWB* 16 (March 16, 1888): 327; W. H. Learned, "Rochester, NY, Sidepaths," *LAWBGR* 29 (March 10, 1899): 343; and Monroe County, *Sidepath Guide*, 69.

14. "The Movement for Sidepaths," *RDC* (May 16, 1896), 19; "Most Popular Sidepath in the County," *RDC* (June 30, 1897): 8; and Monroe County, *Sidepath Guide*, 18–22.

15. "The Movement for Sidepaths," *RDC* (May 16, 1896): 19; "Will Construct Good Ways," *RDC* (May 19, 1896): 14; "A New Association," *RDC* (May 21, 1896): 15; "This Is the Age of Sidepaths," *RDC* (May 29, 1896): 10; and "The Committee's Initial Tour," *RDC* (June 28, 1896): 13. See also Monroe County, *Sidepath Guide*, 18–22.

16. "Side-Paths in and about Rochester," *LAWBGR* 24 (October 2, 1896): 465; W. M. Rebez Jr., "The Cycle Paths of Rochester and Vicinity," in Potter, *Cycle Paths*, 36–41; and "Annual Report of the Park Superintendent," in *Proceedings of the Common Council* (Rochester, NY: Democrat and Chronicle Press, 1896), 767.

17. "City Surveyor McClintock of Rochester Has Found a Way," *EDGFP* (November 29, 1895): 4; "Great Event in Cycledom" *RDC* (June 21, 1896): 13; "Annual Fete Day To Be A Feature" *RDC* (June 26, 1896): 12; "City Wheelmen Capture Fairport," *RDC* (September 27, 1896): 12; "Wheelmen's Meeting," *RDC* (September 18, 1896): 10; "Sidepaths of Monroe County," *RDC* (March 28, 1898): 9; and "The Committee's Initial Tour," *RDC* (June 28, 1896): 13. See also Monroe County, *Sidepath Guide*, 20–26, 36–40.

18. "A New Path for Brooklyn," *RDC* (June 29, 1896): 11; Rebez, "Paths of Rochester"; and "Sidepath Report," *Monroe County Mail* (November 24, 1898), 7.

19. "Tax on Bicycles for the Sidepaths," *RDC* (December 29, 1897): 11; and "Heavy Sidepath Tax and Small Returns," *RDC* (April 22, 1901): 6. See also Monroe County, *Sidepath Guide*, 18, 56–60, 66, 70.

20. "The Committee's Initial Tour," *RDC* (June 28, 1898): 13.

21. "Took Trip over Improved Roads," *RDC* (October 12, 1904): 14; and "Repairs on Sidepaths," *RDC* (April 16, 1899): 20. See also "The Annual Meeting…," *Batavia Daily News* (December 11, 1901): 6.

22. Monroe County, *Sidepath Guide*, 34–36; and "How to Get to the Exposition Awheel," *RDC* (May 13, 1901): 12.

23. Chapter 194, *Laws of New York*, vol. 1 (1899), 357–359; and "Empire State Items," *Holley Standard* (May 17, 1900): 1.

24. "New York Sidepath Bill," *LAWBGR* 29 (January 13, 1899): 52; "Sidepath Bill Is Signed," *AEJ* (April 8, 1898): 10; and "Uniform Bicycle Law," *AEJ* (June 16, 1899): 2. See also "Albany Side-Path Map," *Utica Sunday Journal* (June 2, 1901), 13.

25. John Town, "League Wheelways," *LAWBGR* 22 (November 29, 1895): 21; "Condition of Sidepaths in Albany County," *AEJ* (August 9, 1901): 8; "Temporary Injunction Granted," *AEJ* (November 26, 1900): 2; and "Larger Bridge Is Wanted at Roessleville," *AEJ* (August 19, 1901): 10. Refer also to the appendix of this book under the heading Albany County for additional information.

26. Chapter 224, *Laws of New York*, vol. 1 (1898), 597–600; Chapter 428, *Laws of New York*, vol. 2 (1899), 893–898; and "We Want This Convention," *AEJ* (July 29, 1899): 10.

27. "We Want This Convention," *AEJ* (July 29, 1899), 10. Refer also to the appendix of this book under the heading Albany County for additional information.

28. "Sidepath Badges for 1899," *AEJ* (January 7, 1899): 7; "New Cycle Path for South End," *AEJ* (May 27, 1899): 6; and "Condition of Sidepaths in Albany County," *AEJ* (August 9, 1901): 8.

29. "We Want This Convention," *AEJ* (July 29, 1899): 10; and "Attacks on Sidepath Commission," *AEJ* (September 22, 1900): 12. See also "Builders of Cycle Paths," *RDC* (September 29, 1899): 14.

30. "Attacks on Sidepath Commission," *AEJ* (September 22, 1900): 12; and "Builders of Cycle Paths," *RDC* (September 29, 1899): 14.

31. "Builders of Cycle Paths," *RDC* (September 29, 1899): 14; "The Building of Sidepaths," *UHD* (September 21, 1900): 4; "Cycling: Sidepath Commissioners Meet," *NYDT* (September 30, 1899): 3; "To Extend Sidepath System," *Utica Sunday Journal* (September 2, 1900): 12; "Sidepath Men Coming to Town," *UO* (September 9, 1900): 4; and "Cayuga Was Represented," *Auburn Daily Bulletin* (September 21, 1900): 3.

32. Cycling: Sidepath Commissioners Meet," *NYDT* (September 30, 1899): 3; "To Extend Sidepath System," *Utica Sunday Journal* (September 2, 1900): 12; "Sidepath Men Coming to Town," *UO* (September 9, 1900): 4; and "Cayuga Was Represented," *Auburn Daily Bulletin* (September 21, 1900): 3.

33. *Ryan v. Preston*, 32 Misc. 92, 66 NYS 162 (1900). See also *O'Donnell v. Preston*, 74 AD 86, 77 NYS 305 (1902); and "Suffolk's Side Paths the Finest in the World," *BDE* (October 13, 1900): 15.

34. "Suffolk's Side Paths the Finest in the World," *BDE* (October 13, 1900): 15; "Sidepath Commissioner Samuel Higbie…," *Sag Harbor Corrector* (November 24, 1900): 2. Refer also to the appendix under the heading Suffolk County.

35. "Popular Bicycle Path of 1895 Closed by Long Island Town," *NYT* (January 17, 1932), 1. Refer also to the appendix under the heading Suffolk County.

36. *Road-Book of New York* (1887), Routes (2)1, (2)2, (2)3, (3), (4), and (6); and "Long Island Notes," *LAWB* 4 (June 17, 1887): 451. For macadam roads in Queens and Nassau counties, see "Side Path Tags at LAW Office," *NYET* (July 22, 1899): 7; and "Notes of General Interest—from Cold Spring Harbor...," *Newtown Register* (December 7, 1899): 2. See also "At This Time, when Brooklyn's Wheelmen...," *WCTR* 1 (August 24, 1888): 587. Refer also to the appendix under the headings Nassau County and Suffolk County.

37. "Side Path Tags at LAW Office," *NYET* (July 22, 1899): 7; "Bicycle Tags for 1900," *BDE* (January 20, 1900): 6; "The Suffolk County Sidepath Commissioners Met...," *Newtown Register* (January 17, 1901): 2; "Commissioner Ansel B. Gildersleeve...," *Huntington Long Islander* (September 12, 1902): 3; and "Work for Year Ended," *BDE* (December 17, 1903): 16. See also "Condition of the Roads," *BDE* (July 22, 1899): 6; and "Sidepath Commissioner Samuel Higbie with Eugene R. Smith, Civil Engineer...," *SSCN* (November 16, 1900): 3. The Servoss map is available at the Brooklyn Historical Society. Refer also to the appendix under the headings Nassau County and Suffolk County.

38. For paths prior to 1899, see "To Visit Camp Wikoff at Montauk Point...," *NYS* (August 14, 1898): 5. For sidepath machine, see "Southampton Village Trustees...," *SSCN* (April 4, 1902): 1. For county highway commissioners, see "New Side Paths on Long Island," *NYET* (December 16, 1899): 11; and "The Suffolk County Sidepath Commissioners Have...," *Newtown Register* (November 6, 1902): 2. For mileage estimates, refer to the appendix under the heading Suffolk County.

39. "Now Ride," *SPS* (June 21, 1897): 2; and "Bicycle Paths" *SJ* (May 15, 1902): 8. Refer also to the appendix under the headings Cortland County, Onandaga County, Oswego County, and Thompkins County.

40. "Demand Is Large for Bicycle Tags," *SJ* (May 6, 1904): 6; "Syracuse and Oswego Will Soon Be Connected...," *ODP* (July 30, 1901): 6; and "Seneca County Still Has Some Bicycle Sidepaths," *BE* (May 19, 1907): 17. Refer also to the appendix under the headings Cayuga County, Onandaga County, and Seneca County.

41. Refer to the appendix under the headings Jefferson County, Onandaga County, and Oswego County.

42. "The Wheelmen between Fredonia and Westfield," *WCTR* 14 (December 14, 1894): 35; and *Road Book of New York* (1887), Route (32)5. Refer also to the appendix under the headings Fulton County and Chautaqua County.

43. "On the Boom," *Randolph Register* (June 7, 1899): 1; "If Plans Materialize...," *Otsego Farmer* (January 26, 1900): 1; "Sidepath Map," *Tioga County Record* (June 20, 1901): 1; "That Great Sidepath," *EDGFP* (February 16, 1900): 5. Refer also to the appendix under the headings Allegany County, Broome County, Cattaraugus County, Chemung County, and Tioga County.

44. Chapter 342, *Laws of New York*, vol. 1 (1904), 888; and "The Bicycle Sidepath Craze," *RDC* (August 21, 1905): 5.

45. "Explanation of Sidepath Change," *RDC* (March 27, 1904): 20 1; and "Sidepath System Dead," *BWMR* 51 (September 23, 1905): 623.

46. "Sidepath Law Has Been Changed," *UO* (June 2, 1904): 6.

47. "Proceedings of the Board of Supervisors," *EDGFP* (December 26, 1903): 3; "Sidepath Officials Fickle," *BW* 49 (August 27, 1904): 642; "Sidepaths Abandoned," *SPS* (May 14, 1906): 9, discussing Cortland County paths kept open for workmen in local factories; and "No Longer Needed," *SSCN* (January 25, 1907): 1.

48. "Destruction of Sidepath," *Amsterdam Evening Recorder* (November 28, 1904): 2.

49. Karl Hodges, "Did the Emergence of the Automobile End the Bicycle Boom?" in *Proceedings of the 4th International Cycle History Conference: Boston, October 13–15, 1993* (San Francisco: Bicycle Books, Inc. and the Lallement Memorial Committee, 1993), 39–42. See also "Plan a Campaign," *UO* (September 16, 1902): 4; "Autos Hurt Bicycling," *Binghamton Press* (May 16, 1904): 1; "Cycles vs. Automobiles," *Cycle Age and Trade Review* 27 (May 16, 1901): no page number; and "Scorchers Arouse Long Islanders," *BW* 48 (January 23, 1904): 468. In *Ride to Modernity: The Bicycle in Canada, 1869–1900* (Toronto: University of Toronto Press, 2001), 21–29, 254–256, author Glen Norcliffe offers an economic/cultural theory to explain the decline of cycling, likening the rise and fall of bicycles to a carrier wave that ran its course because consumers on the cutting edge of fashion became fascinated with new sets of innovations.

50. "Explanation of Sidepath Change," *RDC* (March 27, 1904): 20.

51. "Sidepath Commissioner Raymond...," *Holly Standard* (August 10, 1899): 1; "Charles F. Raymond of Niagara County's Sidepath Commission...," *ODP* (August 21, 1899): 1; "A Bill of Interest to All Wheelmen in the State," *EDGFP* (January 20, 1900): 8; and "The Building of Sidepaths," *UHD* (September 21, 1900): 4. See also Section 4, Chapter 640, *Laws of New York*, vol. 2 (1900), 1393–1398.

52. "New Sidepath Idea," *UDP* (October 14, 1901): 5. "Williams Is Appointed," *NFG* (June 29, 1905): 2.

53. "Side Path Legislation," *Otsego Farmer* (September 26, 1902): 1; "Bill to Mulct Bicycle Sidepath Commissioners," *EDGFP* (March 25, 1903): 3; and "Sidepath Bill Approved," *Yonkers Statesman* (May 11, 1903): 4. See also Chapter 465, *Laws of New York*, vol. 2 (1903), 1076.

54. "The Decayed Sidepath," *NFG* (June 30, 1904): 2; and "Williams Is Appointed," *NFG* (June 29, 1905): 2. See also the appendix.

55. "Won't Abandon Sidepaths," *Broome Republican* (August 20, 1904): 1; "Sidepath Bicycle Tags...," *Monroe County Mail* (May 24, 1906): 6; "Meeting Tonight to Decide Fate of County Sidepaths," *EDGFP* (April 1, 1907): 2; and "Keep Up Paths Another Year," *EDGFP* (April 2, 1907): 7. See also "Sidepath Improvement," *Elmira Telegram* (April 30, 1905), 5; and "Bought Wagons with Path Fund," *SJ* (October 7, 1907): 4.

56. "They're Practically Broke," *Auburn Democrat Argus* (May 5, 1905): 5; "To Abandon Sidepaths," *Syracuse Herald* (May 14, 1906): 3; "Bicycle Badges Will Be Cheaper," *Glen Falls Morning Star* (March 3, 1904): 6; "Price of Tags Reduced," *Ithaca Daily Times* (July 17, 1902): 7; "Repairing the Cycle Paths," *BWMR* 53 (July 14, 1906): 455; "Suffolk Revives Cycle Path Tags," *BWMR* 53 (August 4, 1906): 542; and "To Repair Sidepaths," *Fredonia Censor* (July 31, 1907): 5.

57. "Demand is Large for Bicycle Tags," *SJ* (May 6, 1904): 6; "The Bicycle Craze Has Struck Us," *SJ* (May 6, 1904): 9; "Sidepath Commission Submit Annual Report," *SJ* (June 6, 1904): 3; "First Bicycle Run a Complete Success," *SJ* (June 27, 1904): 9; and "Filed Its Report," *SJ* (May 23, 1905): 7. See also "Sidepath Report," *Fulton Times* (March 18, 1908): 1; and "Seneca County Still Has Some Bicycle Sidepaths," *BE* (May 19, 1907): 17.

58. "Try to Get out of Office," *BDE* (January 24, 1906): 2; "No Longer Needed," *SSCN* (January 25, 1907): 1; Chapter 235, *Laws of New York*, vol. 1 (1907), 440–443; and "Lupton Bill Disappointing," *BDE* (May 8, 1907), 3.

59. "County Sidepaths," *Boonville Herald* (December 22, 1904): 1; "Sidepath Commission," *UO* (December 28, 1907): 4; and "Oneida and Rome Road Plans Are Progressing," *SPS* (July 14, 1910), 1.

60. "Oneida County, with Monroe County...," *Otsego Farmer* (May 24, 1907): 1; and "Cycle Side Paths," *BSB* 19 (June 1921), 67.

61. "Popular Bicycle Path of 1895 Closed by Long Island Town," *NYT* (January 17, 1932): 1.

62. "Took Trip over Improved Roads," *RDC* (October 12, 1904): 14.

63. "Cycle Paths in Canada," *WCTR* 23 (February 23, 1899): 38.

64. Chapter 757, *Acts and Resolves: Rhode Island General Assembly* (1900), 58–62; and "The First Bicycle Path...," *Cleveland Plain Dealer* (May 18, 1897): 4 (Little Compton). See also Chapter 180, *Public Acts Passed by the General Assembly of the State of Connecticut* (1901), 1384–1385; "Taxing Bicycles," *MPP* (April 27, 1897), 4; and "Regarding Bicycle Tax," *MPP* (April 28, 1897): 5. See also "The Cycle Path Question," *LAWBGR* 23 (May 29, 1896): 774.

65. Chapter 351, *Acts and Resolves of the General Court of Massachusetts* (1898), 299–300; Chapter 474, *Acts and Resolves of the General Court of Massachusetts* (1899), 533; and Chapter 62, *Acts of the State of New Jersey, 120th Legislature* (1896), 100–101.

66. House Bill 233, "An Act Relating to Sidepaths for Bicycles," in the *Journal of the House of Representatives of the State of Vermont—Biennial Session* (1900): 140 (October 30, 1900); 267, 279, and 281 (November 14, 1900); 293 (November 15, 1900), for committee votes; and 580–588 for introduction of the bill itself on the floor of the General Assembly.

For New Hampshire, see "Cycling Notes," *Monticello (NY) Republican Watchman* (April 27, 1900): 6; and "Cycling Notes," *Monticello (NY) Republican Watchman* (June 22, 1900): 3. For Maine, see "A Side Path," *Washington Hatchet* (May 27, 1900): 3.

67. Act No. 35, *Laws of the General Assembly of the Commonwealth of Pennsylvania* (1899): 36–37; "For Side Paths," *Lake Shore Wheelman* 2 (March 15, 1899): 9; and "Protecting Pennsylvania Sidepaths," *LAWBGR* 29 (May 19, 1899): 704.

68. "Twelve Thousand for Paths," *WCTR* 24 (February 1, 1900): 38; and "To Test Side Path Law," *WCTR* 25 (March 29, 1900): 24. See also "Bradford County Gets in Line," *Tioga County Record* (January 25, 1900): 2. Challenges to Pennsylvania's law developed in the following counties: Bradford County (*Keeler v. Westgate*, 10 Pa. D. 240 [1901]); Erie County (*Porter v. Shields*, 200 Pa. 241, 49 A. 785 [1901]); Dauphin County ("Side-Path Law Unconstitutional," *WCTR* 25 [June 7, 1900]: 20); and Montgomery County ("To Test Side Path Law," *WCTR* 25 [March 29, 1900]: 24).

69. House Bill No. 605, *General and Local Acts, State of Ohio*, vol. 94 (1900), 138–141; "Boom in Cycle Paths," *WCTR* 21 (May 26, 1898): 32 (for the path between Springfield and South Charleston).

70. Potter, *Cycle Paths*, 27–30; "Cycle Paths at Sandusky, Ohio," *LAWBGR* 29 (February 10, 1899): 190; and "Booming Cycle Paths," *Lake Shore Wheelman* 2 (March 15, 1899): 1.

71. Chapter 658, *Laws of the State of Maryland* (1900): 1047–1049.

72. "The Bicycle Path Scheme," *WES* (January 31, 1896): 8; "Bicycle Path to Baltimore," *WP* (October 13, 1896): 4; "The Bicycle Path," *Washington Morning Times* (July 19, 1896): 10; "Club House Half Way," *WP* (November 25, 1896): 7; and "Inter-City Cycle Path," *BS* (January 6, 1899): 6.

73. "For the Intercity Cycle Path," *BS* (January 27, 1899): 6; "Plans for Getting Intercity Path," *BS* (February 4, 1899): 6; "Out for Cycle Paths," *BS* (March 2, 1899): 6; "The Wheelmen," *BS* (March 22, 1899): 6; "Laurel Cyclers Will Help," *BS* (March 22, 1899): 6; "For the Cycle Path," *BS* (March 25, 1899): 6; "Cycle Path Meeting," *BS* (March 29, 1899): 6; and "Intercity Cycle Path," *BS* (April 8, 1899): 6. See also "A Washington-to-Baltimore Path," *WCTR* 23 (February 16, 1899): 48; D. Allen Willey, "Washington–Baltimore Path," *LAWBGR* 29 (May 5, 1899): 628; and "G. J. Oakes, "Bicycle Paths," *LAWBGR* 23 (February 7, 1896): 197.

74. "Washington–Baltimore Cycle Path," *WCTR* 23 (April 13, 1899): 24; "For Sale: 5 Acres, Making 100 Lots," *WES* (May 2, 1899): 13; "The Cyclers," *BS* (May 2, 1899): 6; "First Cycle Path Night," *BS* (July 19, 1899): 6; "Intercity Cycle Path," *BS* (September 7, 1899): 6; and "Cycle Path Movement," *BS* (December 8, 1899): 6.

75. "Legislature Pleased Cyclists," *BS* (April 4, 1900): 6; "Steps for Cycle Paths," *BS* (April 12, 1900): 6; "To Build a Cycle Path," *BS* (August 22, 1900): 6; "Baltimore–Washington Sidepath," *BS* (October 4, 1900): 6.

76. "Judge Sams Out of It," *BS* (December 1, 1900): 6.

77. "The Boulevard Hustlers," *BS* (January 18, 1899): 6; "Speedway Survey," *BS* (February 3, 1899): 6; and "With the Wheelmen," *BS* (February 28, 1899): 8. See also Baltimore Board of Park Commissioners, *39th Annual Report* (1898): 10.

78. "The City Council," *BS* (June 13, 1899): 10; "Road Drivers on Deck," *BS* (December 10, 1900): 6; "Cyclers and Drivers," *BS* (December 11, 1900): 6; and "Road Users Together," *BS* (December 14, 1900): 6. See also "Arlington *Wheelmen*," *WES* (July 3, 1897): 23; and "To Build a Bicycle Path," *WP* (February 25, 1898): 8.

79. "A New National Committee" *LAWM* 1 (July 1900): 2–5; "Cycle Path Legislation," *LAWM* 1 (March 1901): 2; and "Amounting to $3,000," *NYT* (May 25, 1900): 8. See also Rev. Isaac Houlgate, *Guide Minneapolis Bicycle Paths* (Minneapolis, MN: Byron and Willard, 1902).

80. "LAW Drops Racing—Should Boom Sidepaths," *WCTR* 25 (February 22, 1900): 20; "New York-Chicago Side-Path," *WCTR* 25 (March 8, 1900): 17; "The Minneapolis-Chicago Path," *WCTR* 25 (March 22, 1900): 32; "The "Trunk Line" Path," *WCTR* 25 (April 5, 1900): 29; and "Bicycle Path to Omaha," *WCTR* 25 (April 12,

1900): 20. For an 1896 plan, see "From the Pacific to the Atlantic on a Bicycle," *SPS* (June 7, 1896): 11. See also A. B. Choate, "Bicycle Side-Path Trunk Lines," *Outing* 37 (October 1900): 115; and "Cyclists' Great Work," *BS* (May 9, 1900): 6. See also "The Fall of the Mighty," *BWMR*, 44 (December 26, 1901): 282, noting that LAW membership had dropped from one hundred thousand in 1898 to ten thousand in 1901, and from more than forty state divisions to five.

81. Robert Bruce, "Bicycle Side-Path Building in 1900," *Outing* 36 (May 1900): 182; "For Cycling's Grand Armee (Paris)," *WCTR* 18 (January 1, 1897): 48; "Belgian Ruling on Cyclepaths," *BWMR* 48 (January 16, 1904): 438; and "Cycle Paths," *WCTR* 22 (October 6, 1898): 7. See also Ruth Oldenzeil and Adri Albert de la Bruheze, "Contested Spaces: Bicycle Lanes in Urban Europe (1900–1995)," *Transfers* 1 (Summer 2011): 29.

82. James Longhurst, "The Sidepath Not Taken," *Journal of Policy History* 25 (October 2013): 557. Longhurst argues that the failure of the sidepath campaign was primarily one of social class and secondarily one of timing. Separately, Longhurst's discussion about sidepaths in Minnesota and other parts of the country is helpful and expands the contexts for bicycle paths developed here, pointing toward the continuing need to investigate bicycle paths elsewhere in the country through local records.

83. "Revive the Cycle Path," *Bicycle News* 3 (April 1917): 23; Charles E. Weaver, "A Plea for Practical Side Paths for Cyclists," *Bicycle News* 3 (June 1917): 7; and "Side Paths for Bicycles," *Bicycle News* 3 (July 1917): 19.

8 Park Privileges

1. NYBPC, Minutes and Documents (year ending April 30, 1880), Documents 86–87 (October 24, 1879): 241; (February 18, 1880): 381; and (year ending April 30, 1881), Documents 88–89 (May 5, 1880): 14. See also Carl Wiedman, "The Central Park Case" *The Wheelmen* 47 (November 1995): 11-18.

2. Karl Kron, *Ten Thousand Miles on a Bicycle* (New York: printed by the author, 1887), 92–95; NYBPC, *Minutes and Documents* (year ending April 30, 1882), Documents 90–91 (June 29, 1881): 107; and Wiedman, "The Central Park Case."

3. Wiedman, "Central Park Case." See also *In the Matter of the Application of William W. Wright, Conant Foster, and Henry H. Walker*, 29 Hun. 357, 65 How. Pr. 119 (1883).

4. NYBPC, *Minutes and Documents* (year ending April 30, 1883), Documents 92–93 (March 21, 1883): 575; and (April 18, 1883), no page number.

5. NYBPC, *Minutes and Documents* (year ending April 30, 1884), Documents 94–95 (June 6, 1883): 94; "Central Park At Last," *The Wheel* 4 (June 15, 1883): 4; "The First Ride in Central Park," *The Wheel* 4 (June 15, 1883): 7; and "Wheelmen in New York," *Harper's Weekly* 30 (July 17, 1886): 455.

6. NYBPC, *Minutes and Documents* (year ending April 30, 1884), Documents 94–95 (June 20, 1883): 128, and (November 7, 1883): 351; (year ending April 30, 1885), Documents 96–98 (November 21, 1884): 383, and (December 3, 1884): 417. See also "Wheel Gossip," *The Wheel* 4 (June 22, 1883): 8; and Chapter 703, *Laws of New York* (1887): 909–910.

7. NYBPC, *Minutes and Documents* (year ending April 30, 1888), Documents 110–111 (July 20, 1887): 172–173; "The Liberty Bill," *LAWB* 4 (July 1, 1887): 491; "Rights of Bicyclists in the Parks," *LAWB* 5 (July 15, 1887): 23; and "Central Park," *LAWB* 5 (July 15, 1887): 24. See also Chapter 112, *Acts of the State of New Jersey* (1888): 201; and "New Jersey's Liberty Bill," *WCTR* (March 2, 1888): 5.

8. BPC, "Rules and Regulations for Bicycle and Tricycle Riding In Prospect Park, and upon the Parkways and Concourse at Coney Island," in *25th Annual Report* (1885), 39–41; and "Park Privileges Again," *Amateur Athlete* 2 (December 18, 1884): 1.

9. FPC, *1st Annual Report* (December 31, 1868); and *2nd Annual Report* (January 20, 1870).

10. FPC, *Minutes of the Meetings*, vol. 6 (May 24, 1879): 151; ibid. (September 13, 1879): 186; (March 13, 1880): 267; ibid. (November 12, 1881): 463–464; *Minutes of the Committee on Superintendence and Police*, vol. 4 (November 22, 1878 to November 22, 1881), specifically (October 17, 1879): 81, (November 18, 1881): 298, and (April 28, 1883): 59. See also "Historic Dates of Cycling," *BSB* 18 (February 1920): 25, citing the date of May 13, 1882.

11. BABPC, *27th Annual Report* (1887): 25; and BABPC, *28th Annual Report* (1888): 7. See also BABPC, *Book of Proceedings* 5 (June 27, 1888 to December 14, 1892): 65 (meeting of July 11, 1890) and 67–68 (meeting of October 9, 1890); and *Book of Proceedings* 7 (June 11, 1896–1899): 25 (meeting of November 12, 1896).

12. Kron, *Ten Thousand Miles*, 93.

13. BOBPC, *22nd Annual Report* (year ending October 31, 1897): 58–60.

14. Clarence Cook, *A Description of the New York Central Park* (New York: Benjamin Blom, Inc., 1869); and Elizabeth Barlow Rogers, *Rebuilding Central Park. A Management and Restoration Plan* (Cambridge: MIT Press, 1987), 11–13.

15. Witold Rybczynski, *A Clearing in the Distance: Frederick Law Olmsted and America in the Nineteenth Century* (New York: Simon and Schuster, 1999), 335–338; and Kron, *Ten Thousand Miles*, 95.

16. Rybczynski, *Clearing*, 355; and NYBPC, *Minutes and Documents* (year ending April 30, 1884), Documents 94–95 (June 6, 1883): 94; and (June 20, 1883): 128. See also "The League Meet in New York," *The Wheel* 4 (June 1, 1883): 6; and Kron, *Ten Thousand Miles*, 94.

17. Olmsted, Vaux & Co., "Report of the Landscape Architects and Superintendents," dated January 1, 1868, in BPC, *8th Annual Report* (1868): 173–202.

18. Rybczynski, *Clearing*, 354, 401–409.

19. F. L. Olmsted & Co., Plan 1172-3, Plan 1172-33, and Plan 1172-35, "Beacon Street Widening" (1886), Olmsted National Historic Site, Brookline, MA.

20. Cynthia Zaitzevsky, *Frederick Law Olmsted and the Boston Park System* (Cambridge, MA: Belknap Press of Harvard University Press, 1982), 111–113.

21. BOBPC, *20th Annual Report* (year ending January 31, 1895): 54.

22. "Bicycle Path for Commonwealth Avenue," *BW* 29 (September 14, 1894): 519; "Boston's Wheelmen Declare…," *WCTR* 17 (April 24, 1896): 72; and Olmsted, Olmsted, and Eliot, "Letter to Mr. E. C. Hodges," dated May 21, 1896, in BOBPC 22nd *Annual Report* (year ending January 31, 1897): 58.

23. "E. C. Hodges Dead," *BW* 48 (December 19, 1903): 310–311.

24. Olmsted, Olmsted, and Eliot, "Letter to Hodges."

25. Ibid.

26. Frederick Law Olmsted, "The Spoils of the Park: With a Few Leaves from the Deep-Laden Note-Books of a 'Wholly Impractical Man,'" printed pamphlet circa 1882; also in *Frederick Law Olmsted: Landscape Architect, 1822–1903*, ed. Frederick Law Olmsted Jr. and Theodora Kimball (New York: G. P. Putnam's Sons, 1928), 135.

27. Ibid.

28. Daisie, "The Ladies' Eastern Tricycle Tour," *Outing* 13 (December 1888): 260–265.

29. "Buffalo Working for a Cycle Path," *WCTR* 15 (March 1, 1895): 55.

30. Rybczynski, *Clearing*, 285–289; and BUBPC, "Delaware Park," in *27th Annual Report* (January 1897): 12.

31. "Park Cycle Path," *BE* (April 8, 1896): 11; and "It May be Abolished," *Buffalo Courier* March 6, 1895): 5.

32. "Park Cycle Path," *BE* (April 8, 1896): 11; "Park Cycle Path," *BE* (April 15, 1896): 11; and "The Cycle Path Project," *BE* (May 3, 1896): 4.

33. "Park Cycle Path," *BE* (April 15, 1896): 11.

34. "Against the Path," *BE* (May 6, 1896): 8.

35. "Now for the Battle," *BE* (May 7, 1896): 13; "Not Against It," *BE* (May 8, 1896): 8; and "There Will Be a Path," *BE* (May 13, 1896): 8.

36. "That Park Cycle Path," *BE* (May 27, 1896): 8; and BUBPC, *Annual Report* (January 1897): 12, 22, and 71.

37. Louisville Friends of Olmsted Parks, *Louisville's Olmstedian Legacy: An Interpretive Analysis and Documentary Inventory*, ed. Carl Kramer (Louisville, KY: Louisville Friends of Olmsted Parks, 1988), 6–9. See also Samuel W. Thomas, "Louisville's Parks: The Olmsted Myth," *LCJ* (September 15, 1991): travel section, 4.

38. "Report of F. L. Olmsted & Co., Landscape Architect," in LBPC, *1st Annual Report* (1891): 658; also see ibid., 623 and 632; LBPC, *2nd Annual Report* (1892): 627; and Louisville Friends, *Olmstedian Legacy*, 6–9.

39. "Track Nearing Completion," *LCJ* (October 7, 1894): 13; "Bicycle Notes," *LCJ* (November 29, 1896): 8; "The Coming LAW Meeting," *LCJ* (January 23, 1898): A5; "County Bicycle Paths," *LCJ* (January 30, 1898): A2; "The Highwaymen's Path," *LCJ* (July 17, 1898): 7; and "Card From the Highwaymen," *LCJ* (July 31, 1898): A6. See also "Louisville Cycle Paths," *WCTR* 20 (February 4, 1898): 42; and LBPC, *Meeting Minutes*, vol. 5 (December 23, 1895): 144–145; LBPC, *Meeting Minutes*, vol. 6 (December 23, 1896): 51–52; and LBPC, *Meeting Minutes*, vol. 6 (January 7, 1896): 51–52, available at the Filson Historical Society.

40. Charles E. Beveridge and Arleyna Levee, *Louisville's Olmsted Park Legacy: Cherokee, Iroquois, and Shawnee Parks and the Parkways, a History*. (Louisville, KY: Louisville Olmsted Parks Conservancy, 1992, in draft form), 82–88; available at the Olmsted Parks Center. LBPC, *7th Annual Report* (1897): 491–495; and LBPC, *8th Annual Report* (1898): 450; LBPC, *Meeting Minutes*, vol. 6 (July 20, 1897): 225–226; and F. L. Olmsted & Co., *Study for a Plan and Cross Section of Grand Boulevard, Louisville, Kentucky*, Project 1263-9, circa 1892, Olmsted National Historic Site; "Parade Tonight," *LCJ* (October 8, 1897): 6; and "Not Many In Line," *LCJ* (October 9, 1897): 3.

41. Frederick Law Olmsted and John Charles Olmsted, landscape architects, *General Plan for Iroquois Park: Board of Park Commissioners of the City of Louisville, KY* (December 1, 1897), project 1266, National Park Service, Frederick Law Olmsted National Historic Site.

42. Letter from John Charles Olmsted, dated May 6, 1896, in LBPC, *Meeting Minutes*, vol. 5 (May 1896): 223–229, Filson Historical Society.

43. LBPC, *7th Annual Report*, 491–495.

44. Additional field work is needed to compare the plan with the current locations of paths, and to assess the extent to which changes to the park's perimeters in some sections have compromised the proposed locations of those paths.

45. Blake McKelvey, *Rochester on the Genesee. The Growth of a City* (Syracuse, NY: Syracuse University Press, 1973), 112; and Blake McKelvey, *Rochester: The Quest for Quality (1890–1925)* (Cambridge, MA: Harvard University Press, 1956), 174.

46. City of Rochester, *Proceedings of the Common Council* (December 26, 1895): 422; City of Rochester, *Proceedings of the Common Council* (December 29, 1896): 767; and *Plat Book of the City of Rochester, New York and Vicinity* (Philadelphia: G. M. Hopkins Co., 1918), plate 2.

47. City of Rochester, *Proceedings of the Common Council* (December 30, 1897): 665; and City of Rochester, *Proceedings of the Common Council* (December 29, 1898): 621–622; McKelvey, *Quest for Quality*, 183; and "City Surveyor McClintock…," *EDGFP* (November 29, 1895): 4.

48. City of Rochester, *Proceedings of the Common Council* (July 18, 1899): 468; "Park Board's Regular Meeting," *RDC* (September 29, 1896): 12; and "The Repair of Cycle Paths," *BW* 45 (June 18, 1902): 337.

49. "This Is the Age of Side-Paths," *RDC* (May 29, 1896): 10.

50. "New Bicycle Path," *RDC* (May 14, 1899): 16.

51. Frederick Law Olmsted Jr. and John C. Olmsted, "Landscape Architects' Report," (December 1, 1897), in MPC, *Annual Report* (January 1898): 60–61.

52. Olmsted Brothers, "Landscape Architects' Report," in MPC, *Annual Report* (January 1900): 41; "New Park Speedway," *Boston Sunday Herald* (September 3, 1899): 1; and MPC, *Annual Report* (January 1902): 32.

53. MPC, *Annual Report* (January 1898): 61; and "Charles River Athletic Association," *BW* 30 (May 10, 1895): 1100.

54. State Library of Massachusetts, "Index to Special Reports Authorized by the General Court," Card 5-137-2 titled "Bicycle Tracks," dated July 11, 1900, archives of the Metropolitan District Commission; and "Essex County Park Commission, Newark, N.J., Lake Weequahic Reservation Study for Bicycle Track, Etc.," plan 2132 (June 12, 1899), Olmsted National Historic Site.

55. "Cycle Paths in Fairmount Park," *B* 20 (November 19, 1897): 28. See also "Working for Wheelmen," *PI* (January 21, 1899), and "Park Improvement to be Made this Year," *PB* (January 12, 1900), both in a scrapbook of newspaper clippings available at the archives of the Philadelphia Department of Parks.

56. BABPC, *37th Annual Report* (1896): 5, 11; BABPC, *39th Annual Report* (1898): 10; and BABPC, *40th Annual Report* (1899): 8.

57. Charlotte S. Rubinstein, *American Women Sculptors* (Boston: G. K. Hall & Co., 1990), 116–121.

58. LBPC, *7th Annual Report* (1897): 495; LBPC, *Meeting Minutes*, vol. 6 (August 7, 1897): 232; and LBPC, project 1263 (Southern Parkway), plan 148-sh3, National Park Service, Frederick Law Olmsted National Historic Site. The document numbering is probably by John Olmsted, who approved Yandell's plan, and Olmsted may have drawn Wilder Triangle and located the memorial in that park. However, the sketches are by Yandell.

59. "Louisville Cycle Clubs," *LCJ* (August 9, 1896): B4; Carson Torpey, "Wheelmen's Bench," *The Wheelmen* 82 (May 2013): 10–13; and Joe Ward, "Pap Ruff and the Wheelmen's Bench," Louisville Bicycle Club, www.louisvillebicycleclub.org, originally printed in the club newsletter as part of a series in 1988 and 1989. Ward is the club historian and draws reliably from newspaper articles.

60. "Wheelmen's Rest in Central Park," *WCTR* 25 (March 15, 1900): 36; "A Rest in Central Park," *WCTR* 25 (June 21, 1900): 22; and "A Shelter-House for Cyclists," *NYDT* (January 26, 1899), 6. See also *A Facsimile of Frank Leslie's Historical Register of the United States Centennial Exposition* (New York: Paddington Press, Ltd., 1974), 38; originally published in 1876, ed. Frank G. Norton (New York: Frank Leslie's Publishing House); and Rogers, *Central Park*, 115–117.

61. Hartford Board of Park Commissioners, *39th Annual Report* (1899), 12–13.

62. "Albert A. Pope Monument Honors His Generosity," *Hartford Courant* (June 25, 1964): 35; and David F. Ransom, *George Keller, Architect* (Hartford, CT: Stowe-Day Foundation for the Hartford Architecture Conservancy, 1978), 167.

9 Park Way

1. Kara Hanley O'Donnell, "Bowditch, Ernest W. (1850–1918)," in *Pioneers of American Landscape Design*, ed. Charles A. Burnbaum and Robin Karson (New York: McGraw Hill, 2000), 32–35.

2. Bowditch Family Papers, MSS3, Series III, Ernest Bowditch, *Memoirs*, Box 17 and Box 18, Peabody Essex Museum, Salem, MA; and Cynthia Zaitzevsky, *Frederick Law Olmsted and the Boston Park System* (Cambridge: Belknap Press of Harvard University Press, 1982), 37–41.

3. "Jeptha Homer Wade" and "Wade Park" in *The Encyclopedia of Cleveland History*, ed. David D. Van Tassel and John J. Grabowski (Bloomington: Indiana University Press, 1987), 1021; and "Mr. Wade's Princely Gift," *CPD* (June 21, 1881): 4.

4. "Through the Generosity ...," *CPD* (April 17, 1883): 2; CBPC, *Second Annual Report* (1894): 6; and "William J. Gordon," and "Gordon Park," in Van Tassel and Grabowski, *Cleveland History*, 459–460.

5. Bowditch Family Papers, Box 18, Folder 3, 37–48. See also CBPC, *Second Annual Report* (1894): 15, 80–81; "Rockefeller Park," Van Tassel and Grabowski, *Cleveland History*, 838; "Through the generosity ...," *CPD* (April 17, 1883): 2; "New Parkways," *CPD* (July 14, 1895): 1; and "Cleveland's Fine Park System," *CPD* (October 24, 1897): 8.

6. CBPC, *Second Annual Report* (1894): 80–82, 91–92; and CBPC, *Fourth Annual Report* (1896): 27–30.

7. Bowditch, plan titled *Cleveland, Ohio: Department of Public Parks, East Side Park Way, Section 4 and 5, Plan No. 121* (December 7, 1886), Cleveland Public Library; and CBPC, *Second Annual Report* (1894): 91–92.

8. Bowditch, plan titled *East Side Parkway, Section 3—Plan 127* (February 1897), a planting and grading plan for an area near St Clair Street; Bowditch, plan titled *East Side Parkway, Section 4—Plan 129* (February 1897), a planting plan; plan titled *East Side Parkway, Section 6—Plan 133* (February 12, 1897), a paving plan; and Bowditch, plan titled *East Side Parkway Superior Street Bridge, Section 4 and 6—Plan 173* (November 12, 1897). All the aforementioned plans can be found at the Cleveland Public Library.

9. "Jeptha Homer Wade" and "Jeptha Homer Wade, II," in Van Tassel and Grabowski, *Cleveland History*, 1021. In *Ten Thousand Miles*, Kron lists J. H. Wade Jr. as a member of the Cleveland Bicycle Club, at 784, and as a subscriber to the book, at 762. See also CBPC, *Second Annual Report* (1894): 92; and CBPC, *Fourth Annual Report* (1896): 29.

10. "Park Board Plans," *CPD* (January 12, 1894): 8.

11. CBPC, *Second Annual Report* (1894): 92; and CBPC, *Fourth Annual Report* (1896): 27–30; "A Bicycle Path" *CPD* (December 14, 1894): 7; and "Planning a Bicycle Path," *CPD* (December 20, 1894): 8.

12. "New York State Meet and the Cycle Path Celebration," *WCTR* 15 (June 21, 1895): 25–27.

13. "New York State Meet and the Cycle Path Celebration," *WCTR* 15 (June 21, 1895): 25–27; and "The Bicycle Pathway," in BPC, *Thirty-Fifth Annual Report* (1895): 21–24.

14. "New York State Meet and the Cycle Path Celebration," *WCTR* 15 (June 21, 1895): 25–27; and "The New Cycle Path March and Two-Step," *WCTR* 15 (July 19, 1895): 41, credited to F. E. Hutchins.

15. Olmsted, Vaux & Co., "Report of the Landscape Architects and Superintendents," dated January 1, 1868, in BPC, *Eighth Annual Report* (1868): 173–202.

16. BPC, *Thirteenth Annual Report* (1873): 545–546.

17. BPC, *Thirteenth Annual Report* (1873): 545–546; BPC, *Fourteenth Annual Report* (1874): 12–16; BPC, *Fifteenth to Nineteenth Annual Reports* (1875–1879): 44–60; BPC, *Twentieth Annual Report* (1880): 15–16;

BPC, *Twenty-First Annual Report* (1881): 10; and BPC, *Twenty-Fifth Annual Report* (1885): 45–47.

18. "Wheel Gossip," *The Wheel* 10 (April 16, 1886): 4; and "The Brooklyn Club's Road Race, *The Wheel* 11 (October 1, 1886): 5. See also "Editorial," *Wheel and Recreation* 12 (September 9, 1887): 803; and "Path Fund Completed," *WCTR* 14 (December 28, 1894): 34.

19. "From the City of Churches," *The Wheel* 11 (January 28, 1887), 197; "Brooklyn Notes," *Wheel and Recreation* 12 (September 23, 1887): 843; "A Side Path to Coney Island," *WCTR* 11 (April 28, 1893): 44; "A Straight Run to the Sea," *NYT* (August 26, 1894): 24; and "Path Fund Completed," *WCTR* 14 (December 28, 1894): 34.

20. "At This Time…," *WCTR* 1 (August 24, 1888): 587; and "Path Fund Completed," *WCTR* 14 (December 28, 1894): 34. See also "From the City of Brooklyn to the Sea," *BW* (August 31, 1894): 456.

21. "A Side Path to Coney Island," *WCTR* 11 (April 28, 1893): 44; and "The Coney Island Pathway," *WCTR* 11 (May 5, 1893): 38. See also "Brooklyn's Cyclists' Road," *BWLAWB* 26 (May 19, 1893): supplement, no page number; and BPC, *Thirty-Third Annual Report* (1893): 18–19.

22. "Brooklyn's Good Roads Association," *WCTR* 13 (March 30, 1894): 48; "From the City to the Sea," *WCTR* 14 (August 24, 1894): supplement, iii; and "Subscriptions for the Wheelmen's Path to Coney Island," *WCTR* 14 (September 7, 1894): 15.

23. "The Fund for the Cycle Path…," *WCTR* 14 (October 26, 1894): 29; "The Subscription…," *WCTR* 14 (November 9, 1894): 32; and "Path Fund Completed," *WCTR* 14 (December 28, 1894): 34. See also "The Big Cycle Parade," *NYT* (April 8, 1895): 15.

24. "Brooklyn Notes," *The Wheel* 12 (September 23, 1887), 843; "Gossip of the Cyclers," *NYT* (March 31, 1895), 14; BPC, *Thirty-Fifth Annual Report* (1895): 21–24.

25. Chapter 640, *Laws of New York*, vol. 2, pt. 2 (1895), 1418; Chapter 230, *Laws of New York*, vol. 2 (1896), 279; BPC, *Thirty-Sixth Annual Report* (1896): 93–95 and 175–77; "The Coney Island Cycle Path…," *WCTR* 16 (November 1, 1895): 36; and "Woodruff Led Them," *WCTR* 17 (July 3, 1896): 44–45.

26. "Wheelmen Warned Off," *WCTR* 17 (May 8, 1896), 4; and "Wheelway Aftermath," *WCTR* 17 (May 8, 1896): 51.

27. "Wheelmen Warned Off," *WCTR* 17 (May 8, 1896), 4; and "Wheelway Aftermath," *WCTR* 17 (May 8, 1896): 51.

28. "Turtle Soup and Cycle Paths," *WCTR* 17 (March 20, 1896), 55; and "Gossip of the Cyclers," *NYT* (May 10, 1896): 13.

29. "Will Contest the Order," *NYT* (May 9, 1896): 6; "Will Have a Test Case," *NYT* (May 12, 1896): 6; and "Wheelmen Warned Off," *WCTR* 17 (May 8, 1896): 4.

30. "An Official Bluff," *WCTR* 17 (May 15, 1896): 53.

31. "Gossip of the Cyclers," *NYT* (May 10, 1896): 13.

32. "An Official Bluff," *WCTR* 17 (May 15, 1896): 53; and "No Swearer," *WCTR* 17 (May 15, 1896): 56.

33. An Official Bluff," *WCTR* 17 (May 15, 1896): 53; and "No Swearer," *WCTR* 17 (May 15, 1896): 56.

34. "No Special Privileges," *WCTR* 17 (May 22, 1896): 49; "Stand by Old Friends," *WCTR* 17 (May 22, 1896): 49–50; and "Business and Boodle," *WCTR* 17 (June 19, 1896): 48.

35. "Stating His Position," *WCTR* 18 (September 25, 1896): 22; and "Six Hundred Honored," *WCTR* 18 (October 2, 1896): 36.

36. Potter, *Cycle Paths* (Boston: LAW, 1898), 4–8.

37. "The Coney Island Cycle Path," *LAWBGR* 22 (August 23, 1895): 19; and *WCTR* 23 (March 16, 1899): 31.

38. "For the Cycle Path Handicap," *BWMR* 47 (September 5, 1903): 665; "No Cycle Path Handicap," *BWMR* 49 (August 20, 1904): 618; "Cycle Path Race Revived," *BWMR* 52 (October 2, 1905): 71; "Father of Four in Front," *BWMR* 52 (December 2, 1905): 199; "Long Island's Big Road Race," *WCTR* 24 (August 3, 1899): 13; and "Cycle Path Race," *WCTR* 25 (September 6, 1900): 12.

39. "Spoiling the Cycle Path," *BWMR* 47 (September 19, 1903): 712; "Strike at Cycle Paths," *BWMR* 47 (September 26, 1903): 739; and "New York Paths in Bad Shape," *BWMR* 49 (April 9, 1904): 91.

40. "New York's Famous Cycle Path in Peril," *BWMR* 63 (August 19, 1911): 1087; and "Rallying to Defense of Coney Island Cycle Path," *BWMR* 63 (August 26, 1911): 1129.

41. "New York's Cycle Path…," *BSB* 9 (September 1911): 103; and "Labor Day Cycle Parade Proves Huge Success," *BWMR* 63 (September 9, 1911): 1222.

42. New York's Cycle Path…," *BSB* 9 (September 1911): 103; and "Labor Day Cycle Parade Proves Huge Success," *BWMR* 63 (September 9, 1911): 1222.

43. "The New York Side Path Case," *BSB* 19 (March 1921): 29; "Make the World Safe for Cyclists," *BDE* (January 6, 1921): 6; and Chapter 267, *Laws of New York*, vol. 1 (1897), 140.

44. "Ocean Parkway Correspondence," *BSB* 19 (April 1921): 39.

45. "Bicycle Paths," *BSB* 19 (September 1921), 105–106.

46. New York City Landmarks Preservation Commission, "Ocean Parkway, Borough of Brooklyn," LP-0871, no. 3 (January 28, 1975).

47. In "The Path Not Taken: The Rise of America's Cycle Paths and the Fall of Urban Cycling," *Cycle History 20. Proceedings of the 20th International Cycling History Conference*, ed. Gary W. Sanderson (Cheltenham, England: John Pinkerton Memorial Publishing Fund, 2010): 67–72 and in "The Cycling City: Bicycles and the Transformation of Urban America," PhD dissertation, City University of New York (2011), Evan Friss points to the influence of the Coney Island paths. However, interest in building bicycle paths developed in a number of contexts in different parts of the country both before and after the Brooklyn paths became widely publicized, necessitating consideration of those contexts when evaluating the history of specific path projects or programs. For example, apart from ties to the Coney Island paths traceable to J. Y. McClintock in Rochester or Isaac Potter, I have found only a few references to the Brooklyn paths in the multitude of newspaper accounts that chronicle New York's sidepath era, even though many cyclists in upstate New York were aware of Brooklyn's paths. Separately, Friss's central argument—that the cycling city with its varied physical layers occupies a legitimate place in urban history and joins the walking city, the industrial city, and the automobile city—is well stated.

48. "Nathan Franklin Barrett: A Minute on His Life and Service," in *Transactions of the American Society of Landscape Architects (1909–1921)*, ed. Carl Rust Parker et al. (Amsterdam, NY: The Recorder Press), 90–92.

49. "John Bogart Dead," *Engineering News Record* 84 (April 29, 1920): 887.

50. "New York State Meet and the Cycle Path Celebration," *WCTR* 15 (June 21, 1895): 25.

51. John Bogart and Nathan Barrett, "Landscape Architects' Report" (December 22, 1897), in Essex County Board of Park Commissioners, *Second Annual Report* (1897): 26–41.

52. Olmsted Brothers, "Landscape Architects' Report" (December 14, 1899), in Essex County Board of Park Commissioners, *Fourth Annual Report* (1898–1899): 82–83.

53. Bogart and Barrett, "Landscape Architects' Report."

54. Frederick Law Olmsted, "Report of the Landscape Architect on Riverside Park and Avenue" (March 29, 1873), in NYCDP, *Third Annual Report* (1872–1873): 299–303; and "Riverside Park," in NYCDP, *Annual Report* (1898): 18.

55. NYCDP, *Minutes of Meetings* (year ending April 30, 1895): 11 (May 2, 1894); NYCDP, *Minutes of Meetings* (year ending April 30, 1896): 7 (May 8, 1895); NYCDP, *Minutes of Meetings* (year ending April 30, 1896): 205 (February 10, 1896); NYCDP, *Minutes of Meetings* (year ending April 28, 1898): 71 (June 28, 1897); and NYCDP, *Minutes of Meetings* 263 (December 6, 1897).

56. NYCDP, *Annual Report* (1898): 263.

57. BUBPC, *Twenty-Eighth Annual Report* (January 1898): 21–22, 64; BUBPC, *Twenty-Ninth Annual Report* (January 1899): 17–18, 50; BUBPC, *Minutes: Proceedings of the Board of Park Commissioners* 97 (September 6, 1898): 459–460 and 494; and "Park Cycle Path," *BE* (February 27, 1897): 12.

58. Emil Mahlo, "Park Engineer's Report," in LBPC, *Second Annual Report* (1892): 667–668; LBPC, *Third Annual Report* (1893): 230; and LBPC, *Fourth Annual Report* (1894): 814. See also LBPC, *First Annual Report* (1891): 623–629; LBPC, *Third Annual Report* (1893): 194; and LBPC, *Seventh Annual Report* (1897): 491–492. See also "Louisville's Cycling Carnival," *WCTR* 14 (November 16, 1894): 33.

59. LBPC, *Meeting Minutes*, vol. 6 (June 18, 1895): 3–4; and LBPC, *Meeting Minutes*, vol. 6 (March 16, 1896): 190; LBPC, *Fifth Annual Report* (1895): 835; LBPC, *Sixth Annual Report* (1896): 719; LBPC, *Seventh Annual Report* (1897): 491–493; and LBPC, *Eighth Annual Report* (1868): 450.

60. "Parade Tonight," *LCJ* (October 8, 1897): 6; and "Not Many in Line," *LCJ* (October 9, 1897): 3.

61. LBPC, *Seventh Annual Report* (1897): 495–496.

62. CBPC, *Second Annual Report* (1894): 11–13; and Van Tassel and Grabowski, *Encyclopedia of Cleveland*, 752–754.

63. "Planning a Cycle Path," *CPD* (December 20, 1894): 8; "For Special Cycle Path," *WCTR* 13 (March 23, 1894): 34; "A Place for the Bicycle," *LCJ* (July 10, 1894): 6; "Cycle Paths in Cleveland," *WCTR* 15 (March 29, 1895): 34; and "Clevelanders Kick," *WCTR* 21 (May 12, 1898): 36.

64. CBPC, *Fourth Annual Report* (1896): 43. South Side Park, formerly Pelton Park, was later named Lincoln Park. See "Arrangements for Its Celebration in This City," *CPD* (July 3, 1879): 1; and "They Want Water," *CPD* (July 31, 1895): 10.

65. Van Tassel and Grabowski, *Encyclopedia of Cleveland*, 752–754; and CBPC, *Second Annual Report* (1894): 77–82. See also plan identified as "Edgewater Parkway with Bridge 53," undated and unsigned, Cleveland Public Library Map Collection.

66. "Now for More City Parks," *TB* (October 7, 1891): 2; "The Place for a Park" *TB* (November 7, 1891): 6; and "Locating New Parks," *TB* (February 3, 1892): 1.

67. "Nothing but a Rumor," and F. J. Scott, "The Proposed New Park, *TB* (July 11, 1892): 3; "Great System of Parks," *TB* (July 26, 1892): 1; and "Toledo's Park System," *TB* (July 30, 1892): 2.

68. Sylvanus Jermain, "Mental Pictures of My Fifty Years in Public Life," typewritten memoir and "Jermain Scrapbook," an album of newspaper clippings, but without complete dates or names of newspapers; both are available at the Toledo Public Library. See also Shirlie Leckie, "Parks, Planning, and Progressivism in Toledo," PhD dissertation, University of Toledo (1981), 61–86; "Locating New Parks," *TB* (February 3, 1892): 1; "Toledo and Her Parks," *TB* (July 27, 1892): 3; "System of City Parks," *TB* (February 20, 1893): 7; "A Perfect Park System," *TB* (July 15, 1893): 4; "Awarded the Contract," *TB* (June 26, 1894): 7; and "Sunday at Riverside," *TB* (August 27, 1894): 5.

69. Leckie, "Parks in Toledo," 61–86; "Planning for Parks," *TB* (June 2, 1892): 3; "Toledo's Park System," *TB* (July 30, 1892): 2.

70. "The City Park System," *TB* (August 8, 1895): 5; "Toledo Wheelmen in Politics," *WCTR* 25 (March 29, 1900): 24; and Leckie, "Parks in Toledo," 61–86.

71. Leckie, "Parks in Toledo," 61–86. Leckie suggests that Jermain may have created the bicycle path in 1891, but the source cited (an article from the *Toledo Blade* in 1893) does not support that segment of Leckie's otherwise commendable text. See also Jermain, "Scrapbook," clipping dated 1898 and titled "Proposed Improvement of the Popular Wheelmen's Resort—A Cycle Path"; another titled "Our Parks and Proposed Boulevards," approximately pages 82–84; and a third titled "Robinson is President: J. D. Robinson Elected President of the Park Board," regarding the bicycle pavilion. See also an undated photograph of Riverside Park, which may show the pavilion and path. Available at the Toledo Public Library, call no. 88-052.

10 Wheelways

1. "Yes; Call Them Wheelways," *WES* (April 17, 1896): 7.

2. "Cheap Cycle Paths," *WCTR* 21 (March 10, 1898): 36.

3. "The Engineer Department," *WT* (December 4, 1900): 11; "Cycling," *NYDT* (April 12, 1899): 5; William P. Judson, *City Roads and Pavements* (New York: Engineering News Publishing Co., 1909): 103–106; and "The Streets of Buffalo," *LAWB* 3 (November 12, 1888): 497.

4. "Working for Wheelmen," *PI* (January 21, 1899); "Park Improvements to Be Made This Year," *PB* (January 12, 1900); and "Bricks Are Like the Rock of Ages," *Philadelphia Telegraph* (March 21, 1900), all in scrapbooks available at the archives of the Philadelphia Department of Parks. See also "Side Paths for Cyclists," *WCTR* 18 (January 22, 1897): 69; and Judson, *Pavements*, 86.

5. Judson, *Pavements*, 103–126; and "Good Roads Problems in Brooklyn and Queens," *BDE* (April 29, 1900): 16.

6. "New York's Suitable Cycling Streets," *BW* 31 (May 31, 1895): 15; "Plans for Cycle Paths," *NYH* (June 11, 1896): 11; and "Cycle News and Gossip," *NYET* (August 19, 1896): 6.

7. "Plans for Cycle Paths," *NYH* (June 11, 1896): 11; "Street Paths for Wheels," *St. Paul Globe* (June 20, 1896): 4; "Asphalt Strips for Wheelmen," *LAWBGR* 24 (August 14, 1896): 240; and "Bicyclists Have Right of Way on New York's Asphalt Strips," *WCTR* 25 (May 3, 1900): 26.

8. "News of the Wheelmen," *NYS* (July 22, 1896): 4; "Asphalt Strips Not a Success," *NYP* (September 27, 1896): 13; and "Plea for Asphalt Strips," *BDE* (November 3, 1896): 5.

9. "Would Stripe the Boulevard," *NYS* (October 4, 1896): 1.

10. "Good Roads for New York Cyclists," *NYP* (December 17, 1896): 5; "New York State Division," *NYP* (May 8, 1898): 20; "A Battery Park Cycle-Path," *NYEP* (April 27, 1898): 5; and "Uncle Sam's Fine Cycle Path," *WT* (August 6, 1896): 6.

11. "Good Roads for New York Cyclists," *NYP* (December 17, 1896): 5; "Should Not Be a Labor of Love," *BDE* (November 8, 1896): 5; "Endeavoring to Make Good Roads," *NYH* (May 10, 1897): 10; "For Asphalt Strips," *NYH* (June 3, 1897): 5; "Asphalt Strips on Broadway," *BDE* (June 10, 1897): 5; "Third Street," *BSU* (October 11, 1897): 1; and "In the Cycling World," *NYDT* (October 17, 1897): 3.

12. "In the Cycling World," *NYDT* (May 20, 1897): 3; "Wheelmen Have Their Troubles," *NYH* (May 25, 1897): 11; "Information for Bicycle Riders," *NYEP* (June 18, 1897): 4; "Improvements in the City Streets," *NYP* (July 18, 1897): 2; "In the Cycling World," *NYDT* (August 18, 1897): 3; "Street Improvements," *NYH* (October 13, 1897), 15; "Cycling Notes," *BSU* (March 8, 1899): 7; and "Cycleize New York," *WCTR* (May 24, 1900): 12.

13. "Mayor Favors Bicycle Paths," *NYS* (July 8, 1898): 7; "Asphalt Strips," *Brooklyn and Queens Daily Star* (July 8, 1898): 2; "City to Do Its Own Asphalting," *NYH* (September 21, 1898): 7; and "News of the Wheelmen," *NYS* (November 4, 1898): 5.

14. "Bicycle Path for Queens," *NYS* (January 17, 1899): 3; "Asphalt Strips," *Brooklyn and Queens Daily Star* (January 30, 1899): 1; and "The Asphalt Strips," *Brooklyn and Queens Daily Star* (May 19, 1899): 1.

15. Judson, *Roads and Pavements*, 121, 131–137; "Information for Wheelmen," *NYEP* (September 7, 1898): 10; "Cycling," *NYDT* (April 12, 1899): 5; "News of the Wheelmen," *NYS* (April 12, 1899): 8; "To Improve City Streets," *NYT* (April 29, 1900): 10; "Live Topics About Town," *NYS* (June 29, 1904): 7; and "Cycling," *NYDT* (April 12, 1899): 5.

16. "Wheeling Notes," *BDE* (July 27, 1897): 4; "Good Roads for Cycling," *NYH* (October 9, 1897): 10; "Bids for Street Paving," *BDE* (November 24, 1897): 1; and "Improvements for Brooklyn Cyclists," *BDSU* (April 23, 1902): 9. See also "Notes," *NYS* (April 11, 1897): 11 (Jersey City and Hoboken); "To Connect Jersey City's Boulevard and Viaduct," *NYS* (July 15, 1898): 5; "Mount Vernon," *NYDT* (May 3, 1900): 12; "National Meet Arrangements," *RDC* (June 24, 1897): 15 (Philadelphia); "A Bicycle Path," *CPD* (June 29, 1897): 2; "Street Board Matters," *Hartford Courant* (December 17, 1897): 9; "Bicyclists Want the Path," *Worcester Telegram* (August 17, 1895): 1; "Street Paths for Wheels," *St. Paul Globe* (June 20, 1896): 4; and "For a Bicycle Track," *Richmond (VA) Dispatch* (March 1, 1898): 5 (costs comparisons for paving materials).

17. "A Cycle Path Ready Made," and "A Wheelman's Paradise," *NYDT* (March 24, 1895): 6 and 21; "This Man Thought of the Aqueduct Path," *WCTR* 15 (May 31, 1895): 32; and "A Good Friend Gone," *BW* 46 (February 5, 1903): 543. For use of the Croton Aqueduct corridor by cyclists, see New York State Division, LAW, Albert B. Barkman, ed, *Hand-Book and Road Book of New York*, 1st ed (Philadelphia: Stanley Hart & Co., 1887), at unnumbered page titled "New York City Riding District."

18. George H. Rappole, "The Old Croton Aqueduct," *IA: The Journal of the Society for Industrial Archeology* 4 (1978): 15–26; and Larry D. Lankton, "Valley Crossings on the Old Croton Aqueduct," *IA: The Journal of the Society for Industrial Archeology* 4 (1978): 27–42. See also Gerard T. Koeppel, *Water for Gotham: A History* (Princeton, NJ: Princeton University Press, 2000).

19. "Mayor Strong Favors It," *NYDT* (March 27, 1895): 5; and "A Cycle Path Extraordinary," *WCTR* 15 (March 29, 1895): 23 and 26. See also "The Bicycle Path Measure," *NYDT* (March 29, 1895): 3.

20. J. J. R. Croes, "The Bill Unconstitutional," *NYT* (April 2, 1895), 6; "The Aqueduct Pathway," *WCTR* 15 (April 5, 1895): 25; "City End of the Aqueduct May Be Used for Bicycle Path," *NYDT* (April 14, 1895): 5; "The Aqueduct Bill," *WCTR* 15 (April 26, 1895): 43; "Success in Sight," *NYDT* (April 30, 1895): 3; and "The Croton Aqueduct Cycle Path," *BW* (May 3, 1895): 1055.

21. "Success in Sight," *NYDT* (April 30, 1895): 3; "Cycle Path Bill Passed," *NYDT* (May 9, 1895): 5; "Bicyclephobia," *NYW* (May 18, 1895): 4; and "Will Mr. Morton Veto It?" *NYDT* (June 15, 1895): 3. See also "Aqueduct Bill Passed," *WCTR* 15 (May 10, 1895): 22; "Aqueduct Bill

Approved by the Mayor," *WCTR* 15 (May 24, 1895): 39; and "Dead," *WCTR* 15 (June 21, 1895): 32.

22. "LAW Officers Meet," *NYDT* (December 21, 1897): 4; "An Aqueduct Wheelway," *NYT* (November 20, 1898): 24; and "Central Park's Famous Reservoir…," *WCTR* 19 (March 12, 1897): 66.

23. Koeppel, *Water for Gotham*, 289–292.

24. "Plans for a Long Path," *NYT* (July 18, 1895): 6; and "Not All Wheelmen…," *NYT* (July 21, 1895): 14.

25. "Fishing for Wheelmen," *WCTR* 16 (January 17, 1896): 102.

26. "Free Side-Paths: A Proposition to All Wheelmen," *WCTR* 24 (February 8, 1900): 33.

27. "Road for Wheelmen," *WCTR* 25 (July 12, 1900): 18.

28. Olmsted, Olmsted & Eliot, "Landscape Architects' Report," dated December 31, 1894, in MPC, *Annual Report* (January 1895): 41–45; and Olmsted, Olmsted & Eliot, "Landscape Architects' Report," undated, in MPC, *Annual Report* (January 1896): 46–52.

29. John Charles Olmsted, "Classes of Parkways," *Landscape Architecture* 6 (October 1915 to July 1916): 37–48.

30. "Among Local Cyclers," *WT* (June 28, 1896): 11; and "Among Local Wheelmen," *WT* (July 6, 1896): 10. See also National Park Service, Historic American Engineering Record and National Historic Landmarks Program, "Washington Aqueduct," nomination dated June 27, 1973.

31. "Among Local Cyclers," *WT* (June 28, 1896): 11; and "Among Local Wheelmen," *WT* (July 6, 1896): 10.

32. "Among Local Wheelmen," *WT* (July 19, 1896): 10; "The Bicycle Path," *WT* (July 20, 1896): 5; "First Money Subscribed," *WT* (August 4, 1896): 8; "Road Club Boys Are For It," *WT* (August 6, 1896): 2; "With Amateur Wheelmen" and "Times-Wheelmen Bicycle Path," *WT* (August 9, 1896): 10; and "With Amateur Wheelmen," *WT* (August 23, 1896): 10. See also "Fast Driving Checked," *WP* (July 19, 1896): 8; "On the Conduit Road," *WES* (July 18, 1896): 9; and "The Bicycle Path," *WES* (August 22, 1896): 13.

33. "Wheelmen Elect Officers," *WP* (March 31, 1899): 8; "Inspection of Bicycle Path," *WP* (June 4, 1899): 9; "Cyclists at Marshall Hall," *WP* (August 10, 1899): 2; "The Great Falls Cycle Path," *WES* (July 1, 1899): 9; and "Stony Hill Bicycle Path," *WES* (October 8, 1899): 9. See also "Subscriptions to Cycle Path," *BS* (August 26, 1899): 2.

34. "Cyclists at Marshall Hall," *WP* (August 10, 1899): 2; "For A New Bicycle Path," *WT* (September 30, 1899): 6; and "Stony Hill Bicycle Path," *WES* (October 28, 1899): 9.

35. "Cycle Path Over Bridge," *NYW* (November 11, 1897): 11; and "For the Bridge Cycle Path," *NYW* (June 9, 1897): 10.

36. "Room for Cycling" and "Two Opinions on the Bridge Cycle Path," *NYW* (May 20, 1897): 14; "The World Wins a Victory for Wheelmen on Brooklyn Bridge," *NYW* (May 28, 1897): 14; and "Cycle Path Over Bridge," *NYW* (November 11, 1897): 11.

37. "The Wheelmen Combine," *NYW* (November 16, 1897): 8; "Cyclists Ask Trustees," *BDE* (November 29, 1897): 16; "News of the Wheelmen," *BDE* (April 28, 1898): 14; "Cycling," *NYDT* (September 2, 1899): 4; Bridge Trustees' Monthly Meeting," *NYH* (December 14, 1897): 3; and "The Bridge Cycle Path Still Far Away as Ever," *BDE* (April 26, 1899): 2 (discussing a plan by engineer Walter L. Meserole).

38. "Favors Bridge Cycle Path," *BDE* (January 17, 1898): 4; "Bridge Wheelway Plans," *NYH* (January 18, 1898): 10; and "They Favor Wheelway," *NYH* (March 11, 1898): 11; "Cycle Clubs' Blacklist," *BDE* (March 22, 1898): 4; "News of the Wheelmen," *NYS* (May 19, 1898): 8; and "Bridge Cycle Path," *BDSU* (December 14, 1898): 1.

39. "Bridge Cycle Path Up Again," *BDE* (May 10, 1899): 18; "No Prospects of a Bridge Cycle Path," *BDE* (May 24, 1899): 14; "The Bridge Cycle Path," *BDE* (May 30, 1899): 7; "News of the Wheelmen," *BDE* (May 27, 1899): 6; "Bridge Cycle Path Delayed," *NYH* (July 21, 1899): 10; "Martin in Opposition to Bridge Cycle Path," *BDE* (July 21, 1899): 7; "Bridge Cycle Path Dead," *BDE* (August 31, 1899): 15; "No Bridge Wheel Path," *NYT* (September 1, 1899): 12; and "News of the Wheelmen," *BDE* (September 18, 1899): 13.

40. "Cycling," *NYDT* (September 2, 1899): 4; "Path across the Bridge," *NYS* (September 9, 1899): 4; "New Plan for Cycle Path," *BDE* (September 12, 1899): 3; "Brooklyn Bridge Cycle Path," *NYH* (September 13, 1899):14; "Bridge Cycle Path," *BDE* (October 5, 1899): 3; "The Bridge Cycle Path," *WCTR* 24 (September 14, 1899): 17; and "The Brooklyn Bridge Cycle Path," *WCTR* 24 (November 23, 1899): 32.

41. "Bridge Cycle Path Dead," *BDE* (August 31, 1899): 15; "Will Hold Mass Meeting," *BDSU* (September 19, 1899): 9; "At a meeting of the Bridge Cycle Path General Committee...," *NYS* (September 26, 1899): 8; "Theodore Kiendl Replied to," *BDE* (September 30, 1899): 5; "Meeting of the Brooklyn Good Roads Association," *NYS* (December 7, 1899): 9; "Cycle Paths on New Bridge," *NYP* (February 2, 1900): 2; "Wants a Bridge Cycle Path," *NYT* (March 29, 1900): 2; and "For a Bridge Cycle Path," *NYW* (April 21, 1900): 8. See also Edward Hungerford, *The Williamsburg Bridge* (Brooklyn, NY: The Eagle Press, 1903), 105.

42. "Urging the Bridge Path," *BDE* (November 20, 1897): 4.

43. David McCullough, *The Great Bridge* (New York: Simon and Schuster, 1972), 146–147, 479–504, 545.

44. "Cycling Lane Likely for a Major City Street," *NYT* (September 17, 1970): 1; and "Brooklyn Bridge Opens Special Bicycle Ramps," *NYT* (April 1, 1971): 20.

45. In 1896, the Tacoma Wheelmen's Bicycle Club led the campaign to build the Tacoma Bicycle Bridge, also known as the Galliher Gulch Bridge, 440 feet in span length and part of a path leading to the Hood Street Reservoir. Images of the bridge are available at the Tacoma Public Library.

46. "An Engineering Marvel," *LCJ* (August 2, 1896): B4; "East River Bridge Cycle-Path," *NYEP* (August 16, 1898): 10; "Cycle Paths on New Bridge," *NYP* (February 2, 1900): 2; and "Everything from Everywhere," *WCTR* 24 (October 19, 1899): 20.

47. "Plan of the New East River Bridge," *LCJ* (May 13, 1900): B4.

48. "Floor System of the New East River Bridge," *Scientific American* 84 (June 15, 1901): 374; and "Approach to the New East River Bridge," *Scientific American* 89 (July 18, 1903): 46. See also "The New Brooklyn Bridge and Its Exclusive Cycle Paths," *BW* 47 (July 25, 1903): 519–520.

49. "To Steal Bridge Paths," *BW* 48 (October 3, 1903): 48; "Protests to Mayor," *BW* 48 (October 17, 1903): 55; "Use the Bridge Paths," *BW* 48 (November 7, 1903): 140; "Big Bridge Almost Ready," *BW* 48 (November 7, 1903): 145; "Bridge Paths are Safe," *BW* 48 (November 7, 1903): 149; and "First Over the New Bridge," *BW* 48 (January 2, 1904): 383. See also "Cyclists Get Excited over a False Report," *BDSU* (October 19, 1903): 1; and "New Bridge Footpath Open," *NYT* (April 24, 1904): 12. My requests to examine final plans and as-built drawings for the Williamsburg Bridge were not acknowledged by New York's Chief Bridge Officer, likely because of concerns about security. However, the international importance of the bridge in the context of bicycle history is clear, and the quest for complete information should not be abandoned.

50. "Bridge Paths in Danger," *BW* 49 (April 30, 1904): 171; and "To Block Bridge Path Grab," *BW* 49 (May 14, 1904), 231.

51. New York City Department of Records, Municipal Archives, Online Gallery: Bridges-Plant- Structures (BPS): BPS 03419 (April 27, 1912); New York City Department of Records, Municipal Archives, Online Gallery: BPS 04744 (July 7, 1916); and New York City Department of Records, Municipal Archives, Online Gallery: BPS 14803 (December 3, 1931), all by Eugene de Salignac.

52. Fred Bernstein, "Walking the Williamsburg," *NYT* (June 11, 2000): CY21.

53. "An Elevated Cycle Path," *Bearings* 7 (February 24, 1893): 11; "The Proposed Building of an Elevated Bicycle Road...," *Engineering News and American Railway Journal* 34 (July 25, 1895): 56; "Niagara Falls Expo," *LCJ* (July 18, 1897): C4; and Robert A. Reid and the Pan-American Exposition Co., *One Hundred Views of the Pan-American Exposition: Buffalo and Niagara Falls* (Buffalo, NY: Robert Allan Reid, 1901).

54. "Elevated Cycle Path," *NYT* (January 11, 1896): 6; "Rapid Transit for Wheels," *NYS* (January 13, 1896): 6; and "Wheelways," *WCTR* 16 (January 17, 1896): 80.

55. "Cycle Path Over the 'L' Road," *NYT* (April 28, 1896): 6; "Elevated Rapid Transit," *NYT* (April 29, 1896): 9; and "Lawson N. Fuller Dead," *NYT* (July 15, 1904): 7.

56. "Elevated Cyclists," *WCTR* 17 (May 1, 1896): 48.

57. "Gossip of the Cyclers," *NYT* (June 21, 1896): 13; and "News for the Wheelmen," *NYT* (July 9, 1897): 3. See also "Why a Great Plan Failed," *WCTR* 19 (May 21, 1897): 62.

58. William F. Buckley Jr., *The Unmaking of a Mayor* (New York: Viking Press, 1966), 222–223.

59. A. E. Hotchkiss, Elevated Railway, US Patent 488,200, filed December 20, 1892. A number of other inventors attempted to adapt bicycles to traditional railroads, employing a variety of mechanisms. For a summary, see Lorne Shields, "Ridin' the Rails," *The Wheelmen* 79 (November 2011): 18–26.

60. N. R. Ewan, "Holly Shop Owners Reached Smithville by Bikeline in the 90s," *Mount Holly Herald* (January 4, 1946): A5; Kenneth L. Brewer, "Bicycle Railway Was Unique and Fast...But Unprofitable," *Mount Holly Herald* (July 11, 1957): no page number; and "The Great Mount Holly Fair and a Murder Accompany Bike Railway's Delayed Debut," *Mount Holly Herald* (July 18, 1957): 1, 10B. Brewer's articles are in a scrapbook titled "Burlington County Historical Society Scrapbook," vol. 9, 46, 52–53, part of a collection of scrapbooks with newspaper clippings, available at the historical society's library in Burlington, NJ. See also Irving Leonard, "Mr. Smith of the Star," *The Wheelmen* 6 (Summer 1975): 6–8.

61. N. R. Ewan, "Holly Shop Owners Reached Smithville by Bikeline in the 90s," *Mount Holly Herald* (January 4, 1946): A5; Kenneth L. Brewer, "Bicycle Railway Was Unique and Fast...But Unprofitable," *Mount Holly Herald* (July 11, 1957): no page number; and "The Great Mount Holly Fair and a Murder Accompany Bike Railway's Delayed Debut," *Mount Holly Herald* (July 18, 1957): 1, 10B; all in *Scrapbook*, vol. 9, 46, 52–53.

62. N. R. Ewan, "Holly Shop Owners Reached Smithville by Bikeline in the 90s," *Mount Holly Herald* (January 4, 1946): A5; Kenneth L. Brewer, "Bicycle Railway Was Unique and Fast...But Unprofitable," *Mount Holly Herald* (July 11, 1957): no page number; and "The Great Mount Holly Fair and a Murder Accompany Bike Railway's Delayed Debut," *Mount Holly Herald* (July 18, 1957): 1, 10B; all in *Scrapbook*, vol. 9, 46, 52–53.

63. William Bolger, *Smithville: The Result of Enterprise* (Mount Holly, NJ: Burlington County Cultural and Heritage Commission, 1980), 209–215.

64. "Unique Scheme for Wheelmen," *San Francisco Call* (January 23, 1897): 2; "A Bicycle Path for Pasadena," *San Francisco Call* (January 31, 1898), 6; "A Paradise for Wheelmen," *Los Angeles Herald* (July 24, 1898): 21. See also *Articles of Incorporation of the California Cycleway Company*, dated August 23, 1897, recorded August 27, 1897, in the Office of the California Secretary of State, record book 104, p. 10, charter 2401.

65. George Wilson and A. B. Choate, "The Cycle Paths of St. Paul and Minneapolis," in Potter, *Cycle Paths*, 12–21; and Rev. Isaac Houlgate, *Guide to Minneapolis Bicycle Paths* (Minneapolis, MN: Bryon and Willard, 1902). For costs, see "Figures...," *WCTR* 24 (September 28, 1899): 12. For a photograph of the path to White Bear Lake, see "White Bear Lake Path, S. Paul," *LAWBGR* 26 (November 5, 1897): cover. For a more expansive discussion of bicycle path development in Minneapolis and St. Paul, see James Longhurst, "The Sidepath Not Taken," *Journal of Policy History* 25 (October, 2013): 557–586.

66. George Wilson and A. B. Choate, "The Cycle Paths of St. Paul and Minneapolis," in Potter, *Cycle Paths*, 12–21.

67. Olmsted, "Classes of Parkways."

68. "Sixty Miles of Paths," *WCTR* 24 (February 1, 1900): 38.

69. H. R. Huntington, "Side Paths for Bicycles," *LAWBGR* 21 (June 14, 1895): 13; "Cycle Paths in Streets," *LAWB* 24 (October 30, 1896): 581; and "Side-Path Building Day," *WCTR* 25 (March 1, 1900): 38.

70. "A Fine Cycle Path," *LAWBGR* 27 (January 14, 1898): 27; and "The Best Bicycle Sidepath...," *Monticello (NY) Republican Watchman* (May 11, 1900): 3.

71. "Patent Paths Proposed," *WCTR* 18 (January 29, 1897): 74; "The Path Now Assured," *LAWBGR* 29 (April 21, 1899): 544; and "Colorado Wants Side-Paths," *WCTR* 25 (August 2, 1900): 17.

72. A. B. Choate, "Bicycle Side-Path Trunk Lines," *Outing* 37 (October 1900): 115.

Afterword

1. "An Envious Shade," *BWMR* 63 (April 29, 1911): 299.

2. "Referring to the New Title…," *BSB* 8 (November 1910): 133; "The Bicycle News," *BSB* 13 (April 1915): 57; "Return of the Bicycle," *BSB* 18 (December 1920): 180–181; "The Greatest Gathering of Cyclists Since Cycling Ceased to be a 'Craze' and Became a Rational Recreation," *BWMR* 49 (May 7, 1904): 204; and "The Recent Revival Run at Cleveland, Ohio," *BWMR* 49 (June 11, 1904): 354.

3. "The Plans and Scope of the Century Road Club," *WCTR* 8 (January 15, 1892): Supplement, ii; W. T. Farwell, "Pioneer Days with Bicycle Clubs," *Bicycle News* 2 (April 1916): 17–19; "Annual Dinner CRCA," *BSB* 15 (April 1917): 54; and "Amateur Bicycling League of America," *BSB* 19 (February 1921): 18.

4. E. L. Yordan, "Bicycles Roll Back to Favor," *NYT* (October 13, 1935): 21; and David Herlihy, *Bicycle: The History* (New Haven, CT: Yale University Press, 2004), 355–359.

5. Robert Moses to Fiorello H. LaGuardia, August 8, 1938, in NYCDP planning division, *Program of Proposed Facilities for Bicycling* (New York: printed by the author, 1938), a bound pamphlet available at the New York City Hall Library.

6. "Bicyclists Have Their Day Again as Pedals Fly in Park Mall Parade," *NYT* (April 12, 1936): N1.

7. NYCDP, *Facilities for Bicycling.*

8. "Cyclists' Byways Planned by Moses," *NYT* (July 10, 1938): 37; and "New Bicycle Path in Brooklyn," *NYT* (March 23, 1941): 21. See also NYCDP, *Shore Parkway Extension and Marine Parkway* (New York: printed by the author, circa 1936), printed pamphlet available at the New York City Hall Library.

9. William H. Latham to Charles Vogel, March 6, 1939, New York City Municipal Archives-Robert Moses Collection (hereafter NYCA-RMC), in box 102412, folder 17. Box and folder numbers for correspondence and memoranda relating to bicycle paths in the Moses Collection are identified on a list covering the years 1939–1965, inclusive.

10. "Cyclists' Byways Planned by Moses," *NYT* (July 10, 1938): 37.

11. Robert Miller, "The Long Island Motor Parkway: Its Impact on Twentieth-Century Life," a typewritten transcript of a presentation delivered at the Robert Moses Conference at Hofstra University, dated June 10, 1988. Available at the Queens Borough Public Library, Long Island Division.

12. Allyn R. Jennings to Robert Moses, July 21, 1939, in box 102471, folder 24; Francis Cormier to W. C. Johnson, March 19, 1940, in box 102480, folder 25; and William Latham to A. S. Hodgkiss, January 8, 1947, in box 102740, file 30; all in NYCA-RMC. See also "Cyclists' Byways Planned by Moses," *NYT* (July 10, 1938): 37.

13. NYCDP, *Facilities for Bicycling;* and Robert Moses, "Provision for Bicyclists," *NYT* (August 23, 1939): 18.

14. NYCDP, *Facilities for Bicycling;* and NYCDP, *Shore Parkway Extension.*

15. "New Bicycle Path in Brooklyn," *NYT* (March 23, 1941): 21. Southern State Parkway and Southern Parkway are separate corridors.

16. Robert Caro, *The Power Broker* (New York: Alfred A. Knopf, 1974), 515–516. See also Ruth Oldenziel and Adri Albert de la Bruheze, "Contested Spaces: Bicycle Lanes in Urban Europe (1900–1995)," *Transfers* 1 (Summer 2011): 29–49.

17. Moses to LaGuardia, August 8, 1938, in NYCDP, *Facilities for Bicycling.*

18. Clifton Fadiman to Robert Moses, January 23, 1941 and Moses to Fadiman, January 27, 1941, both in box 102540, folder 21, NYCA-RMC.

19. Cecile Meehan, assistant secretary, Cycle Trades of America, "Safety Bulletin For Park Department Executives," May 19, 1942, in box 102591, folder 24, NYCA-RMC.

20. "Highways and Byways," *NYT* (August 14, 1939): 12; Robert Moses, "Provision for Bicyclists," *NYT* (August 23, 1939), 18; Robert Moses to Charles Merz, August 21, 1939, in box 102412, folder 17; and Caro, *Power Broker,* 457.

21. R. C. Geist, Secretary of College Cycle Club, to Robert Moses, May 23, 1942 and Robert Moses to R. C. Geist, May 28, 1942; both in box 102591, folder 24; and J. W. Heaslip Jr. to R. C. Geist, March 26, 1941, in box 102540, folder 21; all in NYCA-RMC.

22. Francis Cormier to W. C. Johnson, March 19, 1940 and memorandum from George Spargo, December 19, 1940, both in box 102480, folder 25, NYCA-RMC.

23. "How many more if…," *BSB* 9 (April 1911): 20.

24. Caro, *Power Broker,* 368–378, 455.

25. Ibid., 484–489.

26. William H. Latham to Charles Vogel, March 6, 1939 in box 102412, folder 17, NYCA-RMC.

27. William H. Latham to Anthony F. Mestice, March 15, 1939 (and accompanying document titled "Bicycling Facilities," a typewritten list) and William H. Latham to Miss J. Wolper, October 9, 1939, both in box 102412, folder 18, NYCA-RMC. See also Elizabeth Barlow Rogers, *Rebuilding Central Park: A Management and Restoration Plan* (Cambridge, MA: MIT Press, 1987), 35.

28. "Bicycling Facilities," typewritten lists dated February 26, 1940 and April 30, 1940 and attached to press release dated July 11, 1940—both in box 102480, folder 25, NYCA-RMC; memorandum from Harold G. Thompson to James A. Dawson, July 15, 1940 and memorandum from Francis Cormier to James A. Dawson, July 19, 1940, both in box 102528, folder 10, NYCA-RMC.

29. Francis Cormier to W. C. Johnson, March 19, 1940, in box 102480, folder 25, NYCA-RMC.

30. William H. Latham to Margaret Keating, dated April 15, 1941, in box 102561, folder 14, NYCA-RMC.

31. NYCDP, "Bicycling Areas Available in New York City," typewritten list dated May 7, 1942, in box 102591, folder 24, NYCA-RMC; Charles G. Bennett, "Special Paths for City's Cyclists," *NYT* (June 21, 1942): 21; and N. E. Gordon, "Letter to the Editor of the New York Times," *NYT* (August 3, 1954): 18.

32. NYCPD, "Bicycling Areas Available in New York City," typewritten list dated May 7, 1942, in box 102591, folder 24, NYCA-RMC; and Bennett, "Special Paths," 21.

33. John W. Heaslip to Miss Evelyn M. Davis, April 19, 1948, in box 102769, folder 25, NYCA-RMC; and John Heaslip to Miss Cecile Meehan, Executive Secretary of the Bicycle Institute of America, April 5, 1946, in box 102710, folder 27, NYCA-RMC.

34. Francis Cormier to W. C. Johnson, March 19, 1940 and Frederick H. Gross to James A. Dawson, October 23, 1940, both in box 102480, folder 25, NYCA-RMC. See also memorandum from Richard C. Jenkins to William H. Latham, September 15, 1943, in box 102624, folder 23, NYCA-RMC; Elbert Cox to Department of Public Parks, New York City, April 8, 1942 and James A. Dawson to Elbert Cox, April 13, 1942, both in box 102591, folder 24, NYCA-RMC; and Stuart Constable to Victor G. Hofer, September 26, 1946, in box 102710, folder 127; all in NYCA-RMC.

35. V. K. Brown to Allyn R. Jennings, February 2, 1940, in box 102480, folder 25, NYCA-RMC.

36. Ibid.

37. Josephine Young Case (Mrs. Everett Case) to Robert Moses, November 26, 1956, in box 102896, folder 31, NYCA-RMC.

38. Robert Moses to Mrs. Everett Case, December 4, 1956, in box 102896, folder 31, NYCA-RMC.

39. Ibid.

40. Public Law 94-210, 94th Congress (February 5, 1976), 90 *U.S. Statutes* (1976), 31–150; see specifically §809 and §810, 144–147. For origins of the Rails-to-Trails Conservancy, see www.railstotrails.org/about/history.

Bibliographic Essay

Readers who are interested in the origins and evolution of the bicycle as a modern, self-propelled machine should begin with David Herlihy's *Bicycle: The History* (New Haven, CT: Yale University Press, 2004). The well-illustrated work is comprehensive but also concisely written—no easy feat for such a broad topic spanning roughly two hundred years—and the book is a useful reference tool for any aspect of bicycle history. Pryor Dodge's book *The Bicycle* (New York: Flammarion, 1996) complements the work by Herlihy (who provides an introduction) with a superbly illustrated focus on the fascinating mechanical innovations that led, ultimately, to the perfection of the bicycle's design. Tony Hadland and Hans-Erhard Lessing have only just finished their work *Bicycle Design* (Cambridge, MA: MIT Press, 2014), which advances that topic to date. An earlier book, *Wheels and Wheeling: The Smithsonian Cycle Collection*, by Smith H. Oliver and Donald H. Berkebile (Washington, DC: Smithsonian Institution Press, 1974), also contributes to our understanding of the bicycle's historical development.

Among its many attributes, Glen Norcliffe's *The Ride to Modernity: The Bicycle in Canada, 1869–1900* (Toronto: University of Toronto Press, 2001), provides an exceptionally clear and concisely written summary of the bicycle's technical development during that period. In addition, although the book's focus is Canada, Norcliffe's observations about cycling and the geographical shifts it influenced have far-reaching implications. Generally, his work opens broad avenues for continued study, particularly with regard to the pursuit of scenic countryside by cyclists (on modern machines) and whether those exploratory impulses represent a form of antimodernism—a reaction to the travails of urban life—or whether cyclists' gathering environmental awareness points them in the direction of progressivism.

For those who are interested in very specific aspects of the bicycle's origins, a number of very good European sources are available, among them *Le Vélocipède: Objet de Modernité (1860–1870)* (Saint Etienne, France: Musée d'Art et d'Industrie, 2008), edited by Nadine Besse and Ann Henry and published for an exhibition coinciding with the Nineteenth International Cycling History Conference. I have also used two older works to trace the early development of bicycles and tricycles: *Cycles and Cycling* by H. Hewitt Griffin (London: George Bell & Sons, 1897) and Luther Henry Porter's series of articles titled "Evolution of the Cycle," published in *LAW Bulletin and Good Roads* during 1898.

In recent years, several studies have traced the story of bicycles through the lens of local history, including Carl Burgwardt's *Buffalo's Bicycles: Reflections on Buffalo's Colossal and Overlooked Bicycle Heritage* (Orchard Park, NY: Pedaling History Bicycle Museum, 2001) and Lorenz Finison's just-published work, *Boston's Cycling Craze (1880 to 1900): A*

Story of Race, Sport, and Society (Amherst: University of Massachusetts Press, 2014). These investigations are important for many reasons, but they hold special promise because the authors uncover patterns of cycling's influence that likely occurred in other parts of the country; thus, the value of these books extends well beyond their defined political boundaries.

Economic historian Bruce Epperson's book *Peddling Bicycles to America: The Rise of an Industry* (Jefferson, NC: McFarland and Company, 2010) also holds importance beyond its stated scope. Epperson deftly unravels the complex machinations of the industry's growth and decline, largely from the vantage point of the Pope Manufacturing Company, yet his penetrating assessments of the economic forces at work also open the door to continued investigation about the multitude of much smaller companies doing business in many parts of the country during the bicycle boom. Those companies represent a cross-sectional view of American light manufacturing at the height of the industrial revolution, and such concerns can tell us much about how American cities and towns of practically every size functioned. Epperson's work enlarges an earlier study by David Hounshell, *From the American System to Mass Production: The Development of Manufacturing Technology in the United States (1800–1932)* (Baltimore, MD: Johns Hopkins University Press, 1984).

For general references to other aspects of bicycle history, a number of sources follow the exploits of cycling's long-distance adventure seekers. In *The Wonderful Ride: Being the True Journal of Mr. George T. Loher, Who in 1895 Cycled from Coast to Coast on His Yellow Fellow Wheel* (New York: Harper and Row, 1978), Ellen Smith transposes her grandfather's travel accounts into a very readable narrative. Similarly, in *An American Cycling Odyssey (1887)* (Lincoln: University of Nebraska Press, 2002) author Keven Hayes recounts the cross-country trek of George W. Nellis Jr., and in *The Lost Cyclist* (New York: Houghton Mifflin Harcourt Publishing Co., 2011) David Herlihy traces the world travels of Thomas Allen, William Sachtleben, and Frank Lenz. Still other historians focus on bicycle racing (seemingly a narrow concentration), but Andrew Ritchie's book, *Major Taylor: The Extraordinary Career of a Champion Bicycle Racer* (Baltimore, MD: Johns Hopkins University Press, 1988), also reveals the influence of bicycles in ways that reach far beyond the racing track. In Andrew Ritchie's *Quest for Speed: A History of Early Bicycle Racing (1868–1903)* (Santa Clara, CA: published by the author, 2011), he adds to our understanding of the influence of racing on the bicycle's mechanical evolution, but the work also points in many other directions, including sport and social history.

For anyone engaged in the study of bicycle history, issues of the *Proceedings of the International Cycling History Conference* are indispensable. The series began publication in 1990, following the Glasgow conference, and over the years contributions have covered a broad range of topics. Presentations often represent ongoing research and are delivered to the academic forum on cycling history. Similarly, one can find scholarly writing on the pages of *The Wheelmen* magazine, published twice each year since 1970 by The Wheelmen, a national organization founded in 1967; the journal is available to members and should not be overlooked. Familiarity with these background readings is essential as a starting point for any modern study of bicycles and their far-reaching influences in American social, economic, geographic, industrial, technological, or cultural history. Although these recent works supersede (and in several instances correct) previous studies, some of those earlier works deserve mention, and for a variety of different reasons. For example, Philip Mason's 1957 PhD dissertation at the University of Michigan, "The League of American Wheelmen and the Good Roads Movement (1880–1905)," became a groundbreaking study that credited cyclists with propelling the country's campaign to improve rural roads.

For readers whose interests turn toward the many challenges that today's bicycle riders face in urban and suburban settings, but who also desire greater familiarity with the historical evolution of cycling, Luis Vivanco's *Reconsidering the Bicycle. An Anthropological Perspective on a New (Old) Thing* (New York: Routledge, 2013), strikes a well-balanced approach and examines the bicycle and its historical, cultural, social, political, environmental, and economic contexts on several engaging levels.

The recently published paper by James Longhurst, "The Sidepath Not Taken," *Journal of Policy History* 25 (October, 2013): 557–586, also explores New York State's sidepath campaign and its influence in other states. Longhurst focuses on tax policy, specifically whether the needs of a small segment of the public (bicyclists) can represent a public good for which taxes are justified. The geographical reach of Longhurst's study is ambitious, and his discussion of path building in the Midwest also points to the need for a geographically comprehensive history of American bicycle paths. The paper is restated in Longhurst's *Bike Battles: A History of Sharing the American Road* (Seattle: University of Washington Press, 2015), which contributes to an important, ongoing dialogue about the moral and legal rights of cyclists to use public roads, and the viability of public taxes as a tool to achieve that end. In particular, his concluding arguments about the predicament of cyclists' present-day path-dependency in cities are forceful.

A much earlier paper by Gary Allan Tobin, "The Bicycle Boom of the 1890's: The Development of Private Transportation and the Birth of the Modern Tourist," *Journal of Popular Culture* 7 (Spring 1974): 838–849, deserves far more attention than it has received in recent years, particularly with regard to the contention that cyclists, in seeking escape from the city, were anti-urban. Instead, Tobin suggests that touring wheelmen and wheelwomen demonstrated an overt pro-urban predilection and developed a complex system of touring aids and guides with the goal of securing pleasant dining and comfortable accommodations at day's end. Astutely, he argues that the bicyclist erased spatial boundaries separating urban and rural America and created travel apparatuses that included satisfactory urban amenities, thereby insulating the traveler from too much nature. As Tobin explains, bicyclists initiated a type of touring that would be perfected during the automobile era.

For the present work and its focus on the cultural imprint of nineteenth- and early twentieth-century cycling on the land, cycling's remarkable collection of periodicals is by far the largest and most important written record of land shaping by cyclists. A restatement of those journals (discussed in chapter 2) is unnecessary here, but readers should be aware that the catalog includes many other serials, both American and European, that deserve continued investigation. Unfortunately, many are rare and are difficult to obtain. As more libraries, historical societies, and other archival institutions digitize their collections of cycling periodicals, access to these materials will become easier. For example, the Boston Public Library has scanned its very valuable collection of *Bassett's Scrap Book*. The review of periodical literature so essential to the study of bicycles in America must also include journals aimed at larger audiences or catering to other very specific fields of interest. In the realm of popular literature, *Frank Leslie's Popular Monthly*, *Scribner's Monthly Illustrated Magazine*, *The Century Illustrated Monthly Magazine*, *Scribner's Magazine*, *Harper's Monthly*, *Harper's Weekly*, and *McClure's Magazine* all capitalized on cycling's popularity during the late nineteenth and early twentieth centuries. On the pages of *Scientific American*, one can learn about prominent bicycle manufacturers or trace the remarkable number of patents issued for bicycles or bicycle-related inventions during that same period; editors of *Iron Age* often devoted attention to bicycle design, manufacture, and repair as well. Various engineering journals, including *Engineering Magazine, Engineering News*, and *Engineering Record*, also embraced the topic on occasion.

Periodicals are the broad avenues that provide access to the places where cycling's influence left imprints on the land, but these journals and magazines are often little more than starting points for investigations that by necessity must turn to local sources, where much of cycling's accurate history is stored—often well hidden. Institutions or offices holding those records include libraries, historical societies, registries of deeds, park boards, municipal archives, city historians, museums, and even bicycle shops, if the owners of such shops have become collectors of ephemera. Depending on the location (New York State, for example), county institutions must be added to the list.

Our ability to find the incomparably valuable information contained in old newspapers has been revolutionized by the digital age and will continue to improve as more institutions scan their newspaper collections. Until that occurs, the tedious process of reading newspapers on microfilm remains essential. Many libraries continue to require membership in order to gain access to digitized collections, unfortunately adding to the long list of fees that historians of local history must bear. I have relied heavily on several free online sources, including Chronicling America: Historic American Newspapers (http://chroniclingamerica. loc.gov) by the Library of Congress; Internet Archive (https://archive.org); the Smithsonian Institution's Digital Library (https://library.si.edu/digital-library); and Thomas Tryniski's Old Fulton Post Cards (www.fultonhistory.com) in Fulton, New York.

Most of this study has been assembled upon a foundation of articles published in journals and newspapers that addressed local events or projects and also upon records in local archives. The daunting task of trying to weave local history into reliable thematic patterns across a broad geographical region has been an ever-present challenge throughout this study (and the challenge continues), requiring constant reckoning. Undoubtedly, information correcting or supplementing the material presented here will surface as more newspapers are scanned.

Adding to the challenge, historical societies and other local institutions have small budgets and limited staff. Understandably, hours available to the public are limited, and that trend will probably continue. In truth, I am constantly amazed at the ability of such organizations to hold together, doing so only through the dedication of their staff. Nevertheless, for someone who is traveling from a distance and who must investigate collections at several institutions in one locale, efficient (and economical) scheduling becomes extremely difficult.

Finally, for those who are interested in the work of artist and toymaker William Blake Luce, whose painting *Which Road* creates a perfect visual setting for this study, author Derin T. Bray's recent book, *Bucket Town: Woodenware and Wooden Toys of Hingham, Massachusetts, 1635–1945* (Hingham, MA: Hingham Historical Society, 2014), offers a biographical sketch of Luce, as well as a fascinating glimpse into that community's Arts and Crafts Society.

A Selected Bibliography of Cycling Sources

Many of the following sources are used throughout the text. Most are useful for any study concerning the ties between cycling and landscape-related studies, but utility will vary according to readers' specific interests.

Beekman, W. S., and C. W. Willis. *Cycle Gleanings, or Wheels and Wheeling for Business and Pleasure and the Study of Nature*. Boston: Skinner, Bartlett & Co, 1894.

Chandler, Alfred D. *A Bicycle Tour in England and Wales*. Boston: A. Williams & Co, 1881.

Chin, George, and Fred E. Smith. *The Wheelman's Hand-Book of Essex County*. Marblehead, MA: Printed by the authors, 1884. Shortened in notes to *Handbook of Essex County* (1884).

Dearmer, Percy, and Joseph Pennell. *Highways and Byways in Normandy*. New York: Macmillan and Co, 1900.

Dwyer, Daniel J. *Prominent Wheelmen and Bicycle Club Directory of Massachusetts*. Boston: Garfield Publishing Co, 1894.

Elliott, Harmon. *The Sterling Elliott Family*. Cambridge, MA: Elliott Addressing Machine Co, 1945.

Fraser, John Foster. *Round the World on a Wheel*. London: Thomas Nelson and Sons, 1899.

Hillier, G. Lacy, and Viscount Bury. *Cycling*. London: Longmans, Green, and Co., 1891. Published for the Badminton Library of Sports and Pastimes.

Howells, William Dean. *Italian Journeys*. New York: Houghton Mifflin and Co., 1901. With illustrations by Joseph Pennell.

James, Henry. *A Little Tour in France*. New York: Houghton Mifflin and Co., 1907. With illustrations by Joseph Pennell.

Kron, Karl. *Ten Thousand Miles on a Bicycle*. New York: Printed by the author, 1887.

Massasoit Cycle Club. *History of the Massasoit Cycle Club (1892–1902)*. Springfield, MA: Printed by the author, n.d. Printed pamphlet available at the Connecticut Valley Historical Museum, Springfield.

Meinert, Charles W. *The History of Bicycling in the Hudson-Mohawk Region of New York State (1880–1900)*. Delmar, NY: Printed by the author, n.d.

Monroe County Sidepath Commission. *Sidepath Guide*. Rochester, NY: Sidepath Guide Company, 1899.

National Publishing Co. *The Standard Road Book: Binghamton-Elmira Section*. Boston: National Publishing Co, 1897.

New York State Division, League of American Wheelmen. *The Higbie-Armstrong Good Roads Law*. Buffalo, NY: Printed by the author, 1898.

Pennell, Elizabeth Robins. *Our Philadelphia*. Philadelphia, PA: J. B. Lippincott, 1914. With illustrations by Joseph Pennell.

Pennell, Elizabeth Robins. *French Cathedrals: Monasteries, and Abbeys and Sacred Sites of France*. New York: The Century Co., 1909. With illustrations by Joseph Pennell.

Pennell, Joseph. *Joseph Pennell's Pictures of the Wonder of Work*. Philadelphia, PA: J. B. Lippincott Co, 1916.

Pennell, Joseph, and Elizabeth Robins Pennell. *Two Pilgrims' Progress*. Boston: Roberts Brothers, 1887.

Pennell, Joseph, and Elizabeth Robins Pennell. *Our Sentimental Journey through France and Italy*. New York: Longmans, Green, and Co, 1888.

Potter, Isaac B. *Cycle Paths*. Boston: League of American Wheelmen, 1898.

Pratt, Charles E. *The American Bicycler: A Manual for the Observer, the Learner, and the Expert. Boston*. Boston: Houghton, Osgood, and Company, 1879.

Rogers, Cline. *Sidepaths—Monroe County*. An album of photographs for the Monroe County Sidepath Commission, 1899. Available at the Offices of the City Historian, Rochester (NY) Public Library.

Stevens, Thomas. *Around the World on a Bicycle*. 2 vols. New York: C. Scribner's Sons, 1887–1888.

Syracuse Herald, sporting ed., comp. *The Syracuse Herald's Road Route Book for Central New York*. Syracuse, NY: Printed by the author, 1897.

Taylor, Frank Hamilton. *Cyclers' and Drivers' Best Routes in and around Philadelphia*. Philadelphia, PA: Printed by the author, 1896.

Thayer, George. *Pedal and Path: Across the Continent Awheel and Afoot*. Hartford, CT: Evening Post Association, 1887.

Webber, John S., Jr. *In and Around Cape Ann: A Handbook of Gloucester, MA, and Its Immediate Vicinity for the Wheelman Tourist and the Summer Visitor*. Gloucester, MA: Cape Ann Advertiser, 1885.

Ward, Maria E. *Bicycling for Ladies*. New York: Brentano's, 1896.

Winder, Tom. *Around the United States by Bicycle*. Elmira, NY: Printed by the author, 1895.

W. L. Chase. *Company. Standard Road Book of New York State*. Boston: W. L. Chase & Co, 1897.

League of American Wheelmen Road Books

The following compilation of road books circulated by state divisions of the LAW is not intended as a complete list. Most state committees published their books in numerous editions beginning during the mid-1880s and continuing through the 1890s, usually with revisions. Most of those selected here are from the author's collection and are representative.

Connecticut Division, League of American Wheelmen, comp. Charles G. Huntington. *The Cyclist's Road Book of Connecticut*. Hartford, CT: Case, Lockwood & Brainard Company, 1888. Shortened in notes to *Road Book of Connecticut* (1888).

Maine Division, League of American Wheelmen. *A Road Book for Cycling and Carriage Driving in Maine*, rev. ed. Printed by the author, 1900. Shortened in notes to *Road Book of Maine* (1900).

Massachusetts Division, League of American Wheelmen, Road Book Committee. *Road Book of Massachusetts*. 4th ed. Boston: Printed by the author, 1892. Shortened in notes to *Road Book of Massachusetts* (1892).

Massachusetts Division, League of American Wheelmen, Road Book Committee, A. D. Peck, chairman. *Road Book of Massachusetts*. 8th ed. Boston: Printed by the author, circa 1895. Shortened in notes to *Road Book of Massachusetts* (1895).

New Hampshire Division, League of American Wheelmen. *Road Book of New Hampshire*. Manchester, NH: A. S. Campbell & Co, 1895.

New Jersey Division, League of American Wheelmen, Road Book Committee, Robert Gentle, chief consul. *Road Book of New Jersey*. Trenton, NJ: Printed by Frank Smith, 1896.

New Jersey Division, League of American Wheelmen, Road Book Committee. *Road Book of New Jersey*. Map work by Frank H. Taylor. Philadelphia: Alfred M. Slocum Co., 1898.

New York State Division, League of American Wheelmen, ed. Albert B. Barkman. *Hand-Book and Road-Book of New York: Containing Also the Principal through Routes of Maine, New Hampshire, Vermont, Massachusetts, Rhode Island, Maryland, Virginia, and Ohio*. Philadelphia, PA: Stanley Hart & Co., 1887. Shortened in notes to *Road-Book of New York* (1887).

New York State Division, League of American Wheelmen, comp. Walter M. Meserole, *Fifty Miles around New York: A Handbook of Cycling Roads and Routes with Maps and Illustrations for Cyclists and Horsemen*. New York: Printed by the author, 1896.

Ohio Division, League of American Wheelmen, comp. T. J. Kirkpatrick. *Hand-Book of the Ohio Division of the League of American Wheelmen*. Springfield, OH: Mast, Crowell & Kirkpatrick, 1886. Shortened in notes to *Hand-Book of Ohio* (1886).

Ohio Division, League of American Wheelmen, State Executive Committee. *The Hand-Book of the Ohio Division L.A.W.* Cincinnati, OH: Charles H. Thomson, 1892. Shortened in notes to *Hand-Book of Ohio* (1892).

Pennsylvania Division, League of American Wheelmen, Road Book Committee, ed. Henry S. Wood. *Road Book of Pennsylvania, New Jersey, Maryland, and Delaware, and the Principal through Routes of New York, Connecticut, Massachusetts, Rhode Island, and Virginia*. 7th ed. Philadelphia, PA: Printed by the author, 1893. Shortened in notes to *Road Book of Pennsylvania* (1893).

Pennsylvania Division, League of American Wheelmen, Road Book Committee, ed. and comp. Carl Hering and Leon Fay. *Road Book of Pennsylvania: Eastern Section*. Philadelphia, PA: Printed by the author, 1900 (copyrighted 1898 and 1900). Shortened in notes to *Road Book of Pennsylvania: Eastern Section* (1900).

Pennsylvania Division of the League of American Wheelmen, Road Book Committee, ed. and comp. W. West Randall and Carl Hering. *Road Book of Pennsylvania: Western Section*. Philadelphia, PA: Printed by the author, 1898. Shortened in notes to *Road Book of Pennsylvania: Western Section* (1898).

Index

Enderle, Charles C., 146
Engineering Record, 56
Essex County (New Jersey). *See* East Orange parkway paths
Estoclet, Alphonse, 75–76
Exploring Circle, 45

Fadiman, Clifton, 283
Fairchild, C. M., 46
Fairfax, Harry, 46
Faulkner, Francis C., 120
Fay, Leon, 83
Fisher, Alvah G., 112, 120
Foster, S. Conant, 187
Frank Leslie's Illustrated Newspaper, 58, 61
Fraser, John Arthur, *37*, 71
Fraser, Sir John Foster, 28, 106
French Cathedrals, Monasteries and Abbeys, and Sacred Sites of France (J. Pennell and E. Pennell), 62
Fuller, Lawson N., 267–268
Fulton County (New York) bicycle paths or sidepaths, 169
Furnas, John H., 134

Gaillard, David D., 256
Gardiner, Richard, 146–147, 172
Garrett, Edmund, *50*, 67–69, 71–72
Germantown Cycling Club (Philadelphia), 64
Geyler, Louis, 49
Gibbstown (New Jersey) region bicycle paths or sidepaths, 121
Gildersleeve, Ansel B., 165
Gilpin, Henry, 22
Girouard, Alphonse, 257
Godfrey, A. H., 39–40
Goodman, Joseph, 325n72
Good Roads, 47, 49, *114*, 137, 142, 150
Good Roads Magazine, 49, 51
Good Roads movement, 108, 113, 137, 139, 146, 155, 177, 181–182, 223
    Arapahoe County Good Roads Association (Co.), 274
    Brooklyn Good Roads Association, 220, 223, 226–227, 249, 258, 260, 262
    Good Roads League of Warren County and Good Roads Wheel League of Warren (Ohio), 177–178, *178*
    Higbie-Armstrong Good Roads Law, New York, 140–141, 143–144, 172
    Monroe County Good Roads Association (New York), 175
    National League for Good Roads, 137
    New Hampshire Good Roads Association, 119–120

relationship to New York's sidepath campaign, 137, 139, 142–43, 150, 175, 182
    Rochester (New York) Wheelmen's League, 158
Gordon, William, 215
Gospel of Good Roads (Potter), 142
Gould, George, 267–268
Gould, Jay, 267
Grand Tours (Withey), 321n36
Graves, John, 198–200
Gray, Charles, 28
Greencastle (Maryland) region bicycle paths or sidepaths, 181
Greenville (New York) region bicycle paths or sidepaths, 254–255. *See also* Appendix—Greene County
Grossman, Emil, 48
Groton Bridge Company, *5*
Gustke, Nancy, 61
Guthrie, George, 197

Hagerstown (Maryland) region bicycle paths or sidepaths, 181
Halpin, William, 252–253
Harman, John, 230
Harper's Monthly, 23, 59, 61, 65, 67–68, 72
Harper's Weekly, 59, 61, 64, 188
Harper's Young People, 72
Harrison, William S., 150
Hartford (Connecticut) region, 86, 128
    bicycle paths or sidepaths, 120, 250
    Pope Park and monument, 211–212, *212*
Hartford Evening Post, *85*, 88
Hassam, F. Childe, *xvi*, *29*, *50*, 67–72, *69*, *71*, *190*, 237
Hawley, Frank W., 125
Hawley (Pennsylvania) region bicycle paths or sidepaths, 111
Hawxhurst, Harry, 146
Hayes, H. W., 79
Hayes, Kevin, 100–101
Hazleton (Pennsylvania) region bicycle paths or sidepaths, or advanced by Associated Wheelmen of Freeland, and by Associated Wheelmen of Hazleton and Vicinity, 116–119, *118*
Heaslip, John, 288
Heck, W. B., 141
Hedges, Samuel, 154–155
Hencke, Albert, 104
Hering, Carl, 77, *82*, 83–84
Hicks, Benjamin, 166
Higbie, Richard, 140
Higgens, H. Stephen, 54
High, Hugh, 100
Hill, A. M., 46–47
Hill, David, 188
Hill, Norman, 280